A CONCISE HISTORY OF PAKISTAN

A CONCISE HISTORY OF PAKISTAN

M.R. KAZIMI

SECOND EDITION

UNIVERSITY PRESS

OXFORD
UNIVERSITY PRESS

Oxford University Press is a department of the University of Oxford.
It furthers the University's objective of excellence in research, scholarship,
and education by publishing worldwide. Oxford is a registered trade mark of
Oxford University Press in the UK and in certain other countries

Published in Pakistan by
Oxford University Press
No. 38, Sector 15, Korangi Industrial Area,
PO Box 8214, Karachi-74900, Pakistan

© Oxford University Press 2009

The moral rights of the author have been asserted

First Edition published in 2009
Second Edition 2024

All rights reserved. No part of this publication may be reproduced, stored in
a retrieval system, or transmitted, used for text and data mining, or used for
training artificial intelligence, in any form or by any means, without the
prior permission in writing of Oxford University Press, or as expressly permitted
by law, by licence, or under terms agreed with the appropriate reprographics
rights organization. Enquiries concerning reproduction outside the scope of the
above should be sent to the Rights Department, Oxford University Press, at the
address above

You must not circulate this work in any other form
and you must impose this same condition on any acquirer

ISBN 978-969-7347-37-7

Typeset in Minion Pro
Printed on 68gsm Offset Paper

Printed by Delta Dot Technologies (Pvt.) Ltd, Karachi

For my grandson
Musi Reza Kazimi

Contents

List of Personality Profiles x
Preface to the Second Edition xi
Preface to the First Edition xii

Part 1: Ancient and Medieval History

Introduction 2

1. Muslim Society in South Asia 19
2. A Comparison of Muslim and Hindu Society 23
3. The Role of the Ulama and the Sufis 32
4. The Fall of the Muslims and the Establishment of British Rule 42

Part 2: History of Muslim Revival Movements

5. Shah Waliullah (1703–1762) 48
6. The Jihad Movement 51
7. Titu Mir (1782–1832) 54
8. The Faraidi Movement 56
9. The Events of 1857 59
10. The Educational Movements 66

Part 3: History of the Political Struggle

11. The Political Aspects of the Aligarh Movement 76
12. The Formation of the All-India Muslim League, 1906 82
13. The Lucknow Pact, 1916 88
14. The Khilafat Movement (1918–1924) 91
15. From Delhi Muslim Proposals to Jinnah's Fourteen Points 96
16. Allahabad Address, 1930: Allama Iqbal and the Ideology of Pakistan 104
17. The Round Table Conferences (1930–1932) 110
18. The Government of India Act 1935 114
19. The 1937 Elections and Congress Rule 117

Part 4: History of the Pakistan Movement

20.	From the Lahore Resolution 1940 to the 1945 Elections	124
21.	The Cabinet Mission Plan, 1946	131
22.	The Partition Plan, 3 June 1947	138
23.	The Radcliffe Award	142
24.	The Role of the Majority Provinces	145

Part 5: Political History of the State

	Introduction: Ideology of Pakistan	156
25.	The Establishment of Pakistan: Early Problems	165
26.	Experiment in Democracy (1951–1958)	174
27.	The First Military Regime (1958–1969)	179
28.	The Second Military Regime (1969–1971)	189
29.	The First PPP Regime (1971–1977)	204
30.	The Third Military Regime (1977–1988)	210
31.	The Democratic Interregnum (1988–1999)	212
32.	The Fourth Military Regime (1999–2008)	217
33.	The Fourth PPP Regime (2008–2013)	225
34.	The Third PML (N) Regime (2013–2017)	230
35.	The Pakistan Tehreek-e-Insaf Regime (2018–2022)	233
36.	The PML (N) Shehbaz Sharif Regime (2022–2023)	241

Part 6: Constitutional History

37.	Constitutional Developments (1947, 1956, 1962, and 1973)	244
38.	The Islamic Provisions of Successive Constitutions	259

Part 7: History of the Institutions

39.	The Bureaucracy	266
40.	The Armed Forces	276

Part 8: Diplomatic History

41.	Introduction: Aims and Objectives	282
42.	Pakistan and the World Powers	286
43.	Pakistan's Relations with SAARC States	324
44.	Pakistan, the Non-Aligned Movement, and the Muslim World	354

Part 9: Economic History

45.	Economic Development	368
46.	Economic Planning	392
47.	Energy	400
48.	Environment	406

Part 10: Cultural History

49.	Culture and Society	416
50.	Language and Literature	422
51.	Human Resource Development and Education	433
52.	Human Rights in Pakistan	437
53.	The Judicial History of Pakistan	456
54.	History of Terrorism in Pakistan	485
55.	75 Years of Pakistan—A Summary	502

Acknowledgements	514
Bibliography	515
Index	518

List of Personality Profiles

1.	Amir Khusro	30
2.	Iftikhar-un-Nisa aka Hazrat Mahal	64
3.	Gopal Krishna Gokhale	86
4.	Chittaranjan (C.R.) Das	94
5.	Mohandas Karamchand Gandhi	102
6.	Chaudhary Rahmat Ali	108
7.	Jawaharlal Nehru	112
8.	Raja of Mahmudabad, Muhammad Amir Ahmad Khan	121
9.	Abul Kasem Fazlul Haq	130
10.	Maulana Abul Kalam Azad	136
11.	Maulana Hasrat Mohani	140
12.	Mohammad Ali Jinnah	163
13.	Nawabzada Muhammad Liaquat Ali Khan	172
14.	Huseyn Shaheed Suhrawardy	177
15.	Field Marshal Mohammad Ayub Khan	187
16.	Sheikh Mujibur Rahman	202
17.	Zulfikar Ali Bhutto	208
18.	Benazir Bhutto	224
19.	Abul Ala Maududi	263
20.	Mahbub ul Haq	398
21.	Hafeez Jalandhari	431

Preface to the Second Edition

I wrote *A Concise History of Pakistan* more than a decade ago. I was then in reasonably good health. In the intervening period, Pakistan has seen a steady decline, first due to the Covid-19 pandemic and then due to unprecedented floods. However, Pakistan has potential, Pakistan has resilience. Presently the history of Pakistan may be required to be written from another vantage, by another author. I have personally suffered a decline, and the resilience of a single individual is quite limited.

I had resumed my teaching career, at the University of Karachi now, and had increased my habit of keeping newspaper clippings. These were thematically and chronologically arranged by two students, Shah Fahad and Muhammad Adeel, who are now teaching History and Pakistan Studies themselves. Our care in documenting what was to be written, led me to petulance, to an intolerance of intellectuals who from time to time repeat their refrain that the written history of Pakistan is fictional. I have countered such critics in the medium they chose. Historians are accountable, whether in class, seminars, conferences or even book launches, and I am the least in a line of most illustrious predecessors.

Another incident adding to my persistence, my ability to complete one update in my lifetime, has been recorded by Lord Acton. When he went to call on Leopold von Ranke in Germany, Lord Acton found him so frail that he thought to himself that the next news he would receive about Leopold von Ranke would be about his death. Then came the first volume of *Universal History*.... Despite my hopelessly lower stature, I was inspired and have lived to write these few words. Whether I shall live to see it in print is entirely up to Providence.

I need to thank Ghousia Bano Gofran Ali, Managing Editor, and Arshad Saeed Husain, Managing Director of the Oxford University Press, Pakistan for their patience and their trust.

Dr Muhammad Reza Kazimi
Editor, *Quarterly Journal of the Pakistan Historical Society*
21 November 2022

Preface to the First Edition

When the United States sought freedom from the British Empire, both countries had a common religion, common language, and common race. Today, no one, least of all, the British prime minister, questions the right of the United States to be independent. If the United States had continued as a British colony, they would not have had the resources or the inclination to side with Britain in the Second World War. The parallel between the American and Pakistani struggles has not totally been lost. A young Lyndon B. Johnson[1] wrote to congratulate the founder of Pakistan, Mohammad Ali Jinnah: 'Not only Pakistan is grateful for your accomplishment, but all people of the world, especially colonials. We in the Western Hemisphere salute you, and are also looking forward to the day of liberation from foreign yoke.'[2]

Governments, unlike individuals, have to deal with exigencies, and if the British prime minister publicly hoped that partition was temporary, it was because the residual interests of Britain lay more with India than with Pakistan. Such attitudes are understandable in politicians, they are not understandable in historians. Arnold Joseph Toynbee was perceptively loath to recognize the new country as a separate entity. In a small note called 'Pakistan as a Historian Sees Her', he commented: 'Yet the pace of the psyche's self-adjustment is so slow that, in AD 1947, the Muslim community in the Indian sub-continent decided that there was still not enough common ground between Muslims and Hindus to enable the two communities to be united under a single government.'[3]

Toynbee who viewed history in terms of civilizations transcending nation-states, mentioned only the challenges faced by Pakistan: 'If, in Pakistan, political allegiance were to be decided on lines of race or language, Pakistan would immediately fall to pieces'.[4] While this is intrinsically true, the fact remains that Toynbee saw greater differences within Pakistan, than between India and Pakistan. A historian of the standing of Toynbee was expected to grade historical developments on the basis of their impact on human rights and on human survival.

How these imperatives appeared in the national perspective was grasped by Bertrand Russell. Writing letters to world leaders regarding the removal of Zulfikar Ali Bhutto as foreign minister, Russell made the following point: 'In Pakistan, the figure most closely identified with the creation of an independent foreign policy for Pakistan has been removed from office.'[5]

At the centre of Z.A. Bhutto's national aspirations has been the issue of Kashmir. The present perception of the Kashmir issue is conditioned by the unipolar configuration, international terrorists, and the nuclearization of the belligerents. The historical coverage of the Kashmir issue is given in the main text, and I hope will contribute to a more realistic appraisal of a dispute that threatens world peace.

In the unipolar configuration, the Kashmir dispute is redundant and Pakistan itself seems expendable. Yet, the outbreak of the Second World War serves to show that the sacrifice of small countries like Poland or Czechoslovakia do not guarantee peace. Apart from the issue of human rights, Kashmir serves as a reminder that had Russia not sold Alaska to the United States, it would not have lost the Cold War. Thus to argue that the dispute is settled because it has been prolonged is not convincing. As for international terrorism, it needs to be recognized that those organizing pogroms with the aid of state apparatus are also terrorists.

There has also been academic neglect in tracing the origins of Muslim militants. No effort has been directed towards studying the rise of the Kharijites, an early group which developed the doctrine of Isti'rad, that is the indiscriminate killing of all non-Kharijite Muslims who came their way. They killed the wives and children of those who crossed their path. It is due to this neglect that rage as a phenomenon remains unexplained. They were highly eulogized by the German historian Julius Wellhausen at the beginning of the 20th century.[6] A re-appraisal is necessary, for it is their offshoots that have the greatest bearing on the third issue.

It is Pakistan which has accepted the UN resolutions on Kashmir; it was Pakistan which proposed that South Asia be a nuclear-free zone, Pakistan had no means to respond to Indian nuclear tests in 1974, but before it responded to the 1998 tests, it sought as an alternative, a nuclear umbrella, which was rudely refused. In the main text, there is mention of two caches of uranium having been stolen in India, by non-state actors. Non-state actors must be pursued wherever they are, for, the surest prescription for proliferation is discrimination.

Pakistan is, as I write, in the midst of a crisis. A transition to democratic rule is underway; but how sincere, and how complete, will be for future historians to record. But, it is a perennial lesson of history, a lesson not confined to Pakistan, that no matter how iron-clad state terrorism may seem, it has the potential to implode. Obliterated from within a framework, bleeding wounds form an alternative vortex. This is how the sands of time keep shifting.

The assassination of Benazir Bhutto on 27 December 2007 is a tragic event which closes a chapter of history, at which point the present narrative should be allowed to conclude. The intervening imposition of emergency as well as its lifting, the setting of an election date, pale into insignificance. The shock and horror over this gruesome act, cut across the political divide, and united former antagonists. Benazir Bhutto had a presence and charisma which far transcended her present status as an opposition leader. The UNSC met and passed a unanimous resolution condemning the dastardly act. The assassin, still unidentified, was an anarchist by intent, if not an anarchist by creed. The news of the assassination was followed, understandably, by an outbreak of violence, in which innocent lives and precious property was lost. However, no one's grief can exceed the grief of her husband, Asif Ali Zardari, and her children, the eldest of whom, Bilawal, has succeeded his mother as Chairman of the PPP. Their dignity in grief is a ray of hope, for a nation which is desolate.

By offering a concise history of Pakistan, I am not unmindful of the suitability of writing a history of Asia, or even South Asia, as indeed, histories of France or Germany have not made superfluous European history as a discipline. The world has evolved different levels of historiography: universal, national, and local. Any one of them helps the reader to arrive at an understanding of history, not possible at the other two levels.

The same can be said of the topic-wise categories: Social history, Cultural history, or Economic history. Since I have been schooled only in some categories, I had to fall back on my wife Dr Anjum Bano, Assistant Professor of Special Education at the University of Karachi, for the section on the history of Education; and my daughter, an IBA student for the section on Economic history. It is only my extreme reluctance to lose political quarrels to them, that I refrain from naming them as co-authors. The faults that remain are, as they will be the first to tell you, mine alone. My son and daughter-in-law have helped me in diverse ways, especially by putting up with my grouchiness. I dedicate this book to my grandson, who not only made me take an optimistic view of events, but because it is children, who without any concern for rights or fairness, celebrate Independence Day with the utmost fervour. I need to record the debt I owe Ameena Saiyid, OBE, Managing Director of the Oxford University Press, Pakistan, and also to Ghousia Bano Ghofran Ali, Managing Editor, for their encouragement.

Notes

1. Lyndon Baines Johnson often referred to by his initials LBJ, was an American politician who served as the 36th President of the United States from 1963 to 1969.
2. Mehrunnisa Ali (ed.), *Jinnah on World Affairs* (Karachi: Pakistan Study Centre, University of Karachi, 2007), p. 521.
3. *Crescent and Green* (London: Cassell and Co., 1955), p. 3.
4. Ibid., p. 2.
5. Reproduced in Kausar Niazi, *Deedawar* (Lahore: Shaikh Ghulam Ali and Sons, 1977), pp. 112–118.
6. Julius Wellhausen, *The Religio-Political Factions in Early Islam*, tr. R.C. Ostle and S.M. Walzer (Amsterdam: North-Holland Publishing Co., 1975), pp. 41, 42.

Part 1
Ancient and Medieval History

Introduction

LAND AND PEOPLE.—Pakistan enjoys several phenomenal features. It has the largest habitat of Green Turtles. It is home to Makli, the world's largest necropolis. Ziarat, Pakistan has the world's largest juniper forest. It is home to the Blind Dolphin. It has in Sukkur, the world's largest man-made irrigation system. It has Tarbela, the world's largest, man-made, earth-filled dam. Pakistan also has the highest metalled road in the world: the Karakoram Highway/Khunjerab Pass.

Pakistan has Haleji, Asia's largest bird sanctuary; in Gilgit is Asia's longest suspension bridge. It has Bolan, Asia's longest railway tunnel, and is among the last refuge of the railway steam engine.

Another indication of Pakistan's prominence is that it has held at various times the world championship in four games: hockey, cricket, squash, and snooker.

LOCATION.—Pakistan is located between 24° and 47° latitude North and between longitudes 61° and 75.31° East. To Pakistan's east is India, to its west is Iran, and to its north-west is Afghanistan. In close proximity are China through Azad Kashmir, and across the Wakhan strip in Afghanistan lies Tajikistan. Pakistan's most strategic feature at present is the Makran coast, with the Gwadar seaport just across from the United Arab Emirates, which has sea access to Basra in Iraq.

CLIMATE AND TOPOGRAPHY.—Few other countries offer such a sharp contrast between climates. In the north are Chitral, Gilgit, and Hunza where the highest mountains and snow-capped areas are located. In the south-east is the Thar desert. In the eastern half of Pakistan lies the Indus Plain. The Balochistan area is a rugged and arid plateau. Khyber Pakhtunkhwa (formerly the North-West Frontier Province)[1] has a similar terrain but is relieved by three valleys.

Area (sq. km.)	Population	Literacy Rates	Manufacturing Sector
Pakistan: 796,096 Islamabad: 906 Punjab: 205,345 Sindh: 140,914 Khyber Pakhtunkhwa: 101,741 Balochistan: 347,190 Gilgit Baltistan: 72,496	Total: 229,320,833 Male: 116,522,7114 (50.8%) Female: 112,798,120 (49.2%) Urban: 90,523,137 (36%) Rural: 138,797,696 (64%)	Remains stagnant at 60% Expenditure lowered by 29.6% Computed population: 225.18 million Male: 70% Female: 48% Urban: 74% Rural: 52%	Large scale 9.37% Small scale 2.12% of the GDP Growth for FY 2021–2022 Automobile Sector: 4.613 tonnes Food, Beverages, and Tobacco 12.370 Textile and Apparel 20.915 Paper and Board 2.314 Pharmaceutical 3.620
Electrical Generation (GWh) July-April 2021	**Agriculture (Major Crops)**	**Energy**	
Thermal: 61,052 (59.42%) Hydel: 31,357 (30.52%) Nuclear: 8,038 (7.82%) Renewable: 2,294 (2.23%) Total: 102,742 (100%)	Cotton 7.064 bales Sugarcane 81,000 tonnes Rice 8.419 tonnes Wheat 27,293 tonnes Maize 8,465 tonnes	Gas Reserves 20.91 trillion cubic feet (50.4% indigenous gas) Oil Reserves 353,500,000 barrels (20%)	

Source: *Pakistan Economic Survey 2021–2022*.

PROFILE OF EARLY SOUTH ASIAN HISTORY.—The land of ancient India is a peninsula, which means that it is surrounded on three sides by water. The fourth side, the north, is covered by high mountain ranges. This means that it is difficult to enter and leave this land from this side. The difficulty of communication made the inhabitants inward-looking. Over time, this tendency became reinforced by religion. The period being referred to is when the Hindu religion dominated India. In Hindu society, if one crossed the sea, even to go from Keamari to Manora, one would lose one's caste. In those days caste was the sole means of identity, therefore, few inhabitants ventured to cross the rough seas or the perilous mountains. This was the effect of the external boundaries.

Internally, distances were vast and travel unsafe because there were no roads, and there was also the danger of being attacked by wild animals or bitten by poisonous insects. The climate of one region, such as cold, mountainous

Chitral, differed sharply from that of Tharparkar, a hot desert area. Just as the external boundaries gave a sense of unity, the internal topographical features pushed India towards diversity. The sense of unity was reinforced by religion: the sense of diversity promoted a rich and varied culture.

Since both unity and diversity had their basis in geography, both impulses were strong. Sometimes one tendency was uppermost, sometimes the other. As has been observed since the Hindu period, how unity was identified with religion, and diversity with culture. These tendencies, moving towards, and away from unity, alternated.

Following the invasion of Alexander (327 BC), this rhythm manifested itself politically. Small local kingdoms and large paramount empires alternated. Small kingdoms gave way to the Maurya Empire and vice versa. This alternation continued in the Muslim era. The Muslims conquered small Hindu kingdoms and ultimately the Delhi Sultanate was established. When the Delhi Sultanate disintegrated, the kingdoms of Bahman, Jaunpur, and Bengal were established. These small kingdoms were succeeded by the Mughal Empire which in turn gave way to the kingdoms of Awadh, Bengal, and Deccan.

This tendency was curbed under British rule. Being foreigners who retained links with their country of origin, they were not affected by these impulses as rulers with local roots were. Another factor was that the British themselves maintained two entities: British India and the Princely States (such as Kashmir and Hyderabad). Once the British withdrew, the divisive forces that had been held in abeyance reasserted themselves.

The partition of South Asia into India and Pakistan created two centres. By centre, it means the seats of a political establishment that influenced the course of development over a large region. Since there were regional and provincial tendencies in both India (e.g. Andhra) and Pakistan (Bengal), a single strong centre in each country would be able to control both tendencies, over-centralization, and regionalism. These are called respectively centripetal and centrifugal tendencies. As mentioned earlier, the outside borders, reinforced by religion (firstly by Hinduism, then other religions), promoted a tendency for unity within the national frontiers. Since regional geography varies as stated above, the languages and lifestyles which evolved in separate regions gave a varied complexion to culture within the same national frontiers. Implying that when the pull of religion was powerful, people favoured unity on that basis. This was witnessed in the creation of Pakistan. On the other hand, when the pull of culture was stronger, then the unity created by religion diminished as a force and cultural distinction led to regionalism.

Following is a brief summary of the phases through which Pakistan has passed.

The cradle of world civilization is Balochistan. By 1954, Kili Gul Muhammad was excavated to yield the remains of a Neolithic settlement. Initially, the inhabitants of this dwelling were so primitive that they could not make pots, though later on, they developed pottery of two distinctive styles: Zhob and

Quetta. The script discovered at Kili Gul Muhammad led Leslie Alcock to describe it as 'what some scholars think' is the oldest alphabet in the world.[2]

The script with angular letters like A, T, and V was found inscribed on pots as single letters. This relates to the middle stage, as the development of pottery allows the tracing of its evolution. The earliest pots were misshapen, thick, and coarse. If the single letters were a primitive version of the alphabet, then, the developed version is yet to be discovered. Of the latter two varieties, the earthenware discovered at Zhob had designs in black on a red background. The earthenware discovered at Quetta had a pale brown background. While Quetta ware had only geometric patterns, Zhob ware had both geometrical forms and animal representations. In Kili Gul Muhammad itself, the model of a house was discovered, the earliest in South Asia.[3] Female statuettes were also a feature of this dwelling. The people who occupied Damb Sadaat 4500 years ago are thought to have come from what is now called Quetta.

The discovery, about twenty years later, of Mehrgarh by Jean-Francois Jarrige proved far more momentous. Jarrige, on the basis of carbon testing dates this civilization from 9000 to 3500 BC. This makes Mehrgarh far older than the Egyptian and Mesopotamian civilizations. The Bolan River was nearby because Jarrige asserts that Mehrgarh did not require any irrigation. The inhabitants used stone implements. The Swamp Deer was hunted, goats and sheep domesticated, and barley and wheat were cultivated. Copper objects have been found, as have evidence of metal, ceramic, and textile industries. The inhabitants buried their dead.[4]

The Mehrgarh populace built large mud brick halls as granaries. Their houses were large, containing many rooms. Mehrgarh has been linked to the succeeding Indus Valley civilization because of common features like long blocks, sophisticated drain systems, canals, and big water tanks. Thus, the discovery of Mehrgarh also proved that the Indus Valley civilization was indigenous and did not originate in Mesopotamia as some archaeologists have speculated.

In between Mehrgarh and Moenjo Daro lies Kot Diji as a possible intermediary phase. Kot Diji and its subsidiary site at Rahman Dehri show that the people could weave, produce pottery, as well as work with bronze and copper.

Both Moenjo Daro and Harappa, twin cities of the Indus Valley civilization were riverside settlements, measuring three miles in circumference; both Moenjo Daro and Harappa have two parts: the higher part consisting of citadels, the lower consisting of small houses. The citadel at Harappa was built on a protective foundation with very high walls of burnt bricks. There are rectangular towers at intervals, especially at the corners. The imposing citadel at Moenjo Daro has a granary, a public bath, and dwellings consisting of many rooms. It is thought that they were the preserve of the rulers or the ruling class, which, from the available evidence, could have been either royal or religious. Architecture had reached the stage of the corbel arch.

In the twin cities, town planning is common to both parts, but the lower part shows uniformity. This uniformity, the smallness and the sameness of the houses has led archaeologists to believe that this was a colony of the lower class, or, that a form of socialism was practiced. The houses consist of one of only two designs, both featuring two small rooms and a courtyard. The roads into which these houses open are symmetrical, geometrically planned roads, consisting of oblong blocks, measuring 400 yards in length 200 or 300 yards in width. There is a drainage system running alongside. The streets are unadorned. This leads Sir Mortimer Wheeler to conclude that: 'sameness, isolation, centralization are the abstract qualities of the Indus Civilization.'[5]

This is the epitaph written on a silent and regimented populace, and until the Indus Script is deciphered, it must be left in place. On the other hand, the fact that though Moenjo Daro had hunting implements, it had no weapons, also speaks for itself. This inspired Faiz Ahmed Faiz to say:

> And their earthen lamps which shed no
> Light on the mysteries of human darkness
> The timelessness of the unicorn.[6]

There are many seals bearing many types of representation, mostly of natural objects, but there is one type of seal that is enigmatic—a three-faced deity with horns, who is seen squatting with folded legs. The background varies. This figure bears a resemblance to the later Hindu images of Shiva, the second member of the Hindu trinity. This so far appears to be the only possible link between the Indus Valley people and the Aryans who later occupied India.

When it was assumed that all excavation at Moen jo Daro had ceased long ago and only preservation was required, newspaper reports on 17 November 2013, revealed the discovery of a pot containing copper coins. Syed Shakir Shah, Director of Archaeology at Moen jo Daro, stated that the copper coins were rusted and stuck to one another. Further details would only be available after additional scientific investigation. What was certain, however, was that the coins dated back to the Kushan period.

The last such discovery had been made by R.D. Bannerji, Sir John Marshall, and their team in 1913. Since it has been known for close to a century that the Indus Valley Civilization lasted well into the Kushan period, dating from 2nd to 5th centuries BC, speculation that the Indus Valley Civilization was destroyed either by a natural calamity or Aryan invaders should have been put to rest. Although the last two discoveries have unearthed coins and not seals, the presence of the proto-Siva seal indicates that some phase of Hinduism had a presence in the Indus Valley Civilization.

With the coming of the Aryans, the evolution of Hindustan can be traced, although this process has been questioned. According to Romila Thapar, 'The evolution of Hinduism is not a linear progression from a founder through an organizational system of sects branching off.'[7] She is partially correct in her view that the evolution of Hinduism was not linear, since the Hindu view of nature, and consequently of the supernatural was not linear.

In the Rig Veda pantheon, there is a deity known as Eka Deva or One God: 'The Vedic Aryans believed that the creation of the universe and the procreation of the human race were the result of a primaeval sacrifice, the self-immolation of a cosmic being.'[8] Despite a superficial resemblance to the Big Bang theory, it is different, since it cannot be called creation *ex nihilo*, as the preceding period is described as between non-being and being. Apart from Eka Deva subsequently being identified with Indra, the next deity in the pantheon is Agni. It was worshipped as fire on earth, as lightning in the sky, and as the sun in the celestial sphere. All these are pure and visible manifestations of nature. But despite showing Agni as the object of worship, the Rig Veda characterizes him as the chief priest, with the implication that the supernatural has a dimension beyond the celestial sphere.

In the later portion of the Rig Veda, a poet searches for the origin of creation, without mentioning any primaeval sacrifice: 'Who really knows? Who shall here proclaim it?—whence came things to be, whence this creation. The gods are on this side, along with the creation. So then, whence it came to be?'[9] In other words, abstraction came after mythology. The progression is not linear, but then, it is also not chaotic, it is cyclic. This is not quite in tune with Romila Thapar's contention: 'The worship of icons was unthought of in Vedic religion, but the idol becomes [a] significant feature of the Puranic religion.'[10] Thus, while the progression is linear between the Vedas and the Puranas, as well as from abstraction to manifestation, abstraction itself did not follow a linear progression.

But what are the Vedas? The Vedas are four in number, Rig Veda, Sama Veda, Yajur Veda, and the Atharva Veda. It is surmised that the Rig Veda was composed between 2000 to 1500 BC. Though the Samhita, a collection of 1028 hymns, was composed later than the other parts of the book, it forms an essential part of the Rig Veda. The Sama Veda was a textbook for rituals to be used by priests during the Sama sacrifice, the Sama being a sacred brew. The Yajur Veda was also a text for ritual purposes, but it extended to rituals beyond the Sama sacrifice. The Atharva Veda is made up of verses, incantations, and charms against evil; it was composed much later than the preceding Veda.

The Vedas were followed by the Brahmanas, the Upanishads and the Sutras. The Brahmanas were basically an exegesis of the Samhita. The Upanishads are a spiritual and mystical treatise. Upanishad means 'sitting at the master's feet'. In its essence, it is about the relation of the individual soul with the universal soul. It is here the doctrine of the transmigration of souls, the ultimate merger of the individual soul, and spells of liberation from the cycle of rebirth are found. This would be the matrix, not only of Hinduism, but Jainism and Buddhism as well. Given below are only two glimpses of the Upanishads. The first is from the Mundaka Upanishad:

> Heavenly, formless is the Person
> He is without and within, unborn,
> Breathless, mindless, pure
> Higher than the high Imperishable.

This concept of God is not mythological; it is compatible with the monotheistic concept. Being unborn has significance, because Hindu doctrine holds that the universe is eternal, not, in other words, born out of nothing. In the Svetasvatara Upanishad, there is a stanza that explains that knowing the One Supreme Person overcomes death:

> Higher than this is Brahma.
> The Supreme, the Great
> Hidden in all things, body by body
> The One embracer of the universe—
> By knowing him as Lord men become immortal.

The process of 'knowing' here is not confined to cognition but is one of a merger of the personal soul into the universal soul. In time the Hindu trinity came to consist of Brahma the creator, Vishnu the preserver and Shiva the destroyer. Distinguishable from Brahma is *Brahman*, the universal soul, i.e. God, and the personal soul, called *Atman*. The soul suffers the consequences of action (*karma*) and according to the nature of deeds performed, is reborn again and again as a human being of either a higher or lower caste. If deeds committed in a lifetime are evil, the soul can find the body of even an animal. To exist is to suffer, and to seek salvation from suffering, the *atman* needs to perform deeds that enable it to escape rebirth by merging with the *Brahman*.

The Sutras were aphorisms, held by some scholars to be the earliest repositories of Indian philosophy. The Sutras require wide reading to yield meaning since they are allusive and symbolic. It is rare to find a Sutra which is self-explanatory. This is intellectually a merit, but socially, it reflects the trend to make higher forms of knowledge inaccessible to the masses.

The Puranas became the text for the instruction of the masses. They are eighteen in number, encompassing a wide range of subjects, mythology, philosophy, history, and laws. The oldest Purana dates to AD 400. Thus came about the dichotomy of Hindus worshipping the concept, and the Hindus worshipping idols. This was discernible even in the 20th century. M.K. Gandhi said that the Rama he worshipped was not the historical Rama, the son of Dasharatha: 'The Rama whom I adore is God Himself, different from any historical Rama. He always was, is now, and will be forever, a God who was unborn and uncreated.'[11] Nevertheless, in carrying his political creed to the masses, Gandhi alluded plainly to the mythology. Similarly, since his creed of non-violence was at odds with Krishna's exhortation to Arjuna, Gandhi interpreted the *Bhagavad Gita* symbolically: 'The battlefield setting of the Gita is allegorical, not historical... The human body is the true chariot, Arjuna the human mind and Krishna the Indwelling Guide... After exhorting repeatedly against anger and hatred in the Gita, why would Krishna ask for killing, a deed inseparable from anger or hatred?'[12]

These allusions bring us to the Epic Age. There are two epics relating to ancient India, the *Mahabharata*, and the *Ramayana*. The *Mahabharata* describes a war between different tribes and factions, notably the battle of Kurukshetra between the Pandavas and Kauravas. The *Bhagavad Gita* referred to above, is a part of the *Mahabharata*. The *Ramayana* tells the story of Rama, the son of Raja Dasharatha, who was exiled for fourteen years at the behest of his stepmother. The purity of Sita his bride, and the loyalty of Lakshman, his brother, have given a sacred aspect to a court intrigue. Rama's battle with Ravana, for the rescue of Sita is the episode that makes the *Ramayana* truly epic. Both Krishna and Rama are considered avatars or reincarnations of Vishnu.

With the Puranas, the forms of worship and the caste system became entrenched in Hindu society. Two successive creeds Jainism and Buddhism challenged the caste system and practised *ahimsa* or non-violence. Jainism remained confined to India but survives here only as an unthreatening minority. Buddhism gained adherents in millions outside India, in the Far East[13] and Southeast Asia,[14] but in the country of its origin, this creed too remains a minority. The main protagonists of the two religions, Mahavira and Siddhartha, were near contemporaries and preached in the same region Magadha (modern Bihar).

Jain tradition holds that the first Tirthankara, Rishabh (aka Rishabhanatha [Sanskrit: 'Lord Bull'] or Adinatha), lived around 6500 BC. Thus, Jainism would predate the coming of the Aryans. While it may not be possible to date the age of Rishabh with precision, the possibility of his having lived in the pre-Aryan era lies in the similarity between Rishabh and the Hindu deity Shiva; both are symbolized by the Bull. Jain theology was codified orally by Indrabhuti Gautama, the direct disciple of Mahavira (aka Vardhamana) as *Dvādasāṅgi* but was committed to writing only a millennium after Mahavira.

The path to liberation under Jainism is called Moksha Marg. It consists of three jewels: correct faith, correct understanding, and correct conduct, and all three are interrelated. These jewels are universal and found in the ethical basis of all major religions. What is new are the Jain concepts of God, Universe, and Time. God is not the creator of the universe, since the universe is considered uncreated and eternal, but God is defined as the souls that have been liberated. This would involve forging the plural into the singular, but it is not surprising that God should be identified with the soul, since Hinduism had already introduced the concepts of the individual soul (*atman*) and the Universal Soul (Brahman). The universe has always existed, according to the Jain doctrine, and shall always exist, but its nature lies in a state between the real and the imaginary. 'Both the spheres, of cognitive sensory soul, and non-cognitive and non-sensory matter exist.'[15]

The Jain concept of time is also noteworthy: 'Time does not operate in the same way everywhere in the universe.'[16] These time zones correspond to real or imaginary parts of the universe. The universe is anthropologically conceived, that is, the universe is in the shape of a human being. This world, in which we live, lies in the waist. This needs further inquiry, since the universe is considered eternal, but the origin of humankind is placed within time.

The life spans of Mahavira and Buddha overlapped, and the area where they carried out their mission is roughly the same. Indeed, Mahavira finds mention in Buddhist literature under the name Nigantha Nataputta.[17] It is generally conceded that the figure of the first Tirthankara, Rishabh, because of belonging to remote antiquity, may have been legendary, but the four Buddhas are rarely mentioned together: Amitabha, Konakamana, Kalachakra and Shakyamuni, the prince of Kapilvastu. Amitabha is the celestial Buddha, Konakamana the ancient Buddha, and Kalachakra, the primordial Buddha. Hui Yuan, a Chinese monk bowed to Amitabha Buddha on 11 September AD 402. Ashoka doubled the size of the brick memorial to Konakamana Buddha in 254 BC, and Kalachakra Buddha was paid homage to by the present Dalai Lama at Bodh Gaya in 1985. However, the scholar introducing these earliest figures to the present generation seems not to believe in the historical existence of the three earlier Buddhas himself. His explanation is 'A nuanced account of Shakyamuni as founder must emphasize his relationship with other Buddhas, because, for Buddhists, Shakyamuni's non-uniqueness as Buddha is central to his status as founder.'[18]

Shakyamuni, Siddhartha, and Gautama are the names by which the founder of Buddhism is known. There is another term Bodhisatta, which has acquired ambiguous shades of meaning, but it was first used in the sense of a previous incarnation of the Buddha. There is also the concept of a future Buddha, foretold by Gautama himself, and called Maitreya, who would, in the future, purify the world.[19] This is an eschatological concept not native to the soil of India. Gautama was a prince enjoying all earthly bounties, but he renounced all worldly pleasures when he encountered disease, old age, and death. He finally struck a middle path between hedonism and asceticism to gain Nirvana or Enlightenment. His four principles are the persistence of suffering, the root cause of suffering (that is existence), that suffering can be brought to an end (by ending the cycle of rebirth) and the measures to be taken to end suffering.

The question that arises is: How did Buddha reconcile his rejection of a Creator with acceptance of the conception of the transmigration of souls? Both involve belief in the supernatural. Even the alleged Buddhist rejection of a Creator contains a supernatural allusion. 'Brahma imagined himself to be the creator, when in fact the world came into existence as a result of natural causes.'[20]

A.L. Basham, after citing a passage from *Pitrputra Sanagama* paraphrases it most lucidly: 'In an illusory world, rebirth is also illusory. The thing man craves, have no more reality than a dream, but he craves nevertheless, and hence his illusory ego is reborn in a new, but equally illusory body. Notice the importance of the last conscious thought before death, which plays a very decisive part in the nature of the rebirth.'[21]

The metaphysical basis of Jainism and Buddhism may have been elusive, but their ethical basis is sound, and in a land where orthopraxy takes precedence over orthodoxy, its contribution to civilization is immense. In the meanwhile, the first kingdoms were making their appearance in the Magadha area. The first was the Shishunaga dynasty (600–317 BC) which had ten kings, out of which Bimbisara (528–500 BC) and his son Ajatashatru (500–475 BC) stand out. Bimbisara was fifth in the line of succession which means that it was midway through their rule that the Shishunaga dynasty was able to assert its power. Bimbisara built Rajagriha where the present-day Rajgir is situated. Bimbisara began a series of conquests and annexed a minor kingdom of Anga. Bimbisara renounced in 500 BC his crown in favour of his son, Ajatashatru, but this act of renunciation could not save him from being killed by his son. His rule was contested by the king of Kosala, the brother-in-law of Bimbisara. Ajatashatru not only defeated the king of Kosala, but he also reduced the entire territory between the Ganges and the Himalayas. Ajatashatru built the city of Pataliputra, modern-day Patna. Pataliputra not only outstripped Rajgir but became the capital of the paramount power in India. All the other kings of this dynasty are known only in name, their deeds or achievements lie in obscurity. The last ruler, Mahanandin, was charged with patricide and was deposed by his son Mahapadma Nanda. The Shishunaga finds mention in the Puranas. The Buddha is said to have visited Bimbisara in 530 BC and died towards the end of Ajatashatru's reign. In the same era, there was also the presence of small aristocratic republics like Vrijians and Mallas.[20] The principality of Sakya was also republican, and the name Shakyamuni for Siddhartha denotes his descent from the Sakyas. In the light of this evidence, Siddhartha's father seems to have been a patriarch, and not actually the king of Kapilvastu. Hemchandra Raychaudhuri cites the Puranas to the effect that Mahapadma, the first of the Nandas was the destroyer of the Kshatriyas, the warrior cast. (The castle system is elaborated in a succeeding chapter.) The Nandas were able to establish an extensive empire in Magadha before being supplanted by Chandragupta Maurya.

Since Magadha in the east, became the political centre of India, the insularity of the country became vulnerable from the west, as the Persian empire extended its borders to the banks of the Indus. Cyrus the Great (558–530 BC) the founder of the Persian empire annexed the territories of Afghanistan and Balochistan. Darius (521–486 BC) belonged to a second line of Achaemenian kings, and though no descendant of Cyrus, occupied the Persian throne and added the territory west of the Indus to his empire. Darius made this territory 'Hindush' the twentieth Satrapy (or province) of the Persian Empire. From here Darius I realized an annual tribute of 360 talents of gold—indirect evidence of the prosperity of this region. One hundred and fifty years later when the Persian Empire faced the invasion of Alexander the Great, Darius III was able to raise a considerable number of soldiers for his defence. Thus, Alexander's invasion of Persia brought him to the bank of the Indus.

Alexander's invasion became a catalyst because he was so different in colour, race language, and weaponry which threw the commonalities of Indian society into relief. Alexander, after his conquest of Iran, entered Afghanistan and probably entered South Asia from a pass in the Northern Areas. He secured an alliance with the king of Taxila and was able to advance to the Jhelum without resistance. Porus (also Raja Puru), king of the lands beyond, decided to resist. He had a large army of 50,000 to Alexander's 20,000. Porus had 200 elephants which were placed eight lines deep. Alexander was able to cross the cold and deep Beas before Porus could anticipate his move. He attacked the rear of the army of Porus and rained arrows on the elephants who stampeded and crushed their own forces. As always Alexander proved to be a better general but found that his adversary had retained his royal dignity. When Alexander asked Porus, 'How would you like to be treated?' Porus replied, 'Like a king'. Suitably impressed Alexander restored Porus's kingdom to him, for this would be his last victory. When he attempted further conquest, his war-weary soldiers refused to advance beyond the Beas. Alexander sailed down the Indus and along the Mekran coast, eventually reaching the mouth of the Euphrates. Soon he would be dead, and his empire would be divided among his generals.

During his advance, Alexander created the First World Empire, and in retreat created the first Indian empire. Alexander's representative Philip was killed in a revolt led by Eudemos. Next, Eudemos treacherously murdered Porus. Seleucus asserted the rule but was defeated by Chandragupta Maurya (320–297 BC) Chandragupta was thus able to acquire territory extending from north India to Afghanistan. Chandragupta is said to have met Alexander, to seek his help in overthrowing the Nandas but nothing came out of this proposal. No meeting between their respective mentors, Aristotle and Kautilya is recorded. The cultural effects of Alexander's invasion would be long-lasting. The defeat of Seleucus gave rise to Central Asian principalities like Bactria situated between the Hindukush mountains and the Oxus River; and Parthia, situated south-east of the Caspian Sea. They achieved independence at the same time (c. 250 BC). Ultimately, these movements would lead to the foundation of the Kushan Empire.

Let us travel with Chandragupta Maurya to Pataliputra. His empire had been established by conquest, after the overthrow of the Nandas, Pataliputra became a city known far beyond South Asia, because of a Greek scribe, Megasthenes, and Buddhist missionaries. According to Jain tradition, Chandragupta Maurya became a Jain renouncing his kingdom and becoming a mendicant. Little is known of his son Bindusara except that his title Amitragatha (the slayer of foes) shows that he continued the course of conquest and could have extended the Mauryan Empire to the south. Bindusara converted to the Ajivikas creed, another non-Brahmanic creed that Megasthenes mentions by the name of Sramanic. His son Ashoka, as the world knows, converted to Buddhism, and became Buddhism's greatest preacher taking Indian traditions far beyond its borders and leading to its eventual supremacy in East and South-East Asia.

The conversions of the Mauryan emperors to the creeds of the Jains, the Ajivikas and the Buddhists, led Romila Thapar to observe that Sramanic creeds were prevalent in Magadha, therefore, exposure to them was not exposure to heterodoxy, but to current religious ideas.[23]

The pacifist policy of Ashoka, in some measure, led to the eventual decline of the Mauryas. Pushyamitra overthrew the last Mauryan and established the Sunga dynasty. Pushyamitra had heralded his accession by offering Ashvamedha, the horse sacrifice signifying the end of the non-violent creeds. Pushyamitra extended his boundaries to the Narbada in the south and successfully repulsed the invasion of Demetrius, the fourth king of Bactria. Little is known of the Sungas, and their successors, the Kanvas.

On the western borders, in the regions of Bactria and Parthia, containing sizeable Greek colonies, a wave of migrations from Central Asia was seen. The Sakas were pushed by the Yueh-Chi or Kushans, due to upheavals in China, and the Sakas then forced the Parthians to move. At Taxila, the Yueh-Chi laid the foundations of the Kushan Empire which straddled Central Asia and the Indus Valley. These constant invasions by Hellenic and Mongoloid people brought about a unique fusion. Many Bactrian coins rank with the finest in existence.[24] These cultural trends gave an impetus to Mahayana Buddhism, which allowed sculptural representation. Thus Buddhism, an oriental creed received a Hellenic style in art. Gandhara, located between the Kunduz and the Indus rivers, was in the proximity of the roads traversing the known world and thus gained a cosmopolitan character.

In 1913, Sir John Marshal discovered the Taxila site, where a university had flourished. In 2005, Muhammad Arif discovered Badalpur, near district Haripur, Khyber Pakhtunkhwa, which seems an extension of Taxila. However, in contrast to Taxila, Badalpur had mud plasters on both sides of a wall. This site held numerous metal objects, large and small, ranging from gold to iron. Also discovered was a building complex of eight cells, which housed Buddhist monks. Fortunately, the western side main entrance is still intact.[25]

The political and military side of this civilization was advanced by the Kushans. The first ruler was known as Miaos (or Heraos). He had to defeat four related tribes to make himself king. Next to gain prominence was Kadphises I who ousted the Parthians. His successor Kadphises II conquered Taxila. It was he who caused Roman gold to flow into his kingdom. In time the third ruler Kanishka would charge cess over the trade and fill the royal coffers with gold. In Kanishka's time, the Kushan kingdom expanded. Bordered by Iran on the west, to the north beyond the Pamir plateau, in the east by the confluence of the Yamuna and Chambal rivers and the Malva plateau in the south. It was under Kanishka that Buddhism acquired a new sect, and he built the Buddhist tower at Peshawar. 'Excavations at Mat near Mathura have disclosed a life-size statue of the great king.'[26] The language used in the Kushan empire was Bactrian from where the Kharosthi script evolved. Newly discovered sites of the Bactrian language are still opening up the secrets of the Kushan dynasty.[27]

Gandhara Art is one of the most valuable assets of Pakistan. It was the first fusion of European and Asian Art following the invasion of the Greeks; it also became the Art style associated with Buddhism—a universal religion. Due to the proselytizing efforts of Ashoka, Buddhism spread more in the Far East and South East Asia, but the territory traversing modern Pakistan and Afghanistan, became important centres as the now-destroyed Bamiyan statues show. New sites continue to be discovered.

An ancient city known as the city of Alexander, Bazira/Barikot in Swat is one such discovery. Dr Luca Maria Olivieri with his team discovered grand bastions, towers, walls, and amazing drain works at Bir-Kot-Ghwandai (Barikot). Another member Dr Michele Minardi said that as the top of Ghwandai Hill was strategically important, four main towers on the corners of the hillocks were built. On top of the tower was a huge water tank and other ancillary structures that were probably built in the Kushan period.[28] However, when the Greeks had re-fortified Bazira, they found a pre-existing structure dating to Maurya times, possibly during the reign of Ashoka.

Dr Olivieri discovered an apsidal Buddhist temple which attested to a new style of Gandhara architecture. Although Sirkap at Taxila has an apsidal. Olivieri terms the 4–meter-high temple at Bazira, the earliest such specimen.[29] Another landmark discovery was that of Fresco paintings dating to the first century. Six murals were discovered intact. The paintings are in different poses including the namaskar pose. Olivieri said that Swat and Gandhara were centres of an important painting school, whose traces have unfortunately faded away.[30]

The discovery of a cave in Kohistan has the potential of unlocking geological mysteries, but since the site was placed under guard immediately after discovery, details are expected to surface later.[31] Some statues, centuries old were discovered at the Thar Heritage site, Nagarparkar City Temple. Here instead of Buddhist, Jain antiquities were found—six statues representing Mahavira and the earlier Tirthankaras.[32]

The Kushan Empire was politically strong, economically rich, and culturally diverse, but it could not withstand the onslaught of the Sassanid dynasty of Persia. In the first year of his reign (AD 240) Shapur I captured Peshawar and extended his writ to the Khyber Pass. The death of Shapur I in AD 271 provided a brief respite, but when Shapur II came of age, the Kushans suffered a massive defeat. Neither the Persian reconquest nor the rise of the Guptas to the east, ended the misery of the Kushan Empire, for another people from Central Asia, the White Huns conquered the region in AD 465. They had a long rule, for the White Huns under Toramana were able to defeat the last of the Guptas. The tables were turned, when Toramana's son, Mihirakula was defeated by the ruler of Malwa, Yasodharman, forcing Mihirakula to seek refuge in Kashmir.

The Gupta dynasty was the first, if not the only paramount power in India to have been Hindu. Six centuries separated the Guptas from the Mauryas when a vibrant civilization flourished. By the time the Guptas came, Sanskrit had passed from common usage and had become the preserve of the priests. It is remarkable that a language which was revived produced masterpieces. Kalidasa embellished the Gupta Age and produced magna operas like *Shakuntala* and *Meghdoot*, which are world classics.

Chandragupta I, the founder of the dynasty was married to a princess of the Licchavi line, and from this position was able to secure his kingdom. His becoming the King of Kings thereafter was due only to his own ability. Although his reign was short, about six years, he extended his territories beyond the Ganges up to Allahabad. These conquests were carried forward by his son Samudragupta (AD 326–327) up to the mountains of Nepal in the north, and the Bay of Bengal in the east. He then turned south and west, taking Khandesh and Maharashtra. It was on his return from these conquests that Samudragupta performed the Ashvamedha, symbolising the revival of Hinduism.

Samudragupta, besides being a poet himself, gathered to his court men of talent and learning. His successor Chandragupta II (AD 375–413) passed into lore as the legendary Vikramaditya and gathered around him Nine Gems (*Navaratnas* or *Nauratan*), individuals embodying the talent and the genius of his age. His conquests took his territory forward to Gujarat from Maharashtra and secured for him the Kathiawar peninsula. Little has been recorded about the last two rulers. From the fact that Kumaragupta (AD 412–455) had held the horse sacrifice, it is deduced that he was militarily and politically, a powerful ruler. His son Skandagupta (AD 455-480) went down before the White Hun invasion.

Because the Gupta empire marked a state revival of Hinduism, its contribution to the flowering of South Asian culture has come in for criticism by revisionist historians. D.D. Kosambi is supported by Romila Thapar in his comment: 'Far from the Guptas reviving nationalism, it was nationalism which revived the Guptas.'[33] It remains unclear under what structure could nationalism make the Guptas its instrument. Moreover, this judgement presumes that nationalism was a force that was stronger than the rulers were. Even if this is so, then religion must be included as a vital ingredient of that nationalism. If this comment is supposed to mean that the Guptas acquired their role only retrospectively, it is an argument that cannot be seriously advanced, since the very fact that the Guptas passed into lore and legend, and were undoubtedly the patrons of great literature, their importance as a factor in the unfolding history of South Asia cannot be discounted.

According to the pattern of South Asian history, the upheaval caused by the inroads of the White Huns brought about a hiatus of fragmentation, before another paramount power, in the present case the empire of Harsha (aka Harshavardhana) could emerge. Harsha had inherited the kingdom of Thanesar which lay between the Sutlej and Yamuna. Rajyavardhana the elder brother of Harsha was killed by the Raja Devagupta of Malwa, who had abducted their sister Princess Rajyashri, after killing her husband Raja Grahavarman of Kannauj. The Raja Shashanka of Gauda who participated in the murder of Rajyavardhana was defeated and his kingdom was overrun. Harsha now became the Raja of Kannauj. The frontiers of the old Gupta empire were restored. Harsha was also a wise and benevolent administrator. Farmers were taxed, about one-sixth of the produce. There was a network of roads, and state-run rest houses, which provided food and medical aid to travellers. In the schools of the empire, both Brahmin and Buddhist teachers were employed.

Harsha was initially a worshipper of Shiva but later converted to Buddhism, yet his conversion brought about no intolerance. Harsha was advised by a Brahmin called Bana, also called Banabhatta, who wrote an account of his patron's reign *Harshacharita* (The Life of Harsha). Bana decried the cynical formulations of Kautilya in the *Arthashastra*. Harsha was himself a scholar and a litterateur. He has left a book of grammar and some plays, one of which *Nagananda* has been translated into English and won acclaim as a world classic. Harsha's empire, built on his personal efforts crumbled when he died at the age of 57.

It was while Harsha was ruling in India that Prophet Muhammad (PBUH) the Messenger of God, his progeny and companions, appeared in Arabia. By the time of Harsha's death, Muslim warriors had conquered Afghanistan.

Notes

1. The name 'Khyber Pakhtunkhwa' was brought into effect for the North-West Frontier Province in April 2010, following the passing of the 18th Constitutional Amendment.
2. Leslie Alcock, 'The Oldest Baluchistan', in *Crescent and Green: A Miscellany of Writings on Pakistan* (London, Cassell, 1955), p. 39.
3. Ibid., p. 44.
4. *Dawn*, Karachi, 14 July 2006.
5. Sir Mortimer Wheeler, 'Pakistan: Four Thousand Years Ago', in *Crescent and Green*, p. 21.
6. One of Faiz Ahmed Faiz's English masterpieces is titled, 'The Unicorn and the Dancing Girl'. In the 1960s Faiz wrote this script in blank verse for a short documentary on Moenjo Daro. It was never produced.
7. Romila Thapar, *Interpreting Early India* (New Delhi: Oxford University Press, 1992), p. 68; Ainslie T. Embree (ed.), *Sources of Indian Tradition* (New York: Columbia University Press, 1998), p. 8.
8. Embree, *Sources of Indian Tradition*, p. 8.
9. Ibid., p. 21.
10. Thapar, *Interpreting Early India*, p. 69.
11. Rajmohan Gandhi, *Mohandas* (New Delhi: Penguin/Viking, 2006), p. 581.
12. Ibid., p. 299.
13. The Far East is used to refer to all the countries of Eastern Asia, including China, Japan, North and South Korea, Myanmar, Thailand, Laos, Cambodia, Vietnam, and Malaysia.
14. A region including Brunei, Cambodia, East Timor, Indonesia, Laos, Malaysia, Myanmar, the Philippines, Singapore, Thailand, and Vietnam.
15. John E. Court, *Jains in the World* (New York: Oxford University Press, 2001), p. 18.
16. Ibid., p. 21.
17. Michel Clasquin-Johnson, 'Will the real Nigantha Nātaputta please stand up? Reflections on the Buddha and his contemporaries', *Journal for the Study of Religion* 28(1) (2015), pp. 100–114.
18. Richard S. Cohen, 'Shakyamuni: Buddhism's Founder in Ten Acts', in *The Rivers of Paradise: Moses, Buddha, Confucius, Jesus, and Muhammad as Religious Founders*, (eds.) David Noel Freedman and Michael J. McClymond (Grand Rapids, MI: Wm. B. Eerdmans Publishing Company, 2000), p. 133.
19. Embree, *Sources of Indian Tradition*, p. 155.
20. Ibid.
21. Ibid., p. 175.
22. Hemchandra Raychaudhuri, *Political History of Ancient India: From the Accession of Parikshit to the Extinction of the Gupta Dynasty* (New Delhi: Oxford University Press, 2006), p. 169; (Calcutta, 1923).
23. Romila Thapar, *Cultural Pasts: Essays in Early Indian History* (New Delhi: Oxford University Press, 2000), p. 423.
24. Tamara Talbot Rice, *Ancient Arts of Central Asia* (New York and Washington DC: Frederick A. Praeger, 1965), p. 138.
25. Mahmood Zaman, 'Badalpur', *Dawn Gallery*, Karachi, 4 November 2006.
26. H.C. Ray Chaudhuri, op. cit., p. 421.
27. B.N. Mukherjee, Commentary on ibid., p. 717.
28. *Dawn*, 19 November 2021, p. 8.
29. *Dawn*, 20 December 2021, p. 4.
30. *Dawn*, 8 February 2021, p. 9.
31. *Dawn*, 1 June 2021, p. 5.
32. *Dawn*, 10 April 2021, p. 3.
33. Romila Thapar, *History and Beyond* (New Delhi, Oxford University Press, 2000), p. 108.

Pre-Historic Partition

It has been sometimes asserted that the territories west and east of the Indus have always constituted two countries and that the religious divide of 1947 was merely incidental. In the preamble, it has been identified that the geographical forces of both unity and diversity, from which it follows that diversity by itself, is not proof of nationhood. The theory that the Indus has been an international frontier has been attributed to Kaniz Fatima Yousuf and Syed Qudratullah Fatimi but developed into a treatise by Aitzaz Ahsan. This author, a celebrity, disarms readers at the outset by saying that he has not examined all trends, nor analysed every historical event or fact. Such a candid and courteous entrant is deserving of full attention, and, if in the process test, not a hypothesis by random sampling, but to determine the universe itself, the contention is well worth probing. Aitzaz Ahsan argues that the *Ramayana* and the *Mahabharata* overlapped. The earliest hymns of the Vedas were composed *c*.1400 BC. The Rig Veda itself from 1500 to 1200 BC. The *Mahabharata* was composed around 900 BC. The *Arthaveda* came later, between 900 to 500 BC. There is no evidence as to where the Vedas were composed. Since they were not composed together in time, the greater probability is that they were not composed together in space (Ahsan, 1996, p. iv). Similarly, to depict the overshadowing of Indra by Krishna as graduating from pastoral life to agrarian production (Ahsan, 1996, p. 43) is most arbitrary. The very size of the granaries in the citadels indicates that the Indus civilization was agrarian. Aitzaz Ahsan himself concedes: 'The Arabs had very little agriculture; Indus had (it seems) never been without it' (Ahsan, 1996, p. 91).

As compared to the east-west difference, the north-south differences are sharper: music and linguistics have different modes; different voice scales. Reportedly, their interpretation of the *Ramayana* also differs. The evidence for the Indus man is slighter than the Indus land. Defiance of imperial authority is not a localized trait; no essential difference exists between Dulla Bhatti and Mangal Pandey.

Note

1. Aitzaz Ahsan, *The Indus Saga and the Making of Pakistan* (Karachi: Oxford University Press, 1996), pp. 11, 12.

Chapter 1
Muslim Society in South Asia

The Arabs came to India as traders long before they came as invaders. Arab seafaring brought traders and even settlers to the west coast of India. It was a one-sided process. Indians could not go to Arabia, for if they crossed the sea, they would lose their caste. Some Indians were forcibly taken to Iraq by the Sassanid rulers of Iran but, this cannot count as a trend. The Coromandel Coast was called 'Ma'bar' by the Arabs, which means 'crossing'. These Arabs established colonies on the west coast of India. When Arabs converted to Islam, these colonies became the outposts of Islam in India. At first, there was little resistance to the Arab settlers. Pandya kings employed Muslims as ministers and ambassadors. Thus, some Muslims were given more importance than Buddhists or Jains.

CONQUEST.—A change in relations came about because of the Arab invasion of Sindh and Multan in AD 711. Even then a complete change in relations seems not to have taken place. The Labbai/Labbay, a west Indian Muslim tribe, claimed to be the descendants of the Hashemites who sought refuge here from Hajjaj bin Yusuf, who, as the eastern viceroy of the caliph, organized the invasion of Sindh.

The Arab invasion of Sindh was not an isolated event; it was part of a wave of conquests which included Spain and Central Asia. The reasons for the invasion of Sindh must be seen within this framework. According to sources, it is quite possible that pirates off the coast of Makran invited the wrath of Hajjaj by kidnapping and looting passengers on their way to Basra from Lanka. It is more probable that Raja Dahir, the ruler of Sindh, was right in pleading that the pirates were beyond his jurisdiction and that he could not be held responsible for their crimes. It is also true that, after the conquest of Sindh, no chastisement of the pirates seems to have occurred. The conquest of Sindh proved to be a momentous event. It is not surprising, therefore, that Hajjaj bin Yusuf, who is considered a villain by the chroniclers of Islamic history, has been portrayed as a hero in Indo-Muslim history.

The image of Mohammad bin Qasim, the conqueror, is different. He is rightly regarded as a hero because he was victorious, whereas his two predecessors, Budail/Bazil and Ubaidullah, battle-worn veterans, were defeated and killed. Mohammad bin Qasim was a youth of 17. His skill, his courage, and his boldness in psychological warfare (such as bringing down the red flag at Debal) all combined to make him a hero. In addition, the imprisonment and execution of this conqueror by his own people, and his evocative poem written in prison made him a legend. Mohammad bin Qasim's execution, like his conquest, was part of a general policy exercised by a caliph and not directed against an individual. All the conquerors under Walid I—Musa bin Nusayr, Tariq bin Ziyad (Spain) Qutaybah bin Muslim (Central Asia) and Mohammad bin Qasim (Sindh)—were punished by his successor, Suleiman.

In time, small Arab kingdoms arose in Sindh and became part of the fragmented entity that India was, when Jaipal, the Hindu Shahi ruler of Kabul and Waihind (near Peshawar), made a pre-emptive attack on the domain of Pirai (or Böritigin), the ruler of Ghazni, setting-off the second series of Muslim conquests led by Sultan Mahmud. Almost two centuries later, Sultan Moizuddin Ghuri and his lieutenants, Qutbuddin Aibak and Ikhtiaruddin Khalji, conquered north India as far as Bengal. Sultan Alauddin Khalji carried Muslim arms to south India in 1296, and two centuries later Babur, the Timurid prince, invaded India to establish the Mughal dynasty. These conquests had long-lasting social consequences. The invasions of Timur, Nadir Shah, and Ahmad Shah Abdali remained intrusions and were regarded as catastrophes by both Hindus and Muslims.

CONVERSION.—The Muslims ruled over the whole of India, but a Muslim majority emerged only in the north-west and north-east; the rest of the country retained its Hindu majority. The question is why Islam spread more in certain parts of India than in others. Many reasons have been advanced to explain this phenomenon. Many reasons have also been advanced to explain why Hindus converted to Islam. The commonly advanced reason is that since Islam is an egalitarian religion, Hindus of the lower castes converted to Islam to escape from the tyranny and humiliation shown to them by higher caste Hindus.

This simple explanation does not consider all the factors. If it were merely a question of escaping the caste system, then Buddhism was at hand. Buddhism was an Indian religion that had challenged the caste system, and the Arabs had liberated Buddhists, so Hindus adopting Buddhism could freely adhere to their creed with a minimum adjustment in theology; Buddha had already been hailed as an avatar of Vishnu. The reasons for the quick spread of Islam west of the Indus and to a lesser extent east of the Indus are many and complex. Richard M. Eaton, who has advanced new explanations for the conversions, admits, 'Clearly, this is a complex phenomenon involving a number of distinguishable processes, some which did not concern conversion at all'.[1]

Who was responsible for the spread of Islam and the assimilation of local elements into its fold, is a debatable issue. Therefore, we must examine the clues that history provides us. There are examples to show that Hindus adopted Islam when the choice was free. Tara Chand relates, on the authority of Vincent, that there were so many Arabs on the Malabar Coast that the people had adopted the Arab religion (probably Sabean). Now whether Arab settlers followed the Sabean or the Pagan religion, the very fact that Indians were receptive to a foreign religion without coercion, is a factor that must be taken into account. When the Arabs themselves converted to Islam, there is every likelihood that the Indians, who had embraced the earlier religion of the Arabs, also embraced Islam.

Sabeans are star worshippers; pagans are idol worshippers who have a closer affinity with the Hindus. The Hindus who converted to Islam could have, instead, followed the more sophisticated idol worship of the Hindus, as had the reconverts from Buddhism. Richard M. Eaton argues: 'A glance at the geographical distribution of Muslims in the subcontinent reveals an inverse relationship between the degree of Muslim political penetration and the degree of conversion to Islam... those regions of the most dramatic conversion of the population, such as eastern Bengal or western Punjab lay on the fringes of Indo-Muslim rule, whereas the heartland of the rule, the upper Gangetic Plain, saw a much lower incidence of conversion.'[2]

Dismissing outright the contention that conversion was forcible, Eaton ascribes it to the influence of living *qazis* and buried saints, arguing that the shrines of the saints who had died, exercised a greater hold on the population than a living saint.

There is much to support Eaton's contention. The sultan could vanquish the raja, but he could not vanquish the *sadhu*. To meet the Indian people at the spiritual level, a Sufi was needed. As we shall see, Khwaja Moinuddin Chishti could enter the domain of Prithviraj Chauhan before Moizuddin Ghuri. Then again, we may challenge Eaton's contention with regard to western Punjab because of its proximity to North-West Frontier and Balochistan, where migration and not conversion had created a Muslim majority; but we cannot challenge it with regard to East Bengal.

The sword of the sultan was double-edged. It created the political space for conversion and simultaneously created ill-will among the Hindus, not a sentiment inducive to a change of religion. Richard Eaton has further argued that Muslim rulers desecrated only royal temples and idols as a form of political vengeance and did not desecrate the temples of the Hindu commoner.[3] It is doubtful whether the Hindus of the Sultanate period could distinguish between political and religious motives. It is true however that the Delhi sultans resisted the fanatical urgings of the ulama to at least humiliate Hindus if they could not kill them.

These urgings were clearly against the injunctions of Islam. The ulama who did not understand this were temperamentally incapable of spreading Islam. Recently, even some Western historians have drawn attention to the following verses of the Holy Quran: 'There is no compulsion in religion' (2:256); 'Had your Lord willed, all the people on earth would have believed. So can you [Prophet] compel people to believe?' (10:99)

ASSIMILATION.—Assimilation took the shape of Hindus and Muslims borrowing from each other's festivals and rituals. This took place even though intermarriage and interdining were taboo. Even now in Pakistan, except for the *nikah*, marriage rituals like wearing a headdress called *sehra* and playing music are of Hindu origin; by and large Muslims borrowed rituals and customs, while Hindus borrowed from the creed.

Notes

1. Richard M. Eaton, 'Approaches to the Study of Conversion to Islam in India', in *Approaches to Islam in Religious Studies*, (ed.) Richard C. Martin (Tucson: University of Arizona Press, 1985), p. 122.
2. Ibid., pp. 107–8.
3. Richard M. Eaton, *Essays on Islam and Indian History* (New Delhi: Oxford University Press, 2000), p. 110 ff.

Chapter 2
A Comparison of Muslim and Hindu Society

Hindu society and Muslim society were different in many ways, but in one respect they were similar. Both had their value system grounded in religion, and both believed that their respective religions, Hinduism and Islam, were a complete code of life, not merely a set of rituals.

Hindus were governed by their religion in two ways. First, Hindu society was structured on the basis of castes. Second, the lifespan of a Hindu has traditionally been divided into four stages. At each stage, he engages in activities appropriate to his age: **Brahmacharya.** The life of a student is marked by learning, discipline, obedience, and celibacy. **Grihastha.** Earn a living for himself, marry, start a family, sustain one's dependents; and fulfil other religious and social responsibilities. **Vanaprastha.** The period of gradual withdrawal from worldly obligations. Pursue activities like studying of scriptures, going on pilgrimages, doing selfless service etc. **Sanyasa.** The period in which one must renounce all his material possessions; and devote himself fully to the realisation of the self.

Some traits of Hindu society became ingrained after a long evolution, particularly those regarding women. Child marriage came to be favoured, monogamy was generally practised, and remarriage for widows was forbidden, as Sati, the burning of wives on the funeral pyres of their husbands, was considered meritorious. Vegetarianism was practised, most probably due to the influence of the Jains and Buddhists since Ashoka had banned eating the flesh of animals.

The Hindus became vegetarians, and venerated cows as a symbol of Mother. This difference became the main cause of conflict between Hindus and Muslims, as Muslims were meat eaters and heartily relished beef.

The Muslims belonged to different racial backgrounds; they were descendants of the conquerors, the Arabs, the Turco-Afghans, and the Mughals. Others were converts or descendants of people who had converted to Islam from Hinduism. Islam prescribed an egalitarian social order in which piety, and not descent, would be the standard of excellence and closeness to God. This provided for greater social mobility than in Hinduism. A low-caste Muslim could attain the highest office. This was witnessed when, following the Ghurid invasion a number of slaves ascended the throne in Delhi. It needs to be emphasized however that Muslim society was not absolutely egalitarian and there were class differences. There was one great difference. The Hindu caste system was prescribed by religion, whereas class consciousness among Muslims in India was not. This was the reason that, although social barriers existed among Muslims, they could be surmounted, whereas in Hindu society the caste system could not.

> **THE FOUR MAJOR HINDU CASTES**
>
> 1. Brahmin: The priest class
> 2. Kshatriya: The warrior class
> 3. Vaishya: The merchant class
> 4. Shudra: The menial class
>
> The caste system evolved over time. The Brahmins and Kshatriyas contested each other's claim to be the highest caste. Caste was determined by profession. Once a family adopted a profession it was confined to it for all time to come. Castes were also determined on the basis of Varna, that is colour, and there were many sub-castes also. There were differences on the basis of creeds, for example between those who gave greater regard to Vishnu or to Shiva, but this difference did not create fissures in Hindu society.

The Hindus were polytheists—worshippers of many gods. It is true that polytheism was interpreted by various savants at different levels. Not only some Hindus, but a Muslim like Amir Khusro defended some features of the Hindu creed. Moreover, Hindus were idol worshippers. This led to a head-on clash between the Muslims and the Hindus after Mohammad bin Qasim brought down the red flag over the temple of Debal.

Jainism and Buddhism had defied Hinduism, especially the caste system, but after a protracted military and spiritual struggle, Jainism practically became a Hindu sect and Buddhism, while it spread over a vast expanse of Asia, became almost obliterated from India—the country of its origin. Hindus conceded that Gautama Buddha was an avatar of Vishnu, and by this means Buddhists were assimilated back into the fold of Hinduism. Such assimilation for the Muslims seemed impossible due to their belief. It was in this light that K.M. Panikkar made his now famous observation that the Muslims brought about a vertical division in Indian society.[1] Previously, Indian society had been divided horizontally on the basis of caste.

When two societies are so different, it is difficult for one to influence the other. It must be recognised at the outset that the impact of Islam on Hindu society was limited in scope. As Tara Chand has said: 'The new ruler was master of the immediate lands, within striking distance of his cavalry encampment; the petty landholder with his retinue was safe within his mud castle and defied the sovereign power.'[2]

In other words, as Muneera Haeri also says, 'Muslim rule was centred around the cities. Hindus were concentrated in the villages and remote areas.'[3] This is the reason why, except for a change in the language, Hindu society re-emerged almost intact, when Muslim rule showed the first sign of decline.

Nevertheless, Hindus and Muslims shared the same land and inevitably there were some areas, especially in the cultural sphere, where Muslims were able to influence Hindu society. This influence was spread over a long period of time and confined to certain aspects of life but on the whole, it culminated in transforming Hindu society.

MUSIC.—Of all the arts, it was in music that Hindus and Muslims had the greatest compatibility. True, their approach was different. For Hindus, music was a sacred art to be performed in temples. Barring the devotional music of the Sufis, Muslims had a secular approach to music. According to Dr Acharya K.C.D. Brahaspati, a well-known musician and musicologist, the *Hindu Gram Moorchana Paduti* gave way to the *Muqam* music of Irani origin. This transition was smooth due to the fact that both Indian and Middle Eastern music were influenced by Hellenic music. Lal Khan Bakhshi has given a very long list of Middle Eastern and Indian compositions which were adopted into the raga form. A short list of Middle Eastern and Indian airs is given below:

	MIDDLE EASTERN AIRS	INDIAN/HINDUSTANI AIRS
1.	Shuba-e-Mukhalif	Ramkali
2.	Eraq	Bhairav
3.	Qandhari Eraq	Malkauns
4.	Nishapur Nihawand	Bilawal
5.	Zangula Chahargah	Asawari
6.	Nawa	Jaijaiwanti
7.	Saghir	Aiman Kalyan

The Muslim contribution to Hindu music was personified in the figure of Amir Khusro (1253–1325) who is credited with creating a new system of musicology called 'Indraprastha Mata' or 'Chaturdandi Sampradaya'. Khusro composed new ragas grafting them on ancient *thaats*, the master melodies on which ragas are based, such as Aiman on Kalyan. Khusro was hailed as a Nayak, one proficient in the theory and practice of present and past music. He contributed equally to the evolution of folk music and qawwali, devotional Sufi music. He is also credited with inventing, among other instruments, the sitar. Amir Khusro was a great poet in Persian, but for his folk and devotional music, he used the local language.

The next major figure in the development of classical music was Husain Shah Sharqi (1458–1505) the last ruler of Jaunpur. He composed ragas including Gaud Shyam, Husaini Todi, Jaunpuri, and Asawari, among a host of others. According to Abdul Halim, Sultan Husain Sharqi's greatest innovation was the evolution of Khayal in which the ascension and dissension of the raga is less gradual. To bring about an alternative to the ancient and stately Dhrupad mode could be best effected by a Muslim and a ruler. Khayal was less rigid and more lively, the result of taking classical music away from the confines of the temple.

The flowering of music took place under Akbar (1556–1605) the great Mughal emperor. His court musician Mian Tansen was hailed by Abul Fazl as the greatest musician in a thousand years. He is credited with the composition of Mian ki Todi, Mian ki Malhar, Darbari Kangra, and a host of ragas. Tansen was a great vocalist but the pandits hailed him only as a Gandharv, one proficient in the practice, but not the theory of music. Tansen was a disciple of Sheikh Ghous Gwaliori, and his elder contemporary, the shadowy Baiju Bawra, was the disciple of Sheikh Adnan Jaunpuri. His compositions include Megh Malhar and Gaud Sarang. Baiju Bawra, like Khusro, was hailed as a Nayak.

Music received patronage from the Mughals, but a further loosening of classical norms took place in the court of Awadh, where Thumri and Dadra, the faster forms of music evolved. Thumri is a shorter form with inflections and arias figuring more frequently than in Khayal. Dadra was still more lively and faster mode. A single raga, for example, Bhairavi, can be sung in the form of Dhrupad, Khayal, Thumri, or Dadra. The composition does not change, the beat, the inflections, and the frequency of notes mark the change.

PAINTING.—Hindu painting is seen at its best in the Ajanta caves. These wall paintings are a mixture of frescos and tempera and cover all the major themes, both religious and secular, of ancient India. The Muslim contribution was mostly miniatures, small-scale paintings on paper, to fill either folios or to illustrate books. There is literary evidence that Hindus painted miniatures and Muslims of the Sultanate period produced wall paintings, but the evidence has not survived. It is to be noted that on the basis of surviving specimens, the evolution of Hindu art and Muslim art was largely based on murals and miniatures respectively.

However, there was one conceptual difference which can be asserted: in ancient India, Shankar Acharya ruled that portraits should conform to traditional norms, and to render faithfully human features was wrong in principle.[4] Under the Mughals, faithful rendering became a requirement. Although Hindus had separate myths from Muslims, both drew upon them, but here also there was a difference between the religious and secular approach, and once they had done with illustrating the *Dastan-i-Amir Hamza* under Akbar, the Mughals, especially under Jehangir, forced painting towards authentic representation in order to preserve scenes for their pleasure as well as for their value as records.

In painting, Muslim influence came about through cooperation. Hindus and Muslims were employed by the same patron to illustrate the same manuscript. Later, again under Jehangir, a single illustration would be painted by different artists; one was responsible for tracing the outline, another would apply the colour, the third would shade the drapes, a fourth the background, another would design the margin and yet another would do the calligraphy. Persian calligraphy was more flowing and cursive than the Nagri/Nagari script, which was angular and in blocks, and therefore did not integrate with the flow of the brush like the Nastaliq Persian script.

The specialists, according to their flair, were trained in each aspect of art. Daswanth, schooled under Abdus Samad, was the earliest artist to gain prominence. Other Hindu artists of natural talent followed, and it is no wonder that, when the Rajput school of painting emerged, it was heavily influenced by the Mughals. The Mughal emperors had portraits painted of their Rajput grandees such as Man Singh, and this further eased the transition. Compared to music, Muslim influence in painting came rather late, and both the Bazar Mughal and the later degenerated and vulgar versions, were overtaken by the influence the British came to exercise over both Hindu and Muslim painters. Since influence came through cooperation, Muslim artists also painted Hindu themes, most notably Abdur Rahman Chughtai who, before he illustrated the poetry of Ghalib and Iqbal, had painted scenes from Hindu mythology.

ARCHITECTURE.—In architecture, unlike in art, there was no close collaboration. Muslims architects appropriated pillars from Hindu monuments while the lower strata of masons were Hindus. Unlike in painting, Hindus were not entrusted with design or planning.

Architecture is governed by the purpose or function of a monument, the building material available, and the climate of the region. Tara Chand characterizes Muslim architecture as conditioned by vast deserts, and Hindu architecture as conditioned by lush and green plains.[5] This is borne out by the fact that except for in the arid areas of Sindh and Balochistan, the glazed tiles used by Muslims in Iran and Central Asia could not flourish in the Indian plains.

Mosques and temples were not entirely different. Both had open courts surrounded by colonnades or chambers (although this is truer of Jain than Hindu temples). The main difference was that temples had dim chambers and sparsely lit passages, while mosques were characterised by clarity and openness to light and air. The most visible difference was that temples had pyramidical spires with a small dome on top, which was either circular or polygonal. Mosques had domes standing on squinches, devices necessary to place round structures on a square base.

Tara Chand has summarised the mutual influence of Hindu–Muslim architecture by saying that 'the simple severity of the Muslim architecture was toned down and the plastic exuberance of the Hindu architecture was restrained'.[6]

The monument he uses to illustrate Muslim influence is the Kantanagar Temple built in Bengal between 1704 and 1722: 'It has three storeys and above the third rises the central tower with its pyramidical spire. The first two storeys have four octagonal towers at the corner'. This has a distinct resemblance to mosques in India. 'The whole surface is covered with terracotta, but no figure sculpture is seen anywhere.' Divesting any part of a temple of sculpted figures is due solely to Muslim influence.

Since Hindus do not bury their dead, the appearance of Hindu mausolea in the 17th century is another manifestation of Muslim influence. The mausoleum of Bir Singh Dev/Deo at Orchha is typical: A large square block with two massive towers and a dome. The facade has three arches in the middle with no sculpture or decoration. In other words, the Muslims had an impact on Hindu architecture at the height of their power, but Muslim influence was limited in scope.

LITERATURE.—The Muslim influence on Hindu literature was again the result of intermingling. Ever since Amir Khusro had composed poetry in both Persian and the early Hindi of his times, this tendency had been marked. Thus, Abdur Rahim Khan-i-Khanan is seen as a great poet of Hindi, and Chandra Bhan Brahman as an important poet of Persian. Muslim rulers patronized local languages. Dinesh Chandra Sen says that if the Hindu kings had continued to enjoy influence, Bengali would never have become a court language. This could be true of other regional languages also.

BHAKTI MOVEMENT.—By noting that Islam and Hinduism were poles apart and that the assimilation of Islam by the Hindu religion was not possible, it is now necessary to inquire whether or not, in the development of Hindu sects under Muslim rule, Islamic concepts played any role, and if so, whether that role was extensive or limited. Tara Chand asserts that Siddharis and Virashaivas were largely influenced by Islam. This may be true, but the influence of Islam seems neither to have been conscious nor pervasive. There is the example of Lingayats, a sect founded by Basava which worshipped one god (Parashiva or Paramshiva). Lingayats had many practices similar to those of Islam, for example, they believed that a bride's consent was imperative for marriage, child marriage was considered wrong, and the remarriage of widows was allowed. They practised burial, not cremation.

On the other hand, Lingayats were emphatic that there should be no sacrifice, no fasts, no feasts, and no pilgrimage, all of which are essential to the practice of Islam. Lingayat beliefs had a mystical bias since they considered love as the first creation of God.

It is from this belief that it is possible to trace the origin of Bhakti to the Bhagavad Gita where it is mentioned as a major path to salvation. Bhakti means faithful devotion. Later, another leader, Ramanuja, ($c.$1025–1137) defined Bhakti as intense long meditation and devotion to God. As Stanley Wolpert states, 'the central tenet of Bhakti became love of God.' It is at this point that reformist Hinduism and mystical Islam meet, for the Sufi calls love for God the real love and love for creatures, temporal love. Another resemblance is in the concept of monism, Hama Oost, 'Everything is He', or the doctrine of Wahdat-ul-Wajood—monism—or unity of existence. We know the Muslim shades of this concept, let us now see it in the creed of Shankara ($c.$780–820). 'God was one and there was no other besides him. God was the only reality, all else was illusion. He was without attributes or qualities. He was not a thinking or knowing being, but thought or knowledge itself.'

Why Bhakti first appeared in the south is not clear. It could be because Muslim conquest was more recent there or because Islam had not penetrated as deep in the south as it had in the north of India. Whatever the cause, there were sincere seekers after truth, and they went beyond Hindu orthodoxy towards Hindu mysticism.

The love of God is a sentiment, and the most powerful outlet of sentiment is poetry. In poetry, Muslims tolerate and even enjoy sayings which do not conform to belief. It was quite natural then that the most celebrated exponent of the Bhakti movement was a poet called Kabir Das (c.1425–1492).

Kabir was first a disciple of Swami Ramananda, who brought the message of Ramanuja to north India, Kabir was a disciple subsequently of Muslim Sufis, beginning with Shaikh Taqi of Manikpur. In his Dohas or Hindi couplets, Kabir preached the importance of love and decried formal and ritualistic creeds. Kabir did not recognize either caste or the four divisions of life as prescribed by Hinduism and refused to recognize the six schools of Hindu philosophy. Kabir refused to consider those aspects of Muslim and Hindu religions which were opposed to each other. Bhakti, or love, was the overriding essence of religion. When he preached at Benares (now Varanasi), he offended both Hindus and Muslims, but when he died at Maghar, both Hindus and Muslims claimed his body.

Notes

1. K.M. Panikkar, *A Survey of Indian History* (Bombay: National Information and Publications, 1947), p. 286.
2. Tara Chand, *Influence of Islam on Indian Culture* (Allahabad: The Indian Press, 1946), p. 136.
3. Muneera Haeri, *The Chishtis* (Karachi: Oxford University Press, 2000), p. 29.
4. Ghulam Abbas Moulvi, *Hindustani Musavvari Ka Irtiqa* (Urdu) (Bombay: Published by the author, 1942), p. 10.
5. Tara Chand, op. cit., p. 240.
6. Ibid., p. 243.

AMIR KHUSRO (b. Patiyali, 1253–d. Delhi, 1325) was a disciple of a saint and the courtier of five kings. He excelled in Indian music and Persian poetry—the most admired accomplishments of the Hindu and Muslim nobility. His mysticism engendered an eclectic outlook. He marked the coming of age of a distinct Indo-Muslim culture; and personified as no other genius did, the spirit of his age.

Orphaned at a tender age, Amir Khusro came under the care of his maternal grandfather. He saw his grandfather apportion a corner of his house to a then unknown and penurious mystic, who would later become a centre of attraction under the name of Shaikh Nizamuddin Auliya (1244–1325). The young boy, himself a dependent, saw his maternal uncle expel the mystic.[1] Amir Khusro's veneration for Nizamuddin Auliya became the hallmark of his life; and the inspiration for both his poetry and music. Amir Khusro dedicated his music to the mystic, just as he dedicated his poems to the kings who patronized him.

In 1280, Prince Muhammad, the son of Sultan Ghiyasuddin Balban, invited Amir Khusro and Amir Hasan Sijzi (both poets, both friends and both devotees of Nizamuddin Auliya) to his court. Prince Muhammad manned the outpost against the Mongol menace, and in the course of an invasion, in 1285, laid down his life. Amir Khusro poured out his heart while composing the elegy of the Martyred Prince, and the bereaved Sultan found the elegy to be an expression of his own grief and frittered his stern and austere life away. From then on, Khusro's presence at the court of Delhi was assured.

Khusro not only became the poet laureate but also the court historian. He wrote one account, *Khazain ul Futuh* (1312) in prose, but all others were in verse. A commissioned work was *Qiran us Sa'dain* (1288) which described the meeting between Sultan Moizuddin Kayqubad and his father, Bughra Khan, the Governor of Bengal. *Deval Rani/Khizar Khan* (1320) was completed after the couple's deposition; hence, it remained not only a romantic tale but also became a social commentary. *Tughluq Nama* (1324) describes the foul murders of the children of the Khaliji household by the usurper, Khusro Khan. Unfortunately, this mature product of his poetic genius fell into comparative oblivion, and hence could not influence forcefully the Indian style (*Sabk-i-Hindi*). This mode was ascribed to Khusro's predecessor, Masud Sa'd Salman (d.1121) and came to be characterized by conceits, involved expressions, metaphors, and unnecessary ornamentation.

According to the eminent literary critic, Syed Mumtaz Husain, Khusro provided a stylistic bridge between the two Shiraz luminaries, Sa'di and Hafiz.

Hailed as a Nayak of classical music, Amir Khusro created a new system of musicology called 'Indraprastha Mata' or 'Chaturdandi Sampradaya', as well as grave and deep *ragas* like Shudh Bilawal, Shudh Kalyan, and Aiman Kalyan. His contribution extended to devotional music, like *qawwali*, as well as folk music, which contained his proto-Hindi lyrics. Today, all three types retain their popularity. A number of musical instruments are said to be his inventions, notably, the sitar. A great deal of this information is shrouded in legend, but Zoe Ansari has discovered an anonymous manuscript, titled *Ghunyat ul Mayna* (1375), which apart from being an expository text, contains illustrations of the musical instruments played in the age of Khusro.[2]

Being a courtier of both Sultan and Saint was a trait that could be reconciled only by a genius of his calibre. In *Nuh Sipihr* (1315), the masterpiece dedicated to Qutbuddin Mubarak Shah, Amir Khusro includes verses praising Nizamuddin Auliya, knowing fully well that his royal patron disliked his spiritual mentor. Khusro approached the Hindu creed sympathetically, even trying to reconcile idolatry with monotheism. Only the Mongols who killed his favourite prince, and had held him captive, aroused the satirist in him. Amir Khusro did not simply reflect the virtues of his age; he contributed to each of them.

Notes

1. Khaliq Ahmad Nizami, *The Life and Times of Shaikh Nizam-U'D-Din Auliya* (New Delhi: Oxford University Press, 2007), pp. 28 and 29.
2. Zoe Ansari, *Khusro ka Zehni Safar* (New Delhi: Anjuman Taraqqi-i-Urdu, 1988/1977), p. 88.

Chapter 3
The Role of the Ulama and the Sufis

Islam is both a spiritual and a social religion. The ulama are the guardians of the Law—the Sharia. The Sufis showed more concern for the spiritual side of Islam. In early Islamic history, there was no distinction between the state and the church, and the ruler himself was the guardian of the law. However, by the time Muslim rule was established in India, the Sultan appointed a Shaikhul Islam, usually a renowned *alim* or scholar, who was given charge of the religious affairs of the kingdom.

> **The Origin of Ulama**
>
> Ulama is the plural of *alim*, the Arabic word for religious scholar. Every Muslim is expected to know the law and act accordingly. However, even in early Islam, Companions of the Holy Prophet (PBUH) were appointed Imams to lead the prayers, and as Qazis or judges to rule according to the Shariah. As specialization took hold, religious functionaries became distinct in society. The emergence of ulama as a class has a sanction in the following verse of the Holy Quran: 'Yet it is not right for all the believers to go out [to battle] together: out of each community, a group should go out to gain [an] understanding of the religion, so that they can teach their people when they return and so that they can guard themselves against evil.' (9:122).

The Sufi was not connected with the court but was the centre of his devotees. This was his distinctive feature. In Sufism (Islamic mysticism) the role of the Shaikh, or spiritual guide was vital. Since the Shaikh was expected to intercede with God on behalf of his followers, therefore, obedience to one's Shaikh is most heavily prescribed in Sufism. The chain connecting the Shaikh with his disciples is called a *silsila* or order.

What distinguishes the Sufi from the Alim is the former's belief in the doctrine of *Wahdat-ul-Wujood*, monism, or the unity of creation. According to this set of beliefs, nothing exists apart from God. It follows, therefore, that all that exists *is* God. Since man obviously cannot be God, some Sufis hold that the existence of human beings was unreal—an illusion—*maya*.

Muslim Revivalism was complicated by this factor: the reformers who defied kings and struggled for the restoration of orthodoxy were ideologically Sufis. This is further elaborated in the section on Mujaddid Alf Thani.

> **THE ORIGIN OF SUFIS**
>
> The word Sufi is derived from *safa*, meaning purity in Arabic. Sufis are mystics who aim for a closer union with God. A dimension to this desire was added when they subscribed to the doctrine of monism, called *Wahdat-ul-Wujood*. The term *Wahdat-ul-Wujood* was coined by Sadruddin Qunavi to describe his teacher Ibn Arabi's theory written in Arabic—*Hama Oost* in Persian. This doctrine is explained in the main text. If all is God, then the union of man's soul with God becomes desirable and attainable. However, monism is a later development. The earliest historical figure to be identified as a Sufi was Hasan al Basri (d. AD 728) reputedly a disciple of the Imam and Caliph Ali bin Abi Talib. It was the figure of Ali which encouraged Sufis to be called *wali* (plural *awlia*). As a consequence, Sufis and disciples could invoke the verses of the Holy Quran in which this term was used. Although the term has greater meaning, it is sometimes translated as 'friend'. Thus *waliullah* would be translated in this verse as: 'But for those who are on God's side there is no fear, nor shall they grieve.' (10:62). Sufis practised what was almost asceticism, living the lives of hermits and founding *khanqah*s or monasteries where their disciples gathered and spread their message. This lifestyle had a particular appeal for Hindus, who were drawn to the Sufis. Sufi saints allowed *sama* or devotional music which induced ecstasy.

Data Ganj Bakhsh (Syed Ali Hujveri, b. Ghazni, *c*. AD 1007–d. Lahore AD 1072) was the first spiritual guide to leave an impression on north India. He came to Lahore from Ghazni with Sultan Masud. Previously he had visited Sultan Mahmud's court infrequently, most probably to participate in religious polemics. He had to leave his books behind in Ghazni, but once he arrived in Lahore (*c*.1039), he proved to be a source of spiritual eminence. He is said to have converted Rai Raju and his companions to Islam and gradually expanded his circle to include more devotees. His book, *Kashful Mahjub*, which is in circulation even today, is the only source which gives the list of the Data's books (which did not survive) and the authentic details of his life. As Qazi Javed has noted, '*Kashful Mahjub* is not a Sufi book usually and commonly written, but a treatise which represents a complete mystical system of thought'.[1]

Data Ganj Bakhsh did not favour neglecting the demands of orthodoxy and observance of compulsory prayers and fasting, although he preferred the attainment of internal bliss to compliance with formal obligations.

During the lifetime of Data Ganj Bakhsh, Lahore was a small town in comparison to Multan. It was due to the spiritual grace provided by Data Ganj Bakhsh that Lahore grew in importance. Although he lived in seclusion, Data Ganj Bakhsh was the first Sufi to have a formative influence on Indo-Muslim society.

Khwaja Gharib Nawaz (Syed Muinuddin Ajmeri, b. Chisht, AD 1141–d. Ajmer AD 1236) hailed from Sanjaristan in Seistan, became the disciple of Hazrat Uthman Haruni and received spiritual favours from Ibrahim Qalandar. He was orphaned at an early age and, impressed by the spiritual powers of Ibrahim Qalandar, gave up all his property. He performed the pilgrimage to Makkah and Madinah. Some historians, notably Juzjani, say that he entered Ajmer as a soldier in the army of Sultan Moizuddin Ghuri. Chishti sources say that he preceded the Ghurid army and settled in Ajmer.

He is said to have converted 700 Hindus to Islam in Delhi before settling down in Ajmer. According to the Khwaja, love was the guiding principle behind creation, and he gave precedence to acts of kindness and charity over rituals. If a destitute person came to him, he would leave optional prayers to help him. This earned him the title of Gharib Nawaz, one who favours the poor. Khwaja Gharib Nawaz is one of the few Sufi saints whose marital life has been recorded.

He chose to remain in Ajmer even after it had lost its central position. He would teach the precepts of Islam to anyone who wished to convert, and he initiated the seekers of spiritual elevation into the secrets of mystic love. It was his love for humanity that won him so many adherents, both in his lifetime and after his death.

The Chishtiyah order had the greatest influence on the masses but ultimately came into conflict with the Delhi Sultans who resented a parallel seat of authority, despite it being devoid of worldliness or political pretensions. Hazrat Farid Ganj-i-Shakar (b. Kahowal, AD 1175–d. Delhi c.1265) made it his conscious policy to maintain a distance between his monastery and the royal court, but his successors, Hazrat Nizamuddin Auliya (b. Badayun, AD 1238–d. Delhi AD 1324) and Khwaja Nasiruddin Mahmud Chiragh Dehlavi (or Chiragh-e-Delhi) (b. Awadh, AD 1277–d. Delhi AD 1356) incurred the wrath of the Tughluq Sultans. Sultan Ghiasuddin Tughluq had ordered Nizamuddin Auliya to leave Delhi before he returned from Bengal. However, the Sultan was killed before he could re-enter Delhi. Sultan Muhammad bin Tughluq tortured Hazrat Chiragh-i-Delhi into becoming his personal attendant. After Muhammad Tughluq's death, the saint is said to have favoured Sultan Feroz Tughluq's accession to the throne, but there is no evidence that he ever received any favour from Sultan Feroz Tughluq. Hazrat Chiragh-i-Delhi did not appoint any successor and the glory of the Chishti order ended with him.

There were two other orders that affected Indo-Muslim society: the Suhrawardi and the Naqshbandi.

Shaikh Bahauddin Zakaria (b. Kotkrur, 1182–d. Multan 1262) belonged to the Suhrawardi order and had visited Hazrat Shahabuddin Suhrawardi in Baghdad. Shahabuddin was the most prominent saint of this order after its founder, Abu al-Najib Suhrawardi. On Bahauddin's return to Multan, the city became one of the spiritual capitals of India. Bahauddin had favoured Iltutmish against the local claimant Nasiruddin Qabacha and was made to suffer for it. However, when Iltutmish defeated Qabacha, Bahauddin was able to pursue his spiritual goals, spread his message, and purify the souls of his followers through the teachings of the Holy Prophet (PBUH).

MUJADDID AND THE MUGHALS.—Thus far, the services of the saints of the Delhi Sultanate era have been recounted. By and large, these Sultans were ideologically, if not factually, subservient to the caliphs and considered their domain part of the Muslim world. They were succeeded by the Mughal emperors who did not recognize the Ottoman Sultans as caliphs. They were inward-looking and took a number of steps to conciliate the Hindu majority of India.

Mujaddid Alf Thani (Shaikh Ahmad Sirhindi, b. Sirhind, AD 1564–d. AD 1624). The most popular account of the relations between the Mujaddid and the Mughals states that Akbar was an infidel, Mujaddid Alf Thani opposed his un-Islamic policies and was imprisoned because he refused to perform *sajdah* or prostrate before Emperor Jehangir. It is further stated that Emperor Aurangzeb, who ruled from AD 1659 to 1707, was a firm adherent of Mujaddid Alf Thani and followed his policy of imposing orthodoxy. There is some truth in the first two statements, the last two are false.

THE MILLENNIAL MOVEMENT.—To understand the activities of both Mujaddid and Akbar we must recall that they took place against the background of the Alfi Tehreek, or millennial movement. As the first thousand years of the Hijri era were drawing to a close, many religious movements were formed, based on a popular Hadith that after every thousand years there shall appear a person who shall renew the faith by reforming the practices prevailing in Muslim societies. This reformer was projected as a Mahdi, a guide. Exaggerated claims were made about the spiritual status of the expected reformers and many claimants came forward and started movements to confuse the common and pious Muslims of that time. Among them was Mahmud of Pasakhwan (d. ad 1492) who led the Nuqtavi Movement in Iran. They believed that the atom, or dot (*nuqta*), was the essence of the universe which was eternal and not created by any being. There is evidence that Abul Fazl and Faizi, courtiers of Akbar, were influenced by this movement.[2]

In India, Syed Muhammad of Jaunpur (b. Jaunpur AD 1443–d. Farah AD 1504) claimed to be the promised Mahdi and founded a movement whose main tenet was *zikr*, a constant repetition of the names of God. Many features of this sect were considered innovations by the orthodox ulama.

Akbar the Great Mughal (Jalaluddin Muhammad, b. Umerkot, 1542–d. Agra 1606) was an intelligent but illiterate member of a highly learned family. Such an unusual combination exposed Akbar to scepticism and eclecticism; that is doubting orthodox beliefs and being quite prepared to borrow from other religions. It is true that from 1580 onwards Akbar walked a path that led him further and further away from Islam, but as the recent writings of Iqtidar Alam Khan indicate, we cannot simply summarize the religious policy of Akbar, we have to understand it chronologically.

Akbar abolished the pilgrimage tax on Hindus	1562
Akbar abolished *jizya*	1564
Akbar proclaimed the conquest of Chittor as a victory of Islam over Hinduism and destroyed temples	1568
Akbar suppressed Shias of Bilgram	1572
Akbar suppressed Mahdavis in Gujarat	1573
Akbar changed the name of Prayag to Allahabad	1574
Akbar reimposed *jizya*	1575
Infallibility Decree or *Mahzar* gives Akbar authority, albeit subject to the Holy Quran	1578
Din-i-Ilahi allegedly proclaimed	1581
Akbar protests to Abdullah Uzbek that he is a Muslim and is falsely reviled by the ulama	1586
Akbar resumes Muslim prayers, reverts to orthodoxy	1601–1605

Some doubts have been expressed by S.M. Ikram as to whether Akbar actually promulgated Din-i-Ilahi as contemporary evidence is slim. This is, however, immaterial since his act of worshipping the sun was patently un-Islamic, therefore one Mulla Yazdi ruled that Akbar had become an apostate. Akbar had Mulla Yazdi killed. It is this factor which complicates the issue: Akbar insisted that he was a Muslim although his conduct and creed were un-Islamic. Yet Khwaja Shirazi and Sharif Amuli called Akbar the Renewer of the Millennium, exactly what the Mujaddid was called.

THE CREED OF MUJADDID ALF THANI.—Even if we consider that Akbar was an apostate, it does not naturally follow that Shaikh Ahmad Sirhindi was orthodox. It was not his refusal to prostrate before Jehangir that caused the emperor to imprison him, but his claim to spiritual excellence over even the first caliph, Abu Bakr (RA), who, moreover, was the fountainhead of the Naqshbandi order. I.H. Qureshi described in muted terms Mujaddid Alf Thani's self-esteem and its consequences: 'He attained the conviction that he held a very high position in the hierarchy of Muslim saints and that he was to bring about a renaissance of Islam. When he made his vision public, he incurred the criticism of several contemporaries of great eminence and also the wrath of Emperor Jehangir, who imprisoned him for what he considered extravagant claims likely to cause mischief. The Shaikh, however, was not deterred from his work, nor was he ready to withdraw his claims.'[3]

Among the contemporaries of great eminence mentioned by I.H. Qureshi was Abdul Haq Muhaddith Dehlavi. It is doubtful that Mujaddid was punished for not prostrating before Jehangir. It must be kept in mind that *sajda*, or prostration before the emperor, was not a Mughal innovation. It was Sultan Ghiyasuddin Balban who initiated this practice.[4] Even the Chishti mystics favoured this practice. Nizamuddin Auliya allowed it, and it was only Hazrat Chiragh-i-Delhi who forbade it.[5]

It is also claimed that the orthodox Islamic policies pursued by Aurangzeb were due to the influence of Mujaddid Alf Thani. This is not true as Aurangzeb had actually banned the works of Mujaddid Alf Thani, as pointed out by Yohanan Friedmann. On the contrary Dara Shukoh, who was the rival of Aurangzeb, had high regard for Mujaddid Alf Thani and mentioned him with great reverence in his book *Safinat-ul-Aulia*.

As in the case of Akbar, so in the case of Sirhindi, we must view his thoughts chronologically. In his youth, when Mujaddid perceived that Akbar was not giving due respect to the station of prophethood, he wrote *Athbat-un-Nubuwwa* (Affirmation of Prophethood). In spite of criticisms, Mujaddid Alf Thani became the champion of orthodoxy in Islam and was responsible for curbing the trend towards Hindu-Muslim integration as seen in the Bhakti movement. According to I.H. Qureshi, the main achievement of the Mujaddid was his ideological opposition to heterodox Sufism in India: 'The cornerstone of his philosophy was the rejection of monism.... It is on the rejection of monism that Shaikh Ahmad Sirhindi's claim for being the Mujaddid of his age is based.'[6]

Actually, Mujaddid did not reject monism in its entirety, as it would have forced him to renounce Sufism altogether. He wished to reform, not reject, monism. He sharply differed with Ibn Arabi (1165–1240) on this point but still respected him. What the Mujaddid did was reject Ontological Monism, that is, *Wahdat-ul-Wajood* or *Hama Oost*. He opted instead, for Phenomenological Monism, that is *Wahdat-as-Shuhood* or *Hama az Oost*. This means that 'all creation is not one, but that God is separate from what he has created, though all that he has created is one'.

Mujaddid Alf Thani was the most prominent person of the Mughal period to emphasize the difference between the Hindus and Muslims and to prevent the intermingling of their creeds. Since this is a question of attitudes it is important to know that he had no influence over Mohammad Ali Jinnah the founder of Pakistan, but had a profound influence over Maulana Abul Kalam Azad, the nationalist and Congress leader who termed the creation of Pakistan a tragedy.[7]

Mujaddid and the Mystics. In order to comprehend fully the mission and personality of Mujaddid Alf Thani we need to recall that he worked within the framework of mysticism. This, in turn, requires that we study his thoughts in relation to the thoughts of Ibn Arabi (1165–1240), where he accepted, and where he rejected or where he modified the views of Ibn Arabi. This interaction was not as simple as his Puritanism. The ethical side of mysticism is simple because it is behavioural. A Sufi lives as spiritual a life as possible without becoming a hermit or an ascetic (since Islam forbids it) and devotes himself to prayers to gain personal closeness to God.

The metaphysical side is complicated. It involves the introduction of concepts which were not present in the original doctrines of Islam. These concepts dealt with the nature of the universe: how it came into being, how God is seen as the only reality, and whatever He created, as an illusion. Although such concepts interfered with the reformist mission of Mujaddid Alf Thani, he had perforce to deal with the views Ibn Arabi introduced in the cosmology of Islam. Ibn Arabi's doctrine of Oneness of Existence does not mean that all existence is one, but that only God exists, and His creation does not exist. This was the concept which impelled Mansur al-Hallaj to proclaim 'An-al-haq' (I am the Truth). A creature's identification with God was held to be blasphemous, and consequently, Hallaj was executed.

Hallaj was answered across the land and time by Rene Descartes (1590–1650) who said *Cogito Ergo Sum* (I think, therefore I am). Hallaj submerged his consciousness in the sea of existence while Descartes held his consciousness afloat. It is only at their starting point that they are divergent. Otherwise, this is where the *Wahdat-ul-Wajood* of the East meets with the pantheism of the West. It was Baruch de Spinoza (1632–1677) who took pantheism one step further. Spinoza resembles Ibn Arabi in an important respect when he speaks of the Divine: 'I hold that God is the immanent and not the extraneous cause of all things. I say All is in God; all lives and moves in God.'[8] Spinoza holds that the process of nature and God are one.[9] He, however, clarified that he did not mean that God and nature—i.e. a mass of corporal matter—are one and the same.[10] However, Spinoza's clarification is not easy to reconcile with his basic contention, just quoted above. Similarly, Mujaddid's modification of Ibn Arabi's views is unable to remove his doctrines from the basic fabric of monism.

This modification of Ibn Arabi's views, the shift from *Wahdat-ul-Wajood* to *Wahdat-as-Shuhood* was affected first by Ala ad-Dawla as-Simnani (1261–1336). Mujaddid merely applied Simnani's criticism to his own milieu. Simnani accused Ibn Arabi of idolizing a verb. Ibn Arabi faced opposition from Ibn Taymiyyah (1263–1328) who held that such a view would absolve mankind of moral responsibility for its deeds. Syed Abul Ala Maududi (1903–1979) focused more on the self-esteem of Mujaddid and Shah Waliullah (see Chapter 5). 'I cannot help saying, irrespective of what the world might say, that it is certainly one of the wrong actions on the part of these two sages to personally proclaim of their being *mujaddid*, and to repeatedly explain this viewpoint on the basis of divine revelations and inspirations.'[11]

> **Equivalent terms:** *Wahdat-ul-Wajood, Hama Oost,* Unity of Being. Ontological monism, the oneness of existence and pantheism. *Wahdat-as-Shuhood, Hama az Oost,* Unity of creation and phenomenological monism.

Shaikh Abdul Haq Muhaddith Dehlavi (1551–1642). Like Mujaddid Alf Thani, Shaikh Abdul Haq was also a pupil of Khwaja Baqi Billah and like him was also concerned that the Millennial Movement was making Muslims oblivious to the pivotal position of the Holy Prophet (PBUH) with regard to both the spiritual and mystical domain. To this end, he wrote a book titled *Madarij-un-Nubuwwa* and questioned even Mujaddid Alf Thani in this regard. Shaikh Abdul Haq received his education in Makkah from Syed Ali Muttaqi, who convinced him that he was needed in India.

In India, Shaikh Abdul Haq concerned himself with the duties an emperor is enjoined with, regarding the Sharia and protection of the faith. He wrote *Nuranniya-i-Sultania* addressed to Jehangir. One tradition relates that Jehangir exiled him to Kabul. On his return, in the reign of Shahjahan (1592–1666), he wrote a monograph consisting of forty Hadiths on the rules of conduct for a good ruler. The science of Hadith, which he had learnt at Makkah, defined his ability and his role. About his historical role, Aziz Ahmad writes: 'From him begins the Indian Muslim tradition of the scholarship of Hadith, which was to culminate in the works of Waliullah and the Ahl-i-Hadith of the late nineteenth century'.[12]

Notes

1. Qazi Javed, *Barr-e-Saghir Mein Muslim Fikr ka Irtiqa* (Urdu) (Lahore: Nigarishat, 1986), p. 10.
2. A.F.M. Abu Bakr Siddiqui, 'Maktubat Imam Rabbani', in *Islamic Studies* (ed.) Zafar Ishaq Ansari et al., Islamabad, vol. 28, Summer 1989, p. 143.
3. Ishtiaq Husain Qureshi, *The Muslim Community of the Indo-Pakistan Subcontinent* 2nd ed. (Karachi: BCCT, University of Karachi, 1999), p. 169.
4. Aziz Ahmad, *Islamic Culture in the Indian Environment* (London: Oxford University Press, 1964; reprinted, Delhi: Oxford University Press, 1999), p. 170.
5. Muneera Haeri, *The Chishtis* (Karachi: Oxford University Press, 2000), p. 165.
6. Yohanan Friedmann, *Shaykh Ahmad Sirhindi* (New Delhi: Oxford University Press, 2000), p. 94.
7. Abul Kalam Azad, *India Wins Freedom* (Complete Edition, London: Sangam, 1988), passim.
8. Will Durant, *Outlines of Philosophy* (London: Ernest Benn, 1962), p. 159.
9. Ibid., p. 152.
10. Ibid., p. 160.
11. Syed Abul Ala Maududi, *Tajdid-o-Ihya-i-Deen* (Lahore, 1952). Cited in Saiyid Athar Abbas Rizvi, *Shah Waliullah and his Times* (Canberra: Ma'rifat, 1980), p. 220.
12. Aziz Ahmad, op. cit., p. 190.

THE THEORETICAL RELATION OF MUJADDID TO IBN ARABI

Orthodox Ulama	Ibn Arabi	Mujaddid Alf Thani
1. The universe has a real and external existence	1. The universe does not have a real existence. It is imaginary. Ghalib has explained this concept in the following verses: When nobody exists except You, Then, o God, what is this clamour? Asad! Do not be taken in by the deception of being. The whole world is encircled by the snare of imagination	1. God Himself created the universe as imaginary. Thus, the universe has no external existence. The existence of the universe is not as real as the existence of God. Unless the Creator and His creatures are not separate, reward and punishment shall remain without justification. Mujaddid reasons that the most unique attribute of God is existence. If we consider the Universe to be as real as God, then, this will be a form of association (*Shirk*).
2. The universe was created *ex nihilo*, i.e. from nothing. The Holy Quran says: When He decrees a thing, He but says to it 'Be', and it is (2:117). The Quran has two terms. *Khalq*: Creation, for mankind; *Amr*: Command, for the soul.	2. The universe is the shadow of God, who is Perfect and Absolute. It exists only in the knowledge of God. It has no external existence.	2. The Universe is imaginary, but to a degree it is eternal.
3. Allah, Who is in need of none and of Whom all are in need, He neither begot any nor was He begotten (112: 2–3)	3. Between God which is the Absolute Entity and the world of mankind, there are six stages, which Ibn Arabi calls the *Tanazzulat-i-Sitta*. The first stage is the Reality of Muhammad (PBUH), and the second stage is *Ae'an-i-Thabita* (Fixed Prototypes of Things)	3. The Reality of Muhammad (PBUH) is less than the Reality of Ka'ba. (Mujaddid considers the reality of the Prophet (PBUH) to be separate from his person, which he holds to be superior to the Ka'ba)
4. This belief does not exist.	4. The six stages which are between God and the world of mankind are all the shadows or the radiance of the attributes of God.	4. These six stages are not the radiance of the attributes of God, but the negation of the attributions of God. This does not mean negation in the normal sense, but that God puts the shadow of His attributes on non-existent things and they become beings. Some beings, among whom Satan is the most prominent, acquire existence from non-existence; and (eventually) become good from evil. According to Ibn Arabi, the object of God is not to obliterate evil, but to transform it.

THE SIX DESCENTS—*TANAZZULAT-I-SITTA*

1. God—The Absolute Being: According to Ibn Arabi, there existed only One Reality. This Reality, however, had two aspects; the Essence (*haq*), the unknowable Being, and the phenomenal world (*khalq*), which had a multiplicity of appearances. The phenomenal world is a mirror or shadow of the Absolute Being. This aspect can be explained, only through symbols.
2. The Reality of Muhammad (PBUH).
3. The sphere of Angels or the sphere of souls.
4. The sphere of similitude. This stage connects the sphere of souls to the sphere of bodies.
5. The sphere of *nasoot*. This is the sphere of bodies in the ideal or conceptual state. From this state proceeds the manifestation of the world of bodies (*ajsam*).
6. The sphere of mankind: Mankind was a mirror that needed polishing in order to become a worthy reflection of the Divine Being.

Chapter 4

The Fall of the Muslims and the Establishment of British Rule

The decline of the Mughal empire led to the downfall of Muslim society in South Asia. Historians differ on the causes that led to the decline but agree that the decline followed the death of Aurangzeb (AD 1707). It is said that the successors of Aurangzeb were inefficient and weak, therefore they could not protect the empire from either the Hindu Marathas or the Muslim governors of Bengal, Awadh, and Deccan. It is nevertheless strange that all the rulers from Babur to Aurangzeb were strong in intellect and character, and all the rulers from Bahadur Shah I (1707–1712) to Bahadur Shah II (1775–1862) were weak and incapable. Thus, impersonal forces should be examined. The structure of society and the events that led to the decline were the wars of succession which began with Jehangir's revolt against his father Akbar.

The structure of the Mughal Empire was agrarian. Akbar and his successors imposed a system called the *Mansabdari* system. Beginning with Akbar's prime minister, Abul Fazl, no historian has been able to explain adequately the intricacies of the *Mansabdari* system. Only one thing is apparent, that the hereditary nature of land ownership gave way to lifelong ownership. *Jagirdars* refused to return their *jagirs* at the end of Aurangzeb's reign. In the feudal system, land or its revenues were allotted so that troops could be maintained and these troops, when called upon by the king or governor, joined the state armies during war. These troops, in normal times, were maintained to collect the *lagaan* or land cess and protect the estate from attacks by outsiders. The produce of the land was needed to pay the soldiers, and the soldiers were needed to protect the produce. This balance was upset by the wars of succession.

When there was war between king and prince, as in the case of Akbar and Jehangir, or between royal brothers, such as the sons of Jehangir or the sons of Shahjahan, loyalties were divided and the holder of one estate would attack the holder of another estate. One of the two estates would be destroyed. As the wars of succession continued there ultimately came a stage when there was no produce to pay the soldiers and no soldiers to protect the crop. This was the vicious circle which replaced the balance of the golden age.

Salaries were often in arrears and if a landlord died without paying them, the soldiers would not allow his funeral prayers to be held. Only if the inheritors were able or willing to pay off the soldiers with jewellery or any other form of wealth, were the funeral prayers performed, otherwise the deceased would suffer the indignity of being buried without religious rites. At one point

The Fall of the Muslims and the Establishment of British Rule 43

a landlord told the troops that he could not pay their salaries. They had his permission to loot and plunder the countryside and keep all of the loot except the gold. This measure tore apart the fabric of society.

Soldiers with swords and horses went from estate to estate, raja to raja and nawab to nawab in search of employment. The soldiers had already mortgaged their shields to feed their children. At a new estate, they would be paid some salary initially, but thereafter payment was stopped. Soldiers were thus uprooted from their original estates and became a floating armed population, further destabilizing society.

Apart from soldiers of fortune, there were the Pindaris, the terrorists of that age. Disenchanted with continuous misery, these were mostly the dregs of society, whether Hindu or Muslim, and out of pure greed or meanness they attacked people savagely. The Pindaris had their hideouts in forests or caves, and emerged to attack the villages or settlements they thought could yield loot. Often, when by hard work and perseverance, cultivators managed to make an economic recovery, the Pindaris used to attack them with a vengeance that defied description. Thus, the decline was sustained.

How did the British take advantage of the Muslim decline? The Europeans, especially the British and the French, set up factories for processing goods to be sent back to Europe. Like the native estates, these factories also needed protection, so they began to hire Indian soldiers. Since the source of its wealth or strength lay outside India, the British East India Company was able to offer the best terms to the best soldiers. Handsome salaries were paid regularly. Soldiers employed by the East India Company were given arms and ammunition as well as fodder for their horses. The British were superior to the Indians in almost all aspects, except that they lacked manpower. By recruiting the best Indian soldiers, the British overcame this disability. In the Battle of Plassey, Lord Clive could bring an army against Nawab Sirajuddaulah which consisted mainly of Indian, not British soldiers. The East India Company, as the name implies, was a trading company. It saw an opportunity to acquire political power in India because of the anarchy which prevailed there.

K.M. Panikkar has described the war between the Mughals and the British as a battle between an elephant and a whale. The Mughals were masters of the land; they neglected to build a navy; only Sher Shah Suri with his vision centred on Bengal and not on Delhi, had set out to build a navy capable of warding off European seafarers. His rule was far too short, and the Mughals did not build on his work. In those days, naval power was as decisive as air power is today, therefore the British had the military edge over the Mughals.

It is true that there was a conspiracy at the Battle of Plassey in 1757. Mir Jafar and his cohorts betrayed Sirajuddaulah on the battlefield, but in the Battle of Buxar in 1764, there was no betrayal and there was no disunity. The Mughal king, the Nawab of Murshidabad, and the Nawab of Awadh had combined forces but were still defeated by the British, who won because of their superior arms and strategy. As at Plassey, so at Buxar, the British army consisted of a majority of Indian troops. Better training and modern strategy were making the difference, not racial characteristics.

Thus, far we have been determining how the British defeated the Indians. One sentence only about how Lord Clive, the British commander, was able to outstrip Joseph-François Dupleix, the French commander. Dupleix was a very capable man but, unlike Clive, he forgot the commercial side of his mission. Clive, even at the height of the war, never neglected trade, and kept on making profits while Dupleix found the war expensive.

There was one other cause of the Muslim decline, recently propounded by Karen Leonard.[1] She implies that the causes of decline did not pertain only to agriculture but extended to banking. She differentiates between moneylenders who gave money to landlords on interest, and the bankers who not only advanced loans but received deposits and dealt with *hundis*. Karen Leonard asserts that by 1750 there were bankers who actually managed to collect land revenue, 'The amount of interest set and the securities demanded by bankers were more critical economic conditions than the revenue demand fixed by a territorial ruler'.[2] These banking firms turned down requests for loans made by Aurangzeb and Farrukhsiyar (r. 1713–1719; the tenth Mughal emperor) but advanced loans to the East India Company. When the East India Company became prosperous, it took over the tasks of revenue collection and advancing loans from banking firms. In two strokes the decline set in: banking firms directed revenue from the Mughals to the British and after 1750 the British displaced the banking firms.

Karen Leonard claims that these financial shifts explain the decline of the Mughals and the rise of the British in economic terms, emphasizing processes rather than events or individuals.[3] Our historians nevertheless give greater importance to events and individuals. The roles of Akbar and Aurangzeb are contrasted and discussed by British, Muslim, and Hindu historians alike.

AKBAR AND AURANGZEB.—There is a tendency to compare and contrast the roles of Akbar and Aurangzeb. The basic premise is that Akbar was responsible for consolidating the Mughal Empire by conciliating the Hindus, while Aurangzeb was responsible for its decline by alienating them. Akbar became the symbol of tolerance and Aurangzeb became the symbol of bigotry. This image has been reinforced by British historians.[4]

The matter is not so simple. Akbar was a most attractive personality but his treatment of his mentor, Bairam Khan, did not do him credit. Aurangzeb is blamed for killing his brothers and imprisoning his father (Shahjahan). It is forgotten that in wars of succession, only the survivor was the king therefore, only the king was the survivor.

As far as their religious policies are concerned, we have mentioned earlier (see Mujaddid and the Mughals) that Akbar did not gain the adherence of the Rajputs by conciliating them, but by his conquest of Chittor which he publicly proclaimed to be a victory of Islam over Hinduism. On that occasion Akbar broke idols and desecrated temples, behaving no differently from Mahmud of Ghazni. The decline of the Mughals is supposed to have been caused when Aurangzeb broke idols and desecrated temples, but as Jnan Chandra pointed out, while Aurangzeb indisputably broke some idols and desecrated temples, he also built and supported others by royal grant.[5]

Aurangzeb is accused of alienating Hindus by reimposing *jizya*. Here again, the facts have not been carefully sifted. We have already seen that at one stage Akbar had reimposed *jizya* (1575). It is, however, not recognized that Aurangzeb reimposed *jizya* after Shivaji's insurrection. It is also alleged that Aurangzeb invaded Bijapur and Golconda because their kings were Shias, but Aurangzeb had a large number of Shia commanders. When asked to appoint one Sunni Bakhshi, Aurangzeb replied: 'What connections have worldly affairs with religion? And what rights have administrative works to meddle with bigotry? For you is your religion for me is mine. If this rule were established it would be my duty to extirpate all rajas and their followers.'[6] It can easily be deduced that the motives of Aurangzeb were imperial, not sectarian.

The emperor was able to annex the kingdoms of Bijapur and Golconda, and he was able to defeat, capture and execute Shambhaji, Shivaji's son, in 1689, but these victories were not decisive. The Marathas rallied under Tarabai and by the beginning of the 19th century were entrenched in Delhi. Chin Qilich Khan (aka Nizam-ul-Mulk Asaf Jah I) founded an independent kingdom in the Deccan in 1724. The real cause of the decline was Aurangzeb's presence in the Deccan from 1681 to his death in 1707. We can recall here Muhammad Habib's comment on Sultan Muhammad bin Tughluq's decision to shift the capital from Delhi to Deogir, 'The south could not be ruled from Delhi, but equally, the north could not be ruled from Deogir'.[7] This long absence from the capital contributed to the decline to a large extent. Secondly, Aurangzeb's son could succeed him only when he himself was old, and then he did not last for more than five years.

I.H. Qureshi speaks of the ideological compulsion of a minority ruling over a majority. He argues that it was wrong to give concessions to the majority. At a later point in history, the British were to apply the same argument. The contrast between Akbar and Aurangzeb was sharp with regard to their temperaments, but in the end, it was their imperial, rather than religious policy, that had long-term effects.

NADIR SHAH.—The collapse of the agrarian system led to the proliferation of soldiers of fortune and to the emergence of the Pindaris which rendered society chaotic. Conditions were appalling but with stable and strong rulership they were still reversible. However, when Nadir Shah of Iran invaded India in 1738 and sacked Delhi, the loss of life and property was staggering, and the process of decline became irreversible. The people of Delhi constituted the intellectual capital of India, and the imperial Mughal treasury could have financed recovery in the outlying provinces. Nadir Shah killed and pillaged indiscriminately and apart from taking the peacock throne and the Kohinoor diamond and other valuables amounting to forty crores of rupees, he also emptied the royal stables of horses and elephants.

The people were still staggering under this calamity when, from around 1756 onwards, Ahmad Shah Abdali (1722–1772) of Afghanistan began his raids. He is historically prominent as the Muslim king who defeated the Marathas in 1761 but his earlier raids caused great devastation. Mirza Sauda in poetry,[8] and Mir Taqi Mir in prose,[9] have described the ravages brought about by his raids.

In 1761, Ahmad Shah Abdali, at the invitation of Shah Waliullah (see Chapter 5), fought the Marathas in the Third Battle of Panipat. The Marathas were defeated and suffered a great setback and the leader, Balaji Baji Rao, died broken-hearted. The defeat of the Marathas could have led to the revival and resurgence of Muslim rule in India, but this did not happen because four years earlier, the British under Lord Clive had defeated Nawab Sirajuddaulah at the Battle of Plassey (1757) and the foundation for British rule in India has been already laid.

Notes

1. Karen Leonard, 'The Great Firm Theory of the Decline of the Mughal Empire', in *The Mughal State*, (eds.) Muzaffar Alam and Sanjay Subrahmanyam (New Delhi: Oxford University Press, 2000), pp. 398–418.
2. Ibid., p. 407.
3. Ibid., p. 417.
4. James H. Gense, *A History of India* (Madras: Macmillan, 1957), pp. 195–6.
5. Jnan Chandra, 'Aurangzeb's Endowments', *Journal of the Pakistan Historical Society*, Karachi, 1959, vol. 7, pp. 99–100.
6. Satish Chandra, *Parties and Politics at the Mughal Court* (Aligarh: Peoples Publishing House, 1959), p. 9.
7. M. Habib, 'Muhammad bin Tughluq', in *Politics and Society during the Early Medieval Period* (New Delhi: Peoples Publishing House, 1981), p. 276.
8. Mirza Muhammad Rafi Sauda, *Kulliyat-i-Sauda*, (ed.) Abdul Bari Aasi (Lucknow, 1932), vol. 1, pp. 367–81.
9. Mir Taqi Mir, *Zikr-i-Mir*, (tr. and ed.) C.M. Naim (New Delhi: Oxford University Press, 1999), pp. 77ff.

Part 2
History of Muslim Revival Movements

Chapter 5
Shah Waliullah (1703–1762)

Shah Waliullah was the first reformer to appear during the period of Muslim decline. Hitherto, kings and governors had dominated the public life of the Muslim community, but the leadership now passed to this intellectual figure, who was both an *alim* and a Sufi, and had made it his life's mission to reverse the trend of Muslim decline. He realized that the Muslim community had to be emancipated both militarily and morally. Militarily and politically the Maratha power was the threat. To this end, he wrote to Ahmad Shah Abdali to remind him of his duty as a Muslim king to liberate the Muslim community, and the result was the Maratha defeat in the Third Battle of Panipat in 1761.

Shah Waliullah was one of the few ulama who realized that war was the lesser jihad, and the greater jihad was against the temptations facing one's own soul. Therefore, the greater and longer part of his mission was to effect a moral reform of his community. Shah Waliullah was the first major figure to analyse the causes of Muslim decline and to suggest remedies. In his description of the rise and fall of societies, he shows his familiarity with the philosophy of history propounded by Ibn Khaldun, illustrating how civilizations rise and fall.

His guiding principles of reform were *adl* and *tawazun*, justice and balance; therefore Shah Waliullah was in favour of an equitable distribution of wealth in society. The concentration of wealth in one class leads to wasteful spending at one level and extreme deprivation at the other. He found it objectionable for anyone to be a burden on society; he wanted every individual to be productive and yet he laid great stress on moral constraints. Wealth, he said should be acquired only by honest and ethical means.

Shah Waliullah forbade the adoption of Hindu customs for two reasons. First, he believed a beleaguered minority needed to assert its distinctive identity. Participating in Diwali, which meant lighting lamps and exploding fireworks, or lighting lamps and fireworks on the Muslim festival of Shab-i-Barat were to be avoided. There were many customs taken from Hindus, such as *sehra* and music during marriage and even on minor occasions, that led Muslims to extravagance and ultimately, to debt.

He gave central importance to Fiqh, or jurisprudence, because he felt that deviation from Islamic norms had led the Muslim community into decline. This deviation he attributed to a lack of direct access to the meaning of the Holy Quran. He took the bold step of translating the Holy Quran into Persian.

By translating the Holy Quran, Shah Waliullah sought to curb the influence of the ulama as a class, and for this reason, he also favoured *ijtihad* over *taqlid*. Usually, *ijtihad* is called innovation and *taqlid* is called imitation. Shah Waliullah explained that these concepts in jurisprudence are not so simple. According to him *ijtihad* 'is an exhaustive endeavour to understand the derivative principles of canon law'—in other words, a jurist must strive hard to find the principles relating to the Quran and Sunnah which must be applied to new situations and problems.

In arriving at this conclusion, Shah Waliullah was aided by his upbringing and his education in Makkah. His father, Shah Abdur Rahim, was a renowned scholar, who founded the Madrassa-i-Rahimiyah where Shah Waliullah studied and taught. During his pilgrimage, he also visited Madinah, where he studied under Shaikh Abu Tahir Muhammad bin Ibrahim and Shaikh Sulayman Maghribi.

One of the most important steps he took was towards conciliation between sects and approaches. He realized the necessity of Muslim solidarity and was able to achieve this because he had humanistic concepts of worship. I.H. Qureshi has pointed out that Shah Waliullah believed what God has revealed is beneficial for mankind: 'God is not a tyrant revelling in getting himself obeyed; such a conception is unworthy and erroneous. In His great mercy, He has shown the way which leads to mundane and spiritual well-being and progress!'[1]

Shah Waliullah detailed the benefits to be gained from such obligations as prayers, alms-giving (*zakat*) and fasting. Although Shah Waliullah was a zealous guardian of Muslim identity, he said that force cannot compel people to accept Islam. The *mujtahid* should persuade people to accept Islam by such means that they should freely adopt it and stand by it even when the *mujtahid* was in no position to impose his belief.[2]

Therefore, he set upon his task of reconciliation with sincerity. First of all, he tried to reconcile both strands of Sufism. He maintained that both the *Wahdat-ul-Wajood* of Ibn Arabi and the *Wahdat-as-Shuhood* of Mujaddid Alf Thani were correct and that there was no meaningful difference between them. In the next stage, he said that all the Sufi orders consist of Tariqat (or spiritual path) and all Tariqat is subordinate to Shariat (religious law). This was also the main platform of his reformist movement, as it was under the cover of Sufism that a number of practices, threatening morality had crept into Muslim society. He further tried to reconcile the Sunnis and the Shias. He wrote a book, *Izalatul Khifa*, disputing their beliefs, but at the same time, he vehemently declared that the Shias were within the pale of Islam.

Shah Waliullah's philosophy of life is contained in his most famous book *Hujjat ullah al Baligha*. No other book of the 18th century has had such a profound effect on the Muslims of South Asia. Shah Waliullah, because of his learning and piety, commanded the respect of kings. It is not merely that

Ahmad Shah Abdali responded to the request of Shah Waliullah to face the Marathas on the field of Panipat. What is important is that Ahmad Shah Abdali heeded Shah Waliullah's warning against tyrannising and terrorising Muslims as had been his habit in all his earlier expeditions.

Notes

1. Ishtiaq Husain Qureshi, *The Muslim Community of the Indo-Pakistan Subcontinent* (Karachi: BCCT, University of Karachi, Reprint, 1999), p. 213.
2. Ibid., p. 67.

Chapter 6
The Jihad Movement

Shah Waliullah was able to defeat the Marathas by invoking the help of Ahmad Shah Abdali, the ruler of Afghanistan. When Maharaja Ranjit Singh established his kingdom over the Punjab and the Frontier, the political landscape changed. Sayyid Ahmad Barelvi (1786–1831), the leader of the Mujahideen, had met the Maratha grandee, Maharaja Daulat Rao Sindhia[1] at Gwalior in 1828. Sayyid Ahmad Barelvi gave Sindhia an assurance that, if successful, the Mujahideen would help restore power to the Marathas, and actively sought his help.

The problem of the position of the Sikhs straddling the route from Afghanistan to India took precedence in their reckoning to those of the growing power of the British and the teeming majority of the Hindus. The mission of Shah Waliullah gave rise, in the following generation, to the Jihadi movement. Sayyid Ahmad Barelvi, with the active cooperation of Shah Ismail Shahid (d.1831), Shah Waliullah's grandson, set out against the Sikhs.

The movement of the Mujahideen has sometimes been called the Wahhabi Movement because of its puritan and strict monotheistic character, but this is a misnomer because in spite of some resemblance in their outlook, the two movements were not identical. The basic tenets of Sayyid Ahmad Barelvi are enshrined in his book *Siratul Mustaqim* (1818) which had as its main theme the denunciation of *bid'at* or innovations which beset Indo-Muslim society. He decried: (1) The use of disrespectful or blasphemous words for God—which were uttered by poets and mystics in ecstasy. (2) Monism, pantheism, or any form of *Wahdat-ul-Wajood*. This put him apart ideologically from Shah Waliullah. (3) Any disputation against fate or predestination being a part of the Sharia is most objectionable, as Sayyid Ahmad Barelvi held predestination to be a fundamental Islamic doctrine. (4) Excessive adulation of one's spiritual guide or *murshid*. (5) Offering food to saints and ancestors (*nazr niaz*) as polytheism (*shirk*). (6) The belief that holy personages could intercede with God on behalf of other mortals; a Muslim should appeal to God directly.

Sayyid Ahmad Barelvi's mission was mistakenly identified with the Wahhabi Movement because he had drawn inspiration directly from Makkah. Setting out for Hajj, Sayyid Ahmad Barelvi reached Makkah in May 1822 and returned to his native town, Rae-Bareli, in April 1824. Both on his way to Arabia and on his way back Sayyid Ahmad had stopped at Patna (the ancient Pataliputra), in Bihar and made it his organizational base. This is the reason why Patna became the centre of Jihadi activities after the martyrdom of Sayyid Ahmad Barelvi.

For his main mission, to dislodge the Sikh kingdom of the Punjab, Sayyid Ahmad Barelvi set out from Tonk and, to avoid a direct route, he traversed the deserts of Sindh and Rajputana to reach Peshawar in 1826. Sayyid Ahmad Barelvi's mission was directed against the Sikhs, but his reformist zeal extended to the Muslims of the frontier region, most of whom regarded his zeal as excessive, therefore he had to face both the Sikhs and the local Muslim chieftains.

The course of his battles with the Sikhs started with the battle of Akora on 20 December 1826, in which 500 Sikhs lost their lives. In the battle of Saidu, the Mujahideen suffered a setback when Muslim tribal leaders were enticed away from the battlefield by the Sikh commander, Budh Singh. After the victory at Hund in August 1829, Sayyid Ahmad told a local Muslim commander that he had reposed his faith in God, not in canons. The friction with frontier tribal leaders continued and Sayyid Ahmad was finally able to secure his base, Peshawar, in the battle of Mayar (1830).

The struggle of the Mujahideen reached its culmination at the Battle of Balakot (8 May 1831). When the battle began, the Mujahideen allowed the Sikhs, under Kunwar Sher Singh, to climb up to their position. The Sayyid's strategy was to attack the Sikhs at the foothills when they were headed towards the hilltop. This strategy failed because the Mujahideen lost contact with each other. Dispersed into small groups they were surrounded by the Sikhs and cut down. Among the martyrs were Sayyid Ahmad Barelvi and Shah Ismail. Both these warriors have been known as 'Shaheed' since that fateful day.

Although the Mujahideen movement ended in destruction, it did not end in failure. The Mujahideen had upheld their principles against all odds and temptations. They left behind a nucleus of Muslim armed resistance which is still active. Another effect of the Mujahideen Movement was to save Sindh from Sikh ambitions. Maharaja Ranjit Singh had extracted tribute from the chieftains of Sindh, but after seeing the ferocity of the battle, they desisted from further adventures.

Sayyid Ahmad had decided to frame a system of leadership because the Mujahideen were ruled by local chieftains during the war. This would impose discipline without detracting from the chieftain's sense of independence. In 1827, Sayyid Ahmad Barelvi was proclaimed the Imam. According to Qeyamuddin Ahmad, this concept: 'envisages the coexistence of the secular authority of the Sultan and the religious authority of the Imam. The former was to function under the general supervision of the latter'.[2] This system could not evolve because Mujahideen lost political power. However, this dualism seems to have resurfaced in contemporary Iran where Khamenei deputises for the Imam and President Khatami is the political leader.

Why did the movement of the Mujahideen fail to dislodge the Sikhs? Firstly the Muslim chieftains of the North-West Frontier considered the Mujahideen to be fanatics and did not subscribe to the harsh system of beliefs they found in *Siratul Mustaqim*. The Mujahideen were able to mollify the Marathas and elude the British but were unable to unite the Muslims. As Qeyamuddin Ahmad admits: 'If one were to judge by the yardstick of battles fought, there was more fighting between the tribal Muslim chiefs than between him and the forces of the Sikh darbar.'[3] The struggle of the Mujahideen lasted a full five years and, seen from that perspective, it was quite admirable.

Notes

1. Also spelt Scindia, Shinde.
2. Qeyamuddin Ahmad, *The Wahhabi Movement in India*, second edition (New Delhi: Manohar, 1994), p. 67.
3. Ibid., p. 301.

Chapter 7
Titu Mir (1782–1832)

With the rise of Titu Mir (Mir Nisar Ali) the reformist and emancipatory zeal of the Muslims shifted to rural Bengal and the grievances of the Muslims became economic rather than military. Titu Mir is supposed to have met Sayyid Ahmad Barelvi at Makkah, either in 1819 or 1822. Whether Titu Mir actually became a disciple of Barelvi is hard to determine, but there is little doubt that his religious ideas were quite in keeping with those of Sayyid Ahmad Barelvi. In Bengal there was a class of Muslims called *Sabiqui* who clung to old customs, including idolatrous customs such as propitiating the Hindu goddess Sitala Devi on the outbreak of smallpox. Titu Mir, like Sayyid Ahmad, was against such concepts of intercession by saints and pilgrimage to the tombs of saints. In addition, he was opposed to the observance of Muharram. Muinuddin Ahmad Khan is of the opinion that since the nawabs of Murshidabad were Shi'ites, Muharram came to have great significance for the Sunni population of Bengal. Bengali literature developed many forms devoted to the tragedy of Karbala, like Puthi and Zarigan. The making of *tazias* and taking them out in Muharram processions was objected to by Titu Mir, and this was the first tension encountered by his followers. The second tension was caused when Titu Mir ordered his followers to keep away from Muslims who did not accept his reforms.

However, Titu Mir's movement was not the result of sectarian dissension, but of the exploitation of the Muslim peasantry by both the Hindu *zamindars* and the British indigo planters. This, unfortunately, was not only an adverse economic equation but an adverse social equation. When Lord Cornwallis imposed Permanent Settlement in 1793, he was ending the temporary settlement or ownership of land. To secure ownership under the new Permanent Settlement, large sums of money were demanded which most of the old Muslim landowners were unable to pay. Their Hindu menials, such as agents and accountants, on the other hand, collected money and multiplied it by advancing loans on interest. In most cases, Muslim landlords became subjugated to their former Hindu employees.

Apart from this antagonism, Hindu *zamindars* began charging tax to spend on expressly Hindu rituals and festivals. Quite apart from the unaffordable nature of such taxes, the puritan persuasion of Titu Mir's followers prevented them from paying such taxes to their landlords or *zamindars*. In retaliation Hindu *zamindars* began taxing Muslim cultivators for the beards they grew and the mosques they built. Attempts to collect such taxes from Poorna and Sarfarazpur led to violence.

Meanwhile, the European indigo planters appeared on the scene and became another source of exploitation. Muslim cultivators wanted to grow rice and other grains, but European (mostly British) planters found the export of indigo to be the most lucrative and forced the cultivators to reserve their most fertile land for indigo.[1] They forcibly advanced about two-and-a-half rupees for the cultivation of indigo. If a farmer or cultivator refused, the planter would take away his cattle and starve them until the cultivator relented. Once he accepted the advance, he could never repay the debt due to the corruption of the police and would forever be under the yoke of the planter. Only Titu Mir and his followers had the courage to resist this double exploitation. The economic exploitation reinforced feelings of Muslim identity and popularised reforms.

Titu Mir made Narkelberia, a village in twenty-four Parganas (a district next to Calcutta), his headquarters. From here he prevented the collection of cess from Sarfarazpur, which resulted in a riot in which people were killed and a mosque was burnt. In retaliation, the followers of Titu Mir attacked Poorna (1831). In the riots which ensued a temple was defiled, and a Brahmin and a Christian were killed. The British realized that the movement was no mere insurgency; it had deep social and economic implications for British rule and the social order they had imposed. Accordingly, one Alexander, an employee of the Government Salt Agency was ordered to advance from Barasat to Narkelberia on 18 March 1832. In the fighting that ensued, Titu Mir was killed while fighting gallantly.

Note

1. Muinuddin Ahmad Khan, *Fara'idi Movement* (Karachi: Pakistan Historical Society, 1965), p. cxi.

Chapter 8
The Faraidi Movement

The Faraidi Movement centred in rural East Bengal was an organized religious movement that set up a hierarchical system of control. It was a militant movement that met violence with violence and succeeded in both religious and social reform. The leaders of the Faraidi Movement, Haji Shariatullah (1781–1840) and his son Dudhu Miyan/Mohsinuddin Ahmad (1819–1862), responded to the same challenges of Hindu *zamindars* and British indigo planters as Titu Mir had, but avoided outright confrontation with the British. Some scholars have tried to emphasize the difference between the movements of Titu Mir and Haji Shariatullah but their similarities are more apparent. It is said that Dudhu, on his way to Haj, had met and paid his respects to Titu Mir. There were certain doctrinal differences between Titu Mir and the Faraidis, but there was only twelve years' difference between the two movements, the first centred in West Bengal while the second was focused on East Bengal. To their Hindu and British adversaries, their resemblance was more apparent than their differences.

The religious tenets of the Faraidis were different from those of Titu Mir and the Jihadis, only in the sense that in jurisprudence the Faraidis were strict Hanafis and believed in *taqlid* rather than *ijtihad*. They were called Faraidis because they gave primacy to the five basic pillars of Islam—the declaration of faith (*shahada*), prayer (*salah*), alms-giving (*zakat*), fasting (*sawm*), and pilgrimage (*hajj*). They wished to return to the pristine purity of Islam and waged a war against what they termed *bid'at* (innovation) and *shirk* (polytheism). As with other reformers, they considered visiting the graves of saints and seeking their intercession with God to be polytheistic. They were also against un-Islamic rituals and customs during marriage and other ceremonies. The *zamindars*, who were mostly Hindu, had imposed as many as thirty-two Hindu religious cesses on Muslim peasants (for the reasons discussed in the chapter on Titu Mir). In retaliation, the Hindu *zamindars* subjected the Faraidis to different types of torture and imposed the beard tax. It should be noted that the Faraidis insisted on cow slaughter on Eid-ul-Azha, because, in the words of Muinuddin Ahmad Khan, 'it was less expensive and more convenient in Bengal'.[1] The Faraidis differed from other reformers in insisting that under British rule congregational prayers like those on Fridays and the two Eids could not be held. Scholars have insisted that unlike Titu Mir, the Faraidi leaders, succeeded in keeping their movements away from politics. This is true only to the extent that they avoided armed reprisals by the British, but their doctrinal position, that congregational prayers were not allowed in Dar-ul-Harb, the domain of war, as they characterized British rule, was undeniably a political stance.

Apart from propagating their beliefs, the Faraidis were successful in communal organization and imposed a system of control and interaction which they called a 'khilafat' system. The head, next to the *ustad* (Dudhu Miyan) were the Uparastha Khalifahs, next to them were the Superintendent Khalifah, followed by the Gaon (village) Khalifah, who was in charge of around three hundred families. Thus a whole network was at the disposal of the Faraidis, making it easier to combat the *zamindars*. In addition, they had a Panchayat system where disputes were settled. Muslims were discouraged from approaching the British judiciary. However, if they were summoned by the courts they had to attend, as did Dudhu Miyan who himself faced a number of cases filed by *zamindars* or planters.

One positive action they took was to combat the caste system within the Muslims' own professions or even the professions of their forefathers which had led to discrimination and segregation. Even fishmongering was looked down upon. The Faraidis abolished this evil and social organization helped in inculcating egalitarian values. Since the Faraidi leadership, like Titu Mir's family, came from the lower middle class, class parity was all the more necessary.

Such a radical class movement invited the hostility of the vested interests of the Hindu *zamindars* and British plantation owners. However, it should be noted that this situation did not pertain to the rest of India. In neighbouring Bihar, the Muslim landlords were quite prominent, and they had Hindu tenants. Some Muslim landlords were licentious, but they were not tyrannical like the *zamindars* in Bengal.

Haji Shariatullah was in and out of police custody, because of his resistance to the *zamindars*' oppression, and his insistence on cow slaughter, but he was never convicted. During the leadership of Dudhu Miyan, the incidence of confrontation increased. During the lifetime of Haji Shariatullah, Dudhu Miyan had raised a cadre of club-wielding men, who used their blunt instruments to combat the hirelings of the landlords and planters.

Since the Faraidis were organized, the *zamindars* took strong and sweeping measures to suppress them. They inflicted various forms of torture, of which the least was sprinkling chilli powder on their beards, to prevent their tenants from joining the Faraidis. In retaliation, Dudhu Miyan led his club-bearing men in two major encounters against *zamindars*. The first was against the Sikdar (also Shiqdar) of Kanaipur in 1841. In this case, merely a show of strength was sufficient. The Shiqdar agreed to cease torture and exempted Muslim tenants from cess intended to fund Hindu festivals.

During the following year, Dudhu Miyan led a campaign against the prominent landlord Joynarain Ghosh. According to the police who investigated this incident, the landlords had degraded their tenants, including the females. The Faraidis attacked the landlord and carried off his younger brother, Madan Ghosh. Subsequently, Madan was cut to pieces and his body was buried under the riverbed of Padma. The Faraidis next turned their attention to an indigo planter, Andrew Anderson Dunlop, who had attacked Dudhu Miyan's house, killed four watchmen, severely wounded others, and stole one-and-a-half lakh of rupees.

On 5 December 1846, the Faraidis killed Anderson's agent, Kali Prasad Kanjhi Lai. Dudhu Miyan was convicted of murder by the lower court, but the appellant court, Diwani Adalat, acquitted him because his presence at the site was not proved. The British kept a watch on him and during the 1857 War of Independence, he was placed under 'protective custody'. On 24 September 1862, Dudhu Miyan died peacefully at his Dhaka residence. His grave has been declared a historical site. All reformist movements were eventually overtaken by the events of 1857.

Note

1. Muin-ud-Din Ahmad Khan, *History of the Faraidi Movement* (Karachi: Pakistan Historical Society, 1965), p. 17.

Chapter 9
The Events of 1857

The War of Independence of 1857 was the last attempt to dislodge the British by force of arms. This attempt failed, but in the process, all the parties committed and suffered great atrocities. Since these events affected the fortunes of all three communities involved, it must be considered a key point in history. Whether it should be considered a Sepoy Mutiny, as the British called it before 1947, or the First War of Independence as most South Asians called it after 1947, is still the subject of debate. During the centennial celebrations in 1957, two eminent Indian historians, Surendranath Sen and Ramesh Chandra (R.C.) Majumdar, were of the view that events were not as widespread as to be called a national struggle, nor so constricted as to be called a mere Sepoy Mutiny.

However, the question cannot be settled merely by invoking the magnitude of the events because they were governed by opportunity. The Punjab and the Deccan did not support the uprising, but they made attempts to join the war. The NWFP was not insensitive to the crisis and attempts to rebel were made by sepoys at Nowshera and Mardan on 21 and 22 May 1857. In the Punjab, Jalandhar revolutionaries marched to Delhi, and in the Deccan, there was a partial mutiny at Aurangabad on 13 June 1857.

Although both Hindus and Muslims participated and suffered, the Muslims were singled out for punishment, because of a misconception, shared by all three communities: Muslims were bitter because they had lost power to the British while the Hindus were lukewarm because they had only suffered a change of masters. The point was that the British had to struggle more against the Marathas than the Mughals to gain power in India. This misconception spread to the British because the mutineers had made the last Mughal ruler, Bahadur Shah Zafar, the titular head of their movement. The mutineers asserted the legitimacy of the Mughal empire to counteract the claims made by the British East India Company and both Hindus and Muslims were united in pursuing this course. This was an ideological stand involving an acceptance of Muslims as insiders as against the British who were considered to be, and conducted themselves as, outsiders. The proclamation by the mutineers, among whom the Hindus were in majority, of Bahadur Shah II as the emperor of India shows that the two communities were not just fighting a common enemy but were struggling for a common cause. During the mutiny, Hindus and Muslims forgot their differences, and in the aftermath of 1857, neither community can be blamed for bringing about disunity. Their unity did not last as not all Indians were united in the cause of dislodging the British.

Just as the battle of Plassey was won with a majority of Indian soldiers,[1] the Sepoy Mutiny was overcome with the help of Indian allies. Maharashtrian and Sikh soldiers joined in suppressing the mutineers in Awadh and Rohilkhand.[2] The transformation of Sepoy attitudes which took place between 1757 and 1857 was the cause of the mutiny.

CAUSES.—The causes of the mutiny were political, economic, and religious. Although sepoys had joined the British, they had not forgotten patriotism. In 1806, sepoys at Vellore (South India) showed visible sympathy for Tipu Sultan. In 1824, sepoys in Barrackpore (Bengal) refused to serve in the campaign against Burma because perquisites for past services were not being offered.[3] The British underestimated the effects of this and were unprepared for the magnitude of the outbreak of hostility. The annexation by the British of Awadh in 1856, added to the unrest. The steps the East India Company took were insufficient to prevent a rising but aroused suspicion. The number of British troops was increased, and the artillery was kept away from the sepoys.

Wittingly or unwittingly, the social reforms that the British favoured, the abolition of *sati*, abolition of child marriage, and provision for the remarriage of widows aroused suspicions that the British intended to spread Christianity by force. This impression was further strengthened by an act passed by the viceroy, Lord Charles John Canning, in 1850, which allowed converts to other religions to inherit the property of their Hindu or Muslim parents or ancestors. The sepoys were made to sign contracts that they would not refuse to cross seas and would remove their earrings while in uniform.

The induction of greased cartridges for the regulation of Enfield rifles triggered the mutiny. Soldiers were required to bite the cartridge before loading, and it was widely rumoured that these cartridges were smeared with the fat of pigs and cows so that both Hindus and Muslims were defiled. The East India Company denied these rumours and cancelled the provision of biting the bullet, but suspicions had been so widely aroused that these measures came too late. This was coupled with the fact that, over the century, British high-handedness had increased.

The Sepoys noted that the salary and emoluments of Europeans were higher than theirs. Another cause of disaffection was the system of pensions and land grants for invalid soldiers or survivors of those slain. The Company maintained detailed records of sepoy families, and on this basis had the right to determine the heirs entitled to a pension. This was Lord James Dalhousie's 'Doctrine of Lapse' according to which no adopted heir could inherit in the absence of true issues. This was a cause of discontent, 'which eventually culminated in the mutiny—rebellion of 1857.'[4]

EVENTS.—On 22 January 1857, sepoys stationed at Dum Dum showed their unease about the Enfield cartridges. The discontent simmered from January to March and broke out at Barrackpore and Berhampore. Sepoys then tried to communicate with their colleagues in other cantonments by sending lotus flowers as a symbolic message asking fellow troopers to rise up. Civilians communicated through *chapatis* (a flatbread).

The mutiny proper began at Meerut on 10 May 1857. Sepoys overpowered their officers and indulged in arson and killing of European inhabitants. The mutineers marched to Delhi and on 11 May 1857, proclaimed a reluctant Bahadur Shah Zafar as the emperor of India. This step was taken to prove that the rebels had legitimate power in the land whereas the East India Company was an outright usurper. The mutineers established their rule at Delhi, forcing all European survivors to take refuge in Karnal. On 16 May, fifty European prisoners, including women and small children, were massacred in Delhi.

The mutineers moved quickly and ruthlessly but neglected to cut the telegraph wires. This alerted loyal forces far sooner than the rebels had anticipated. On 4 July 1857, Europeans were massacred at Rampur. The Lucknow residency had also been besieged and on the same day, Sir Henry Lawrence, the chief commissioner of Awadh, succumbed to his wounds. Meanwhile, the common people of Rohilkhand, Awadh, and Bihar joined the mutineers. The agricultural tax was excessive and the money-lenders rapacious, therefore both landlords and peasants had been seething with disaffection. At the same time, it should be noted that the sepoys lost the sympathy of the common people when they started taking revenge on the infirm, women, and children among the British.

The tide turned against the rebels in July. On 16 July 1857, Nana Sahib, one of the main leaders, was defeated at Fatehpur. In retaliation he ordered all 'Bengali babus' to be apprehended. On 16 August 1857, Nana Sahib Peshwa II was again defeated at Bithur. On 28 May 1859, the Nana Sahib was reported to be in Butwal (Nepal), with Hazrat Mahal, the Begum of Awadh, who had taken up arms against the British. On 20 April 1859, Nana Sahib sent a message to Queen Victoria hoping to be reconciled with the British but was unsuccessful. He reportedly died in Nepal sometime in September 1859.

As early as 1857, the British captured Bahadur Shah II at Delhi, killed two of his sons and a grandson, and sent their severed heads to the king for breakfast. This was on 22 September 1857 and two days later the Lucknow Residency was relieved by General Henry Havelock. Two prominent British generals were killed along with 600 Englishmen.

In 1858, Lakshmi Bai, the Rani of Jhansi, declared war against the British. Early in April, Jhansi was stormed and sacked but the Rani escaped. On 1 June the Rani of Jhansi, along with Tatya Tope, Rao Sahib, and the Nawab of Banda succeeded in capturing Gwalior. On 17 June, the Rani of Jhansi was killed in battle. Another revolutionary, Mahbub Khan, was hanged at Aligarh on the same day. Later, Tatya Tope was captured and hanged on 18 April 1859.

Not all events can be recounted here, but one aspect is apparent: this was an uprising in which both Hindus and Muslims participated. It was a deliberate policy of the British to blame the Muslims for playing the leading part, being convinced that they were the main leaders because the British had seized power from them. In their view Hazrat Mahal of Awadh proved to be more heroic than either her husband, the deposed Wajid Ali Shah, or even Bahadur Shah II who at one stage was more concerned with protocol than independence.

CAUSES OF FAILURE.—If we examine the reasons for the failure of the mutiny, we can see that firstly the revolutionaries had not been able to plan or synchronize their uprising. Naturally, their means of communication were not safe and reliable and being clandestine were also not very effective. Secondly, the Sikhs and the Marathas with whom the British had fought wars, sided with the British in attacking the rebels. The problem of lack of manpower, the one weakness of the British, was solved by the Sikhs and Marathas and the soldiers of the Nizam of Deccan who also came to the rescue of the British. Great valour and, at the same time, great bestiality was shown on both sides. Had Bakht Khan not been deserted while defending Delhi, the rebels would have given a better account of themselves. In the end, access to the ports and to ammunition secured victory for the British.

Nevertheless, it had been a close call for the British. A reappraisal of their rule in India was thought necessary, and though there was a widespread call for revenge, the viceroy, Lord Canning, adopted a policy of conciliation.

THE EFFECTS.—Queen Victoria was a constitutional monarch and was guided by parliament. The events of the mutiny pained her, and she did not take a one-sided view. The prime minister also decided that it was an opportune moment to end the constitutional anomaly of a trading company conducting the trial of a king (Bahadur Shah II) for treason. The first casualty of the 1857 revolt was the East India Company itself. The British Crown abolished the Company's rule and governed India directly. It was officially recognized that it was Lord Dalhousie's Doctrine of Lapse, (which provided for the annexation of a state if the ruler did not have a direct heir) that was the cause of the revolt. Lord Canning toured India and assured all princes that the British had no wish for further acquisitions. Thus about 500 states, including Kashmir and Hyderabad, were left out of British India and formed separate autonomous entities. They recognized Britain as the paramount power and ceded defence and foreign affairs to Britain but in internal matters they were quite free, having only to accommodate a British officer, 'the Resident'. J.H. Gense explains, 'That during the rising most of the states ruled by Indian princes had proved exceptionally loyal; so that it was better to have a laudatory prince than an annexed state.'⁵ An Imperial Legislative Council was formed in British India and a number of princes were admitted to the council.

Notes

1. Nirad C. Chaudhuri, *Clive of India* (Bombay: Jaico Press, 1977), p. 269.
2. Burton Stein, *A History of India* (New Delhi: Oxford University Press, 2001), p. 226.
3. Ibid.
4. Seema Alavi, *The Sepoy and the Company* (New Delhi: Oxford University Press, 1999), p. 9.
5. James H. Gense, *History of India* (Madras: Macmillan, 1957), p. 374.

IFTIKHAR-UN-NISA; HAZRAT MAHAL (b. Faizabad, Awadh, c. 1825–d. Nepal, 1879). Her maiden name was Mohammadi Khanum. She was a dancing girl who caught the eye of the king, Wajid Ali Shah. She entered the royal harem, and on the birth of her son, Birjis Qadar, she was granted the status of queen. In the upheaval of 1857, defending the honour of her nation, she emerged as a natural leader of men. She had the charisma to galvanize both the nobility and the masses, who had taken the 7 February 1856 annexation of Awadh lying down. Not conversant with the arts of war herself, she commanded brave and experienced generals, like Raja Jai Lal Singh which is another indication of the communal harmony fostered by British expansionism.

As a first step, she had her 12-year-old son, Birjis Qadar, crowned king of Awadh (July 1857). Wajid Ali Shah was somewhat taken aback by this supersedence of his position, but Bahadur Shah II ratified this investiture. It was taken for granted that Hazrat Mahal would rule in the name of her son. The siege of Lucknow was efficiently organized and left an indelible imprint on British memory. When the British rallied, the desertions were mainly from the nobility. Hazrat Mahal confiscated the property of Raja Man Singh, who after initially siding with Awadh, went over to the British.

When the British inflicted reverses, Hazrat Mahal held court, and after recounting the treason of Sikh militias, and the rajas loyal to the British, she exhorted her subjects: 'The whole army is in Lucknow, but it is without courage. Why does it not attack Alumbagh [where the British had regrouped]? Is it waiting for the English to be reinforced and Lucknow to be surrounded?'[1] She lost the Battle of Musabagh, despite the great courage and gallantry displayed by her troops, but she did not lose heart. She emerged as a politician through tumultuous events—the first in South Asia after the ancient Chanakya. This was most evident in her rejoinder to the proclamation of Queen Victoria, on 1 November 1858, ending the rule of the East India Company. The proclamation provided an opening to end the uprising.

In her counter-proclamation, issued on the next day, Hazrat Mahal said that the British were not to be trusted. She reiterated that the British never forgive a fault, be it great or small. 'What is the use of accepting the idea that the Company is dead, and that now the Queen rules; when the laws, settlements and judicial are all unchanged?' She went on to give details of when and where the British had broken pacts and treaties. Citing Queen Victoria's intention of rebuilding India, Hazrat Mahal issued her rebuttals. 'It is worthy of little reflection that they have promised Indians no better employment than making rocks and digging canals.'[2]

Unlike the Rani of Jhansi, who was born to a learned and cultured father, who was respected for his attachment to the Peshwa's house, Hazrat Mahal originally belonged to a profession responsible for the streak of frivolity pervading Awadh culture, therefore, historians, not without malice, mention the men in her life. The first is Mammu Khan, her pre-marital paramour, and adviser after her assumption of the throne. She finally dismissed Mammu Khan for cowardice. Mammu Khan surrendered to the British, but was, nevertheless, hanged, tragically vindicating the presentiments of his queen. The second man was, of course, her husband, Wajid Ali Shah (b. Lucknow, 30 July 1822–d. Calcutta, 21 September 1887)—who has been painted heavily as a debauched sensualist—but, who, nevertheless, displayed courage. Even his antagonist, Major-General Outram, wrote, 'I am told that his conduct at the time of annexation astonished our officers; that is, it was characterized by dignity and propriety.'

At the outbreak of the Mutiny, Wajid Ali Shah was placed under custody at Fort William. He consistently refused to sign a treaty legitimizing the annexation of his kingdom.[3] The British perceived negative opposition and passive resistance in him, which they would later encounter manifold under Gandhi. The third man was Maulvi Sikander Shah, of Faizabad; he had come on stage as a rival because of his military expertise. He came under Hazrat Mahal's service but they lost the battle of Nawabganj together. She retreated to Nepal, where she died in 1879. It was a sign of the times that the cleric could not replace the courtesan.

Notes

1. P.J.O. Taylor (ed.), *A Companion to the Mutiny of 1857* (Delhi: Oxford University Press, 1996), p. 42.
2. Ibid., p. 273.
3. Ibid., also see Mirza Ali Azhar, *King Wajid Ali Shah of Awadh*, vol. 1 (Karachi: Royal Book Company, 1982), p. 463.

Chapter 10
The Educational Movements

SIR SYED AND ALIGARH.—The first Indian reaction to the failure of the 1857 uprising was the realization that it was not possible to dislodge British rule by force of arms. The second was to seek the causes of British superiority, and the third was to prescribe modern education as the remedy for political decline. The quest for exploring non-military means of emancipation led to reform in religious thought and to the adoption of Western scientific education.

The trailblazer was Raja Ram Mohan Roy (1772–1833), who called for a reform of the Hindu religion. He claimed he was returning Hinduism to ancient Vedic purity (just as the Muslim revivalists aimed at restoring Islam to the purity of the early or right-guided caliphate). In practice, Raja Ram Mohan Roy favoured belief in one god (monotheism), repeal of the caste system, the abolition of *sati* and child marriage, and recommended the remarriage of widows. He formed an organization called the Brahmo Samaj which, though influential in the intellectual circles of Bengal, caused it and the creed of Raja Ram Mohan Roy, in general, to be cast outside the pale of Hinduism. In truth, his creed came closer to Christianity and Islam than to Hinduism as it was practised. The Bengali intelligentsia was discerning and while it rejected the prescriptions of Raja Ram Mohan Roy, it heeded his advice to adopt Western education and to qualify for service under the British.

The reaction of Sir Syed Ahmad Khan (1817–1898) to the trauma of 1857 was similar to that of Ram Mohan Roy and ran into similar difficulties. Sir Syed tried to modernize Muslim beliefs. He sought a natural explanation for every phenomenon and denied the incidence of miracles recounted in the Holy Quran and Hadith. He said every law is according to nature and that there can be no contradiction between the work of God and the word of God. Every belief had to be subordinate to science. No wonder then that he too was branded a heretic. This was, in fact, also a great psychological reaction because, in his youth, Sir Syed had written a pamphlet to 'prove' that the sun revolved around the earth! Amid all these controversies, Sir Syed published a refutation of Sir William Muir's *Life of Mahomet*, a scurrilous attack on the Holy Prophet (PBUH), and carried his inquiry to the Western side by subjecting the Bible to theological scrutiny. This represents the first aspect of Sir Syed's contribution.

The second aspect was political. He had saved British lives at Bijnor in 1857, therefore there was a hard core of Englishmen who paid attention to what he said. Sir Syed wrote several pamphlets and books, the most prominent among them being *The Causes of the Indian Revolt*, which he sent to the members of the British Parliament. To a great many, whose arrogance had increased by their success in 1857, this book, in itself constituted treason, but others, as reflective of 1857 as the Indians, gave it their serious attention.

There were two main strands in the writings of Sir Syed Ahmad: first, to explain that Muslims were not obliged, by their belief, to oppose British rule. In the second strand, he maintained that the main cause of the 1857 uprising was the absolute lack of communication between the British and the natives, between the rulers and the ruled. Sir Syed said that had there been any means of bringing Indian aspirations to the notice of the British, the 1857 war would not have erupted.

The last observation, it is said, led Allan Octavian Hume (1829–1912), to lay the foundation of the Indian National Congress (1885) as a forum for forming Indian aspirations and airing them. However, Sir Syed emerged as the foremost critic of the Congress. It is important to recall the circumstances under which the Congress was founded; it had a British convenor(Hume) and the blessings of the British. Sir Syed could have been expected to go along with it, but he did not. As Aziz Ahmad has explained, at first Sir Syed remained silent, but he spoke out in 1887 when a Muslim, Badruddin Tyabji, was elected as the Congress president.

Earlier, Sir Syed had not taken a separatist stance, but in 1867, just ten years after the mutiny, a language controversy between Hindi and Urdu arose, when Hindus said Hindi should replace Urdu as the language of instruction and of the courts. Hindi was the language of the majority, but the Muslim elite regarded Urdu as representative of the joint Indo-Muslim culture, therefore this demand came as a shock to them. Both an Indian and a Pakistani historian, Tara Chand and Farman Fatehpuri have concurred that the Muslim reaction to Hindi was conditioned by the fact that Hindi had not naturally evolved as a language; the British through Fort William College, Calcutta, patronized *Prem Sagar* by Laloo Lalji to create deliberately a Sanskritized version of Hindi which was different from the spoken language.

The result of this cultural shock was that Sir Syed, who had previously said that India was a bride with one Hindu eye and one Muslim eye, now said that Hindus and Muslims were separate nations. He said that if the British withdrew, Muslims would not share power with the Hindus but would lead a life of subjugation. With these presentiments, Sir Syed opposed Muslim participation in the Indian National Congress. He forecast that despite being favoured by the British, the Congress was a political party and at some juncture, it could come into conflict with the British; if the Muslims participated in it, they would again face punishment as they had after 1857. His fears were justified as even Pandit Jawaharlal Nehru has written that Muslims suffered more than Hindus after 1857.

Sir Syed had the example of Raja Ram Mohan Roy before him and knew fully well that his own religious views were considered heretical, therefore he consciously sought to separate his religious outlook from his educational reforms. It was to this end that he inducted the services of Shibli Nomani (1857–1914) to teach Islamic studies at Aligarh.

Sir Syed's first venture was to open a school at Muradabad, in 1858 just one year after the mutiny. Sir Syed had embarked on his career of imparting Western education while the mutiny was still in the news. The next step was to establish a translation society at Ghazipur, in January 1864. Later it was renamed the Scientific Society because its purpose was to translate scientific literature into Urdu. It was in Aligarh that Sir Syed gave expression to his main ambition in education. In 1866 he founded the *Aligarh Institute Gazette* a magazine devoted to the cultural needs of Muslims having an English education. Also at Aligarh, Sir Syed started a primary school on 24 May 1875, Queen Victoria's birthday, and on 1 January 1877 the viceroy, Lord Lytton, laid the foundation stone of the college. The All-India Muhammadan Educational Conference was founded at Aligarh in 1866, a society that held its sessions all over the country and was the means of spreading the spirit and the message of Aligarh to all corners of the country. It was the All-Indian Muslim Educational Conference (as it was later known) that proved to be the parent body of the All-India Muslim League in 1906.

It was twenty-two years after Sir Syed's death, in 1920, that Aligarh College was raised to the status of a university. Lord Macaulay, the great historian, had favoured the spread of Western education in India, with English as the medium of instruction, but to get conservative Indians to accept this was quite another matter. Raja Mohan Roy persuaded the Hindus and Sir Syed Ahmad Khan persuaded the Muslims. It was only due to their efforts that Hindus and Muslims began to demand from the British the fruits of modern Western education.

Sir Syed held communal and class interests supreme and did not favour modern education being imparted to the lower classes. He also did not favour the emancipation of Muslim women. These criticisms have substance, but if one considers the progress that Western education made due to Sir Syed's efforts, one realizes the extent of Sir Syed's contribution to the Indo-Muslim Renaissance. Peter Hardy offers an objective appraisal of Sir Syed's movement: 'What Aligarh did was to produce a class of Muslim leaders with a footing in both Western and Islamic culture, at ease both in British and Muslim society and endowed with a consciousness of their claims to be the aristocracy of the country as much in British as in Mughal times.'[1]

It was this last-named trait that gave the Muslim community the morale necessary to voice the demand for Pakistan. Jinnah was to call the Muslim University, Aligarh, his arsenal. Two heads of the new Pakistani state, the first prime minister, Liaquat Ali Khan, and the second president, Mohammad Ayub Khan, were graduates of the Muslim University, Aligarh.

DEOBAND.—Sir Syed had been inspired not only by Lord Macaulay but by Shah Waliullah as well. Sir Syed's mission was to preserve the future of the Muslim community. There were conservative elements, opposed to him, who were anxious to ensure the religious identity of the community, and the premier traditional institution where this need was nurtured was the Darul Uloom at Deoband. Aligarh was considered loyal to the British, and Deoband was hostile. Aligarh worked against the Congress, and Deoband did not favour separatism. Aligarh and Deoband were to exercise profound influences on the Muslim mind from opposite directions.

Deoband lies in the Saharanpur district of the United Provinces. The Darul Uloom (seminary) began as a small *maktab* (a primary school where the three Rs are taught). It was founded on 30 May 1867 by Maulana Fazlur Rahman, the father of Maulana Shabbir Ahmad Usmani, and Maulana Zulfiqar Ali, the father of Shaikh-ul-Hind, Maulana Mahmud-ul-Hasan. Later, the Darul Uloom was run by Maulana Muhammad Qasim Nanotvi (1832–1880) and Maulana Rashid Ahmad Gangohi (1828–1905).

Since Aligarh was founded to further the material progress of the Muslims, the ulama of Deoband pointedly illustrated their reliance on the bounty of Allah by refusing to plan, and therefore refused all grants and sources of fixed income. Neither the government nor rich patrons were allowed to contribute to the funding of the Darul Uloom. Apart from showing their reliance on God for their day-to-day sustenance, by refusing large grants they preserved their intellectual and ideological freedom. Despite such strict screening of funds, the buildings of the seminary were completed in good time through small donations from the people. At the end of the first year, seventy-eight students had enrolled. Today it is the largest seminary after the Al Azhar University in Cairo. It is a residential university and students from all over the world study there.

The seminary of Deoband follows essentially the syllabus of the Madrasah-i Rahimiyah founded by Shah Abdur Rahim (father of Shah Waliullah), where Shah Waliullah himself and his sons, Shah Abdul Aziz (1746–1824) and Shah Abdul Qadir (d.1813) had taught. The syllabus was consequently traditional, Arabic including prosody and rhetoric, logic, indirectly obtained from the Greeks, *kalam* (religious discourse), jurisprudence, Quranic exegesis, Hadith, and its subordinate disciplines and, somewhat surprisingly, *tibb* or traditional medicine. Urdu was the medium of instruction. The students were trained in very few vocations and the result was that the graduates of Deoband spread out all over the country to seek positions in mosques and madrassas. It was this practice that made Deoband not the name of a seminary, but the name of a creed.

This creed was derived from the Mujahideen, the followers of Sayyid Ahmad Barelvi, Titu Mir, and Haji Shariatullah. They forbade belief in the intercession of saints, and prescribed limits beyond which adulation of the Holy Prophet (PBUH) himself transgressed the concept of *tauhid* (or monotheism). Visiting the graves of saints and Sufis was forbidden as was *nazr* and *niaz* (religious food offerings) and of course, *azadari* in Muharram was forbidden.

Maulana Qasim Nanotvi wrote a book, *Tasfiyatul Aqaid*, to counteract and refute the religious thought of Sir Syed Ahmad Khan. In this work, he asserted that reason was subordinate to Hadith. The Deobandis held that 'which God commands is good, rather than God commands what is good'.[2] The ulama of Deoband wrote tracts against Judaism, Christianity, and Hinduism and carried out *jihad* against Ahmadis. On the political plane, the ulama of Deoband, especially Maulana Rashid Ahmad Gangohi, issued a *fatwa* that it was permissible to associate with the Congress under certain circumstances, but under no condition was it possible to cooperate with Aligarh. In the 20th century, Deoband continued its relations with Congress and opposed the Muslim League. This did not prevent the Congress government of independent India from closing down the Deoband Seminary. The ban was brief, but it was a sad comment on the political stance of Deoband. Of the prominent ulama of Deoband, only Allama Shabbir Ahmad Usmani (1885–1949) was a supporter of the Pakistan Movement.

MADRASSA MANZAR-E-ISLAM, BARELVI.—The Deobandis and Barelvis are the two major denominations of Sunni Islam in South Asia. The Deobandi persuasion was the successor of all the revivalist movements beginning with Shah Waliullah. Although Sayyid Ahmad Barelvi, Titu Mir, and Haji Shariatullah did not identify themselves with the creed or movement of Shaikh Muhammad bin Abdul Wahhab (1703–1792) there was nevertheless sufficient resemblance for the British to label all South Asian revivalist movements of Sunni Islam as Wahhabi, though it did not represent the majority of Sunni Muslims—who were shocked by the Wahhabi desecration of holy tombs in Madinah and its attack on Karbala. To the Sunni Muslims with Sufi tendencies, who venerated Sufi saints and who flocked to the tombs of the Sufis, the revivalism of Deoband was sacrilege. They believed in offering *fateha* for the departed and believed in the intercession of saints and other holy personages for the salvation of their souls. Ever since Shah Ismail *Shaheed* had published *Taqwiyat-ul-Iman* there had arisen a tendency to decentralize the love and veneration for the Holy Prophet (PBUH) in the revivalist creeds. To correct this, Maulana Ahmad Raza Khan of Barelvi (1856–1921) made his appearance. He founded the Madrassa Manzar-e-Islam in his hometown. Ahmad Raza Khan was a spellbinding orator and a good poet, writing *na'ats* in praise of the Holy Prophet (PBUH) and other holy personages of Islam. He believed in the Qadiri Silsila and believed that Shaikh Abdul Qadir Jilani was at the apex of spiritual authority, below the Holy Prophet (PBUH). Ahmad Raza Khan believed in the intercessory power of the Holy Prophet (PBUH) and the venerated Sufi saints. He had a high regard for the Syeds. Usha Sanyal sums up his mission: 'In all he did or wrote, love of the Prophet was the motivating factor.'³ Of all the madrassa founders, Ahmad Raza Khan was the only one to expound the two-nation theory. This is contained in his book *al-Hujjat al-Muwtammah*. As such Ahmad Raza Khan can also be considered one of the spiritual founders of Pakistan.

NADVAT-UL-ULAMA, LUCKNOW.—Many dignitaries within the Muslim community were concerned about the contrast between Deoband and Aligarh. Deoband focused solely on the afterlife, while Aligarh only cared about worldly matters. To address this imbalance, there was a need to establish an institution that catered to both the spiritual and temporal needs of the Muslims.

The proposal to establish the Nadvat-ul-Ulama was floated in Kanpur by Maulana Muhammad Ali Mongeri in 1892. It received an impetus when Maulana Abdul Hye joined the Nadva and undertook a tour of Bareli and Fatehpur to seek support for this institution, and on 2 September 1898 Nadvat-ul-Ulama was transferred to Lucknow.

A new life was infused into the Nadva when Shibli Nomani joined it after the death of Sir Syed. His celebrity shed lustre on Nadvat-ul-Ulama. Shibli Nomani had been a protégé of Sir Syed but, over the years, he felt that Sir Syed had become more loyalist and communal than the circumstances warranted. His background in traditional Arabic education and his exposure to modern education at Aligarh made him the most suitable person to head Nadvat-ul-Ulama, but this was only in theory. In practice, and despite the stated purpose of founding the Nadva, Shibli faced resistance from a group of his colleagues led by Safdar Yar Jung when he tried to introduce a minimum of English and science into the Nadva syllabus.

Later, when Maulvi Abdul Karim challenged Shibli's concept of *jihad* in an article, Shibli dismissed him from service. At this, a storm of protest was raised and Shibli had to leave the Nadva. When asked what the achievement of the Nadva had been, he replied that the production of a scholar like Syed Suleman Nadvi alone justified the establishment of the Nadva. However, Syed Suleman Nadvi was not alone; a galaxy of scholars like Riyasat Ali Nadvi, Najeeb Ashraf Nadvi, Abdul Hye Nadvi, Muzzafaruddin Nadvi, and Abul Hasan Nadvi were among the ulama produced by the Nadva. They excelled in historiography, literary criticism, and theology. Shibli's successor and official biographer, Maulana Syed Suleman Nadvi, was also a pupil of Maulana Ashraf Ali Thanvi, the renowned *alim* from Deoband. Due to his influence, the Nadva began to lean more towards Deoband than towards Aligarh. Shibli's impact on his first generation of disciples was limited, but he was able to influence considerably the second generation. This was no mean achievement.

ANJUMAN HIMAYAT-I-ISLAM.—The Anjuman Himayat-i-Islam was founded against the backdrop of Christian missionary activity in the Punjab. It was not a policy of the British Raj to convert the natives to Christianity, but missionaries, mostly European, were engaged in converting the poorer section of society. Another challenge came from the Arya Samaj who had made it their mission to reconvert to Hinduism the descendants of those who had converted to Islam. The Anjuman represented a beleaguered minority when it was formed. The initiative to establish a society to support Islam and prevent conversion was taken by Qazi Khalifa Hameed ud Din, a scion of a noble family of Lahore. The Anjuman was founded on 24 September 1884. The other office bearers were Maulvi Ghulamullah Qasuri (honorary secretary) Munshi Chiragh Din and Munshi Pir Bakhsh (joint secretaries) and Munshi Abdur Rahim Khan (treasurer).

By the end of December 1885, there were 600 members. Their office was set up in the Haveli of Sikander Khan. The Anjuman raised its funds in a novel manner; every member would put a handful of wheat flour in an earthen vessel every day. The volunteers would collect this flour and go from door to door selling the flour for one-and-a-half rupees. In this way the Anjuman raised Rs 754 per month but spent only Rs 344.

There were four aims of the Anjuman as determined by the founders: to counter the propagation of Christian missionaries and Arya Samajists, to preserve Islamic values, to spread religious and modern education to the youth of the community, and to further social and cultural development. The last aim was taken very seriously. The Anjuman not only founded educational institutions for boys and girls but also for adults. It founded orphanages and shelters for women. It founded seven boys' schools, two girls' schools, and also the famous Islamia College which became no less an 'arsenal' than Aligarh during the Pakistan Movement. Muslim politics in the Punjab took many turns, but it was the Anjuman Himayat-i-Islam that gave the Muslim cause its constant attention.

Only after the Anjuman had established its credentials by collecting funds from its members, did the rulers of the princely states, like the Nizam of Hyderabad, the Amir of Bahawalpur, the nawabs of Bhopal and Rampur, start sending their contributions. King Habibullah of Afghanistan had the Habibiya Hall of Islamia College built. One feature of the Anjuman was to have its annual sessions presided over by literary luminaries such as Sir Syed Ahmad Khan, Maulana Shibli Nomani, and Maulana Zafar Ali Khan. However, the most distinguished personage was Allama Iqbal. Allama Iqbal had stopped reciting at the *mushairas* but recited his long poems from 1903 onwards. The first such poem was *Nala-e-Yateem* (The Lament of an Orphan). Copies of Allama Iqbal's poems were sold on the spot, thereby generating more funds.

Other dignitaries who served the Anjuman as presidents were Sir Muhammad Shafi, Nawab Sir Zulfiqar Ali Khan, Sir Abdul Qadir, and Sir Fazl-i-Hussain. They ensured not only quality education for Muslims but also performed social and political services when the political forces of Punjab such as the Unionist government, were hostile. It was the students of Islamia College who brought Jinnah safely to Minto Park in a procession for the historic Lahore session in the very tense atmosphere created by the Khaksars. It was on the grounds of Islamia College that Jinnah hoisted what was to become the national flag of Pakistan, and it was the students of Islamia College who canvassed for the votes which brought Punjab—the very province whose adherence was most vital to the creation of Pakistan—to the Muslim League. This was the institution that brought together the services of Allama Iqbal and Mohammad Ali Jinnah.

SINDH MADRESSATUL ISLAM, KARACHI.—Sindh was the first province to demand separation based on its Muslim majority, and the first province to call for separate Hindu and Muslim federations. Sindh's assembly was the first to demand partition, and Sindh's premier institution, the Sindh Madressatul Islam, was the alma mater of the founder of Pakistan. All these achievements were made possible by the founding of the Sindh Madressa.

Sindh Madressa owed its existence to the efforts and vision of a great benefactor, Hasan Ali Effendi (1830–1895). He conferred directly with Sir Syed when he went to Aligarh to admit his children. Sir Syed was impressed by this devoted man and advised him not to be content with founding a school but to aim at establishing a college and a university too. Hasan Ali Effendi also came into contact with Syed Amir Ali, and it was under the auspices of the National Muhammadan Association, that the Sindh Madressa was formed.

Hasan Ali Effendi opened the Sindh Madressa on 1 September 1885 and had it formally inaugurated by the viceroy, Lord Dufferin, on 14 November 1887. Not only did Sindh Madressa spread education and political awareness throughout Sindh, but it also produced the most illustrious students including Quaid-i-Azam Mohammad Ali Jinnah, Sir Shahnawaz Bhutto, Sir Ghulam Hussain Hidayatullah, Haji Sir Abdullah Haroon, Dr Umar Muhammad Daudpota, Dr I.I. Kazi and a host of other luminaries.

The Sindh Madressa body, also established, one after the other, the S.M. Science College, S.M. Arts and Commerce College, and S.M. Law College, institutions which had luminaries among their faculty and students. Sindh was known as Babul Islam, the gate of Islam in India, and this gate was opened for the emancipation and the glory of Pakistan by the students of Sindh Madressatul Islam, Karachi. Sindh Madressatul Islam became a university in 2012.

ISLAMIA COLLEGE, PESHAWAR.—Like the Punjab, the NWFP also had an association called the Anjuman Himayat-i-Islam that founded an institution that grew to be Islamia College, Peshawar. Over time it became the University of Peshawar. In 1890, Babu Haider Thakedar and Mian Abdul Karim set up the Anjuman. An Englishman, George Roos-Keppel (d.1919) collaborated with Nawab Sahibzada Abdul Qayyum and according to Sir Olaf Caroe: 'Together they created the Islamia College, now grown into the University of Peshawar. That is their joint and visible monument, the tribute to their foresight and wisdom. No man who was not great, whose imagination did not soar, would have established a great place of learning on the very margin of the cultivated land, overlooked by the black jaws of Khaibar, open maybe to raiders, on the very site of the furious battle between Akbar Khan and Hari Singh.[5]

This vision infused life into the intellectual and cultural body of the Pathans. In the 1940s, Islamia College had a very distinguished and effective principal, Sir Ian Dixon Scott, who later, as a member of the viceroy's staff, was to contribute to the uplift of this institution. It is a matter of significance that the founder of Pakistan chose Sindh Madressa, Karachi, Islamia College, Peshawar, and Muslim University, Aligarh to bequeath his wealth in recognition of their contribution to the Pakistan Movement.

Notes

1. Peter Hardy, *The Muslims of British India* (Cambridge University Press, 1972; Reprint, New Delhi, 1998), p. 103.
2. Ibid., p. 171.
3. Usha Sanyal, 'Pir, Shaikh and Prophet', in T.N. Madan (ed.), *Muslim Communities of South Asia* (New Delhi: Manohar, 1995), p. 442.
4. Olaf Caroe, *The Pathans* (London: Macmillan, 1965), p. 424.

Part 3
History of the Political Struggle

CHAPTER 11
The Political Aspects of the Aligarh Movement

Political activity began at the turn of the 20th century. When Urdu was curtailed, Muslims formed the Urdu Defence Association on 2 May 1900 at Aligarh. The next stage was the Partition of Bengal on 16 October 1905 at Calcutta (now Kolkata), which led to violent Hindu protests. As a reaction, the conservative section of Muslims formed the Simla (now Shimla) Deputation on 1 October 1906, while the radical element established the All-India Muslim League on 30 December 1906 at Dhaka.

The Muslim community of India had developed its centre at Aligarh in the aftermath of the 1857 uprising. Only two years after the death of their leader, Sir Syed Ahmad Khan, the Muslims of the United Provinces (UP) received a cultural setback with the introduction of Hindi by the British in 1900. Since the use of Urdu had been actually banned in Bihar, the UP Muslims were alarmed. Although Sir Syed had warned Muslims against political activity against the British, the resurgence of the Hindi–Urdu conflict forced the Muslims to disregard his advice: after all, it was the 1867 Hindi–Urdu conflict that had originally led Sir Syed to formulate his Two-Nation theory. Muslims began to organize themselves politically and to protest against the official decision. Nawab Mohsinul Mulk, the new secretary of Aligarh College, organized the Urdu Defence Association on 2 May 1900.

Urdu replaced Persian as the official language in 1837. Thirty years later the Hindi–Urdu conflict broke out. Four years later, on 7 November 1871 at Muzaffarpur, the Lt. Governor of Bihar, George Campbell banned the use of Urdu in offices and schools. On 13 May 1872, the Muslims organized a public protest at Aligarh followed by a meeting on 18 August 1872 in Lucknow.

These activities invited the wrath of Sir Antony McDonnell, the Lt. Governor of UP. He had moved the Hindi resolution and, feeling that he had been defied, forced Mohsinul Mulk to resign from the Urdu Defence Association. These measures politicized the Muslims even more. In October 1901, a meeting of Muslim notables was called at the Lucknow residence of Hamid Ali Khan. It was here that the Mohammadan Political Organization was formed.

THE PARTITION OF BENGAL.—The earliest associations that the Muslims had formed were in Calcutta. On 31 January 1856, the Mohammadan Association was founded with Fazlur Rahman as president and Mohammad Mazhar as secretary. The Mohammadan Literary Society was founded in 1863 by Nawab Abdul Latif. The first open political body was established in 1878 by Syed Amir Ali, called the National Mohammadan Association. In Bengal, the British had first established themselves and built their capital city, Calcutta, which led the rest of India to adopt Western education, manners, and fashions.

It should be noted that political activity as such was a British importation. The native rule for centuries had been autocratic; what passed for politics was intrigues and conspiracies. The democratic ideals of Europe came along with Western education. Politics as a public activity began with the founding of the Indian National Congress with official encouragement from a British convenor, Allan Octavian Hume. But in 1905, Lord Curzon, the viceroy, was exasperated with the Congress.

Bengal was a large, thickly populated area and Calcutta had to administer not only British India but the Bengal presidency itself. Lord Curzon, for reasons of facilitating administration, divided Bengal into two parts, West and East. As a consequence of the partition of Bengal in 1905, Assam was tagged with East Bengal to form the province of East Bengal. Although both parts of Bengal were to be under British rule, the creation of a new province in the east led to sharp Hindu protests.

Bengal was a Muslim-majority area, the Muslims were unaware of this, as in West Bengal, where Calcutta was located, there was a concentration of Hindus. Muslim rule under the nawabs of Murshidabad practically ended in 1757 and in the 1857 upheaval, the vestige of Muslim revivalist movements like those of Titu Mir and the Faraidi had been wiped out.

The reason why there was such uproar was that West Bengal became predominantly Hindu and East Bengal predominantly Muslim. The Hindu reaction was visibly religious. The protest meeting on 16 October 1905, the day the partition took effect, was organized at the Kali temple. The protest was swiftly and efficiently arranged because the vested interests of the professional classes were in danger.

The professional classes in the main cities grew as a result of Western education. These classes were led by lawyers. During the Hindi–Urdu controversy of 1900, it was noted that most of the leaders from both sides had been lawyers. Knowing the law of their masters they could plead for their clients in the courts and for their country in the assemblies. They had large incomes and independent status, therefore, they could afford to enter the political arena. Lawyers practised in the chief court in Calcutta which had jurisdiction over all of Bengal, thus they had clients throughout Bengal.

Next came the doctors who were highly educated and, since they could cure a number of diseases that traditionally trained *hakims* or *vaids* could not, they were highly regarded. Sometimes the doctor would be the only educated person in an entire village, therefore his opinion, even on political matters, carried weight. Third in line were the professors at Calcutta University. Though they were employed by the government and were not allowed to participate in political activities, they enjoyed an autonomous status and could influence students indirectly. When Sir Ashutosh Mukherjee became vice-chancellor of Calcutta University, he prescribed Lord Byron's poem *The Childe Harold's Pilgrimage* in the syllabus. This poem filled the students with revolutionary fervour.

Following the 1905 partition, the new Muslim-majority provinces of East Bengal and Assam threatened the wealth and influence of the professional classes. The new province would have a new chief court, a new medical college hospital, and a new university, all located in Dhaka. The Calcutta lawyers would lose half their briefs, and the Dhaka lawyers would gain them along with the money and influence. The doctors of Calcutta would lose half their patients who would, for reasons of convenience and economy, seek doctors and hospitals closer at hand. Doctors from the region would have greater opportunities for education and practice. The University of Dhaka would cater to students not able to obtain admission in Calcutta, and teaching posts would go to local people.

Because of the lead the Hindus had in all three professions, all the new posts and opportunities would initially go to them. But they saw all the implications and looked ahead. Dominance in Calcutta, in undivided Bengal, seemed to them the more secure policy. The people of Bengal were united by language but divided by religion. At that juncture, religion became the overriding sentiment, and the Kali temple in Calcutta became the starting point of agitation against partition.

The Indian National Congress, thoroughly disliked by Curzon, was still under the control of the moderates led by Gopal Krishna Gokhale (1866–1915). But a radical group supporting the protest sprang up led by Bal Gangadhar Tilak (1856–1920) and Lala Lajpat Rai (1865–1928).

Leaders of the Agitation. Sir Surendranath Banerjee (1848–1925); Jatindramohan Tagore (1831–1908); Rai Bahadur Norendranath Sen (1843–1911); Motilal Ghose (1847–1922); Bipin Chandra Pal (1858–1932).

Very early in the term of the new province, its lieutenant governor, Sir Joseph Bampfylde Fuller (1854–1935), was forced to resign. He had been dealing with the agitation firmly and was widely considered pro-Muslim and was indeed looked up to by the Muslims whom the partition had benefited. Fuller had disaffiliated two schools in Sirajganj because their students had taken part in the agitation. This was disallowed by Lord Minto (1847–1914) the new viceroy, and Fuller resigned. The Muslims of Bengal mourned the removal of Fuller just as the Muslims of UP had rejoiced over the retirement of McDonnell. It seems that rather than adopting a policy of 'Divide and Rule', British functionaries were themselves divided into pro-Hindu and pro-Muslim groups. Fuller's resignation was seen with foreboding by Bengal Muslims. They had been encouraged by policy statements of the British that the partition of Bengal was a settled issue. Sir Bampfylde Fuller's resignation showed that this resolve could weaken.

The resolve was broken because the agitation was marked by violence. This violence was uninhibited, it was directed against the highest dignitaries and not confined to India. Sir Curzon Wyllie, political secretary to John Morley, secretary of state, was killed in London on 1 July 1909. Two successive viceroys were attacked along with their wives but survived. Lord and Lady Minto were attacked in Ahmadabad on 13 November 1909. After the partition was annulled, on 23 December 1912, Lord and Lady Hardinge were attacked in Delhi; Lord Hardinge survived but was severely injured.

In Bihar, a public prosecutor and a deputy superintendent of police were assassinated. A judge in Muzaffarpur escaped when he was attacked but a European lady and her daughter were killed. Trains and telegraph lines were a constant target of terrorism. Three attempts to derail trains were recorded and twelve attempts were made to bomb them.

As a result of these activities, two groups of Muslim politicians emerged. One, centred in Bengal, grateful for the creation of the Muslim province of East Bengal and Assam, was concerned to see that it was not undone. Another group, centred mostly in UP, realizing that the British, exasperated with the Hindus, might be sympathetic to their plight, decided to approach Viceroy Lord Minto at his summer residence at Simla.

THE SIMLA DEPUTATION.—The Simla Deputation that called on Viceroy Lord Minto, on 1 October 1906, was led by Sir Aga Khan III. The Aga Khan was chosen with the confidence that the British would listen to him. As secretary of the Aligarh College, Mohsinul Mulk was the successor of Sir Syed and it was expected that the Muslim community would listen to him. Mohsinul Mulk had to incur a personal loan of Rs 2000 from Kings & Kings Company. The memorial was drafted by Nawab Imadul Mulk (1844–1926) and was signed by 1,461,183 Muslims. The deputation stressed that the Muslims were a large and distinct community in India and formed at least one-fifth of the total Indian population. They said their importance should not be measured only by their population, but by their cultural and historical role. They mentioned that Muslims had been the rulers of India barely a century before.

Their four demands were for separate electorates for Muslims, weightage, a larger share in government service, and the status of a university for Aligarh College.

In his reply, Lord Minto expressed profound sympathy for the Muslims especially their plea that their importance extended beyond their numbers. He mentioned that the partition of Bengal was a settled issue, although the deputation did not directly mention this. He did not mention any other demand, for example, giving more government and judicial posts to Muslims or elevating the Aligarh College to the status of a university.

Contrary to the general impression, Lord Minto did not accept any of the demands of the delegates. He was sympathetic but did not commit himself to any step whatsoever.

> **THE DEMANDS OF THE SIMLA DEPUTATION**
>
> 1. *Separate electorates.* This meant that Muslim voters would be registered separately from the Hindus and would vote only for Muslim candidates. The candidates could be independent or belong to any party.
> 2. *Weightage.* This meant that minorities would be given more representation than their population proportion. For example, the Muslims of UP were 13 per cent of the population; they would get 20 per cent representation.
> 3. *Government and Judicial Service.* This was the most sought-after employment. It brought handsome salaries, power, and influence in society at large. People adopted Western education mainly to qualify for such posts. Appointments as judges were even more prestigious. Judges were supposed to judge impartially between the government and the people. They enjoyed an autonomous status which even English officers had to respect.
> 4. *Aligarh* was the nerve centre of the Muslim political revival. As long as the college was subordinate to a university for examinations and award of degrees, it could not freely prescribe its own syllabus or award post-graduate degrees. The college acquired university status in 1920.

The demands for separate electorates were based on practical considerations. The Muslims of Bengal, who comprised more than 50 per cent of Indian Muslims, had a little over 10 per cent representation in provincial councils.[1]

The demand for separate electorates was not achieved at Simla but was the means by which the demand for Pakistan was ultimately achieved. Two years later, on 27 November 1908, Lord Morley (1838–1923), the secretary of state for India, suggested a new system for Muslim representation: reservation, but not separate electorates. Lord Minto did not object to the new scheme and the Muslims began to display anxiety. The honorary secretary of the Muslim League, Syed Hasan Bilgrami, commented that under Morley's scheme, all the Muslim votes of a constituency would be insufficient to elect the candidate of their choice. The reservation of seats would only ensure that the Hindus could elect any Muslim they nominated. When Muslims raised a storm of protest, Morley said in effect that there could be separate electorates but no weightage. Still later, after Syed Hasan Bilgrami and Syed Amir Ali had applied pressure, Morley conceded separate electorates at all levels. Bilgrami had argued on 23 February 1909 in parliament, that separate electorates were already practised in some constituencies; the Muslims only wanted the law to be applied all over India. It was the deputation that met Morley on 23 February 1909 in London that made separate electorates a part of the constitution in 1909 [see Chapter 12].

THE CONSPIRACY THEORY.—It is often alleged that the Simla Deputation was a British conspiracy to subvert the movement for Indian independence. The Simla Deputation was called by the viceroy following the announcement of the acceptance of separate electorates which divided the Hindus and Muslims, it was alleged.

Fuller's departure caused discomfiture to Muslims. Mohsinul Mulk wrote to William A.J. Archbold, principal of Aligarh College to ask if Lord Minto would receive a delegation of Muslims. Archbold contacted the viceroy's secretary, Dunlop Smith, in Simla who, after using persuasion, replied to Mohsinul Mulk that a delegation would be welcome. Archbold's reply was quoted but Mohsinul Mulk's letter was suppressed to create an impression that the initiative came through Archbold. While insisting that a conspiracy existed, Peter Hardy wrote that 'The members of the Simla Deputation knew in advance that they would not, to say the least, meet with a hostile reception from Lord Minto, and that this preknowledge powerfully influenced the requests they made and the manner in which they made them.'

Francis Robinson, on the other hand, refutes this argument by observing that, 'Yet in October 1906 Minto promised and intended to promise nothing except sympathy'.[2] The correspondence between Morley and Minto also confirms that the initiative had not come from the British, nor did the Muslims gain anything from sending this deputation. It has assumed importance only because it was seen as a step leading to the foundation of the Muslim League.

Notes

1. R.A. Zakaria, *Muslims of India 1885–1905* (London University Thesis, 1948), p. 155.
2. Francis Robinson, *Separatism Among Indian Muslims* (Delhi: Oxford University Press, 1994), p. 147.

CHAPTER 12
THE FORMATION OF THE ALL-INDIA MUSLIM LEAGUE, 1906

BACKGROUND.—Political parties are the gift of British rule in India. Britain has a constitutional monarchy which means that the actual conduct of government is not carried out by the monarch but by elected members of parliament. When the British decided to introduce their own system of education into India, they were also introducing their concept of democracy. They did not introduce their political practices and concepts because they had conquered India by force of arms and naturally wished to rule autocratically. In Britain, on the other hand, there were statesmen who forced the East India Company to act responsibly and respect the human rights of the conquered people. This can be illustrated by a brief summary of the Acts in the constitutional history of India on page 83. These were not constitutions in the normal sense, because a constitution contains the terms according to which a people wish to live together. Since these were imposed by foreign rulers these Acts did not have this feature. A constitution is also a law which is the basis of all other laws.

When Sir Syed Ahmad Khan analysed the causes of the 'Indian Revolt' of 1857, he stressed that the uprising occurred because there was no communication or contact between the British and Indian races. The only way known to the British for removing this barrier between the ruler and the ruled was through parliamentary democracy run by political parties. People who shared similar opinions about public matters came together and formed political parties. These parties participated in elections and sought votes on the basis of their programmes. Whichever party secured a majority in parliament formed the government. It was up to the people to retain or reject the party in power during the next elections.

THE INDIAN NATIONAL CONGRESS.—It was with the object to have representative institutions that the British actively sponsored the formation of the Indian National Congress in Bombay (now Mumbai) in 1885. Its first president was Womesh Chandra Bonnerjee. Gokhale later admitted that without British patronage, the Indian National Congress would not have succeeded. The Bengal Councils Act which practically introduced the principle of self-government came seven years after the formation of the Congress, in 1892.

With British support and Indian participation, Congress would have been the most natural means to attain self-government. This did come about, but not as fully as expected for two reasons.

The Formation of the All-India Muslim League, 1906

Democracy Suitable to India. The first reason was that the British wished to transfer power gradually, not completely, and not immediately. The second reason was that Sir Syed, who had advocated communication between the British and the Indians, challenged the representative character of the Congress, saying that it did not represent the Muslims. In 1887, Sir Syed publicly asked Muslims not to join the Congress. Since the Hindi–Urdu conflict of 1867, he had asserted that Hindus and Muslims were different nations. The Congress would represent the majority community, the Hindus; and Muslim representation would be by default as the Muslims were outnumbered four to one and were unable to secure adequate representation.

When Sir Syed told the Muslims not to join the Congress, he also discouraged them from joining or forming any political party. He explained that it was in the nature of political parties to confront the government sooner or later. Some Muslims, knowing that the British were themselves patronizing the Congress, found this hard to believe. But it was true, and within twenty years of its founding, Lord Curzon had become totally alienated from the Congress, so much so that the very concept of a political party became distasteful to the British. This is how it came about that the Congress, which was patronised by the British, was seen by them as being hostile, while the All-India Muslim League, which was formed against the wishes of the government, came to be seen as pro-British.

Who Founded the Muslim League? It is generally assumed that the same leaders of the Simla Deputation also founded the All-India Muslim League (AIML). This is far from true. It was mentioned earlier that the conservative section of Muslims led the Simla Deputation, while the radical, that is the more revolutionary and extreme, section of Muslims formed the AIML. The interests of both sections, the conservative, led by Aga Khan III and Nawab Mohsinul Mulk, and the radical section led by Nawab Viqarul Mulk (1841–1917) and Nawab Salimullah (1871–1915) were similar but not identical.

The Muslims of Bengal, led by Nawab Sir Khwaja Salimullah Bahadur of Dhaka, were concerned mainly that the partition of Bengal should not be undone. Sir Bampfylde Fuller's removal had sounded a warning bell and Bengali Muslims were apprehensive that the British might yield to violence. The leaders of the Simla Deputation had made no direct mention of Bengal's partition. The Muslims from minority provinces were concerned mostly with separate electorates. The Nawab of Dhaka was not present in Simla and Sir Aga Khan was not present in Dhaka. The Aga Khan was of the opinion that the issue of forming a political party should be left to a future generation of Muslims. The annual session of the All-India Muslim Education Conference was to be held in Dhaka in December. The secretary of the conference, Mohsinul Mulk, who was also the secretary of the Simla Deputation, wrote an article in the *Aligarh Institute Gazette* forbidding any political discussion at Dhaka. The delegates to the Muslim Educational Conference completely disregarded Mohsinul Mulk's article and founded the AIML at Dhaka on 30 December 1906. Nawab Viqarul Mulk presided. The British, who were averse to the creation of a new party, were given the excuse that if Muslim youth were not given a political party of their own, they would flock to the Congress. However, when the aims and objectives, rules, and regulations of the party were being framed, the older generation gained the upper hand. *From Consultation to Confrontation* is the title Matiur Rahman gives to his book covering these events.[1]

In retrospect, the anxiety or anger of the British over the formation of a new political party seems to have been somewhat exaggerated; but it seemed very real then. The aims and objects of the AIML were therefore expressed in terms of abject loyalty. No doubt, some members felt the need to placate the British so that the partition of Bengal would last. For some, this may have been only a stratagem to overcome British disapproval by showing their loyalty. Both factions felt the need to show unity and the above-stated objectives were adopted. Being pro-British was one criticism that the AIML faced, the other was that the party was an elite organization, not representative of the people. In 1906, this was quite true.

The main development following the foundation of the AIML was the passage of the Morley–Minto Reforms, or India Councils Act 1909. The demand for separate electorates was finally accepted in these Reforms. From the notes on the Simla Deputation, it is evident that Lord Minto had not actually accepted the Muslim demand, and that the honorary secretary of the Muslim League, Syed Hasan Bilgrami, had to struggle to have it accepted in London. In the end, it took three years from the placing of the demand to its acceptance. In his presidential address to the first AIML session in Karachi in 1907, Sir Adamjee Peerbhoy (1845–1913) admitted that the viceroy had made no commitment. Lord Minto himself wired Morley on 2 May 1909 that: 'If interpreted literally that would involve separate Muslim electorates within the various electorates proposed.... This is manifestly impractical and has never been suggested.'

Seven months later Morley wrote to Minto saying that his reply to the Simla Deputation had first raised the hopes of the Muslims. Perhaps it was the intention of the Viceroy to convey this impression but to offer nothing concrete.

Note

1. Matiur Rahman, *From Consultation to Confrontation: A Study of the Muslim League in British Indian Politics, 1906–12* (London: Luzac, 1970).

The Formation of the All-India Muslim League, 1906

AIMS AND OBJECTIVES OF THE ALL-INDIA MUSLIM LEAGUE (AIML) 1906

a) To promote among Musalmans of India, the feeling of loyalty to the British Government and remove any misconceptions that may arise as to the intention of the Government with regard to any of its measures.
b) To protect and advance the political rights and interests of the Musalmans of India and to represent their needs and aspirations to the Government.
c) To prevent the rise among the Musalmans of India of any feeling of hostility towards other communities without prejudice to the other objects of the League.

PROFILE OF THE AIML

The membership of the All-India Muslim League was limited to 400 members. Members had to be over 25 years of age, as well as:
- literate in an Indian language,
- have an annual income of more than Rs 500,
- be able to pay Rs 25 as entry fees, and
- Rs 25 as an annual subscription.

REVISED AIMS AND OBJECTS OF THE AIML 1912

1. To maintain and promote among the people of India feelings of loyalty to the British Crown.
2. To protect and advance the political and other rights of the Muslims of India.
3. Without detriment to the foregoing objectives, to attain under the aegis of the British Crown, a system of self-government suitable to India through constitutional means.

Gopal Krishna Gokhale (b. Kotluk, 9 May 1866–d. Poona, 19 February 1915). By caste, Gokhale was a Chitpavan Brahmin. He opted for the teaching profession and joined the New English School, Poona, at a salary of Rs 35, in January 1885. The following year he was appointed lecturer at Ferguson College, Poona. He caught the attention of the eminent leader, Mahadev Govind Ranade, who put social reform ahead of political emancipation. Ranade appointed him the secretary of Poona Sarvajanik Sabha. Later in 1897, Ranade sent Gokhale to London to appear before the Lord Welby Commission on Indian Expenditure. Gokhale entered electoral politics in 1899, becoming a member of the Bombay Council, and in 1901, he was elected to the Imperial Legislative Council.

It was as a parliamentarian that Gokhale excelled. Lord Curzon, who had grown impatient of the Congress, was unflinching in his praise for its leader. Ten years after he had left India, within a month of Gokhale's death, Lord Curzon recalled that he had never met a man of any nationality more gifted with parliamentary capacities. 'Mr Gokhale would have obtained a position of distinction in any parliament in the world, (16 March 1915).

This was no ordinary praise: Parliamentary practice was introduced to India by Britain, and excellence as a legislator meant that the white man was finding a native capable of self-government. Other leaders of India had received high praise, but no other received it universally.

The phrase 'ambassador for Hindu Muslim unity', for M.A. Jinnah, had been picked up by Sarojini Naidu, from Gopal Krishna Gokhale. However, Gokhale realized how daunting the task was. When Sarojini Naidu expressed her opinion that Hindu–Muslim unity would be achieved in five years; Gokhale replied, 'Child, you are a poet, but you hope too much. It will not come in your lifetime or mine.'[1]

Two English sympathizers of Congress, William Wedderburn and Henry Cotton, sent Gokhale to appear before parliamentary candidates, in London. The other delegates were Sir Surendranath Banerjee, Mohammad Ali Jinnah, and Lala Lajpat Rai. This was the highest quality of leadership, to inspire a whole generation of leaders to work together. Another Congress delegation, of whom Jinnah was the spokesman, urged that one-third of the members of the India Council be elected by Indian legislators. Gopal Krishna Gokhale had deliberated that, 'The India of the future could not now be only a Hindu India or a Muhammaden India; it must be compounded of all the elements which existed in India-Hindu, Muhammaden, Parsee, Christian, and aye, the Englishman who adopted India as his country.'[2]

For ensuring communal harmony, Gokhale put greater responsibilities on the Hindus: 'They had the advantage of numbers, education and wealth. It was their duty to understand the genuine fears of the Muslim minority, and to treat it with tact and forbearance.'[3] The advice Gokhale gave Muslims was also sound: 'You must remember that the British, who love patriotism and liberty, cannot but despise you. There may be small favours, but when a certain limit is reached, you too will not be allowed to go further.'[4]

He was honoured for his sincerity. In Lucknow, he was feted separately by Nawab Mohsinul Mulk and the Maharaja of Mahmudabad. 'At Aligarh, the Muslim youth unhorsed his carriage and pulled it through the streets to the College Hall, amidst shouts of 'Gokhale Zindabad.'[5] Unfortunately, Gokhale died at 48, an early age for a statesman, while all the politicians of the succeeding generation reached their three score years and ten. Even his distant hopes for unity vanished in the coming years.

Notes

1. Stanley A. Wolpert, *Tilak and Gokhale; Revolution and Reform in the Making of Modern India* (Delhi, Oxford University Press, 1991), p. 249.
2. B.R. Nanda, *Gokhale: The Indian Moderates and the British Raj* (Delhi: Oxford University Press, 1977), p. 442.
3. Ibid., p. 341.
4. Ibid.
5. Ibid., p. 339.

CHAPTER 13

THE LUCKNOW PACT, 1916

The period from the Delhi Durbar in 1911 to the Nehru Report of 1928 is seen as one of Hindu–Muslim cooperation. The Lucknow Pact, the Khilafat Movement, the Delhi Muslim Proposals, and the Simon Commission all came about during this period.

DELHI DURBAR, 1911.—The King of England was the emperor of India. For most of his Indian subjects, however, he was a distant and awe-inspiring figure. Only King George V visited India. He held court at Delhi. Durbar is the Indian word for Court, his presence was recalled as the Delhi Durbar.

King George V used this ceremonial occasion to make two announcements: that the partition of Bengal was annulled and that the capital would be shifted from Calcutta to Delhi. The British had repeatedly called the partition of Bengal a 'settled issue' but within six years it was undone. A common reaction was that the result of this reversal would be for Indians to think that agitation was the only way to change British decisions and that just their word was not reliable.

This was also the reaction of Indian Muslims. The partition of Bengal had so far been the only British decision which had benefited the Muslims. It was to uphold this decision that Dhaka was chosen as the venue for the formation of the All-India Muslim League (AIML). The announcement that the capital would be shifted to Delhi, the old Muslim capital, made no impression because it was considered to be an empty gesture.

The violence forced the British to undo the partition of Bengal. This gave rise to a slogan, 'No bombs, no boons'. The shock led Muslims to a major policy reconsideration. Fortunately, there were some Muslim Congressites for whom the independence of India was the primary goal, and communal safeguards were secondary. These politicians had previously refused to join the Muslim League because they thought it pro-British. Most prominent of these leaders were Sir Wazir Hasan (1874–1947), Maulana Mohammad Ali Jauhar (1878–1931), Maulana Abul Kalam Azad (1888–1958), and Mohammad Ali Jinnah (1876–1948). These leaders helped Wazir Hasan, the honorary secretary of the Muslim League to change the party's creed, transforming it from a loyalist to a revolutionary party.

These were far-reaching changes. Allegiance to the British Crown instead of the British government implied a vast constitutional difference. Allegiance to the British Crown meant that Indians would be self-governing like other dominions of the British Commonwealth such as Canada and Australia. The provision for self-government 'suitable to India' meant that a joint freedom struggle would still be based on separate electorates. Thus, some difficulties remained in the way of Hindu–Muslim cooperation since not only Hindus but some prominent Muslim leaders including Mohammad Ali Jinnah and Liaquat Ali Khan had spoken against separate electorates. These leaders were able to create goodwill which enabled Hindu–Muslim cooperation to last from the Delhi Durbar in 1911 to the Nehru Report in 1928.

LUCKNOW PACT, 1916. The era of Hindu–Muslim harmony overlapped with the duration of the First World War (1914–1918). This cooperation was formalized by a pact midway through the war which was to be the high point of Hindu–Muslim rapprochement. The leaders who affected it were Mohammad Ali Jinnah and Wazir Hasan on one side and Ambica Charan Mazumdar (1851–1922) and Bal Gangadhar Tilak (1856–1920) on the other. The pact, which was signed in Lucknow on 30 December 1916, provided for a joint struggle against British rule and the attainment of a representative government in India. The Congress, given the changed creed of the Muslim League, agreed to both separate electorates and weightage.

For the Congress, it was an achievement that the Muslim League would be a partner and not a rival in the freedom struggle. For the Muslim League, Congress support for separate electorates and weightage was of equal importance. Indeed, the British had finally accepted these demands under the Morley–Minto Reforms, but Congress support was more reassuring. The partition of Bengal and its annulment had shown that whatever the British gave, they could take back under Hindu pressure.

Within the Muslim community, however, the Lucknow Pact did not enjoy equal popularity. In the Muslim-majority provinces of the Punjab and Bengal, it caused resentment.

There was a general agreement over separate electorates. We have seen how, despite being a majority in Bengal, Muslims were not a majority in the council. Weightage was also producing the same result. In the minority provinces of UP, for example, Muslims constituted 14 per cent of the population but were given 30 per cent representation. In Madras, Muslims made up less than 7 per cent of the population but were given 15 per cent representation. This enhancement did not bring any concrete benefits as the Muslims were a minority, and they remained a minority. In return the Bengali Muslims surrendered 25 per cent, and in Punjab 10 per cent of their entitlement. This reduced the Muslim majority to a minority and proved detrimental to the Muslims.

Weightage was tied to separate electorates, and separate electorates were desired by all Muslims. This disadvantage was not immediately apparent as Congress agreed to extend this principle to the Punjab and Central Provinces where it had not been imposed by the British.

On the larger Indian stage, the Lucknow Pact marked a culmination and not a new beginning. By signing the Lucknow Pact, Jinnah was playing the role of 'Ambassador of Hindu-Muslim Unity'. This phrase was first coined for Jinnah by Gopal Krishna Gokhale and given currency by Sarojini Naidu (1878-1949). Jinnah could play this role because, at that time, he enjoyed equal eminence in both the Congress and the Muslim League.

However, this phase did not last because a year earlier, in 1915, Gopal Krishna Gokhale had died and Mohandas Karamchand Gandhi (1869-1948) had returned to India. Gandhi was present in Lucknow when the Lucknow Pact was signed, but had 'no high opinion of it'. The pact had the approval of Congress, but since it lacked endorsement by Gandhi, this instrument of Hindu-Muslim cooperation did not last long.

Chapter 14
The Khilafat Movement (1918–1924)

The Muslims of India had an emotional attachment to the Khilafat (Caliphate). Powerful sultans were proud to receive investiture from the caliphs of Cairo who were little more than prisoners of the Egyptian sultan. In the 20th century, this attachment took on a different aspect: the Muslims of India, deprived of power themselves, looked up to the Ottoman caliphate as the only surviving symbol of Muslim glory.

For most of the British rule in India, Britain and Turkey were allies. This partly helped to reconcile Muslims to British rule. During the First World War, there was a complete reversal of alliances; Turkey became an ally of Germany against Britain and when Germany lost the war, it was proposed that the Ottoman caliphate be deprived of all its territories. This caused an uproar among the Indian Muslims, and when the Treaty of Sèvres was imposed, the protest became organized.

THE ROLES OF GANDHI AND JINNAH.—The events in the Middle East caused some dramatic and permanent changes in Indian politics. Towards the end of the war, the British badly needed Indian cooperation. Tilak and Jinnah withheld cooperation until the British allowed Indian soldiers to be commissioned into the army. Stanley Wolpert states that Gandhi frustrated them by offering the viceroy, Lord Chelmsford unconditional support. When the war ended, Gandhi joined the Muslim agitation over the Khilafat.

Jinnah, on the other hand, discouraged discussion of the Khilafat issue in the AIML Council but was overruled. Jinnah wrote to Gandhi, warning him against raising the religious sentiments of the masses, but Gandhi would not agree even though the religious sentiments would be those of Muslims and not Hindus. Above all, Jinnah wanted both the Congress and the Muslim League to concentrate on Indian issues. This caused him and the Muslim League to be side-lined exactly at the time when Hindu–Muslim unity was touching new heights.

The leaders of the Khilafat Movement, as a gesture of goodwill, agreed not to slaughter cows because cows are sacred to the Hindus. For the first time a large number of leaders, mostly from the ulama class, came forward to join the Khilafat Movement.

THE EVENTS.—The Khilafat Committee was formed on 20 March 1919 in Bombay. As a follow-up, the All-India Khilafat Conference was founded on 23 November 1919, in Delhi, with 300 members. The following day, Gandhi was elected leader of the joint Hindu–Muslim Committee. On the same day, Hasrat Mohani moved a resolution calling for a progressive boycott of European goods. The resolution was passed by a majority but was opposed by Gandhi personally.

Later, however, Gandhi supported the same resolution and started a Non-Cooperation Movement. First in Calcutta and then in the Nagpur Congress session of 1920, a seven-point resolution was passed. When Jinnah opposed the resolution, he was shouted down, and as a consequence, he resigned from the Congress.

NON-COOPERATION.—In principle, Jinnah supported some form of non-cooperation but was against extreme and impractical measures. He agreed with the provisions which called for surrendering titles given by the British, refusal to attend official durbars or to serve in Mesopotamia (Iraq). What he opposed was the boycott of schools, colleges, and law courts and the boycott of foreign goods. Jinnah said these measures would only harm Indians as they had no replacements for these goods and services.

The high point of the movement was the trial of the Ali Brothers at Khaliqdina Hall in Karachi. After their arrest, and in front of thousands of their compatriots, their mother Bi Amman made her appearance, rallying women folk to join the movement.

THE END OF THE MOVEMENT. This movement, because of its fervour, had a fair chance of success since the British had been weakened by the First World War, but the following external factors brought it to an end:

1. **The Moplah's Uprising of August 1921:** Taking national liberation to mean social liberation, the Muslim Moplahs of Malabar set upon their Hindu landlords, killing, and looting them. This damaged both Hindu–Muslim relations and Gandhi's creed of non-violence. However, leaders from both sides controlled the extent of the damage.
2. **The Chauri Chaura Incident of 5 February 1923:** Police fired on unarmed protesters in the village of Chauri Chaura. In retaliation, twenty-two policemen were rounded up and burnt to death. Terming this act as an end to non-violence, Gandhi called off his Non-Cooperation Movement leaving the Khilafat cause in the lurch.
3. **The Abolition of the Caliphate—October 1924**: The grand national assembly of Turkey itself abolished the office of caliph or *khalifa*. One leader of the Khilafat Movement, Maulana Abul Kalam Azad, agreed with the Turkish decision and advised Indian Muslims to leave Turkey to its fate and to concentrate on matters closer to home. Thus, what Jinnah said at the beginning of the Khilafat Movement, Azad conceded at its end.

RESULTS OF THE MOVEMENT.—Among the negative results of the movement, the greatest disaster was the Hijrat Movement when Maulana Jauhar asked Muslims to migrate to Afghanistan in February 1921, but Afghanistan closed its borders. Many Muslims who had sold their property cheaply were ruined while many others died.

Secondly, Dr Saifuddin Kitchlew and some other Khilafat leaders spoke out against the Lucknow Pact, saying that it was unnecessary since Hindu-Muslim amity would last forever. In this, they were joined by Hindu leaders. Thus separate electorates, the only political victory gained by the Muslims, became controversial.

Finally, the All-India Muslim League was weakened.

However, all the above negative aspects were counterbalanced by the experience gained in mass agitation: organizing processions, conducting strikes, and going to jail. Had such a cadre not been available to the Muslim League in the years following 1940, the struggle for Pakistan would have been impossible.

The Leaders of the Khilafat Movement

Haji Jan Mohammad Chotani (1873–1932); Maulana Abdul Bari (1878–1926); Maulana Shaukat Ali (1873–1938); Maulana Mohammad Ali Jauhar (1878–1931); Maulana Abul Kalam Azad (1888–1958); Dr Saifuddin Kitchlew (1888–1963); Maulana Hasrat Mohani (1881–1951).

CHITTARANJAN DAS (b. Calcutta, 5 November 1870–d. Darjeeling, 16 June 1925), fondly called '*Deshbandhu*' (friend of the nation) by his followers, was a poet and lawyer, before he was a politician. He graduated from Presidency College, Calcutta, in 1890, and was called to the Bar from the Inner Temple, in 1892. The books he authored were *Malancha*, *Mala*, *Kishore-Kishori*, and *Antaryami*. Being a contemporary of Rabindranath Tagore and Sarat Chandra Chatterjee, he needed to have extraordinary literary merit merely to gain recognition. His reputation as a lawyer was made in 1908 when he conducted the defence of Sri Aurobindo Ghosh, then editor of *Bande Mataram* (however, as a lawyer he was outstripped by his brother, P.R. Das).

C.R. Das came into contact with M.K. Gandhi, in 1919, during the Khilafat/Non-cooperation Movement. For his part, he was arrested by the British—not alone, but along with his wife, sister, and son. He called a successful meeting at the Calcutta Town Hall, to protest against the Rowlatt Act. He strongly denounced the Montagu–Chelmsford Reforms: 'Wholly inadequate, unsatisfactory, disappointing.'[1] During the Non-cooperation Movement, he initially opposed Mahatma Gandhi's resolution, but ultimately, at the 1920 Nagpur session of the Indian National Congress, he supported it.

Two years later, however, in 1922, along with Pandit Motilal Nehru, he founded the Swaraj Party. They favoured council entry—a move that Mahatma Gandhi opposed. It was because of this association that Jawaharlal Nehru could observe C.R. Das closely. 'Mr Das, in spite of being a lawyer, was a poet and had a poet's emotional outlook. He is reputed to have written fine poetry in Bengali. He was an orator, and he had a religious temperament.'[2]

It was precisely this religious temperament that endeared C.R. Das to the Muslims. Magnanimity and sacrifice were the two guiding principles of his faith. He did not profess to be secular. He clearly said: 'I am not a Brahmo. I am a Hindu, and I claim to be a sincere Hindu…My point of view is the Hindu point of view.'[3]

C.R. Das said that Hindu-Muslim unity was vital for Swaraj.[4] This was commonplace. What was lofty in his perception was his credo: 'Life is certainly greater than dogma and logic, and I want you to be men—whole men—who will obey none but the will of God.'[5]

C.R. Das became the first mayor of Calcutta and gave effect to the Bengal Pact.

This gave Muslims representation in the Bengal council on the basis of their population, with separate electorates, even in places where they formed the majority. They would have 60 per cent of local bodies; 55 per cent of government posts. There was to be no interference with cow killing for sacrificial purposes. No law relating to cow killing for food was to be taken up. Cow killing was to be carried out in a manner as not to wound the feelings of Hindus![6] C.R. Das had stood the Faraidi Movement on its head. To his opponents, C.R. Das replied: 'You can delete the Bengal Pact from the resolution, but you cannot delete Bengal from the Indian National Congress.'[7] The pact resulted in C.R. Das winning the November 1923 Council elections.

Concessions only whet the appetite, but generosity overwhelms. The reverence that C.R. Das received from H.S. Suhrawardy, Maulana Abul Kalam Azad, and even

Chaudhry Mohammad Ali shows that C.R. Das had touched their hearts with his nature, and not just his proposals.

Notes

1. S.R. Bakshi, *C.R. Das: Congress and Swaraj* (New Delhi: Anmol Publications, 1990), p. 3.
2. Jawaharlal Nehru, *An Autobiography* (Delhi: Allied Publishers, 1962), pp. 10, 105 ff.
3. S.R. Bakshi, op. cit., p. 20.
4. Ibid., p. 15.
5. Ibid.
6. Ibid., p. 13.
7. Ibid., p. 14.

Chapter 15
From Delhi Muslim Proposals to Jinnah's Fourteen Points

DELHI MUSLIM PROPOSALS, 1927.—The Lucknow Pact contained the first constitutional proposals put forward jointly by Hindus and Muslims. Since it was based on separate electorates, which had become controversial during the Khilafat Movement, a new constitutional formula was required to replace it. The Muslim League had lost its appeal by this time and the Congress had not fared much better. Srinivasa Iyengar, the Congress president found that his party had become ineffectual in the Indian legislative assembly. He approached Jinnah in the hope that cooperation between the two parties might speed up the process of liberation. Jinnah responded by convening a meeting of thirty Muslim notables on 20 March 1927 in Delhi. Briefly stated, the following proposals were formulated: (1) Sindh should be separated from Bombay and form a new province. (2) Reforms should be introduced in NWFP and Balochistan, making them full provinces. (3) Weightage for Hindu minorities in Muslim provinces should be equal to weightage given to Muslim minorities in Hindu provinces. (4) In the central legislature there should be a one-third representation of Muslims.

In return for these provisions, Muslims would agree to joint electorates. A two-thirds majority being traditionally required for any constitutional amendment, and a one-third majority at the centre was sufficient for safeguarding arrangements within the provinces.

These proposals presuppose a federal form of government in which the maximum number of subjects (e.g. finance, education etc.) would be vested in the provinces. In a unitary form of government, the centre would have overriding control of the provinces. Muslims wanted power concentrated in the provinces where they would have access to it rather than at the centre where they had no access. Hindus would have no serious objections because traditionally the key federal areas such as defence, foreign affairs, and communications would, for the time being, be controlled by the British. Six Muslim provinces, out of a total of thirteen, while Muslims constituted one-fifth of the population, would be a very favourable arrangement.

Replacing separate electorates with joint electorates meant that the distribution of power between Hindus and Muslims would be aggregate and not watertight. It would provide a healthy atmosphere for the economic and cultural progress of Muslims. There was a feeling of relief when the Congress, in its 15 May Bombay session, accepted the Delhi Muslim Proposals. The Congress ratified its acceptance of the proposals in its 30 December 1927 Madras meeting.

Apparently, India was now securely set on the path to freedom. Only the absence of Gandhi from the Madras Congress provides a hint of what the future held.

Two factors impeded the culmination of this process of reconciliation. First was the opposition of the Mahasabha, the fundamentalist Hindu party. The Hindu Mahasabha had accepted only the renunciation of separate electorates and rejected all the other clauses of the proposals (23 March). However, those members of the Hindu Mahasabha who were also members of the Congress did not raise any objection in the Congress sessions.

The Congress was aware of this opposition, but guided by Iyengar and Motilal Nehru, it stayed firm. At one stage they even offered a concession not contained in the original proposals: 'No bill or resolution on any communal matter would be passed or even considered if three-fourths of the concerned community were opposed to it.'

The Hindu Mahasabha carried out insidious propaganda against Motilal Nehru saying that he was a beef eater. In the end, he had to yield to this propaganda.

The second factor was British opposition; the Simon Commission was appointed to supplant the new Congress-Muslim League proposals.

THE SIMON COMMISSION, 1927.—A new constitution to replace the Montagu–Chelmsford Reforms had been demanded by political parties and discussed within official circles well before the Delhi Muslim Proposals were formulated, yet the timing of the announcement on 8 November 1927, that an Indian Statutory Commission had been set up, was disruptive.

Statute means a law passed by a legislature, and a statutory commission means a body set up by a statute. An Indian Statutory Commission was formed to review the prevailing Government of India Act 1919. It was due in 1929 but was advanced by two years. This commission was called the Simon Commission after its chairman, Sir John Simon (1873–1954).

Since no Indian was included in the commission, the majority of Indian leaders and parties boycotted its proceedings. An All-India Leaders Manifesto issued on 16 November 1927 plainly stated this position. Among the signatories of this manifesto were Jinnah and Sir Tej Bahadur Sapru (1875–1949).

The Madras Congress of December 1927 took three interconnected decisions: (i) to ratify the Delhi Muslim Proposals (ii) to boycott the Simon Commission, and (iii) to set up an All-Parties Committee under Pandit Motilal Nehru to draft a constitution for India. All three steps were positive in nature and had they been acted upon in unison and harmony they would have led to a free and united India.

The All-India Muslim League, in contrast, was a house divided. Its president, Sir Mohammad Shafi (1869–1932) was in favour of cooperating with the Simon Commission, while its honorary secretary, Dr Saifuddin Kitchlew, was firmly in favour of boycott. This caused a rift in the Muslim League on 11 December 1927. Sir Mohammad Shafi had with him as honorary secretary and associate secretary Allama Sir Mohammad Iqbal and Maulana Hasrat

Mohani, both revolutionary poets, the latter of the fire-brand variety. This was a notable alliance since Hasrat looked down upon even dominion status and insisted on full independence. He was expected to side with Kitchlew but sided with Shafi instead.

Kitchlew, the original honorary secretary, had with him as president first Sir Mohammad Yaqub (1879–1942) and then M.A. Jinnah. Sir Mohammad Shafi presided over the session of the Muslim League in Lahore from 30 December 1927 to 1 January 1928. Sir Mohammad Yaqub presided over his faction's session at Calcutta from 31 December 1927 to 1 January 1928.

The Simon Commission visited India twice (i) from February to March 1928 and (ii) from October 1928 to April 1929. The members included Clement Atlee, the future prime minister of Britain who saw for himself the intensity of the boycott when he landed in Bombay on 3 February 1928. Leaders from the Muslim aristocracy such as the Maharaja of Mahmudabad (1879–1931) and Sir Abdur Rahim (1867–1947) had become banner-carrying protesters shouting 'Simon Go Back'.

Why did the Muslim aristocracy of the Punjab side with the Simon Commission and go against the political mood of the country? To please their British masters? The answer is not that simple. The group, represented by Shafi, had advised the viceroy, Lord Irwin, that the time was opportune to appoint a statutory commission and it was at this group's repeated insistence that the Simon Commission was kept all white.

The Shafi Group, as David Page has established, was supporting its own scheme, not its masters'. This faction influenced the viceroy through Sir Malcolm Hailey (1872–1969), governor of the Punjab. They took the stance that the induction of Indians into the commission would encourage Indian representation in the central government in New Delhi while the Punjab Muslim aristocracy, having its leverage in the provincial power structure, was not willing to weaken it by having to defer to Indians at the centre instead of to the British. How they chose to clothe their objectives was to tell the viceroy that provincial administrations were closer to the Indian people than the central administration which the viceroy governed.

Lord Birkenhead, the secretary of state who had infuriated Jinnah by stating on 24 November 1927 that the induction of Indians would create divisions, did not himself believe in this argument. Unknown to the public, Lord Birkenhead had tried to convince Lord Irwin of the folly of excluding Indians from the commission, first as far back as August 1926 and then again in March 1927.

Jinnah, unaware of Birkenhead's actual opinion took his rebuff personally and undertook to produce an agreed constitution for the Indians, by the Indians. Jinnah was confident that since a basic constitutional agreement already existed under the Delhi Muslim Proposals, all that the Congress and Muslim League would have to do was to supply the details, to answer Birkenhead's challenge. For Jinnah, national pride came before personal prestige. He forgot his humiliation at the 1920 Nagpur Congress and preferred a split in the Muslim League to leaving the Congress in the lurch. During the time Jinnah led the agitation, Gandhi adopted a low profile.

When the recommendations of the Simon Commission were published, they were strongly biased towards empowering the provinces. The provinces would decide what form the federation would take at the centre. Against this background, the Simon Commission recommended that provincial boundaries be redrawn. Various objections were raised against the separation of Sindh and reforms in the NWFP and Balochistan.

The unkindest cut was the recommendation that at the centre, separate electorates be replaced progressively with proportional representation. In the Punjab, separate electorates which would ensure a Muslim majority were rejected. This naturally caused a chorus of protests led by Allama Iqbal. The Simon Commission's recommendations were never implemented and, therefore, it never served its constitutional purpose, but it served the political purpose of derailing the Hindu–Muslim joint struggle.

THE NEHRU REPORT, 1928.—The Nehru Report was the first attempt by the Indians to frame a constitution for themselves. Previously they were limited to trying to influence or modify British-imposed constitutions. In view of the challenge given by Lord Birkenhead, the 1927 Madras Congress appointed a committee under Pandit Motilal Nehru to frame a constitution. In the same session, his son Pandit Jawaharlal Nehru had moved a resolution calling not for a dominion status but for complete independence. Gandhi considered this an extreme and impractical demand. It seems from the direction the Nehru Committee took, that the younger Nehru was forcing the hand of both his mentor Gandhi and his father Motilal. According to David Page: 'The determination of the author to face the problem and solve it, his condemnation of communal organizations for not wanting to change the existing structure of society, and his faith that in a free India political parties would be formed on an economic basis, all smack strongly of Jawaharlal and not his father.'[1]

This midway change in policy reflects a change in personalities. Motilal was harassed by Hindu Mahasabha propaganda, not Jawaharlal. He caused the committee to resile from the Delhi Muslim Proposals not due so much to communal considerations as to a liberal outlook that considered communal safeguards out of date.

Recommendations of the Nehru Report. According to the recommendations of the Nehru Report, the new central governments were to control all departments without reserving any for the British. A governor-general and a prime minister would be appointed by the king. A six-member cabinet would be appointed by the governor-general but recommended by the prime minister. This system would be repeated in the provinces with governors and chief ministers.

The new features were that (i) the cabinets would be responsible not to their appointing authorities but to their respective assemblies which (ii) would be elected by direct adult franchise.

The distribution of responsibilities between the centre and provinces suggested that the form of government would not be federal. This meant undercutting the very basis of the Delhi Muslim Proposals. As for the creation of new provinces, only conditional support was given to the separation of Sindh. Balochistan would have the same status as the NWFP, which would remain the same, lower than that of a full province, without a governor or legislature.

Consideration of the Nehru Report. When the All-Parties Committee met at Lucknow on 28 August 1928, it was apparent that of all the safeguards for minorities that had earlier been agreed upon, not a trace remained. Jinnah suffered a blow when his close friend, the Maharaja of Mahmudabad, and his closest disciple, M.C. Chagla, signed the Nehru Report. Abul Kalam Azad tried unsuccessfully in Calcutta to obtain a majority in favour of the Nehru Report from within the Muslim League.

At a larger All-Parties Conference, called on 22 December 1928, it was principally Jinnah who prevented the Muslim League from accepting the Nehru Report. As a politician, Jinnah was an idealist, but as a lawyer he was prudent. He was in favour of written guarantees not vague expressions of goodwill. Thus the era of Hindu-Muslim détente was over.

THE FOURTEEN POINTS, 1929.—The efforts at Hindu–Muslim reconciliation which began with the Delhi Durbar in 1911 ended with the publication of the Nehru Report in 1928. The All-India Muslim League, which had split over cooperation with the Simon Commission, was reunited. The original body led by Sir Mohammad Shafi was for cooperation and against giving up separate electorates. The group led by Jinnah had been against cooperation with the Simon Commission and in favour of joint electorates with some guarantees in exchange. Jinnah tried to move a three-point amendment to the Nehru Report. The points were: (i) One-third representation of Muslims in the central assembly; (ii) Muslim majority in Bengal and the Punjab be maintained on the actual population ratio for ten years, and (iii) The provinces should have residuary powers, which meant a federal and not a unitary scheme.

All three amendments were turned down by the All-Parties Conference even though they demanded considerably less than the Delhi Muslim Proposals. The reunited Muslim League, under Jinnah's leadership, issued the Fourteen Points as the basis of any future constitution for India. The Delhi Muslim Proposals had been an alternative to separate electorates. The Fourteen Points emerged as the Delhi Muslim Proposals in addition to separate electorates. They were:

1. The form of the future constitution should be federal, with the residuary powers vested in the provinces.
2. A uniform measure of autonomy shall be granted to all provinces.
3. All legislatures in the country and other elected bodies shall be constituted on the definite principle of adequate and effective representation of

minorities in every province without reducing the majority in any province to a minority or even equality.
4. In the central legislature, Mussalman representation shall not be less than one-third.
5. Representation of communal groups shall continue to be by means of separate electorates as at present, provided it shall be open to any community at any time to abandon its separate electorate in favour of a joint electorate.
6. Any territorial re-distribution that might at any time be necessary shall not in any way affect the Muslim majority in the Punjab, Bengal, and the NWF Province.
7. Full religious liberty, i.e. liberty of belief, worship and observance, propaganda, association, and education, shall be guaranteed to all communities.
8. No bill or resolution or any part thereof shall be passed in any legislature or any other elected body if three-fourths of the members of any community in that particular body oppose such a bill, resolution, or part thereof on the ground that it would be injurious to the interests of that community or in the alternative, such other method is devised as may be found feasible and practicable to deal with such cases.
9. Sindh should be separated from the Bombay presidency.
10. Reforms should be introduced in the NWF Province and Balochistan on the same footing as in other provinces.
11. Provision should be made in the constitution, giving Muslims an adequate share along with the other Indians in all the services of the state and in local self-governing bodies.
12. The constitution should embody adequate safeguards for the protection of Muslim culture and for the protection and promotion of Muslim education, language, religion, personal laws, and Muslim charitable institutions and for their due share in the grants-in-aid given by the state and by local self-governing bodies.
13. No cabinet, either central or provincial, should be formed without there being a provision of at least one-third Muslim ministers.[2]
14. No change shall be made in the constitution by the central legislature except with the concurrence of the states constituting the Indian Federation.

These demands formed the basis of negotiation by Muslims in the Round Table Conferences, but they were overshadowed by the demand of Allama Sir Mohammad Iqbal.

Notes

1. David Page, *Prelude to Partition: The Indian Muslims and the Imperial System of Control, 1920–1932* (Karachi: Oxford University Press, 1987), p. 172.
2. Durga Das, *India From Curzon to Nehru and After* (London: Collins, 1969), pp. 144, 145. The author claims he authored point number 13 at the behest of Jinnah so that the number of points would be increased to 14.

Mohandas Karamchand Gandhi (b. Porbandar, 2 October 1869–d. New Delhi, 30 January 1948) lived for the emancipation of India and died for the survival of Pakistan. Described by two eminent historians[1] as the greatest Indian after Gautama Buddha, Mahatma Gandhi was—by any criterion—a most remarkable man. To the West, with its notion of India as a land of maharajas, tigers, and the rope trick, this 'half naked *faquir*' acquired a mystical aspect—a Hollywood film bringing this image to a climax. Unfortunately, the vacillations of this great man brought about results contrary to his aims. Gandhi's role in the Khilafat Movement led Gail Minault to describe him as: 'This "simple" man who was the most complex character imaginable, and treated them as their own, though he had had an advantaged youth, a foreign education and a career away from India.'[2]

Gandhi's mindset was medieval, his schemes were visionary, and his strategies whimsical, yet there had to be a wellspring from where the intense and widespread influence he exercised, proceeded. Whatever his personal limitations, his political stature was gigantic. Stanley Wolpert has closed in on the main feature of Gandhi's genius; his greatest and elemental contribution to the awakening of India: 'He equated cotton spinning with his own quest to see God face to face.'[3] This alone among all other items of his protest and boycott was neither impractical nor medieval; its economic and social potential being immense.

That said, we have to inquire whether his vision and his approach were a reliable basis for communities seeking emancipation. Gandhi's interaction with the Depressed/Dalit castes provides a precedent. As early as 1915, Gandhi had lodged three low-caste inmates in his *ashram*, being undeterred by the threats of the upper castes. But when, on 17 August 1932, Ramsay Macdonald announced separate electorates for the depressed castes, Gandhi was outraged. A mystified British premier wrote to Gandhi that since the Communal Award had doubled low caste votes, he had expected Gandhi to approve, rather than to undertake a fast. Gandhi's reply was that the depressed castes must be emancipated by their oppressors—and not by the British. Instead of separate electorates, Gandhi offered a double reservation of untouchable seats. This resulted in the untouchables losing each and every seat in the next elections. Gandhi was verbally contrite but offered no practical remedy; leaving them ultimately to face caste wars and riots.

This, in essence, was Gandhi's approach to the Muslim problem, and this is what the Muslims rejected, much to the chagrin of those who would judge India in the light of her professions, not her actions. However, in contrast to his conduct towards the depressed castes, Gandhi tried to make amends with the Muslims. His last interaction with Jinnah was that of concurrence; they both desired a united Bengal, independent of India and Pakistan. In this, Gandhi was frustrated by Jawaharlal Nehru. When Nehru withheld Pakistan's share of her financial assets, Gandhi undertook a fast until death to make India release the funds. This in turn led a Hindu fanatic Nathuram Godse to assassinate him. Only ten days earlier, Gandhi had refused police protection, saying that if he had to die by an assassin's hand, he must do so without anger or fear.[4]

For three days all the programmes of Radio Pakistan were dedicated to his memory. These bulletins consisted of descriptions of the tragic events, statements by Jinnah and Liaquat, and provincial heads. The next day's transmission opened with Gandhi's favourite *bhajan*, 'Raghupati Raghav Raja Ram' followed by other *bhajans*. The third day's transmission covered condolence meetings in Lahore.[5] Pandit Nehru was moved enough to say that the best programmes on the Mahatma, were done by Radio Pakistan.[6]

Notes

1. Stanley Wolpert, *Gandhi's Passion: The Life and Legacy of Mahatma Gandhi* (New York: Oxford University Press, 2001), p. 263; Michael Brecher, *Nehru: A Political Biography* (London: Oxford University Press, 1959; New Delhi, Reprint, 2004), p. 387.
2. Gail Minault, *The Khilafat Movement: Religious Symbolism and Political Mobilization in India* (New Delhi: Oxford University Press, 1999), p. 124.
3. Stanley Wolpert, op. cit., p. 124.
4. Michael Brecher, op. cit., p. 384.
5. *Dawn*, Karachi, 12 February 1948.
6. Sabeeh Mohsin, *Dastan Kahte Kahte* (Karachi: Maktabai-i-Jamal, 2006), p. 49.

Chapter 16

Allahabad Address, 1930: Allama Iqbal and the Ideology of Pakistan

The most often quoted passage from Iqbal's presidential address to the 1930 Allahabad session of the All-India Muslim League is: 'I would like to see the Punjab, North-West Frontier Province, Sindh and Balochistan amalgamated into a single State. Self-government within the British Empire, or without the British Empire, the formation of a consolidated North-West Indian Muslim State appears to me the final destiny of Muslims, at least of North India.' This is substantially as Pakistan emerged and how it presently exists. These words of Allama Iqbal promoted for the first time, from the platform of the All-India Muslim League, the idea of a separate Muslim state in India.

Two aspects need attention. Firstly, this address is not the sum total of Iqbal's contribution to the Pakistan Movement. Secondly, in this Allahabad address, Iqbal was proposing both long-term and short-term solutions. The following passages from the Allahabad address also deserve to be considered: 'The life of Islam as a cultural force in this country very largely depends on its centralization in a specified territory.'

He went on to emphasize that his demand was 'actuated by a genuine desire for free development, which is practically impossible under the type of unitary government contemplated by the nationalist Hindu politicians with a view to secure permanent communal dominance in the whole of India'. Iqbal further underlined that 'The problem of India is international, not national.'

This address is an important landmark in the Pakistan Movement but it should also be realized that Iqbal's entire life and work was a contribution to the Pakistan Movement. To begin with, Iqbal's poetry, both Urdu and Persian, struck the most responsive cord of Indo-Muslim consciousness. We cannot separate the message from the style in Iqbal's poetry as both were inspired by the same zeal. Apart from his poetry, Iqbal wrote a number of articles and essays intended to reform Muslim society and give it a clear political direction. In 1904, he wrote an article on national life, pin-pointing the aspects that needed reform. In 1909 he wrote on 'Islam as a Moral and Political Ideal'. In 1910, he addressed the students of Aligarh on their patriotic duty. In 1931, he delivered his lectures on *The Reconstruction of Religious Thought in Islam* where he stated that the concept of Islam is bound up with majesty, which has the state as its manifestation. Finally, in his letter to M.A. Jinnah dated 21 June 1937, Iqbal wrote: 'A separate federation of Muslim provinces, reformed on the lines I have suggested above, is the only course by which we can secure a peaceful India and save Muslims from the domination of non-Muslims. Why should not the Muslims of North-West and Bengal be considered as nations entitled to self-determination, just as other nations in India and outside India are?'

Iqbal's Allahabad address has an added importance because it was a public statement from a representative platform. All the leaders of the Pakistan Movement, Mohammad Ali Jinnah, Nawabzada Liaquat Ali Khan, and the Raja of Mahmudabad had publicly acknowledged the contribution of Iqbal even before Independence in 1947.

IQBAL AND HIS IDEOLOGY.—Shaikh Mohammad Iqbal was born in Sialkot on 9 November 1877. He was educated in his hometown, Government College, Lahore, and Trinity College, Cambridge. He passed his Bar examinations from London and obtained his PhD from Munich University. He became a professor at Government College and later practised law before the Punjab High Court. Iqbal was briefly honorary secretary of the All-India Muslim League and a member of the Punjab legislative council. He was knighted in 1922.

Iqbal earned international acclaim as a poet in both Urdu and Persian. Very few poets who have written on philosophic themes in a grand style like Iqbal have become a favourite of the masses. Iqbal died in Lahore on 21 April 1938 after having published poetic collections in Persian and Urdu, as well as prose works in English. He was also a literary critic, having written a tract in English on the Indo-Persian poet Bedil Azimabadi.

> **THE PHILOSOPHY OF ALLAMA IQBAL.** The philosophy of Allama Iqbal is contained in both his Urdu and Persian poetry as well as in his English prose. It is very difficult to summarize his philosophy as it is very complex. However, the high points of his metaphysics have a bearing on his political thought and are summarized here.
> 1. The central concept of Iqbal's philosophy is *Khudi*. In English, it can be translated as *Self* or *Ego*. Unlike its general meaning, *Khudi* in Iqbal's philosophy does not mean pride. It means *self-awareness* and *loftiness of character*. Iqbal's concept of *Khudi* is partly a reaction to the traditional creeds where the *Self* is a mere delusion of the mind. In Islamic mysticism as well as Hindu and Buddhist philosophy, *self-negation* is the dominant trend.
> *Khudi* is not merely personal but is divided into three basic realities (a) *Unique Self*, that is God (b) *Creative Self*, that is man (c) and *Larger Self*, that is society. According to Iqbal, a harmonious working of man and society produces a durable human civilization, which fulfils the purpose of God.
> 2. It follows, as Iqbal stated in Allahabad, that religion is not the private affair of an individual.
> 3. For both science and religion the way to pure objectivity lies through the purification of experience.
> 4. Because Iqbal's concept of the larger self is social, he makes a distinction between spirituality—*Ruhaniyat* and monasticism—*Rahbaniat*.

5. The reconstruction of Muslim society is possible only through democracy.
6. An Islamic state is based on a social contract; therefore, non-Muslims have nothing to fear in an Islamic state.
7. Belief in Monotheism, the One-ness of God, brings about three values in human society; liberty, equality, and stability.
8. Iqbal's concept of Islam is bound up with Majesty (or power). If majesty is the objective of Islam, its manifestation is the state.
9. God does not give different principles for different nations but chooses a certain nation and trains it spiritually to make it a model for other nations and thus gives universal rules for human society.
10. The state is the territorial specification of Islam.
11. Religious experience is a state of feeling with a cognitive aspect.
12. Thought is not a principle that organizes and integrates its material from the outside but is a potency that is formative of the very being of its material.
13. Iqbal holds that there are potential types of consciousness lying close to human consciousness. These have the ability to impart life-giving and knowledge-giving experiences. These concepts of consciousness, Iqbal derived from Mujaddid Alf Thani who describes three stages, *Ruh* or Soul, *Sirr-i-Khafi*, the lesser mystery, and *Sirr-i-Ikhfa* the greater mystery. In this sense, it is possible that religion can become the source of a higher experience.
14. In this manner, Islam is socially, morally, and spiritually rewarding. This is why Iqbal stresses the need for cultural independence more than economic independence. This is the ideological aspect of Iqbal's demand for a separate Muslim state, different from the political aspect which was shaped by the attitude of the Hindu majority and British autocracy towards the Muslims as a minority.

THE SOCIAL CONTRACT THEORY

This was a theory designed to replace the theory of the Divine Rights of Kings. The thinkers who preceded the French Revolution in 1789 had begun to advance theories that spoke of the sovereignty of the people. Among these theorists, the most prominent were Thomas Hobbes (1588–1679), John Locke (1632– 1704), and Jean-Jacques Rousseau (1712–1778).

According to Thomas Hobbes, nature was a state of perpetual strife because people were governed by (1) competition (2) distrust and (3) glory. These traits are inherent in human nature but are redeemed by Reason. Reason leads all citizens to make a contract with one another. Every person gave up his/her right to govern him/herself, provided other people did likewise. Thus, citizens made a contract among themselves to delegate their authority to the ruler. The ruler himself was not a party to the contract, therefore, his actions could not be questioned. Although Hobbes held the ruler to be above the social contract, he negated the Divine Right of Kings and upheld the will of the people as the basis of the King's authority.

Historically, speaking, such a contract was never actually signed. Its signing is hypothetical and a supposition. Hobbes was fascinated by Geometry in which a theorem begins with one supposition and leads to another.

John Locke maintained that the state of nature was benign and peaceful, not of conflict or disorder, yet it was unsatisfactory because there was no judge or common authority to interpret the laws of nature. Locke emphasized that one man's freedom stopped where it could injure another man's freedom. Hence, freedom in political society is freedom under the law. Locke said men enter society to preserve their property. Individuals surrendered their natural rights to a properly elected ruler, so that the ruler may protect their remaining rights. In an advance over Hobbes, Locke held that the ruler was also party to the contract, and therefore answerable to the people. The people could resist, even change their ruler.

Jean-Jacques Rousseau said, 'Man was born free, but is everywhere in chains.' Nature was paradise, but with the growth of population, complications, and problems arose, therefore people contracted among themselves to create a civil society. Society secured the freedom of individuals. Since each gave himself to all, he gives himself to none. (They all become an abstraction.) There is gained the equivalent of what is lost, with greater power to protect what is left.

According to Rousseau, the contract was not one between the people and the ruler, it was among the people themselves, and sovereignty belonged to the General Will,which can be expressed in an assembly. The ruler is a mere agent of the people. General Will is not the sum total of all selfish or particular wills. Rousseau objected to delegation of power at all, as sovereignty cannot be surrendered. Rousseau claimed that the General Will emanates from the community as a whole, so sovereignty must reside in it.

The Social Contract Theory as we have seen, passed through an evolutionary process. When Iqbal assured minorities of an Islamic state of their rights, he was announcing that there would be no Divine Right for the sultan. Rousseau did not equate General Will with Majority Will, therefore, the rights of the minorities would remain inalienable.

 CHAUDHRY RAHMAT ALI (b. Balachaur, Hoshiarpur [East Punjab], 16 November 1897–d. Cambridge, UK, 3 February 1951) did his MA from Cambridge in 1940, and was called to the Bar from the Middle Temple in 1943. Ten years earlier, on 28 January 1933, he published *Now or Never*. Later in the same year, he published *What Does the Pakistan National Movement Stand For?* Thus, the word 'Pakistan' was coined by Chaudhry Rahmat Ali. He introduced this name in a pamphlet called *Now or Never*. He explained the composition of the word in the following manner: 'Pakistan is both a Persian and Urdu word. It is composed of letters taken from the names of all our homelands—'Indian' and 'Asian'. That is Panjab, Afghania [North-West Frontier Province] Kashmir, Iran, Sindh (including Kutch and Kathiawar) Tukharistan, Afghanistan and Balochistan. It means the land of the Paks—the spiritually pure and clean. It symbolizes the religious beliefs and ethnical stocks of our people and it stands for all the territorial constituents of our original Fatherland.'

His pamphlet was launched from the platform of an association the Pakistan National Movement that he had founded the same year. Chaudhry Rahmat Ali urged Muslim delegates at the Round Table Conference not to recognize the Indian Union. Jinnah had then called Pakistan an impossible dream.

The British Parliament and Hindu organizations took Chaudhry Rahmat Ali's proposal far more seriously than Jinnah had done. On the same day as *Now or Never* was issued, the British Parliament took notice of what it termed the testimonial of Chaudhry Rahmat Ali and his associates, and the following August, a Joint Parliamentary Select Committee queried a number of Muslim leaders about their views on a separate Muslim State.

The reaction of Hindu organizations was quite sharp. Mahr Chand Khanna of the Hindu Conference declared Rahmat Ali's proposal 'dangerous'. In 1935, Chaudhry Rahmat Ali published another pamphlet, calling for the separation of Pakistan, just as Burma was being separated from India, and by 1937 the *Encyclopedia of Islam* had featured Chaudhry Rahmat Ali and his scheme for Pakistan.

Chaudhry Rahmat Ali was a very sincere and devoted servant of the Muslim community, however, his scheme for Muslim separatism was impractical. Apart from Pakistan, in which he wished to include Lucknow, Delhi, and Aligarh, he named the second entity 'Bang-i-Islam' comprising Bengal and Assam. This at least had an overall Muslim majority, the third entity was to be Usmanistan, the domain of Usman Ali Khan, Nizam of Hyderabad, who ruled over a Hindu majority state.

When Jinnah and the Muslim League accepted the 3 June Plan Chaudhry Rahmat Ali broke out in invective. He accused Jinnah of shattering the foundations of Muslim nationhood and sabotaging the future of 100 million Muslims living in India. He called the creation of Pakistan 'the blackest and the bloodiest treachery in our history!'[1]

Chaudhry Rahmat Ali has an indelible place in our history. His demand loomed so large in the Hindu and British imagination that even though the Lahore Resolution had not mentioned Pakistan by name, the press designated it as the 'Pakistan' resolution, and later M.A. Jinnah thanked them for this name. The disappointment that

Chaudhry Rahmat Ali felt was severe, but his outburst was most intemperate. Jinnah had not actively wanted a divided Punjab and Bengal, he had himself termed such a Pakistan, 'truncated and moth-eaten', but when an ideal solution is not forthcoming, the next best solution has to be accepted. Since Chaudhry Rahmat Ali was a very zealous votary of setting up a Muslim state, he was deeply disappointed that the Pakistan that emerged fell far short of the Pakistan he had proposed. Still, he should be remembered with gratitude for giving Pakistan its name.

Note

1. Khalid Hasan, 'The Quaid's Detractor,' *The News International*, Karachi, 14 April 1998.

Chapter 17
The Round Table Conferences (1930–1932)

FIRST SESSION (21 November 1930–19 January 1931).—The Round Table Conferences were held partially to support the Simon Commission, and partially to meet the objection that it contained no Indian members. A series of Round Table Conferences (RTCs) were held between 1930 to 1932. The first session was opened by King George V in London on 10 November 1930. A fifty-eight-member Indian delegation led by Aga Khan III representing diverse interests; Muslims, liberals, and the Chamber of Princes was present. Only the Congress, the largest political party in India, was absent. During this session, a Federal Structure Subcommittee was formed under Lord Sankey. The communal question could not be resolved. Edward Thomson, on the prompting of some quarters he did not name, proposed that the communal question be submitted to the arbitration of three members, one Hindu, one Muslim, and one British. Thomson also observed that the younger Muslims were not as communal as the older ones. This remark was resented by the Muslim delegates and this proposal found no favour.

At the conclusion of the first session, 19 January 1931, British Prime Minister Ramsay Macdonald (1866–1937) made the commitment that if the Indian legislature was formed on the basis of a federation, the British would recognize the principle that the executive would be responsible to the legislature. During this session, the princes gave their assent to joining a federation.

Meanwhile in India, both the Congress and the Muslim League were voicing their demands. It was during this session that Sir Muhammad Iqbal delivered his Allahabad address. Motilal Nehru demanded full dominion status by 31 December 1931; his son Jawaharlal Nehru demanded full independence. On 5 April 1930 Gandhi broke the Salt Law, heralding another Civil Disobedience Movement.

SECOND SESSION (7 September–1 December 1931).—This session saw Sir Muhammad Iqbal and Pandit Madan Mohan Malaviya as new delegates with Mohandas Karamchand Gandhi as the sole representative of the Congress. Communal differences could not be resolved despite the initial conciliatory gestures of Gandhi. Liberals like Sir Chimanlal Setalvad, Vitthal Bhai Patel, Sir Srinivasa Shastri, and Sir Tej Bahadur Sapru were in favour of a settlement, but Mahasabhaites like Madan Mohan Malaviya were not. At the first RTC session, a formulation by M.A. Jinnah had been vetoed by M.R. Jaykar (1873–1959) of the Mahasabha party. Gandhi had to announce to Sir Muhammad Shafi on 8 October that his mediatory efforts had failed and that he had his limits. In this session, the princes withdrew their assent to join a federation. The role of Jinnah was described as 'unique'. According to a British journal: 'The Hindus thought he was a Muslim communalist, the Muslims took him to be pro-Hindu, the princes deemed him to be too democratic, the British considered him to be a rabid extremist—with the result that he was everywhere but nowhere. None wanted him.'

This is a correct assessment and is also ironic because it was Jinnah who had originally written to Macdonald on 19 June 1929 that only a conference of Indian delegates in London could break the political impasse. Since Jinnah was denied a leading role, the efforts of the Muslim delegates became ineffective. Allama Iqbal disagreed with Sir Akbar Hyderi during the RTC and on his return to India criticized the role of the Muslim delegates as well as the British government.

The Depressed Classes (Untouchable Hindus), led by Dr Bhimrao Ramji Ambedkar (1891–1956), had asked for separate electorates like the Muslims. Gandhi asked the Muslim delegates to oppose this demand. The Muslims agreed to abide by any agreement reached between Gandhi and Ambedkar but said that they could not reasonably oppose the extension of the same right they had claimed for themselves.

THIRD SESSION (17 November–24 December 1932).—This session of the conference was almost inconsequential; only the White Paper embodying recommendations of all three sessions was of consequence. Gandhi and Jinnah were both absent. There was a change of viceroy and Lord Willingdon, who had succeeded Lord Irwin, had Gandhi arrested. The Gandhi–Irwin Pact was undone and the Congress started another Civil Disobedience Movement. Jinnah was not invited to this session because he had accused Lord Sankey, chairman of the Federal Structure Subcommittee, of partiality. He explained that his insistence on the Fourteen Points was the reason for his exclusion from this RTC session.

JAWAHARLAL NEHRU (b. Allahabad, 14 November 1889–d. New Delhi, 27 May 1964) was a Kashmiri Brahmin by lineage, an agnostic by belief, and an aristocrat by upbringing. As one of his admirers remarked shortly before independence, '[Nehru] is explosive in speech, disciplined in action, impulsive in gestures, deliberate in judgement, revolutionary in aim, conservative in loyalty, reckless of personal safety, cautious about matters affecting Indian welfare'.[1]

If we refuse to bicker about the mutual incompatibility of these stated qualities, we must admit that they mark out greatness in his makeup. Alas, Nehru lacked the humility which underscored greatness. In the words of his latest biographer, Nehru 'interiorized this complex sense of superiority'.[2] Another chronicler has been more explicit: 'A little greater humility, a little less certainty of righteousness, might conceivably have saved their ideal of a united India'.[3]

This trait may have sprung from Jawaharlal's psychological reserve regarding his father, Motilal. Michael Brecher, one of Nehru's earliest biographers, commented that 'respect and affection were there, but Motilal Nehru could not draw out his son's emotional response to the same extent or in the same way as the Mahatma'.[4]

Judith Brown, who approached Nehru after her momentous study of Gandhi, has noted, 'As his attitude sharpened, he became increasingly critical of his father's political stance, and this created tension between them'.[5]

Now Mohammad Ali Jinnah, a friend of his real father, but a rival of his political mentor became the focus of Nehru's ire. How close Motilal and Mohammad Ali had been can be glimpsed from one of Jinnah's speeches: 'Will you bring Motilal Nehru to bow before the throne at Viceregal Lodge? What has Pandit Motilal Nehru been doing in the Assembly? Has he not been cooperating with you? Have you no eyes, have you no ears, have you no brains?'[6] This was five years after Jinnah left Congress.

Jinnah was chiding the British for being unable to discern policy from posture. His exasperation went unnoticed by not only the Viceroy, but by Motilal's son. Even after a rift with Jinnah, Motilal remarked: 'We can afford to fight like Kilkenny cats and still be friends'.[7] Once, when Jawaharlal Nehru, as Secretary of the Congress, offended a Muslim League delegation, Motilal rushed to conciliate Jinnah. Soon after Motilal's death, Jawaharlal Nehru referred to 'my dear friend Mohammad Ali Jinnah'.[8] To describe one's father's friend as one's own went against the grain of Indian culture, and did not bode well for the future.

In the ultimate analysis, Nehru's sophistication overcame his pragmatism. When, despite a tacit electoral understanding, Nehru forbade Govind Ballabh Pant from bringing the Muslim League into the 1937 UP cabinet, he did not characterize it as a communal or even religious party, but as a 'small' party. His next decision was to sabotage the Cabinet Mission plan. Latter-day apologists have justified Nehru's 10 July 1946 press conference on the ground that acceptance would have led to the creation of Pakistan. Certainly, this defence would have been justified had Nehru's refusal prevented the emergence of Pakistan. Nehru spurned Jinnah's demand for a corridor between West and East Pakistan, even though it was accompanied with an offer of common defence—a step that would have prevented the nuclearization of Pakistan.

More inexplicably, Nehru turned down President Ayub Khan's offer of a common defence against China—not pausing to reflect on how his acceptance would have isolated Pakistan. Shortly after, Nehru was cheered by a nostalgic Pakistani crowd when he came to sign the Indus Water Treaty (1960). When Nehru died, Inder Malhotra reported from Pakistan, that the grief was sincere.

Notes

1. Michael Brecher, *Nehru: A Political Biography* (London: Oxford University Press, 1959; Delhi: Oxford University Press, reprint, 2004), p. 596.
2. Judith Brown, *Nehru: A Political Life* (New Delhi: Oxford University Press, 2004), p. 36.
3. H.V. Hodson, *The Great Divide: Britain–India–Pakistan* (Karachi: Oxford University Press, 1989), p. 182.
4. Michael Brecher, op. cit., pp. 608–09.
5. Judith Brown, op. cit., p. 39.
6. Ian Bryant Wells, *Ambassador of Hindu–Muslim Unity: Jinnah's Early Politics* (Delhi: Permanent Black, 2005), p. 157.
7. Ibid., p. 138.
8. Ibid., p. 144.

Chapter 18
The Government of India Act 1935

The constitutional history of India began with British rule. Before British rule, there were only monarchies under whom the rights or obligations of the subjects were not defined. When British rule began, there started a struggle between the unscrupulous and rapacious East India Company and the liberal and idealistic ruling classes of Britain. Even though the parties kept changing, the policy towards India remained contentious. Following the RTCs there began a tug of war, with the Congress demanding a swift and complete transfer of power, and members of the British Conservative Party led by Winston Churchill, who were strongly opposed to Home Rule in India. The British Labour Party sympathized with the Congress Party and joined it in its boycott of the third RTC. The Muslim League also wanted Home Rule but with safeguards so that the transfer of power would not simply result in a change of masters.

A constitution is normally the set of conditions according to which a people agree to live with each other, as well as the basic law, which is the source of all other laws. The various Acts of the British parliament which determined how India was to be governed, was not a set of rules freely arrived at by the people, because the rules were imposed from above, by outsiders.

However, these Acts were constitutions in the sense that they were the basic law in India which became the source of subsequent legislation. Under both definitions, a constitution determines the structure and nature of government and lays down how power is to be shared by the different segments of society. A constitution is easy to propose, and also easy to impose, if the concerned population is homogenous; that is, if the people follow one religion, belong to one race, speak one language, and have a common culture. This was not the case in India. Apart from Hindus and Muslims, there were Sikhs, Christians, Parsis, Buddhists, and Jains. Ethnically they were descended from Aryan, Dravidian, Mongol, and aboriginal races. The variety in climate created a variety in culture, causing diversity in food, clothing, language, and the arts. These taken together, made reaching a constitutional agreement a daunting task in India.

There was another entity, not normally found in other countries; this was the princely states. When the British conquered India, they annexed some territories, leaving some rajas and nawabs holding territories ceded by them to the British under different treaties. This made them constitutionally the vassals of the British crown as all matters of defence, external affairs, and communications were given under British control. In all other matters, these rulers exercised freedom. Their subjects enjoyed even fewer human rights than the citizens of the British-ruled provinces. There were many princely states some as large as Kashmir and some as small as Porbandar. Half of the Indian population lived in these princely states. They were not contiguous, therefore, they formed a Chamber of Princes to represent their interests collectively.

Under the Government of India Act of 1935, the British wanted both the provinces and princely states to come together under a federation. The British themselves had a unitary form of government with one parliament and one government.

At the first RTC, the princes had shown their willingness to join the federation, but later they changed their minds because of the fear of losing their wealth and privileges. Their fears were not unfounded. The Congress did not wish to join the federation because it preferred a unitary system since the British were withholding most of the power. Liaquat Ali Khan explained the Muslim League's stand: 'Inadequate safeguards for the Muslims is an additional grievance of the Musalmans to other fundamental objections to the scheme (1935 Act) namely that it does not give any real power and control in vital matters to the Federal Legislature or the Minister that may be appointed'. The Government of India Act 1935 shifted dyarchy from the provinces to the centre. Some subjects were transferred to Indians who were responsible to their legislatures and some were reserved for British officials responsible to no one. This dyarchy had been introduced in the provinces through the Government of India Act 1919 and had proved unpopular. It was proposed to remove dyarchy from the provinces and introduce it in the centre; therefore the Congress and Muslim League were willing to work on the provincial part of the 1935 Act but not on the federal part.

This decision had two consequences, one immediate and one long-term. The immediate consequence of the 1935 Act was that in 1937 elections were held for provincial legislatures, but not for the federal legislature (which had until then been held under the 1919 Act). The long-term consequence was, as H.V. Hodson states, that both India and Pakistan adopted the Government of India Act of 1935 as their basic law before promulgating their respective constitutions.

While all parties condemned the federal part, the AIML led by M.A. Jinnah, expressed willingness to work 'the scheme of provincial autonomy for what it was worth.' Therefore, elections were held only for provincial legislatures in 1937.

Main Features of the Government of India Act 1935

a. Federal Part: Reserved federal executive was to be constituted of a governor-general and a council of ministers. The following portfolios would be described as reserved: defence, foreign affairs, tribal area affairs, and ecclesiastical affairs that is administration of Christian churches. Transferred were: education, finance, home, law, railways, commerce, industries and labour. A bicameral legislature was proposed. The upper house known as the Council of State was to consist of 250 members. The lower house to be known as the House of Assembly was to consist of 375 members.

b. Provincial Part: Dyarchy was removed and a measure of autonomy was introduced; the governor except in the case of 'special responsibility', was to act on the advice of the elected chief minister. Six provinces, i.e. Bengal, Bihar, Assam, UP, Bombay and Madras had bicameral legislatures. The upper house was known as the Legislative Council and the lower house was called the Legislative Assembly. In the remaining five provinces only the lower house existed. Three new provinces were created. NWFP was made a full-fledged province with a legislative assembly and a governor. The same condition applied to Sindh which was separated from Bombay, and Orissa which was separated from Bihar.

c. A federal court was to be set up to decide disputes between the federal government and provincial governments.

d. The Council of the Secretary of State (or India Council) was abolished.

Chapter 19
The 1937 Elections and Congress Rule

The elections of 1937 were the first broad-based elections in which the representative status of political parties was tested. The tone of the campaign was set by Jawaharlal Nehru's statement that 'there were only two parties in India, the British and the Indian National Congress, all the others must line up'. To this, Jinnah rejoined: 'I refuse to line up with the Congress. There is a third party in this country and that is the Muslims. We are not going to be dictated to by anyone' (Calcutta, 8 January 1937). However, when the elections were held, the Congress won and the Muslim League lost, though under separate electorates the Muslim League had to face only Muslim voters.

The Muslim League could win only 104 out of 489 Muslim seats. The position of the Muslim League was worst in the Muslim-majority provinces. In NWFP, the pro-Congress Khudai Khidmatgars won by a large margin. In the Hindu-majority provinces, the Muslim League had a respectable win only in UP and Bombay. In UP out of 66 Muslim seats, AIML won 27, and in Bombay, out of 30 Muslim seats it won 20.

The Congress had won less than half the general votes; 711 out of 1585, but its results were still better, and the distribution of seats allowed it to form the government in 7 out of 11 provinces in India.

CAUSES OF THE AIML FAILURE.—There were three main reasons for the defeat of the All-India Muslim League in the 1937 elections:

1. The Muslim League suffered a setback during the Khilafat Movement. Since this was an emotional issue for the Muslims, they set aside political considerations and came out against the British, under the Congress. Muslims sidelined Jinnah and the Muslim League to join Gandhi and the Khilafat cause. Although the Khilafat could not be saved, this trend of bypassing the AIML could not be completely reversed.
2. Since elections were held only for provincial legislatures and provincial autonomy was the most attractive feature of the GOI Act 1935, regional and provincial tendencies surfaced in Muslim parties. Even Sir Khwaja Nazimuddin, who was to become the second governor-general and second prime minister of Pakistan stated on 30 July 1936 that no All-India party could select proper candidates from rural areas. Provincial parties like the Unionists in Punjab and the Muslim United Parties of Sindh, Bengal, and Bihar were proving more popular.

3. The organization of a party, especially during elections, is the responsibility of the honorary secretary. On 12 April 1936, Liaquat Ali Khan was first elected honorary secretary of the AIML, and on 11 November 1936, he resigned from the AIML Parliamentary Board and stood as an independent candidate. The combination of all these factors contributed to the defeat of the AIML in 1937.

MUSLIM LEAGUE EXPECTATIONS.—The Congress had won sufficient seats in UP and Bombay to form a government, yet the AIML insisted that it should be included in the government and given representation in the cabinet. It did not believe that it would have to sit as the opposition. What was the basis for the Muslim League making this extraordinary demand, which was particularly strong in the UP?

One reason was that the manifestos of the Congress and Muslim League in social and economic terms were compatible. The Congress wanted the abolition of Zamindari. The Muslim League was not in favour of outright abolition but was strongly in favour of land reforms.

A second reason was that in UP, the Congress and Muslim League had a tacit understanding against the National Agriculturist Party, a party sponsored and favoured by the British and representing the landlord class. Fearing the influence of the Royal party, both Congress and the Muslim League opposed it. This agreement lasted beyond the general elections. Rafi Ahmad Kidwai, the main Congress candidate on the Muslim list had lost the elections. He was elected in a by-election when the Muslim League agreed not to put up any candidate against him.

Thirdly, during the period between the elections and the assumption of ministries by Congress, the Muslim League sided with Congress and refused all British offers of ministries. The 1935 Act had vested special responsibility in the governor according to which he could over-rule the ministry, therefore, the Congress, despite winning the elections, refused to assume office unless this condition was removed.

Meanwhile, a minority government backed by the British was formed by the Nawab of Chhatari. He offered ministries to Muslim League members including Liaquat Ali Khan. If the Muslim League had cooperated with the National Agriculturist Party, the Congress could have been made to sit as the opposition. However, the Muslim League refused all offers and Liaquat Ali Khan stated that to form a minority government, one not supported by the majority of members, was undemocratic, and in principle, the Muslim League would not support it. In expectation of having their members included in the UP cabinet, by the Congress, the Muslim League refused British offers to join the government. On the refusal of Congress to include them the Muslim League reacted with bitterness.

MUSLIMS UNDER CONGRESS RULE.—The Congress ministries alienated the Muslims of their provinces by their conduct. Some practices were symbolic; Muslims resented the singing of the song *Vande Mataram* taken from Bankim Chandra Chatterjee's virulently anti-Muslim novel *Anand Math*. Moreover, Muslim schoolboys had to salute Gandhi's portrait and Hindi replaced Urdu in schools. Other features were far more threatening. In UP, Hindu–Muslim riots doubled in number. This was put down to Congress's neglect or connivance because incidents of armed robbery had increased by 70 per cent and those of murder had gone up by 30 per cent.

It must be recalled that because of separate electorates, Muslim League candidates had been defeated by Muslim voters, not Hindu voters. It was because of the Congress's attitude that the Muslims began to regret having caused the defeat of the Muslim League. The Muslim League published three reports about Congress's misrule. The 'Pirpur Report' covered UP, the 'Sharif Report' covered Bihar, and the 'Fazlul Haq Report' covered the Congress rule in general.

Foreign writers called these reports Muslim League propaganda. It is not explained why Muslims should believe the propaganda of a party they had themselves recently rejected at the polls. Moreover, recently published (2003) correspondence between Jinnah and Liaquat shows that both leaders were initially reluctant to blame Congress and only did so when the evidence mounted.

REVIVAL OF THE MUSLIM LEAGUE.—The Muslims, not only of minority provinces but of majority provinces like Bengal and Punjab, came to the realization that if this was the behaviour of the Hindu majority, while the British still controlled the central government, what would be their conduct if the British withdrew, and the Congress controlled the centre as well?

AIML LUCKNOW SESSION, 15–18 OCTOBER 1937.—This meeting was organized by the treasurer of the Muslim League, the Raja of Mahmudabad (1914–1973). Besides paying the expenses of the session from his own purse (Rs 30 lakhs), he toured the nearby districts of Agra and Muzaffarnagar inviting every Muslim to attend the session and led Jinnah's carriage procession when he arrived. It took the procession four hours to cover a distance of three miles. In his welcome address, the Raja of Mahmudabad stated, 'We are here not to follow history, but to create it'.

The Muslim premiers of the Punjab, Bengal, and Assam, Sir Sikandar Hayat, Fazlul Haq, and Sir Muhammad Saadullah, attended the 1937 Lucknow session. In their provinces, they and their parties had prevailed over the Muslim League, but now they closed ranks. They wanted the Muslim League, not the Congress to represent them at the centre. In early 1937, the Muslim League was in decline; in October 1937 it was resurgent and only because, as Jinnah said at the Lucknow session 'the Congress have shown their hand that Hindustan is for the Hindus'.

DAY OF DELIVERANCE.—The Second World War broke out on 3 September 1939. The same day, Lord Linlithgow announced that India was also at war. The Congress protested that they were not consulted. On 15 September 1939, the Congress said that India would not participate in the war unless the British accepted the principle of full and immediate independence for India. The British refused but instead offered full dominion status at the end of the war. On 22 September the Congress resigned all its ministries.

Even after such a bitter experience, M.A. Jinnah first offered terms to the Congress rather than to the British. He asked for Muslim League–Congress coalitions in the provinces, an end to anti-Muslim moves, and acceptance of the principle that no legislation affecting the Muslims would be passed unless two-thirds of Muslim members voted for it. Only when Congress did not respond did Jinnah go ahead with a programme to observe 22 December 1939, as a 'day of deliverance' from Congress rule.

At this juncture, the Congress president, Jawaharlal Nehru, approached Jinnah saying that he had asked the British to express their war aims, agree to Indian independence, and the right to frame its own constitution, 'as the Muslim League has the same declared object there should be no difference of opinion about them'. Nehru expressed these sentiments when Congress ministers had already resigned, and not when the ministries were being formed in 1937 or even when Jinnah had recently made an offer of cooperation.

On 22 December 1939, Muslims rejoiced over their deliverance and what is more, were joined by small non-Muslim parties as well. The Congress had made a strategic mistake by resigning. The British were relieved that they would be able to fight the war with Indian soldiers and resources but without any hindrance from Congress. This gave an opening to the Muslim League to consolidate their political gains.

RAJA OF MAHMUDABAD, MUHAMMAD AMIR AHMAD KHAN (b. Mahmudabad, 1914–d. London, 1973) The Raja of Mahmudabad was the third of the triumvirate that created Pakistan. As treasurer, he ranked immediately after the president and honorary secretary of the AIML. A prince who would be pauper, he sacrificed his fabulous wealth for the cause of Pakistan, and on the success of his mission, refused to partake of its fruits and retired from politics. He was the only member of the AIML hierarchy to undergo ideological stress. He personified the transition from movement-oriented to state-oriented politics in Pakistan.

The Raja of Mahmudabad's endeavours towards the establishment of Pakistan consisted mainly of financing and organizing the movement. We have already mentioned, under the 1937 Lucknow session, the contributions made by the Raja. This session was only the beginning. According to Chaudhry Khaliquzzaman, the Raja opened his purse strings to meet election expenses—whatever the amount.[1] The Raja's efforts reversed the 1937 defeat by winning 86 per cent of the seats in the by-elections. Apart from elections, the Raja's recorded contributions were to *Dawn*. All these efforts won him the appreciation of the Quaid-i-Azam who hosted, in Bombay, the largest-ever dinner of his life, inviting 400 guests to honour the Raja of Mahmudabad. 'The Raja of Mahmudabad, although young in age' Jinnah told his guests, 'is a great man in wisdom and capacity'.[2] This was a momentous tribute, but it, unfortunately, marked the point from where the tide ebbed.

Although he held the largest estates in UP, he led an abstemious life, following the precepts of the holy personages of Islam. Another outcome of his religious idealism was his espousal of an Islamic state. It was this idealism which would cause him ideological stress. On 28 July 1940, he wrote to the Quaid-i-Azam: 'When I say an Islamic state, I do not mean a Muslim state.'[3] According to Isha'at Habibullah, when the Raja reiterated his stand in Jinnah's presence, Jinnah responded: 'Did you realize that there are over seventy sects and differences of opinion regarding the Islamic faith, and if what the Raja was suggesting was to be followed, the consequences would be a struggle of religious opinion from the very inception of the State leading to its very dissolution...'[4]

Jinnah's objection to an Islamic state was not ideological but empirical, but it was only in 1970, that the Raja wrote that Jinnah had been right, and he had been wrong.[5] Apart from the issue of an Islamic state, the Raja wished Jinnah to bide his time, and not accept the partition of Bengal and Punjab. When the Raja went to NWFP, buying up arms in the aftermath of the 1946 riots, Jinnah reprimanded him sharply. No wonder the Raja had refused to go to Karachi on 14 August 1947, in spite of being in Hyderabad (Sindh). In all three issues—his insistence on an Islamic state, his insistence that Jinnah risk the creation of Pakistan to prevent the bifurcation of provinces, and taking recourse to violence during the riots—Jinnah was right and the Raja was wrong. This did not detract from the emotional crises the Raja underwent. On 16 December 1943, the Raja had written to Jinnah: 'But I have nobody except you whom I regard in place of my father and the prodigal son in trouble returns only to his father.'[6] In 1947, the son was prodigal and there was no father to return to. The only meeting that the Raja had with Jinnah after independence was when he was forcibly made to disembark, at Karachi. The scene was stormy, but the governor-general exercised restraint: 'Amir! You have no idea of the situation here, I am surrounded by traitors. I cannot entrust the fate of Pakistan to them.'[7]

The Raja came to Pakistan after a decade, in 1957, and left again after ten years, in 1967, when he was asked to show his passport. Within that decade, he shunned offers of high office given by Presidents Iskander Mirza, Ayub Khan, and Yahya Khan. He also refused to build up a constituency. In a Karachi public meeting, on 19 March 1958, he told the *muhajir* audience that they—and not Bengalis or Punjabis—were responsible for the spread of racial prejudice.[8] When Princess Abida Sultaan visited him when he was on his London deathbed, he recalled bitterly that he was being cared for by the very British against whom he had struggled.

Notes

1. Chaudhry Khaliquzzaman, *Pathway to Pakistan* (Lahore: Longman, 1961), p. 159.
2. Shaiq Ahmad Usmani (ed.), *Asr-i-Jadid*, Calcutta, 24 January 1938.
3. Rizwan Ahmad Collection, Baitul Hikmat, Hamdard, p. 74.
4. Isha'at Habibullah, "Memories of British and Feudal India," *Dawn* 27 September 1991 pp. 3–9.
5. Raja of Mahmudabad, 'Some Memories', in Mushirul Hasan (ed.), *India's Partition: Process, Strategy and Mobilization* (Delhi: Oxford University Press, 1994), p. 426.
6. Shamsul Hasan Collection.
7. Dr Afzal Iqbal, 'The Young and Fiery Raja of Mahmudabad', *Dawn*, 11 November 1983.
8. *Imroze*, 20 March 1958.

Part 4
History of the Pakistan Movement

CHAPTER 20

FROM THE LAHORE RESOLUTION 1940 TO THE 1945 ELECTIONS

The 1937 elections were the lowest point for the Muslim League. The 1937 Lucknow session was the highest point of resurgence. The attendance of the premiers of Muslim-majority provinces where the Muslim League had lost, showed that the damage had been controlled, and the Muslim League was on its way to success. Between 1937 and 1942, the Muslim League won 46 out of 56 seats in by-elections.

The reason behind this resurgence is not simply that the Muslims felt that they had to unite to face the prospects of a central government headed not by the British, but by the Congress, as could easily be foreseen, but also because the Lahore Resolution gave Muslims, as Khalid B. Sayeed states, 'a clear aim and direction'.[1] It meant that Muslims had forsaken seeking guarantees for themselves as a minority and now asserted their rights as a separate nation. In constitutional terms it meant that the Muslims would not be subject to the law of the land, as all minorities are, but to international law. Under international law, being smaller in numbers than the Hindu population or in occupied territory did not matter; Hindus and Muslims would form equal sovereign states.

There are a number of individuals who were already thinking along these lines. Dr Syed Abdul Latif of the Deccan put forward a scheme in 1939, proposing four zones for Muslims in India. Professors Syed Zafarul Hasan and M. Afzal Qadri of the Aligarh University proposed three federations: one each in the north-west and north-east, and one centred in Hyderabad Deccan. However, no scheme which envisaged the creation of a Muslim entity over areas where Muslims were in a minority could be seriously considered.

It was the Sindh Muslim League which, on 10 October 1938, adopted a resolution moved by Sir Abdullah Haroon which called for a division of India into two federations, Hindu and Muslim. G.M. Syed said Hindus and Muslims were two separate nations. On 25 March 1939 at Meerut, Liaquat Ali Khan voiced his preference for division. Less than a year later, the AIML held its historic session in Lahore.

THE TWO-NATION THEORY.—The Lahore session is noted for the formal adoption of the Two-Nation theory by the AIML. Presiding over the session, M.A. Jinnah said: 'The Hindus and Muslims belong to two different religious philosophies, social customs, and literature[s]. They neither intermarry nor interdine together, and indeed they belong to two different civilisations which are based mainly on conflicting ideas and conceptions.'[2]

The theory raised a storm of controversy. The first question was, is Jinnah sincere in formulating this theory? Durga Das, a journalist, asked Jinnah in Lahore whether Pakistan was a serious demand or merely a bargaining stance. The reason behind such speculation was that firstly, early in his career Jinnah had opposed separate electorates and was called 'Ambassador of Hindu–Muslim Unity' by Gopal Krishna Gokhale. Secondly, on achieving the goal set by the Lahore Resolution, Jinnah partially weakened the Two-Nation theory. On 11 August 1947, in his first address to the Constituent Assembly of Pakistan, Jinnah said: 'You may belong to any religion or caste or creed—that has nothing to do with the business of the State... We are starting with this fundamental principle: that we are all citizens, and equal citizens, of one State.'

Thus, the Two-Nation theory was an intermediary position adopted by Jinnah. He was careful to emphasize that the Two-Nation theory was held also by some Hindus, notably Lala Lajpat Rai. The differences Jinnah pointed out between Hindus and Muslims, were, and are, real. The question is whether they were capable of political integration despite these fundamental differences.

The question that needs to be answered is, why did Jinnah formulate the Two-Nation theory in 1940 and discard it in 1947?

Here we have to study the essence of the Two-Nation theory. Not only Lala Lajpat Rai but other Hindu leaders elaborated on this theory. Gandhi, while inspecting the extremist Rashtriya Swayamsevak Sangh (RSS) camp in Wardha, had supported their creed by saying: 'Every community is entitled, indeed bound to organize itself, if it is to live as a separate entity.'[3] Of course he did not foresee then that a few years later the RSS would bring his life to its violent end. Even Jawaharlal Nehru inadvertently upheld the Two-Nation theory when Bengali nationalism made a bid to assert itself in 1947. Therefore, we have to examine whether the Two-Nation theory was valid as an instrument of partition or not.

The Two-Nation theory in India was put forward to protect a minority from a majority. In Pakistan, the same Two-Nation theory would encroach on the rights of minorities. This can be explained by a single example. The Muslims, being a minority in India, struggled to achieve separate electorates. Without these, they felt that their voice would not be heard. In Pakistan, General Zia ul-Haq imposed separate electorates against the wishes of the minority. The minorities struggled to have this provision removed because they felt that separate electorates were marginalizing them and because of this provision they were unable to make their voice heard.

Therefore, the essence of political emancipation is securing measures for survival, the essence is not any theory. The religious parties in Pakistan have held that since Partition had been achieved by separate electorates, it should be retained, whether the minorities demand it or not.

A resolution was moved on 23 March 1940 at Lahore by Maulvi Abul Kassem (A.K.) Fazlul Haq who represented Bengal, a Muslim majority province, and was seconded by Chaudhry Khaliquzzaman representing UP, a Muslim minority province. It was this resolution of the AIML which was responsible for the creation of Pakistan.

The main resolution stated: 'No constitutional plan would be workable in this country or acceptable to the Muslims unless it is designed on the following basic principles, viz., that geographically contiguous units are demarcated into regions which should be so constituted with such territorial adjustments as may be necessary, that the areas in which the Muslims are numerically in a majority, as in the north-western and eastern zones of India, should be grouped to constitute 'Independent states' in which the constituent units shall be autonomous and sovereign.'

The text of the resolution is ambiguous. The name Pakistan is not mentioned. The areas which were to constitute the state demanded by the Muslim League are not mentioned by name, nor are they clearly demarcated. By using the word 'states' (in the plural) it is not clear whether Pakistan would consist of one state or more. Furthermore, 'autonomous' and 'sovereign' are not equal terms; states can be autonomous without being sovereign. whether this ambiguity was inadvertent or deliberate is also not clear.

Whatever the ambiguity, it definitely rules out a unitary state and points to a federal state. Even Fazlul Haq, as a politician, and Khaliquzzaman, as a historian proved to be revisionists. Fazlul Haq, as governor of East Bengal, and Khaliquzzaman in *Pathway to Pakistan*,[4] later expressed their reservations about Pakistan as a country and as a solution to the communal problem in India. The reality is discussed under the Cabinet Mission Plan.

Jinnah cleared some of the ambiguity in an interview with the Associate Press of America. He said that Pakistan was to be a democratic federal state comprising the existing provinces of the North-West Frontier, Balochistan, Sindh, and Punjab in the west and Bengal and Assam in the east. From 1940 onwards, the Muslim League observed 23 March as Pakistan Day. The Muslim League had now introduced a new factor in the politics of India at a time when the British were fighting for survival in the Second World War.

THE CRIPPS MISSION, 1942.—The Second World War was determining every move of the British. On its part, the Congress had realized its mistake in resigning from provincial ministries. Being in office would have been tactically beneficial to the Congress at a time when they thought British rule would collapse before the Japanese onslaught which had taken Singapore and Burma (now Myanmar), and which was bombing Calcutta. The British were relieved that the Congress was not there to hinder their war efforts, but their ally, the United States of America, insisted that Britain enlist the active cooperation of Indian politicians. President Franklin Delano Roosevelt (1882–1945) expressed this view personally to Prime Minister Winston Churchill (1874–1965) and the result was that Churchill had to send Sir Stafford Cripps

(1889–1952) to India to seek a solution that would induct the political leadership of India into the war effort.

Sir Stafford Cripps had been the British ambassador to the USSR and was widely credited with bringing the USSR into the war on the side of Britain and against Germany. He was a socialist, a member of the Labour Party, and a personal friend of Jawaharlal Nehru, the Congress leader. The president of the United States wanted Cripps to succeed in enlisting the Congress and Muslim League cooperation, while the British prime minister prayed that he would not.

The outcome of the Cripps Mission has become controversial. Some say that Cripps initially assured the Congress that they could enter the Viceroy's Executive Council which, by convention though not by constitution (Government of India Act 1935), would be a cabinet, or a quasi-cabinet in the phrase of Sir Reginald Coupland. According to this version, Viceroy Lord Linlithgow complained of being side-tracked and Cripps had to modify his offer which the Congress then rejected. At one stage Cripps had assured Nehru that he would not let any British official, no matter how high, hold up an agreement: an obvious reference to the viceroy.

There was much bickering over whether an Indian or a British representative would exercise control over the conduct of war. A draft declaration was officially endorsed by Winston Churchill on 11 March 1942. Cripps declared on 29 March, that as soon as the war ended, an elected body would be charged with framing a new constitution for India. Cripps offered dominion status to India after the war with the option to leave the British Commonwealth. Congress turned down the proposal and wanted immediate power. *Roy's Weekly* described the Cripps offer as a 'post-dated cheque on a crashing bank', a comment popularly but wrongly attributed to Gandhi.

At one stage Cripps wondered why Nehru did not understand that even if he brought the Congress into government without changing the Constitution, as a 'quasi-cabinet' the viceroy would not be able to override it. It is reasonable to infer that the real reason behind Congress's refusal was the non-accession clause. Peter Clarke, who has had access to the private papers of Sir Stafford Cripps, does not think so, and there was actually a Congress resolution that said that the Congress committee would not force any territorial unit to remain in India against 'their declared and established will'. However, during a private discussion that Cripps had with Maulana Azad and Nehru, it surfaced that the Congress leaders were contemplating a Pakistan which could secede five or ten years hence. The Congress was demanding immediate powers from the British and offering deferred (or delayed) power to the Muslim League. In 1946, Congress was prepared to offer the Muslims even less.

The non-accession clause of the Cripps offer meant that provinces that wished to remain outside the proposed Union of India could do so, and if the non-acceding units wished to form a union of their own, this union would be at par with the Union of India; a constitutional and roundabout way of saying that the British would concede Pakistan. M.A. Jinnah thanked Cripps for recognizing the principle of Pakistan, but still did not accept the Cripps offer because the non-acceding provinces would have to vote in a joint electorate system, and not through separate electorates. Thus, for different reasons, both the Congress and the Muslim League turned down Cripps's offer.

THE QUIT INDIA MOVEMENT, 1942.—Since great expectations had been initially raised by Sir Stafford Cripps, the disappointment was deep. Cripps had made his offer in the expectation that Congress and the Muslim League would cooperate in Britain's war against Germany. Gandhi persuaded Congress to adopt a Quit India Resolution. At first Nehru and Sardar Patel resisted but finally agreed with Gandhi.

In the Muslim League, the Quit India Movement was fanning differences of opinion in the working committee. The Raja of Mahmudabad and G.M. Syed moved a resolution calling for the Muslim League to join the Quit India Movement. Ultimately, the Raja of Mahmudabad abstained and only G.M. Syed voted for the resolution. It must be mentioned that the Quit India Movement created an emotional crisis. Police had fired upon students in Allahabad, Nehru's hometown, and Hindu students appealed to their Muslim classmates to join them. However, Jinnah did not want to participate in the Quit India Movement and instead coined the slogan 'Divide and Quit'.

Why the Muslim League chose to remain aloof from the Quit India Movement is a question often asked. Jinnah viewed the Quit India Movement with suspicion, considering it a Congress effort to force the British to transfer power only to Congress, thereby leaving the Muslim League in the lurch. His suspicion was based on past experience. Jinnah recalled how, during the First World War, when he had opposed cooperation with the British, it had been Gandhi who had thwarted him by extending unconditional cooperation to the British. In 1918, Gandhi had written to Jinnah that independence would soon be achieved if their party became a recruiting agency for the British army. Jinnah had not understood Gandhi's logic then, and he did not understand his motives in 1942. While speaking on the war efforts, Jinnah recalled Gandhi's phrase, saying that: 'I could not play the role of a recruiting sergeant'. However, he added that the Muslim League was not non-cooperating. In other words, the non-cooperation of Gandhi was active, and Jinnah's non-cooperation was passive. He said he could give the British much more trouble than Congress but the result of that would be either a change of masters or the fragmentation of India. He meant that if the British quit, the advancing Japanese would take over India, or some parts would fall as Burma (now Myanmar) and Singapore had. Even now Jinnah was showing concern for the unity of India, but he opposed the Quit India Movement because he thought it was meant to pressurize the British into handing over power to the Congress alone leaving the Muslim League high and dry.

The British eventually subdued the Quit India Movement, the Japanese advance on India was halted, and the war ended in victory for the British and their allies.

SIMLA CONFERENCE AND THE 1945 ELECTIONS.—In 1943, British Prime Minister Winston Churchill replaced Viceroy Lord Linlithgow and appointed the Commander-in-Chief, Lord Wavell, in his place. Churchill had expected that being a military man, Lord Wavell would take no political initiative but the new viceroy, a conscientious man, made an attempt to break the political deadlock in the country by installing an interim government representative of Indian political parties. In his scheme, the viceroy and the commander-in-chief would continue to be British while all the members of the Viceroy's Executive Council would be Indian.

Unlike at the time of the Cripps offer, Congress did not raise any objection to the conduct of war being directed by the British. The viceroy made it clear that this arrangement would last as long as the war with the Japanese continued. The interim government would function under the existing constitution, i.e. Government of India Act 1935.

The viceroy broadcast his proposals on 14 June 1945, simultaneously announcing the release of Gandhi and other Congress leaders. The Simla Conference opened on 25 June, and on 14 July Lord Wavell announced its failure apportioning the blame to himself. The Conference had actually failed because M.A. Jinnah, as president of the AIML, had said that since his party was the sole spokesperson for the Indian Muslims, no other political party had the right to nominate any Muslim to the Viceroy's Executive Council. This contention was unacceptable to the Congress and the viceroy and thus the Conference failed, and no interim government could be nominated.

Objectively the stand of the Muslim League could not be upheld in the light of its dismal performance in the 1937 elections. Before the AIML delegation left Simla, it called for fresh elections. These were held in December 1945 and January 1946. In the elections to the (central) Indian Legislative Assembly, the AIML secured all 30 Muslim seats. In the elections to the various provincial assemblies, it won 446 out of a total of 495 Muslim seats. Thus, the claim the AIML made in Simla, that it was the sole spokesperson of Indian Muslims, was vindicated.

Notes

1. Khalid bin Sayeed, *Pakistan: The Formative Phase* (Karachi: OUP, 1978), pp. 179, 197.
2. Address by Quaid-i-Azam Mohammad Ali Jinnah at Lahore Session of Muslim League, March 1940 (Islamabad: Directorate of Films and Publishing, Ministry of Information and Broadcasting, Government of Pakistan, Islamabad, 1983), pp. 5–23.
3. *Young India*, 6 January 1929.
4. Chaudhry Khaliquzzaman, *Pathway to Pakistan* (Lahore: Longman, 1961).

ABUL KASSEM FAZUL HAQ (b. Barisal, 1873–d. Dacca, 1962) moved the 23 March 1940 Resolution which culminated in the creation of Pakistan. In 1954, he stated at a Calcutta meeting that he could not understand the *raison d'être* of Pakistan.[1] In 1916, he fervently advocated the Lucknow Pact, although weightage to the Hindus would make the Muslim majority precarious in Bengal, and in 1931, he opposed it. In 1918, Fazlul Haq became president of the All-India Muslim League; and in 1941, he resigned from it. In 1939, he denounced Shyama Prasad Mookerjee as being communal minded. In 1941, he included Mookerjee in his Bengal cabinet. Thus, Fazlul Haq had a vacillating disposition and in consequence, suffered the most chequered career in the political history of South Asia. He also sometimes got what he had given. In 1954, he was denounced as a traitor for his Calcutta statement, and in 1956 he was appointed Pakistan's Minister of Interior.

Behind all these political moves was a most charismatic personality. He was the exemplar of the indigenous Bengali elite; intellectually exasperating, he had a heart of gold. He helped anyone who approached him, not hesitating to incur heavy debts in order to succour the needy. It was this trait that shone brightly amidst the ruins of his political career. Also, his volatile personality presented a spectacle rarely witnessed in the political arena. A case in point is the manner in which his Krishak Sramik Party, by ousting the rival Muslim United Party provided a reopening to the Muslim League in Bengal. According to M.A.H. Ispahani, he had briefed Fazlul Haq minutely on how to disrupt the All-Bengal United Muslim Conference of August 1936. As the plan unfolded, Fazlul Haq reacted first with suspicion, then with disbelief, and finally with amusement. According to the script, immediately after the Muslim United meeting, Fazlul Haq, head of the rival Krishak Sramik started to address the meeting: 'As expected, shouts from the dais were first heard calling upon him to sit down and to shut up. The more he was reprimanded, the more he insisted on speaking at the top of his voice. These shouts and counter-shouts made the conduct of serious business impossible. Appeal for silence was made, and I addressed the gathering with words to this effect: That as a dispute had unfortunately arisen, it was necessary that it be resolved and for that purpose that a neutral person of national status, namely Mr Mohammad Ali Jinnah, be invited to Calcutta immediately.'[2]

In Pakistan, all his appointments, barring one, were provincial. As advocate general, chief minister, and governor during the crucial Language Movement, Fazlul Haq had remained uncommitted. That is why he did not enjoy the measure of success Huseyn Shaheed Suhrawardy enjoyed, even though it was brief. Fazlul Haq has also suffered for not having an influential biographer: Shaista Ikramullah wrote about the life of her cousin Huseyn Shaheed Suhrawardy, but she scarcely mentions that Fazlul Haq was her uncle. Her father and Fazlul Haq had married sisters.[3]

Notes

1. H.S. Suhrawardy, *Memoirs* (Dhaka: The University Press, 1987), p. 86.
2. M.A.H. Ispahani, *Quaid-e-Azam Jinnah as I Knew Him*, 3rd ed. (Karachi: Royal Book Co., 1976), pp. 23–4.
3. Rajmohan Gandhi, *Eight Lives: A Study of the Hindu-Muslim Encounter* (New York: State University of New York Press, 1986), p. 190.

CHAPTER 21
THE CABINET MISSION PLAN, 1946

> **MEMBERS OF THE CABINET MISSION**
>
> Secretary of State for India, Lord Frederick Pethick-Lawrence (1871–1961); President of the Board of Trade, Sir Richard Stafford Cripps (1889–1952); and First Lord of the Admiralty, Albert V. Alexander (1885–1965).

Against the background of unfolding events at the end of the Second World War, Britain, with the help of her Allies had won the war, but in the effort had lost her economic ascendancy, a section of her population, and its imperialist sentiments. The Conservative Party led by Winston Churchill still nurtured hopes of an empire and great power status but was defeated in the 1945 elections.

The Labour government under the new Prime Minister, Clement Atlee (1883–1967), was more conscious of the economic plight of Britain, and also more sympathetic to the cause of Indian independence. They realized that they had to transfer power to India. The question was, to whom should power be transferred? Left to itself, the Labour Party would have transferred power to the Indian National Congress as the overall majority party, but the Conservative Party, especially its leader, was aware of the pledges the British had given to the minorities and the Chamber of Princes. Recognizing that Muslims numbered 90 million, Churchill held the opinion that the word 'minorities had no relevance or sense when applied to masses of human beings numbered in many scores of millions.' He was later to publicly state this in parliament. The Conservative Party was then in opposition, but in the strong two-party system the opposition was powerful, and in the House of Lords, the Conservative Party had greater influence.

The Viceroy, Lord Wavell, desired a united India because it would serve the residual strategic and commercial interests of Britain. The Congress had its own justifications for wanting India to remain united. Both, thus, disagreed with Jinnah. However, Wavell realized that the Congress did not represent Muslims, and wanted Muslims to be given safeguards in the future constitution. Congress considered safeguards unnecessary. They wanted a unitary government with a strong centre. The viceroy felt that the Muslims would be better protected in a federal system with a weak centre. The viceroy's fair-mindedness was proving to be a hindrance in the transfer of power, therefore Clement Atlee agreed to send three members of his cabinet to India. They were to seek an agreement among the parties, and if no agreement was forthcoming, to transfer power on the terms demanded by the Congress. On 20 February 1946, M.A. Jinnah disapproved of the decision to send a Cabinet Mission to India but cooperated with it, nevertheless.

Congress leaders M.K. Gandhi and Jawaharlal Nehru dominated the proceedings from the beginning. Gandhi had anticipated that the Cabinet Mission would ultimately produce a document and he extracted a commitment from Frederick Pethick-Lawrence that such a document should be in the nature of a recommendation and not an award which would be binding on the parties. Lord Pethick-Lawrence did not disclose this to Lord Wavell, nor to the Congress president, Maulana Azad, and the question of his confiding in M.A. Jinnah did not arise. There was confusion during the negotiations and the secret undertaking was revealed to King George VI only after the Cabinet Mission had failed.

According to Sir Penderel Moon (d.1987), the Cabinet Mission decided that the Muslim League was to be offered two options: (1) Pakistan—with six provinces, which would be part of a common union with India and without sovereignty. (2) A fully sovereign Pakistan with the partition of Bengal and Punjab. The Pakistani Punjab would not include Gurdaspur.

These two options were disclosed to M.A. Jinnah except for the clause pertaining to Gurdaspur. He considered both options: a sovereign Pakistan, which would result in dividing the Muslim community; an autonomous Pakistan which would consist of six provinces, but which would keep the Muslim community intact within one country. The Cabinet Mission pressed this option on him and sent Chief of the General Staff, General Sir Arthur Smith, to convince him. Smith told Jinnah that Indian security would be endangered if the country was divided. Jinnah said both Pakistan and Hindustan could have a military pact when there was war with outside forces, but not during peacetime.

Nevertheless, there are indications that the defence of South Asia weighed on him. It is worth recalling that during the Quit India Movement, Jinnah had said that he neither wanted a change of masters (i.e. the Japanese) nor the fragmentation of India. Perhaps this sentiment was stronger in him than he realized. There is a body of scholars, led by Ayesha Jalal, which holds that Hindu–Muslim parity within a united India was Jinnah's real demand. The Muslim provinces would be grouped together and derive maximum autonomy. However, Gandhi had let it be known to the Cabinet Mission on 8 May 1946 that he did not favour grouping, and parity was worse than a sovereign Pakistan.

Sir Stafford Cripps and Lord Pethick-Lawrence insisted that the acceptance of 'grouping' by the Congress, and the acceptance of a common Union of India by the Muslim League would be a fair basis for agreement between the two parties. Therefore, on 12 May 1946, the Muslim League sent its constitutional proposals conceding a union that would deal with defence and foreign affairs but would have no legislature and no powers of taxation. There would be a Pakistan group of provinces and a Hindustan group of provinces that would contribute voluntarily towards the expenditure of the union. Even such a vital concession by the Muslim League was not appreciated, and the Cabinet Mission published its own plan on 16 May 1946, in which the Muslim League proposals had been further diluted.

Thus, it seems that the Cabinet Mission incorporated the essence but not the safeguards that the AIML had proposed four days earlier. After the Cabinet Mission Plan was published, Liaquat Ali Khan sent M.A. Jinnah, on 21 May 1946, some typed objections to it. Far from proving to be a stepping-stone for Pakistan as the Muslim League leadership asserted, Liaquat Ali Khan argued that the Congress, as the majority party, would control the coercive apparatus of the state, the armed forces, and the police; it would not only physically prevent secession, but also wipe out the given safeguards. However, M.A. Jinnah favoured acceptance. M.A.H. Ispahani has revealed that the Cabinet Mission told the Muslim League that it would have to accept its 16 May 1946 plan without change or face the consequences, which were riots. It transpired that the Cabinet Mission was willing to let Congress modify its plan. On 17 May, Gandhi wrote in his journal, the *Harijan*, that there was 'no take it or leave it business about the Plan, and the provinces were free to reject the very idea of grouping'. This he could write because of the undertaking he had extracted from Lord Pethick-Lawrence. The Muslim League disregarded this editorial of Gandhi's, thinking that the British would uphold their own scheme, regardless of whatever anyone wrote.

On 6 June 1946, the AIML council voted to accept the Cabinet Mission Plan, saying that it could be a stepping-stone to Pakistan. Jinnah later explained that the AIML had accepted it as it would give Muslims sufficient autonomy to develop economically and culturally.

The Congress had always criticized the demand for Pakistan; it did not believe in dividing the country. M.A. Jinnah and the Muslim League had accepted the formula of 16 May 1946 according to which India was not to be divided. Instead, Hindu-majority and Muslim-majority provinces were grouped so that zonal sub-federations were created. The Congress and Mahasabha ridiculed the AIML for its weakness and said that 'Mr Jinnah had come to his senses.' It is not known why they pushed the Muslim League after having gained a united India. Why did they object to the grouping of Muslim-majority provinces when the Congress would dominate the Union? Another enigmatic question is, even if the Congress disliked grouping, why did they not wait for the British to leave before saying so?

The AIML was aware that Congress did not like the grouping clause, but they thought that the British would uphold their Plan. However, on 10 July 1946, Jawaharlal Nehru told a Bombay press conference that the Congress did not accept grouping and was not bound by any agreement except that it had decided, for the moment, to enter the Constituent Assembly.

Now the AIML had no choice. All the safeguards it had accepted in lieu of a sovereign Pakistan were proving illusory. The AIML council reassembled in Bombay on 29 July 1946 and withdrew its acceptance of the Cabinet Mission Plan. It also announced Direct Action. There were two Muslim leaders of India, M.A. Jinnah, who wished to see India divided, and Abul Kalam Azad who wished to keep India united. In his book, *India Wins Freedom*, Abul Kalam Azad calls the Cabinet Mission Plan a scheme that would have preserved the unity of India and still solved the communal problem. He blames Nehru, not Jinnah, for wrecking the Plan. The latter's interpretation he accepted as correct. Jinnah had given united India a chance, but Congress ruined that chance. In view of Azad's admission, it is wrong to imply that Jinnah and Azad held opposing views because both had reached the same conclusion.

DIRECT ACTION.—At the 29 July 1946 Bombay meeting, Jinnah had said that he was now bidding farewell to constitutional methods and calling for Direct Action. This came as a surprise to the Congress because Jawaharlal Nehru had written to Sir Stafford Cripps that the Muslim League was incapable of Direct Action.

At a press conference, Liaquat Ali Khan said that Direct Action meant any action against the law. The AIML fixed 16 August 1946 as Direct Action Day. All over India the day passed peacefully but in Calcutta, where Huseyn Shaheed Suhrawardy led the provincial government, a holiday was declared. This resulted in the Great Calcutta killings. When the viceroy visited Calcutta, he upbraided H.S. Suhrawardy for starting the Hindu–Muslim riots. Suhrawardy politely told the viceroy to set up an inquiry committee under the Chief Justice, Sir William Patrick Spens. This was done, and in his report, the chief justice exonerated Suhrawardy, or the Muslims, of having started the riots. It was clear, however, that once Hindus started the riots, the Muslims also retaliated most fiercely. As a result of the Calcutta riots, Muslims of Noakhali in East Bengal killed Hindus and the Noakhali riots spread to Bihar where the Muslims suffered most.

In the midst of this bloodshed, Congress formed the Interim Government on 2 September 1946. It was only on 26 October that the AIML bloc, led by Liaquat Ali Khan joined the Interim Government. Nehru's official designation was vice-president of the Viceroy's Executive Council, but he insisted on being called the prime minister of India although he had accepted office on the condition that the Government of India Act 1935 be retained as the constitution for India. In the meantime, a parliamentary delegation from Britain led by Professor Robert Richards visited India, and on its return met with Clement Atlee and pressed him to accept the Pakistan issue.

Early in 1947, Congress members of the interim government insisted that the Muslim League members be expelled because they were not attending the Constituent Assembly of India which had started functioning in December 1946. Once again, the question of whether Congress had accepted the 16 May 1946 Cabinet Mission Plan came up. Congress had said that it accepted the Plan but would not accept the grouping clause. On 6 December, when both Congress and Muslim League leaders were in London, the British government conceded that the AIML interpretation of the Plan was correct; in other words, the grouping of provinces was an essential feature of the 16 May Plan and the Congress interpretation, that the Cabinet Mission Plan could be accepted without grouping, was wrong. Nevertheless, since the AIML had formally withdrawn its acceptance, Congress said it had no right to remain in the government.

While participating in the interim government, Liaquat Ali Khan had taken the lead in the division of the armed forces. Lord Mountbatten who succeeded Lord Wavell as viceroy in 1947, had intended to divide the country without dividing the armed forces. He hoped to be the governor-general of both India and Pakistan and by this method undo partition. Liaquat Ali Khan told Lord Mountbatten that Hindu officers of the Indian army were planning a coup, a development that would prevent partition. When Mountbatten did not believe Liaquat Ali Khan, Jinnah accompanied him to meet the viceroy and convinced him of the impending coup. Following this meeting, Mountbatten agreed to divide the army.

On 28 February, Liaquat Ali Khan, as finance member, presented the last budget of United India. He had imposed a business profit tax of 25 per cent on all profits exceeding Rs 100,000. Liaquat Ali Khan said he was following Islamic principles by taxing the rich and providing relief to the poor. The people of India termed it the 'Poor Man's Budget'. Actually, Liaquat had drawn up an anti-British budget, but because it hurt the rich of every community, the largest community, the Hindus, complained. Among the plutocrats who were being taxed were those who provided funds to the Congress. They were angry. There were many more rich Hindus than rich Muslims, but despite having a majority in the Indian Legislative Assembly, Congress did not dare defeat the budget because they knew that there were many more poor Hindus than there were poor Muslims. Abul Kalam Azad has written that Sardar Vallabhbhai Patel was so annoyed with Liaquat's budget that he was willing to consider partition seriously. According to Hugh Tinker, Sardar Patel said that 'If the Muslim League did not accept the Cabinet Mission Plan, then the Congress desired Partition'.

Eventually, the Congress agreed to the creation of Pakistan. Why the Congress preferred partition of the country rather than grouping of provinces is not clear unless we accept the view that the Congress thought that partition would be temporary. They thought that Pakistan without industries would not be economically viable and would collapse. Whatever the reason, Independence and Partition were to come about simultaneously under the 3 June Plan.

MAULANA ABUL KALAM AZAD's (b. Khem Kharan, 1888–d. New Delhi, 1958) real name was Mohyuddin Ahmad. Azad is the exemplar for those intellectuals who hold that the partition of India was a mistake since it weakened India, as well as the Muslims of India. Such people think that if Abul Kalam Azad and not M.A. Jinnah had been followed, all bitterness and strife would have been avoided. Here we consider this line of argument.

Azad began his career as a journalist in Calcutta, editing *Nairang-i-Alam*, in 1900, and *Al-Misbah*, in 1901. Early in his life, Azad came under the influence of Sir Syed Ahmad Khan, and wrote a poem, in 1901, to commemorate the coronation of King Edward VII. He made his revolutionary impact with the launch of *Al-Hilal* (1912–1915). When the British closed it down, he launched *Al-Balagh* (1915–1916). These journals established him as a stylist of high repute, and his political commentaries began gaining him admirers. At around this time, he joined Congress. His journalism saw him interned at Ranchi, from 8 July 1916 to 27 December 1919. On his release, Azad met Gandhi for the first time. During the same time, Azad made a bid to become Imam-ul-Hind. Maulana Abdul Bari said: 'Azad is ready to accept, I have no objection.' However, his candidature did not find general acceptance. He then floated the idea of having an Amir-i-Hind. The CID report of 1 April 1920 stated that Azad wished for the position.[1]

Earlier in 1913, Azad had joined the Muslim League and remained a member till 1929, and resigned only when his efforts to obtain a party majority in favour of the Nehru Report failed. Azad has suppressed mention of his membership of the Muslim League from both his memoirs *India Wins Freedom* and *Azad Ki Kahani, Azad Ki Zabani*.

In 1923, at the age of 35, Azad became the youngest president of the Indian National Congress. Azad was jailed from 1942 to 1945, for participating in the Quit India Movement. It was during deliberations over the Quit India Movement that Azad first ran afoul of Gandhi who called for his resignation for not supporting the Non-cooperation proposal. From then on his high profile presence in the Congress was only a façade. On 13 July 1942, Gandhi wrote to Nehru with regard to Azad: 'I do not understand him, nor does he understand me. We are drifting apart on the Hindu–Muslim question as well as on other questions. Therefore I suggest that the Maulana should relinquish Presidentship.'[2] Gandhi's assessment was correct, as he was taking Congress solicitude about Muslims at face value. During the visit of the Cabinet delegation, in 1946, Azad's solution to the communal problem coincided with that of the Muslim League: maximum autonomy to the provinces, with a centre having only defence, foreign affairs, and communications; substantially what M.A. Jinnah had proposed on 12 May 1946. Azad wrote a letter to the Cabinet ministers embodying these proposals but denied it to Gandhi while Gandhi held his letter in his hand.[3] Azad next wrote to say that the Congress would not nominate a Muslim to the interim government.[4] In this also, he exceeded his brief, and his undertaking was disowned by the Congress. He was extricated from this imbroglio by Nehru, yet he unfairly singled out Nehru for denunciation for wrecking the Cabinet Mission plan on 10 July

1946. In *India Wins Freedom*, Azad passes over his own, and Gandhi's role in opposing the Cabinet Mission Plan.

After independence, Azad remained minister of education till his death. Thirty pages of his memoirs—that Azad had withheld for thirty years—were published, in 1988—the year of his birth centenary. As a religious scholar, Azad was both erudite and enlightened. His *Tarjuman-al-Quran* (1932 and 1936) was a landmark in exegesis. He enjoys an enviable position as an Urdu litterateur: his belle letters—written in the grand style, are highly esteemed. These are evident in *Tazkira* (1919) and *Ghubar-i-Khatir* (1946).

Notes

1. G.I. Home Poll 180/1921, CID Report on Bihar *Ulama* Conference, 25, 26 June 1921 in David Page, *Prelude to Partition*.
2. Stanley Wolpert, *Gandhi's Passion* (New York: Oxford University Press, 2001), p. 203 vide Gandhi to Nehru dated 13 July 1942.
3. Sudhir Ghosh, *Gandhi's Emissary* (London: Cresset Press, 1967), p. 108.
4. Ibid., p. 167.

Chapter 22
The Partition Plan, 3 June 1947

The 3 June 1947 Plan was announced simultaneously in the House of Lords, the House of Commons, and at the Viceregal House in New Delhi. It is also known as the Mountbatten Plan because it was announced by Lord Mountbatten, the last viceroy. M.A. Jinnah on behalf of the AIML, Jawaharlal Nehru on behalf of the Congress, and Sardar Baldev Singh, on behalf of the Sikh community followed the viceroy in speaking to the nation over the radio.

Under the 3 June Plan, the British would transfer power to two successor authorities, the Congress and the Muslim League, meaning in territorial terms the dominions of India and Pakistan, which would remain within the British Commonwealth. The 565 princely states in India included Kashmir and Kurwai which comprised a territory of 144 square miles. British paramountcy over them would not be transferred to the two dominions and consequently would lapse constitutionally. Thus, the third option of remaining independent, and not joining either dominion was kept open for the princely states while it was denied to provinces, as in the case of Bengal.

The Indian Independence Act of 1947 received King George VI's assent on 18 June 1947. This Act expressly provided for the partition of Bengal and the Punjab. The Act also provided for the continuation of the Government of India Act 1935 until such time as the two dominions framed their own constitutions. Until then the governor-general could adapt the Government of India Act 1935 to suit the peculiar requirements of his dominion. The office of the secretary of state for India was abolished. Lord Listowel was the last secretary of state.

The Congress was the first to accept the 3 June Plan by demanding the partition of the Punjab and Bengal and in this indirect way, they made known their agreement to the partition of India. Conversely, it was the partition of the two provinces which prevented the Muslim League from accepting the Plan immediately. Jinnah could concede only a personal and provisional nod of acceptance. Lord Mountbatten told Jinnah it would be impossible to hold the Plan until such time as the AIML council assembled. (He thought the Congress would retract, as it had from the Cabinet Mission Plan). Mountbatten, in this way, threatened Jinnah with the permanent loss of Pakistan if he did not give an immediate and firm acceptance, but even this threat did not work. Lord Mountbatten then took it upon himself to speak for the AIML council and expressed his willingness to accept the blame if the AIML council did not ratify his Plan.

The partition of the provinces caused the 3 June Plan a rough passage in the AIML council. Prominent members said that the Plan should be rejected because the territory being offered was almost the same as what was offered by C. Rajagopalachari in 1944. Maulana Hasrat Mohani protested the loudest and said that a truncated Pakistan should not be accepted. Jinnah replied that he had not accepted the Plan and that it was the AIML council's privilege to accept or reject it. He added, however, that there could be no modification of the Plan, which had to be either completely accepted or completely rejected. Some members said the Muslims left behind in India would suffer, and some members who would be left behind said that at least a section of Muslims would be free; Abdul Hamid of Assam was one of these. The most memorable words were spoken by Sir Ghulam Hussain Hidayatullah, the chief minister of Sindh: 'We will rapidly industrialize our country and provide a haven of refuge to Muslim traders and craftsmen who would choose to migrate to Sindh from the Muslim minority provinces. We have removed the consideration of Sindhi and non-Sindhi from our province, and we will see that Sindh will soon progress far.'

Abul Hashim, the general secretary of the Bengal Muslim League, was disappointed that the 3 June Plan did not provide for the independence of Bengal. At a later date, the Congress wanted the provision of independence to be given to the NWFP, but Lord Mountbatten said that since the Congress had rejected that option in the case of Bengal, it could not be reintroduced in the case of the NWFP.

The AIML council session was held *in camera*. The AIML council accepted the 3 June Plan under protest and authorized its President M.A. Jinnah, to take 'further necessary action'. This was unacceptable to the Congress leaders, particularly Nehru and Sardar Patel, who wanted a clear-cut acceptance of the 3 June Plan before the Congress ratified it. Liaquat Ali Khan countered Sardar Patel by reminding him that after the AIML had accepted the Cabinet Mission Plan, Congress had defeated them by proposing so many reservations that AIML had to withdraw its acceptance. Lord Mountbatten accepted undertakings from both the Congress and the AIML simultaneously. The AIML also undertook to term their acceptances 'a compromise settlement'. The stage was now set for the creation of Pakistan.

MAULANA HASRAT MOHANI (b. Mohan, Unnao district, UP, India, 1878–d. Lucknow, 1951) was the maverick and gadfly of the South Asian freedom struggle. He was an extremist in politics, a romantic in poetry, and an ascetic in character. By all criteria, Hasrat was a remarkable man, and had he been made of sterner stuff, his image would have been as well-known as Gandhi's. In the 1907 Surat session of the Congress, Hasrat proposed the policy which proved to be the precursor of non-violent protest. Of the three courses available, Hasrat said that we should not accept the humiliation of being beggars, neither should we risk violence, but rather we should take the path of defensive resistance. Hasrat also championed Bolshevism, refusing to accept that it was in conflict with Islam. He convened a session of the All-India Communist Party, at Kanpur, in 1925. When the Khilafat Movement began, Hasrat joined it fervently. On 23 November 1919, he moved a resolution calling for a progressive boycott of European goods. His resolution was passed over the opposition of Gandhi and Haji Jan Muhammad Chotani, popularly known as Seth Chotani. On 1 June 1920, at the Allahabad Khilafat Conference, Hasrat horrified non-Muslim delegates when he vowed to join any Afghan army, in order to drive the British from India. On 23 October 1921, at the Agra Provincial (Khilafat) Conference, Hasrat not only called for people to resign from the army and the police but also for a declaration of complete freedom. On such occasions, Hasrat's stand was exasperating to the Congress, as indeed, it was to the Muslim League. Once, in 1942, when Hasrat was violently opposing the Cripps proposals, Fatima Jinnah was infuriated. Jinnah pacified his sister by saying that Hasrat was incorruptible.

This attribute of Hasrat's remained unquestionable. Jinnah's tribute had come in the aftermath of severe political differences. When the Simon Commission was formed and the Muslim League was split, Hasrat sided with the pro-British faction of Sir Muhammad Shafi, rather than the anti-British faction of Jinnah. Hasrat later explained his conduct, by saying that he had wished for all Muslims to be united in one organization; and the expectation that if the conservative element did not support complete independence, 'it will at least not dilute the demand by calling for dominion status'.

Hasrat's expectation that he would be able to prevail over the loyalist majority was unrealistic in view of his own conduct. Hasrat's editorial, on 25 February 1930, for the *Mustaqbil*, Kanpur, was quite uncalled for: 'As far as participation in the Round Table Conference and negotiating with the British is concerned…Jinnah, Shafi and [Sir Muhammad] Yaqub are capable. Hasrat will not be able to do this, and he will not interfere in this matter—on the condition, that in the matter of complete independence, they should also not interfere and should leave it to Hasrat, Muhammad Ali and Abul Kalam….'

With all his concern for complete independence, there came a stage when Hasrat was willing to settle for even less than dominion status.[1] He was a man of principle; he suffered rigorous imprisonment from 1910–1912, for not revealing that the anti-British articles included in his edited *Urdu-i-Mualla* were written by Syed Sulaiman Nadvi and Iqbal Ahmad Suhail. More terms in prison would follow. But Hasrat was like a Greek hero imbued with the defect of inconsistency. After taking the lead in promoting non-violent agitation, he proposed the use of violence in the joint Congress/Muslim League/Khilafat meeting, in December 1921. In mid-March 1922, Hasrat favoured dropping non-cooperation altogether. Inconsistency can be detected in all the great leaders of the freedom struggle, but the tragedy is that Hasrat's inconsistency was not anchored to any great political vision. Hasrat never lost his courage. In the Indian Parliament, he strongly criticized the invasion of Hyderabad.

The strong support Hasrat received from his wives, caused his lyrics to be as sweet as his political invectives were bitter. He performed the last of many Hajjes, in 1950, and in the following year faced death with complete composure.

Note

1. Ahmad Salim (ed.), *Hasrat Ki Siyasat* (The Politics of Hasrat) (Karachi: Pakistan Study Centre, University of Karachi, 2000), p. 452.

Chapter 23
The Radcliffe Award

Only one step remained before the British withdrew from the subcontinent. This was the demarcation of boundaries between India and Pakistan, running through the Punjab and Bengal, as well as the district of Sylhet in Assam. The terms of reference were drafted by Congress and sent to the viceroy on 12 June 1947. They were: 'The Boundary Commission is instructed to demarcate the boundaries of the two parts of the Punjab on the basis of ascertaining the contiguous majority areas of Muslims and non-Muslims. In doing so, it will also take into account other factors.' The same terms were repeated for Bengal with the word 'Bengal' being substituted for 'Punjab'.

The nominees to the commission were two Congress and two Muslim League members of high judicial standing, under a chairman. The members for Punjab were Justice Mehr Chand Mahajan, Justice Teja Singh (Congress) and Justice Din Mohammad, and Justice Mohammad Munir (Muslim League). The members for Bengal were Justice Bijan Kumar Mukherji, Justice C.C. Biswas (Congress), Justice Saleh Muhammad Akram, and Justice S.A. Rahman (Muslim League). Sir Cyril Radcliffe was the chairman of both commissions.

Sir Cyril Radcliffe's name was first proposed by Lord Listowel, the secretary of state for India. It was then conveyed to the Congress and Muslim League by Lord Ismay, the chief of the viceroy's staff. When Lord Mountbatten first mentioned Radcliffe's name to Jinnah, he made a non-committal comment that he would need time to consider Radcliffe's nomination. Lord Ismay in his memoirs asserts that Radcliffe's conduct was unassailable because he did not accept any payment for his work. This is contradicted in the Transfer of Power Papers which show that high fees were negotiated between Lord Listowel and Lord Jowitt. Radcliffe's awards became controversial when, in Punjab, Muslim-majority areas Gurdaspur, Ferozepur, and Zira were given to India. A series of documents has long been available to show that Radcliffe, almost at the last moment, departed from his judiciously considered award, under pressure from 'authorities in Delhi'.

With respect to Gurdaspur, which provided India an all-weather access to Kashmir, suggestions had been pouring in, before Lord Mountbatten's appointment as viceroy, more than a year before Partition. Vappala Pangunni (V.P.) Menon (1899–1966) wrote to Lord Wavell on 17 July 1946 to stress the strategic importance of Gurdaspur to India. Menon next wrote to George Abell (private secretary to the viceroy) asking for Gurdaspur to be excluded from Pakistan.[1] Sir Penderel Moon revealed in 1973 that the Cabinet Mission proposed giving to Jinnah the Muslim majority areas of the Punjab excluding Gurdaspur.

On 4 June 1947, Lord Mountbatten told a press conference that the accession of Gurdaspur to Pakistan was unlikely. Not satisfied with this, Vengalil Krishnan (V.K.) Krishna Menon (1897–1974) Nehru's confidant, wrote to Lord Mountbatten that Anglo–Indian relations would suffer if Pakistan was strengthened with the accession of Kashmir.[2] V.K. Krishna Menon had asked Mountbatten to destroy his letter, but Mountbatten chose to preserve it. On 17 June Nehru wrote to Mountbatten directly asking for Kashmir to be given to India. 'It is absurd to think that Pakistan would create trouble if this happens', reasoned Nehru. These letters which are still preserved, clearly prove that India's claim of obtaining an Instrument of Accession from the Maharaja of Kashmir was false. Alastair Lamb has shown such an Instrument does not exist.[3] The reason for the tribal incursion which India cited, was to save the Muslims of Poonch from annihilation.

On 25 February 1948, Philip Noel-Baker, secretary of state for commonwealth relations wrote to Prime Minister Clement Atlee that there was reason to believe that Radcliffe had altered his award after showing the first draft to 'authorities in Delhi'. Baker, in a hand-written paragraph, sought Atlee's permission to 'warn' Sir Zafrullah Khan, Pakistan's foreign minister, from pursuing an inquiry regarding the role of Lord Mountbatten.[4] In spite of these sentiments Baker was dismissed by Atlee on Nehru's complaint that he was unsympathetic to India. Many years later he told Richard Symonds that he would write the true story of the Kashmir dispute, even if it meant going to jail.[5]

FEROZEPUR AND ZIRA.—On 11 August, Chaudhry Mohammad Ali saw a map in Lord Ismay's study which showed Gurdaspur as part of India, but Ferozepur and Zira still as parts of Pakistan. Nehru and the Maharaja of Bikaner put pressure on Mountbatten to have this award withdrawn. With two strokes, the injustice to Pakistan was done and with this loss, Pakistan lost control of its rivers.

THE ROLE OF H.C. BEAUMONT.—Herbert Christopher Beaumont, private secretary to Radcliffe in 1947, issued a statement on 24 February 1992, that Radcliffe had altered the awards of Ferozepur and Zira at the last moment at the behest of Mountbatten. 'Grave discredit to both', said Beaumont. His own conduct during Partition caused Justice M. Munir to complain of Beaumont's pro-India bias. Beaumont had tried to mislead Radcliffe into believing that there was no bridge on the River Beas that would allow Sikhs access to Amritsar from East Punjab.

The 9 August 1947 diary entry of W.H.J. Christie, P. Noel-Baker's admission to Atlee in 1948, and H.C. Beaumont's confession of 1992 all confirm that the Radcliffe Awards were grossly unfair. Though termed unfair and even 'perverse' by Jinnah they were accepted because Pakistan was honour-bound to do so. There is no other document of the 20th century that has caused more wars, repression, and human misery than the Radcliffe Award.

Notes

1. On 23 January 1946 in S.M. Burke and S.A.D. Qureshi, *The British Raj in India* (Karachi: Oxford University Press, 1995). Appendix B, p. 3.
2. Alastair Lamb, *Kashmir: A Disputed Legacy* (Karachi: Oxford University Press, 1992), p. 108.
3. Burke and Qureshi, op. cit., p. 562.
4. Alastair Lamb, Incomplete Partition (Karachi: Oxford University Press, 2002), pp. 143, 157, 164, and 165 deal with this matter exhaustively.
5. Richard Symonds, *In the Margins of Independence* (Karachi: Oxford University Press, 2001), p. 96.

Chapter 24
The Role of the Majority Provinces

Neither the role nor the aspirations of the Muslim majority provinces and the Muslim minority provinces were identical. The differences were nuanced but they were apparent. The Muslims in the provinces in which they were in a majority, and the Muslims in the provinces in which they were in a minority were situated separately, and since the beginning of their political struggle, this became noticeable. The Simla Deputation was inclined to the demands of the minority provinces, while the foundation of the All-India Muslim League (AIML) was geared to the aspirations of the majority provinces. In the 1916 Lucknow Pact, while the demand for Separate Electorates was common the demand for weightages was not equally shared. While weightages to Muslims in minority provinces, no matter how generous, did not affect their status materially, the reciprocal weightage provision in the majority provinces had the effect of reducing the Muslims of Bengal and Punjab to minorities.

On the issue of cooperating with the Simon Commission, the AIML split up with the original president Sir Mohammad Shafi favouring cooperation, the factional president Mohammad Ali Jinnah was leading the boycott. When Jinnah formulated the Delhi Muslim Proposals, most Muslim provinces resisted the move to supersede Separate Electorates. When the trust placed by Jinnah in the Congress was belied in the shape of the Nehru Report, all Muslims came together under Fourteen Points.

Provincial imperatives were strong during the 1937 elections, and the AIML could show a presence in only two minority provinces, UP and Bombay. It was only in the 1937 Lucknow session of the AIML that leaders from the majority and minority provinces shared the same platform, having become uncomfortable at the prospect of Congress replacing the British at the centre. Even then, the Jinnah–Sikandar Pact proved to be a drag and weakened Jinnah's bargaining position during the Second World War

Two nation theories had been floated by leaders both Hindu and Muslim, from time to time, but the empirical quotient derived only from the Muslim majority areas, the partition of Bengal in 1905, and the separation of Sindh in 1937. These territorial demarcations proved more convincing than verbal theories and had the Punjab undergone a religious divide at the same time as the separation of Sindh, the borders would have been more equitably drawn and would have been less contention than in 1947 when the dividing line provoked a holocaust.

Since one of the major problems besetting Pakistan at its establishment, was the continuous influx of refugees having suffered pogroms in minority areas, the contribution of the Muslim-majority provinces did not immediately impress itself on the historian. However, within the last two decades, a number of works have appeared, and the reader is enabled to view the contribution of the majority provinces more clearly.

Sindh has been called the gateway to Islam in South Asia and has also proved to be the gateway to Pakistan. Sindh offered the greatest military resistance to the British and had always displayed battle-ready defiance. In this preparedness, the Hurs, the followers of the Pirs of Pagaro, formed the core. In 1826, the then Pir Pagaro Sibghatullah Shah Rashidi ordered the Hurs to aid the Mujahideen of Syed Ahmad Barelvi against the Sikhs. The Hurs as a permanently armed cadre was a constant thorn in the side of the British, and from the beginning of the Khilafat Movement to the Second World War the Hurs kept up a progressively increasingly armed resistance. Finally, the movement of the Hurs had to be put down concertedly, the only military distraction the British suffered during the Second World War when South Asian troops were fighting for the British in far-off lands. In 1943 a nonchalant Pir Pagaro was executed by the British. This created great resentment as Muslims compared this execution with the mild treatment of Gandhi, who had been in open rebellion since 1920.

The next momentous development, already covered, was the setting up of the Sindh Madressatul Islam in Karachi by Hasan Ali Effendi on 14 November 1887. The alumni of the Sindh Madressa constituted the cadre of political leaders—led by Jinnah which achieved partition. The first issue before these leaders was to secure the separation of Sindh from the Bombay presidency. Ironically this demand was first put forward from the platform of the Congress in 1913, as Hindu Sindhis at that time resented the dominance of their co-religionists in Bombay and Ahmadabad. It was only later, when the political atmosphere was charged with communalism, that this demand was taken over by the Muslim League, most pointedly in the Delhi Muslim Proposals and the Fourteen Points during the Round Table Conference. This objective was pursued with great persistence by Sir Shahnawaz Bhutto. In the Government of India Act 1935 this demand was conceded. The separation was affected on 1 April 1936.

The Muslim League did not have a strong presence in the aftermath of the Sindh separation in 1937. Sindh Muslims like their counterparts in Bengal and Bihar had a number of small parties. On the eve of the 1937 elections, Jinnah was able to persuade only four politicians, all from urban Sindh to contest on the Muslim League tickets. In the 1 February 1937 elections there were upsets, and both stalwarts, Sir Shahnawaz Bhutto and Sir Abdullah Haroon lost. Consequently, two ministries were formed, under Sir Ghulam Hussain Hidayatullah (March 1937–March 1938) and Allah Bux (March

1938–March 1940) which were dependent on Congress members for their majority.

It was during this period of exclusion that the Sindh Muslim League held a conference in Karachi (8–12 October 1938). Delegates from all over India attended including Jinnah, Liaquat, and Raja of Mahmudabad. Resolution No. 5 proved to be the operative one, calling upon the All-India Muslim League to devise a scheme of constitution under which Muslims may attain full independence. The Director of the Intelligence Bureau characterized their resolution, on 16 November 1938 as going 'Further than the Pakistan scheme'. It was again during this session that Jinnah stated that he was proud to be a Sindhi, and also that he had been born in Sindh.[1]

In 1939 the communal polarization was accentuated by the Manzilgah Mosque controversy, an old monument at Sukkur, claimed by both Hindus and Muslims. This claim led to Muslim demonstrations against Allah Bux and ultimately caused the fall of his ministry. It was their perception of the Congress's attitude as communal that led leaders like G.M. Syed to resign from Congress and join the Muslim League. As an adherent or adversary, G.M. Syed cast a long shadow over Muslim politics in Sindh. Concerned now over these developments, the Congress sent Abul Kalam Azad to negotiate a pact with Sindhi leaders which called for cooperation, especially in the Sindh assembly.

The Azad pact was signed in November 1940 by G.M. Syed and M. Ayub Khuhro but denounced by Hidayatullah. It was only on 22 October 1942, that Sir Ghulam Hussain Hidayatullah was able to form a full-fledged Muslim League ministry in Sindh. This ministry lasted till independence, Hidayatullah's fortitude earning him the ire of Jawaharlal Nehru. Most crucially, the Muslim League ministry remained intact while negotiations with the Cabinet Mission were in progress.

On 3 March 1943, G.M. Syed moved a resolution in the Sindh Assembly, endorsing the 23 March 1940 Lahore Resolution. Unfortunately, during a clash between the Sindh Muslim League Party and Ministry, Hidayatullah and Syed fell out. In the ensuing 1946 elections, the Muslim League won 27 out of 35 seats in the Sindh Assembly. When re-election was ordered the Muslim League seats increased to 34. On 24 June 1947, the vote for partition was won by 33 votes in favour and 20 votes against. The Speaker of the Sindh Assembly aptly remarked: 'Sindh has arrived at the portals of Pakistan first. Congratulations'.

The Punjab was the most indispensable province for Pakistan the most elusive, yet in the end suffering the most. Punjab held a member of advantages, it had a canal system which made it the granary of India, a feudal structure subordinate to educational progress, and the area which provided most of the soldiers. All these factors gave Punjab a predominant position. While rejecting the Cabinet Mission Plan, Pandit Nehru speculated that Sindh would not like to be dominated by the Punjab. True to Nehru's fears the eastern half of the

Punjab which fell to India was divided into three provinces Punjab, Haryana, and Himachal Pradesh.

For a long time, cultural cohesion translated into communal harmony. We need to understand the process whereby the Unionist Party founded in 1923 by Sir Fazl-i-Hussain and Sir Chhotu Ram dominated Punjab politics till the very eve of partition, and finally made a place for the Muslim League after a display of street power. In the elections of 1937, only two members of the Punjab Assembly had been elected on the Muslim League ticket, Malik Barkat Ali and Raja Ghazanfar Ali Khan, but the latter almost immediately defected to the Unionist Party. In the elections of 1946, the situation changed dramatically, with the Muslim League winning 75 out of 86 seats we need to understand the process whereby this transformation was effected.

Ian Talbot the pre-eminent authority on pre-partition Punjab first offered the solution that the Second World War transformed Jinnah's status and enabled him to dispense with Unionist backing.[2] This is hardly tenable since the same war which enhanced Jinnah's status enhanced the status of Sir Sikandar Hayat, Chief Minister of the Punjab. Jinnah's position over the war efforts was far more constricted than Sikandar's. When the Punjab body sent in a requisition for a special meeting of the AIML Council to move a resolution supporting the war efforts, both Jinnah and Liaquat balked. The Raja of Mahmudabad was enlisted to counter this move, and in 1941 the AIML expelled those of its members who joined the Viceroy's Defence Council over its head.

The Unionist Party under both Fazl-i-Hussain and Sir Sikandar Hayat had an uneasy relationship with the Muslim League. The Unionist Party supported not only communal harmony but also the British. After an acrimonious relationship with Jinnah stretching over decades, Fazl-i-Hussain wrote to him on 15 May 1934: 'Muslim India cannot afford to lose you. Men of clear vision, independent judgment and strength of character are very few.'[3]

Yet, two years later Fazl-i-Hussain sent the same Jinnah empty-handed, warning him to keep his fingers out of the Punjab pie. Sir Sikandar Hayat under a pact with Jinnah allowed the Unionist Muslim members of the Punjab legislatures, to form a Muslim League, so for all intents and purposes, the Unionist Party doubled as the Muslim League in the Punjab, despite the efforts of Iqbal, Malik Barkat Ali, and Ashique Hussain Batalvi, to form a provincial body independent of the Unionists. Why the Muslim League, though being subordinate, remained so close to the surface, is explained by Ian Talbot that the Unionist Party never achieved a mass base of political support. It owed its success in 1937 to strategic local factional alliances.[4]

There can be no other explanation for why the Muslims of Punjab demonstrated so violently against Sikandar Hayat during the 1940 Lahore Session of the AIML. The very fact that the AIML held its most momentous session in the Punjab capital, refusing to be distracted by police violence on the Khaksars, is a strong indication of strong local support. The following eyewitness account of Ashique Hussain Batalvi was endorsed by the Punjab governor in his secret report.

The people were listening quietly and calmly to Nawab Shahnawaz Khan Mamdot, who was presenting the address of welcome, but when he mentioned the efforts of Sir Sikandar Hayat in restoring the Badshahi Mosque, '... there was consternation from one end of the ground to the other. From all corners the cries came: We won't listen, "don't take the name of Sir Sikandar" "sit down" and "shame shame". Sir Sikandar... saw the demonstration of the people's unhappiness and anger with his own eyes he went out from the back-door of the podium.'[5]

The stage had been set for the Muslim League victory in the 1946 elections; it won 75 out of the 86 Muslim seats. Still, Sir Khizr Hayat Tiwana, who had succeeded Sikandar Hayat in 1942, who had only 18 seats out of 175 was called upon by the governor, Sir Bertrand Glancy to form the government. Muslim League volunteers, half of whom were ladies, led demonstrations, braved police brutalities and jail but succeeded in forcing the resignation of Sir Khizr Hayat on 2 March 1942.

Two days later the Sikhs demonstrated against the decision under the leadership of Master Tara Singh. Riots started in Amritsar spread to Rawalpindi and then the whole province was up in flames. The presence of the Sikhs in the Punjab was an element not found in other provinces. The treatment of the Sikhs by the Mughals had been brutal, and it was natural that in the cauldron of 1947, the Sikhs veered towards the Hindus, brushing aside their affinities to the Muslims as a minority. The Muslim League had achieved power too late and after a very bitter struggle for the party to attempt reconciliation with the Sikhs.

This was the reason why, when the Muslim League leadership attempted an approach to the Sikh leadership, it proved futile. M.A. Jinnah handed over a blank paper to the Maharaja and Diwan of Patiala to inscribe their conditions for accession to Pakistan. At the 17 August 1947 meeting, Liaquat Ali Khan asserted his right to speak for the Sikhs of Pakistan, just as Pandit Nehru was speaking on behalf of the Sikhs of India. The Muslim League wanted neither a homogeneous population nor communal dislocation. The amorphous nature of the land and people admitted only approximation, but the communal flareup of 1947 denied the Sikhs a balancing role. Even if Khalistan had emerged, it could have acted as a buffer state between India and Pakistan, and the upshot was that the people of Punjab had to go through fire and blood to achieve Pakistan.

NWFP is a nameless province inspiring nameless fear. Sir Olaf Caroe, a former governor of NWFP, in his defining work *The Pathans*, has devoted a whole chapter to Waziristan, by which he sought to characterize the whole region. 'No empire of which we have any record has ever succeeded in making subjects of the tribes of Waziristan.'[6]

Perhaps this was one of the reasons why the British delayed reforms in the NWFP. It was only through the logic and persistence of Lord Curzon that NWFP was separated from the Punjab on 9 November 1901 and made a Chief Commissioner's Province, i.e., a province with no governor and no assemblies. The first demand that came forward was from the Arya Samaj. It was to re-amalgamate the NWFP to the Punjab. When Lala Lajpat Rai came to inaugurate the Peshawar Arya Samaj School, he promised to support re-amalgamation.[7]

Thus, despite the overwhelming majority of Muslims, the NWFP was not entirely free of communal troubles, and Muslims could have seen that their majority status needed vigilance to be maintained. On 23 April 1930, Hindu–Muslim riots took place in Peshawar, but certainly communalism was not an issue as it was in the Hindu majority areas. The NWFP continued to progress, we have already mentioned the establishment of the Islamia College, Peshawar, through the efforts of three dedicated notables George Roos-Keppel (Chief Commissioner), Sahibzada Sir Abdul Qayyum, and Nawab Akbar Hoti, but it was only in 1932 that the NWFP was raised from a Chief Commissioner's to Governor's province, and under the Government of India 1935 another instalment was received. Sir Abdul Qayyum became Minister of Transferred Subjects (see under Montagu–Chelmsford Reforms).

The Congress established itself firmly in the NWFP, strangely through religious means. Since the Khilafat and Non-Cooperation Movements were being run together by Gandhi, the Congress inducted the Khudai Khidmatgars led by Khan Abdul Ghaffar Khan. They believed in non-violence, but the British did not. The British fired at unarmed Khudai Khidmatgars at Qissa Khawani Bazaar, Peshawar on 23 April 1930. This was the Frontier version of the Jallianwala Bagh tragedy, but unlike in the Punjab a massacre did not have a sobering effect; it was followed by firing on unarmed protestors in a number of smaller Frontier towns. The Khudai Khidmatgars had established a firm moral basis and it would have taken a party with utmost probity and efforts to dislodge it. Unfortunately, the Muslim League government which had a brief tenure from 1943 to 1945 could not effect this.

The AIML established its presence in 1912, under Mian Abdul Aziz (barrister) but as the First World War erupted in 1914, the British promptly suppressed the AIML, and it disappeared. In October 1936, M.A. Jinnah travelled to the NWFP but was not able to persuade any politician to contest elections on the Muslim League ticket. It was only in September 1937 that Sir Abdul Qayyum facilitated the foundation of the Frontier Muslim League, and during the following month, the Peshawar City Muslim League was established putting the party in a position of vantage.

The next step was placed forward but proved unfortunate; when Sir Abdul Qayyum died (6 December 1937) Sardar Aurangzeb Khan (1892–1953) was chosen as his political heir. He had served as Sir Abdul Qayyum's secretary during the Round Table Conferences. He presided over the first session of the All-India States Muslim League on 23 March 1940 at Lahore.⁸ Because of his prominence; he had to be persuaded to join the Muslim League. In 1939 he became the leader of the opposition in the NWFP Assembly. Even when Congress resigned in late 1939, the Muslim League under Sardar Aurangzeb Khan was unable to form a ministry, and governor's rule had to be resorted to. When ten Congress legislators were jailed on 25 May 1943, Aurangzeb was invited to form a ministry. Aurangzeb was able to win four more seats for the Muslim League in by-elections, but his position remained so fragile that he resorted to large-scale corruption.

It is true that the Muslim League was faction-ridden. Khan Bahadur Sadullah Khan was an inveterate rival of Aurangzeb, but his complaints of corruption and nepotism to Jinnah were genuine. Large-scale corruption meant large-scale discontent, even within the ranks of the Muslim League. When Congress legislators were released from jail, it was natural that Aurangzeb faced a no-confidence movement. Three members of the Muslim League, led by Sadullah Khan, voted against Aurangzeb. On 14 March 1945, Aurangzeb resigned.

The outgoing chief minister refuelled the charges against himself by offering the defence that 'Corruption started with Adam and will end on doomsday.'⁹ Far from being a means of consolidating the Muslim League, the Aurangzeb ministry had the opposite effect. In the elections of 1946, the Muslim League won only 17 of the Muslim seats to the Congress figure of 30. These results were contrary to the country-wide trend, but these results, conditioned by the corruption of the Muslim League did not prove to be stable. The visits by Pandit Nehru to the NWFP signalled a reverse in attitudes. As Maulana Abul Kalam Azad was later to recall: 'The actual position in 1946 was that the Khan brothers did not enjoy as much support in the Frontier as we in Delhi thought. When Jawaharlal reached Peshawar, this discovery came to him as an unpleasant shock.'¹⁰

Jawaharlal Nehru faced a hostile black flag-waving demonstration at the Peshawar airport. The Khan brothers themselves needed police protection, they were in no position to protect Nehru. On his way back from Landi Kotal, he had stones thrown at his car. The sentiments of the public had been made clear. On 28/29 April 1947 Lord Mountbatten, the new Viceroy arrived in the Frontier, and what he saw and heard convinced him that the results of 1946 no longer held.

A medical team from the NWFP had visited Bihar, and when they saw the riot-stricken Muslims, the religious divide was brought home to them in a manner that the Muslim majority of their province had prevented than from seeing. Two months after Nehru's departure (December 1946), tribesmen attacked Hindus and Sikhs, uprooting them from Hazara. In the Referendum of 20 June 1947, Pakistan received 50.49 of the votes effectively doubling the

AIML's performance since the 1946 election. An explanation of this reversal is provided by Ian Talbot: 'The Muslim League's claims that the choice was either *Akhand* Hindustan or Pakistan, overnight look on a reality that had been missing during the earlier provincial elections.'[11]

To gauge the intensity of the feeling, we need to recount the efforts of the brave Pakhtun ladies who led the demonstrations against the Congress ministry. A delegation of the Zanana Muslim League led by Lady Nusrat Haroon arrived in Peshawar on 17 October 1945. Besides addressing public meetings in purdah, they visited other cities of the province, especially Mardan, at the invitation of Begum Zari Sarfaraz. By early 1947 Zanana League offices had been opened in all urban centres.

On 14 April 1947, members of the Zanana Muslim League lay down on the railway tracks, the 58 Down Bombay Express did not stop, knocked down three women, and injured thirty more. The AIML high command prevented them from risking their lives any further.[12] On 3 June 1947, Jinnah paid them tribute: 'I cannot but express my appreciation of the sufferings and sacrifices made by all the classes of Musalmans and particularly the great part the women of the Frontier played in the fight for our civil liberties.'[13]

Balochistan served as a reminder of the brief occupation of its territory by the Persian Empire. Balochistan was partitioned between the British and Persian empires in 1875. At the first opportunity that presented itself, Baloch people rebelled against the British, in 1914, siding with the Germans. This movement was crushed militarily by the British but initially, the concern of Baloch leaders remained irredentist. Baloch sardars organized the Anjuman-i-Ittehad-i-Balochistan, and by the beginning of the Second World War, they held public meetings to demand the separation of Balochistan from British India. This move naturally alarmed the Muslims of India, and they pleaded against such a move.

One year earlier, a young man Qazi Muhammad Isa, met Jinnah in Bombay and asked him to establish the Muslim League in Balochistan. Qazi Isa first inducted Allama Abdul Ali Akhunzada Khanozai, and thereafter the two of them toured the length and breadth of the vast province, establishing local branches. The Balochistan Muslim League held its first conference at Quetta on 10 and 11 June 1939. It was in this conference session that Qazi Isa was elected President. After holding forth on the poverty in his province, and the lack of educational opportunities, Qazi Isa declared: 'We are Muslims first, Baloch next, and Indians third.'[14]

The Balochistan League was affiliated to the AIML in September 1939. Speaking on that occasion Jinnah said: 'About six months ago, I had commissioned Qazi Isa to do the work. He has performed a great miracle in such a short time.'[15]

Thereafter the activities of Qazi Isa increased. He held a meeting at Quetta on 19 April 1940 to observe Muslim Independence Day. Four years later he published a booklet called *Balochistan: Case and Demand*. Qazi Isa had succeeded in setting the direction of Baloch Muslims to the East instead of the West. Since he had proved to be an effective orator, Jinnah sent him to NWFP at the time of the by-elections. Thereafter he was sent to Aligarh, where, contrary to his expectations, he discovered great affinity, and soon he became familiar with the students at Aligarh.

From 26 to 28 July 1940, the Annual Session of the Balochistan was held. Liaquat Ali Khan who presided said in his address: 'The British government has treated the province most unjustly, so much so that its parallel cannot be given anywhere else in India.'

Writing privately to Jinnah, Liaquat Ali Khan gave him a detailed report of the Conference, ruing the fact that Jinnah himself was not there: 'The Conference was a great success. There were large gatherings every night, and people stayed on till 2 o'clock in the morning at every meeting. It was encouraging to see what wonderful progress a backward province has made in such a short time. Of course, the credit is due to the untiring zeal and enthusiasm of Isa.'[16]

On 1 July 1943, the Balochistan Muslim League held a meeting to honour Jinnah who spent two months in Balochistan. From 10 to 14 July, he was the guest of the Khan of Kalat. Jinnah paid another visit in September 1945 and addressed a number of meetings. In 1945 Nawab Mohammad Khan Jogezai of the AIML defeated Abdus Samad Achakzai of the Congress by 61 votes to 13.

In the Shahi Jirga that followed 54 members voted en bloc for Pakistan. The Jirga had been scheduled for 30 June 1947, but since an overwhelming number of members were present, the Shahi Jirga gave its verdict one day earlier. On 4 August 1947 Ahmad Yar Khan, the Khan of Kalat in the presence of Lord Mountbatten, M.A. Jinnah, Liaquat Ali Khan, Pandit Nehru, Sardar Patel, and Sir Sultan Ahmad, Legal Remembrances of the Chamber of Princes, signed a standstill agreement with Pakistan. This agreement accepted Kalat as an independent state, with the privilege to decide whether British Balochistan would be part of Kalat or Pakistan. The allocation of subjects like Defence, Foreign Affairs, Communications, and Currency was to be decided by mutual consultations.

Negotiations with Kalat were prolonged. On 17 March 1948, other Balochistan states, Lasbela, Kharan, and Makran acceded to Pakistan. Being isolated, Kalat acceded to Pakistan on 28 March 1948, and its independent status ended. Only one aspect of Balochistan's services to Pakistan remains to be recalled. In his last tour, Children's Muslim Leagues were formed at Sibi and Loralai. Jinnah had saluted them. Had he been alive Jinnah would salute the children today. It is they who celebrate Independence Day with great enthusiasm and patriotism.

Notes

1. D.A. Pirzada, in M.A. Shaikh (ed.), *The Role of Sindh in the Creation of Pakistan* (Karachi: Sindh Madressatul Islam, 1998), p. 171. I am grateful to D.A. Pirzada for answering my queries.
2. Ian Talbot, *Provincial Politics and the Pakistan Movement* (Karachi: Oxford University Press, 1988), p. 91.
3. Ian Bryant Wells, *Ambassador of Hindu Muslim Unity* (New Delhi: Permanent Black, 2005), p. 235.
4. Ian Talbot, *Freedom's Cry: The Popular Dimension in the Pakistan Movement and Partition Experience in North-west India* (Karachi: Oxford University Press, 1996), p. 84.
5. Ashique Husain Balalvi, *Our National Struggle January 1940 to December 1940* (Lahore: Altaf Husain, 1975), pp. 17, 18.
6. Olaf Caroe, *The Pathans* (London: Macmillan, 1965), pp. 390–91.
7. Himayatullah, 'Jinnah Muslim League and the Introduction of Reforms in the NWFP', in Riaz Ahmed (ed.), Papers Presented at the Three-Day International Conference on All India Muslim League (Islamabad: NIHCR, 2006), vol. 1, p. 275.
8. Ahmad Saeed, *Muslim India, 1857–1947: A Biographical Dictionary* (Lahore: Institute of Pakistan Historical Research, 1997), p. 91.
9. Altaf Ullah, 'Sardar Mohammad Aurangzeb Khan', in Riaz Ahmad, op. cit., p. 18.
10. Abul Kalam Azad, *India Wins Freedom* (Calcutta: Orient Longmans, 1959), p. 171.
11. Ian Talbot, *Provincial Politics*, op. cit., p. 21.
12. Lal Baha Ali, in Riaz Ahmed, op. cit., p. 143.
13. Ibid., p. 145.
14. Inam ul Haq Kausar, Famous Personality of BML, Qazi Isa in Riaz Ahmed, op. cit., p. 12.
15. Ibid., p. 13.
16. Muhammad Reza Kazimi (ed.), *Jinnah–Liaquat Correspondence* (Karachi: Pakistan Study Centre, University of Karachi, 2003), p. 99.

Part 5
Political History of the State

Introduction
Ideology of Pakistan

In this section, we shall first discuss the political developments resulting from the creation of Pakistan. Thereafter we shall discuss the Ideology.

On 14 August 1947, the Dominion of Pakistan came into existence. A movement led to the establishment of a state. In a state, the rights and duties of citizens have to be defined, as has their loyalty to the state. In the context of Pakistan, it is important, at the outset, to learn what a state is, and what is the nature of its relations with the government and society.

The State. Political scientists hold that the state is a politically organized community, and the government is its agency. The government is only one part or constituent of a state. The state is permanent, the government is temporary. In democratic states, people are asked to vote every five years or so. The people, by voting, either retain the government or change it. This change of government does not affect basic principles such as national security or territorial integrity.

The Government. The state is abstract, but the government is concrete. A government has the following components: Executive, Legislature, and Judiciary.

The Executive. The executive is headed by a President or Prime Minister. It consists of the cabinet ministers, the bureaucracy, and other officials. They implement the policies of the government. These policies either originate from the legislature or they originate from the government and are sanctioned by the legislature.

The Legislature. It is a body of members elected by the people to represent them primarily in their function of framing laws, but also to project their aspirations and protect their rights generally. Theoretically, the legislature can change the executive. Legislatures exist at the district, provincial, and national levels. The national parliament is bicameral consisting of the National Assembly and the Senate.

The Judiciary. Described collectively, the judiciary means the judges of a state. The judiciary exists at the district, provincial and national levels. The judiciary decides disputes between citizens or between citizens and the government on criminal, civil, or constitutional matters. There is also a Shariat Court which decides cases according to Islamic law.

Society is wider than the state. The state is territorial whilst society is not. The state is organized while society is not necessarily organized. The state has coercive forces while society has moral forces.

The above represents the basic concepts in the abstract. Whether they have remained the same in practice is explained in the following sections.

IDEOLOGY OF PAKISTAN.—The term *idéologie* (English: ideology) was coined by Antoine Destutt de Tracy in 1796 as a name for his own 'science of ideas'. Without making any direct reference to De Tracy, Justice Mohammad Munir explained that ideology is the science that deals with beliefs, notions, and theories. These in turn have their origin in the fundamental assumptions held by a people. These ideas may be naturally acquired; sometimes they may be consciously spread.

The ideology of the French Revolution (1787–1799) could be summed up as equality, fraternity, and liberty. It overthrew the theory of the divine rights of kings. It also modified the still unfolding law of social contract. According to Charles E. Bressler, ideology refers to the collective or social consciousness of culture.[1] This is opposed to the material reality on which an experience is based. This means that though the ideology of Pakistan has been derived from the Two-Nation theory, it is not identical to it. In other words, the ideology of Pakistan is enshrined, not in the Lahore Resolution, but in the Objectives Resolution.

This needs an explanation. An ideology is expressed in absolute, not relative terms. The Two-Nation theory is relative because it depends on the existence of the 'other'—in our case, the Hindu majority of undivided India. If the Hindus did not exist—or if they existed as a minority—there would have been no need to propound the Two-Nation theory according to which Hindus and Muslims form different nations.

Islamic ideology means to order our individual and collective behaviour in accordance with the Islamic concepts of justice, morality, human rights, and tolerance. Human rights in Islam are an important component of its ideology. The rights of God and the rights of worshippers are clearly demarcated. There are sins against God, such as neglecting prayers, fasting, and pilgrimage. There are sins against human beings, such as killing them, stealing from them, and even backbiting—against which the Holy Quran has passed the severest of strictures. Islamic ideology is a matter of personal conscience, but social behaviour.

IDEOLOGICAL HISTORY.—The nature of Islamic ideology was hotly debated during the process of framing constitutions. The place of Islam in state polity was viewed differently by the Pakistan Muslim League, Pakistan National Congress, and the Jamaat-i-Islami. It is undeniable that while religious majorities prefer an ideological state, religious minorities prefer a secular state. This was witnessed between 1937–1939, when Muslims objected to the Congress practices like the Wardha scheme of education, singing of the anti-Muslim song, *Vande Mataram*, and the practice of saluting the portrait of Gandhi. It is also undeniable that minorities sought mainly to safeguard human rights.

If the majority guarantees freedom of conscience and belief, then, the ideology so practised can be acceptable to minorities.

With regard Jinnah, under Ideology we thought it proper to confine ourselves to his public speeches, however, in the testimony of the Raja of Mahmudabad[2] and Isha'at Habibullah, he had objected to Pakistan becoming an Islamic state,[3] on the ground that there were over seventy sects, and 'the consequences would be a struggle of religious opinion from the very inception of the state leading to its very dissolution'. What Jinnah wanted was a 'Liberal Democratic State.'

It should be noted that Jinnah's objection to an Islamic state was not ideological, but empirical. There is one strand of ideology, on which—not only Jinnah and Mahmudabad—but the entire leadership of the Muslim League agreed, and that is Islamic socialism.

ISLAMIC SOCIALISM.—This concept has a long Middle Eastern pedigree, with its origins in the so-called fundamentalist circles with Syed Qutb, and Mustafa al-Sibai at its head. Syed Qutb said, in 1948, that Islamic socialism avoided the pitfalls of Christianity's separation of religion and society and those of communism's atheism.[4] Maulana Hasrat Mohani espoused Islamic Communism—Jinnah mentioned it as an ideal in Chittagong on 26 March 1948.[5] Liaquat Ali Khan projected it as a state ideology. He said, at Lahore, on 3 September 1949: 'For us, there is only one "ism"—Islamic Socialism.'[6] Fatima Jinnah, while disagreeing with Liaquat Ali Khan on a number of issues, agreed with him on the issue of Islamic socialism, stating in a February 1951 speech, that 'Islamic Socialism did not allow any class struggle.'[7] The Raja of Mahmudabad argued cogently in favour of Islamic socialism at the Katrak Hall, Karachi, in 1967.[8]

With this consensus among the Muslim League stalwarts, it is not possible to exclude Islamic socialism from the ideological history of Pakistan. However, two questions arise: First, how is it possible for leaders to differ on the need for an Islamic state, but to agree on Islamic socialism? Second, when there was a consensus among the founding generations, why was it never implemented?

As to the first question, the latitude given by the Holy Quran in the political sphere is more than that given in the economic sphere. The Holy Quran (68:7–14) specifies the types of persons who should not be obeyed: 'Your Lord knows best who strays from His path and who is rightly guided. So do not yield to those who deny the truth--they want you to compromise with them and then they will compromise with you--do not yield to any contemptible swearer, to any backbiter, slander-monger, or hinderer of good, to anyone who is sinful, aggressive, coarse, and on top of all that, an imposter. Just because he has wealth and sons.'[9] This is a formidable list, but it does not proscribe any political system, presidential or parliamentary. Ideally, a republican caliphate encompassing the entire world would be preferred, but nation-states cannot be termed un-Islamic, because even welfare societies formed to regulate the affairs of localities, or apartment blocks cannot be proscribed, because they help in fulfilling social requirements obligatory under Islam. Regulating water supply, sanitation, and security are bare necessities and are not dependent on the larger ideological dispensation of the state. The Holy Quran 4:92 says that belivers can belong to distinct, even hostile nations (Qawm).

On the other hand, strictures against economic crimes are not only more severe but determine to a greater extent the nature of the state Muslims can adopt. These are usury, hoarding, gambling, and cheating in weights and measures. All the economic crimes listed here affect the ethical mores of society, but the proscription of usury, conjoined with the payment of *zakat*, or the tithe meant for charity, determines the nature of the state. This aspect became most conspicuous during the Cold War (1945–1990).

Islam grants the right of private ownership but simultaneously dislikes the concentration of wealth in some hands. This is to avoid the exploitation of the masses. Islam preceded both the capitalist nation-state as well as the communist state, so while Islamic socialism may be a new term, the concept of social justice is old. The West had also not allowed interest until John Calvin legalized it. As long as usury is practised, only a capitalist system can exist. This is the reason why, in answer to our second question, Islamic socialism remained a pious hope and was never implemented.

During the era following Liaquat Ali Khan, Islamic socialism was rarely mentioned, however when the movement against Ayub Khan began, Maulana Abdul Hamid Khan Bhashani (president, National Awami Party), and Zulfikar Ali Bhutto (chairman, PPP) raised the slogan of Islamic socialism. Bhashani did not contest the 1970 elections, but Bhutto did and eventually came to power. In reply to a question by Abul Hashim, Z.A. Bhutto explained in this author's presence that 'Islamic socialism means that part of socialism, which is not in conflict with Islam'. During the 1970 election campaign, about 122 ulama issued a decree that socialism was *haram* (religiously forbidden), and that Islamic socialism was a contradiction in terms. This decree was ignored by the electorate, but in the 1977 Pakistan National Alliance (PNA) Movement, it gained credence.

Partly due to the constraints of the 1971 defeat, partly because of a feudal background, and partly because of his temperament, Z.A. Bhutto was unable to implement his programmes. He nationalized industries, banks, and insurance companies, and even introduced land reforms, but veered sufficiently away from the left to alienate the socialist component of his party, but not sufficiently to mollify the religious parties forming the PNA, who, in 1977, launched a movement to enforce Nizam-i-Mustafa or an Islamic order.

Islamization.—General M. Ziaul Haq who staged a coup d'état, in the wake of the PNA movement, made Islamization the ideological basis of his regime. The aim, and even the destiny of the people of Pakistan is Islamization, but it should be made clear what Islamization means. It cannot be coercion because the Holy Quran forbids it. Moreover, it cannot be applied selectively. Islamic laws were imposed for all crimes except murder, because under Islamic law, Zia would have had to release the prime minister he had overthrown. Again, Islamic provisions in the laws of evidence and adultery created an anomaly not permissible in Islam. For example, in 1983, two victims of rape were convicted of adultery. As women, their evidence was not considered sufficient to convict the perpetrators, but their complaint was construed as a confession to unlawful sex. Women's rights and the rights of minorities suffered due to discrimination.

It is not that the ulama—even those who had agitated for an Islamic order—did not realize the implications of this type of Islamization. Firstly, when Nawaz Sharif learnt that the Shariah court, set up under Zia, had outlawed usury, including interest, he appealed against this decision. Again, when Nawaz Sharif moved the Fifteenth Amendment to make Shariah the supreme law of the land, even the religious parties did not support him. They feared that this would be a device to subordinate the constitution, which means he would gain unbridled power. It is manifest to all that Islamic laws can come into operation only when social anomalies are not created.

A side effect of the Islamization process was an increase in sectarian violence. If the extreme verdict of Abu Musab al-Zarqawi of Al-Qaeda is accepted, Shaikh Hassan Nasrallah of Hezbollah cannot be considered a Muslim. It was after the capture of Afghanistan by the Taliban that Islamization had come in for condemnation by the West. After the events of 9/11, this hostility has increased immeasurably. Islam does not allow militancy—either in the preaching of Islam or even in times of war. Islam enjoins Jihad but has strict rules governing Muslim conduct. The old, infirm, women, infants, and other non-combatants are not to be harmed. Even trees are not to be cut down, or fields devastated.

ENLIGHTENED MODERATION.—The regime of General Pervez Musharraf eschewed the militancy attached to the fair name of Islam and opted for what he called 'Enlightened Moderation'. This is all for the good. The challenge from without is weak. The challenge from within is strong. When custom is allowed to supersede Sharia, then Islamization is indeed remote. Islam is a religion of mercy, the Holy Quran begins in the name of Allah, Who is Compassionate and Merciful. We repeat these verses in our prayers. Yet a mother had her daughter, Saima Sarwar, killed in her presence because she had sought divorce—a right that is guaranteed to her in Islam. Honour killing should be punishable by death in accordance with the laws of Islam. We must reiterate that Islamic laws cannot be applied selectively. It is those village or tribe elders who sentence women to gang rape, who are impeding the imposition of Islamic laws. Those who kill and rape are rebels unto

God, and it is their audacity which explains why Islamic punishments are harsh.

There is no denying that Muslims all over the world are subject to oppression, but they are not subject to the type of oppression our Holy Prophet (PBUH) had to face—the oppression he forgave when he conquered Makkah. The Holy Quran (2:143) has honoured Muslims by designating them as *Ummatan Wasatan*: 'We have made you [believers] into a just community, so that you may bear witness [to the truth] before others and so that the Messenger may bear witness [to it] before you.'

Midmost, medium, middle—all these words can be used to translate *wasatan*. It means above all that the Muslim community should not be extremist, and must not be seen as extremist by the other people to whom it must bear witness. Militancy and extremism are un-Islamic. The laws of God cannot be subject to human passion. The repression of Muslims in Chechnya is horrible. This does not justify the gruesome murder of innocent schoolchildren in Beslan (2 September 2004). Unless such means are condemned, the ends shall be despised. Islam permits retaliation, but the retaliation must be strictly measured. The Holy Quran (81:8-9) warns of the time when the buried infant shall be asked for what sin she was slain. It is clear that the burying alive of the girl child was a pagan practice, not a Muslim practice. Here the Holy Quran is decrying the slaying of non-Muslim children. Yet the ulama did not condemn the Beslan massacre. Islamic norms cannot be trampled upon, even in the pursuit of what is seen as Islamic causes.

If ideology is the value commitment of a people, as Eqbal Ahmad (1933-1999) once said, then values take precedence over rituals. The Holy Quran (2:177) says: 'Goodness does not consist in turning your face towards East or West. The truly good are those who believe in God and the Last Day, in the angels, the Scripture, and the prophets; who give away some of their wealth, however much they cherish it, to their relatives, to orphans, the needy, travellers and beggars, and to liberate those in bondage; those who keep up the prayer and pay the prescribed alms; who keep pledges whenever they make them; who are steadfast in misfortune, adversity, and times of danger. These are the ones who are true, and it is they who are aware of God.'

Allama Iqbal, writing in the context of the above verse, comments: 'The form of prayer ought not to become a matter of dispute. Which side you turn is certainly not essential to the spirit of prayer.'[10]

Islam is a religion in which human rights are not infringed upon by Divine Right. If a person commits a crime against a fellow being, God, in His divine mercy shall not forgive the culprit over the head of the victim. Just above, we have mentioned the law of retaliation. We are encouraged to forgive, but the right of retaliation is not taken from us.

Notes

1. Charles Bressler, *Literary Criticism: An Introduction to Theory and Practice* (New Jersey: Prentice Hall, 1994), p. 172.
2. Raja of Mahmudabad, 'Some Memories', in *India's Partition*, ed. Mushirul Hassan (New Delhi: Oxford University Press, 1994), p. 425.
3. Isha'at Habibullah, 'Memories of British and Feudal India', *Dawn*, 27 September 1991, p. 3, graciously given to me by the author's daughter, Muneeza Shamsie, pp. 108–109.
4. John Esposito, *Unholy War: Terror in the Name of Islam* (Oxford University Press, 2000), p. 57.
5. M.A. Jinnah, *Speeches and Statements as Governor-General* (Karachi, 2000), p. 182.
6. Richard Symonds, *The Making of Pakistan*, 2nd edition (Islamabad: National Book Foundation, 1976), p. 182.
7. Khan Salahuddin Khan, *The Speeches and Statements of Mohtarma Fatima Jinnah* (Lahore: Research Society of Pakistan, University of the Punjab, 1976), pp. 25–26.
8. Muhammad Ali Siddiqui, 'Foreword', in *The Life and Times of the Raja Sahib of Mahmudabad*, ed. Syed Ishtiaq Hussain (Karachi: Mehboob Academy, 1998), p. 18.
9. M.A.S. Abdel Haleem (trans.), *The Qur'an* (Oxford World's Classics). First published, with corrections, as an Oxford World's Classics paperback, 2005.
10. Muhammad Iqbal, *Reconstruction of Religious Thought in Islam* (Lahore, Sang-e-Meel, 2004), p. 85.

MOHAMMAD ALI JINNAH (b. 25 December 1876–d. 11 September 1948) was a campaigner for India's freedom. M.A. Jinnah was an instrument of India's partition. Both claims are valid. Whether this represents an advance or a derailment, depends on the meaning of the word 'freedom'. The Hindus had not gained freedom after the defeat of the Muslims. Would the Muslims gain freedom on the withdrawal of the British?

The first step in the direction of partition was taken when the Congress leadership transitioned from Jinnah to Gandhi. Both had emerged together as champions of India's freedom, both were disciples of Gopal Krishna Gokhale, and both gained prominence by protesting against the plight of Indians in South Africa; Gandhi with his novel *satyagraha*, and Jinnah by confronting the viceroy face-to-face. Then, was their later divergence an outcome of their vision, or their circumstances? These were not insuperable, and may not have come about without the fateful intervention of Motilal Nehru who primed Jinnah to oppose Gandhi's non-cooperation resolution at Nagpur, in 1920, and then resiled from his stand.[1] Only ten days before, Jinnah had spoken of his belief in the ideal of non-cooperation; and even at Nagpur (where he resigned), Jinnah had not opposed the principles, but he had opposed the impractical portions of Gandhi's resolution.

His resignation from Congress brought about a personality change. Dewan Chaman Lal, who knew Jinnah as a young man, described his 'uninhibited laughter and general bonhomie'.[2] Jinnah's formality and reserve developed as a reaction to the social treatment he received from his Congress compatriots—which was strange considering his close friendship with Nehru's father, and Patel's brother. Again, had Gandhi not gone against Jinnah's pleas, by raising the religious sentiments of the (Muslim) masses during the Khilafat Movement, the role of the Muslim League would have been limited to being a moderating influence in Indian politics.

His reserve also developed when his marriage with a young girl—whom he had pursued tempestuously—broke down. Kanji Dwarkadas—a mutual friend—was called home by Jinnah, the day after the heart-rending scene of his wife's burial: 'Never have I found a man so sad and so bitter. He screamed his heart out, speaking to me for over two hours, myself listening to him patiently and sympathetically, occasionally putting in a word here and there. Something, I saw, snapped in him.'[3]

A number of freedom fighters were widowers: Gandhi, Jawaharlal Nehru, Vallabhbhai Patel, and Abul Kalam Azad, but only Jinnah's wife, Ruttie, had been politically active.

Jinnah had resigned from Congress politically, not psychologically. Jinnah caused a split in the Muslim League over the composition of the Simon Commission, rather than abandon Congress (which he had left) in its struggle. Viceroy Lord Willingdon found Jinnah more Congress than Congress, but Jinnah was alienated time and again by Congress; by the abjuration of the Lucknow Pact, by resiling from the Delhi Muslim Proposals, by disregarding the tacit UP 1937 electoral understanding, and finally by reneging on the grouping clause. Without these rebuffs, Jinnah would not have faced a choice between territorial loyalty and communal survival.

Jinnah was not elitist in politics. He led a mass demonstration against Lord Willingdon. He dealt with tough hecklers and their political patrons in a Bombay meeting held to promote the candidature of R.P. Paranjype.[4] Ian Bryant Wells has quoted Jinnah's speech on the Elementary Education Bill: 'Are you going to keep millions and millions of people under your feet for the fear that they may demand more rights'? In spite of these sentiments, Indian historians favour a Jinnah who would bow before Nehru—not a Jinnah who would stand up to Lord Mountbatten. Only one reviewer, T.W. Hutton, has identified Jinnah's fear of emotion as central to both his politics and personality. This trait eluded his Congress contemporaries. Speaking at the All-Parties Conference, in 1928, Jinnah said: 'Every country struggling for freedom and desirous of establishing a democratic system has had to face the problem of minorities...minorities cannot give anything to the majority and the majority alone can give...'

Twenty years later, addressing the Constituent Assembly of Pakistan, Jinnah said: 'You may belong to any religion, cast or creed, that has nothing to do with the business of the state. We are starting with this fundamental principle that we are all citizens and equal citizens of one state.'

Jinnah was upholding a lifelong principle ignored equally by the citizens of India and Pakistan.

Notes

1. Kanji Dwarkadas, *India's Fight for Freedom, 1913–1937: An Eyewitness Story* (Bombay: Popular Prakashan, 1966), pp. 286–87.
2. Dewan Chaman Lal, 'The Quaid-i-Azam as I knew him', in Jamiluddin Ahmad (ed.), *Quaid-i-Azam as seen by his Contemporaries* (Lahore: Ashraf, 1976), p. 171.
3. Kanji Dwarkadas, *Ruttie Jinnah: The Story of a Great Friendship* (Bombay: Kanji Dwarkadas, 1963), p. 58.
4. V.N. Naik, *Mr Jinnah: A Political Study* (Bombay: Sadbhakti Publications, 1947), pp. 38–41.

Chapter 25

The Establishment of Pakistan: Early Problems

On independence, Pakistan was without any infrastructure to set up a new state. It had neither of the two capital cities, Calcutta or New Delhi, developed by the British in India. It established its capital at Karachi, which had become a provincial capital only ten years previously. It had no office buildings, furniture, or stationery whereby the administrative machinery for the seat of a government could be set up. People sat under trees, bringing furniture from wherever they resided, and the government started functioning. Even Lord Mountbatten, then the governor-general of India, described Karachi as a 'tent' compared to the splendour of New Delhi.[1]

Apart from the practical difficulty of setting up government machinery, there was the political difficulty that the provincial government of Sindh resented the declaration of Karachi as the capital. The Sindh Muslim League began to function as an opposition party. The cash-strapped government of Pakistan promised financial compensation, but the provincial government did not consider the amount adequate.

RIOTS AND REFUGEES.—The partition of India was accompanied by widespread riots throughout the subcontinent. Since the boundary awards had been delayed, rioting was most rampant in the Punjab. The riots were started by the Sikhs and the RSS, the militant Hindu organization, and were followed by a Muslim reprisal which was also swift and brutal. There was widespread murder, rape, and arson on both sides. Partition resulted in the largest human migration in recorded history. According to Pakistani estimates, approximately, 6,500,000 Muslims reached Pakistan from India; 5,200,000 came from East Punjab, including the princely states where rioting was severe. 500,000 lost their lives or were abducted. From Pakistan, there was an exodus of about 5,500,000 Hindus and Sikhs. According to Richard Symonds, writing in 1950, the population of Pakistan increased by about 100,000 people.[2]

In the face of unspeakable atrocities, writers from all three communities, Hindu, Muslim, and Sikh, led by Krishan Chander, Sa'adat Hasan Manto, and Rajinder Singh Bedi rose to the occasion and most impartially showed that the riots were crimes not against communities but against humanity. Books are a poor defence against bullets, but these writers provided a bridge to mental reconciliation and normalcy. At first, numbers proved deceptive. Inevitably as news of atrocities spread in Karachi, there was rioting against the Hindus. On 9 January 1948, Jinnah warned the Muslim refugees 'not to abuse the hospitality that has been extended to them'.[3]

DIVISION OF ASSETS.—Field Marshal Sir Claude Auchinleck, the British commander-in-chief of India had taken the position that regardless of the partition of India, the armed forces should not be divided. However, when a political decision to divide the armed forces was taken, he testified that the Indian government wanted to prevent the establishment of Pakistan. He did not admit that he had delayed the decision to physically divide the military assets before Partition.

As far as financial assets were concerned, India was prepared to pay Pakistan only 5 per cent of the total capital on the condition that Pakistan accept the liability of 20 per cent of the debt. In November 1947, Hirubhai M. Patel (finance secretary, India), and Chaudhry Mohammad Ali (secretary general, Government of Pakistan) agreed that the disputed portion of Pakistan's share of the cash balances in sterling would be 17.5 per cent. In terms of cash, it worked out to Rs 750 million. But even this agreed amount was not transferred to Pakistan. Nehru wrote to Liaquat Ali Khan that India could not release the money because Pakistan planned to use it against India in the ongoing Kashmir war. When Junagadh, with a Muslim ruler and Hindu majority, had acceded to Pakistan, India forcibly occupied it, saying that Junagadh's accession to Pakistan was against the principles of the religious divide. India had occupied Kashmir, which had a Hindu ruler and a Muslim majority, against the principle it had recently expounded. Nehru's linking of the division of assets with the Kashmir war was a hollow argument that deprived India of its moral ground. Gandhi started a fast unto death, forcing the government of India to transfer Pakistan's share. Lord Mountbatten and Nehru had side-lined Gandhi, therefore, they resented his intervention but were forced to pay an instalment of Pakistan's share of assets to induce Gandhi to break his fast. Gandhi was assassinated on 30 January 1948 by an RSS member, Nathuram Godse. Gandhi had rendered ineffective the Cabinet Mission Plan but had now paid with his life for helping Pakistan.

The payment of this instalment did not end Pakistan's crisis. The Nizam of Hyderabad sent a cheque for a large amount, but since it was based on Indian securities, Nehru did not allow it to be encashed. At this, Sir Adamjee Haji Dawood arranged for a loan on his guarantee from Mohammad Ali Habib, the founder of Habib Bank, thereby preventing the financial collapse of Pakistan.

THE KASHMIR WAR.—Nehru had made a public reversal of the principle of Partition by occupying first Junagadh and then Kashmir. This diplomatic gamble could have only been taken on the expectation that Pakistan would not survive the blow. Pakistan had been denied its share of military and financial assets. The reorganization of the Pakistan Army was still underway when the Kashmir war was thrust on it. Within Kashmir, the state forces had started a massacre of Muslims in Poonch. These Muslims had relatives in the tribal areas of Pakistan who invaded Kashmir hoping to rescue their relatives.

The Pakistan Army did not have the resources to halt their advance. They were unable to control the tribals even when they looted Muslim property in Rawalpindi. Secondly, had Pakistan taken action against the tribesmen, it would have popularized the demand for Pakhtunistan—an independent Pathan state, a demand supported by the Congress leaders.

The Government of India made the plea that it entered Kashmir because Maharaja Hari Singh had signed an Instrument of Accession to India. The Instrument of Accession has never surfaced, and Alastair Lamb has proved that it was never signed. Nehru promised the people of Kashmir and the whole world that the fate of Kashmir would not be decided by the accession but by a free and impartial plebiscite of the people of Jammu and Kashmir.[4] India has since reneged on this promise and this is one of two issues which still beset Pakistan–India relations.

THE INDUS WATER DISPUTE.—The Indus Water dispute, like the Kashmir war, had its origin in the Radcliffe Award. Just as the award of Gurdaspur to India was responsible for giving India access to Kashmir, the award of Ferozepur and Zira to India resulted in the Canal Waters dispute. All three were Muslim-majority districts and were given to India for a purpose.

The British had developed the upper Indus basin as an integrated unit having a vast irrigation network. The Radcliffe Award gave India the Ferozepur Headworks that controlled the Sutlej River as well as the Madhopur Headworks controlling the Ravi River. An arbitral tribunal was set up under Sir William Patrick Spens, which recommended that the flow of water to Pakistan should not be stopped. Immediately after the tribunal was wound up in April 1948, the Indian government actually cut off the flow of water to Pakistan. Since this was in breach of international law which holds that an upper riparian country cannot interfere with the existing irrigation of the lower riparian country, the supply was partially restored. This long-standing dispute was apparently resolved in 1960 when Nehru came to Karachi to sign an agreement with President Ayub Khan and Eugene Black, vice-president of the World Bank.

In 1999, when India began its Baglihar project and despite Pakistan's protests continued with it, this threatened to upset the Indus Basin Treaty of 1960. After several rounds of unsuccessful talks on the design of the project, in 2005, the World Bank was asked to arbitrate between India and Pakistan. In 2007, in its final verdict, the World Bank Swiss neutral expert, Raymond Lafitte, conceded three of Pakistan's objections but upheld India's design to build spillway gates, to which Pakistan vehemently objected. In June 2010, India and Pakistan resolved the issue relating to the initial filling of the Baglihar dam and decided not to raise the matter further. The decision was taken at the meeting of the Permanent Indus Commission.

THE JINNAH ERA.—One of the greatest setbacks to Pakistan in its early days was the death of Jinnah, barely thirteen months after Independence. His presence as governor-general had been vital to the survival of Pakistan. Lord Mountbatten had publicly admitted that had he become the common governor-general of India and Pakistan, partition would have been temporary. In this design, he had the support of his Prime Minister Clement Atlee who while speaking on the Independence Bill, had expressed his hope that Pakistan would not last. It was to prevent this outcome that the AIML nominated M.A. Jinnah to be the first governor-general of Pakistan.

In these peculiar circumstances, the Independence Act was amended to make the governor-general and not the prime minister the chief executive of Pakistan. From 30 December 1947, all vital policy decisions would be taken by the governor-general in the cabinet. M.A. Jinnah also became the chief executive of the Balochistan province. There had been no political reforms in Balochistan up until Independence, i.e. there was no governor and no assembly.

M.A. Jinnah envisaged Pakistan as a modern state, not as a theocracy. He chastised Muslim migrants from India on 9 January 1948 for the anti-Hindu riots in Karachi.[5] His 11 August 1947 speech giving equal rights to minorities was the result of years of deliberation. On 5 November 1941, he told H.V. Hodson that minorities would be represented in the cabinet. His only reservation then had been that the Hindus being a minority 'could not dictate policy'.[6]

In the domain of foreign policy, he held out friendship to all upholding the Charter of the United Nations. He believed in leaning towards the West without going out of the way to annoy the USSR. He noted later that the USSR was the only country not to congratulate Pakistan on its creation. He undertook a personal initiative with regard to Afghanistan, the only country to oppose Pakistan's membership of the UN. On 3 December 1947, the Afghan ambassador presented his credentials to the governor-general of Pakistan as the result of negotiations conducted by the special representative, Nawab Saeedullah Khan. Jinnah also strongly supported the Palestinian cause and upheld the independence of Indonesia.

In terms of internal politics, although the Congress ministry in NWFP had lost its representative status in the referendum, the governor-general let Dr Khan Sahib head the provincial administration. However, when Dr Khan Sahib refused to salute the Pakistani flag and persisted in his refusal, the governor-general was obliged to dismiss his ministry on 22 August 1947.

Jinnah was able to visit East Bengal only once as governor-general. In his speech at Curzon Hall, Dhaka, he reiterated the decision of the AIML Delhi Legislators Convention in March 1946, that Urdu would be the official language of Pakistan. In his speech on 20 March 1948 at Dhaka, on 12 April 1948 at Peshawar, and on 15 June 1948 at Quetta, he warned the people against provincialism.

He advocated Islamic socialism and Islamic social justice, although Pakistan had to depend on its few plutocrats for its solvency. Jinnah prescribed industrialization as the key to development. On 1 April 1948, he hailed the issuance of Pakistan's own currency as an assertion of Pakistan's economic viability and independence. On 1 July 1948, while inaugurating the State Bank he called upon it to undertake research to make banking compatible with Islamic principles. He told the youth to choose a career in commerce over one in civil or government service.

At the Chittagong meeting on 25 March 1948, he told gazetted officers that the country would no longer be ruled by the bureaucracy and that they should have nothing to do with party politics. Addressing the military staff college at Quetta on 14 June 1948, he reminded the military of the oath which they were required to take, the text of which he read out.

By 12 April 1948, Jinnah's illness had overtaken him. In June he had to reside at Quetta and Ziarat in Balochistan. He was brought to Karachi without protocol on 11 September 1948. His ambulance broke down, A second ambulance was rushed, with Prime Minister Liaquat Ali Khan following it in his car,[7] and though his physicians said that Jinnah had not suffered due to the breakdown, he died the same evening. The scene is recounted by two historians hostile to Jinnah: 'At ten minutes to ten that evening, his doctor bent close to the dying Quaid and whispered "Sir, I have given you an injection. God willing you are going to live." Jinnah fixed his unwavering glare on the last sight his eyes would ever see, his doctor's face. "No, I am not," he firmly replied. Half an hour later he was dead.'[8]

The death of Jinnah created a sense of uncertainty. Sensing this, on 13 September 1948, India invaded the Princely State of Hyderabad, and within four days Hyderabad's accession to India was achieved.

By all standards, the achievement of Pakistan was momentous. Jinnah had rarely displayed emotion, but his followers shed uninhibited tears, feeling the weight of history while carrying his coffin.

THE LIAQUAT ERA (1948–1951).—Prime Minister Liaquat Ali Khan had been an honorary secretary of the AIML and leader of its bloc in the interim government. Due to his role in the Pakistan Movement, he had the magnetism to pull the country out of its despondency over Jinnah's death and the consequent Indian attack on Hyderabad, Deccan. The challenges of nation-building were still immense, and Liaquat Ali Khan was able to meet only some of them. As far as the framing of the constitution was concerned, Liaquat Ali Khan presented the Objectives Resolution on 12 March 1949. This is a valuable document that has been retained in all subsequent constitutions. The interim report of 28 September 1950 proved so unpopular that it had to be withdrawn in November. In the interim report, the prime minister had recommended the concentration of power in the future president. Other major impediments such as differences over the constitutional role of Islam and the quantum of East Bengal's representation were not removed.

Liaquat Ali Khan's policy of giving precedence to the Muslim League over parliament increased the tension between the centre and provinces and resulted in the formation of twenty-one opposition parties. Since one party was given overwhelming importance, opposition elements began forming new parties. Liaquat Ali Khan was popular with the masses, but the political forces were aligned against him. Jinnah himself complained of rising provincialism and Yusuf Haroon, as Sindh chief minister, also warned against this trend on 27 July 1947. Liaquat dismissed both the Punjab governor, Sir Francis Mudie and the Punjab Assembly, and the situation did not improve till the end of 1950 when the Muslim League won the elections to the NWFP and West Punjab. This success did not extend to East Bengal because of their outstanding demand to declare Bengali one of the national languages of Pakistan.

The constitution and the Kashmir problem remained unresolved, but Liaquat Ali Khan obtained favourable resolutions on 13 August 1948 and 25 July 1951 from the UN, calling for an impartial plebiscite. Till today these resolutions are the bedrock of Pakistan's stand on Kashmir.

Liaquat Ali Khan made rapid strides towards industrialization. He formed two Pakistan Industrial Development Corporations, one for large and one for small-scale industries. He did not wait for private entrepreneurs but kept provisions for their partnership. Pakistan was the largest jute producer in the world, but at the time of Independence, it had no jute mill. It had a large cotton crop but only fourteen cotton mills. Liaquat's boldest decision was his refusal to devalue the rupee following the British and then Indian devaluation on 15 September 1949. India refused to buy jute and other commodities at the new rate. Liaquat was demonstrating Pakistan's financial viability with a vengeance. This caused the greatest stress to the jute growers of East Bengal. Liaquat travelled to Dhaka to assure them that if the Indians did not buy jute at the new rate, the government of Pakistan would buy the entire crop. Since Liaquat Ali Khan was a man of unassailable character, the peasants relied on him and refused to sell at the old price.

Liaquat Ali Khan accelerated Bengali recruitment in both the armed and civil services. The government gained financial respite because of the Korean War which gave a boost to Pakistani exports. This may have been a modest and ephemeral respite for Pakistan's economy, but it was a much-needed one. Similarly, Liaquat's efforts to achieve economic independence may have taken its toll on institution building. Liaquat could not decentralize power when immense efforts had gone into building a centre.

Liaquat Ali Khan constructed the 107–mile-long BRB canal on the Punjab border and in July 1951, he de-escalated tension by a show of strength. He negotiated the Liaquat–Nehru Pact giving protection to minorities in both countries. Liaquat Ali Khan had put Pakistan on the road to progress when, in Rawalpindi on 16 October 1951, he was assassinated. His last words were: 'May God protect Pakistan'.

Notes

1. Allen Campbell-Johnson, *Mission with Mountbatten* (London: Robert Hale, 1972), p. 87.
2. Richard Symonds, *The Making of Pakistan* (Islamabad: NBF, 1976; Original 1950), p. 87.
3. *Jinnah: Speeches and Statements 1947-1948* (Karachi: Oxford University Press, 2000), p. 92.
4. Jawaharlal Nehru, AIR broadcast, 2 November 1947.
5. Waheed Ahmad (ed.), *The Nation's Voice* (Karachi: QAA, 2000), pp. 831–43.
6. Ibid.
7. Brigadier Noor A. Hussain, *The News*, 23 March 1995, Supplement. I am indebted to Khurram Ali Shafiq for providing this reference.
8. Larry Collins and Dominique Lapierre, *Freedom at Midnight* (Delhi: Vikas, 1997), p. 572.

Nawabzada Muhammad Liaquat Ali Khan (b. Karnal, 1 October 1896–d. Rawalpindi, 16 October 1951) was the last honorary secretary of the AIML, the leader of the AIML block in the interim government, and the first prime minister of Pakistan. More worth recalling is that the Pakistan High Commission, in India, is housed on Liaquat Ali Khan's property. He did not file any claim for any property left behind in India, nor did he exchange any property. The chief minister of Sindh had cut off the water supply to his official residence. When his mother asked for a car to bring her from the border to Karachi, Liaquat Ali Khan respectfully declined, saying that she would have to come in 1947, like any other refugee. When he was assassinated, he was discovered to be wearing a patched shirt. His bank balance was meagre. His sacrifices for the cause of Pakistan were second to none, yet he remains the most maligned Prime Minister of Pakistan.

Both in the 19–21 December 2006 centennial of the AIML, under the Quaid-i-Azam University, and in the 19–20 February 2007 Punjab University Conference on Peace and Security, Liaquat Ali Khan was blamed for derailing the destiny of Pakistan. His ambition, his flawed foreign policy, and his neglect of democratic norms are cited. As for his ambition, on 27 December 1947, he sent in his resignation: 'You are the architect of Pakistan and, as such, I feel that it is but fair that you should have only such persons around you in building it up who can command your complete confidence and goodwill. I would never dream of doing anything that would, in any way injure Pakistan in the slightest degree, but as everyone knows, my health has not been well for the last two months; my slipping out quietly will not create any misunderstanding or difficulties.'[1]

Liaquat's relations with Jinnah need comment. Jinnah often heeded Liaquat's suggestions: they worked out strategies and itineraries together and entertained each other's objections. Yet, there seems to have been something elusive; Liaquat wrote to Jinnah, on 29 May 1940: 'In reality, it is the Congress alone which is responsible for this unsatisfactory state of affairs. You have hit the nail on the head by issuing your statement.'[2] Which is all perfectly true, yet the fact that he had to spell out explicitly the position of the Muslim League to Jinnah is an oddity. It is also enigmatic that their correspondence tells us more about the reserved and reticent Jinnah, than about the amiable and affable Liaquat Ali Khan.

How much Liaquat was his own master needs to be reconsidered now. Giving an interview to Nicholas Mansergh, in March 1947, Liaquat proposed that there be a capital in each wing: one administrative, one parliamentary ('I have made his suggestion.'[3]) Yet, when Shaista Ikramullah made the same proposal in the Constituent Assembly, Liaquat opposed it.[4] In the same interview, about the United States, Liaquat said: 'We did not dislike them, we just feel that there is nothing in common. Therefore we are likely to think of Britain as an associate since we know her. The Soviet Union is an uncertain factor and her materialism is repugnant to Muslims.'[5]

That the materialism of the USSR was repugnant was a point reiterated by Jinnah on 7 September 1947. By the phrase 'uncertain factor,' Liaquat could not then have meant that the USSR would collapse, rather, that its policy with regard to a new

Muslim country, near Central Asia, would be uncertain. The Pakistan Cabinet pre-empted Liaquat by retaining his reservations about the USSR but discarding them with regard to the US. The stage was set for spreading a myth about the Moscow visit. It was the USSR which had advanced the original date 20 August 1949 to 14 August, the independence day of Pakistan and there after never set a date. Liaquat had thwarted two military coups—one in India (1947), and one in Pakistan (1951). His reputation was bound to suffer.

Notes

1. Roger Long, 'Jinnah and his Right Hand', in M.R. Kazimi (ed.), *M.A. Jinnah: Views and Reviews* (Karachi: Oxford University Press, 2005), p. 138.
2. Muhammad Reza Kazimi (ed.), *Jinnah–Liaquat Correspondence* (Karachi: Pakistan Study Centre, University of Karachi, 2003), p. 88.
3. Nicholas Mansergh, *Independence Year* (New Delhi: Oxford University Press, 1999), p. 245.
4. Shaista Ikramullah, *From Purdah to Parliament* (Karachi: Oxford University Press, 1998), p. 229.
5. Nicholas Mansergh, op. cit., p. 246.

CHAPTER 26
EXPERIMENT IN DEMOCRACY (1951–1958)

The assassination of Liaquat Ali Khan was followed by a period of instability. No less than six prime ministers served during the next eight years.

Khwaja Nazimuddin stepped down as Pakistan's second governor-general to become the second prime minister. He was temperamentally unsuited to combat the intrigues of the new governor-general, Ghulam Mohammad, who had given himself overriding powers. Khwaja Nazimuddin became the target of criticism due to a shortage of food, and his ineffectual handling (initially) of the anti-Ahmadi riots in the Punjab. Being a Bengali, his opposition to the declaration of Bengali as a national language, brought the Language Movement to a head. By and large, he retained the esteem of the masses and the confidence of the Constituent Assembly. This did not prevent Ghulam Mohammad from dismissing Khwaja Nazimuddin as prime minister on 17 April 1953. The success of this coup signalled the fragility of parliamentary democracy in Pakistan.

Mohammad Ali Bogra was inducted as prime minister. The induction of a nonrepresentative Bengali prime minister did not pacify the Bengalis, and in the ensuing 1954 provincial elections in East Bengal, the ruling Muslim League was defeated by the United Front. A.K. Fazlul Haq, the new chief minister of East Bengal stated on 3 May 1954, in the Indian city of Calcutta, that he did not believe in Pakistan. According to H.S. Suhrawardy, this statement sparked off protests in his own province, one led by his erstwhile ally Maulana Abdul Hamid Khan Bhashani. Fazlul Haq promised to retire from politics and was eventually removed. Later he was appointed governor of the province.

The governor-general, emboldened by Nazimuddin's removal, dissolved the Constituent Assembly on 24 October 1954. The prime minister acquiesced to the decision, but the speaker, Tamizuddin Khan (1889–1963), challenged the action in the Sindh High Court. The court upheld the stand of the speaker, but the Federal Court, in a majority decision on 10 May 1955, decided against the speaker and in favour of Governor-General Ghulam Mohammad. This was the first verdict to uphold the dissolution of an assembly. Since Prime Minister Mohammad Ali Bogra had already tried, in 1954, to curtail the powers of the governor-general, and because he was without a popular base, he too was eased out of office on 10 August 1955.

The new Prime Minister, Chaudhry Mohammad Ali, was a bureaucrat having served as secretary general in 1947. He supported the move to merge the four provinces of Pakistan into One Unit which came into effect on 5

Experiment in Democracy (1951-1958) 175

October 1955. Chaudhry Mohammad Ali became the first Prime Minister to give Pakistan a Constitution on 29 February 1956. Pakistan remained within the British Commonwealth but was designated an Islamic Republic. This achievement did not prove sufficient to prevent his fall. The newly created Republican Party forced Chaudhry Mohammad Ali's resignation on 8 September 1956.

The next Prime Minister, Huseyn Shaheed Suhrawardy was the only seasoned politician after Liaquat Ali Khan to hold this office; he had the credentials to bring about the now much-needed stability to Pakistani politics. He was a leading barrister of his time, and the most successful since Jinnah. He was also chief minister of Bengal during the great Calcutta killing and had stayed with Gandhi to keep peace in Calcutta during Partition. He, along with Kiran Shankar Roy (1891-1949), the leader of the opposition in Bengal, and with Sarat Chandra Bose, had drafted a scheme for a united and independent Bengal, which M.A. Jinnah had immediately accepted.[1] Later, Gandhi and Liaquat Ali Khan also voiced acceptance but Nehru, the prime minister-designate, turned down this scheme saying that the Hindus of Bengal could not live under a perpetual Muslim majority.[2] He refused the offer of becoming the governor-general's personal roving ambassador or rehabilitation minister and insisted on becoming deputy prime minister.[3] Jinnah interpreted this as a lack of confidence in Khwaja Nazimuddin, then chief minister of East Bengal. Later his membership of Pakistan's Constituent Assembly was cancelled because he had decided not to take up permanent residence in Pakistan. The result was that H.S. Suhrawardy ceased to be a member, while Kiran Shankar Roy remained a member of the Pakistan Constituent Assembly.

With the Language Movement, Suhrawardy's political role was enlarged, and he (quite rightly) called himself the last bridge between the eastern and western wings of Pakistan. Earlier his observation that East Bengali demands were largely met by parity representation in the National Assembly and the recognition of Bengali as a national language of Pakistan (under the 1956 Constitution) held out hope for national integration. Unfortunately, he became prime minister when he espoused a most unpopular cause. The Suez Crisis had resulted in the invasion of Egypt in 1956 by Britain, France, and Israel and while the people of Pakistan were outraged by the invasion, H.S. Suhrawardy justified his desertion of the Arab cause by describing Muslim countries as 'zeroes'. This phrase was earlier employed by President Iskander Mirza on 26 July 1956 but was noted largely when echoed by the prime minister. His foreign policy initiatives and the impact left by this charismatic leader both on foreign affairs and interior politics were weak and temporary. He was the first prime minister to state that the Two-Nation theory had lost its validity after the creation of Pakistan and his main success was the induction of joint electorates in Pakistan. The defection of Maulana Bhashani from his party and thereafter, the desertion of the Republican Party enabled President Iskander Mirza to force his resignation.

The next Prime Minister, I.I. Chundrigar (15 September 1897–26 September 1960), had been a stalwart of the Bombay Muslim League. In the interim government, he had been member for commerce. He was ambassador to Afghanistan and governor of NWFP. His was the shortest term as prime minister (18 October to 16 December 1957). He resigned over the question of separate or joint electorates.

The seventh Prime Minister, Sir Feroz Khan Noon (7 May 1893–9 December 1970), had even more impressive political credentials. He became the first native to become defence member of the Viceroy's Executive Council (1942–45) and was the Indian High Commissioner to Britain (1936–41). Sir Feroz Khan Noon remained prime minister for only nine months (11 December 1957–7 October 1958) when he was removed in Pakistan's first military coup.

This democratic but unstable era saw progress in the industrial sector. The economy had survived the recession following the end of the Korean War (1952). The democratic dispensation was severely inhibited by Governor-General Ghulam Mohammad and President Iskander Mirza, who had the support of the bureaucracy and perhaps some elements in the armed forces. The franchise base was too narrow to provide succour to prime ministers and parliaments, but the politicians cannot be absolved of the charge of discrediting democratic rule.

On 20 September 1958, Abdul Hakim, the speaker of the East Pakistan assembly was physically expelled from the House amidst loud allegations that he was insane! On 23 September 1958, the deputy speaker, Shahed Ali, who had to preside over the proceedings, unfortunately, died as a result of the violence in the assembly.

Such incidents, coupled with allegations that Kalat was preparing to secede created alarm. President Iskander Mirza abrogated the 1956 constitution, dismissed the prime minister, and dissolved the assemblies.

On 7 October 1958 martial law was proclaimed. The Commander-in-Chief, General Mohammad Ayub Khan was appointed chief martial law administrator, and on 24 October, General Ayub was designated prime minister. On 27 October, he exiled President Iskander Mirza and occupied the office of the president. The despondent public widely and sincerely hailed the military coup, and President Ayub, regarded as a saviour, began his rule with expressions of approval from the public.

Notes

1. H.V. Hodson, *The Great Divide*, 2nd ed. (Karachi: Oxford University Press, 1989), p. 246 (First edition London, Hutchinson, 1969, was published when Bengal separatism had gathered momentum).
2. S.M. Burke and S.A.D. Qureshi, *The British Raj in India* (Karachi: Oxford University Press, 1995), p. 513.
3. Ata Rabbani, *I was the Quaid's ADC* (Karachi: Oxford University Press, 1996), p. 171.

Experiment in Democracy (1951-1958)

Huseyn Shaheed Suhrawardy (b. Midnapur, 8 September 1892–d. Beirut, 5 December 1963) was born to Sir Zahid Suhrawardy, a judge of the Calcutta High Court, and Khujesta Akhtar Bano—a pioneer of the Urdu novel. Suhrawardy was educated at Oxford, became a barrister, and as a practising lawyer, led the profession in Pakistan. As a politician, he rose to become chief minister of Bengal and prime minister of Pakistan (12 September 1956–13 October 1957), but in his personal life he suffered tragedies, and as a consequence, he took refuge in humour. His first wife died three years after marriage. His second marriage—to a Russian—was also brief. The greatest tragedy was the death of his son, Shahab, a graduate of Christ Church College, Oxford, in 1940, at the age of 20. Suhrawardy adopted a fast lifestyle—even indulging in pranks. Khwaja Nazimuddin shuddered when he recalled how Suhrawardy brought a toy Panda—which squeaked—to a cabinet meeting.[1] Towards independence, he admitted to the viceroy that he had lied to Jinnah.[2]

His heart led his head. He minted money as a lawyer but frittered it all away by doling it out to the deserving as well as the undeserving. In Calcutta, Sheikh Mujibur Rahman discovered that Suhrawardy made monthly payments of over Rs 3000 to the needy.[3] Such a man does not start riots, and although Suhrawardy suffered obloquy for the Great Calcutta killings of 1949, Chief Justice Sir William Patrick Spens, exonerated him. In order to avoid a repetition of the holocaust at partition, Suhrawardy persuaded Gandhi to join him in a mission to promote communal harmony. This mission induced him to refuse high office in Pakistan: 'Jinnah had been kind enough to offer me, successively, the refugee ministry, permanent representative to the UN, ambassador to the countries of the Middle East, and even the defence ministry.'[4]

Ever since Suhrawardy defended the leftist stalwarts in the Rawalpindi Conspiracy case, 1951, whom Liaquat prosecuted, his reputation had become coloured. Syed Jaffar Ahmad writes: 'Liaquat Ali Khan did not hide his dislike of Suhrawardy, who was humiliated when he was voted out of membership, while he was present on the floor of the house.'[5] What Liaquat had said was: 'My honourable friend is having a very mistaken sense of his importance if he thinks this amendment has been brought forward only for the purpose of eliminating Mr Suhrawardy from the constituent assembly of Pakistan. Mr Suhrawardy, if he so desires, can become a permanent resident of Pakistan tomorrow.'[6]

H.S. Suhrawardy was evasive in his address: 'I think that there is no anomaly in a member, in a citizen of the Indian Dominion being a member of the constituent assembly of Pakistan…and I feel, Sir, that the greatest loyalty is a loyalty to humanity, which transcends all parochial loyalties.'[7]

There is no doubt that Suhrawardy was the most able and popular prime minister after Liaquat Ali Khan, but he had compromised himself even before assuming office. He issued a statement in support of Urdu as the state language of Pakistan, also saying that Urdu be taught as a compulsory second language in East Bengal.[8] On 17 April 1953, he publicly endorsed the dismissal of Khwaja Nazimuddin.[9] As prime minister, he had to uphold the most unpopular foreign policy by supporting the invasion of Suez and added insult to injury by calling the Arabs a collection of zeroes.

His exchange of visits with Zhou Enlai was a resounding success, but on his visit to the US, he dissipated its effect by lampooning China. Consider also his denunciation of Russia: 'The frequent purges, executions and massacres for political reasons the concentration camps, the farcical trials of alleged foreign spies...'[10]

Not even Liaquat (who has been accused time and again of alienating Russia) had used such strong language. It is no wonder, then, that his premiership occupies barely three pages in Suhrawardy's own memoirs.

Notes

1. Shaista Ikramullah, *Huseyn Shaheed Suhrawardy* (Karachi: Oxford University Press, 1991), p. 12.
2. L.A. Sherwani, *The Partition of India and Mountbatten* (Karachi: Council of Pakistan Studies, 1986), p. 161.
3. S.A. Karim, *Sheikh Mujib: Triumph and Tragedy* (Dhaka: The University Press, 2005), p. 96.
4. M.H.R. Talukdar (ed.), *The Memoirs of Huseyn Shaheed Suhrawardy* (Dhaka: The University Press), p. 106.
5. Syed Jaffar Ahmad, 'The Bengali Trio,' *Dawn*, 30 December 2006, p. 34.
6. M. Rafiq Afzal (ed.), *The Speeches and Statements of Quaid-i-Millat Liaquat Ali Khan* (Lahore Research Society, University of the Punjab, 1967), p. 157.
7. Shaista Ikramullah, op. cit., p. 153.
8. Badruddin Umar, *The Emergence of Bangladesh* (Karachi: Oxford University Press, 2004), p. 217.
9. Ibid., p. 243.
10. M.H.R. Talukdar, op. cit., p. 115.

CHAPTER 27

THE FIRST MILITARY REGIME (1958-1969)

The Ayub Khan era began as a benevolent despotism but ended as a discredited polity. In the beginning, the military regime succeeded in cracking down on corrupt civil servants, black marketeers, and notorious smugglers. It also strictly imposed traffic regulations and civic rules, thereby earning the gratitude of the common man. This success was not replicated in East Pakistan, causing the General Officer Commanding, Maj.-Gen. Umrao Khan to admit that in his province, martial law had been a failure. In the exuberance following the reforms, people forgot that elections under the 1956 Constitution, scheduled for early 1959, had been relegated to oblivion.

Instead of general elections based on adult franchise, Field Marshal (since 1959) Mohammad Ayub Khan introduced a system of indirect elections called Basic Democracy (BD). Eighty thousand members (120,000 since 1967) would be directly elected to form the electoral college. Basic Democrats would then elect the president (which they did on 17 February 1960) and thereafter, the members of the national and provincial assemblies. These BDs would also run local government and union councils. Structurally, this system was designed to provide services to the people. Members would be available locally and be accessible throughout their term instead of only in the election season. Culturally it was a different story since a limited electorate was open to coercion and corruption. Martial law punishments were harsh, some unwarranted, but as the presence of the military was not resented, reprisals were not vicious.

On 8 June 1962, President Ayub Khan lifted martial law and promulgated Pakistan's second constitution, which was presidential, not parliamentary. The four-year calm was broken by anti-constitution demonstrations led by former Prime Minister H.S. Suhrawardy. The political and student protests could then be contained because of the great popularity enjoyed by the governor of East Pakistan, Lt.-Gen. Azam Khan. The first major rift between the ruler and ruled had been created and would only widen with time.

President Ayub Khan initiated a number of reforms in the law, education and population planning sectors. The president took several steps which he believed would accelerate economic progress in East Pakistan and the backward regions in West Pakistan. Contrary to the socialist tendencies then prevailing in Asia, the Pakistan Industrial Development Corporation set up units in the public sector and sold them to the private sector. Industrial development took long strides under Ayub, and even today, the development achieved in his era remains the mainstay of Pakistan's economy. Being conservative by nature, Ayub did not see the need for spreading wealth socially as much as regionally. Ultimately, because the distribution of wealth was not equitable socially, it proved to be unbalanced regionally. After he had resigned, Ayub told foreign journalists that there was a lack of managerial capacity in East Pakistan, which caused wastage of investment.[1] This may have been partially true then, but amidst the production of wealth, labour law was weighted heavily in favour of the capitalists. The chief economist of the Planning Commission, Dr Mahbub ul Haq, revealed that the wealth of the nation was held by only twenty-two families. Another aspect was that the free import of capital goods gave an impetus to the consumer goods industry while retarding the development of heavy industries. In trade, a scheme of Bonus Vouchers (which could be purchased in the open market) was launched, which would subsidize imports. Despite the boom of the 1960s, the import of some articles, especially books, was severely curtailed.

In the agriculture sector, the labour force was not properly organized, and Ayub's reforms were less effective than in industry. A Green Revolution was achieved using mechanized farming, chemical fertilizers, and the sinking of tube wells. The signing of the Indus Water Treaty with India in 1960, and the construction of the Warsak and Mangla dams increased the extent of irrigation. Water logging and salinity were tackled on a war footing. However, because of social constraints, most of the benefits were appropriated by the landlords and did not trickle down to the peasants.

On the diplomatic front, because of the arms imbalance, Ayub Khan told the American Congress that Pakistan was a country where US troops could land at any time. He withstood bravely the U2 crisis in 1960 when a US spy plane took off from Badaber base in Pakistan and was shot down over USSR territory. The US arming of India in the wake of the 1962 Sino–Indian War came as a rude awakening. Friendship with China grew, and President Ayub became the first Pakistan head of government to visit the USSR in 1964. To offset Western anger over Pakistan's wooing the Communist giants, a Regional Cooperation for Development (RCD)—was signed with Iran and Turkey, who were already pro-US CENTO allies. These were the conditions when the first presidential elections under the new 1962 constitution were announced.

Ayub Khan had a distinct advantage over the opposition: the only politician of consequence, H.S. Suhrawardy had died in 1963. Lt.-Gen. Azam Khan, a rival from within the military establishment, spoke out before the elections were scheduled and was countered tactically. The weakness of the disparate combination of the opposition was exposed when Fatima Jinnah, was chosen as the presidential candidate of the Combined Opposition Parties (COP). Despite social disparities, stability had brought progress to Pakistan. The urge for democracy brought forth impressive rhetoric, but except in the politically charged cities of Karachi, Dhaka and Chittagong, Ayub won with a majority of 64 per cent. Had the 1965 war not intervened, political stability would have brought greater economic gains to Pakistan.

The 1965 war was preceded by the Rann of Kutch conflict, an area where the borders had not been demarcated at Independence. The Pakistan Army gave a good account of itself but yielded to British advice to submit the dispute to arbitration.

THE 1965 WAR—Causes. Indian Prime Minister Jawaharlal Nehru went back on his repeated public promises of a UN supervised plebiscite in Jammu and Kashmir on the ground that Pakistan had become a military ally of the United States. Resentment had been simmering in Kashmir when Jawaharlal Nehru arrested Sheikh Abdullah who he had himself appointed the prime minister of the disputed territory. Then the Hazratbal incident took place in which a relic—a hair believed to be that of the Holy Prophet disappeared from the shrine causing demonstrations. Then came the Rann of Kutch war. The upshot was that Indian troops crossed the Cease-Fire Line and occupied Kargil.

Fearing that unless Pakistan reacted now, its case on Kashmir would be lost by default. The UN had forced India to vacate Kargil, on 15 June 1965 but the step was so limited that Pakistan felt that if it again appealed to the UN, it would again be frustrated by the Russian veto. If it simply sat back and let the ceasefire line become the international border (as some Pakistanis are now proposing) then constitutionally it would mean surrendering claims also to Azad Kashmir.

These were the circumstances, Pakistan had to break the deadlock by sending infiltrators to Kashmir, which was not a novel step. President John F. Kennedy had recently sent infiltrators into Cuba. The leaders of Britain, Sri Lanka, Indonesia, even far-off Brazil, and the majority of the world said that India was the aggressor when it crossed the international frontier on 6 September 1965

Unfortunately, some very prominent Pakistani leaders have attributed the outbreak of war to a miscalculation made by Pakistan. Air Marshal Asghar Khan said that the Foreign Office had assured President Ayub that if the operation was confined to Kashmir, India would not cross the international frontier at Punjab.[2] This in spite of the fact that the Indian Prime Minister Lal Bahadur Shastri had publicly proclaimed that India would retaliate at a place of her choosing.

Altaf Gauhar, in his Foreword to Air Marshal Asghar Khan's book *The First Round*, made this accusation naming Aziz Ahmed as the person who had given such an advice to President Ayub Khan,[3] but Aziz Ahmed the war time Foreign Secretary lost no time in refuting this accusation, 'I never made any such statement, nor, to my knowledge, did any other functionary of the Foreign Office. What I had actually said was naturally qualified and invariably coupled with a note of caution that we must be prepared.'[4]

Contrarily, it was in India that the Foreign Minister, Sardar Swaran Singh and Chief of Army Staff General J.N. Chaudhuri initially had reservations over crossing the international border.[5]

The only rational explanation for the Pakistani initiative is that it was prompted by the Chinese leadership and was based on Chinese intervention. In early 1965, the Chinese premier Zhou Enlai said to Ayub that a just settlement of the Kashmir dispute required sacrifices. On 4 September 1965, the Chinese Foreign Minister Chen Yi was told of the Pakistani sacrifices.[6] One Pakistani informant, Shamsuddin, told Keith James of the British high commission that the suggestion that regular troops be disguised as Kashmiri freedom fighters was a Chinese one.[7]

The Indian response to these moves was to take Kargil on 15 August 1965. This did not cause an international outrage as did the Pakistani occupation of Kargil in 1999. Both the 1965 and 1999 actions were for the same reason, to cut Srinagar–Leh communications. Kargil was returned after the Tashkent Declaration and remained on the Pakistan side till the 1971 war. The fall of Kargil to India created a situation where surrender would lead inexorably to the ultimate liquidation of Pakistan or else Pakistan would have to disregard the arms imbalance, which could only grow worse with time, and defend itself.

Events. On 6 September 1965, the Indian forces crossed the international border and tried to capture the two cities of Lahore and Sialkot. The capture of these cities was calculated to break Pakistan's resistance. The assault on Lahore was halted with the help of the BRB canal. The defenders fought recklessly. A great battle was fought at Chawinda which Pakistan won. Pakistan had initially made headway in the Khem Karan sector, but beyond that line, the Indians flooded the area so that Pakistani tanks were bogged down. In Kashmir, the Pakistan advance was hampered by a midway change of command. Lt.-Gen. Akhtar Malik was replaced by Lt.-Gen. Yahya Khan. A spectacular aspect of the war was the superiority displayed by the Pakistan Air Force. The Pakistan Navy, though ill-equipped, took the Indian port of Dwarka. Pakistan performed well considering all the odds.

Results. The 1965 war is one of the most curious wars in history. Initially, both sides claimed victory, and subsequently, both sides admitted defeat. By 1990, Admiral Jayant Ganpat Nadkarni of India and General Mirza Aslam Beg of Pakistan had stated that their respective countries had fared badly in the war. India was unable to take Lahore and Pakistan was unable to take Kashmir. After seventeen days of war, first India, and then Pakistan accepted a ceasefire.

THE ROLE OF FOREIGN POWERS. — All Third World countries with the solitary exception of Malaysia sided with Pakistan. Indonesia supplied a submarine and there were demonstrations favouring Pakistan in Iran and Turkey. Even Brazil showed solidarity with Pakistan. The British Prime Minister, Harold Wilson, stated that India's crossing of the international border was an act of aggression. Thereafter, all his efforts were centred on Pakistan accepting a ceasefire without securing a political settlement of

The First Military Regime (1958–1969)

Kashmir; above all, Britain was most anxious that Pakistan should eschew Chinese intervention. The British High Commissioner, Sir Morrice James, assured President Ayub that 'the world would not, repeat, not in the foreseeable future revert to the position that the future of Kashmir was a closed issue'.[8] In other words, James was cajoling Ayub into accepting a ceasefire without political progress in Kashmir. In his memoirs, he justly claimed that he had played a vital role in persuading Ayub to accept the ceasefire[9] without accepting Chinese help.

US President Lyndon B. Johnson's initial reaction was to halt arms supply to both India and Pakistan, though fully conscious that India had an alternative source of supply from Russia, while Pakistan had none. The US had replied to Pakistan's invocation of the 1959 Mutual Defence Treaty with the charge that Pakistan had sent infiltrators on 5 August 1965. In the face of the Chinese factor, the US state office displayed a more measured response. US Secretary of State Dean Rusk told the Indian envoy on 18 September that in case of Chinese intervention, the US would need Congressional sanction to commit its troops, an outcome Rusk said was unlikely.[10] US Under Secretary George Ball and Assistant Secretary William Bundy said, on 23 September, that the Chinese movement would give the US greater leverage over India.[11] Amid the US recrimination was embedded Dean Rusk's statement upholding the principle of the plebiscite.[12]

The Chinese role, as stated above, began before the hostilities broke out. The Chinese foreign minister was in Pakistan on 4 September. On 7 September, China declared that India's invasion of Pakistan was an act of naked aggression. On 8 September it sent warnings against Indian intrusions into Chinese territory. On 16 September, China issued an ultimatum that unless India dismantled its military posts in Chinese territory, stopped intrusions and undertook to refrain from hostile acts across the border, it would take appropriate action. On 19 September, the Chinese extended their ultimatum by three days and at the end of the period announced that India had complied with their demands.

It is obvious that the first Chinese ultimatum was to give Pakistan time to decide its course and the announcement of Indian compliance signalled that Pakistan had finally decided against taking advantage of this ultimatum. The Chinese condition for helping Pakistan was that Pakistan remain steadfast and not succumb to pressure,[13] but being conservative by temperament and training, Ayub was forced to give in to British blandishments, and threw away an opportunity. The American assessment was clear in analysing the chances of winning by the combatants. While they calculated that Pakistani ammunition (which the US had supplied) would run out before Indian ammunition did, the US also reckoned that if Pakistan won a major battle in the Punjab, it could win the war. Another power to play a major role was the USSR. Its role could be best understood in the context of the Tashkent peace talks of 10 January 1966, which were called by the USSR.

TASHKENT DECLARATION PROVISIONS. — The Tashkent Declaration was finally signed on 10 January 1966. It provided for (a) the reaffirmation by both sides of their obligation under the United Nations Charter, to settle disputes by peaceful means; (b) the withdrawal of all armed personnel by 25 February 1966 to positions held prior to 5 August 1965; (c) discontinuance of hostile propaganda; (d) restoration of full diplomatic representation; (e) machinery to continue joint India/Pakistan discussions on other issues of direct concern.

The only mention of the cause of the conflict was as follows: 'It was against this background that Jammu and Kashmir was discussed, and each of the sides set forth its respective positions.'

This was a disappointing outcome, and though the Soviet Union had been protective of India's occupation, Kosygin realised that the solution he had imposed did not have portents for peace. After the Tashkent Declaration was signed Kosygin asked Shastri to solve the Kashmir problem. Shastri offered minor adjustments along the ceasefire line, which Pakistan rejected.

REACTIONS. — The Indian reaction to the Tashkent Declaration was naturally favourable. The death of Lal Bahadur Shastri in Tashkent sanctified the Declaration. In Pakistan, anti-Tashkent demonstrations were set off by a war widow who appeared at the Punjab University campus with her fatherless infants. These demonstrations swelled into a widespread movement. On 10 June 1966, Foreign Minister Z.A. Bhutto advocated overstepping the Tashkent Declaration to obtain a solution to the Kashmir problem.[14] Eventually he came to lead the movement. The killing by police gunfire of a student, Abdul Hamid, on 7 November 1966 accelerated the movement. The arrest of Z.A. Bhutto on 13 November 1968 only served to inflame the masses, and the movement was sustained for three years, leading ultimately to Ayub's resignation on 25 March 1969.

Another factor which led to disenchantment with Ayub was the prominence given by the government-controlled press to his son, Captain Gohar Ayub. This bred the suspicion that he was being groomed for succession. Gohar Ayub's unpopularity was due to a January 1965 victory procession he had led in Karachi that had turned violent. There were wild rumours that Gohar Ayub was buying up every profitable enterprise. This rebounded on a president who had been elected to put an end to corruption. In 1967, Ayub published his political autobiography *Friends Not Masters*[15] which took away the mystique of his reforms and caused the 'Decade of Development' which could have justly been celebrated, to become an occasion for derision.

In East Pakistan, the cause of disaffection was not Tashkent which most opposition leaders had hailed. During a Lahore meeting in 1966, of opposition leaders, the Awami League President Sheikh Mujibur Rahman (1920–1975), presented his Six Point programme: a confederal formula for East and West

Pakistan. Agitation for this programme, further inflamed by the Agartala Conspiracy trial, led to violent demonstrations, entailing what was called *Gherao Jalao* (Besiege and Burn) operations. If Ayub had resigned on 21 February 1969 instead of just saying that he would not again run for president, the momentum towards disintegration could have been contained. He resigned on 25 March 1969 when anti-government demonstrations became anti-state demonstrations. People calling for regime change began calling for secession. Thus, while Ayub's removal was inevitable and of course popular, it was mistimed, because it created uncertainty.

Notes

1. *Morning News*, Karachi, 2 April 1972, p. 4.
2. Anwar H. Syed, *China and Pakistan: Diplomacy of an Entente Cordiale* (Amherst; The University of Massachusetts, Press, 1974) p. 117.
3. *Dawn*, 4 May 2001, p. 6.
4. Air Marshal (retired) M. Asghar Khan, *The First Round, Indo-Pakistan War 1965* (London: Islamic Information Services, 1979). Altaf Gauhar's Foreword, pp. iii–xviii.
5. Aziz Ahmed, 'The First Round-A Rejoinder', *Dawn*, 22 June 1979, pp. 7 and 17.
6. Durga Das, *India from Curzon to Nehru and After* (London: Collins, 1969), p. 394.
7. Roedad Khan (ed.), *The British Papers* (Karachi: OUP, 2002), p. 422.
8. Ibid., p. 388.
9. Sir Morrice James, *Pakistan Chronicle* (Karachi: OUP, 1993), p. 153.
10. *The British Papers*, p. 372.
11. Ibid., pp. 375, 410.
12. Ibid., p. 384.
13. Khan, *The First Round*, p. 22.
14. *The British Papers*, p. 573.
15. Mohammad Ayub Khan, *Friends Not Masters* (Karachi: Oxford University Press, 1967).

THE TASHKENT DECLARATION.—President Ayub led the Pakistani delegation, Prime Minister Lal Bahadur Shastri, the Indian delegation and Alexei N. Kosygin, Chairman, Council of Ministers, the USSR delegation. Tashkent is the capital of Uzbekistan, then in the USSR. The talks lasted from 4 to 10 January 1966. India had opposed the drawing up of an agenda.

The outcome of the 1965 war was that Pakistan spurned the offer of help from China which had consistently supported it and accepted the good offices of the USSR which had consistently opposed it. The statements of US Secretary of State Dean Rusk and his deputies show that Chinese intervention would have given more time to Pakistan, thus demoralizing India before the US counter-intervention took place. Even in the British estimation 'India had come off best on the ground but had no great victory to announce'.[1] To create an air of neutrality, the USSR Prime Minister, Alexei Kosygin, remarked that Kashmir was a disputed area.[2]

This explains why Prime Minister Lal Bahadur Shastri was apprehensive and sought Anglo–American clearance before accepting the USSR invitation to talks in Tashkent.[3] President Ayub was, on the other hand, aggressively defiant, terming the Russian offer a propaganda stunt. He openly said that if he and Shastri met face to face, they would merely restate their cases and depart without reaching an agreement. Ayub favoured arbitration under UN Security Council as has been the case with the Rann of Kutch engagement.[4] Thus, Ayub went to Tashkent against his better judgement and, had the US not put its weight behind the Soviet initiative, Ayub would not have attended the peace talks. As we now know, he would have been able to prevent his fall.

It was Pakistan that had imposed conditions for accepting a ceasefire on 11 September 1965. Foreign Minister Bhutto told Sir Morrice James that the UNSC resolution of 4 and 6 September favoured India by asking for a return to the 5 August position without providing for a Kashmir settlement.[5] The British stated that the problem could be approached in four stages: (i) Both sides stop fighting (ii) both sides agree to return to the status quo (iii) measures be taken to neutralize and quieten the situation within Kashmir and (iv) future settlement of the whole problem of Kashmir.

Britain approached the problem it had created, gingerly. The first two stages would be unacceptable to Pakistan unless followed by the last two.[6] This was the objective Pakistan pursued at Tashkent and this was the objective that eluded it.

The Indian objective was to secure a No-War Pact from Pakistan so that the Kashmir dispute was permanently put into cold storage. At one point in the negotiations, Shastri prevailed on Ayub to inscribe in his own hand on the typed draft, a renunciation of force. Z.A. Bhutto had the undertaking cancelled. Kuldip Nayar, an Indian journalist who retained Ayub's inscription, surmises that this was the secret clause in the Tashkent agreement to which Z.A. Bhutto later referred.[7]

The only pressure the USSR exercised over India was to return the Kargil area, and it is on this point that Ayub was forthright. Otherwise, the pressure was on Pakistan, as Kosygin stated that if no accord was signed, the world would get the impression that disputes could be settled only by force. According to another version, Kosygin stated that he would not allow the meeting to be unproductive. Kosygin also dismissed a proposal for independent Kashmir, citing the ethnic diversity of the state.[8]

It was India that was dependent on the USSR for arms and money, not Pakistan. Therefore, it was held anomalous that Pakistan, and not India, yielded to Soviet pressure. Meanwhile, China issued another ultimatum to India on 6 January while negotiations were in progress.

Notes

1. Roedad Khan, (ed.), *The British Papers* (Karachi: Oxford University Press, 2002), p. 410.
2. Mahboob A. Popatia, *Pakistan's Relations with the Soviet Union* (Karachi: Pakistan Study Centre, University of Karachi, 1988), p. 95.
3. Roedad Khan, (ed.), *The British Papers*, p. 395.
4. Ibid., p. 408.
5. Ibid., p. 326.
6. Ibid., p. 321.
7. Kuldip Nayar, *India: The Critical Years* (New Delhi: Vikas, 1971), p. 245. In his later publication *Distant Neighbours* (New Delhi: Vikas, 1972), p. 136, Kuldip Nayar reproduced Ayub's handwritten concession.
8. Iqbal Akhund, *Memoirs of a Bystander* (Karachi: Oxford University Press, 1997), p. 118.

FIELD MARSHAL MOHAMMAD AYUB KHAN (b. Rehana, 1907–d. Islamabad, 1974) had a dominating presence, but a vulnerable personality. He was educated at Aligarh and Sandhurst. As president, he brought stability, and in its wake unequalled economic prosperity. Ayub's prescription for prosperity however proved to be too conservative, giving rise to a backlash from which Pakistan has never recovered. Ayub was the first military ruler of Pakistan, and while the novelty lasted, he was more popular than the ephemeral prime ministers he replaced. His was the only military regime which brought about a respite from corruption to a degree that surprised even him. 'Take the example of how readily people declared their untaxed hidden wealth—they declared Rs. 1,700 million. I asked a businessman "Why did you do it?" He said, "In one of your photographs, I saw you with your finger pointed like this, and your mouth screwed up like this." I said to myself, "This man will not leave us alone".'[1] Even more revealing is his analysis of the prospects of a military coup d'état in India: 'The fools don't realize that even if he [General Kondar Maddapa Cariappa, 1899–1993] was inclined that way, he being a retired man, has no power or influence to do such a thing. I told him that even if circumstances warranted, take over of seventeen provincial governments and a central government was not a feasible proposition. However what is possible is that someone like Yashwant Balwant Rao Chavan may take over with the backing of the army.'[2] In other words, the necessary ingredients were either a military personality capable of overshadowing politicians, or conversely, a political personality capable of dominating the military, and a compact administrative apparatus, simple to take over. In connection with capitals, Ayub's critical faculty went on and off. He objected that Lahore as the capital of the west wing was too close to the border.[3] This idea did not cross his mind while determining the location of Islamabad.

It is apparent that in his later years, his protégé Zulfikar Ali Bhutto became quite an obsession with him, and Altaf Gauhar explains why. In Tashkent, 'When Ayub was relating how Shastri kept saying that he was answerable to the people, Bhutto interrupted quite sharply, "But you too are answerable to the people".'[4]

Even in his diary, his reason for Bhutto's removal appears as an afterthought: 'His real trouble was that he started running a personal policy assisted by a few elements in the foreign office, instead of the national, also, he was distrusted and disliked in most capitals.'[5]

What Ayub considered 'national' policy was telling the Chinese Ambassador, just one year after the 1965 war, that the Chinese government's treatment of Muslims would have repercussions in Sinkiang, Central Asia, and Pakistan![6] The following April 1987, he criticized the past action of Bhutto and Aziz Ahmad for bending over backwards to establish close relations with Nepal, and even Sikkim and Bhutan.[7]

During the 1971 crisis, he received information—which he believed Bhutto shared—that many PPP men had sworn allegiance to Mujibur Rahman. He conceded that Bhutto's stand was logical given Mujibur Rahman's uncompromising attitude, but his object was difficult, as indeed it was.

Ayub was innately a gentleman—very patriotic—but his days at Sandhurst had rendered him incapable of taking the plunge at crucial times. In this trait, he was not followed by his son, Gohar Ayub (d. 2023), who proved to be an intrepid Foreign Minister.

Notes

1. Mohammad Ayub Khan, *Friends not Masters* (Karachi: Oxford University Press, 1971), p. 76.
2. Craig Baxter (ed.), *The Diaries of Field Marshal Mohammed Ayub Khan* (Karachi: Oxford University Press, 2007), p. 165.
3. Ibid., p. 91.
4. Altaf Gauhar, *Ayub Khan, Pakistan's First Military Ruler* (Karachi, Oxford University Press, 1996), p. 262.
5. Baxter, op. cit., p. 3
6. Ibid., p. 10.
7. Ibid., p. 84.
8. Ibid., p. 452.

CHAPTER 28

THE SECOND MILITARY REGIME (1969–1971)

On 25 March 1969, Field Marshal Mohammad Ayub Khan (1908–1974) imposed martial law, abrogated the 1962 Constitution, and transferred the offices of chief martial law administrator and president to Gen. Yahya Khan (1917–1980). He temporarily banned all political activity, vowing to lead the country back to sanity, as the demonstrations against Ayub Khan had assumed violent proportions. The 1962 Constitution had provided for the transfer of power to the speaker of the National Assembly, Abdul Jabbar Khan, a Bengali leader who had not spared even his son Rashid Khan Menon for his revolutionary activities. Constitutionally and personally, Abdul Jabbar Khan had a better chance than anyone else to address the tide of Bengali nationalism, but he was never given the chance.

General Yahya Khan asserted that he had neither staged a coup d'état nor was he the elected representative of the people. He was instead, a soldier on 'deputed duty'. Later, with the encouragement of political parties, he took two decisions in advance of the constitution-making process. On 28 November 1969, he announced the dissolution of One Unit; the restoration of the three West Pakistan provinces and the creation of Balochistan. He also announced that parity between the two wings was being revoked. This had meant an equal number of seats in the National Assembly for both wings. Yahya Khan affirmed the principle of one man, one vote which meant that East Pakistan would have a majority in the next assembly. The Legal Framework Order (LFO) had made a simple majority sufficient for framing the constitution.

The LFO was promulgated on 30 March 1970. This prescribed the limits in which elections would be held and within which the constitution was to be framed. The LFO provided that: 'Pakistan shall be a Federal Republic to be known as the Islamic Republic of Pakistan in which the Provinces and other territories which are now and may hereafter be included in Pakistan shall be so united in a Federation that the independence, the territorial integrity and the national solidarity of Pakistan are ensured and that the unity of the Federation is not in any way involved. (para 20).' In addition, the LFO provided that the constitution was to be framed within 120 days, failing which the National Assembly would be dissolved.

Shorn of constitutional terms, federating unit meant West Pakistan on one hand, and East Pakistan on the other. After the break up of One Unit, the term federating unit would apply equally to Sindh, Punjab, NWFP and Balochistan. All provinces, according to the Six Points would have separate currencies, separate foreign currency accounts and separate militias. The politicians immediately understood that the LFO and the Six Points were not compatible. Sheikh Mujibur Rahman, the Awami League president said, on 2 May 1970 at Hatiya, that the Constituent Assembly should be made sovereign. He pointed out that 'the coming elections were not for achieving power, but to frame the country's constitution…' He regretted that certain provisions in the LFO had negated the principles of democracy.[1] On 3 May Awami League leader Tajuddin said that the Six Points were a must.[2] On 8 May 1970 Sheikh Mujibur Rahman reiterated that there was no possibility of compromise on the Six Points.[3] Thus we see that the incompatibility between the LFO and Six Points was glaringly apparent even before the 7 December 1970 general elections. On 14 August 1970 Independence Day, students of Dhaka University, in a meeting presided over by the Vice-Chancellor Abu Saeed Choudhry displayed a new map and flag of Bangladesh.[4] Former professor and chair of Political Science at Dhaka University and a member of Yahya's cabinet G.W. Choudhry later commented that Mujib's scheme of a centre with only two responsibilities, defence and foreign affairs, was devoid of financial or administrative means to carry out its obligations.[5]

Mujibur Rahman had stressed that the elections were for framing a constitution and not for achieving power. There would be no provision under constitutional law to limit the Six Points to only one province. The Awami League insisted that the constitution be framed only by the simple majority it enjoyed and vehemently rejected the suggestion that the constitution be passed by a 61 per cent majority. This figure was proposed as a compromise since it is a universal convention to frame or amend a constitution by a two-thirds majority. The importance of the Six Points became clear after the Awami League won the 1970 elections.

THE SIX POINT PROGRAMME

1. The character of the government shall be federal and parliamentary in which the election shall be direct and on the basis of universal adult franchise; the representation in the federal legislature shall be on the basis of population.
2. The federal government shall be responsible only for defence and foreign affairs and, subject to conditions provided in (3), below, currency.
3. There shall be two separate currencies mutually freely convertible in each wing for each region, or in the alternative, a single currency with regional federal reserve banks to prevent the transfer of resources and flight of capital from one region to another.
4. Fiscal policy shall be the responsibility of the federating units (provinces). The federal government shall be provided with requisite revenue resources for meeting the requirements of defence and foreign affairs.
5. Constitutional provisions shall be made to enable separate accounts to be maintained of the foreign exchange of each of the federating units, under the control of the respective governments.
6. The government of the federating units shall be empowered to maintain a militia or para-military force in order to contribute effectively towards national security.

THE ELECTIONS OF 7 DECEMBER 1970.—These were the first-ever general elections to be held on the basis of direct and universal adult franchise throughout Pakistan. The framing of the constitution had been an elusive exercise, therefore the enthusiasm of the voters to secure a lasting constitution for Pakistan was unprecedented. It was generally recognized that the conduct of elections had been free and fair. For this, Yahya Khan was rightly praised. In East Pakistan, the Awami League won 167 out of 169 seats. Out of the 144 seats allotted to the west wing, the PPP, led by Zulfikar Ali Bhutto won 81 seats initially. After independent members joined the PPP, its representation grew to 88. The Awami League had not won a single seat outside East Pakistan, and since One Unit had been done away with, the PPP, on the same basis of regional representation, represented only the Punjab and Sindh; as in Balochistan and NWFP the National Awami Party, led by Khan Abdul Wali Khan (d.2006), had the majority representation. Thus three parties represented three regions: East Bengal, Sindh and Punjab, and Balochistan and NWFP. The party caught in the middle, the PPP set off the constitutional crisis.

The Awami League leader Sheikh Mujibur Rahman was also making disquieting observations but was neither loud nor categorical. He told Ardeshir Zahedi and Ihsan Sabri Cagliyangil, the foreign ministers of Iran and Turkey, that 'he would rather be the father of a new nation than the Prime Minister of Pakistan.'[6] On 14 January 1971, Yahya Khan declared that Sheikh Mujibur Rahman was the next prime minister of Pakistan. On 17 January, Yahya went to Larkana to confer with Z.A. Bhutto. This created a bad impression since Yahya had not visited Mujibur Rahman at his house, but called him to the Governor's House, Dhaka. According to Bhutto, he expressed to Yahya, his misgivings about the Six Points.[7] Bhutto, thereafter, went to Dhaka to confer with Mujibur Rahman about the Six Point formula from 27 to 30 February 1971. These talks proved inconclusive, and, on his return, Bhutto asked Yahya to delay convening the Constituent Assembly.

THE CONSTITUTIONAL CRISIS.—Yahya did not accede to Bhutto's request and fixed 3 March 1971 as the date when the Constituent Assembly would be convened at Dhaka. At this, Z.A. Bhutto set off the constitutional crisis by stating, on 15 February 1971 in Peshawar, that he would not attend the Constituent Assembly on 3 March. In Bhutto's own words, 'unless assured that our point of view would be heard, and if found reasonable, accepted by the Awami League',[8] he would not attend. On 28 February in Lahore, Bhutto said he was willing to go to Dhaka if the pre-condition of framing the constitution within 120 days was lifted. Bhutto's position was equivocal; he had denied at Peshawar that he was boycotting the session, but this was only a play of words because his refusal to attend, and, moreover, his refusal to let his party members attend was, in effect, a boycott.

In East Pakistan, Mujibur Rahman told the *New York Times* on 4 March 1971, that each wing should have its own prime minister. As M. Rafique Afzal aptly says: 'No one took notice of this extreme statement, but ten days later, a similar statement by Bhutto evoked an uproar'.[9] Whatever the objective situation, Bhutto's ambition is a factor which nobody is willing to discount. Whether Bhutto was justified in depicting the Six Points as secessionist can be judged by tracing the history of Bengali nationalism.

THE COURSE OF ETHNIC VIOLENCE.—On 25 March 1971, General Tikka Khan (1917–2002) ordered military action which was indiscriminate and reprehensible but not unprovoked. The violence was initiated by Bengali militants and not by the Pakistan Army. In fact, there were two broad phases of violence, a limited phase dating from 1954 and a second phase beginning in 1966. The first ethnic riot took place on 23 March 1954 at Chandraghona Paper Mills (near Chittagong), and the second took place in the Adamjee Jute Mills at Narayanganj (near Dhaka) on 15 May 1954. The majority of victims were non-Bengalis, lumped together under the name of *Biharis* as most of them had sought refuge from anti-Muslim riots in Bihar.

The next round of ethnic riots took place in Chittagong early in May 1966, when a Khoja family refused to allow their daughter to marry a Bengali boy, (for sectarian rather than ethnic reasons).[10] Following Yahya's martial law, on 7 August 1969, there were attacks on non-Bengali localities in Dhaka,[11] and another attack on 1 November 1969.

On 1 March 1971, when General Yahya Khan announced that the Constituent Assembly session scheduled for 3 March was being postponed, Mujib held a press conference and called for a strike and civil disobedience. This was the signal for widespread genocide against the non-Bengalis. This was a pogrom during which around 30,000 non-Bengalis, men, women and children, were killed.[12]

HISTORY OF BENGALI NATIONALISM

Following are excerpts from different books and journals that trace the various stages of Bengali nationalism:

1. Since the dawn of history, Bengal had been a problem, demanding political independence against imperial domination whether Hindu or Muslim since the age of Harsha down to the age of Akbar.[1]
2. Ethnic animosity between Bengalis and Biharis, especially, Hindu Bengalis and Hindu Biharis surfaced before Partition. The Congress Working Committee formed a sub-committee to deal with this problem. It finally adopted Dr Rajendra Prasad's proposal of doing away with ethnic distinction, by abolishing the provision of Domicile Certificates.[2]

3. Netaji Subhash Chandra Bose was forced by Gandhi to resign as Congress President in 1939. To show his solidarity with the great Bengali leader, the great Bengali poet Rabindranath Tagore hosted a reception in honour of Bose and delivered the welcome address.[3]
4. In 1947, H.S. Suhrawardy, then chief minister, and Kiran Shankar Roy, then leader of the opposition in the Bengal Legislative Assembly, presented a scheme for a United and Independent Bengal. Jinnah,[4] Liaquat Ali Khan, Sarat Chandra Bose and even Gandhi agreed, but the Congress President, Jawaharlal Nehru refused, saying that 'there was no chance of Hindus there agreeing to put themselves under permanent Muslim domination.[5]

This led to Nehru endorsing the Two-Nation Theory, which he had otherwise detested and ridiculed. It was wrong for Hindus to be permanently subjugated in Muslim-majority Bengal, but it was acceptable for Muslims to be permanently subjugated in Hindu-majority India. Nehru had realised that if a single province, Bengal, was allowed independence, other provinces would make the same demand, and the Princely states would be encouraged to retain their freedom.[6]

In 1947, Nehru blocked the independence of Bengal to preserve the integrity of India. In 1971, Yahya blocked the independence of Bangladesh to preserve the integrity of Pakistan. Three out of five provinces, East Bengal, NWFP and Balochistan had voted for pro-USSR parties (Awami League in the post-Suhrawardy era and NAP). While Jinnah could agree to an independent Bengal, there was no constitutional device by which he could refuse the accession of East Bengal to Pakistan.

Notes

1. Kalikaranjan Qanungo, *Sher Shah and His Times* (Calcutta: Orient Longman, 1965), p. 303.
2. *Star of India*, Calcutta, 16 January 1939, p. 6.
3. Stanley Wolpert, *Gandhi's Passion* (New York: Oxford University Press, 2001), p. 188. Shakeel Ahmad Zia, *Sindh Ka Muqaddama* (Sindh's Case), Karachi, April 1987, p. 25.
4. H.V. Hodson, *The Great Divide* (Karachi: Oxford University Press, 1989), p. 246.
5. Nicholas Mansergh et. al (eds.) The Transfer of Power, London, HMSO 1981, vol. x, 1013.
6. Sailesh Kumar Bandyopadhyay, *Quaid-i-Azam Mohammad Ali Jinnah and the Creation of Pakistan* (New Delhi: Sterling, 1991), p. 323.

A British technician who crossed the border on 6 April 1971 reported the massacre in Dinajpur. 'After the soldiers had left, the mobs set upon the non-Bengali Muslims from Bihar. I don't know how many died, but I could hear the screams throughout the night'. The European manager of a Chittagong bank said, 'It was fortunate for every European living here that the Army arrived when it did; otherwise, I would not have lived to tell the tale'. Most of the non-Bengalis were killed before 25 March.[13]

All these atrocities are well-documented. The effect of the violence was to shape the outcome of the three-sided negotiations being carried out between Yahya Khan, Mujibur Rahman and Zulfikar Ali Bhutto.

The negotiations began on 22 March 1971. Tajuddin conveyed the Awami League decision that it would not allow any central or national cabinet and demanded that power be transferred to the two wings directly.[14] This meant that the Awami League, which had already called for martial law to be lifted, wanted not a transfer but an abdication of power. The next day—Republic Day—Kamal Husain submitted the final proposal of the Awami League to Yahya Khan.[15] According to G.W. Choudhry, who personally saw the draft, the Awami League set forth the procedure for framing two constitutions by two sovereign constitutional conventions. 'In fact, the Mujib plan was nothing but an unqualified scheme for splitting the country into two separate entities, Bangladesh and Pakistan.'[16] Although G.W. Choudhry is critical of Z.A. Bhutto throughout, his analysis of the Six Points is the same as Bhutto's.

Thus the crisis had nothing to do with transferring power to the majority party. It was a constitutional crisis. As Bhutto had explained, the Six Point programme was a confederal not federal scheme. In a confederal set up, the majority party of one unit cannot become the majority party of another federating unit,[17] for example, both Britain and Australia are members of the Commonwealth, and both have Queen Elizabeth II as their head of state, but the majority party of Britain cannot form a government in Australia. If the Awami League wished for power at the centre, it would have had to compromise on the Six Points. Mujibur Rahman could not become the prime minister and yet retain a Six Point mandate.

Bhutto became the main adversary for pointing this out. The slogan chanted by the Awami League protesters was *'Bhuttor Mukkhe Lati Maro'* (Kick Bhutto's face). It is clear from the conclusion reached by all political analysts that the Six Point programme was a scheme of secession. Why did Mujibur Rahman not make a direct declaration of independence? G.W. Choudhry's explanation is that Mujibur Rahman wished to employ a weak confederal link to extract financial benefits. He writes: 'While the Central Government was denied any financial powers or resources as far as Bangladesh was concerned, it might be liable to pay dues to the Bangladesh Government on the basis of the 1970–71 budget'.[18] This marked the end of the talks and was the signal for action by the Pakistan Army on 25 March 1971.

PAKISTAN ARMY ATROCITIES.—G.W. Choudhry, a Professor of Political Science, was present during the crisis and was able to depict unerringly the events that unfolded. He concedes that armed rebellion had to be encountered, but condemns the action taken by the army and then asks: 'But could there be any justification or rationale for the killing of thousands of innocent villagers who had not the slightest idea of the issues involved?'[19] The atrocities cited in the Hamoodur Rahman Commission Report are sufficient to convey a sense of the trauma: 'There was a massacre in Comilla Cantonment on 27 March 1971, ordered by Lt.-Gen. Yaqub Malik. Seventeen officers, nine hundred and fifteen soldiers were killed. In Salda Nadi another five hundred persons were killed'. Brigadier Arbab also asked Lt.-Col. Aziz Ahmad Khan to destroy all houses in Joydebpur, who carried out the order to a great extent.

In May, Brigadier Abdullah Malik gave a written order to kill Hindus. Lt.-Gen. Gul Hassan used to ask the soldiers 'how many Bengalis have you killed?'[20]

The Hamoodur Rahman Commission stated that there was indiscriminate killings of Bengalis.[21] While it is to the credit of West Pakistanis that no Bengalis were killed in the west wing, it is a matter of grave discredit that the terrorists were allowed to escape and innocent people were killed.[22] When asked, about the army action, General Tikka Khan said, 'it was a complete distortion of history to believe as everyone in the world does, that we started everything. Mujib wanted a showdown'.[23]

As far as this statement goes, it is true. He complained about exaggeration by the Awami League. His own estimate of the number of Bengalis killed was 30,000! The Hamoodur Rahman Commission estimated 26,000 Bengalis were killed. The verdict of the Hamoodur Rahman Commission Report is that: 'No amount of provocation by the militants of the Awami League or other miscreants could justify retaliation by a disciplined army against its own people'.[24] It is in the background of this verdict, perhaps, that President Pervez Musharraf apologized on 29 July 2002, in Dhaka for the army action.

WEST PAKISTAN ARROGANCE.—Just as important as recounting the history of Bengali nationalism, is the need to analyse the mindset of West Pakistanis. The history of Bengali nationalism and the language issue encompasses policy, but not conduct, as all the portents of nationalism could have remained latent, possibly even contained, even after having emerged from the Calcutta and Noakhali communal riots. The arrogance of the ruling elite towards the Bengali population had a cumulative effect in creating alienation.

The language factor had led the Bihari refugees to side with the Urdu-speaking West Pakistan, but this was a purely sentimental attitude of a largely lower middle-class community. In practice, the Biharis were fluent in Bengali and only needed to learn the script. This involved effort since the scripts were so different and there were few facilities for on-the-job training.

The Bengali population was overwhelmingly responsive to rulers who showed sensitivity to their feelings. The popularity of Lt.-Gen. Azam Khan as governor of East Pakistan is irrefutable evidence that the population of East Pakistan was actively constructing Pakistan nationalism. It is in the governorship of Azam Khan that we find the factor that kept East Pakistan loyal to Pakistan. His term and style as governor should be studied in any analysis of the crisis. In spite of being a military governor and a Pathan, and ethnically poles apart from the Bengalis, he identified with the masses.

On the occasion of the state visit of Queen Elizabeth II, while the road connecting Dhaka airport to the city was under repair, Azam Khan shared food and drink from the earthenware vessels of the labourers, squatting with them during visits which were round-the-clock. Apart from labourers, he identified with fishermen and farmers. Even after braving the shock of his removal and a presidential election which was bitterly contested in 1965, the population of East Pakistan had solidly supported the 1965 war. It was apparent, but not expressed then, that there was not a single anti-aircraft gun in the whole of East Pakistan.

It was this spirit of patriotism that had to be broken before a secessionist plan could succeed. The Fourteen Points of 1954 had similarities to the Six Points of 1966. When, in 1954, the popular and newly-elected Chief Minister, A.K. Fazlul Haq, made a statement in Calcutta decrying the creation of Pakistan, there were widespread protests in the province and the largest protest was led by Maulana Abdul Hamid Khan Bhashani (1885–1976). The same man called for outright secession in 1970. It was only after the 1965 war that politicians waiting in the wings could bring secessionist feelings into the mainstream of Bengali politics.

It is now admitted that the east wing was treated as a colony. This is true only of the urban areas; the rural areas were treated worse than the colonies. It is also ridiculous to blame, as some authors do, Hindu teachers for spreading disaffection. By 1965 Hindu teachers were in a minority and did not feel as secure as their Muslim colleagues, who were the ones preaching secession. It is also true that the literary and cultural bias of the East Wing was different from that of the West Wing but this was not an insuperable problem. The killing of Dr Govind Chandra Dev, and Prof. Jyotirmoy Guhathakurta were tragedies.

CROSS-BORDER TERRORISM.—By 1970, the Bengali militant cadre had been organized. The Indian government took advantage of the ethnic unrest to train saboteurs. The Indian Prime Minister, Indira Gandhi, admitted in an interview with Oriana Fallaci that Indian help to the Mukti Bahini (Liberation Army) marked the beginning of the 1971 war; she openly admitted that India started the war.[25] The Indian general who trained and led the Mukti Bahini was Shahbeg Singh, who shaved his beard for the purpose.[26] In order to give ideological cover to cross-border terrorism, Indira Gandhi began to negate the sovereign status of Pakistan. She stated in London on 1 November 1971, that India and Pakistan were not equal, and that India would not accept such treatment.

In a further development, the USSR and India concurred that 'if Pakistan attacked India in retaliation against Indian assistance to the Mukti Bahini, it would be considered aggression. USSR regarded the Mukti Bahini as a liberation movement, and its support was just and defensible'.[27]

THE ROLE OF FOREIGN POWERS.—The concord between the USSR and India reflects on the role of foreign powers in the 1971 war. Paradoxically, Pakistan's relations with the USSR had improved considerably. On 15 June 1970, the USSR and Pakistan signed a pact for cultural and scientific cooperation.[28] Relations thereafter were deliberately worsened, to take advantage of the 25 March 1971 military crackdown. Only three days later, USSR Prime

Minister Alexei Kosygin expressed his concern about the situation in Pakistan and on 2 April, USSR President Nicolai Podgorny threatened Yahya Khan with dire consequences. Yahya called it a blatant interference in Pakistan's internal matters. The same day, the US State Department issued a statement that the Awami League insurgency was an internal matter. This would be the first and last time the US State Department would issue a statement openly supporting Pakistan. Both President Richard M. Nixon (1913-1994) and the National Security Advisor, Henry Kissinger (1923-2023), mention in their memoirs that the Secretary of State, William Rogers, was pro-India and obstructed the efforts of President Nixon.

In April, the Chinese prime minister told a Pakistani delegation that China would side with Pakistan, but would not be able to support military measures.[29] When Henry Kissinger made his clandestine trip to China on 11 July 1971, he said that the US would support Pakistan in the crisis but could not take military action.[30] Thus, though Pakistan won the diplomatic support of the US and China, it was unable to secure military guarantees for its integrity. At different times each country would encourage the other to intervene militarily on Pakistan's side, but this never materialized.

Henry Kissinger's secret trip to China and the announcement that President Nixon had accepted an invitation to visit China created quite a stir. Pakistan had suffered badly in the 1965 war and the Tashkent negotiations because of US and USSR collusion with the aim of containing China. With this change in world alliances, there was hope for Pakistan. This hope was not fulfilled. As a counterpoise to the thaw in US-China relations, India and the USSR signed a Treaty of Friendship and Cooperation on 9 August 1971, which included military collaboration.

Instead of showing solidarity with Pakistan or China, the US State Department chose to contradict the contention of Benjamin Oehlert Jr., a long-serving US Ambassador to Pakistan, that the US had obligations towards Pakistan.[31] By issuing this statement, the US State Department undermined the joint efforts of the US and China to support Pakistan. The US had not still formally recognized China, and the secret assurances of Henry Kissinger were not considered reliable enough by China to take a military initiative. Later, on 11 December, Z.A. Bhutto carried the intelligence that the Chinese were confused by the split in the US establishment.[32]

Thereafter, the pace of events increased. On 2 December 1971, President Yahya Khan invoked the 1959 Mutual Defence Treaty. On 3 December war began on the western front. On the same day, the Washington Special Action Group (WSAP) held a meeting in which President Nixon's wish to tilt towards Pakistan was raised. William Rogers continued to be obstructive but George Bush Sr. then US envoy to the UN, condemned India as the aggressor. The UNSC considered a resolution for a ceasefire and withdrawal of forces to their own countries, but the USSR vetoed it. On the following day, 6 December,

India formally recognized Bangladesh. On 7 December, the UN General Assembly called for a ceasefire and withdrawal from each other's territory. The 104 against 11 votes for the motion reflected international support for Pakistan. There is no veto in the UN General Assembly, but its resolutions are not binding.

The US State Department deplored Indian intervention the same day, but Henry Kissinger confided that when Maj.-Gen. Rao Farman Ali's offer of ceasefire was received at the UN, the State Department personnel were jubilant.[33] On 9 December, Nixon said he reprimanded the State Department. However, Nixon accepted the State Department's assessment that the independence of East Pakistan was both inevitable and desirable.[34] Nixon and Kissinger violently disagreed with another assessment of the US State Department. The State Department held that India had no designs on West Pakistan. India gave the US an undertaking that it would not invade West Pakistan but, much to the chagrin of India, Nixon insisted that this undertaking would have to include Azad Kashmir.

Henry Kissinger explained, first to Huang Hua and then to Bhutto, that the military conditions on the ground were deteriorating so fast that if efforts were directed at saving East Pakistan, Azad Kashmir and West Pakistan would meanwhile fall.[35] India could mount a single air attack with a hundred planes. Kissinger took the precaution of telling General A.N. Raza, the Pakistani ambassador, that Pakistan should insist that any ceasefire proposal should include a ceasefire in West Pakistan as well. On 9 December, *after* East Pakistan was a lost cause, President Nixon ordered the Seventh Fleet's USS *Enterprise* to move towards Bengal.[36] At about the same time the USSR moved its troops to the Chinese border. The USSR ambassador assured India that they would divert Chinese troops and would not allow the Seventh Fleet to intervene.[37] Another explanation of how the USSR prevailed over the US and China is provided by a Yale professor. In 1971 the USSR deployed nuclear submarines off the east coast of the USA, from where they could attack US targets in eight minutes.[38] In view of the lengths to which the USSR had gone to dismember Pakistan, it was no consolation to be told by its deputy foreign minister that: 'The game is being played for high international stakes. It has nothing to do with you. You are the victims of an objective situation.'[39]

THE OUTBREAK OF WAR.—On 22 November 1971, without a formal declaration of war, India started an all-out offensive in East Pakistan. On 3 December 1971, to relieve some pressure on the eastern front, Yahya Khan ordered a counter-offensive in the west. The total result was the loss of Kargil to India. The defeat of Pakistan was expected. With the simultaneous US arms embargo on Pakistan and the Russian supply of arms to India, no other result, short of foreign intervention, could be expected. President Yahya Khan was to complain that his orders on the western front were not being carried out, while the soldiers complained of not receiving orders. President Yahya Khan attempted to retain power even after the surrender in Dhaka on 16 December but, by 20 December, he was forced to resign. His comment on the outcome of the war was: 'There was always the possibility that events in East Pakistan might take the course they have taken, but I had no alternative. People would not have excused me if I had allowed East Pakistan to secede.'[40]

THE POLAND RESOLUTION

On 15 December 1971, when surrender had already been agreed upon, Poland, then a Russian satellite, moved a resolution, which called for (a) Power to be transferred to Sheikh Mujibur Rahman as the elected representative of East Pakistan (b) After the Awami League had been installed, there would be an initial ceasefire of seventy-two hours (c) Thereafter, steps would be taken to evacuate Pakistani troops to pre-set positions (d) West Pakistan civilians would be allowed to go home, through the auspices of the UN (e) Indian armed forces shall start their withdrawal after the Pakistan troops, at a time fixed in consultation with the Awami League government.

According to Clause D, civilians were to be sent home, but the ultimate destination of the Pakistan Armed under C was not stated as an ominous omission. Thus we see that contrary to popular belief, the Poland Resolution was not acceptable. Moreover, the Poland Resolution having been rejected earlier was not even on the agenda. On 15 December 1971, only the Anglo-French Resolution was under consideration. The paper Z.A. Bhutto tore was the UNSC agenda.[1]

The Pakistani permanent representative to the UN rejected the resolution on the ground that it provided for Pakistan to first withdraw from its own territory. Only then the occupying Indian forces would begin to withdraw.[2] Other analysts have pointed out that (1) the resolution mentioned no ceasefire in the west[3] (2) it was the most stringent and specific of all the drafts so far moved.[4]

Notes

1. *The New York Times*, 16 December 1971, p. 1. Also the *Sunday Times*, London for the same date.
2. Sultan M. Khan, *Memories and Reflections* (London: Centre for Pakistan Studies, 1997), p. 384.
3. Iqbal Akhund, *Memoirs of a Bystander* (Karachi: Oxford University Press, 1997), p. 203.
4. Hasan Zaheer, *The Separation of East Pakistan* (Karachi: Oxford University Press, 1994), p. 414.

1971 IN RETROSPECT.—Of late, some new material about the 1971 crisis has surfaced. More papers from the US archives have been declassified, but they do not add substantially to what has been revealed in the *American Papers* (1999) and *The White House and Pakistan* (2002) or in the memoirs of Richard M. Nixon and Henry Kissinger (see Bibliography).

Bangladeshi writers like Badruddin Umar[41] and S.A. Karim[42] have written that Sheikh Mujibur Rahman was indeed involved in the Agartala Conspiracy but as Karim relates Mujib would not call it a conspiracy but 'a striving for independence'. While Pakistani writers like Syed Shahid Husain have argued that the Six Points were not secessionist[43] Bangladeshi writers do not bother to argue. But here also the honours go to Bangladeshi writers. While B. Umar and S.A. Karim mention some killings of non-Bengalis; Pakistan HRCP director, I.A. Rehman, says killings of non-Bengalis is 'not relevant'.[44] More than documents, retrospection has been valuable. Sarmila Bose, an Indian Bengali belonging to an illustrious political family, gave a verdict that all the combatants of 1971 should consider. After stating that allegations of Pakistani atrocities were grossly exaggerated, she added: 'The Civil War of 1971 was fought between those who believed they were fighting for a united Pakistan and those who believed their chance for justice and progress lay in an independent Bangladesh. Both were legitimate political positions. All parties in this conflict embraced violence as a means to the end, all committed acts of brutality outside accepted norms of warfare, and all had their share of humanity. Their attributes make the 1971 conflict particularly suitable for efforts towards reconciliation, rather than recrimination'.[45]

Notes

1. *Dawn*, Karachi, 2 May 1970, p. 1.
2. Ibid., 4 May 1970, p. 3.
3. Ibid., 9 May 1970, p. 1.
4. G.W. Choudhry, *The Last Days of United Pakistan* (Karachi: Oxford University Press, 1998), p. 99.
5. Ibid., p. 135.
6. Sultan M. Khan, *Memories and Reflections* (London: Centre for Pakistan Studies, 1997), p. 288.
7. Zulfikar Ali Bhutto, *The Great Tragedy* (Karachi: PPP, 1971), p. 28.
8. Ibid.
9. M. Rafique Afzal, *Pakistan: History and Politics 1947–1971*, Karachi: Oxford University Press, 2001, pp. 416–417.
10. Roedad Khan (ed.), *The British Papers* (Karachi: Oxford University Press, 2002), p. 535.
11. *Pakistan Times*, Lahore, 18 August 1969, p. 1.
12. *Times*, London, 6 April 1970.
13. Lawrence Ziring, *Bangladesh from Mujib To Ershad* (Karachi: Oxford University Press, 1992), p. 64. A.O. Mitha, *Unlikely Beginnings* (Karachi: Oxford University Press, 2003), pp. 402–410. Tajul Islam Hashmi, 'The Bihari Minorities in Bangladesh', in Mushirul Hasan (ed.), *Islam, Communities and the Nation* (New Delhi: Manohar, 1998), pp. 392–398. Raunaq Jahan, *Pakistan: Failure of National Integration* (New York: Columbia University Press, 1972), p. 202.
14. *The New York Times*, 11 May 1971.
15. Ibid., 28 April 1971.
16. G.W. Choudhry, op. cit., p. 176.
17. Zulfikar Ali Bhutto, op. cit., p. 19.
18. G.W. Choudhry, op. cit., p. 173.
19. Ibid., p. 182.
20. Hamoodur Rahman Commission Report (HRCP), *Dawn*, Karachi, 14 August 2000 and 6 February 2001.
21. Ibid., p. v.
22. Ibid.
23. Safdar Mahmood, *Pakistan Divided* (Lahore: Jang, 1984), p. 143.
24. HRCP, op. cit., p. vi.
25. Oriana Fallaci, *Interview with History* (Boston: Houghton and Muffin, 1976), p. 160.
26. Khushwant Singh, *Truth, Love and a Little Malice* (New Delhi: Viking, 2002), p. 315.

27. Pran Chopra, *India's Second Liberation*, 2nd ed. (Cambridge Massachusetts: MIT Press), 1976, p. 100.
28. *Dawn*, Karachi, 16 June 1970, p. 1.
29. Sultan M. Khan, op. cit., p. 308.
30. Henry Kissinger, *The White House Years* (London: Weidenfeld and Nicolson, 1979), p. 862.
31. Ibid., p. 893.
32. Ibid., pp. 905 and 908.
33. Richard M. Nixon, *The Memoirs of Richard Nixon* (New York: Grosset and Dunlop, 1978), p. 526.
34. Henry Kissinger, op. cit., p. 907.
35. Richard Nixon, loc cit.
36. S.M. Burke and Lawrence Ziring, *Pakistan's Foreign Policy*, 2nd ed. (Karachi: Oxford University Press, 1996), p. 404.
37. *The New York Times*, 11 January 1972.
38. Paul Bracken, *Fire in the East* (New York: Perennial, 2002), p. 102.
39. Sultan M. Khan, op. cit., p. 380.
40. Hasan Zaheer, *The Separation of East Pakistan* (Karachi: Oxford University Press, 1994), p. 409.
41. Badruddin Umar, *The Emergence of Bangladesh* (Karachi: Oxford University Press, 2006), Vol. II, p. 137.
42. S.A. Karim, *Sheikh Mujib: Triumph and Tragedy* (Dhaka: The University Press, 2005), p. 111.
43. Syed Shahid Husain, 'Of Lessons Not Learnt', *Dawn*, 11 December 2005.
44. *Newsline*, Karachi, February 2001, p. 49.
45. Sarmila Bose at a New York seminar, *Dawn*, 7 July 2005.

SHEIKH MUJIBUR RAHMAN (b. Tungipara, 1920–d. Dhaka, 15 August 1975) was the leader who founded Bangladesh, and in the process dismembered Pakistan. What was his precise role during the last round of negotiations remains unclear, even after the release of US State Department papers. One report says that Mujib reneged on an agreement with Yahya Khan which called for (a) the immediate establishment of provincial governments, (b) temporary continuation of the central government under Yahya, and (c) a constitutional scheme in which the central government would deal only with defence, foreign affairs and currency.[1]

A subsequent report stated that Mujibur Rahman wanted confederation, not separation.[2]

Sheikh Mujibur Rahman began his political life in Mission High School, Gopalpur, when he told A.K. Fazlul Haq and H.S. Suhrawardy, who were jointly on inspection, that the roof leaked. The principal thought he had spoken out of turn, but in the years ahead, Mujib's encounter with the two leaders would continue. He went on to Islamia College, Calcutta and the University of Dhaka. He became an ardent Muslim Leaguer, and in the 1946 Bihar riots, played a leading role in rehabilitating the refugees in East Bengal.

It was in the wake of the 1948 Bengali Language Movement that Mujibur Rahman gained prominence. He was able to persuade H.S. Suhrawardy to retract his statement favouring Urdu as the sole national language but was unable to associate Fazlul Haq with the Language Movement. This defined his attitude towards them. On 5 January 1956, he criticized Fazlul Haq for challenging the leadership of HS Suhrawardy.[3]

The number of times Sheikh Mujibur Rahman was sent to jail needs to be noted: (i) he was arrested while picketing the Dhaka Secretariat on 11 March 1948; (ii) he was again arrested while agitating for better working conditions in the Dhaka University; from 10 April to 29 July 1949; (iii) he was jailed on 1 January 1950 for two years; (iv) he was already in jail when he was indicted under the Agartala Conspiracy Case. This writer saw him being tried by a magistrate in 1965. He was released in 1968 to participate in the Round Table Conference. (v) The last time he was arrested was after the Army Action on 25 March 1976. He looked at the (burning) skyline and asked the commanding officer: 'Was it necessary to do all this?' Sheikh Mujibur Rahman had courted arrest to avoid a crackdown: other than him, each and every Awami League legislator had escaped.

Sheikh Mujibur Rahman remains a living factor in the politics of Pakistan. This is because most Pakistanis blame only Yahya and Bhutto for the 1971 debacle.

He has more ardent supporters in the country he divided than in the country he emancipated. While his Bangladeshi biographer has accepted that Mujib had indeed gone to Agartala,[5] and that the militants who killed the Dhaka intellectuals on 14 December 1971 were Bengalis and not Biharis,[6] his Pakistani reviewer complained: 'Mr Karim's considerable capacity to respect the truth is likely to deepen a Pakistani majority's miscomprehension of the events of 1971.'[7]

In those fateful days, Z.A. Bhutto recalled Mujib saying: 'If they (the army) destroyed him first, they would also destroy me.'[8] What Bhutto said to the army commander was far more poignant: 'In spite of what Sheikh Mujibur Rahman stood for, he was a leader of the people and merited respect.'[9]

Notes

1. *Daily Times*, Karachi, 11 May 2005.
2. *Dawn*, Karachi, 7 July 2005.
3. S.A. Karim, *Sheikh Mujib: Triumph and Tragedy* (Dhaka: The University Press, 2005), p. 63.
4. Ibid., p. 200.
5. Ibid., p. 110.
6. Ibid., p. 284.
7. I.A. Rehman, 'Anatomy of a Tragic Hero', *Newsline*, October 2006, p. 111.
8. Zulfikar Ali Bhutto, *The Great Tragedy* (Karachi: Pakistan People's Party, 1971), p. 43.
9. Ibid., p. 50.

Chapter 29
The First PPP Regime (1971–1977)

On 20 December 1971, the office of the chief martial law administrator and president was transferred to Zulfikar Ali Bhutto (1928–1979) as the elected representative of what remained of Pakistan. Under the cover of martial law, which was then the basic law of the country, Bhutto nationalized all heavy industrial units except textiles. This created an environment in which educational institutions were nationalized. The nationalization of education was not in the original Pakistan People's Party manifesto but took place under pressure from teachers' unions guided by recommendations made by the Nur Khan Commission (1969). Labour reforms could be effected as capital and labour were drawn from different ethnic groups.

Stringent agricultural reforms were announced but not strictly implemented as Zulfikar Ali Bhutto had previously cabled Yahya Khan against the imposition of agricultural tax.[1] After keeping commerce and business in suspense, the government nationalized banks and insurance companies on 1 January 1974.

Bhutto was the first populist leader of Pakistan since the generation of the founders. He adopted the creed of Islamic socialism which was considered anathema by over a hundred ulama representing fundamentalist Islamic parties, although Islamic socialism as a concept was favoured by Allama Iqbal and Maulana Hasrat Mohani (1881–1951). The term itself was used by Jinnah,[2] and projected as the state ideology by Liaquat Ali Khan,[3] the Raja of Mahmudabad (1913–1973)[4] and Fatima Jinnah[5] as we have seen in the ideological history of Pakistan.

After the trouncing of conservative parties by the Awami League, PPP and National Awami Party (NAP), Chaudhry Mohammad Ali, the former prime minister, and Maj.-Gen. Sher Ali Khan Pataudi, Yahya's information minister, had urged Yahya to cancel the results of the 7 December 1970 elections. Some officers solemnly contemplated transferring power to Air Marshal (retd.) M. Asghar Khan who had lost his own seat in the elections.[6] The electoral victory of the PPP had broken the traditional patterns of results and many feudals and other entrenched politicians had lost.

In the urban constituencies, especially in Karachi, Bhutto faced opposition even from the liberal sector, when he recognized Sindhi as the official language of Sindh. This decision resulted in rioting between Urdu- and Sindhi-speaking groups. It had great destabilising potential, but Z.A. Bhutto overcame it by making a direct sentimental appeal to all contenders. The industrial and commercial interests having already been alienated, Bhutto next eliminated radical elements from his party.

Bhutto eschewed revolution and veered around to reaction, but the war of attrition between the political and economic forces of the country, begun by his reforms, did not end. The nationalization of industries was accompanied by handcuffing and briefly detaining the top industrialists Ahmad Dawood and Fakhruddin Valika. The psychological impact was greater than the economic, as the units taken over had marginal production.

The nationalized sectors gradually showed a dismal performance. The nationalized banks performed professionally during Bhutto's term and only later faced bankruptcy when huge loans were advanced without collateral and even written off under political pressure. On the whole, however, security of service combined with lack of incentive had a detrimental effect on services for which the major and moral responsibility is vested in the employees.

Bhutto had an uneasy relationship with the NAP-JUI coalitions in the NWFP and Balochistan provinces. On assuming power he lifted the ban on the NAP imposed by the Yahya regime and even gave them governors appointed by their party. An arms cache was discovered in the Iraqi embassy; becoming suspicious of their intentions, Bhutto dismissed the government of Balochistan, in consequence of which the NWFP government also resigned. There was army action in Balochistan, and the nationalist trend in that province and NWFP was heightened, but Bhutto pre-empted them diplomatically by engaging with Afghanistan which had supported the NAP-JUI irredentist claim, which means that parts of Pakistan should have been part of Afghanistan. At the height of the 1971 war, King Zahir Shah had been in Moscow and had refused to endorse the USSR policy of dismembering Pakistan. Even when Zahir Shah was ousted by Daud Khan, Bhutto visited him while he incarcerated the NAP leaders.

In the domain of foreign policy, there was a see-saw pattern. In the beginning, Bhutto had to contend with the USSR and towards the end of his term he had to contend with the US which was infuriated at Bhutto's attempt to counteract India's nuclear explosion of 1974. Bhutto leaned to the left, pulling out of CENTO and SEATO and extending recognition to North Korea, North Vietnam, and East Germany. Bhutto had a signal success with the Muslim world; following the 1973 Arab-Israeli war, Bhutto allegedly advised the policy of an oil embargo and in 1974 he hosted the second Islamic Summit at Lahore, taking time out to recognize Bangladesh.

Bhutto's most enduring legacy is the near-unanimous Constitution promulgated on 12 August 1973, under which Bhutto became prime minister. He also laid the foundation of the nuclear programme which enabled Pakistan to test in 1998. Bhutto was to complain that this initiative caused his overthrow. However, in 1976 Bhutto felt confident enough to schedule general elections for March 1977. Almost overnight, large urban centres became bastions of opposition; a nine-party opposition alliance called the Pakistan National Alliance was formed. There was a hard-hitting campaign in which the opposition promised to establish an Islamic order. Claiming that inflation was due solely to the extravagance of the ruling clique, the PNA vowed to bring prices back to 1970 levels. They also termed their campaign a movement for democracy.

There were reasons behind the bitterness of the campaign, apart from ideological, class and ethnic conflict. Zulfikar Ali Bhutto was imperious by nature, and there were many, who became victims of his fits of rage, the most prominent among them being J.A. Rahim, the secretary general of the PPP and a federal minister, who was dismissed, beaten and humiliated. Bhutto veered more to state power than people's power, and while welcoming feudals into the PPP fold, he alienated the committed socialist radicals of his party. Yet he retained sufficient oratorical skill to strike a direct rapport with the masses.

There matters stood when the 1977 general elections were held. The PPP won more seats than Bhutto expected. The Pakistan National Alliance refused to accept the results claiming that the polls had been rigged. That there were glaring and striking polling irregularities is quite evident, yet it is doubtful that they extended to an actual controversion of the public mandate. That is why Bhutto's military successor, General Ziaul Haq kept on postponing elections. Two surviving members of the three-man PNA team, Abdul Ghafoor Ahmed and Nawabzada Nasrullah Khan stated on national television on 5 July 1989 that the PPP and PNA had reached an agreement and that General Ziaul Haq's coup of 5 July 1977 had been unwarranted. On 4 April 2011, Saeed Mehdi, then Deputy Commissioner, Rawalpindi that seven days before the execution, he was sent to the death cell to get Zulfikar Ali Bhutto to sign a Mercy Petition, Z.A. Bhutto refused.

Z.A. Bhutto regained popularity immediately after his removal. To neutralize his popularity the military regime tried Bhutto for aiding and abetting in the murder of a political opponent. Despite discrepant ballistics evidence and a divided bench, Z.A. Bhutto was executed on 4 April 1979. With his all too human failings Bhutto possessed a political mystique. On 18 September and 5 October 2004, Z.A. Bhutto's lifetime opponents joined in paying him tribute.

THE SIMLA AGREEMENT

The Simla Accord signed between India and Pakistan on 2 July 1972 had as its main provisions: (i) That the principles and purposes of the Charter of the United Nations shall govern the relations between the two countries (ii) That the two countries are resolved to settle their differences by peaceful means through bilateral negotiations or by any other peaceful means mutually agreed upon between them. Pending the final settlement of any problems between the two countries, neither side shall unilaterally alter the situation (iv: ii) In Jammu and Kashmir, the line of control resulting from the ceasefire of 17 December 1971 shall be respected by both sides without prejudice to the recognized position of either side. (*The numbering is from the original document*)

This agreement was the greatest challenge to be faced by Zulfikar Ali Bhutto since his popularity had been based on his denunciation of the Tashkent Declaration. Had he failed in Simla,'despite the military defeat, his tenure would have immediately ended.

Predictably, both sides gave different interpretations of the text. On 4 April 1995, P.N. Dhar, who had been secretary to Indira Gandhi, claimed that there had been a secret clause in Simla. This is a tacit admission that the official Indian interpretation was unsupported by the text. Opposition leaders in both countries, including Mahmud Azam Faruqi of Pakistan's Jama'at-i-Islami, upheld the Indian interpretation that the Simla Agreement precluded a reference to the UN, while Atal Bihari Vajpayee the future Indian Prime Minister said that Z.A. Bhutto had achieved regaining the territory under Indian occupation, securing the release of the prisoners of war and reopening the Kashmir issue.[1] Vajpayee's interpretation was supported by party man Bhai Mahavir.[2] Abdus Sattar from the Pakistan side pointed out that P.N. Dhar was not present at the one-to-one talks between Indira Gandhi and Z.A. Bhutto; he recalls that Indira Gandhi had denied any secret clause in the Simla Agreement. He also quotes Z.A. Bhutto's speech in the National Assembly that by bifurcating and delinking the international boundary from the ceasefire line in Kashmir, Kashmir had been acknowledged as a disputed area.[3] Lately, the United Nations Secretary-General Antonio Guterres has urged Pakistan and India to come together and seriously discuss their problems, reminding the two nuclear-armed countries that any military confrontation would be 'a disaster of unmitigated proportions'. At his first briefing of 2021 in New York, the UN Chief also emphasized the need to 'fully respect' human rights in the India-occupied regions of Jammu and Kashmir. Mr Guterres was responding to a question by APP. The question also referred to Mr Guterres's August 2019 statement which called for a resolution of the Kashmir dispute in accordance with relevant UN resolutions and the UN Charter.[4] The Secretary-General was stressing, it seems, that the *principles and purposes* of the UN Charter cannot be reconciled with the suspension of Human Rights in any region, for any period of time. The Simla Agreement says that the two countries are *resolved*, it does not say that they are *compelled*. The Simla Agreement calls for *negotiations*, not for a monologue. The clause that neither side shall unilaterally alter the situation was violated by the 1985 Indian occupation of the Siachen Glacier.

Notes

1. G.S. Bhargava, *Success or Surrender: The Simla Summit* (New Delhi: Sterling 1972), p. 68.
2. Ibid., p. 70.
3. Abdus Sattar, 'Simla Agreement-IV', *Dawn*, 5 July 1995, p. 12.
4. *Dawn*, 30 January 2021, p. 12.

Notes

1. Roedad Khan (ed.), *American Papers* (Karachi: Oxford University Press, 1999), p. 632.
2. *Jinnah Speeches as Governor-General* (Karachi: Oxford University Press, 2000), p. 166.
3. On 26 March 1948, M. Rafique Afzal, *Speeches and Statements of Quaid-i-Millat Liaquat Ali Khan* (Lahore: Research Society, 1976), p. 267.
4. Ishtiaq Husain, *The Life and Times of the Raja Saheb of Mahmudabad* II (Karachi: Mahboob Academy, 1998), p. 18.
5. 25 December 1961, in Khan Salahuddin Khan (ed.), *Speeches, Messages and Statements of Mohtarma Fatima Jinnah* (Lahore Research Society, 1976), passim.
6. A.R. Siddiqi, *East Pakistan: The Endgame* (Karachi: Oxford University Press, 2004), p. 211.

> ...The noble Brutus
> Hath told you Caesar was ambitious.
> If it were so, it was a grievous fault,
> And grievously hath Caesar answered it.
> – William Shakespeare, *Julius Caesar*, Act III, Scene II

Zulfikar Ali Bhutto (b. Larkana, 5 January 1928–d. Rawalpindi, 4 April 1979). No other lines apply more aptly to the dramatic course of Z.A. Bhutto's political career. Shock and grief over his death touched new depths, while exultation over his execution opened a new, sordid dimension in the politics of Pakistan. Even, thirty years after his deposal, Z.A. Bhutto remains Pakistan's most controversial figure and except for Jinnah, he is the subject of more studies than any other leader of Pakistan.

A federal minister at the young age of 30, Bhutto held diverse portfolios before becoming foreign minister, in 1963, which proved to be his real metier. On his removal from this office, he produced a treatise on foreign affairs, called *The Myth of Independence*. This contains his concept of bilateralism and his dicta on the survival of small states against great powers. It is hazardous to deduce from theoretical principles, the guiding elements of a practising statesman, but in this case, they not only apply, they guide. Bhutto postulated that barring glaring exceptions, the great powers sought to unite former colonial states to better exploit them.[1] As regards India-Pakistan relations, Bhutto's main plank of resistance was elaborated in the following words, which eerily recall the present situation: 'It has been suggested that Pakistan should become realistic and seek *rapprochement* with India without the settlement of outstanding disputes...It would mean capitulation by instalment and eventual liquidation[2]...In exploring the possibilities available in capitulation by instalment, it must be remembered that it is a function of diplomacy to look for various approaches and to avoid abrupt decisions which sound like an ultimatum.'[3]

Even with finesse, a search may not yield a solution. This point is reiterated in Bhutto's aphorism: 'Pressure is a worm if you stamp on it, but it becomes a monster if you recoil.'[4] Bhutto was indeed under pressure on the nuclear issue, as declassified documents from the national security archives of the George Washington University testify. Safeguards are not enough, he was told, because one side could break an agreement,[5] an argument not followed in the 2006 India–US nuclear agreement, Bhutto's prescription on pressure is a reminder that character is destiny. He was successful in foreign policy because, in that domain, one cannot be a feudal lord. The pages of this book attest that during the East Pakistan crisis, which brought him into power, his choices were constricted, and during the Pakistan National Alliance agitation, which ushered him out, he had none. Were both events portents of a greater design? The transfer of power to Bhutto, as the elected representative, held an element of defiance resembling post-Great War Hungary, where Prime Minister Michael Károlyi had brought out from prison Bela Kun, and transferred his office to him. Bela Kun promulgated a Soviet constitution, nationalized land, paid unemployment wages, and accepted health and education as state responsibilities. When these measures resulted in national awakening and revitalization of the proletariat, Bela Kun was exiled, and the Romanian army was unleashed on Hungary.[6] Bhutto's fate was deferred, but in the end more tragic. It is curious that in the long gallery of role models suggested for Bhutto, extending as it does from Napoleon to Nehru, Bela Kun has found no place.

There is an esoteric element which links his tyranny to his charisma. As Stanley Wolpert discovered, none of his behaviour, even when well documented, seemed to diminish his political appeal for most Pakistanis.[7]

He regained his popularity when he was deposed, and his passion—much more than his discourse—made him a legend.

Notes

1. Zulfikar Ali Bhutto, *The Myth of Independence* (London: Oxford University Press, 1969), p. 10.
2. Ibid., p. 177.
3. Ibid., p. 106.
4. Ibid., p. 13.
5. *Dawn*, Karachi, 28 May 2006.
6. J. Hampden Jackson, *The Post-War World: A Short Political History 1918–1934* (London: Victor Gollancz, 1935), pp. 36, 37.
7. Stanley Wolpert, *Zulfi Bhutto of Pakistan* (New York: Oxford University Press, 1993), p. 314.

CHAPTER 30
THE THIRD MILITARY REGIME (1977–1988)

The clash between the PPP and PNA had polarized the nation, destabilized the state and ruined the economy. A beleaguered Z.A. Bhutto had banned night clubs and liquor, horse racing, and gambling and declared Friday as the weekly holiday instead of Sunday, but these concessions to Islamic sentiments proved to no avail. Only while the PPP and PNA teams negotiated, was the violence suspended.

General Muhammad Ziaul Haq (1924–1988) said he was staging his coup so that the army could act as a neutral force between the PPP and PNA, hold elections within ninety days and retire to the barracks immediately afterwards. In his inaugural address to the nation, Zia said that he supported the movement for Islamization. It was this pronouncement that dispelled the notion that the coup had been staged at Bhutto's behest. Zia imposed the *Zakat* and *Ushr* ordinance which allowed the government to deduct the Islamic tithes on savings and land revenue. Zia introduced Islamic punishments for all crimes except murder since Islamic laws would ensure Z.A. Bhutto's release. Zia alteration of the law of evidence resulted in legal perversities. A victim of rape would be convicted of adultery while the perpetrator would be let off for lack of evidence.

Zia, in need of a political anchor, gave a boost to religious parties which hitherto had been badly mauled in every election. This led to heightened sectarian militancy. Soon the banning of political activity resulted in the emergence of ethnic parties. The influx of Afghan refugees fleeing their country in the wake of the Soviet invasion added to the chaos. The cumulative effect of all this was an unprecedented brutalization of society and the introduction of Kalashnikov and drug cultures. Drugs, till then almost unknown, registered widespread consumption.

Yet, despite these crippling social defects, Zia policy of containing and combating the Soviet presence in Afghanistan was basically sound. For Pakistan to refuse aid against the Soviet presence on Pakistan's borders would have tempted the Soviet army to extend its presence to Pakistan and add a warm water port to its possessions. The social consequences of the Soviet invasion alone could have hardly been worse than the result of the Afghan influx.

Under cover of the Afghan crisis, Ziaul Haq was able to replenish both the coffers and the arsenals of Pakistan and, more vitally, he was able to continue Pakistan's nuclear programme, notwithstanding the 28 April 1977 statement of his predecessor Z.A..Bhutto that he was being punished for pursuing nuclear deterrence. In the domain of defence, the loss of Siachen to India in 1985 can be weighed against him. The Soviet invasion of Afghanistan was an ad hoc situation and as such led to ad hoc results in terms of Western support. The liberal parties in the US and Europe had muted, but not dropped, their demand, for democracy in Pakistan. In 1983, Ziaul Haq was able to militarily crush the Movement for the Restoration of Democracy (MRD) but realized that at least a cosmetic exercise in democracy had become unavoidable. As a first step, he held a referendum on his Islamization policy, so worded that it meant validation of Zia's term for a further five years. There was a low turnout in the referendum, but in February 1985 the electoral response was greater.

A parliament based on non-party polls was ushered in. Mohammad Khan Junejo (1932–1993) was appointed prime minister on 23 March 1985. General Zia made the restoration of parliament conditional on the passage of the Eighth Amendment. The amendment had a clause 58(2)(B) which empowered the president to dismiss the prime minister and dissolve the parliament. After initial resistance from a group headed by Muhammad Saifullah Khan (Haji Saifullah), the legislature capitulated and enacted the Eighth Amendment giving constitutional cover to martial law regulations. On 31 December 1985 martial law was lifted but Zia remained president as well as chief of army staff.

Mohammad Khan Junejo, contrary to General Zia expectations, wished to pursue an agenda of his own.[1] He signed an accord in Geneva which paved the way for Soviet withdrawal from Afghanistan. Although this conformed to Pakistan's official policy, in reality, Zia had hoped to prolong the withdrawal process, thereby retaining a front-line state status for Pakistan, for a longer period. Mohammad Khan Junejo practised and imposed austerity in government expenditure. He put both military and civil officers in small cars. His character was impeccable, but since he was perceived as a product of the military regime, his sterling qualities were recognized only retrospectively. The National Assembly was showing restlessness and Syed Fakhr Imam was elected speaker against Zia's favoured candidate.

Ojhri Camp, a munitions depot in Rawalpindi, blew up with considerable loss of life on 10 April 1988. The prime minister launched an inquiry resented by the military top brass. Public bickering between young military officers and ruling party legislators added to the tension. On 29 May 1988, President Zia dismissed his own hand-picked prime minister and dissolved the National Assembly which was elected on a non-party basis under clause 58(2)B of the Eighth Amendment. This proved to be a more complicated course of action than an outright coup since the president was forced to order fresh elections within ninety days. Before the world could discover whether this second promise would be kept, President Zia was killed in an air crash on 17 August 1988. In accordance with the 1973 Constitution, the Chairman of the Senate, Ghulam Ishaq Khan (1915–2006) assumed the office of president.

Note

1. K.M. Arif, *Working with Zia* (Karachi: Oxford University Press, 1995), p. 395.

Chapter 31

The Democratic Interregnum (1988–1999)

From 3 December 1988 to 12 October 1999 Pakistan witnessed a partial respite from autocratic rule. This period also saw an increase in ethnic and sectarian strife. With the role of political parties having previously been constricted, ethnic and sectarian forces acquired greater public space. Since sectarian strife raised the spectre of greater violence, the heightening of ethnic feelings was grasped as an alternative involving lesser violence. Due to discriminatory legislation regarding employment and education quotas Muhajir ethnic feeling cut through sectarian fanaticism which led to the emergence of the Muhajir Qaumi Movement (MQM).

In the November 1988 elections, the PPP emerged as the party with the largest number of seats, but President Ghulam Ishaq Khan was visibly reluctant to name its leader, Benazir Bhutto, as prime minister. He only did so when all efforts to set up a counter-coalition against her failed. On 3 December 1988, Benazir Bhutto became the first woman prime minister in the entire Muslim world. She had become a world celebrity as well because of the courageous struggle she had waged against despotism. Power was transferred to her under stringent conditions including signing a pre-negotiated IMF agreement.

In her first press conference, Benazir Bhutto made it clear that she was not a free agent and that she had to work under a system. The largest province, Punjab, in an almost overnight turnaround between the national and provincial elections, voted her political rival Nawaz Sharif into power. The establishment headed by President Ghulam Ishaq Khan, and the Punjab government headed by Nawaz Sharif, kept her in a crucible. Her parliamentary coalition with the MQM fell apart revealing the precarious nature of her government.

The MQM clandestinely broke its alliance with the PPP on 6 October 1989 and made its hostility public only when a no-confidence motion was tabled against the prime minister. Her response was more impolitic than the MQM's and the shooting down of women protestors in the Pucca Qila in Hyderabad tarnished her image as a champion of democracy and human rights. No other domestic strife has had a more disastrous fall-out. The MQM demonstrations drew blood and obfuscated the Kashmir *intifada* which led also to her falling out with General Beg. In his biography, General Beg testified that at the beginning of 1990, the USA, India, and Israel decided to invade Pakistan's atomic installations. When the information was surely confirmed, Benazir Bhutto sent a message through Foreign Minister Sahibzada Yaqub Khan: 'Refrain from your designs otherwise your nuclear installations shall be destroyed'. To the COAS she ordered that land forces and navy be put on red alert. The PAF was ordered to arm their aircraft with nuclear missiles and a squadron was sent to the Mauripur airbase to await further orders. These activities were observed by American satellites, and they were shocked.[1]

The disaffection against Benazir Bhutto in the main cities of Karachi, Lahore and Quetta set the stage for her dismissal on 6 August 1990, on charges of misrule and corruption attributed to her husband. A sympathetic biographer admits that Benazir Bhutto had been distracted by her opponents and had not fulfilled her promises.[2]

The damage to the nascent democracy could have been contained if an impartial interim prime minister had been appointed ahead of the new elections, but President Ghulam Ishaq Khan took the novel step of transferring power to the Leader of the Opposition, Ghulam Mustafa Jatoi who had lost his seat in the elections and had to be inducted to the National Assembly through a by-election in a different constituency. The dismal showing of the PPP coalition (only forty-five seats) was immediately seen by PPP supporters as the result of rigging.

Later, when the then-ruling clique was out of office, it did not contradict allegations of rigging. Nevertheless, Nawaz Sharif had an electoral base in the Punjab, and it was expected that his government would be stable. For no rational or vital reason, this expectation was belied. The term of Nawaz Sharif saw the first Gulf War which clearly showed up the contradictions of Pakistan's polity. President Ghulam Ishaq Khan, Mirza Aslam Beg (COAS), and Begum Nusrat Bhutto (Chairperson of the main opposition party, the PPP) issued statements favouring Iraq. Nawaz Sharif and Benazir Bhutto (leader of the parliamentary opposition) were firmly on the side of Kuwait, fully realizing that Muslim solidarity took second place to national sovereignty and understanding all the implications of supporting an invasion of a sovereign state.

With Nawaz Sharif inclining towards reconciliation with the PPP and stating openly his intention of scrapping the Eighth Amendment, the president moved to prevent curtailment of his powers, dismissed Nawaz Sharif, and dissolved the National Assembly on 18 April 1993. On 26 May 1993, the Supreme Court restored the parliament and premier; the only instance when the Supreme Court ruled against the plea of 'state necessity'. President Ghulam Ishaq Khan stuck to office despite this judicial rebuff, but a situation in which the relations between the president and prime minister were openly strained was proving detrimental to the state, and on 18 July 1993 each had to resign his office.

This term of Nawaz Sharif's PML (N) also saw heightened tension in Sindh province. The president had imposed a ruthless minority government under Jam Sadiq Ali to keep the PPP (which had an enhanced presence in the Sindh Assembly) out. In this, the chief minister had the enthusiastic support of the MQM. When it was perceived that the MQM was irrevocably cut from its

Sindh moorings, it was subjected by its allies to military action. Although its fortunes went on fluctuating, the MQM never fully recovered from this blow, and for a long time, Karachi remained a city of insecurity and economic stagnation.

Benazir Bhutto won the 6 October 1993 elections by securing eighty-six seats. This time, the Punjab Assembly as well as the office of the president went to her party members, making her second term as prime minister seemingly more secure. Benazir Bhutto was able to improve the economy by increasing inward investment and trade. This was only to the extent permitted by the ethnic strife which continued to plague her administration. Military action against the MQM continued, with the MQM retaliating with strikes, damaging the economy. On 1 September 1996, an opposition leader, the prime minister's only surviving brother, Murtaza Bhutto, was killed in a police shootout. After offering formal condolences, President Farooq Leghari had the Supreme Court opened on a holiday[3] to file a case against the bereaved prime minister, and she was finally dismissed on 5 November 1996 on grounds of extra judicial killings and corruption. Benazir Bhutto's petition for the restoration of her government was dismissed by the Supreme Court.

During his second term, Mian Nawaz Sharif took pre-emptive legislative measures to secure his government. On 4 April 1997, the anniversary of Z.A. Bhutto's execution, the National Assembly unanimously, and in a matter of minutes, passed the Thirteenth Amendment partially repealing the Eighth Amendment, i.e. the power of the president to dismiss the prime minister and dissolve the assemblies. On 1 July 1997, the Fourteenth Amendment was passed preventing floor-crossing or flouting of party discipline by legislators. The Chief Justice of Pakistan, Sajjad Ali Shah, had his court stormed by the PML-N (ruling party) members while he was hearing an appeal to strike down the Thirteenth Amendment. This would have enabled the president to dismiss the prime minister. Frustrated at being unable to dismiss Nawaz Sharif as he had dismissed Benazir Bhutto, Farooq Leghari resigned as president on 2 December 1997.

Some destabilizing factors intruded from external sources. On 25 May 1997, Pakistan, along with US allies including Saudi Arabia and the United Arab Emirates, recognized the militant Taliban regime in Afghanistan. This was later to be the cause of friction with the US. On 11 May 1998, India conducted a series of nuclear tests and threatened to occupy Azad Kashmir. Since India had already demonstrated its nuclear capacity in 1974, the new threats were taken very seriously. Pakistan responded on 28 May, after international guarantees of security were not forthcoming.

Unfortunately, simultaneous with the announcement of nuclear success, the prime minister, also announced the freezing of foreign currency accounts and the construction of the Kalabagh Dam which was opposed by three out of four provinces of Pakistan. This dissipated the political advantage gained by the prime minister.

After the nuclearization of both countries, the Indian Prime Minister, Atal Bihari Vajpayee, visited Lahore on a bus on 20 February 1999 and held talks with his Pakistani counterpart in an atmosphere of cordiality. It was noted that the joint statement of the two prime ministers sidelined the Kashmir issue. Frustrated by this omission and the stalled talks on the Siachen issue, Pakistani irregulars, supported by regulars, crossed the Line of Control, and took up positions in the Kargil sector. Kargil, as mentioned above, had been part of Pakistan till 1971, and after the 1971 war, it was India which had pressurised the UN to withdraw its observer group from that sector.

Tactically, the Kargil episode was the consequence of, in the words of a high-ranking Pakistani diplomat, 'unstructured, personalised decision making'. The propaganda war was lost by Pakistan because the nuclearization of the adversaries had focused world attention away from the causes to the consequences. Attention, in other words, shifted from the evasion of UNSC resolutions by India to the issue of cross-border terrorism by Pakistan. Nawaz Sharif travelled to the US to announce Pakistan's withdrawal from Kargil; this was in exchange for the vaguest of promises made by President Bill Clinton to use his influence to solve the Kashmir dispute. It was transparently clear that the promise was not to be taken seriously.

On the domestic side, the prime minister tabled the Fifteenth Amendment designed to make the Quran and Sunnah the supreme law of the land.[4] Even the religious parties would not support this bill, although on the surface it met their longstanding demand. They understood it to be a measure to completely undermine the constitution and give a free hand to Nawaz Sharif. The constitution was inadvertently undermined when Nawaz Sharif attempted to dismiss the army chief, General Pervez Musharraf, while he was on an incoming flight from Sri Lanka. The attempt rebounded on him and on 12 October 1999, Nawaz Sharif was ousted in a coup led by General Musharraf in retaliation for the prime minister's attempt to dismiss him and endanger the lives of all the passengers.

Notes

1. Col. Ashfaq Husain, *Compulsions of Power: Biography of General Mirza Aslam Beg* (Lahore: Adabiyat, 2021), pp. 227–228. In the previous edition, it was stated on the authority of Mehtab Ali Shah, *The Foreign Policy of Pakistan* (London: I.B. Tauris, 1997), vide *Dawn*, 17 February 1994 that Benazir Bhutto had handed over a list of Sikh dissidents to India. In video clips surfacing after her assassination both Benazir Bhutto and her Interior Minister Aitzaz Ahsan denied this accusation.
2. Diane Sansevere-Dreher, *Benazir Bhutto* (New York: Bantam Skylark, 1991), p. 74.
3. Ajmal Mian, *A Judge Speaks Out* (Karachi: Oxford University Press, 2004), p. 203.
4. On 9 October 1998, this bill was passed by the National Assembly, but not the Senate.

The Nuclear Choice

'Your money or your life', said the marauder to the traveller. 'Take my life' said the traveller, 'I am saving my money for my old age.' Here was a man who knew his priorities, a man who would have opted for economic aid and international goodwill. Don't go nuclear and we will reward you. We shall deliver to you the F-16s you have already paid for. No, the F-16s are no deterrent against nuclear attack but have faith in us. After you have been destroyed in a nuclear attack, we shall reschedule your debts and offer you new loans on soft terms.

This nice old lady told her son's class teacher: 'My child is very sensitive when he is naughty, slap the boy next to him.' The teacher agreed. Ever since India exploded a nuclear device in 1974, Pakistan has had country-specific sanctions slapped on her. This comes out of experience. If the US had been as mature at the outbreak of the Second World War, they would have imposed sanctions on Britain immediately after Hitler invaded Poland. Already the Kashmiris feel that the description of a terrorist has begun to fit Gilbert du Motier, Marquis de Lafayette.

When Pakistan lost her moral advantage by carrying out her own tests, Prem Shankar Jha expounded the theory that Pakistan's nuclear explosions carried out later were a justification for India's nuclear explosions carried out earlier. In the immortal words of the sensitive child: 'It all started when he hit me back.'

Chapter 32

The Fourth Military Regime (1999–2008)

Pakistan's second democratic interregnum ended when General Pervez Musharraf (1943–2023) reacted to his mid-flight dismissal as COAS by Prime Minister Nawaz Sharif, by staging a coup d'état. His was the first military regime which did not declare martial law. General Musharraf chose initially the designation of Chief Executive. The United States accepted the legitimacy of the military regime on 6 December 1999. The Supreme Court gave its final judgement on the legitimacy of the military regime on 12 March 2000. General Musharraf's coup was justified but the Supreme Court ruled that he was bound to hold elections within three years.

Gradually, General Musharraf was able to sidestep his constitutional obligations. On 20 June 2001, he assumed the office of President after obtaining the resignation of President M. Rafiq Tarar. On 30 April 2002, Pervez Musharraf held a referendum to confirm himself as president. He later admitted that there were flaws due to 'over-enthusiastic officials'. However, the crisis ran deeper. Had the Supreme Court struck down the referendum programme as unconstitutional, the people of Pakistan would have been absolved of responsibility, but since the legality of the referendum was upheld, the people had no choice but to participate in it, as an unrepresentative government at such a sensitive security juncture was a high risk.

Again the blame for enabling President Musharraf to transform constitutional provisions, in stages, is shared by the gullibility of the religious alliance Muttahida Majlis-e-Amal (MMA), whose concessions to the military, over the constitution, in effect, weakened the position of the centrist Alliance for the Restoration of Democracy (ARD) opposition. Elections were held as per the Supreme Court verdict on 10 October 2002, but General Musharraf only shared power with the parliament and did not effectively transfer power to it.

The first prime minister under Pervez Musharraf was Mir Zafarullah Khan Jamali (1944–2020) who held office from 23 November 2002 to 26 June 2004. Chaudhry Shujaat Hussain (b.1946) served as prime minister for forty-five days. There is no provision for an interim prime minister in the constitution, but Chaudhry Shujaat Hussain served as interim prime minister to pave the way politically for his successor. Prime Minister Shaukat Aziz (b.1949) took office on 23 August 2004 as the twenty-third incumbent.

A National Security Council (NSC) was inducted which alone would be empowered to dismiss prime ministers or dissolve parliaments. The NSC would include the leader of the opposition. Superficially this is fraught with risk as he or she would have the incentive to replace the prime minister, but in normal conditions, it could be a forum where continuity and briefing could be imparted to the leader of the opposition. At present it is a supra-cabinet. Its membership consists of the president, prime minister, leader of the opposition, all service chiefs, the chairman of the joint chiefs of staff committee, governors, and chief ministers of all four provinces, and of course the defence and foreign ministers and secretaries.

The real challenge to the regime had been the Afghanistan problem. General Zia had sown the wind of terrorism and General Pervez Musharraf has reaped the whirlwind. As the Zia policy was sound for halting the Soviet advance, despite the disastrous social fallout, the policy of Pervez Musharraf of joining the US war against terror was also sound. During the democratic interregnum, the military establishment allegedly attempted to bring Afghanistan into an alliance to obtain defence in depth. This military establishment was slow to realize that although defence in depth had value in conventional warfare, in nuclear warfare it can prove a liability.

During the Zia era, the Mujahideen had been trained, armed, and financed by the US. After the Soviet withdrawal from Afghanistan, these religious warriors were left to their own devices and took fanaticism and militancy to their extreme limits. The Taliban regime of Afghanistan, which personified these tactics, was initially given tacit Western support because it provided a sectarian counterpoise to the 1979 Irani revolution. It was like the support given in the 1980s to Iraqi leader Saddam Hussain on the other flank of Iran.

Following the terrorist attacks on US targets on 11 September 2001, Pakistani support for the fanatical Taliban regime was withdrawn. Pakistan had been one of only three countries to recognize the Taliban regime in Afghanistan, the other two being Saudi Arabia and the United Arab Emirates. Since these were traditionally pro-US countries, there was widespread speculation that Pakistan had recognized the Taliban regime with US approval. Thus, Pakistan's turnaround on the Taliban regime was not an isolated step. Neither was it harmful. Pakistan's pro-Taliban policy had strained the country's relations with its most benign neighbours—China and Iran. Most usefully, its alliance with the West on this issue secured the support of the US during the 13 December 2001 to 16 October 2002 military standoff with India, which started with a terrorist attack on the Indian parliament.

As with the Zia regime, the Musharraf regime faced a domestic backlash over a foreign policy option. This was centred in the South Waziristan vicinity of Wana. Wana had been the recurring scene of the battle against the British in 1894, 1919, and 1937. In 1947, Wana was the scene of revolt against newly established Pakistan by the Faqir of Ipi. Since April 2003, roughly, Wana again became the centre of armed resistance to the pro-US policy of the government. There were air attacks on 11 June and 9 September 2004. Militants laid down their arms on 20 April and 5 August 2004, but this did not stem the violence. The economic blockade imposed on Wana was lifted by Prime Minister Shaukat Aziz on 25 September 2004 but to no avail. On 9 October 2004, two Chinese engineers were kidnapped by the tribals one of whom was killed. Wana continues to bleed, and a major initiative is required to restore peace there.

Pervez Musharraf's alliance with the West allowed him to ride out the storm over the Dr Abdul Qadeer Khan (1936–2021) affair. A.Q. Khan, the father of the Pakistani bomb, came under pressure for nuclear proliferation when Libya admitted to US authorities that it had received help from him. At the time of the first Gulf War of 1990, Iraqi scientists had also named A.Q. Khan as the architect of their nuclear programme. In 1995, the Government of Pakistan put Dr Khan on the exit control list, but he was soon exonerated because of his national standing. Pakistani commentators were quick to point out that even the US had to pardon J. Robert Oppenheimer, the architect of the US bomb. The cases were dissimilar, and even if there had been similarity, proliferation was too alarming a prospect to induce judicial review, and without US support President Musharraf would not have been able to stand between A.Q. Khan and international agencies, especially after his televised confession on 1 February 2004.

According to the eminent historian Stanley Wolpert (1927–2019): 'The positive achievements of General Pervez Musharraf's regime have included stabilization of the economy and overall improvement in Pakistan's relations with other countries—notably with the USA, with whom Pakistan is allied in the "War against Terror", and with India.'[1]

President Musharraf was also able to withstand pressure to commit Pakistani troops to Iraq. The American war in Iraq and Afghanistan is unpopular in Pakistan, but all diplomacy requires give and take, and an appreciation of the differences between the West's Middle East policy and South Asia policy; the USSR consistently supported the Arabs against Israel but that did not prevent it from dismembering Pakistan.

On the economic front, the investment climate did not seem to have improved; there was friction when retailers observed a three-day strike beginning on 19 May 2000. Nevertheless, stability and the control of ethnic conflict had a salutary effect. It was reported that Pakistan's economy had grown by 4.9 per cent in the 1999–2000 financial year. Principally because of the War on Terror, Pakistan had not been able to cope with sectarian violence so effectively. The regime had to contend with an almost new dimension to religious strife. Christians and their churches were attacked; most notably the church in the Islamabad Diplomatic Enclave (17 March 2002), a boarding school at Murree (4 August 2002), and a Christian charity office in Karachi (25 September 2002).

There were signs of national reconciliation too. Asif Zardari, the husband of Benazir Bhutto, originally incarcerated by Nawaz Sharif, was finally released after eight years, on 22 December 2004. Benazir Bhutto made guarded references praising Musharraf for increasing women's representation in legislatures and for the 26 October 2004 bill for enhancing punishment for so-called honour killings.

It was Sam Goldwyn who wanted 'a story that starts with an earthquake and works its way up to a climax.'[2] This is essentially the story which has unfolded since 8 October 2005, when an earthquake hit the northern part of Pakistan leaving 100,000 dead, 70,000 injured, and 3.5 million homeless. Initially, the nation was united in grief, but when the relief measures proved hopelessly inadequate: fissures began to appear. The homeless endured two winters in the high mountainous areas that are naturally exposed to frost.

In a terrain of another type, the simmering discontent in Balochistan erupted. In the first crisis, under Ayub Khan, Balochistan was bombed and Nawab Akbar Bugti was sentenced to death. The death sentence was commuted at the behest of Z.A. Bhutto, and when the National Awami Party led an insurgency in Bhutto's own time, Akbar Bugti (and after him the Khan of Kalat) were made governors to deal with rival tribes. During the Musharraf regime, Nawab Akbar Bugti and a number of associates, who had taken refuge in a cave, were blasted to death on 26 August 2006. It needs reflection that this round of protest and defiance had started with the rape of a lady doctor, Shazia Khalid. Balochistan is the province with the lowest population, but it has the largest area, the largest energy reserves, and the largest mineral resources. A rationalization of returns from its resources may even now, pave the way for national reconciliation. This is vital if the strategic value of Balochistan is to be appreciated, both as the littoral of the Gwadar seaport being built with Chinese cooperation, and the transit area of the lucrative Iran-Pakistan-India pipeline.

The events moved from a calamity to a catastrophe, when on 9 March 2007, the president, on the advice of the prime minister, moved a reference against the Chief Justice of Pakistan, Iftikhar Muhammad Chaudhry. The suspension sparked protests led by lawyers and increased calls for Musharraf's resignation. On the other hand, the regime's move was not whimsical: it was driven by desperation. The chief justice overturned the privatization of the Pakistan Steel Mills and was pursuing, with unprecedented assiduity, the cases of people who had gone missing, and whose dependents had accused the intelligence agencies of causing their disappearance. It is true that the Pakistan Steel Mills had been grossly undervalued, but any setback to privatization could be viewed as a setback to IBRD/IMF conditionality. Similarly, the US/NATO's ever-rising refrain to do more to contain acts of terrorism caused the concerned agencies to use high-handed methods, putting suspects into the Pakistani equivalent of Guantanamo Bay. The government's methods lacked finesse, thus making its position difficult to defend on 27 March 2007.

The government blamed Jihadi groups for the disappearances.³ It could hardly be imagined that the situation could get worse, yet when the chief justice accepted an invitation to address the Karachi Bar Association on 12 May 2007 and the MQM scheduled a rally on the same day, trouble was clearly anticipated. In the National Assembly, the former Prime Minister, Zafarullah Jamali, made a humble request to the MQM to postpone their rally. The response of the MQM leader, Nawab Mirza, was chilling: 'No one will be allowed to do anything in Karachi. The country belongs to everyone, but Karachi belongs to us.'⁴ This position was not only extra-constitutional but ensured the MQM's political isolation. The violence on the following day set the course for the events that were to follow.

On 10 July after a prolonged stand-off, and fruitless rounds of negotiations, the Lal Masjid (the Islamabad stronghold of the militants) was finally stormed. The leading *alim* Abdur Rashid Ghazi with a number of die-hard supporters perished in the assault. The other *alim* Abdul Aziz (brother of Abdur Rashid), had earlier been caught trying to escape. Not only Pervez Musharraf but George W. Bush were reaping the whirlwind, while Jimmy Carter, who had sown the wind unjustly arraigned the incumbent president. Muslim militants were given a boost above their electoral standing to destabilize the first PPP regime in 1977. Later Jimmy Carter rewarded India for its 1974 nuclear explosion and imposed sanctions on Pakistan two days after Bhutto's execution. This impelled even Bhutto's adversaries to seek the nuclear option.

On 20 July 2007, the Supreme Court bench reinstated the chief justice, putting the seal of futility on a concerted campaign by government supporters. These supporters mainly consisting of the members of the Pakistan Muslim League (Q) received a jolt when it surfaced that President Musharraf had held direct talks with Benazir Bhutto, on 26 July. It further transpired that this had been the second such meeting. Another former prime minister, Nawaz Sharif received an apparent reprieve on 23 August when the Supreme Court ruled, he could return to Pakistan. The political import of this verdict was that Nawaz Sharif could participate in the forthcoming elections.

To offset this contingency, the Saudi Intelligence Chief, Muqrin bin Abdul Aziz and Sa'ad Hariri son of the slain Lebanese Premier Rafiq Hariri produced on 8 September 2007 the original of the signed undertaking of Nawaz Sharif to stay away from Pakistan for ten years. Earlier Sharif had denied the existence of this document, and when confronted with it, said that the ten-year exile had verbally been reduced to five years. Whether this admission dampened the ardour of his supporters, who were unable to prevent his re-deportation when Nawaz Sharif arrived on 10 September, is not known. The only notable development in this connection is that the former Prime Minister

Chaudhry Shujaat Hussain, and the ruling PML (Q) resolved by a majority that Nawaz Sharif be allowed to return to Pakistan.[5]

Simultaneously, it decried a possible deal between the president and the PPP. The party leadership present in Pakistan bravely kept on reiterating its principled stand against dictatorship, but their dissonance with Benazir Bhutto's attempts to find a negotiated transition to democracy was audible. On 1 September 2007, Benazir Bhutto said that she had not reached an agreement with Musharraf and when, on 5 September, emissaries resumed talks, she called for a direct meeting with the president. However, their differences were unbridgeable, and negotiations petered out.

On 3 November 2007, General Pervez Musharraf proclaimed a state of emergency sending back the superior judiciary for the second time. Almost immediately seven judges of the Supreme Court led by Chief Justice Iftikhar Muhammad Chaudhry overturned the Provisional Constitutional Order under which the emergency was proclaimed. If the amendments are *ultra vires* (beyond the power) of the basic provision of the constitution, even a two-thirds majority provides no remedy.

President Pervez Musharraf doffed his uniform on 28 November 2007 and the National Assembly completed its five-year tenure, amidst congratulations that it had not been dissolved. The lifting of the emergency should have instilled confidence, but the caretaker government did not appear neutral. The assassination of Benazir Bhutto on 27 December 2007 caused a violent backlash which destabilized the government. On 21 January 2008, President Musharraf reacted to foreign press criticism by asking Western nations to stop their 'obsession with democracy'.[6]

The regime of General Pervez Musharraf came to a gradual end. First, he was held to his word that he would doff his army uniform. The assassination of Benazir Bhutto on 27 December 2007, and the Lawyer's Movement for the restoration of Chief Justice Iftikhar Muhammad Chaudhry created the momentum under which elections were ordered and held on 18 February 2008. Both the parties Musharraf had wished to keep out of the election process were returned in large numbers. On 6 March 2008, Chief of Army Staff General Ashfaq Parvez Kayani announced his support for the incoming government. On 30 March 2008, President Pervez Musharraf administered the oath of office to Prime Minister Syed Yusuf Raza Gilani and his cabinet.

Another feature of Musharraf's last year in office was the sharp increase in the incidents of terror, mostly by organizations Musharraf had banned. There were thirty-one acts of terror which caused the US Chairman, the Joint Chiefs of Staff Committee to visit Islamabad on 12 July 2008 to exhort the Pakistani leadership to act 'decisively' against the militants. The Americans were fully cognizant that the terrorists were their own creation, as were the three million Afghan refugees on Pakistan's soil, who were responsible for the violence. However, they chose to lean on Pakistan, which had been weakened by their own sanctions, and Pakistan realized it was unable to respond. Finally, finding a hybrid administration too stressful, or just futile, Pervez Musharraf resigned as President of Pakistan on 18 August 2008.

Notes

1. Stanley Wolpert, 'Pervez Musharraf', in Hafeez Malik and Yuri Gankovsky (eds.), *Encyclopedia of Pakistan* (Karachi: Oxford University Press, 2005), p. 183.
2. Sam Goldwyn, *Dictionary of Modern Quotations* (Harmondsworth: Penguin, 1980), p. 134.
3. *Dawn*, 28 March 2007.
4. *Newsline*, Karachi, June 2007.
5. *Dawn*, 27 January 2007.
6. *Dawn*, 22 January 2008.

BENAZIR BHUTTO (b. Karachi, 23 June 1953–d. Rawalpindi, 27 December 2007). She was the only politician to suffer the trauma of her father's execution. She held no State office at the time of her death, yet the United Nations Security Council was convened to condemn her assassination. She had represented hope. In her autobiography *The Daughter of the East* she noted that: 'Pakistan is no ordinary country. And mine has been no ordinary life'.[1] To this, to our regret, we have added that she had no ordinary death. She openly spoke that her life was at risk, but she had to undertake the risk to rid Pakistan of the militants. In another context, she said: 'We had heard rumours that the [Zia] regime was going to get the Afghan *mujahideen* to kill me.[2]

Of lasting impact are the reactions of people who had been subordinate to her Kamran Shafi wrote: 'She came out as someone from one's own family: relaxed, easy, and eager to put her guest at immediate ease...Benazir was a very decent person at heart'.[3] Another journalist M. Ziauddin wrote of his experience: 'I had gone to the meeting after hearing many stories about her arrogance, hot temper, and [a] short fuse. But the Benazir I met was a person one could communicate [with], enter into [a] heated debate and argue with'.[4]

She did not excise from the second edition, Faisal Hayat's account of his resistance to torture and his refusal to abandon her cause, even though, in between, he had joined the cabinet of General Musharraf. This is symptomatic of people having resisted Ziaul Haq and having joined Pervez Musharraf. But the shrinkage of dictatorial space has been greater. After Benazir Bhutto's assassination, an array of generals, admirals, and air marshals gathered together asking President Pervez Musharraf to step down.[5]

She spent most of her life in jail or exile. Her years in power were not her years of triumph. She fought an uphill battle to become Prime Minister twice. She fought a losing battle both times, unable to complete her terms. Her husband suffered terms of imprisonment. His mettle showed when he could handle the crisis of her assassination with more responsibility than the regime.

Instead of stressing that Pervez Musharraf had met Benazir Bhutto twice in Dubai and that he and she shared common enemies, her death was put down not to the assassin, not to the suicide bomber, but to a lever on her vehicle. The manufacturers of the vehicle threatened to sue.

In contrast, Asif Zardari, her widower, responded by saying 'We have decided to turn our grief into our strength'.[6] This is the strand of hope that her legacy holds out.

Notes

1. Benazir Bhutto, *Daughter of the East*, 2nd ed. (London: Simon and Schuster 2007), p. xi.
2. Ibid., p. 328.
3. *Dawn*, Karachi, 28 December 2007.
4. Ibid., 30 December 2007.
5. Ibid., 23 January 2008.
6. *Newsline*, Karachi, January 2008, p. 24.

CHAPTER 33
THE FOURTH PPP REGIME (2008–2013)

Following a pattern, a long period of military rule was succeeded by a PPP regime. Having lost Benazir Bhutto to a terror attack on 27 December 2008, the PPP rallied. In the elections held on 18 February 2008, the PPP won 118, the PML (N) 89 and PML (Q) 50 seats. Thus, the ruling party lost, and the least favoured party won yet another term. Pervez Musharraf continued as president till 18 August 2008 and administered the oath of office to PPP nominee Yusuf Raza Gilani as prime minister. Subsequent to Musharraf's resignation, Benazir Bhutto's widower Asif Ali Zardari served as President from 9 September 2008 to 8 September 2013

During this term, apart from frayed relations with political forces, the PPP faced three internal challenges: from the judiciary, from power outages, and from unemployment. The PPP was able to bring in the Eighteenth Amendment to the Constitution, undoing the Eighth Amendment, and reducing the powers of the President, especially Article 58 2(b) under which prime ministers were dismissed and parliaments dissolved.

Following up on the Charter of Democracy, the PPP and the PML (N) agreed on 21 February to form a coalition, but there was underlying tension over the restoration of Supreme Court judges, who had been dismissed by Pervez Musharraf. While Nawaz Sharif was wholeheartedly in favour of their restoration, Asif Ali Zardari was vocally reluctant. This ultimately led to the break-up of the coalition, but this development took place in stages.

On 24 March 2008, immediately after being elected prime minister, Syed Yusuf Raza Gilani ordered the release of the Supreme Court judges, but not their restoration. On 1 March 2008, both parties agreed to restore the judges, but on 11 May the talks collapsed and the next day the PML (N) pulled out of the coalition. With its democratic credentials in the balance, the PPP relented and on 20 September four deposed judges took fresh oaths of office. It was not till 15 March 2009 that Iftikhar Muhammad Chaudhry was re-installed as chief justice.

On 13 February 2009, Chief Justice Iftikhar Muhammad Chaudhry took *suo moto* notice of President Zardari's decision to appoint judges without the approval of the Supreme Court and suspended the official notification. On 17 February 2009, Prime Minister Gilani said that all the recommendations of the Chief Justice regarding the appointment of judges had been approved.

On 30 March 2010, the Supreme Court gave the National Accountability Bureau (NAB) 24 hours to implement the court verdict.

At the core of contention were the allegations of corruption against Asif Ali Zardari. On 6 December 2009, the Supreme Court re-opened the National Reconciliation Order (NRO) cases which had given immunity to politicians and declared the amnesty unlawful. The Court ordered fresh action by approaching the Swiss courts that had made the allegations of corruption. Upon inquiry, it was found that the Swiss courts had closed the corruption cases against the Zardaris, but the Chief Justice ordered Prime Minister Gilani to write a letter to the relevant Swiss authorities asking to re-open the cases. This Gilani refused to do, citing the constitutional immunity enjoyed by the President.

This refusal, the Supreme Court refused to countenance, and on 12 June 2010 the Supreme Court rejected the government's summary on the NRO verdict and on 25 July reserved judgment. The Chief Justice was insistent that the Prime Minister write a letter to the Swiss authorities following a draft it had approved. On 31 October the Supreme Court began hearing the Review Petition in the NRO case. On 10 January 2013 issued a short order on the NRO case. On 16 January 2012, Prime Minister Gilani was charged and on 26 April convicted of Contempt of Court. The Parliament had sought to give immunity to the Prime Minister, but on 19 June 2012, he was unseated. The PPP on 22 June 2012 elected Raja Pervaiz Ashraf as the new Prime Minister. These developments were taking place simultaneously with a sit-in led by Imran Khan the cricketer and Maulana Tahir-ul-Qadri, a cleric flown in from Canada.

As a remedy, the National Assembly on 9 July 2012 passed the Contempt of Court Bill (COCA 2012) amending the powers of contempt, but the Supreme Court struck down the legislation as unconstitutional and on 15 September, annulled it. On 10 October, the Supreme Court approved the draft of the letter it wished to write to the Swiss courts.

Apart from its pursuit of corruption cases against the President, the Supreme Court delivered other judgments that could not have been relished by the Executive. On 28 April 2010, the Supreme Court struck down the Prime Minister's orders promoting fifty-two bureaucrats. On 14 January 2011, the Supreme Court removed Syed Ali Raza as President of the National Bank. On 21 April 2011, the Supreme Court acquitted all the accused in the widely publicised Mukhtaran Mai gang rape case. On 30 March the Supreme Court scrapped the Executive's agreements with private power plants. As we shall presently see, power outages had become a political issue. On 12 October 2012, the Supreme Court issued an interim order on the Balochistan situation, where unrest had become compounded by sectarian massacres.

Not content with annulling the COCA 2012 Bill passed by the Parliament, the Supreme Court began proceedings against the Eighteenth Amendment, which had repealed the Eighth Amendment, in order to restore the parliamentary form of government and to curtail the powers of the President, which had increased during the previous military regime. The Eighteenth Amendment bill had been adopted unanimously by the National Assembly on 8 April 2010 and by the Senate on 15 April. On 12 May 2010, a full bench began hearing petitions against the Eighteenth Amendment on 21 October, it passed an interim order.

The only Supreme Court judgment which could have been welcomed by the government was its detailed judgment in the Asghar Khan case wherein it was held that the PPP had been unfairly deprived of representation in the 1990 elections.

During the fourth PPP regime, relations with the United States plummeted because of three incidents, the Raymond Davis affair, the US Seal raid that killed Osama bin Laden in Abbottabad, and the Salala incident when NATO forces bombed to death twenty-eight Pakistani soldiers.

According to his memoirs, *The Contractor*, Raymond Davis killed two Pakistanis Faizan Haider and Muhammad Fahim, whom he said were carrying guns and seemed to threaten him. As there was no remedy for the act of murder, American functionaries headed by Senator John Kerry claimed diplomatic immunity for him, a claim that Foreign Minister Shah Mahmood Qureshi rejected. The following passage from his Preface characterizes the nature of his revelations: 'If I withhold anything, it is only to ensure that I don't divulge information that could compromise our national security, or put any American service personnel or contractors in harm's way.'[1]

Finally, recourse was taken to a Sharia court to obtain his release by paying $130,000 for each, for a total of $2,340,000 the largest amount of blood money ever awarded in Pakistan.[2] What Davis does not withhold, is that the US's concerns were not confined to the safety of an American citizen, and a larger consideration had prevailed: 'Those responsible for my welfare needed to get me out of the country first, and they needed to do it fast before Bin Laden could slip away once again.'[3]

From Davis's account, it appears that the CIA had traced Osama bin Laden to a house in Abbottabad but could not carry out its mission of killing him, lest the presence of Raymond Davis in Pakistan complicated the situation. President Barack Obama reveals: 'Although Pakistan's government cooperated with us on a host of counterterrorism operations and provided a vital supply path for our forces in Afghanistan, it was an open secret that certain elements inside the country's military, and especially its intelligence services, maintained links to the Taliban and perhaps even al-Qaeda, sometimes using them as strategic assets to ensure that the Afghan government remained weak and unable to align itself with Pakistan's number one rival, India.[4]... When I reached him [President Zardari], however, he expressed congratulations and support. "Whatever the fallout," he said, "it's very good news".'[5]

Barack Obama says that the US had considered bombing Osama bin Laden's hideout but, in that case, the death of Osama bin Laden could not have been proved. Consigning his corpse to the sea, however, also had the effect of leaving lingering doubts.

The 'fallout' anticipated by Asif Ali Zardari became a reality but with an unconventional twist. The discovery of Osama bin Laden in the proximity of the Pakistan Military Academy had put the Army Chief General Ashfaq Parvez Kayani and the ISI Chief Lt.-Gen. Ahmed Shuja Pasha on the defensive. The fact that the US had made a lightning SEAL strike on Pakistan undetected by them, lay them open to charges of either complicity or negligence.

However, one act of indiscretion by Pakistan's Ambassador to the US, Hussain Haqqani, put the shoe on the other foot. Haqqani in a memo to Admiral Mike Mullen allegedly wrote to his hosts asking them: 'To set up in Pakistan, a security team more friendly to Washington'. The judicial fallout was prolonged and outlasted the regime. Chief Justice Saqib Nisar resurrected the 'Memogate' case on 1 February 2018. Finally, Chief Justice Asif Saeed Khosa closed the case on 14 February 2019 by ruling that it was the responsibility of the State of Pakistan to arrest Hussain Haqqani if it so wished. The Chief Justice noted that the petitioners were not present in court and the case had been pending for eight years.

With two high-profile cases involving the United States fresh in mind, Pakistan's attitude during the third, the Salala incident, was hard. In November, NATO forces bombed twenty-eight Pakistani soldiers to death. On 22 December 2011, the US issued a statement that 'The killings resulted in mistakes from both sides.' It was alleged that Pakistani troops had fired first but Maj.-Gen. Athar Abbas challenged NATO to prove that Pakistan had fired first. In retaliation Pakistan shut down the Shamsi Airfield and the road supply line of NATO to Afghanistan. The apology of Anne W. Patterson, the US Ambassador to Pakistan, was not considered enough and, finally, on 3 July 2012, Secretary of State Hillary Clinton apologised, and the supply line was restored.

What President Barack Obama had termed an *open secret* was formally conveyed to the American ambassador by the Pakistani Chief of Army Staff on 23 September 2009. 'Fear that the ISAF mission will end without the establishment of a non-Taliban, Pashtun-led government friendly to Pakistan adds to the Pakistani establishment's determination not to cut its ties irrevocably to the Afghan Taliban. General Kayani was utterly frank about this'. Ambassador Anne Peterson's advice to the State Department was that 'resolving the Kashmir dispute which lies at the core of Pakistan's support to terrorist groups would dramatically improve the situation. Enhanced USG [United States Government] efforts in this regard should be considered.'[6]

General Kayani's presentiments have proved to be well-founded, but despite heightened Congress support for the Kashmir liberation struggle, the USG is not willing to let this option come to the table. In 2009, Pakistan was unhappily in the crossfire. There were more than forty drone attacks on Pakistan, in which besides designated targets innocent men, women, and children were killed. In response, from the other side, there were enhanced terror strikes on military installations. On 22 May 2011, Naval Base PNS Mehran was attacked; on 27 January 2012, the Pakistan Military Academy at Abbottabad was attacked. On 16 August, it was the turn of Kamra airbase and on 20 December 2012 the Peshawar airbase was targeted.

Sectarian killings went side by side, with the distinctive Hazaras being the main targets. There were eighteen sectarian attacks in 2011 culminating in ninety-three Hazaras being killed in Quetta on 10 January 2013 and another sixty-seven being killed on 10 February. Sporadic bomb attacks against minority sects became routine. There were other challenges as well on the home front. Inflation was attributed by the Hazaras solely to the corruption of the ruling party. According to Imran Khan of Pakistan Tehreek-e-Insaf expensive petrol, inflation, and high electricity rates, meant that the prime minister was a thief.

Shehbaz Sharif of the PML (N) complained that the PPP-led Sindh government was withholding electricity from the Punjab, and once in power, his party would end power outages in a fortnight. Power riots in the Punjab took place on 2 October 2011 and 18 June 2012. In between, on 30 March 2012, the Supreme Court scrapped the regime's agreements with private power plants. The suffering people of Pakistan believed in these accusations. The end of the fourth PPP tenure on 25 March 2013 provided relief to both, the ruler and the ruled.

Notes

1. Raymond Davis, *The Contractor* (New York, Ben Bella Books, 2017), p. 8.
2. Ibid., p. 133.
3. Ibid., p. 119.
4. Barack Obama, *A Promised Land* (New York, Crown Publishing Group, 2020), p. 679.
5 Ibid., p. 696.
6. *Dawn*, 29 May 2011.

Chapter 34
The Third PML (N) Regime (2013–2017)

The third term of Nawaz Sharif as Prime Minister did not have the sanction of his earlier terms. He was identified as a part of the Zia legacy. When President Ghulam Ishaq Khan dismissed him under 58(2b), the Supreme Court under Chief Justice Nasim Hasan Shah restored his government. A restored prime minister and a fuming president affected the normal functioning of the state; with the result that the COAS General Abdul Waheed Kakar brokered a deal under which both resigned. The second term of Nawaz Sharif ended when he dismissed the COAS General Pervez Musharraf mid-flight from Colombo and jeopardized the lives of the airline passengers by refusing to let the aeroplane land. The armed forces intervened, the first coup made necessary by a matter of life and death. Nawaz Sharif's equation with the armed forces broke down in the wake of the Osama bin Laden operation. He called the army a 'holy cow', the burden of his stricture being: 'End your domination of foreign policy [making] if you wish the criticism to end.'[1]

Paradoxically, upon coming to power in 2013, Nawaz Sharif did not even appoint a full-time foreign minister. Ostensibly holding the portfolio himself, Nawaz Sharif made two appointments: Sartaj Aziz as Advisor to the Prime Minister on National Security and Foreign Affairs and Syed Tariq Fatemi as Minister of State for Foreign Affairs. With regard to foreign policy, the priority of Nawaz Sharif was to improve relations with India.

Abdul Basit, then Pakistan's High Commissioner to India has described the parleys between the Indian Prime Minister, Narendra Modi, and the Pakistani Prime Minister, Nawaz Sharif, in the following words: 'The meeting between the two prime ministers was suffused with incredible amicability... the prime minister also talked about enhancing bilateral trade and people to people contact and moving from confrontation to co-operation. He, however, did not raise the issue of Kashmir and restricted himself to proposing that the foreign secretaries should meet as early as possible to work out modalities for resuming the bilateral dialogue process.'[2]

Such a weak stance served no purpose. It encouraged India in the hope that beneficial relations could be obtained with Pakistan circumventing the Kashmir dispute. On 9 July 2015, both Pakistan and India became members of the Shanghai Co-operation Organization (SCO) and the prime ministers of the two neighbours met on the sidelines of the summit/ these overtures proved utterly insubstantial. On 9 December 2015, Sushma Swaraj (1952–2019) the Indian Minister of External Affairs paid a surprise visit to Lahore and met the Pakistani Premier. Nothing came of this visit, or Prime Minister Narendra Modi's visit to Lahore on 27 December 2015 to meet his Pakistani counterpart. Because, about a year later, on 30 September 2016, India put off the SAARC Summit indefinitely.

Relations with Russia improved though, as without Russian support, Pakistan's entry to the SCO would not have been possible. On 20 November 2014, a Defence Co-operation Pact was signed. On 16 October 2015, the two countries signed an LNG Pipeline Accord. Two years later the Russian representative Zamir Kabulov was vocally critical of the Indo-Afghan hostility to Pakistan, at the Heart of Asia Conference at Amritsar (4 December 2016) and even had praise for Pakistan's foreign policy.

Relations with the United States, on the other hand, deteriorated. On 2 July 2017, US Senator John McCain (chairman of the Senate Armed Services Committee) arrived in Islamabad with another 'do more' tough message. More arm twisting was done by Secretary of State, Rex Tillerson, on 24 October 2017. And on 4 December Secretary of Defence, James Mattis, arrived with a similar message. A month later, on 5 January 2012, the United States suspended aid to Pakistan. Pakistan retaliated after fifteen days by demanding American help in sending Afghan refugees back to their country.

On 26 January 2018, the United States and Pakistan were at odds over another drone attack. The United States said it had targeted terrorists, while Pakistan pointed to 'collateral damage' which meant the killing of non-combatants, especially women and children. Nawaz Sharif termed drone attacks a violation of Pakistan's sovereignty, but they continued unabated. Drone attacks served only one purpose; they provoked terrorists, who would plan their attack in US-held Afghanistan and after the incidents disappear into the Afghan refugee camps, for the removal of which, Pakistan was pressing the United States.

Pakistan retained the support of China, and Nawaz Sharif visited China in July 2013 and November 2014. President Xi Jinping arrived in Pakistan on 20 April 2015. Relations were maintained also with the Muslim world. On 3 March 2015, Nawaz Sharif visited Saudi Arabia and on 25 March 2016, the President of Iran, Hassan Rouhani, arrived on a two-day visit.

On the home front, the terror continued to strike with regularity, with three incidents seared on the Pakistani psyche. On 16 December 2014, the Taliban attacked the Army Public School in Peshawar massacring 141 persons mostly students and teachers. The Principal Tahira Qazi who had been rescued went back inside the school, refusing to abandon her students, and shared their fate. The Taliban accused Pakistan of excesses to the same extent the United States considered Pakistan's efforts inadequate. The Taliban had hit where—according to their statement accepting responsibility—it would hurt most. They wanted the Pakistan Army to mourn their children. Such inhuman acts would make the rehabilitation of the Taliban an emotional crisis.

On 13 May 2015, forty-five residents of Al Azhar Garden housing complex, belonging to the Shia Ismaili community, were gunned down in a bus near Safoora Goth in Karachi. On 8 August 2016, the Taliban killed Balochistan Bar Association President Bilal Anwar Kasi. When his body was taken to the Civil Hospital, Quetta, more than seventy lawyers who had gathered there in protest were blown up by a suicide bomber. On 24 October, again in Quetta, terrorists stormed the Police Training Centre, killing sixty-two cadets. These are only the most devastating incidents. Terror attacks in which the casualties were lower are too many to be detailed.

In addition to the above, the PML (N) regime faced challenges and sit-ins organized by Imran Khan of the Pakistan Tehreek-e-Insaf and Tahir-ul-Qadri of Pakistan Awami Tehreek. During the first sit-in, a violent clash ensued between the Punjab Police and Pakistan Awami Tehreek activists on 17 June 2014 resulting in several protesters being killed by the police. On 28 August a First Information Report was registered against Prime Minister Nawaz Sharif, and his brother Shehbaz Sharif, the Chief Minister of the Punjab. The sit-in ended on 16 December 2014, only when the Army Public School, Peshawar tragedy took place.

Another source of trouble was the judiciary. The Supreme Court judges Nawaz Sharif had campaigned to have restored, and for whose cause he had left the ruling coalition in 2008, within a fortnight of becoming prime minister, the Swiss authorities declared the cases against the Zardaris time barred. The political scene became more interesting when the Supreme Court served a Contempt of Court notice on Imran Khan on 21 July and absolved him of contempt on 28 August 2013.

Finally came the discovery of the Panama Papers which listed Nawaz Sharif among the individuals who had stashed money offshore. The Supreme Court took up the so-called 'Panama Gate' case on 1 November 2016 and on 28 July 2017 disqualified Nawaz Sharif from being Prime Minister. The operative part of the judgment was: 'It has not been denied that Respondent #1 as Chairman of the Board of Capital SZE was entitled to salary, therefore the statement that he did not draw the salary would not prevent the undrawn salary from being receivable, hence an asset.'[3]

In sum, the Prime Minister was disqualified for not mentioning a salary he had not drawn. On 1 August, Shahid Khaqan Abbasi was elected Prime Minister. Thus in both, the PPP and the PML (N) regimes, the party would complete their constitutional terms, but not the prime ministers.

Notes

1. *Dawn*, 11 June 2011, p. 1.
2. Abdul Basit, *Hostility: A Diplomat's Diary on Pakistan-India Relations and More* (Karachi: Lightstone Publishers, 2022), p. 66.
3. Anwer Shaheen (ed.), *Pakistan Perspectives*, Vol. 22, no. 2 July–December 2017, p. 211.

Chapter 35
The Pakistan Tehreek-e-Insaf Regime (2018–2022)

Imran Khan has been Pakistan's star cricketer. He was the captain of the cricket team which won the World Cup in 1992. Coming into power after what he described as a '22-year struggle' Imran Khan promised change—a New Pakistan. Later, he would describe it as the State of Madinah, the dispensation under the Holy Prophet (PBUH) himself.

During the terms of his two immediately preceding regimes, Imran Khan would address the crowds at the sit-ins he had organized denouncing inflation as man-made and ascribing it solely due to corruption.

Another Oxford man to become the Prime Minister of Pakistan, he did not know what were the market forces and the US sanctions that precluded Pakistan from buying fuel and power from neighbouring Iran. During the second year of his term, Imran Khan had to contend with the Covid-19 pandemic, an international increase in oil prices and a US dollar gain against the Pakistani rupee.

Normally, a leader already popular in another field, leading a government elected by the people generates sufficient goodwill to ride out such crises. Imran Khan, an all-rounder did not realize that by raising the ante by bowling aggressively, he was preparing the pitch for bouncers. When such a team wins the toss and elects to bat, the batsmen face balls in which line and length have been pre-determined. In a triangular match, the batsman faces a fast bowler at one end, and a spinner at the other. The selection of the team was another problem. The prime minister promised change and had a cabinet liberally filled with former members of the PPP, including both the foreign and finance ministers.

Had Imran Khan not, at the top of his container, at the top of his voice proclaimed that if there was inflation and the power tariff was high, 'the Prime Minister was a thief,' he would not have been judged too harshly. When Imran Khan could not prevent prices of everyday goods from spiralling, when he could not control rapid increases in fuel prices, the people too disregarded the normal economic forces at work. Prime minister Raja Pervaiz Ashraf who had suffered Imran Khan's harangues turned around in parliament to call the incumbent prime minister 'a thief'. The Speaker expunged the remarks, but the video went viral. The consequence was that the prime minister kept away from parliament as long as possible.

Regardless, Prime Minister Imran Khan, and his spokespersons, kept a brave face. On 26 August 2021, Imran Khan in a 251-page document highlighted the achievements of his government over the last three years. This provides us with a convenient document to tabulate his accomplishments. In his introductory remarks, Prime Minister Imran Khan said: 'When we came to power, [the] current account deficit was $20 billion, but today it has declined to $1.8 billion. In 2018 foreign exchange reserves were $16.4 billion, which are now over $27 billion. Total tax collection in the previous government was $3,800 billion, now it is $700 billion. Similarly, foreign remittances were $19.9 billion in 2018 and now they are $29.4 billion.'[1] The main document has another list.

ECONOMIC SECTOR.—Establishment of N-ovative Health Technologies (NHT) Pakistan's first facility for indigenous manufacturing of cardiac stents, angioplasty balloon catheters and other life-supporting medical devices; the launch of the country's first Green Bond (saving facilities); a people-friendly budget and upward economic trajectory; Roshan Digital Account (banking facility); Roshan Apni Car (car hire-purchase facility); and Roshan Samaji Khidmat (social service facility).[2] No one shall take issue with stent production, as it is an expensive component of heart surgery. All the above being mostly at the planning stage cannot really be termed as achievements, nevertheless so far so good, but 'people-friendly budget' has proved to be 'fighting words' as inflation has hit the common man harder than ever before. When in opposition Imran Khan had taunted his adversaries for approaching the IMF, but now his own budget was being termed an IMF budget. The 'upward economic trajectory' shall be measured by social indicators. The power tariff was already 40 per cent since July 2018 but on 8 October 2021, a further increase was ordered at the behest of the IMF to cut down circular debt.

Other details can be given in the Economic History section; at present we are presenting the Fuel prices of 1 October 2021 as compared to 1 July 2018. Fuel prices push up the transport price of almost every good or service making them more expensive. On the left are the present prices and on the right are the prices as they stood in the previous regime:

E10 Gasoline	Rs 125.32	Rs 97.00
Premier Euro	Rs 127.30	Rs 99.50
High-Octane Diesel Euro	Rs 120.04	Rs 119.31
LDO	Rs 99.51	Rs 80.91
SKO	Rs 99.31	Rs 87.70
JP-1	Rs 100.63	Rs 76.18

The inflation rate in 2021 is 19.9 per cent while in 2018 it was 3.93 per cent. In addition, there is the unusual figure of six chairmen of the Federal Board of Revenue having resigned within a period of three years. Shabbar Zaidi claimed that he had not been allowed to tax the lucrative poultry sector. Thus, political clout is still resisting the horizontal extension of the tax net and forcing a vertical increase which directly hurts the masses. Dr Kaiser Bengali named unnecessary import of luxury goods such as cat and dog food and also cited instances of parallel services. He named Coast Guards and Maritime Security Agency both having the responsibility of securing the coastal areas of Pakistan. Kaiser Bengali added: 'My personal conspiracy theory is that it [the Financial Assistance Task Force—FATF] is a tool to bring Pakistan to the point where they will force us to hand over our nuclear weapons'.[3]

FOREIGN AFFAIRS.—The next item on the achievement scoreboard: Kashmir cause; Palestine cause; Afghan Peace Process; and countering Indian propaganda. Naming the Kashmir cause first is ironic. No other ruler of Pakistan has damaged the Kashmir cause more than Imran Khan. For decades the main struggle before Pakistan has been to garner international support for the Kashmir dispute. The Kargil war was unable to achieve it, nor was Pervez Musharraf's contrary Four-Point formula (giving Kashmir autonomy and diarchy instead of freedom) have any effect and mercifully was allowed by India to lapse.

During the 1965 Indo-Pak war, Malaysia was the only country with which Pakistan had severed diplomatic relations for siding with India in the Kashmir dispute. On 18–20 December 2019, Malaysia under Prime Minister Mahathir Mohamad, held an international conference in Kuala Lumpur to discuss the situation arising out of India's revocation of Article 370 of the Indian Constitution which formally gave a special status to Kashmir, igniting fresh and more widespread protests in India-held Kashmir. Unlike Kofi Annan, this time, the Secretary-General of the United Nations Antonio Guterres was protesting over Human Rights violations in Kashmir.[4] Even American legislators, despite the US–India Nuclear Strategic Partnership were vocal about the atrocities being committed by Indian troops on unarmed even non-combatant Kashmiris (men, women, and children). Thus, at last, Pakistan was given a wide and sympathetic hearing. But the most prominent absentee at the Kuala Lumpur Conference was the Prime Minister of Pakistan, Imran Khan. A career diplomat pointed out: 'Kashmiris and Pakistanis raised questions of how a country which so quickly buckled under the Saudi pressure would fight the long and difficult battle for the cause of Kashmir.'[5]

As for the Palestine cause, it is difficult to determine why it was listed at all. During the last months of the Donald Trump Presidency, Secretary of State Mike Pompeo induced a number of Arab states to establish diplomatic relations with Israel. With their compliance, there is hardly any *locus standi* left for Pakistan. As far as the Afghan Peace Process is concerned, Pakistan is showing prudence because in 2000, it along with Saudi Arabia and the United Arab Emirates had recognized the Taliban regime, this time round, it is playing a waiting game. It was Senator Chris van Hollen, incidentally, who saved Pakistan from being made the scapegoat for American failure in its twenty years war in Afghanistan.

Countering Indian propaganda has been successful to a large extent, due to alliances between Russia, China, Iran, and Turkey, but has not made any difference on the ground as yet. Despite India's Nuclear Defence Alliance with the United States, she still buys war machines from Russia, this probably determines the extent of support that Pakistan receives from Russia.

CONSTITUTION.—Apart from the listing of achievements the PTI government has become involved in constitutional imbroglios concerning the Chief Election Commissioner and the NAB Chairman. The PTI government vowed on 1 September 2021 to bring a bill introducing Electronic Voting Machines (EVM) through its majority in parliament. On 7 September the Election Commission of Pakistan (ECP) posted thirty-seven objections to the induction of EVMs in the forthcoming 2023 elections. The basic objection was: It is nearly impossible to ensure that every machine is honest. Lack of ballot secrecy, lack of capacity at all levels and lack of ensuring security and chain custody for the machines at rest and during transportation. It also pointed out that there would be no evidence available in case of an election dispute. The ECP said that EVMs could not prevent low voter turnouts, low women's turnout, misuse of state authority, election fraud, and electronic ballot stuffing.

The next day, on 8 September 2021, the government rejected these objections. The Minister for Science and Technology, Shibli Faraz, stated that twenty-seven of the thirty-seven objections were not about machines, but related to the capacity of the Election Commission. Babar Awan (now in PTI) asked: 'Why do we feel threatened by technology?' To that the ECP had already responded by mentioning that Germany, Holland, Ireland, Italy and Finland had abandoned EVMs due to the lack of security. Why Imran Khan was averse to an electoral process that had brought him into power was not addressed.

The government's initial response was sober, but on 10 September 2021, Azam Swati, the Minister of Narcotics Control and Railways accused the ECP of accepting bribes and regularly rigging elections. He even suggested burning down such institutions. Fawad Chaudhry, Federal Minister for Information and Broadcasting, also criticized the ECP, calling it a mouthpiece for the opposition. Chaudhry noted that the Election Commission lacked legislative authority and attempted to blame Chief Election Commissioner Sikandar Sultan Raja for raising objections. Predictably, a PPP and ANP delegation waited on the Chief Election Commissioner promising to support him. The PPP Vice-President Senator Sherry Rahman termed the induction of EVMs as 'preparation for pre-poll rigging.'

On 16 September 2021, the Election Commission issued notices to the two ministers Swati and Chaudhry asking them to substantiate their allegations that the ECP had taken bribes or rigged elections. The same day *Dawn* published a letter addressed to NADRA by the ECP: 'The ECP is of the view that in the first instance, NADRA may inform us the fate of the previous project; that why NADRA is going to abandon the previous system and on what grounds and on which considerable sum of money equal to Rs. 66,500, 000 has already been dispensed with...'. Still, on the same day, 16 September 2021, a related development took place. The ECP had ahead of the Karachi Cantonment Board elections, served a show-cause notice to the Federal Minister for Maritime Affairs, Ali Haider Zaidi, over the violation of the election code of conduct. After more than a week, the minister retaliated by writing: 'In view of the above, I call upon you to tender [an] unconditional apology within 14 days of receiving the date of this letter,' making specific reference to the letter issued on 12 September 2021. Ali Zaidi went on to say that he would file a defamation suit on the ECP failing an apology.

On 19 September 2021, Fawad Chaudhry and Shibli Faraz asked the two junior members of the ECP to review the decision of the Chief Election Commissioner. Fawad Chaudhry also asked the CEC to resign. Predictably the PML (N) spokesperson Marriyum Aurangzeb urged punitive action against the ministers under Article 10 of the Election Act for inciting members to act against their chairman. The next day Azam Swati accused the Chief Election Commissioner of 'messing around' with the government. The PTI tried to remove the Chief Election Commissioner and sought to retain the NAB Chairman, Javed Iqbal.

After the NAB chairman's constitutional term expired, the government did not follow the prescribed procedure of consulting with the Leader of the House and the Leader of the Opposition. Fawad Chaudhry argued that consulting with the accused (Leader of the Opposition) on the appointment of his prosecutor would be inappropriate. However, Farogh Naseem, the Federal Minister of Law and Justice, publicly stated that they would consult with the Leader of the Opposition, Shehbaz Sharif.

Ultimately, the government took recourse to have President Arif Alvi, issue an ordinance on 6 October 2021 extending Javed Iqbal's tenure. PPP Vice-President Sherry Rahman described the person-specific ordinance as unconstitutional. On 8 October 2021, the Opposition requested a National Assembly session to discuss the Presidential Ordinance. Additionally, the Pakistan Bar Council and Supreme Court Bar Association stated that they would challenge the ordinance in the Supreme Court.

In a parallel development the Election Commission of Pakistan's (ECP) Scrutiny Committee while hearing the Foreign Funding case lodged against Imran Khan and the PTI, Prime Minister Imran Khan's lawyer had the original copy of the Habib Bank Ltd. account removed. Despite reminders, the ECP staff—deputed to scrutinize PTI's accounts—expressed their inability to provide the petitioner Akbar S. Babar's lawyers with the relevant documents. The petitioner's lawyer, Dr Syed Ahmad Hasan Shah, blamed the Committee for obstructing the perusal process. On 6 April 2021, the ECP reserved its ruling in the case against the prime minister.

Similarly, the cabinet refused to disclose details of the Toshakhana.[6] The government took the stand that disclosure of the details of the Toshakhana jeopardizes international ties. In his application, Rana Abrar Khalid an Islamabad-based senior journalist specializing in economic issues had asked the Pakistan Information Commission about the gifts received by Prime Minister Imran Khan.[7]

NO-CONFIDENCE MOTION.—When Imran Khan had first sought a vote of confidence, he had asked his party members to vote according to their conscience, but when the Opposition tabled a no-confidence motion, he invoked Article 63, which is an act against defection or floor crossing. After deferring twice the no-confidence motion, Deputy Speaker Qasim Khan Suri, who was presiding, termed the no-confidence motion unconstitutional, as it was inspired by a foreign conspiracy (by the United States). The accusation that a majority of the National Assembly was acting at the behest of a foreign power is extremely hard to credit.

On 3 April 2022, President Arif Alvi acted on the advice of Prime Minister Imran Khan and dissolved Pakistan's National Assembly. The intention behind this move was to thwart the scheduled no-confidence motion that aimed to depose Khan from his position as PM.

Thus considered, the deputy speaker's ruling was *prima facie* against a basic provision of the Constitution. The Constitution under Article 58, even in its first publication, contains the following explanation: 'Reference in this Article to "Prime Minister" shall not be construed to include reference against whom a resolution for a vote of no confidence has been moved in the National Assembly, but has not been voted on, or against whom such a resolution has been passed, or who is continuing in office after his resignation or after the dissolution of the National Assembly.'[8] This, the Supreme Court upheld in its judgment of 7 April 2022. It restored the National Assembly, the Prime Minister and the Cabinet and fixed 9 April for the no-confidence vote to proceed. The National Assembly passed a no-confidence motion on 10 April, with 174 (172 were needed) out of 342 votes in favour. As a result, Khan was removed from the position of prime minister, making him the first prime minister of Pakistan to lose a no-confidence vote.

Apart from the judiciary, this move has involved Pakistan, at a vulnerable time in a diplomatic row among world powers. A US representative denied involvement in the no-confidence resolution[9] and the Russian representative asserted that the US was punishing Imran Khan for taking a balanced approach to the Russia–Ukraine War. Further claiming that it was tabled at the inception of Imran Khan's visit to Russia on 23 February and his parleying with President Vladimir Putin on 24 February—the day Russia moved its troops into Ukraine.[10] On the same day, the United States reiterated its denial of any role in the political crisis in Pakistan.

Although the DG ISPR issued a statement that the army was not behind the no-confidence vote, Chief of the Army Staff, General Qamar Javed Bajwa, speaking at the Islamabad Security Dialogue, apparently took a different stance on the Russia–Ukraine crisis, 'despite legitimate security concerns of Russia, its aggression against a smaller country cannot be condoned'. 'Relations with Russia were "cold" for a long time because of numerous reasons. However, some positive developments in this regard had taken place recently.... Pakistan enjoyed close strategic ties with China. "Equally, we share a long and excellent strategic relationship with the US which remains our largest export market," he added.'[11]

Three Congressmen, namely Scott Perry, Gregory Steube, and Mary E. Miller, pushed for sanctions against Pakistan. Furthermore, the President of the United States skipped the customary phone call to the Pakistani Prime Minister. General Bajwa's description fits loosely. Nonetheless, it appears improbable that the no-confidence resolution against Imran Khan could have been influenced by the US. It is hard to believe that Opposition members of the National Assembly committed treason.

The no-confidence resolution was a result of accumulated grievances and not a sudden move. The misgovernment, partial accountability especially the directive given to the National Accountability Bureau to not investigate businessmen or ventures, and mounting inflation was a matter badly affecting the constituents. None of these could be swept under the rug of American interference. Why would the United States wish to change a pro-Russian regime that was incompetent?

The economic challenges faced by Pakistan, largely attributed to the IMF's policies, have led to growing dissatisfaction with the United States. Inflation has been a persistent issue in the country, but the current PTI government saw an unprecedented level of hyperinflation, with the US dollar reaching a high of Rs 187. Public debt also skyrocketed to over Rs 18 trillion, surpassing the combined liabilities accumulated in the past seventy-five years. According to the State Bank of Pakistan, the total debt amounts to Rupees 42.8 trillion, not including liabilities incurred as of March 2022.[12]

It is also very unlikely that the United States would want to remove a regime that was following its economic dictates. This is a publicly stated American and not Russian objective.

We must reiterate, however, that Imran Khan's visit to Russia and his meeting with President Vladimir Putin was an act which we must admire. Our relations with Russia do not allow any excuse to postpone a visit to Russia (see Part 8: Diplomatic History). By the same token, the menacing attitude of the United States towards Pakistan does not admit of a rebuff to the Russian Federation.

Notes

1. *Dawn*, 27 August 2021, p. 1.
2. Ibid., p. 3. Where exact dates are mentioned, the following day's *Dawn* and other newspapers provide the references.
3. Masooma Hasan (Editor-in-Chief), *Pakistan Horizon*, vol. 73, no. 1, January 2021, pp. 28, 33.
4. *Dawn*, 30 January 2021, p. 12.
5. Abdul Basit, *Hostility*, p. 271.
6. The Toshakhana Department was initiated in 1974 during the ministry of Zulfikar Ali Bhutto. It is controlled by the Cabinet Division of the Government of Pakistan. Its main purpose is to collect and keep gifts offered to members of parliament, ministers, foreign secretaries, bureaucrats, the President, the Prime Minister, military personnel, and other officials by the heads of other states, governments, and international dignitaries.
7. *Dawn*, 21 September 2021, pp. 1, 3.
8. *The Constitution of the Islamic Republic of Pakistan, 1973* (Lahore: Mansoor Book House, 1973), p. 42.
9. Lisa Curtis, cited in *The Express Tribune*, Karachi, 5 April 2022, p. 1.
10. *The Express Tribune*, 2 April 2022, p. 1.
11. *The Express Tribune*, 3 April 2022, p. 6.
12. *The Express Tribune*, 6 April 2022, p. 11.

Chapter 36

The PML (N) Shehbaz Sharif Regime (2022–2023)

Twelve days after the PTI government led by Imran Khan was removed through a No-Confidence Movement, the Pakistan Democratic Movement (PDM) coalition government took charge on 11 April 2022. This coalition included PML (N) with Shehbaz Sharif as the prime minister and the Pakistan People's Party with Bilawal Bhutto-Zardari as the foreign minister. President Arif Alvi, associated with PTI, refrained from administering the oath.

Imran Khan's decline in popularity was primarily attributed to escalating inflation. Contrary to expectations, the PDM regime not only failed to control inflation but witnessed its acceleration, surpassing the previous regime's pace. By the end of June 2023, the inflation rate had soared to over 21.03 per cent, marking the highest in thirteen years.

Not allowed by the US to complete the Iran-Pakistan gas pipeline, led to a substantial and debilitating increase in petroleum prices for Pakistan. Additionally, elevated transportation charges contributed to a 31 per cent surge in food prices, a situation deemed unimaginable just a few years prior. The dissatisfaction with the regime was exacerbated by politically hostile private television channels. The looming threat of default became the paramount concern for both the government and consumers, largely driven by International Monetary Fund (IMF) conditionalities. Dr Ashfaque Hasan Khan expressed discontent, stating, 'This is the most brutal IMF program ever given to any country in the world.'[1]

Although the statement holds true, a crucial point to consider is that the tax net consistently expands in a vertical manner rather than a horizontal one. In other words, government employees and individuals with taxes deducted at the source experience an additional tax burden, while those in sectors or individuals not directly subjected to taxes find themselves in a more favourable position. It is worth noting that agricultural tax has evolved into a provincial cess, and though it is imposed, landowners can potentially evade it if the enforcement system is lenient.

Two noteworthy observations demand attention. Despite increasing food prices, the lines of customers at upscale restaurants increased, and the fervour for branded clothing shows no signs of diminishing. On the other side, more people have become destitute. In a book of history, it is unavoidable to allude to the French Revolution. The revolution was triggered by the oppressive taxation of the poor and the ancient regime's preferential treatment of the rich. In 1774, Controller-General of Finances Anne-Robert-Jacques Turgot attempted to reverse this trend by taxing the rich and sparing the poor, only to incur the disapproval of Queen Marie Antoinette. He was subsequently replaced, and in 1777, Jacques Necker, who enjoyed popularity at court, inadvertently fuelled discontent leading to a revolution.

Hence, there are limitations to the potential benefits of privilege, particularly for those who have concealed their wealth abroad. An evident consequence of this practice is the depreciation of the rupee, dropping from Rs 65 per dollar to the current rate of around Rs 300 per dollar. It is imperative for the affluent to remember a historical precedent: during Independence, when the Nizam of Hyderabad attempted to send a cheque to Pakistan, Prime Minister Jawaharlal Nehru prevented its encashment, citing its reliance on Indian securities. Even after seventy-five years, the unresolved matter remains before the British courts. In the event that withholding wealth from the country jeopardizes the sovereignty of the nation, the Government of India retains the authority to seize such assets.

Kaiser Bengali and Syed Shabbar Zaidi have consistently alerted us to the fact that the import of super luxury items and the duplication of services are depleting our resources, with privilege acting as a shield for financial stability. While genuine trade and industry associations often place advertisements lamenting that certain levies or reductions are negatively impacting their profitability, their situation remains comparatively better than those facing homelessness. If the affluent contribute their fair share in taxes, they could potentially enjoy freedom from taxes on products instead of on income. This point is crucial to highlight, particularly in the context of the 16-month tenure of Shehbaz Sharif, which has been marked by inflation.

The challenges extended beyond issues such as an unsympathetic judiciary and large-scale demonstrations, exemplified by the events on 7 May following Imran Khan's arrest. Despite avoiding the challenges posed by the COVID-19 pandemic and climate change disasters during the PTI regime, they continued to be deeply immersed in political intrigues and strategies. As the constitutional term of the National Assembly concluded, the regime mercifully came to an end on 9 August 2023.

Note

1. *Arab News*, 1 July 2023.

Part 6
Constitutional History

CHAPTER 37
Constitutional Developments (1947, 1956, 1962 and 1973)

The Constitutional History of British India

1. *Regulating Act 1773*: The East India Company was required to submit all material correspondence to the King's ministers.
2. *Pitt's India Act 1784*: Company affairs subordinated to a Board of Governors appointed by the Crown (6 members). This system of dual government, with more amendments in 1813, 1833 and 1853 continued till the Company's rule ended.
3. *An Act for the Better Government of India 1858*: It abolished the Company's rule and appointed a Secretary of State for India with a council of 15 members. The Governor-General was given the additional designation of Viceroy.
4. *Indian Councils Act of 1861*: A 5th member was added to the Viceroy's Council. Between 6 to 12 members were added to act as a legislature. The portfolio system was introduced, and a measure of decentralization was adopted. Indians were included in the Council and provinces were given legislative councils.
5. *Indian Councils Act of 1892*: Enlarged the Imperial and Provincial Councils memberships. Although direct elections were not the norm, the councils became more representative, as the chambers of commerce, university bodies, municipal bodies and district boards sent their nominees, though the official majority was retained. The powers of criticism of the councils increased.
6. *Indian Councils Act 1909*: Morley–Minto Reforms. Central and provincial legislatures were enlarged, their functions extended, and the principle of election was legally recognized. An official majority was maintained in the centre but not in provinces. Separate electorates were ceded.
7. *The Government of India Act 1919*: (Montagu–Chelmsford Reforms) Central and provincial subjects were divided. Central subjects were foreign affairs, defence, communications, and taxation. Provincial subjects being education, health, agriculture, law & order, and justice. Bi-cameral legislature in the Centre. In the provinces, there were two categories. Reserved subjects were under nominated members with no responsibility to the House whereas transferred subjects were under directly elected members. This was known as Dyarchy. Separate electorates were extended to Sikh and Christian groups.
8. *Government of India Act 1935*: The Federal Act was never carried out as the Congress, and Muslim League, and Princes opposed it. It sought to impose Dyarchy in the centre. However, it gave greater power to the provinces. Dyarchy was removed from the provinces, Assemblies replaced councils in the provinces. Burma was separated from India. Sindh was separated from Bombay and NWFP was given full provincial status with an Assembly.

Framing a constitution for Pakistan has been an uphill task, while preserving the constitution has proved to be a daunting task. Simply put, Pakistan enacted three constitutions, in 1956, in 1962 and in 1973; there are also some documents preceding the 1956 constitution and a series of amendments succeeding the 1973 constitution, which have to be taken into account in tracing the constitutional development of Pakistan. It is unusual for a country to have had more than one constitution. That we have had so many, with so many amendments, speaks volumes for political instability in Pakistan. While describing the constitutional history of British India, it was explained that a constitution embodies the set of rules according to which people agree to live with each other. The *Oxford English Dictionary's* definition is 'The system or body of fundamental principles according to which a nation, state, or body politic is constituted and governed'. It is thus the basic law from which other laws proceed. Constitution-making has proved elusive and contentious because of the inability to arrive at a consensus on two issues: the role of religion in the state and the degree of autonomy to be granted to the provinces. Both issues are covered under separate headings below. But first, we need to trace the early history of constitutions in Pakistan.

EARLY CONSTITUTIONAL HISTORY.—Pakistan gained independence as a Dominion of the British Commonwealth of Nations. Two documents governed the dominion: the Indian Independence Act of 1947 and the Government of India Act of 1935 (GOI Act 1935), which was to function as an interim constitution. There was a departure from the norm when the Jinnah chose to be governor-general, instead of prime minister, who is usually the chief executive in a parliamentary democracy.

The reason why Jinnah assumed the office of governor-general was to preempt the appointment of Lord Mountbatten, who wished to undo partition as governor-general. The GOI Act 1935 gave discretionary powers to the viceroy/governor-general; the British withdrew this provision when they handed over power. It has been pointed out[1] that Provision C to Section 8(2) of the Indian Independence Act precluded the governor-general from exercising personal discretion and individual judgement and made it mandatory for him to follow the advice of the prime minister.

On the other hand, Pakistan was being governed by the Provisional Constitution Order 1947. The centre had full power to alter the interim constitution under Section 9(1) of the Indian Independence Act. Until 1949, the governor-general was personally entitled to alter the interim constitution and after 1949, the Constituent Assembly was so empowered. Jinnah died before 1949 and thus he was able to alter the interim constitution. His first act was to change the form of the oath to be taken by the governor-general. It originally read: 'to bear true faith and allegiance to His Majesty (the King of England). Jinnah had it changed to 'bear true allegiance to the Constitution'.

It was under this amended form of the interim constitution that Jinnah took his oath of office as governor-general of Pakistan. Until 1949, the governor-general rather than the prime minister had been the chief executive of

Pakistan. To enforce this further, on 30 December 1947, the cabinet decided that no matter of policy or principle could be decided unless its meeting was presided over by the governor-general. This provision was personal to Jinnah since much depended on the prestige of the office holder. Had Jinnah been bound by decisions taken by Liaquat Ali Khan, it would have been a reversal of their pre-independence equation. This factor was also illustrated by the fact that Liaquat Ali Khan did not have to wait till 1949 to become chief executive. He became prime minister and chief executive following Jinnah's death in 1948 because, in the freedom movement, he had been far more prominent than the new governor-general, Khwaja Nazimuddin. The division of power at the centre did not become a constitutional issue at that time, but later it was held responsible for weakening the tradition of parliamentary governance.

The first contentious issue was the role that religion was to play in the polity of Pakistan. Since protagonists of both a secular and a religious state quote Jinnah. His statements are detailed below:

1. 'Let us lay down the foundations of our democracy on the study of truly Islamic ideals and principles.'[2]
2. 'You are free to go to your temples, you are free to go to your mosques or to any other place of worship in this State of Pakistan. You may belong to any religion, caste or creed—that has nothing to do with the business of the State...we are starting with this fundamental principle that we are all citizens and equal citizens of one State.'[3]
3. 'The constitution of Pakistan has yet to be framed by the Pakistan Constituent Assembly. I do not know what the ultimate shape of this constitution is going to be but I am sure that it will be a democratic type, embodying the essential principles of Islam...In any case, Pakistan is not going to be a theocratic state—to be ruled by priests with a divine vision. We have many non-Muslims they will enjoy the same rights and privileges as any other citizens.'[4]

The first quotation is cited by protagonists of an Islamic state and the second by the secularists. It is the third quotation that needs to be considered most. It is within one speech that we have a reference to Islamic values as well as a denunciation of theocracy. By considering both parts together, it emerges that Jinnah considered *liberty, equality,* and *fraternity* to be Islamic values that had to be followed. Democracy and Islam, according to him, were identical. Theocracy means the rule of the priests, and this certainly is a concept opposed to democracy. He also knew that there is no provision for an ordained priesthood in Islam. Jinnah spoke simultaneously against theocracy and in favour of Islamic norms because the majority was Muslim. No constitutional guarantee could neglect this aspect of Pakistan's polity. The form was secular, but the content was religious, and both these realities had to be reconciled. Then there is another vital aspect of Jinnah's third speech: The Constituent Assembly as a body, and not its president as an individual, would determine the nature of the constitution. Much of these statements reflected Jinnah's experience as the champion of minorities.

The Role of Minorities. Jinnah knew from experience that if a minority community of whatever following was discriminated against, it led to disintegration. He observed that it was Hindu–Muslim discord which had been responsible for India's enslavement. He also noted that there were caste and sectarian differences among Muslims and Hindus. These internal dissensions had to be contained. Then again, the role of the minorities was of more than symbolic value.

Jogendra Nath Mandal presided over the inaugural session of the Pakistan Constituent Assembly. The casting vote of S.P. Singha, the Christian Speaker of the Punjab Assembly enabled it to join Pakistan. H.S. Suhrawardy and Kiran Shankar Roy were co-authors of the united and independent Bengal scheme. H.S. Suhrawardy was denied his seat in the Constituent Assembly because he did not take up permanent residence in Pakistan. Kiran Shankar Roy took up residence and made one of the most moving speeches in support of Pakistan. Therefore, in any constitutional dispensation, the representation of minority communities could not be denied an honourable place.

The contribution of the Parsi community to the development of Pakistan is immense. They too have contributed to civic life and education, and their expertise in commerce has stood Pakistan in good stead.

The Role of the Ulama/Objectives Resolution. The demand that Pakistan be declared an Islamic State was put forward by Maulana Abul Ala Maududi, the founder of the Jamaat-i-Islami, who had earlier opposed the creation of Pakistan. He addressed meetings all over Pakistan and asserted that the future constitution should embody the following principles: (1) The sovereignty of Pakistan belongs to Allah alone and the Government of Pakistan has no right other than to enforce the will of Allah. (2) The basic law of Pakistan is the Shariah of Islam. (3) All those laws which are repugnant to Islam are to be revoked and in future, no such law should be passed. (4) The Government of Pakistan will exercise its authority within the limits prescribed by Islamic Shariah.

Apart from the fact that Jinnah was opposed to theocracy, some practical problems came in the way of applying the Shariah smoothly. Shariah has four legal systems, Hanafi, Maliki, Shafii and Hanbali. Since there is no accord on what constitutes Shariah, the law prescribed by one school of thought could be proscribed by another. As an example, the Hanafi Fiqh does not make the consent of a guardian binding on a bride; other *fiqhs* do. The social fallouts are the 'honour killings' which clearly transcend the Shariah. This movement of the Jamaat-i-Islami gathered wide support and momentum, and the Objectives Resolution tabled by Liaquat Ali Khan represented an attempt by the prime minister to defuse this tension. The Objectives Resolution was passed by the Constituent Assembly on 12 March 1949. It served as a preamble to the constitutions of 1956, 1962, and 1973 and has proved to be the most resilient document in the constitutional history of Pakistan.

> **OBJECTIVES RESOLUTION**
>
> 1. Whereas sovereignty over the entire Universe belongs to Allah Almighty alone, and the authority which He has delegated to the State of Pakistan through its people for being exercised within the limits prescribed by Him is a sacred trust.
> 2. This Constituent Assembly representing the people of Pakistan resolves to frame a constitution of the sovereign independent state of Pakistan; wherein the state shall exercise its power and authority through the chosen representatives of the people.
> 3. Wherein the principles of democracy, freedom, equality, tolerance, and social justice as enunciated by Islam shall be fully observed.
> 4. Wherein the Muslims shall be enabled to order their lives in the individual and collective spheres in accordance with the teaching and requirements of Islam as set out in the Holy Quran and the *Sunnah*.
> 5. Wherein adequate provisions shall be made for the minorities to freely profess and practice their religions and develop their cultures.
> 6. Whereby the territories now included in or accession with Pakistan and such territories as may hereafter be included in or accede to Pakistan shall form a federation wherein the units will be autonomous with such boundaries and limitation on their powers and authority as may be prescribed.
> 7. Wherein shall be guaranteed fundamental rights including equality of status, of opportunity before law, social economic and political justice and freedom of thought, expression, belief, faith, worship, and association subject to law and public morality.
> 8. Wherein adequate provision shall be made to safeguard the legitimate interests of minorities and backward and depressed classes.
> 9. Wherein the independence of the judiciary shall be fully secured.
> 10. Wherein the integrity of the territories of the federation, its independence and all its rights including its sovereign rights on land, sea and air shall be safeguarded.
> 11. So that the people of Pakistan may prosper and attain their rightful and honoured place amongst the nations of the world and make their full contribution towards international peace and progress and happiness of humanity.

The points on which the Objectives Resolution departed from the Jamaat-i-Islami formula are:

> **Point 1** meant that sovereignty was to be exercised by the people, reintroducing democratic principles. The rights other than to enforce the will of the sovereign was removed. **Point 2** specifically mentioned tolerance. **Point 3** says that Muslims shall be 'enabled', not compelled to order their lives in accordance with the Shariah. The Objective Resolution is in accord with the 256th Verse of the Quran (Surah Baqra) where 'there is no compulsion in religion'. **Point 4** mentions minority rights and **Point 6** mentions fundamental human rights, both of which were not part of the Jamaat-i-Islami demand. **Point 8** reiterates the rights of minorities and backward classes.

The Jamaat-i-Islami found Jinnah's declaration at the Sibi Durbar that the foundation of democracy would be on the basis of truly Islamic ideals and principles, inadequate. Since it did not support Jinnah's view of equal rights for minorities, as soon as it entered government, it imposed separate electorates on the minorities against their will. Maulana Abul Ala Maududi was arrested under the Safety Act on 4 October 1948. Some ulama such as Allama Shabbir Ahmad Usmani and Umar Hayat Khan, who had supported the Pakistan Movement, joined hands with them and the Jamaat-i-Islami, far from being deterred by the arrest of its leaders, widened its base and mounted intense pressure on the government. Points 6 and 9 to 11 are not directly concerned with religion but with the distribution of power between the centre and provinces, but even these were related to the demands made by the ulama.

Provincial Autonomy. East Pakistan was larger in terms of its population than all the provinces of West Pakistan put together. In any democratic dispensation, the representatives of East Bengal would command a majority. This, the politicians from West Pakistan, wished to avoid. The point was raised that East Bengal was greater in population by virtue of its Hindu community, otherwise, the Muslim population of both wings was equal. By cutting down minority rights it was possible to reduce the franchise of the East Wing.

Basic Principles Committee Report. The next document to be produced after the Objectives Resolution was the Basic Principles Committee Report. The committee, consisting of twenty-five members, was headed by Maulvi Tamizuddin Khan, president of the Constituent Assembly. Its interim report was submitted on 7 September 1950, but it pleased no one. The religious faction was angry because of the provision that the head of state could be a non-Muslim and the Bengalis were angry because their language was not given national status. The interim report indemnified the governor-general, prime minister, and legislators from appearing in court. On this score, the indignation of the ulama was justified, as the pious caliphs had readily appeared before courts when summoned. Since the interim report drew on the GOI Act 1935 it gave sweeping powers to the head of state, who could assume control of the provinces and, in case of emergency, could suspend the constitution in part or fully. This provision was circulated in advance of any constitution being framed! The interim report provided, moreover, for the head of state to be indirectly elected by the legislature. The form of government would be federal, as provided by GOI Act 1935. A federal form has more than one level of government, one at the level of the federation—in the centre—and the other governing the federating units or the provinces. The legislature was to be bicameral, having two houses, the lower being directly elected and the upper being indirectly elected. The upper house was to give equal representation to all the provinces. Thus, if East Bengal had a majority in the lower house, it became a minority in the upper house. Since the powers of both houses were equal, the majority of East Pakistan would be neutralized in this manner.

The final report of the Basic Principles Committee was presented during the term of Khwaja Nazimuddin's prime ministership in July 1952. Both the east and west wings were to have equal representation. Unlike the interim report, which mentioned Urdu as the only national language, the final report made no mention of any national language. One provision was made to conciliate the ulama. An ulama board was formed, at both the federal and provincial levels to prevent legislation which was un-Islamic. This fell short of conciliating the ulama as the government would have the power of nomination. Prime Minister Khwaja Nazimuddin withdrew the final report on 21 January 1953 without informing Maulvi Tamizuddin Khan, president of the Constituent Assembly. On 17 April 1953, Khwaja Nazimuddin was dismissed by Governor-General Ghulam Mohammad. Constitution framing, which had hitherto been contentious, had now assumed the proportion of a crisis.

1954 Draft Constitution. In 1954, Mohammad Ali Bogra, who was appointed prime minister in place of Khwaja Nazimuddin, formulated his constitutional proposals. He represented nobody but hailed from East Bengal. When he came across West Pakistani opposition to allow his province a majority, he proposed a solution to overcome it. His solution was given the name of the Mohammad Ali Bogra Formula. The federation was to have a bicameral legislature (two houses of Parliament). In the upper house, each of the 5 provinces would have 10 seats, in the lower house the total membership would be 300 of which 165 would be from East Bengal. Thus, in both houses taken together, each wing would have 175 seats. This parity between the two wings offered a workable compromise and had there been the political will to enforce this formula, there would have been no insurmountable crisis in the future. After a hectic and prolonged session, the Constituent Assembly took a recess on 14 November 1953. During the recess the Muslim League lost the provincial elections in East Bengal, causing some to observe, with justice, that the Constituent Assembly had become unrepresentative.

When the Constituent Assembly reconvened on 14 March 1954, it carried on business as usual. On 7 May, Mohammad Ali successfully moved a resolution making Bengali a national language along with Urdu. The Constituent Assembly stood poised to give the country a constitution, but trouble was brewing in another quarter. Governor-General Ghulam Mohammad was not satisfied with the Bogra Formula. He felt that some smaller provinces like NWFP or Balochistan could join hands with East Bengal and pass measures not to the liking of his Punjab constituency. He, therefore, planned a merger of all four West Pakistan provinces, Sindh, Punjab, NWFP, and Balochistan to be called One Unit. Another piece of legislation which the Constituent Assembly was enacting surreptitiously, but of which Ghulam Mohammad learnt, was to curtail the powers of the governor-general.

On 21 September it was enacted that the governor-general would have no powers to dismiss the prime minister or dissolve assemblies. The prime minister would hold office as long as he enjoyed the confidence of the house, and not at the pleasure of the governor-general. One day earlier the Constituent Assembly had repealed the Public and Representative Officer (Disqualification) Act (PRODA), which was the main weapon the governor-general could use to coerce individual politicians. Therefore, when the Constituent Assembly had almost passed the constitution, the governor-general intervened and dissolved the Constituent Assembly on 24 October 1954.

THE 1956 CONSTITUTION.—A constitution for Pakistan was finally enacted in 1956 when Ghulam Mohammad retired. Prior to his retirement, the One Unit Scheme had been put into effect in 1955. Therefore, the first difference between the 1954 draft and the 1956 Constitution was that it had a unicameral legislature, that is, having only one chamber, but 150 or an equal number of seats was allotted to the two wings which meant parity (total of 300). Bengali was declared a national language alongside Urdu.

The constitution had an involved system in relation to the head of state and government. According to the constitution, the country was to be known as the Islamic Republic of Pakistan. The president would be a Muslim male adult of at least 40 years of age. He would be indirectly elected by the federal and provincial assemblies for a period of five years and be eligible for re-election only once. The president could be impeached by two-thirds of the National Assembly. He was required to act on the advice of the cabinet. On the other hand, the president could veto any legislation, subject to the provision that two-thirds of the members could override the veto.

The president could issue ordinances when the National Assembly was not in session. No money bill could be introduced without the consent of the president. The president possessed the power to proclaim an emergency and suspend human rights. The list of human rights was long, but as one commentator has remarked, compromised by the proviso[5] 'subject to any reasonable restrictions imposed by law'. Not only was 'reasonable' very imprecise but what 'law' would apply was also ambiguous. The only guarantee of human rights in the constitution was an independent judiciary. Although proclaimed a republic, Pakistan would remain a member of the British Commonwealth.

In spite of the provision that the president would act on the advice of the cabinet, the position of the president was far more secure than that of the prime minister. The last Governor-General Iskander Mirza had become the first president, but he outstayed a number of prime ministers: Chaudhry Mohammad Ali (who gave the constitution), H.S. Suhrawardy, I.I. Chundrigar, and Feroz Khan Noon. President Mirza complained about the polity but abrogated the constitution. Only when the 1956 Constitution was abrogated, Mirza's new prime minister and chief martial law administrator, General

Mohammad Ayub Khan was able to oust him and take his place. (Islamic provisions of the three constitutions are listed separately in Chapter 38).

THE 1962 CONSTITUTION.—Two years after staging his coup, on 17 February 1960, President Ayub Khan appointed a constitution commission. It was entrusted with examining the causes of the failure of the parliamentary system, implying that, as if the constitution had abrogated itself. It was charged to suggest a form of democracy suited to 'changed circumstances'. A cabinet committee was appointed to study the recommendations of the constitution commission. On the submission of this committee's report, a two-member team was appointed to study the administrative problems which the introduction of the new constitution would bring. Finally, on 1 March 1962, President Ayub Khan broadcast features of his one-man constitution. He had disregarded the recommendations of his own constitution commission, which had recommended a strong presidency, but an equally strong parliament. Ayub retained the first and rejected the second.

The 1962 Constitution replaced the parliamentary system with the presidential system. Rather than go through the tedium of frequently changing prime ministers, the post was abolished altogether. Direct Adult Franchise was done away with for an electoral college of Basic Democrats, themselves directly elected, in February 1960. They totalled 80,000–40,000 in each wing. They constituted four tiers of local government and formed the electoral college for the president and the members of the national and provincial assemblies. The legislature was unicameral and there was no vice-president. The president appointed judges, chiefs of the armed forces, and ministers. Two-thirds of the National Assembly could impeach the president. One redeeming feature was that the president could not dissolve the National Assembly without losing his own office as well. As we have seen in the political section, Ayub Khan effectively abrogated his own constitution on 25 March 1969 by transferring power to the army chief instead of to the speaker of the National Assembly.

THE CONSTITUTIONAL CRISIS 1969–71.—There was a conflict between the Legal Framework Order (LFO) of General Yahya Khan and the Six Points of Sheikh Mujibur Rahman. There were some decisions taken in advance of electing the Constituent Assembly which were at the behest of the political forces, such as the restoration of direct adult franchise, the parliamentary system, and the abolition of One-Unit.[6] No constitutional commission was appointed to probe the causes of the failure of the presidential system. Only one (and the most) contentious issue remained: the degree of provincial autonomy. On 11 January 1970, Sheikh Mujibur Rahman asked Yahya Khan not to grant autonomy in advance of the election.[7] On 7 March Mujib said that he would launch a movement after elections to achieve autonomy.

The constitutional crisis over the degree of autonomy could not be resolved until Indian armed intervention caused the secession of the East Wing. The power of the chief martial law administrator and president was transferred to Zulfikar Ali Bhutto on 20 December 1971. Although Z.A. Bhutto emerged as the elected representative of residual Pakistan, the transition could only be made by transferring the office of the chief martial law administrator under the only basic law in the country.

Martial Law was lifted and an interim constitution, enacted on 17 April 1972, came into force on 21 April. The presidential form was retained. It was strongly rumoured that Bhutto preferred a presidential system for the permanent constitution as well, and it was this discord which ultimately led to the resignation of the Law Minister, Mian Mahmud Ali Kasuri.

The National Assembly doubled, as before, as the Constituent Assembly. On 17 April 1972, a committee to draft the permanent constitution was appointed. On 20 October 1972, a draft bill was signed by all parties represented in the Assembly. On 2 February 1973, a constitution bill was moved, and the bill was passed almost unanimously on 10 April 1973 and promulgated on Independence Day 1973. Zulfikar Ali Bhutto stepped down to become prime minister, and the speaker, Fazal Ilahi Chaudhry became the fourth president of Pakistan.

> **WHAT IS A FEDERATION?**
>
> This question is relevant to deciding whether the Six Points were federal, or confederal, which is a loose arrangement. This also forms the basis whereby Z.A. Bhutto sought consensus on the 1973 constitution. Federation is a term of American origin when thirteen States who found themselves individually weak against Britain or France, came together in a federation for mutual security. Alexander Hamilton, formulated on 18 December 1787 the purpose and functions of a federation: 'The principle purposes to be answered by Union are these—the common defence of the members—the preservation of the public peace as well against internal convulsions as external attacks—the regulation of commerce with other nations and between the States—the superintendence of our intercourse, political and commercial, with foreign countries.' The Federalist Papers No. 27.

Efforts for Consensus. Zulfikar Ali Bhutto was conscious of the fact that firstly, constitution framing in Pakistan had been delayed, and secondly, it could be abrogated because it had no firm foundation. Pakistan had recently been dismembered ostensibly because no consensus could be built between the Awami League and the PPP. Now the PPP–NAP/JUI equation in residual Pakistan was the same as that between the Awami League and the PPP. The National Awami Party (NAP) chief, Khan Abdul Wali Khan, said as much. Consequently, opposition parties were brought together and on 20 October 1972, a constitutional accord was signed effecting a compromise. Z.A. Bhutto thanked the opposition for its cooperation.[8]

The dismissal of the NAP-JUI government in Balochistan and its resignation in NWFP intervened between the accord and the passage of the constitution. Without giving in on the political issue, Z.A. Bhutto was still able to gather their support for his draft 1973 Constitution.

The Constitution was to be a federal and parliamentary system of government. For the first time, a bicameral legislature was brought into being. The upper house was called the Senate and the lower house would be called the National Assembly. Members of the National Assembly would number 200, elected directly by the people. The Senate would consist of 63 members to be indirectly elected. Each provincial assembly would elect 14 members, 5 would be elected by the Federally Administered Tribal Areas (FATA) and 2 by the federal capital area. The Senate would not be subject to dissolution. The term of their office would be four years, with half the members retiring after two years. The National Assembly members would have a tenure of five years.

The president would act on the advice of the prime minister. He could exercise the power to pardon prisoners condemned to death. Only a male Muslim of more than forty-five years of age would be eligible to stand for office. The president would be elected by the members of the National and Provincial assemblies. The prime minister would be elected by a majority of the National Assembly.

Since the first era of parliamentary government had seen a succession of prime ministers, it was provided that any motion of no-confidence against the prime minister would have to name his successor. Since it is easier to secure agreement on the removal of a serving prime minister, than to agree upon a common candidate to succeed him, this provision was designed to give stability to the prime minister's office.

In the provinces, the governor would be the nominee of the federal government, while the chief minister would be elected by a majority of the provincial assembly, to which he was accountable. The structure of the federal system was replicated in the provinces.

There was a list of human and provincial rights but those were used to secure a consensus and sadly, compromised later, by the majority enjoyed by the ruling party.

AMENDMENTS TO THE 1973 CONSTITUTION.—The constitution can be amended by a two-thirds majority of both houses of parliament. Seven amendments were moved by Z.A. Bhutto, the architect of the 1973 Constitution. (1) The First Amendment allowed the government to ban political parties from operating in a manner prejudicial to the sovereignty or integrity of Pakistan. This decision had to be confirmed by the Supreme Court. This was the amendment Bhutto used in banning the NAP. (2) The Second Amendment declared the Ahmadis as non-Muslims. (3) The Third Amendment softened safeguards against arrest and detention and facilitated the continuation of a Proclamation of Emergency under which basic human rights could be curtailed. (4) The Fourth Amendment curtailed the writ powers against arrest and detention. The high courts were largely precluded from granting freedom or bail to people who were detained. (5) The Fifth Amendment further curtailed the power of the higher judiciary. Their terms of office were to be determined not solely by age, but by a fixed term. Judges could be transferred from one High Court to another for one year without their consent. (6) The Sixth Amendment clarified the retirement age of judges. (7) The Seventh Amendment provided for a referendum. This was to avoid re-election after the 1977 allegations of poll rigging. Politically, Bhutto was unable to use this amendment, but two military rulers, General Zia and General Pervez Musharraf, used it.

Except for the First Amendment, which was subject to the decision of the Supreme Court, and the second, which was thrust upon him, there was no real necessity for Bhutto to subject his own constitution to so many amendments. They were aimed mainly at human rights and the judiciary which would uphold them. The amendments followed a constitutional procedure and were passed by a two-thirds majority but weakened the moral force behind the near consensus that the 1973 Constitution had achieved, and compromised the sanctity of this document when it was challenged by extra-parliamentary forces.

Later Amendments. (8) President Zia made the passage of the Eighth Amendment a condition for lifting martial law. By this amendment, the electoral college for the president came to include the Senate in addition to the national and provincial assemblies. It contained Article 58 2(b) according to which the president could dismiss the prime minister and dissolve the assemblies. President Zia exercised this power once, President Ghulam Ishaq Khan twice and President Farooq Leghari once. When President Leghari was unable to dismiss his second prime minister and the Eighth Amendment had been repealed, he had to resign. This amendment increased the strength of the Senate from 63 to 87; five seats from each province were reserved for ulama, technocrats or professionals. The number of seats reserved for women increased from 10 to 20. The Federal Shariat Court was set up. Its task was to rule whether any existing law was in accord with Islamic laws and pass verdicts on government measures in any domain of life. (9) The intent of the Ninth Amendment was to make the Quran and Sunnah the supreme law. It was passed by the Senate, but because of the dismissal of Prime Minister Junejo in 1988, the amendment did not become effective. (10) The Tenth Amendment provided that the interval between two National Assembly or Senate sessions should not exceed 130 days. (11) The intent of the Eleventh Amendment was to revise the number of seats reserved for women in the National Assembly. This was enacted in the Seventeenth Amendment with the number of reserved seats increased. (12) The Twelfth Amendment provided for the setting up of speedy trial courts. (13) The Thirteenth Amendment was enacted by the PML (N) government to repeal the Eighth Amendment, especially 58 2(b). It simultaneously struck down the provision by which governors could dismiss chief ministers and dissolve provincial assemblies. The president's powers to appoint judges and the three chiefs of the armed forces were curtailed. He would have to make these appointments on the advice of the prime minister. (14) The Fourteenth Amendment prevented floor-crossing or horse-trading by elected members. (15) The Fifteenth Amendment was again meant to make the Quran and Sunnah the basic law of the land. Since this would have resulted in drastic curtailment of the constitution, even the religious parties did not oblige Nawaz Sharif. This amendment was passed by the National Assembly on 9 October 1999, but not by the Senate. (16) The Sixteenth Amendment related to extending the quota system in the services for another forty years from August 1993. This was to amend Article 27 of the constitution which provides for safeguards against any form of discrimination including domicile or place of birth.

LEGAL FRAMEWORK ORDER (LFO).—General Pervez Musharraf took over the government on 12 October 1999. The Supreme Court justified his takeover on 12 May 2002 in the Zafar Ali Shah case on 30 April 2002. General Pervez Musharraf held a referendum to justify his assumption of power on 20 June 2001. On 21 August 2002, he promulgated the Legal Framework Order (LFO). Again, by this LFO, the president and not the prime minister would have the power to appoint the three chiefs of the armed forces and judges of the supreme and high courts. The office of the prime minister would be restored, but the constitution would, in its orientation, become presidential rather than parliamentary.

The LFO originally provided for the establishment of a National Security Council.[9] General Musharraf extended his term as president by five years, secured indemnity for all his orders since his take-over and reinstated the rule that the president and not the prime minister would have the power to appoint armed forces' chiefs and members of the higher judiciary.

Some features of the LFO were positive and political leaders have not stinted from characterizing them as such. These are the reduction of the voting age from 21 years to 18, increasing the number of National Assembly seats from 217 to 342, and of Senate seats from 87 to 100. Women's representation was increased. Candidates for assemblies had to be at least graduates and finally, separate electorates for minorities were abolished. This was to fulfil a long-standing demand of the minorities.

After the 10 October 2002 elections, some modifications to the LFO were deemed advisable. The treasury benches contended that the LFO was a part of the constitution whereas the opposition benches disagreed. One opposition alliance, Muttahida Majlis-i-Amal (MMA), to the exclusion of another component the Alliance for the Restoration of Democracy (ARD), negotiated with the government and the resultant compromise was enacted as the Seventeenth

Amendment on 29 December 2003. The Seventeenth Amendment had originally required the president to resign as chief of army staff on 31 December 2004, but the parliament passed a dual offices bill before that date enabling the president to retain his uniform.

As a compromise, the pre-LFO retirement age of the higher judiciary was restored; this resulted in the retirement of the chief justice and a number of other judges. Under this amendment, the local government system would function for a further six years. The local government system had been inducted under a Devolution of Power Plan on 23 March 2000 which was put into operation through the National Reconstruction Bureau. The regime criticized the earlier local government systems on the grounds that the provincial administration had controlled it through bureaucrats at every stage. As a result, the post of divisional commissioner was abolished, and the deputy commissioners were re-designated as district coordination officers.

Two innocuous amendments to the LFO were made. The president would retain the power to appoint the military chief, but in doing so would consult the prime minister. The invocation of 58 2(b) would be referred to the Supreme Court, a recourse which, with a solitary exception in 1993, was found ineffective. A former judge of the Supreme Court, and a former Attorney General, Fakhruddin G. Ebrahim, has observed that the Supreme Court gave three years to General Musharraf when he had not even asked for it, and the power to amend the constitution even though the constitution was in abeyance for three years. This judgement, dated 12 May 2000, gives judicial cover to the Seventeenth Amendment.[10]

Later Amendments. (18) The Eighteenth Amendment was passed on 8 April 2010, to do away with the Eighth Amendment. It reduced the powers of the president and did away with Article 58 2(b) under which prime ministers had been dismissed and assemblies dissolved. Under the same amendment powers from the federation were delegated to the provinces, mainly education. (19) According to the Nineteenth Amendment assented to by the president on 1 January 2011, the tribal areas adjacent to Tank and Laki Marwat districts became part of FATA. This amendment also related to the appointment of judges. A parliamentary committee would send the names of the nominees to the prime minister, who in turn, would forward them to the president. (20) The Twentieth Amendment 2012 substituted the words 'Election Commission of Pakistan' for Chief Election Commissioner. (21) The Twenty-First Amendment was for the purpose of establishing speedy military courts. This was in the wake of the Army Public School massacre. (22) The Twenty-Second Amendment was related to defining the powers of the Election Commission of Pakistan and that of the Chief Election Commissioner. (23) The Twenty-Third Amendment was passed to extend the provision of military courts till 6 January 2019. (24) The Twenty-Fourth Amendment was for the adjustment of seats in Parliament. While the total number remained unchanged,

Punjab lost some seats while NWFP and Balochistan gained some seats. Sindh was unaffected. This reallocation was made in view of the National Census 2017. (25) By the Twenty-Fifth Amendment FATA was merged with Khyber Pakhtunkhwa. (26) The Twenty-Sixth Amendment was introduced to amend the 1973 Constitution with regard to federation-provinces subjects. It was never passed. (27) The Twenty-Seventh Amendment related to electoral reforms and comprised the Draft Election Bill. (28) The Twenty-Eighth Amendment was for the purpose of restoring military courts in Pakistan. (29) The Twenty-Ninth Amendment bill was to enable the trial of terrorists under the Pakistan Army Act 1952.

Notes

1. *Dawn*, Karachi, 5 October 2002.
2. Sibi Durbar speech, 14 February 1947.
3. *Jinnah: Speeches and Statements 1947–1948* (Karachi: Oxford University Press, 2000), p. 28, (11 August 1947).
4. Ibid., p. 125, Broadcast to the USA, February 1948.
5. Louis D. Hayes, *The Struggle for Legitimacy in Pakistan* (Lahore: Vanguard, 1986), p. 92.
6. Abdur Rahman Siddiqi, *East Pakistan: The Endgame* (Karachi: Oxford University Press, 2004), p. 225.
7. Ibid.
8. Rafi Raza, *Zulfikar Ali Bhutto and Pakistan 1971–1977* (Karachi: Oxford University Press, 1997), p. 176.
9. Charles H. Kennedy and Cynthia A. Botterton (eds.), *Pakistan 2005* (Karachi: Oxford University Press, 2006), p. 2.
10. *Dawn*, 14 January 2005.

CHAPTER 38
THE ISLAMIC PROVISIONS OF SUCCESSIVE CONSTITUTIONS

The definition of religious jurisdiction is not unique to Pakistan. In Britain, the mother of parliaments, the constitution of Clarendon (1641), set the limits of civil and ecclesiastical (church) jurisdictions. The king or queen is designated Defender of the Faith. Originally, Defender meant the Defender of the Roman Catholic Church, and, after King Henry VIII, the British sovereign became the Defender of the Church of England.

This example has been given to show that the original intent of the founder is capable of being altered. Taking the dicta of Jinnah together, we can reach the conclusion that he expected secular principles to devolve from Islamic values. Such a concept needs adjustment. However, as much as we deplore the induction of religion as a coercive force, we must acknowledge that the demographic composition kept the door ajar for Islamization.

THE 1956 CONSTITUTION.—(1) The country was named the Islamic Republic of Pakistan. (2) The Objectives Resolution 1949 was adopted as a preamble indicating State policy. (3) The moral teachings of Islam would be encouraged and vices such as gambling, drinking and prostitution would be curbed. (4) *Zakat* and *Auqaf*. The government was instructed to collect and administer alms and trusts. (5) Article 24 of the constitution obliged Pakistan to maintain friendly relations with Muslim countries. (6) No law repugnant to Islam was to be passed. Existing laws (inherited from the British) would also be examined with a view to making them conform to Islamic laws. (7) The government was required, under Article 197 to set up an Islamic Research Institute to examine laws. During the period the 1956 Constitution remained in force, such an institute was not set up. (8) The president was required to be a Muslim male adult. However, the speaker of the National Assembly who was to officiate in the president's absence, or infirmity could be a non-Muslim. No non-Muslim speaker has ever been appointed save Joginder Nath Mandal who inaugurated the Constituent Assembly of Pakistan.

1962 CONSTITUTION.—(1) Initially the country was called the Republic of Pakistan, but by its first amendment on 25 December 1963, the words Islamic has been added. (2) The Objectives Resolution was again retained as the preamble, only the word Islam was substituted for 'Quran and Sunnah'. (3) The government would provide for the compulsory education of the Quran and Islamiat to Muslim students. (4) Under an amendment the 1956 provision of bringing existing laws in conformity with Islam was restored. (5) An Islamic Advisory Council was to be set up consisting of no less than five and no more than twelve members. It was meant to answer the queries of the president and legislators. Its advice was not binding. (6) For the framing of Islamic laws, an Islamic Research Institute was set up with the head office in Islamabad and provincial offices in Lahore and Dhaka.

THE 1973 CONSTITUTION.—(1) This was the first constitution in which Islam was declared to be the state religion. (2) The Objectives Resolution was adopted. (3) All legislation was to be in conformity with the Quran and Sunnah. All existing laws were to be brought into conformity within nine years. Personal law for non-Muslims was according to their respective creeds. (4) Both the president and prime minister were required to be adult Muslims. The president would be male. (5) The government of Pakistan would take the responsibility of printing the Holy Quran. Article 31 required copies to be free of all types of printing errors. (6) The government would provide maximum facilities for the promotion of the Arabic language. (7) A Council of Islamic Ideology (CII) would be formed having eight to fifteen members. Two had to be either serving or retired judges of the supreme or high courts. The chairman would also have to be a serving or former judge of the Supreme Court. At least one member had to be a woman, and all sects were to be represented. The CII had to complete Islamization within seven years. (8) The second amendment declared all Ahmadis as non-Muslims.

The framing of the existing constitutions was reflective of a desire to Islamize the government and society. Islamization is called the destiny of Pakistan, and indeed it is a natural and noble goal. However, we must be vigilant against those versions which are not in accordance with the beneficial spirit of Islam.

RESULTS AND CONSEQUENCES OF THE ISLAMIC PROVISIONS.— One of the initial impediments to the framing of the constitution was the controversy over the degree and role of Islam in the collective lives of its citizens. The 1973 Constitution had more Islamic provisions than the previous constitutions; it was the first constitution to declare that Islam was the state religion, but this did not mollify the ulama. Instead, a movement for complete Islamization of the legal system was started. During the 1977 Pakistan National Alliance (PNA) campaign, Z.A. Bhutto banned gambling and drinking, closed down night clubs and from 1 July, Friday was declared the weekly holiday instead of Sunday. These measures did not halt the PNA Movement and as a result of this movement, General Zia declared Martial Law and took further steps towards Islamization.

The first measure was to introduce separate electorates for minorities. In British India, Muslims obtained separate electorates because of their demand. In Pakistan, minorities had consistently opposed separate electorates. Since Zia sensed that minorities would vote for the PPP whom he had overthrown, he imposed separate electorates on the minorities. A non-Muslim voter could only vote for non-Muslim candidates. It was finally rescinded by General Pervez Musharraf in the seventeenth amendment which was enacted on 29 December 2003.

On 21 June 1980, *Zakat* and *Ushr* were introduced in the domain of Public Law. *Zakat* is paid at the rate of 2.5 per cent of annual savings. This is compulsory in Islam, but now it is not left to personal conscience but collected and administered by the state, with the donor having no say over its utilization. *Ushr* is land tax; it literally means one-tenth of the produce of the land. This, like *Zakat*, is levied on Muslims only.

On 1 January 1981, interest-free banking and risk-free insurance were introduced. Islamic banking became the model, but in reality, a profit-and-loss system was launched, in which interest was introduced under another name. When the Shariat Court ruled that Interest was Usury and un-Islamic, the Nawaz Sharif government appealed against the judgement. However, some public good resulted from this measure: widows and orphans were exempted from paying interest on the loans they had taken from the House Building Finance Corporation, which is a public sector institution.

Islamic punishments (*Hudood* in Arabic) were introduced. Bhutto's June 1977 measures were deemed insufficient, and Islamic punishments and Islamic laws of evidence were prescribed for every major crime except murder, specifically for theft, adultery, and false accusation of adultery. The prohibition on drinking was strictly applied and severely punished. Non-Muslims were allowed drink on ceremonial occasions, as were foreigners, behind closed doors.

The Council of Islamic Ideology (CII) was enlarged to 19 members and the terms of its reference were extended to oversee all laws of the land and to rule which existing law was Islamic or not. This applied mostly to the laws inherited from the British. Parliament could seek the opinion of the CII on any legislation being considered or reviewed.

In December 1977, a Federal Advisory Council was also established to accelerate the pace of Islamization.

A federal and four provincial ombudsmen (*Mohtasib*) were appointed. Apart from probing charges of corruption, the ombudsmen could issue directives to government functionaries, if they felt that a decision was unwarranted. Usually, retired members of the higher judiciary were appointed to this post.

A Shariah Appeal Bench was set up, composed of both *ulama* and lawyers. Any decision of the Shariah Appeal Bench could not be challenged in the Supreme Court or High Courts.

The Islamic Research Institute was rejuvenated and its task of conducting research was enhanced.

A faculty of Shariah was introduced at Quaid-i-Azam University, Islamabad, and Peshawar University. The International Islamic University, Islamabad also has a large faculty of Shariah.

Under the Educational Reforms of 1979, the teaching of Islamic and Pakistan Studies was made compulsory for all faculties of Science, Arts, Commerce, Engineering and Medicine.

Some constitutional aspects of Islamization are covered in the chapter on Human Rights. It must be acknowledged that Islamization is a noble purpose. If it is carried out with honest intent, it would result in the moral uplift of society.

 ABUL ALA MAUDUDI (b. Aurangabad, 25 September 1903–d. Buffalo, 25 September 1979). It is true that Maulana Maududi opposed the Pakistan Movement. That he anathematized the founder of Pakistan is also true. That he refused to characterize the 1947–48 Kashmir war as Jihad is even truer. What is equally true is that while he opposed the Muslim League, he also denounced the Congress, and by doing so, he endorsed the Two-Nation Theory. This sets him apart from the other *ulama* who opposed Pakistan. It needs to be conceded that he is not the only party leader in Pakistan to make a volte-face. This apart, Maulana Maududi has been one of the most influential citizens of Pakistan; his works have been absorbed by such Islamic ideologues as Syed Qutb of Egypt, and Ayatullah Khomeini of Iran. During the drafting of the Objectives Resolution (1949), his party—Jamaat-i-Islami—represented street power in Pakistan, forming the nucleus of the Lal Masjid—the Islamabad-based fanatical agitation, which now, in May 2007, threatens the state foundations of Pakistan.

Maududi was the maternal grandson of Qurban Beg Salik, who is familiar to all Ghalib scholars. Maududi composed poetry, and during the course of his literary and journalistic endeavours, came into contact with Josh Malihabadi and Niaz Fatehpuri—the poet and the critic who were most vociferously denounced as free thinkers. Maududi started his career in journalism as editor of *Medina* (Bijnor), and *Taj* (Jabalpur). He went back to the Deccan, in 1928, from where he launched the *Tarjuman-ul-Quran*, which is still under publication. In 1941, Maududi founded the Jamaat-i-Islami (JI) in Lahore with 75 members. The membership of the JI was to be graded according to piety and belief. At a later stage, this had an adverse effect when the JI's street power did not translate into electoral victory. Maududi was sentenced to death for his part in the 1953 anti-Qadiani agitation, but the sentence was commuted to three years imprisonment. He was arrested once more, in 1964.

Since Maududi came to the forefront at the time when the Objectives Resolution was being drafted, he faced a dilemma in trying to resolve the readiness of the Islamic state (which was the ideal) and the readiness of an Islamic constitution (which was to be the instrument). For Maududi, the Islamic State was not an evolving model, but an already perfect one, requiring no change.[1] On the other hand, about the Islamic constitution for which the immediate battle was raging, he said: 'When we say that this country should have an Islamic Constitution, we do not mean that we possess a constitution of the Islamic state in a written form and the only thing that is required to be done is to enforce it. The core of the problem is that we want an unwritten constitution to be transformed into a written one. What we term an Islamic constitution is in reality an unwritten constitution. It is contained in certain specific sources, and it is from that we have to evolve a written constitution in keeping with the present-day requirements of our country.'[2]

This was actually a post-colonial exercise. Previous to this, law and jurisprudence had existed. The theoretical formulations of an Islamic state, as set down by such writers as Abul Hasan al-Mawardi, were ex post facto. No wonder a category such as *imarat al-istila* (the emirate of conquest), existed. The JI had adopted a hierarchical form of membership, and when it called for the sovereignty of Allah, it *ipso facto* marginalized the electorate—the only method of constituting a government known to classical Islam. An analysis of all ideological arguments put forward by Maududi points to a religious oligarchy, as recently witnessed in Iran, where a council of guardians reduced an elected president (Muhammad Khatami) to the state of the leader of the opposition. Some mechanism is visibly necessary to prevent the enjoining of virtue and forbidding of evil from being reduced to compelling virtue and extirpating evil, the challenge being issued from Lal Masjid, Islamabad, on 2 April 2007, which proclaims that only six Taliban enforced Islamic law in Afghanistan, and we are 10,000.[3]

Notes

1. Seyyed Vali Reza Nasr, *Maududi and the Making of Islamic Revival* (New York: Oxford University Press, 1996), p. 89.
2. Ibid., p. 96 vide Abul Ala Maududi, *First Principles of the Islamic State* (Lahore: Islamic publications, 1983), p. 1.
3. *Dawn*, 3 April 2007, p. 1.

Part 7
History of the Institutions

Chapter 39
The Bureaucracy

'Can you really rule India?' asked the Viceroy Lord Irwin. 'My lord', replied Sir Sultan Ahmed, 'Your post can be taken instantly, Governors will not be a problem, and we can take over these posts. We will have problems administering the districts.'[1] A former prime minister of Pakistan, Sir Feroz Khan Noon also calls the Deputy Commissioner the lynchpin of administration.[2] This, we shall see presently, is a situation that still obtains from 1947 to 1973, Pakistan was administered under the Government of India Act 1935 adopted as Article 8 of the Indian Independence Act 1947. A year ago the grand total of civilian employees was 955,000. Ninety-five per cent of the federal employees belong to Basic Pay Scale 1 to 16 and they are being paid over 80 to 85 per cent of the total Wages Bill.

This means the majority of the employees are what can be termed clerks. One bureaucrat wrote, 'Reduce a secretary to the level of a clerk, and then he will realize how much work the clerk does. Ask a Chief Secretary to find a file and he will be merely wasting his time. Ask the clerk and he will find it quickly. It is the clerks that run Pakistan.'[3]

The term Bureaucrat originated in France. Bureau means desk (it also means office) in French, and people who worked at desks were called bureaucrats. In time this term became associated with certain characteristics: it denoted a body of public servants who devised and followed certain set rules which slowed the process of implementation, who sought to make policy subservient to their rules and had passed a lifetime in their careers, knew all the rules, and could implement, reject, delay or hasten a decision or verdict. This power could make a section of the bureaucracy open to corruption. These characteristics also apply to the clerks.

It is often said that Pakistan inherited its bureaucracy from the colonial model, which had a different set of characteristics. The colonial model was the Indian Civil Service (ICS) cadre. To this cadre, at first, no natives could be admitted and the examination for recruitment was for a long time, held only in England, and in India only after great agitation. After Indians appeared in centres in India, they became a class of their own. This exclusiveness stemmed from the fact that Western education, and by implication, Western culture, was considered superior.

The superiority of Western culture, in time, overtook the notion of the superiority of Western education. What India needed most to learn from England were the sciences and commerce. For centuries these had been taken away from the formal syllabi of Muslim India. Yet the class to whom the highest echelons of service were entrusted were those with a classical or general education. Even when the system of patronage was extended, scions of well-connected native families needed to acquire a Bachelor of Arts (BA) degree, to be appointed honorary magistrates. In those days, no Indian rose higher than a deputy commissioner. The ICS officers were exceptionally brilliant and, by inclination or by training, learnt to distance themselves from the people they ruled.

This distance was distinct from ignorance. A candidate passing the ICS examination was sent as a probationer to one of four institutions: the universities of Oxford, Cambridge, and London or Trinity College, Dublin. Once in India, the first appointment would be as an assistant district officer serving under a district officer with seniority between seven to twenty years and who served under a commissioner who headed a division comprising a number of districts. Normally an ICS officer would retire from this post.

Those ICS officers who staffed the central or provincial secretariats had to start their careers in the provinces and were seconded from their district offices. In the words of one officer: 'This constant interchange was in my opinion one reason for the general excellence of the Indian administration, since a great many personal relationships were formed and desk bound bureaucrats were never too far away from the way things were worked in the provinces.'[4]

Service in the provinces involved a great deal of touring, mostly on horseback, but this same officer mentions that a superior advised him against mixing with Indians even if they were also ICS officers.[5] The Pakistani successor to the ICS were members of the Central Superior Services (CSS), having a number of cadres, the first being an addition. The Pakistan Foreign Service trainees were sent to the Fletcher School of Diplomacy at Duke University, USA. The nearest cadre to the ICS was the Civil Service of Pakistan (CSP). The CSP followed the ICS formula for postings in the central secretariat, 'For the first six years the trainees were rotated in the districts and only then were they posted in the secretariat as under-secretary. Nine years as under-secretary qualified a civil servant to be posted as deputy secretary.' The deputy secretary is the lynchpin of the administration; this is quite understandable as the deputy secretary was halfway between the junior and the senior officers. The deputy secretary would be promoted to joint secretary, and only the few at the top would be posted to the highest post of Secretary to the Ministry.

At the time of Independence, the Civil Service was headed by Chaudhry Mohammad Ali, as secretary general. This experience stood Chaudhry Mohammad Ali in good stead when he became the prime minister of Pakistan.

A deputy secretary in the secretariat was equivalent to the deputy commissioner in the district. It has been remarked that he too was the lynchpin of the operation although the British had no corresponding post in Britain.

The CSS included cadres such as the Information Service, Military Accounts Service, Income Tax Service, Office of the Controller of Imports and Exports, (which has been abolished) Police Service (where the recruitment was central and posting was provincial) in addition to the Foreign and Civil Service. Medicine, Education, Archaeology or Geological Survey perhaps did not merit admission to these superior services.

A change was brought about in the Ayub era when the post of additional secretary was added between the posts of secretary and joint secretary. During the first PPP government, Z.A. Bhutto abolished the service cadre. The CSP became the District Management Group, the Secretarial Group, and so on. There was a unified pay scale, and the grades were from 1–23. Grade 23 was for the secretary. What had previously been Class One Service began in Grade 17. There was no great shake-up except that the nomenclature had changed, and inter-cadre posting was somewhat easier. Bhutto also made a provision for lateral entry into the superior services by examination.

This came about because Z.A. Bhutto had ordered a 'screening', that is a major purge of civil servants who numbered 1330.[6] Bhutto was the third president to screen officers. This process had begun with President Ayub and continued with Yahya Khan. The reasons for the purges were said to be corruption and inefficiency. On the whole, both inefficiency and corruption had crept in, but there was some dispute about particular bureaucrats. For example, Abbas Khalili was dismissed by Ayub but re-instated by Bhutto and made secretary of defence production. On the other hand, others who had died or had already retired from the service found their names on Bhutto's lists. This affected the morale of the officers and made them more subordinate to the rulers than the rules.

The administrative structure at the centre was replicated in the provinces—except for purely central departments such as Defence and Foreign Affairs. The chief secretary of a province headed its administration with secretaries of various ministries under him. The purges affected even the provincial cadres, and the overall effect of insecurity was increased corruption.

Corruption, not inefficiency, has been the main bane of Pakistan's bureaucracy despite the quota system. No inefficient officer can be corrupt, but in analysing the causes of corruption one cannot repeat the Actonian cliché. When the bureaucracy was invaded by corruption, provides the answer to why. At the time of independence, there was a shortage of bureaucracy at all levels, gazetted and non-gazetted. Officers were given the option to serve in Pakistan, and in those early years, no one cared to know the ethnic composition or even the sectarian composition of any cadre. Everyone served not only selflessly but paid from his own pocket for the stationery and furniture. Without the honesty, dedication, and efficiency of the first batch of officers, Pakistan would not have survived. It was political instability in the first instance, and long periods of non-political regimes, which created the corrupt practices. Mahbub ul Haq estimated that millions of rupees were syphoned off from government funds by bureaucrats. As recently as 2020 it was revealed that malpractices in the office of the Accountant General Pakistan Revenues cause a loss of Rs 175 billion annually.[7]

Reforms under President Musharraf, in the form of the local government system, have affected the District Management Group. A Devolution of Power Plan was announced on 23 March 2000 and was put into operation through the National Reconstruction Bureau, newly set up by the military government. The regime took the position that the previous local government systems were governed by the provincial administration. Also criticized were the separate provisions for local governments in the city and town areas as opposed to local government in the rural areas.

As a first step, divisions and the connected posts of the commissioner were abolished. The district or deputy commissioner's post was retained along with that of assistant commissioner, but they were redesignated as district coordination officers etc., and their direct jurisdiction was curtailed. The administrative structure of local government was formed at three levels (i) District or *Zila*; (ii) Subdistrict or *Tehsil*; and (iii) Union (a subdivision of subdistrict). Each level is headed by a Nazim or administrator and Naib Nazim or deputy administrator. These officials are responsible to a legislative council and have to work in conjunction with an administrative unit headed by a bureaucrat (e.g. the district coordinator).

This system of bypassing divisions has led to political criticism that by devolving power to the districts directly, provincial autonomy is being circumvented. It is undeniable that local bodies are revived and empowered under dictatorships, and either made to lapse or to weaken under democratic regimes.

The police officer has also been re-designated the town police officer, but the extent of his jurisdiction is at present being debated. The local governments at present deal with a very long list of departments, agriculture, works and services, health, education, literacy and community development. Provincial governments have appointed a director general, implementation, monitoring and evaluation cell. This may serve as a link between local and provincial governments. How much the people are empowered, and how much the local government, remains to be seen.

As is usual in Pakistan, a scheme lasts as long as its author does. When Ayub Khan resigned in 1969, Basic Democracies were wound up, first as an electoral college, then as administrative units. Similarly, when Pervez Musharraf resigned his system of local governments was wound up. The main grievance against Musharraf's system was that it had divested the deputy commissioner, the most powerful bureaucrat of his/her power. The powers enjoyed by the deputy commissioner were administrative, judicial and revenue collection. It would be against human nature to expect the bureaucracy to transfer such powers to the people.

To define the status of local bodies it must be recalled firstly that it was the constitutional preserve of provincial governments to determine the composition and responsibilities of local governments. Safdar Javaid Syed said of the Musharraf model that they combined the institutions of district-level governance and the structure of self-government within the district and overlooked the principle of subsidiarity.[8]

As a first step, the 5 districts of Karachi were restored by appointing deputy commissioners; later 26 sub-divisions were restored, thus implementing the Commissionerate system along with the local government system of 1979.[9] Since it was their preserve, provincial governments in Pakistan one by one dealt with the districts. In Khyber Pakhtunkhwa, when the local government was notifying budget rules it provided for all three tiers, district, tehsil, and union council to give their respective deputy commissioner powers of oversight and guidance. The deputy commissioner would be the principal accounting officer of the district.

The Supreme Court had to order the restoration of local government institutions; Holding that their absence amounted to a violation of Article 140A of the Constitution. In Karachi only, leaving the rest of Sindh aside, audit teams revealed this year (2022) that 70 per cent of allocated amounts were spent on salaries and other administrative purposes, with only 30 per cent left for development. The only exceptions were the South and Korangi districts which spent more on development than salaries. This means that there is no structural fault and here too, over-staffing seems to be the cause of retarded development.[10] Local government polls are scheduled to be held in Sindh after a lapse of seven years.

PROMOTION CRITERIA.—Lately, promotion criteria have changed. The greatest weight is given to the opinion of the Central Selection Board (CSB) headed by the Chairman of the Public Service Commission. Previously, there were 50 marks for Annual Confidential Report (ACR), 35 for professional courses and 15 for the CSB. Thus, if an officer obtained 80% marks, he/she would be promoted despite reservations by the CSB. Now, according to Civil Servants Promotions (BPS 18 to BPS 20) Rules 2019, the CSB had 30 marks instead of 15 marks, 40 for ACRs, and 30 for professional courses. What is more the CSB, according to the report could take into account intelligence reports.[11]

The Civil Servants Efficiency and Discipline Rules 2020 provided that the promotion of a civil servant could be deferred if he/she was facing any criminal proceedings. Recently it was conceded that promotion could be recommended if a case had dragged on for more than three years.[12] Promotion criteria remained unchanged. Personal Evaluation Reports a reincarnation of ACRs were 40 per cent, professional training was 30 per cent, and CSB was

30 per cent. Personal Evaluation Report has an additional criterion giving marls for addressing public complaints.[13]

The Supreme Court has moved against the refusal of the Establishment Division to disclose the assets held by civil servants.[14]

CIVIL SERVANTS DEMONSTRATE.—In February 2021, the federal All Government Employees Grand Alliance clashed with police in the Red Zone of Islamabad. The government servants were demanding a raise in salaries of employees till grade 22, a demand that the government did not find possible to meet. The matter was resolved the next day when Basic Pay Scales 1 to 19 were increased by 25 per cent. Sheikh Rasheed Ahmed said the pay scales of Grades 20 to 22 would be increased in the next budget.[15]

PUBLIC/PRIVATE SECTORS.—The Federal Cabinet allowed serving bureaucrats to take contractual jobs in the lucrative management position scales (MP-I, II, and III).[16] However reversing the position was not favoured. The proposal to allow private sector employees to join the civil service as technical advisers was turned down on the plea that such a step would harm the government's efforts to reform the bureaucracy.[17]

STATE-OWNED ENTERPRISES.—SOEs as they are called have been running at a loss for decades. The railways are a case in point. Passengers throng the stations, and bookings have to be made a month in advance, yet the Railways are running at a loss. Pakistan International Airlines (PIA) was rated in the 1960s as one the world's best airlines with an impeccable punctuality record and new destinations such as Beijing, demanded bailouts from the federal government year after year. During a heated debate in the Senate, Farhatullah Babar proposed a three-point formula: (1) preparing a plan for revival; (2) entering into 'code sharing' arrangements with other airlines for sharing the traffic; (3) replacing the Board of Directors with a board comprising professionals of the aviation industry.[18]

Members of the Pakistan Air Force also debated the decline of PIA. Captain Afaq Rizvi wrote on 6 February 2016 that 'the fall of PIA began when the Civilian Aviation Authority (CAA) was married to the Pakistan Air Force.' Air Vice Marshal Abdus Sami Toor rejoined that PIA reached its zenith under Air Marshal Nur Khan's tenure. Air Marshal Khurshid Anwar Mirza revamped the CAA. The Open Skies policy was not framed by the PIA but by the government. In his rebuttal Capt. Rizvi said Air Vice Marshal Abdus Sami Toor's letter gives the impression that 'Air Marshals worked wonders for PIA and CAA.' He argued that 'everyone is not Nur Khan who had the ability to raise the pinnacle anything he touched PAF or PIA'.[19] One should keep in mind that Air Marshal Nur Khan had two terms. The first was exemplary. During his second term, he replaced Mian Mohammad Rafiq Saigol and was not as effective as in his first term. An insider explained 'the first time he had come from the military, the second time he came as a civilian.' One irate correspondent inquired within this debate, how is it that the Pakistan Broadcasting Corporation is running at a loss while tiny Frequency Module (FM) radio stations run on profit? This is the question which hangs over the once profitable but now unsustainable state entities.

> **STUDIES ON STATE OWNED ENTERPRISES**
>
> The government has been seeking a solution to this question. Given below are a few glimpses:
>
> > '...it is equally important that SOEs, whether these are retained in the long run or are retained till these are liquidated, divested, or privatized, are managed through introducing appropriate governance framework and oversight mechanisms.'[1]
> > 'All the interviewees unanimously asserted that employee issues and bad governance are the most leading factors behind the failures of these public enterprises...'[2]
>
> On 4 April 2020 the Pak-China Investment Company (PCIC) was given the first draft of human resources, financial and tax due diligence by the Privatization Commission,[3] but till now, despite CPEC, nothing substantial has emerged. Privatization as an option has also receded, because when this October (2023) the Pakistan Steel Mills were put up for sale there were no buyers.[4] The only solution is that state owned entities need updated and professional management skills.
>
> **Notes**
>
> 1. *State-Owned Enterprises Triage: Reforms & Way Forward*, Finance Division, Government of Pakistan, 3 March 2021, p. 12.
> 2. Abdul Khaliq, *Performance Evaluation of State-Owned Enterprises in Pakistan* (Islamabad: Pakistan Institute of Economic Development, 2022), p. 43.
> 3. *Dawn*, 5 April 2020, p. 9.
> 4. *PT Profit*, 26 October 2023.

FOREIGN SERVICE.—Pakistan's Foreign Service is in the main manned by career diplomats. However, the post of ambassador under whom career diplomats have to serve, is, not only in Pakistan but the world over shared by politicians. While some, because of their high profile and familiarity with ruling classes become assets, sometimes they become an embarrassment. Thus the appointment by the fourth PPP government of Husain Haqqani as Ambassador to the United States culminated in what came to be known as the 'Memogate Scandal' Husain Haqqani started his career with the Islami Jamiat-e-Talaba ended up in the liberal PPP.

He should not have been chosen in the first place because he was the author of a book which claimed to show that there was a nexus between the Military and Mullahs. US personnel knew of course, that they were themselves responsible for inducting religious fanatics first in the Islamization Movement of 1977 and after the Soviet invasion of Afghanistan, but Indian diplomats were playing up the card that the liberation movement in Kashmir was terrorism by Pakistan and they had a number of US legislators amplifying that charge. In such a situation he should not have been chosen to represent Pakistan in the United States. The 2 May 2010, the Abbottabad raid was an embarrassment and at this juncture Husain Haqqani reportedly wrote a memo to a US official, asking the US to intervene in case the military decided to take over again. He was replaced by Sherry Rahman, but seven years down the road his having been a PPP appointee was raked up by the then ruling PML, the PPP especially Khurshid Shah not only disowned him but called a recent article written by Haqqani 'an act of treason'.[20]

This is an extreme and rare case, but it goes to show how carefully diplomats need to be chosen, and that to choose career diplomats is the safer option. Foreign Office members apart from pursuing their country's foreign policy have to cater to Pakistani expatriates, especially in the Gulf countries. On this count, Prime Minister Imran Khan chided envoys for failing to serve the expatriates and for failing to attract foreign investment for Pakistan.[21] Retired diplomats retaliated. They stated that the Prime Minister had himself mentioned that most complaints pertained to the issuance of passports and Identity cards which were under the domain of the Interior Ministry. 'Angst in the Foreign Office is palpable'.[22]

Even as far as Saudi Arabia and the UAE the respective missions helped evacuate thousands of Pakistanis in difficult home country's environment during the Covid-19 pandemic. When the Yemen War began, the Pakistani missions did not hesitate to evacuate Indians along with Pakistanis. Finally realizing that his rebuke was undermining the diplomatic efforts of the Foreign Office the Prime Minister retracted his statement.[23]

Zahid Husain made the comment, 'The spectacle of religiously inspired extremist groups rampaging through the streets and demanding the expulsion of a foreign envoy will not make investors, domestic or international comfortable…Our foreign missions cannot be expected to build an image of the country that is completely the opposite of what exists at home.'[24]

What Zahid Husain was alluding to was the demand of a religious party Tehreek-e-Labbaik, Pakistan for the expulsion of the French Ambassador for the *Charlie Hebdo* (French satirical magazine) affair. Critics still harped on the services of the Interior Ministry. Our diplomats have to contend against very powerful lobbies and very resourceful adversaries. Under the circumstances they deserve appreciation.

POLICE.—Police is a federal service, but it is administered according to provinces. The police of each province are headed by an Inspector General (IG), with Deputy Inspector Generals (DIGs) serving under him/her, for violent crimes, traffic, investigation and the like. The Police Act 1861 was the colonial era legislation under which the police functioned. It was replaced by the Police Act 2002 which in turn was replaced in 2016. There are high profile cases such as the 1 September 1996 death of Murtaza Bhutto, an opposition leader but the brother of the sitting Prime Minister Benazir Bhutto.

Punjab has a police force of 180,000, Sindh has 150,000, Khyber Pakhtunkhwa has 80,000 and Balochistan has 40,000. The Police have a reputation for brutality and corruption, but nevertheless, the law takes its course unless weak prosecution or absence of witness protection in criminal cases hampers it. Dr Shoaib Suddle a retired IG called the colonial era Act oppressive and favoured the 2002 Act. According to him, the 2002 Act had been an ideal way of handing over the tasks of registering the First Information Reports (FIR), investigation, carrying out investigation, gathering evidence and prosecution. Dr Suddle complained that the tenure of Station House Officers (SHOs) was a mere three months which was a major hindrance in police work.[25]

Another former IG Tariq Khosa complained that an honourable and honest Director General of the Federal Investigation Agency (FIA) was shown the door just because he was trying to do his duty in accordance with the law. Political executives, he said cannot digest this behaviour, as they want the law of the ruler to prevail. Another retired IG Afzal Ali Shigri also complained about the politicization of the police. To him, the security of the tenure of a police commissioner is the key to effectiveness, but in practice, political parties do not guarantee this.

The posting of the IG in a province can become contentious if the federation and the province are governed by different political parties. In 2016, IG Allah Dino Khawaja was sent on forced leave and later IG Syed Kaleem Imam lasted two months after the Sindh government let it be known that it wanted his transfer. On 28 February 2021, Syed Kaleem Imam was transferred as IG of the Motorway and Highway Police. He was succeeded as IG by Mushtaq Ahmad Mahar. These two cases loomed large in the public eye although from 2018 to 2020, five IGs have been posted in the Punjab and four in Khyber Pakhtunkhwa.

The most publicised case was that of retired Captain Muhammad Safdar whose apartment was raided. This led to the siege of IG Mushtaq Ahmad Mahar's official residence and his kidnapping by the ISI and Rangers. Along with IG Mahar, twenty-five DIGs and thirty SSPs asked for a hundred days' leave simultaneously. The COAS intervened and had the concerned ISI and Ranger personnel removed.

There are many instances of gallantry which need acknowledgement. IG Abdul Aziz Bullo was killed by terrorists in Balochistan. The Police Training Centre at Saeedabad, Karachi is very innovative. This author is well-known to the police. Forensic laboratories and DNA testing are working, and the manuals are being published. *Basic Investigation Handbook* by Abdul Khalique Shaikh (Bar-at-Law) and Muhammad Akbar is the first in a series of police training manuals. The system is fine, the implementation is a problem.

Notes

1. Syed Tanvirul Hasan, *Freedom and Partition Life and Times of Sir Sultan Ahmed* (New Delhi: Commonwealth Publishers 2007), p. 27.
2. Feroz Khan Noon, *Chashm Deed* (Lahore: Takhliqat 2022), p. 54.
3. *Dawn*, 2 July 2018.
4. Denis Judd (ed.), *A British Tale of Indian and Foreign Service: The Memoirs of Sir Ian Scott* (London: The Radcliffe Press, 1999), pp. 39, 40.
5. Ibid., p. 36.
6. S. Irtiza Husain, *Compromise with Conciliation* (Karachi: Pak-American Commercial, 1997), p. 197.
7. *Dawn*, 12 July 2020.
8. *Dawn*, 7 September 2009.
9. *The Express Tribune*, 10 December 2011.
10. *The Express Tribune*, 13 July 2022.
11. *Dawn*, 11 December 2019.
12. *Dawn*, 21 July 2021.
13. *Dawn*, 10 July 2021.
14. *Dawn*, 9 April 2021.
15. *Dawn*, 12 February 2021.
16. *Dawn*, 5 May 2021.
17. *Dawn*, 10 May 2021.
18. *Dawn*, 11 February 2016.
19. *Dawn*, 13 February 2016.
20. *Dawn*, 14 March 2017.
21. *Dawn*, 6 May 2021.
22. *Dawn*, 7 May 2021.
23. *Dawn*, 12 May 2021.
24. *Dawn*, 12 May 2021.
25. *Dawn*, 11 February 2016.
26. *Dawn*, 24 December 2019.
27. *Dawn*, 11 November 2020.

Chapter 40
The Armed Forces

One of the causes of Muslim decline was the fact that the Mughal army lacked organization. Naval superiority ensured the triumph of Britain over India, and no ruler, with the exception of Sher Shah Suri, had devoted attention to the strengthening of naval forces in India. The lack of organization had also impeded modernization, and the actual military worth of the youth became apparent when they provided manpower to the British forces. We have discussed how the East India Company was able to recruit the cream of military talent and turn it into such an efficient fighting machine as to make the numerical superiority of natives a liability rather than a source of strength.

Even to die-hard imperialists, it was apparent that India needed to consolidate her defences before British control loosened.[1] It suited the British to create regiments by purposely mixing Hindus and Muslims of different castes. When Britain needed Muslim troops from India to station in Egypt in 1882, the Indian General Headquarters informed London that such a dispatch would not be possible because the Indian army was deliberately not organized on religious lines. However, the exigencies of the vast British Empire were many and from 1892 onwards recruitment was on the basis of caste and creed.[2]

With the advent of the 20th century, this phase was over. The recruitment was no longer on religious lines. Up until the First World War (1914-1918), native soldiers were refused commissions and it was this point that led to the first clash between M.K. Gandhi and M.A. Jinnah. Gandhi was in favour of unconditional cooperation with the British, even going to the extent of making the offices of the Home Rule League a recruiting agency, while Jinnah and B.G. Tilak took the position that unless Indian troops were given Royal Commissions (as they were then called), the Home Rule League would not cooperate with the British. Jinnah was then championing the cause of an Indian and not a Muslim army, but by the time of the Second World War (1939-1945), the Muslim presence in the British Indian army brought great political benefits to the Muslims of India. The Muslim soldiers hailing mainly from the Punjab and NWFP were so important to the British war effort that their aspirations could not be disregarded during the course of the war, and even after, they were such a major factor that even the Labour government could not override these aspirations. British Intelligence had intercepted the letters of Muslim soldiers to M.A. Jinnah.

This debt, we tend to overlook when we complain about the political or administrative role of the armed forces. Indeed, the image of the privileged few obscures the hardship and privation officers have to endure for the defence of the country. The armed forces were of the essence and both M.A. Jinnah and Liaquat Ali Khan had refused to accept power in Pakistan unless they were given an army immediately. Since the British were of the view that Pakistan would be temporary, they delayed the division of the armed forces when they decided to divide India. As it was, although there were pure Hindu and Sikh units there were no all-Muslim units, which according to Stephen Cohen was a result of British distrust dating back to 1857.[3]

At Independence, the officer corps of the Pakistan Army consisted of one major general, two brigadiers, and fifty-three colonels. The rest of the required officers were British, and it was from this small corps of officers that the Pakistan Army developed. The present strength of the Pakistan Army is 520,000. It was earlier headed by a commander-in-chief, but since 1971 it is headed by the chief of army staff. Below him are lieutenant generals each of whom heads a corps made up of two or more divisions. The divisions are headed by major generals and consist of three or more brigades. A brigade is headed by a brigadier. Also below the chief of staff are four central command officers (i) chief of general staff (ii) adjutant general (iii) quartermaster general and (iv) master general of ordnance.[4]

THE NAVY.—The present strength of the navy is 22,000. It is headed by the chief of naval staff. The next senior officer is the vice-chief of the naval staff who is responsible for maritime operations and planning. The deputy chief of naval staff is responsible for recruitment, administration, and planning. There are three principal staff officers responsible respectively for operations, personnel, and material.[5] At present there are ten surface ships and nine submarines. A most vital adjunct is the Navy's aviation wing.

THE AIR FORCE.—The Pakistan Air Force (PAF) has a strength of 45,000 men. The chief of the air staff is assisted by five principal staff officers, each responsible respectively for (i) operations, (ii) engineering (iii) administration (iv) training and (v) personnel.[6]

CIVIL ACTIVITIES OF THE ARMED FORCES.—The armed forces are often called upon to perform civilian functions, such as managing airlines and other institutions, building roads in difficult places such as the Karakoram Highway, and conducting rescue operations at times of natural calamities such as the earthquake of October 2005. They have also taken over the running of the whole country several times in the history of Pakistan. The armed forces take on all these responsibilities because it is felt that civilians are too corrupt, undisciplined, and untrained to perform these functions well.

It needs to be noted that nuclearization has not decreased Pakistan's dependence on conventional forces. Pakistan is a country that has had its nuclear response opposed. Another factor is the 3.5 million Afghan refugees whose camps provide a hideout for the perpetrators of terrorist acts. No foreign concern over this situation is needed. The Pakistan Army is charged with guarding and shifting its nuclear arsenal.

COLD START DOCTRINE.—The nuclear stalemate in South Asia caused India to come up with what it called a Cold Start Doctrine. This is an operational plan devised by the Indian Army in 2004. It provides for rapid penetration of Pakistan territory by the Indian Army 'that would enable India to enact swift retribution for a Pakistan attack.'[7] Couched though it is in the language of defence the Cold Start Doctrine makes sense only if it is adopted as a surprise attack. Lt.-Gen. (retd) Khalid Kidwai said that the Cold Start Doctrine had prompted Pakistan to develop short-range missiles to counter such a move.

Pakistan's indigenous defence production reached $1.5 billion it was revealed on 15 December 2014. By 30 August 2016, the Pakistan Navy had developed its *third* state-of-the-art Regional Air Transport aircraft and Scan Eagle Unmanned Aerial System. The Navy had initiated its air arm in the early 1970s. Admiral M. Zakaullah (2014–2017) termed the delivery a new era in the capabilities of the Pakistan Navy. The Pakistan Air Force had begun the manufacture of JF-17 advanced fighter aircraft with the help of China but by December 2016 the Pakistan Aeronautical Base at Kamra had achieved the target of producing sixteen JF-17 aircraft in a year. Another model the JF-17B dual carriage fighter jets equipped with a long-range superior radar system and advanced firing capabilities was produced in Pakistan; fourteen in quantity. Thus, technology transfer is showing its benefits.

What looms in the public eye are the coups d'état carried out by the Pakistan Army. The blame, however, should be shared. The 1958 Martial Law was promulgated by President Iskandar Mirza and the Martial Law of 1969 was promulgated by President Ayub Khan. Only the 1977 coup was initiated by the Pakistan Army, with all its tragic consequences.

The coup of General Pervez Musharraf also had the excuse of saving the lives of the PIA passengers flying with him from Colombo when Prime Minister Nawaz Sharif would not allow the aircraft to land on Pakistani soil, with its fuel running out. It is significant that the PML government charged Pervez Musharraf for his 2007 action of launching another state of emergency than for his 1999 takeover.

The greatest criticism that the Army has faced has been over the execution of Zulfikar Ali Bhutto. General Mirza Aslam Beg has pleaded that this decision was not institutional in nature: 'We are unfortunate to see this day when decisions about us are taken somewhere else. Our rulers have different gods. Had Bhutto not been hanged, we would not have seen the political turmoil prevailing since 1990. General Musharraf would not have come into power, Benazir would not have been murdered. Zardari would not have become the president and this political labyrinth would not have been our fate.'[8]

We can take General Beg at his word when we notice that Maj.-Gen. Majid Malik resigned over this decision and the largest demonstration against Z.A. Bhutto's execution, was led in Lahore by retired General Tikka Khan. Nawaz Sharif's main criticism of the Pakistan Army was its role in framing the foreign policy of Pakistan.[9] Surely this is an exaggeration. No syllabus of international relations across the world is devoid of a paper on Strategic Studies. It is wrong on the part of the military to monopolise the formulation of foreign policy, but no foreign policy can be formulated without input from the military.

The harshest criticism of the Pakistan Army has come from Dr Ayesha Siddiqua on the basis of Armed Forces bodies being involved in economic activities: 'Commercial or profit-making ventures conducted by the military with the involvement of armed forces personnel, or using the personal economic stakes of the defence establishment, constitute a major part of the political economy that has not been analysed systematically.[10]... Its most significant component is entrepreneurial activities that do not fall under the scope of the normal accountability procedure of the state.[11]... The driving force is not loyalty or ideology, but vested interests. Therefore it is not possible to get the military out of politics, or for the military to strengthen democratic institutions, even if some claim to bolster democratic institutions.'[12]

The seed money for the Fauji Foundation came from arrears due from the Second World War. This windfall was put to a collective purpose. In a country where after the 1972–1974 nationalisations, capital has remained shy and investment is not forthcoming, the fact that military entities are willing to invest is not a measure to be scorned at. Dr Shahida Wizarat is of the opinion: 'Another innovation would be to introduce and promote public-private coalitions. State institutions like the Pakistan Army, Pakistan Air Force and Pakistan Navy can constitute companies in the private sector. These companies can participate in the development of physical infrastructure. For example, an entity owned by the Pakistan Army can be involved in building roads, one owned by the PAF can build airports and one owned by the PN can build ports etc. Profits made by these firms can then be transferred to the parent company. This way the defence of the country can be self-financed to some extent.'[13]

It should not be assumed that Shahida Wizarat is an apologist for the armed forces. She is quite the opposite. In a chapter that is hauntingly relevant to our present plight 'Why IMF is Not an Option', she writes: 'Increase in foreign debt/GDP ratio has led to the interruptions to the democratic process and installations of technocratic governments.... International Financial Institutions subscribe to the New Political Economy approach which labels politicians statesmen and women as corrupt, insincere and therefore, ineligible to govern. As the stakes of the IFIs [International Financial Institutions] in a country rise, they feel comfortable when the country is governed by its own officials and consultants.'[14]

Not everyone agrees though. The Senate wanted the military's role in commercial activities. Concerns over accountability and quality were voiced. The National Logistics Cell had built a bridge in Karachi that collapsed one day before it was to be inaugurated by President Pervez Musharraf.[15] The judiciary too agrees. In a case pertaining to encroachments in the Margalla Hills National Park, the Islamabad High Court held that the armed forces neither had the power nor the jurisdiction to engage in business ventures directly or indirectly outside its composition.[16]

A major crisis occurred when the United States was able to carry out its action against Osama bin Laden (2 May 2011) without detection. The Armed Forces were accused of either complicity or negligence. The military offered itself for accountability, for intelligence failure, mainly its inability to track the four US helicopters used in the raid. Lt.-Gen. Ahmed Shuja Pasha, chief of Inter-Services Intelligence (ISI) during a five-hour-long briefing to parliament offered to resign. He explained that the Shamsi airbase had been given under UAE command and it was the base from where drone attacks were carried out.[17]

A very novel situation was created when former President Pervez Musharraf blamed his successor as COAS General Ashfaq Parvez Kayani for his reluctance—not his poor judgment—that prevented him from launching an operation against the Taliban.[18] The former President was not privy to General Kayani's conversation with Anne Patterson the American ambassador on this topic.

Thus, there is an accountability mechanism within the military enclave. The Pakistan Ex-Servicemen Society (PESS) stated that the military should not be above accountability.[19] The National Accountability Bureau had three years earlier on 1 November 2012 summoned retired Lt.-Gen. Javed Ashraf Qazi, Lt.-Gen. Saeed-uz-Zafar and Maj.-Gen. Hamid Hasan Butt for a probe.

When Lt.-Gen. Asad Durrani, former DG ISI co-authored the book *The Spy Chronicles: RAW, ISI and the Illusion of Peace*, with his Indian counterpart Amarjit Singh Dulat and journalist Aditya Sinha. The ISPR reported that retired Lt.-Gen. Asad Durrani had been summoned on 28 January 2021 to the GHQ to explain his position.

The rank and file of the Armed Forces are known for their devotion, dedication, and spirit of sacrifice.

Notes

1. Arthur Vincent, *The Defence of India* (Bombay, 1922), p. 91.
2. M.E. Chamberlain, *Britain and India* (Devon, 1974), p. 160.
3. Stephen P. Cohen, *The Pakistan Army* (Los Angeles, University of California Press, 1984), p. 5.
4. Pervaiz Iqbal Cheema, *The Armed Forces of Pakistan* (Karachi Oxford University Press, 2003), p. 46.
5. Ibid., p. 86.
6. Ibid., p. 104.
7. Andrew Small, *China–Pakistan Axis* (London, Hurst and Co., 2015), p. 45.
8. General Mirza Aslam Beg, *Compulsions of Power* (Lahore. Idara Matbu'at-i-Suleimani 2021), p. 128.
9. *Dawn*, 11 June 2011.
10. Ayesha Siddiqua, *Military Inc.* (Karachi Oxford University Press, 2007), p. 1.
11. Ibid., p. 2.
12. Ibid., p. 249.
13. Shahida Wizarat, *Fighting Imperialism Liberating Pakistan* (Karachi: Centre for Research and Statistics, 2011), p. 77.
14. Ibid., p. 175.
15. *Dawn*, 19 December 2017.
16. *The Express Tribune*, 14 July 2022.
17. *Dawn*, 14 May 2011.
18. *Dawn*, 28 January 2015.
19. *Dawn*, 22 June 2015.

Part 8
Diplomatic History

Chapter 41
Introduction: Aims and Objectives

The terms on which a state wishes to conduct its international relations is called its foreign policy. The purpose of foreign policy is to gain for the state such a place in the comity of nations that it has no difficulty in sustaining its sovereignty and integrity, to give it a voice in the formulation of international principles conducive to its interests, and to extend its influence beyond its frontiers and within international fora.

FORMULATION OF FOREIGN POLICY.—The formulation of foreign policy has three structures. The first of them is within the executive: (i) The president or prime minister of a country. For example, US President Harry Truman said, the 'President makes foreign policy'. In 1956, the British Prime Minister, Sir Anthony Eden did not consult his full cabinet before the invasion of Egypt. (ii) The foreign minister. If the head of government lacks any special interest in foreign policy, or if the foreign minister is the head of a coalition party, he may play a more decisive role. The classic example is the British Foreign Minister, Ernest Bevin under Prime Minister Clement Atlee. (iii) The Foreign Office. This is the government department responsible for the formulation and execution of foreign policy. It has many sections known as 'desks' which deal with specific countries or groups of countries. Because of close focus and specialization, they provide inputs of detailed, even secret, information and give expert opinions on this basis. The bureaucracy along with career diplomats provides continuity to foreign policy when the elected government changes.

Sometimes foreign policies can cause tension. In 1971, for example, the pro-Pakistan policy of the US president was nullified by the state department headed by the Secretary of State.

Apart from the foreign office, the military establishment and scientists also formulate foreign policy in some measure. The military brings security considerations to the foreign ministry's notice. Scientists have a better insight into the scientific capacity of contending countries, and their expertise can increase the options a government can exercise. Nuclear capability is the most obvious example. Between the Executive and the Foreign Office, an intermediary body like the National Security Council (NSC) can intervene. The Defence Committee of the Cabinet also has a strong bearing, but the NSC can have information on a wider spectrum of both political and technical interests.

There is the intermediary structure consisting mainly of parliaments. These are usually multiparty bodies; therefore they are usually unable to initiate foreign policy, but they monitor it closely. 'Their main power lies in the ratification of treaties.'[1] The US Congress is the most prominent example of the exercise of this power. In 1919, it refused to ratify the Treaty of Versailles by which the League of Nations would be formed. The US President, Woodrow Wilson had taken the initiative in its foundation, but Congress would not allow the US to join. The Comprehensive Test Ban Treaty (CTBT) is a treaty that the US urged other countries, including Pakistan, to sign. In 1999, the US Congress itself refused to ratify it, thereby relieving Pakistan of pressure. The Symington, Pressler, and Brown Amendments of the US Congress played a leading role in the maintenance of US relations with Pakistan.

The outer structure reflects Public Opinion and/or Ideology. If there had not been a strong public opinion in favour of carrying out retaliatory nuclear tests in May 1998, the government would have succumbed to world pressure. Similarly, the Tashkent Declaration (1966) went against public opinion and a movement was unleashed which toppled the Ayub regime. During the Simla Summit (1972) public opinion was sober because Pakistan had lost the 1971 war.

This brings us to instances where public opinion is strong, but since all other elements formulating foreign policy are united, the government goes against public opinion. For example, Pakistan took an anti-Arab stance in the 1956 Arab–Israel War. Public opinion was in favour of Iraq in the 1990 Gulf War; but since the underlying principle, that the invasion of a neighbouring state was obviously dangerous, Prime Minister Nawaz Sharif, against much of the establishment and with the solitary support of the former Prime Minister Benazir Bhutto, was able to pursue an anti-Iraq policy. Ideology is often bound up with public opinion but not necessarily. Pakistan does not recognize Israel out of ideological differences, practical incentives notwithstanding. This is not because of anti-Zionism but because Israel is perceived to be established on Arab lands. Pakistan has ideological sympathy with the people of Chechnya but nevertheless recognizes it as a part of Russia.

In addition to the above three structures, there are politicians and academics who have theories on foreign policy but have no means to impose them. Mehtab Ali Shah states that the provincial bodies should have an input. He further states that Pakistan's policy on Kashmir is only for the benefit of Punjab and not the remaining three provinces of Pakistan. He advocates a compromise over Kashmir and says that Pakistan can live without it if it can live without East Pakistan.[2] M.B. Naqvi advocates accepting Indian hegemony.[3] This policy would be very sound if the disappearance of Pakistan could also guarantee the disappearance of India. Previously East Pakistani intellectuals expressed the opinion that the Farakka Barrage issue was raised by West Pakistani politicians to embitter the relations between Bengal and India. Now, thirty-four years after the liberation of Bangladesh, the Farakka Barrage is again a very contentious issue between Bangladesh and India. Therefore, goodwill alone does not lead to solutions to international disputes.

HISTORICAL PERSPECTIVE.—Pakistan came into being when its name was unfamiliar, when the notion of a state founded on religion was unpopular, and when, almost simultaneously with its creation, it was forced into a war over Kashmir with India—the same country which had withheld its military and financial assets. Moreover, Pakistan came into existence when the Cold War had already begun.

Pakistan had barely formulated the principles of its foreign policy when it was forced to define its objectives which were security and sheer survival. The principles of Pakistan were broadcast by its Founder as honesty and fair play, the extension of moral and material support to oppressed and suppressed nations (e.g. Indonesia), and the upholding of the United Nations Charter.

There was some dissonance in the beginning; while the Governor-General, Mohammad Ali Jinnah, although stressing neutrality as a principle, gave preference to the USA over the USSR on ideological grounds. The Prime Minister, Liaquat Ali Khan also stressed neutrality but voiced his preference for Britain over the United States. While the regimes of Jinnah and Liaquat lasted, Pakistan remained officially neutral, but under Governor-General Ghulam Mohammad, Pakistan entered into military alliances with the West, CENTO and SEATO.

Pakistan's alliances with the West gave the Indian Prime Minister, Pandit Jawaharlal Nehru the excuse to renege on his repeated promises to hold a plebiscite in Kashmir ('Pakistan has brought the Cold War to India's door') and since Russia gave India all-out support against Pakistan, our intelligentsia has bitterly regretted this decision. In reality, Pakistan stayed neutral for a longer time than its resources warranted. As Francesco Guicciardini stated early in the 16th century, while neutrality was good for a powerful state, it was dangerous for a weak state. Pakistan was weak, it badly needed arms to secure itself against India, and its strategic location was also suited to American strategic interests, most notably for bases suited to the surveillance of the USSR (such as one established later at Badaber), bases for which the US had approached the British before Independence.

During the 1965 war, Zulfikar Ali Bhutto characterized India's non-alliance as a double alliance, as it indeed was, but Pakistan could not match the resources and market potential of India and it was sheer naivete to suppose that the standards which were being applied by the US and the UK to India would be applied to Pakistan. From the 1960s to the 1980s, Pakistan's, relationship with China was the cornerstone of Pakistan's foreign policy. Relations with the Muslim world, which were initially uneasy, plummeted during the 1956 Suez War. Some improvement was achieved during the 1967 Six-Day War, but the solidarity Pakistan sought remained elusive. Relations with the newly independent Central Asian States provided a real opportunity for Pakistan to extend its influence, but Pakistan's policy over Afghanistan, apart from causing tension with its most friendly neighbours China and Iran, actually led to a resurgence of Russian influence in central Asia.

Pakistan regained its non-aligned status after the 1971 war when India and the USSR jointly acted against Pakistan, making its eastern wing (East Bengal) the only state since the Second World War to have successfully seceded. Having lost a war and a province, in 1971, Pakistan also lost strategic posts like Kargil in the conflict. When, eighteen years later, and subsequent to the loss of Siachen, Pakistan reoccupied Kargil, it led to a crisis in which world opinion went against Pakistan. The re-focusing of world opinion away from UN resolutions on Kashmir to cross-border terrorism was the greatest-ever foreign policy failure of Pakistan. In the previous year, Pakistan had finally tested and proved its nuclear capability but the diplomatic advantage of going nuclear was dissipated by integrating the announcement with two very contentious domestic issues, the Kalabagh Dam, and the freezing of Foreign Currency Accounts. The 12 October 1999 coup initially compounded Pakistan's difficulties, but when Pakistan joined the US-led alliance against terror following the 9/11 terrorist attack it was able to emerge from isolation. Pakistan was therefore successful in containing the fall-out of the revelation that Pakistani scientists had been engaged in clandestine nuclear proliferation, but this has been a fragile success, and to emerge victorious from this crisis will require the highest order of vigilance and confidence-building.

Notes

1. Joseph Frankel, *International Relations* (London: Oxford University Press, 1964), p. 37.
2. Mehtab Ali Shah, 'Soul Searching on Kashmir', *Dawn*, Karachi, 4 September 1999.
3. M.B. Naqvi, 'Portents of the 1996 Indian Polls', *Dawn*, Karachi, 3 October 1995.

Chapter 42
Pakistan and the World Powers

Countries which can influence decisions and events in most parts of the globe are called world powers. These powers are the United States of America, Russia, China, and Britain. We shall trace the relations of Pakistan with these powers in turn. In the background, we must consider the relations these powers maintained mutually.

During the entire course of the Cold War from 1946 to 1999, there was an ideological war between the countries led by the US which stood for democracy and market economy on the one side, and the Union of Soviet Socialist Republics (USSR), which subscribed to a dictatorship of the proletariat and a planned economy, on the other. These were described as the two worlds, capitalist and communist, and those countries which kept themselves away, and were, incidentally, developing countries, were said to belong to the Third World. This was called the Bipolar Age.

From the beginning of the Cold War which encompassed the Korean and the Vietnam Wars, relations between the US and China were hostile right until 1970, when ideological differences were subserved to strategic considerations as both confronted the USSR. There is no mutual hostility, but there is also no warmth between the two powers.

The Cold War lasted as long as the USSR remained a communist power and held sway over the Central Asian states. Since 1991, the USSR as such has ceased to exist and no longer remains an ideological adversary of the US. It is still a large country with immense resources and still retains, like the US and China, a huge nuclear arsenal. Russia may not have lost its importance, but since it was then no longer opposed to the US, what had emerged is called a Unipolar world, as opposed to the Bipolar phase when the two world powers were dominant.

Britain too has seen its status reduced but had anticipated this reduction and planned accordingly. It has retained sufficient heirlooms of the Empire, and from the time of the partition of India in 1947, to at least the 1956 War, when its invasion of Egypt was disliked by both the US and the USSR, it remained, for practical purposes, a world power. It also has a nuclear arsenal, but this alone does not account for its world power stature. France, which also has a nuclear arsenal and, like the world powers mentioned above, is a permanent member of the United Nations Security Council (UNSC), has not been able to exercise the same measure of influence as Britain. With this brief introduction, we come to world power relations with Pakistan.

PAKISTAN AND THE UNITED STATES OF AMERICA.—The year 2003 is a good point from which to view the nature of US–Pakistan relations. On 15 March 2003, the US waived democracy-related sanctions against Pakistan. On 24 March the US imposed sanctions on the Khan Research Laboratories nuclear facility in Pakistan. On 3 April the US waived the $1 billion debt payable by Pakistan. On 4 April the majority view at a Johns Hopkins University seminar was that Pakistan was a greater challenge than Iraq. On 10 April, Secretary of State, Colin Powell rebutted the assertion of the Indian Foreign Minister Yashwant Sinha that there was a stronger case for military action against Pakistan than against Iraq. However, Powell also stressed that the situation across the Line of Control (LoC) in Kashmir was difficult and painful, in other words accusing Pakistan of cross-border terrorism in Kashmir. In 2004, Pakistan was granted the most favoured non-NATO ally status and was enmeshed in the A.Q. Khan nuclear proliferation scandal.

These developments show that there are no other two countries in the world whose relations are as chequered as those of the US and Pakistan. There is no sustained cordiality and there is no sustained hostility. From Colin Powell's 10 April 2003 statement it can be concluded that bilateral concerns are not adverse, but they follow an erratic course because of third-party considerations. An example of this is the divergence, indeed deflection of views regarding the Arab–Israeli conflict. During the Cold War, Pakistan detested the role of the USSR in South Asia but applauded its role in the Middle East. Since the Cold War has ended, Pakistan must give precedence to US support in South Asia and not make US policy in the Middle East an overriding concern.

When the US and Pakistan established relations in 1947, they had different reasons for doing so. Pakistan needed help against India which had withheld its military assets, while the war had broken out in Kashmir; the US wanted Pakistan's assistance in encircling the communist states of the USSR and China. The lead taken in establishing relations on a discordant basis was taken by Pakistan, not the US.[1] In October 1947, a Pakistani delegation led by Mir Laiq Ali, offered the country's services to halt the progress of communism for the sum of $2 billion.

That amount of money was not forthcoming, but the US viewed Pakistan sympathetically and supported its position on Kashmir in the UN. Liaquat Ali Khan, as the first prime minister of Pakistan made a successful visit to the US but still held back from committing troops to Korea. On his return from the US, Liaquat announced that Pakistan was completely neutral because it was not beholden to any country. After Liaquat's assassination during Ghulam Mohammad's tenure as governor-general, Pakistan signed SEATO and CENTO (originally Baghdad Pact) accords in 1954, and a Mutual Defence treaty in 1959. The implications of these have already been covered. Briefly, India went back on its promise to hold a plebiscite in Kashmir, and the USSR vetoed every UNSC resolution that urged action on the plebiscite.

These pacts with the US enabled Pakistan to assemble a large arsenal, especially in the air force. During the 1950s, Pakistan was called the 'most allied ally'. President Dwight D. Eisenhower visited Pakistan on 8 December 1959. President Ayub Khan told the US Congress on 12 July 1960 that the US could land its troops in Pakistan whenever it wished. In the same year a U2 American spy plane, which had taken off from Badaber in Pakistan, was shot down over the USSR territory and the pilot, Gary Powers, was captured alive. Ayub remained placid in the face of a direct threat from Nikita Khrushchev, the Soviet Premier.

Even at the outset of the 1959 Sino–Indian tension, President Ayub left his country aghast when he proposed a joint India–Pakistan Defence Pact against China. Luckily for Pakistan, the Indian prime minister turned this offer down. Two successive foreign ministers, Mohammad Ali Bogra and Zulfikar Ali Bhutto, were able to secure the support of China. Pakistan's growing relations with China crossed what the US termed 'acceptable limits', and the American action of arming India became a source of contention during which Pakistan's Foreign Secretary, Sami Khan Dehlavi, was removed from his post. Relations remained cold when the 1965 India–Pakistan war broke out. The US imposed an arms and aid embargo on both India and Pakistan, but harmed only Pakistan, as India had an alternate source of supply in the USSR.

Relations remained sour until 1970 when the US revised its anti-China policy and sought Pakistan's help in establishing contact with it. This Sino–US detente raised Pakistan's hopes but these hopes were countermanded by the Indo–Soviet Treaty of Friendship of 1971. Although the Sino–US partnership was active in the UNSC, India and the USSR moved swiftly to pre-empt it and dismembered Pakistan. Only one side of the atrocities had been reported in the US, consequently, members of Congress as well as the State Department thwarted the attempts of President Richard Nixon to prevent the secession of East Pakistan. The new president, Z.A. Bhutto, publicly acknowledged that President Nixon had saved West Pakistan and Azad Kashmir.

The US's so-called 'tilt' towards Pakistan lasted until the beginning of the Jimmy Carter era, when Pakistan, in response to the 1974 Indian nuclear explosion, started its own defensive programme. Pakistan's pursuit of a defensive nuclear armoury seemed unreasonable to the Carter administration. This phase continued until 1979 when the USSR invaded Afghanistan.

Pakistan became a front-line state and under both Jimmy Carter and Ronald Reagan received massive military and financial aid. The Pakistani government under General Zia took complete advantage of the lifting of American pressure and went ahead with the nuclearization programme. One other consequence of the Afghan war for both the US and Pakistan was the induction and arming of Islamic military groups from Afghanistan itself and the Middle East, against the Soviet Union. After the Soviet withdrawal from Afghanistan, this policy was to have catastrophic consequences for both countries.

Once Pakistan lost its front-line status, events moved at a fast pace. Within two years the USSR was fragmented and with the end of the Cold War the US resumed its nuclear non-proliferation pressure on Pakistan with a spate of legislation. First came the Symington Amendment of 1975, passed to stop aid to non-nuclear countries who were importing uranium enrichment technology. It was followed by the Glenn Amendment of 1977 which sought to bar assistance to countries importing nuclear reprocessing technology. (A French Nuclear Reprocessing Plant had been negotiated by Z.A. Bhutto). These amendments were first invoked by President Jimmy Carter on 6 April 1979 (two days after Z.A. Bhutto's execution) but soon had to be suspended in view of the Soviet invasion of Afghanistan. It should be noted that this situation was more critical for Pakistan than for the US, since Pakistan could hardly have been able to survive had Russian troops advanced into Pakistan.

It was to seek suspension of the earlier amendments and to help Pakistan that the Pressler Amendment was passed in 1985. Only later did it work against Pakistan. This provided for the reaffirmation of the 1959 Mutual Assistance Treaty relating to aggression from a communist country. It also had a provision that the US president had to certify annually that Pakistan did not possess a nuclear explosive device. When, after the end of the Cold War, President George Bush refused to issue such a certificate, the Symington and Glenn Amendments came into operation against Pakistan.

The restoration of democracy brought about a thaw in mutual relations. President Bill Clinton said, on the occasion of Benazir Bhutto's official visit, that it was wrong on the part of the US to retain both the F-16 aircraft and the money paid for it. In November 1995, Senator Hank Brown moved his amendment which restored US economic and non-military aid. The Brown Amendment did not repeal or modify the Pressler Amendment, but this was done by the Harkin–Warner Amendment on 17 July 1997.

When Pakistan responded to the Indian nuclear tests in 1998, the US did not question the rationale of Pakistan's nuclear tests but was nevertheless unhappy. Relations plunged again during the 1999 Kargil crisis. US officials issued no statements when India seized Kargil from Pakistan in 1965, nor when India violated the LoC by taking Siachen in 1985, but the nuclearization of both combatants had an alarming effect when Pakistani irregulars occupied Kargil in 1999. Pakistan was forced to withdraw under international military pressure led by the US.

When Pakistan once again came under military rule in 1999, President Bill Clinton showed his displeasure by condescending to spend only a few hours in Pakistan on 26 March 2000, when he delivered a homily on television. The succeeding George W. Bush administration indicated that it would objectively review bilateral relations. By an ironic twist, Pakistan was being held responsible for the puritanical deeds of the Taliban regime in Pakistan. The Taliban were the residue of the Islamic militant groups jointly fostered by the

US and Pakistan to combat Soviet occupation. After the Soviet withdrawal, these groups turned against the US. Pakistan's support for the Taliban alienated all and conciliated none. This was a serious aberration. According to an American chronicler, Dennis Kux, the initial US response to the Taliban regime had been positive and saw 'nothing objectionable' in the steps the Taliban had taken to impose Islamic law.[2]

It is not simply that the US were taking ad hoc measures. They planned to raise whole generations of Jihadis. In her book, *I is for Infidel: From Holy War to Holy Terror*, Kathy Gannon shows how small children were given books to indoctrinate them. Francis Robinson pertinently commented, 'It is well known that the rise of the Taliban was in part the outcome of Western measures in Pakistan and Afghanistan to resist the Russian invader.'[3]

The 11 September 2001 terrorist attacks gave Pakistan an opportunity to cut its Taliban connection. The US ultimatum and Pakistan's opportunity to withdraw from a most unpopular alliance were the flip sides of a coin. Pakistan again became a front-line state and an ally in the war against terror. President Pervez Musharraf was received warmly in the US on 12 February 2002, and a number of times thereafter.

The succeeding PPP regime elected following the assassination of Benazir Bhutto (27 December 2007) though democratic, had a much more troubled relationship with the US. There were three high-profile cases which coincided with the Barack Obama administration. First, the case of Raymond Davis an undercover American agent who killed two Pakistanis in Lahore. The diplomatic immunity claimed for him by the US was denied by Pakistan and ultimately recourse had to be taken to the Sharia which permitted a *lex talionis* (blood money).

Second, Raymond Davis revealed that the US government's anxiety to get him out of Pakistan was due to its having traced Osama bin Laden to Abbottabad. Attacking him on Pakistani soil, while an American was being held prisoner in Pakistan would complicate matters. In his own memoirs, President Barack Obama reveals that when he called Pakistan's President Asif Ali Zardari about having killed Osama bin Laden the fact that the US had violated Pakistan's sovereignty was uppermost in his mind rather than the fact that Pakistan had been harbouring a fugitive, the knowledge of whose whereabouts it had consistently denied. So prone to blame Pakistan, the US giving Pakistan a clean chit in the Osama bin Laden affair stands out.

Third, the Salala incident took place on 26 November 2011, in which ISAF/US forces killed twenty-eight Pakistani soldiers in a bomb attack. Already incensed, Pakistan cut off the US supply line to Afghanistan through its territory. The supply line was re-opened finally after 3 July 2012 when US Secretary of State Hillary Clinton apologized to Hina Rabbani Khar, the foreign minister of Pakistan. However, during the third PPP regime, Pakistan received more than forty drone attacks which killed more 'collateral' than the designated targets. Collateral means non-combatants, the elderly, women, and children.

Nawaz Sharif was near the end of his third tenure when Donald Trump took over as president of the US on 20 January 2017. Relations plunged. President Trump repeated the worn-out mantra, 'We can no longer be silent about Pakistan's safe havens for terrorist organizations, the Taliban and other groups...We must prevent nuclear weapons and materials from coming into the hands of terrorists'.[4]

The Secretary of State Rex Tillerson took a broader view, 'There are areas where perhaps even India can take some steps of rapprochement on issues with Pakistan to improve stability and remove some of the reasons why they deal with these unstable elements inside their own country.'[5]

It was after Imran Khan's election as the prime minister on 21 July 2018 that President Trump loosened. He offered to mediate on the Kashmir dispute, saying that Indian Prime Minister Narendra Modi had asked him to. Although Modi denied having made such a request, Trump repeated his offer. On 16 August 2018 when asked to address India's denial, a senior presidential aide responded, 'The US President does not make up things.'

Earlier, on 5 August 2019, India revoked Article 370 of its constitution which gave Kashmir its special status. Simultaneously, India clamped down a curfew. A US State Department official noted that 'Stripping Kashmir of its special status has implications that go beyond the Indian borders.[6] After a UNSC meeting of 16 August 2019 ended without a joint communique (which would have been actionable) the American media weighed in on the side of Pakistan. What helped was the favourable impression of Imran Khan that Donald Trump carried, 'We have a good friendship, a good feeling, good chemistry I think Pakistan will help us.'[7]

By late August, American legislators protested the shutdown in Kashmir. They reminded India that: 'transparency and political participation were the cornerstones of representative democracies.' Congresswoman Yvette D. Clarke from New York said, 'Modi has no right to do what he is doing to the people of Kashmir.'[8] Indian American Congresswoman from Washington state, Pramila Jayapal, said 'Deeply troubled by reports of Indian government's arrests of 2,000 in Kashmir....'

On 4 October 2019, Senator Christopher van Hollen was denied entry into India-held Kashmir. Senator Bob Menendez decried Indian repression in Kashmir. Kamala Harris (49th Vice-President of the US) stated that 'we have to remind the Kashmiris that they are not alone in the world.' Senator Elizabeth Warren said that the rights of the Kashmiris must be respected. Senator Bernie Sanders termed India's 5 August 2019 action unacceptable and called on President Trump to support a UN-backed peaceful resolution that respects the aspirations of the Kashmiri people.[9] The most pointed question came from Abigail Spanberger, a former CIA operative, 'How is the State Department accepting that at this time India, a close strategic partner for the United States on everything from trade to military cooperation is telling us that we cannot allow U.S. diplomats to enter Kashmir?' In a similar vein, Congressman David Trone from Maryland also questioned India's refusal to allow delegations to Kashmir and wanted to know what the official reason cited for such refusal was.[10]

All this would change when President Joe Biden assumed office as the US president. Biden had resolved that all American troops would be withdrawn from Afghanistan on 9 September 2021, the twentieth anniversary of the American invasion. By announcing a firm date Joe Biden precipitated a disorderly withdrawal and the sudden collapse of the Afghanistan regime propped up by it. At first, it sought to make Pakistan the scapegoat for the failure. The previous Secretary of State Rex Tillerson had stated the US position rather carefully. He said that Pakistan was important for the US because Washington wanted to engage the Taliban in peace talks whenever the conditions permitted that.[11]

What this comes down to is that the US while wanting Pakistan to do more wiping out Taliban sanctuaries from its soil, yet it must hold its punches, so that the Taliban remained in one piece to engage in talks. It also meant that at the end of the conflict, the US should retain enough goodwill to engage in peace talks with Afghanistan, but neighbouring Pakistan should not. It was due to the close questioning of Senator Chris van Hollen that such facts were revealed after the US withdrawal and Pakistan escaped being made the scapegoat of a war which a former Pakistani COAS General Mirza Aslam Beg had predicted would end in the victory of the Taliban.[12]

The US drone attacks were meanwhile having a blow-back effect on war-weary pilots: 'But this mission killed someone because of incorrect information... We got the wrong guy... I had just killed someone's dad. I had watched his kids pick up the body parts. Then I had gone home and hugged my own kids.'[13] It did not occur to anyone that Americans being basically very decent people, didn't need counselling. Their leaders did. Their concerns were exacerbated when it was learnt that Russian President Vladimir Putin had invited Prime Minister Imran Khan. Ned Price, State Department spokesperson had earlier issued a statement: 'Pakistan is a strategic partner of the United States. We have an important relationship with the government in Islamabad, and it's a relationship that we value across a number of fronts... Islamabad does not have to strain its relations with China to maintain ties with Washington.'[14]

This evidently, did not apply to Pakistan's ties with Russia, and anyway, Admiral Michael Mullen, 17th chairman of the Joint Chiefs of Staff, put forward a different view on China: 'I think that we have clearly distanced ourselves from Pakistan over the last decade and Pakistan has more and more fallen under the umbrella of China.'[15]

That means that the Russian visit of Imran Khan did enrage the US. US Department of State spokesperson Ned Price said that it is the responsibility of all nations to voice concern over Russia's actions in Ukraine. Despite the presence of the Pakistani prime minister in Moscow, Pakistan had publicly regretted the escalation of hostilities, and the US had simultaneously on 24 February announced a $20.4 million penalty against the National Bank of Pakistan.[16]

There were scholars in Pakistan who saw the Russian invasion of Ukraine, as a mirror image of the 1962 Cuban Missile Crisis. The Soviet Union had planted nuclear warheads in Cuba a sovereign country, but President John F. Kennedy had taken the position that the presence of Russian missiles in the proximity of the US was a security risk. Similarly, at least since 2015, President Vladimir Putin has been voicing concerns over the European Union and NATO expansion to Ukraine. Moscow could be hit in less than four minutes he had explained. Pakistan having sided with the US in 1962, could not, on principle, avoid siding with Russia.

Seeing that such considerations are removed from realpolitik, the incoming Minister of State for Foreign Affairs Hina Rabbani Khar voiced the opinion that Pakistan should have sought an excuse to postpone Imran Khan's visit to Moscow. When we turn to the section on Pakistan–Russia relations it shall be clear that Pakistan's relations with Russia do not admit of a postponement and even more so our relations with the US do not admit of a rebuff to Russia.

As soon as the incoming PML (N) government had settled down the chargé d'affaires ad interim for US Mission Pakistan, Angela Price Aggeler, met Hina Rabbani Khar and US–Pakistan relations were on the mend. On the same day Prime Minister Shehbaz Sharif threw all diplomatic proprieties to the wind and stated that Pakistan cannot afford the enmity of the US.[17]

Outstanding Issues. The US dominates the unipolar world, therefore the issues between it and Pakistan and the attitudes taken by citizens of both countries are not only the most urgent foreign policy concerns of Pakistan but central to Pakistan Studies itself.

Cross-Border Terrorism. The Secretary of State Hillary Clinton admitted: 'Let's remember here...the people we are fighting today we funded them twenty years ago...and we did it because we were locked in a struggle with the Soviet Union... They invaded Afghanistan... and we did not want to see them control Central Asia and we went to work... and it was President Reagan in partnership with Congress led by Democrats who said you know what it sounds like a pretty good idea... let's deal with the ISI and the Pakistan military and let's go recruit these mujahideen... And great, let them come from Saudi Arabia and other countries, importing their Wahabi brand of Islam so that we can go beat the Soviet Union... And guess what... the (Soviets) retreated... they lost billions of dollars and it led to the collapse of the Soviet

Union... So there is a very strong argument which is... it wasn't a bad investment in terms of the Soviet Union, but let's be careful of what we sow because we will harvest... So then, we left Pakistan... We said okay fine you deal with the Stingers that we left all over your country... you deal with the mines that are along the border, and... by the way we don't want to have anything to do with you... in fact, we're sanctioning you... So we stopped dealing with the Pakistan military and with ISI and we now are making up for a lot of lost time.'[18]

The Soviet invasion of Afghanistan ended in 1989 and all that happened has been described above. Now that it can revert to friendship with India, the US shows concern over cross-border terrorism by Pakistan in Kashmir. It believes that the uprising in Kashmir is not indigenous but the result of infiltration from the Pakistan side.[19] One way of verifying this claim is to have the UN monitor the border. Pakistan proposed this not only in the 1990s but in 1971 as well.

Referring to allegations that East Pakistan guerrillas were operating from Indian soil, Indira Gandhi said, 'How can we check it? Our border with East Bengal is so long that even if India deployed her entire army it would not be able to stop them.' Indira Gandhi indicated that she was opposed to a plan proposed by Pakistan for posting UN (forces) in East Pakistan. She could see no purpose in it.[20]

The Soviet stance was more belligerent: If Pakistan attacked India for Indian assistance to the Mukti Bahini, the Soviet Union would consider it an act of aggression.[21] If Pakistan's plea for UN monitoring had been accepted, there would be no invasion of East Pakistan in 1971 and no Kargil crisis in 1999. The following words of Bill Clinton are worth pondering over: 'Essentially I believe a policy that causes so many civilian casualties without a political solution ultimately cannot succeed.'[22] This he said with reference to Chechnya; it would apply more aptly to Kashmir. The testimony of an independent US photographer and filmmaker, Martin Sugarman, who constantly reports on the human rights violations in Indian-held Kashmir, could be heeded.[23]

Democracy. Since both the US and India are huge democracies, they are allies, much to the discomfiture of Pakistan. India's definition of a democracy should be taken into account. According to the *Dawn* of 12 November 1971, Indira Gandhi said, on 11 December 1971: 'India was hurt to discover that certain countries which called themselves democracies had preferred to ignore the repression in East Pakistan during the last eight months.'

Accordingly, countries that take recourse to repression cannot be called democracies. Indian repression in Kashmir exceeds eight months, it also exceeds eight years, and 700,000 Indian troops are stationed in Kashmir.

Nuclear Proliferation. For this issue also we have the declassified comments of Secretary of State Henry Kissinger. When US diplomat Philip C. Habib

(1920–1992) complained on 9 July 1976 that Z.A. Bhutto was making a bomb, Kissinger replied: 'If you were in his place, you would do the same thing. I must say I have some sympathy for Bhutto on this. We are doing nothing to help him on conventional arms, we are going ahead and selling nuclear fuel to India even after they exploded a bomb and then for this little project (French Nuclear Re-processing Plant) we are coming down on him like a ton of bricks... An imbalance is being created in which Pakistan is totally dependent on India. There is no question we can break Pakistan's back; they have made the mistake of allying themselves with us.'[24]

To the US public, the Dr Abdul Qadeer Khan scandal highlights their proliferation fears. This episode, as Henry Kissinger has explained above, has a history. During the 1991 Gulf War, Americans discovered that A.Q. Khan had been helping Iraq with its nuclearization programme. In a little-publicized move, the Government of Pakistan placed A.Q. Khan on its exit control list on 21 January 1995. This points to the proliferation role of the Pakistani scientist. But the press and public opinion play a very potent role here. The day after the Pakistani president issued a pardon to A.Q. Khan, two leading columnists rushed to print the case of J. Robert Oppenheimer, father of the US bomb, who was deprived of security clearance.[25] The words used for Oppenheimer were found to fit A.Q. Khan squarely: 'Although the US owed a "great debt of gratitude for his magnificent service, his continuing conduct and associations reflected a serious disregard for the requirements of the security system".'[26]

The A.Q. Khan affair acquired an intriguing aspect when Ruud Lubbers, former Netherlands prime minister, revealed on 9 August 2005, that his government could not arrest A.Q. Khan in 1975 because of CIA intervention. Again in 1979, the CIA prevented the Netherlands from further investigation. The next day, an American State Department spokesperson refused to comment on the report on the grounds that it dealt with long past events and intelligence matters. Thus, there is more to the A.Q. Khan affair than meets the eye.[27]

While hardly anyone ever refers to the fact now, and the US is known as the only power to use the bomb, the Manhattan Project was actually a race with Yoshio Nishina's (1890–1951; 'father of nuclear physics in Japan') laboratory in Japan, where efforts to build an atomic bomb were underway. Oppenheimer and his team pre-empted an atomic attack on the US. The principle is that a difference must be made between a bomb for hegemony and a bomb for survival. If the US had not turned a blind eye to Indian efforts to go nuclear, Pakistan would not be in possession of a bomb. The only way to stop proliferation is to stop discrimination. No country other than India has needled and goaded another country into nuclear retaliation. It was Pakistan that proposed a nuclear-free South Asia, and it was India that opposed it.

In contrast to fears of proliferation by Pakistan, the news that a container carrying uranium was stolen in India was almost ignored. The Chief Minister of Jharkhand, Madhu Koda revealed three weeks after the theft: 'It was not highly enriched but neither was it just yellow cake.'[28] A year earlier, police had arrested two uranium thieves in Assam. Thus, there are non-State actors in India as well, where religious fundamentalists organize pogroms.

The China Factor. Pakistan's friendship with China became the first cause of friction between the US and Pakistan. Yet when world power configurations changed, a Sino–US rapprochement was favoured. Relations between the US and China still remain intact, yet there is a lobby that projects China as the long-term adversary of the US. This is calculated on the basis of China's size, population, and nuclear capacity. Ideological differences between China and the US did not impede a strategic alliance during the Cold War. With ideology now scaled down, no cause of conflict is apparent. As far as purely strategic factors are concerned, the same potential for conflict that exists between the US and China also exists between the US and India. From China there emanates no intent of hostility; from India, it has been frankly conveyed: 'Soon, predict some BJP seers, India must come into conflict with the US and China for possession of Mideast oil. India must be militarily prepared.'[29]

The Pakistani Perception. While it is necessary to clear up some American perceptions about Pakistan, it is equally imperative to clear the Pakistani perception of the US. It is usually thought that the US is only a fair-weather friend, and we would have fared better by being neutral or with an alliance with Russia. The accusation of being a fair-weather friend was made by Foreign Minister Gohar Ayub (1930–2023) to Strobe Talbott (Deputy Secretary of State).[30] On other occasions, US emissaries like Bill Gates[31] and Anthony Zinni[32] have been blunt; this means that when the US feels it is on weak ground, it listens. Most of Pakistan's complaints relate to the 1965 and 1971 wars. The complaints are valid but nevertheless warrant closer inspection. The US did not abide by the 1959 treaty during the 1965 war. Secretary of State Dean Rusk cited the reason that Pakistan had sent infiltrators into Kashmir.[33] Since this charge has been repeated by Air Marshal Nur Khan, then PAF chief and subsequently by a former foreign secretary, Humayun Khan,[34] there remains no ground to censure the US on this point. However, this statement is not representative of the US efforts during the 1965 war. How the China factor influenced reactions needs to be set out. Dean Rusk told the Indian ambassador that in the unlikely event of sizeable Chinese intervention, the US would first ask India to stop the fighting, moreover, there was little chance of the US committing troops to the conflict.[35] US Ambassador Walter P. McConaughy said that the destruction of Pakistan's military capacity would not be in US interests. Under Secretary of State George Ball and Assistant Secretary of State William Bundy advanced the view that were the Chinese to indulge in some mild harassing action, it would give the US leverage over India. The consequences of the US stopping arms supplies were immense and were appreciated later by Henry Kissinger but on balance, the US was supportive, even though behind the scenes, and publicly, Dean Rusk endorsed the plebiscite principle.[36]

As for the 1971 war, we have already seen that the Russians had stationed two nuclear submarines off the US coast in 1971.[37] In spite of having a hostile Congress and an insubordinate State Department, the US saved both West Pakistan and Azad Kashmir. Again when we see *Pakistani* journalists blaming Henry Kissinger for condoning the genocide of Bengalis in 1971 and say that Kissinger's advice to Nixon to tilt towards Pakistan was 'infamous', we can well imagine the extent of the US feeling against him.[38]

Finally, we must note that no matter how low our relations have plunged, there have been strong votaries of Pakistan in the US. Senators Dan Burton, Tom Harkin, John W. Warner, Hank Brown, and Sam Brownback have vigorously supported Pakistan. Congressman Dana Rohrabacher criticized his government for inaction on Kashmir and savaged the Indian representative and called for a plebiscite.[39] In no other country, do we have such eloquent spokespersons. We have already noted the later friends of Pakistan like Ilhan Omar, Sheila Jackson Lee, and Chris van Hollen.

Prospects. After years of sanctioning Pakistan, and raining drones on it, the US finally awoke on 4 February 2022 to the realization that Pakistan was a strategic partner. On 20 November 2022, the US spelt out its policy on South Asia: 'India is a global partner, while Pakistan is a valuable partner in a sensitive region...India is an invaluable partner, not just in the region but as it relates to a lot of the United States' shared priorities across the world...The United States values our long-standing cooperation with Pakistan and has always viewed a prosperous and democratic Pakistan as critical to US interests.'

The following statement made by Subrahmanyam Jaishankar, Indian Minister for External Affairs in Australia, illustrates the nature of American priorities: 'India has had a long-standing relationship with Russia, including military co-operation, dating to the times when Western countries didn't supply weapons to India and saw Pakistan as the preferred partner.'[40]

This is the extent to which Indo-American Nuclear Strategic Partnership goes. The US was treating India and Pakistan differently, but India and Pakistan were treating the US similarly, by abstaining from voting in favour of a UNGA resolution condemning Russia's action in Ukraine.

In mid-February 2023, the US and Pakistan resumed defence dialogue in Washington to enhance coordination on strategic issues and explore various options for ramping up bilateral military and security ties. These were held against the backdrop of increased militant activities in Pakistan by insurgents coming from Afghanistan.[41] The same meeting addressed Pakistan's economic woes. US State Department Counsellor Derek Chollet said: 'For the US, it's going to be about how we can deepen the partnership further and help Pakistan as it's trying to deal with what is an unquestionably challenging economic situation.' On this aspect, the US has remained somewhat ambivalent, as the IMF cannot be brushed aside. In April, When Pakistan's Ambassador to the US urged the restoration of Foreign Military financing and Foreign Military sales suspended by the Donald Trump administration, He was urged to work with the IMF: 'The reforms that Pakistan and the IMF agreed to, are not easy. But it is crucial that Pakistan take these actions to bring the country back to sound financial footing, avoid falling into further debt, and grow Pakistan's economy.'[42]

Despite such a discouraging response, the US undertook to provide Pakistan with a grant of $445.6 million under a new five-year bilateral agreement.[43] Two days later the USAID said that 'Pakistan needed to follow a reform agenda and adopt solid macro-economic policies to put back the national economy on a strong footing. USAID has been investing in Pakistan's economy for many years, but no amount of USAID funds is going to deliver that; it is the reform agenda that should come from the Government.'[44] A rebuke richly deserved.

The latest development is that sixty-six US Congressmen wrote to Secretary of State Antony Blinken to protect democracy in Pakistan, a reference to Pakistan's crackdown on the PTI for its 9 May 2023 demonstrations. Somewhat bizarre, as a comparison to Donald Trump's 6 January 2021 assault on the Capitol looming large. The Secretary of State responded that his department 'maintains close communication with the Government of Pakistan, and strongly supports the upholding of democratic principles and the rule of law for all.'[45] On this optimistic note, our relations rest.

THE USSR AND PAKISTAN.—On 25 May 2002, Russia invited the leaders of India and Pakistan to attend a peace conference.[46] Pakistan agreed, and India refused. Russia blamed Pakistan.[47] This exchange defines the relations between Pakistan and the USSR. These relations began in the Cold War when not only strategic but ideological rifts existed. While Jinnah found no ideological affinity with the USSR, he made the proviso that Pakistan should not go out of its way to annoy Moscow. In a meeting on 11 September 1947, he noted that the USSR was the only country not to congratulate Pakistan on its creation. Moscow was informed that the British embassy would represent Pakistan's interest in the USSR. There seems to be a behind-the-scenes move in this decision; prior to independence, Muslim League leader, Yusuf Haroon had attempted to contact Soviet Foreign Minister V.M. Molotov to secure the emergence of Pakistan, but the central leadership of the Muslim League later disowned his representative status, most probably under British pressure as *Dawn,* Delhi, the All-India Muslim League organ had published news of Yusuf Haroon's departure for Paris for this purpose (26 September 1946). It was decided that the British Embassy in Russia would represent Pakistan's interests. A.M. Dyakov, a Russian expert on India had written: 'There can be no doubt that many Hindu political leaders who are against Pakistan, are reflecting the strong urge of the bourgeoisie to rule fully over the whole of the Indian market. These circles are not only against Pakistan but do not even acknowledge the elementary democratic rights to self-determination in Muslim majority areas.'[48]

When the Indian Prime Minister Jawaharlal Nehru was invited to the US, the USSR looked for an opening in South Asia. On 2 June 1949, Joseph Stalin invited Liaquat Ali Khan to the USSR and on 7 June Liaquat announced acceptance and proposed 20 August as the date of the visit. It was against the background of these moves that Liaquat stated, on 10 June, that, 'Pakistan cannot afford to wait. She must take her friends where she finds them.' But from then on, the USSR backpedalled. On 19 July, Liaquat was informed that the date of his visit had been advanced, and he must arrive on 14 August. Since this would have meant his absence from Pakistan during its first Independence Day since the death of Jinnah, Liaquat proposed 18 August, but from then on until Liaquat's assassination on 16 October 1951, no date was set.[49]

A section of the intelligentsia has blamed Liaquat Ali Khan for strained relations with the USSR, maintaining that he obtained an invitation from Moscow only to use it for soliciting an invitation from the US. There is no factual foundation, no archival basis, for this story. Hasan Zaheer who has seen the Pakistani records, and Mansoor Alam who has seen the Soviet records, are among those writers who have sought to destroy this myth. In 1956, Anastas Mikoyan, then deputy foreign minister, came to Karachi and issued another invitation, but this invitation was not accepted. This was after Pakistan had become a military ally of the West, and Soviet leaders had publicly sided with India over Kashmir.

It was during this phase that, on 7 May 1960, a U2 American spy plane that had taken off from Badaber near Peshawar, was shot down over USSR territory. The Soviet Prime Minister, Nikita Khrushchev, directly threatened Pakistan with reprisals. The following year, however, Z.A. Bhutto, then fuel and power minister, successfully negotiated with the Soviet Union an oil and gas exploration agreement (4 March 1961). The Sino–Indian war of 1962 and the Western arming of India created dissatisfaction with a pro-West policy. President Ayub Khan made a state visit to the USSR in April 1965. In the same year the India–Pakistan war broke out. Now the new Soviet Prime Minister Alexei Kosygin inched closer to Pakistan, acknowledging that Kashmir was a disputed issue. After the ceasefire, the USSR hosted the Tashkent conference. Ayub visited Moscow again in 1967. Kosygin visited Pakistan in April 1968 and May 1969 and concluded a token arms deal.

Even as late as 1970, relations were on the upswing and the USSR had signed a cultural pact with Pakistan. But as soon as military action began in East Pakistan, President Nikolay Podgorny threatened President Yahya Khan. In his reply, Yahya referred to Soviet military suppression of Hungary and Poland. A meeting between the two presidents in Tehran was not cordial. An

Indo–Soviet treaty of friendship was signed under which any action against cross-border terrorism by Mukti Bahini from Pakistan would be treated as an act of war.

During the December 1971 debates in the UNSC, the USSR vetoed every proposal for a ceasefire and made Pakistan's withdrawal from its own territory a condition for peace. After the war, the new president, Z.A. Bhutto, made an official visit to Moscow from 16–18 March 1972 but was told plainly by his hosts that the USSR would again act in a similar manner in a similar situation as had prevailed in East Pakistan. This was interpreted as a Soviet invitation for the secession of NWFP and Balochistan provinces. Z.A. Bhutto's second visit from 24–26 October 1974 was far more cordial. Nevertheless, Leonid Brezhnev's Plan to include Pakistan in a security arrangement with what he called the 'States of Hindustan' showed that Indian hegemony over South Asia was the lynchpin of Soviet policy.

Meanwhile, some progress was witnessed in trade and economic cooperation including an agreement to build a steel mill which eventually became operational in 1980.

Relations deteriorated sharply again when the USSR invaded Afghanistan in 1979. In this crisis, the US again helped Pakistan against the USSR. President Zia tried to maintain relations regardless of the Afghan crisis, but his visits to Moscow for state funerals proved fruitless. Finally, the Soviet withdrawal began after the 14 April 1988 Geneva Accord, and they vacated Afghanistan on 15 February 1989.

This was actually a prelude to the break-up of the Soviet Union which provided an opportunity to review relations. On 24 December 1995, the Russian ambassador, A.I. Alexeyev stated that state and national interests and not ideology would guide Russo–Pakistan relations. No change was perceptible in practical terms. There were two irritants: Pakistan's support of the Taliban regime in Afghanistan, and Russia's conviction that the Taliban were behind the resistance in Chechnya, despite Pakistan's stated position that it considers Chechnya to be a part of Russia. There was a meeting between President Putin and President Musharraf at the UN in 2000, but no concrete result was obtained.

In October 2000, President Putin visited India and signed a new Defence Pact which was described by the Indians as more comprehensive than the 1971 Treaty of Friendship. The only perceptible thaw in relations between Russia and Pakistan was when Russia helped Pakistan launch a satellite in 2003. There are irritants between Russia and India, but never to the advantage of Pakistan. On 2 December 2004, Indian sources reported that Russia had imposed conditions on India for the continued supply of arms. However, during President Putin's visit to India, all such conditions were withdrawn. Indeed, Russian support for India has never been conditional. On 3 January 2005, the Pakistani ambassador to Russia said that economic relations between the two countries would improve.[50] The Russian ambassador to Pakistan made no corresponding statement.

A ripple was created in the uneventful relations between Russia and Pakistan, when Prime Minister Mikhail E. Fradkov arrived on 11 April 2007 at Islamabad at the head of a large delegation. Apart from delivering a formal message from President Putin to President Musharraf, he held a joint press conference with Prime Minister Shaukat Aziz on 12 April 2007 advocating economic diplomacy and expanded cooperation in the war against extremism and terrorism. Shaukat Aziz said that both sides had agreed to promote trade ties, using Iran as a corridor for this purpose. The delegation accompanying the Russian premier offered Pakistan high-speed locomotives and train coaches.

How relations began improving in the 21st century is framed in two observations. Firstly, the Russian ambassador to Pakistan, Danila Ganich, called for multilateralism. He said that with the rise of China, lasting shifts are taking place in the global economy. The US and Europe which pioneered globalization now seem to be turning to protectionism. The ambassador stated that: 'We are not a superpower as the USSR used to be.' Still, he was resentful of the US treating Russia as a marginal player.[51]

In actual fact after the economic dislocation in the last decade of the 20th century, a more compact but vast Russian Federation has been regaining ground. The rise of China, unlike in the Cold War era has been to the advantage of Russia. Now for the second observation: 'If Russia returns to superpower status, one reason will be that the world needs energy and Moscow has it to burn.'[52]

This has been painfully apparent after the Ukraine war, but Pakistan–Russia relations began with energy. In 1960, as stated Pakistan concluded an oil agreement with the Soviet Union.[53] For reasons of lucidity then we shall study Russo–Pakistan relations under the following heads: energy, military cooperation, the China factor, the Indian factor and finally the Ukraine war 2022 and the American factor.

Gas and Oil. On 30 May 2012, Zamir Kabulov special envoy on Afghanistan told Prime Minister Yusuf Raza Gilani spoke about the 'enormous commonalities' between Russia and Pakistan over regional issues and apart from supporting Pakistan's full membership of the Shanghai Cooperation Organization also supported the Iran–Pakistan Gas pipeline project. That is it was aware of the American objection to this project and recognized the energy needs of Pakistan. The next initiative, on 26 August 2012 was not about exporting gas to Pakistan but was about obtaining Russian help in building a pipeline from Karachi to Lahore. The next step was line Understanding, an accord for Russian oil exploration and production accord on 9 September 2015 worth $2.5 billion of which 85 per cent of the equity would be Russia's and 15 per cent Pakistan's. On 8 June 2018, both countries agreed that Russia carry out a feasibility study for laying down an underwater gas pipeline to Pakistan.

The next step was the signing of an agreement on 6 February 2019 for the offshore exploration of gas and oil. This time Pakistan undertook to import 500 million to 1 billion cubic feet of gas from Russia through a sea link. The project would take four years to complete. Among other items of discussion, Russian Foreign Minister Sergey Lavrov said in Islamabad: 'Energy is a promising area of business partnership.' The Karachi to Lahore gas line proposal became an accord on 15 July 2021 and on 17 January 2022 assured Vladimir Putin that Pakistan's interest in the Karachi to Lahore pipeline was very much alive. So far only initial steps seem to have been taken because of US sanctions on Iran and then on Russia. The gas cooperation has the potential of providing relief to Pakistan which has seen power riots break out.

Military Cooperation. Military cooperation received an impetus from Russia's re-assertion of its superpower status. Russia strongly condemned the US seal operation against Osama bin Laden in Abbottabad calling it an unacceptable violation of Pakistan's sovereignty.[54] The mere fact that Russia respected Pakistan's sovereignty was quite reassuring. The next year, from 4 to 7 October 2012, Pakistan's COAS General Ashfaq Parvez Kayani visited Moscow and held meetings with Colonel General Vladimir Chirkin. General Chirkin returned the visit on 5 August 2013. During the same month, 31 August 2013, Foreign Secretary Jalil Abbas Jilani travelled to Moscow. All these moves culminated in a Russia–Pakistan Defence Cooperation accord being signed on 20 November 2014.

Russia was still sensitive to Indian concerns and on the eve of his visit to India, President Vladimir Putin (10 December 2014) stated that the scope of the Russia–Pakistan Pact was limited, elaborating that it aimed at improving Pakistan's counterterrorism and anti-drug operations. 'In my view' the president said, 'this kind of co-operation served the long-term interests of all countries in the region, including India.' Next, on 20 February 2018, Khwaja Asif and Sergey Lavrov formed a panel to step up military cooperation. Later, Additional Foreign Secretary Tasneem Aslam said that Pakistan wished to purchase military equipment, as well as seek Russian investment in infrastructure development such as the construction of dams.[55]

In Moscow on 16 April 2015, Pakistan's Defence Minister Khawaja M. Asif and Russian Defence Minister Sergei Shoigu called for a multipolar world, as it would ensure peace and balance in international relations. The implications of this announcement were explained to a home audience by Sartaj Aziz, the prime minister's advisor on foreign affairs. 'The rise of China and Russia's growing interests in South Asia are very important developments for Pakistan.' Not forgetting to add, however, that these were counter-balanced by India's ambition to become a major power with Western help (12 September 2015). But only a month earlier (19 August 2015) had signed an agreement for Russia to sell Pakistan four Mi-35M (Hind E) attack helicopters.

On 23 September 2016, Russian soldiers arrived in Pakistan for a fortnight's military exercise. Lt.-Gen. Asim Bajwa commented: 'The first joint exercises being held by Pakistan and Russia is a testimony to our improving relations.'[56] During General Qamar Javed Bajwa's first visit to Moscow both countries agreed to boost cooperation.[57] The first development to follow was an agreement for Pakistani troops to be trained at the Russian Military Academy (8 August 2018). The two countries began joint counter-terrorism drills. By November they had concluded their third counter-terrorism drill Druzhba-III.[58] Only two days later Russia and Pakistan signed an agreement to enhance naval cooperation aimed at maritime security (8 November 2018).

On 2 July 2019, General Oleg Salyukov called on General Bajwa at Rawalpindi GHQ and expressed his desire to forge strong and broad-based relations with Pakistan. The Shanghai Cooperation Organization forum provided for increased interaction and on 5 September 2012 General Nadeem Raza discussed defence ties in Moscow with General Valery V. Gerasimov. As far as exercises drills went, Russia would participate in naval exercises off Pakistan's coast notwithstanding the presence of NATO navies also.

The following year saw many strides being taken the Pakistan Air Force and Pakistan Navy both brought their air crafts to participate in anti-surface and anti-air warfare. Sufficient joint actions had by then been taken for Shafqat Ali Khan (Pakistan's ambassador to Russia) to say that Pakistan and Russia have gradually built strategic trust. The director of the Russian Institute of Foreign Affairs said on the occasion that Russia and Pakistan enjoyed geo-political importance both at the regional and global levels (30 March 2021). Discussions about military drills and exercises went on, and on 14 November 2021, the national security advisors of both countries broached enhanced defence ties, especially cyber security cooperation. All this was however interrupted by the Ukraine war, when General Bajwa took a stand contrary to that of the prime minister and said that Russia's aggression against Ukraine could not be condoned. While describing US–Pakistan relations as close, he called relations with Russia 'cold' except for recent developments.

Policy Frame. It was the induction of both Pakistan and India into the Shanghai Cooperation Organization that provided the two countries with opportunities for closer interaction. Pakistan had had an observer status in Shanghai Cooperation Organization since 2005 but Pakistan (and India) joined as full members at Astana on 9 June 2017. Prime Minister Nawaz Sharif who led the Pakistan delegation acknowledged that this was due to the efforts of both China and Russia. From a unilateral world which had resulted from the collapse of the Soviet Union in 1989 onwards, the world was moving to a multilateral world. In December 2014, President Vladimir Putin protested that NATO's expansion was upsetting the strategic Balance of Power. This caused increasingly closer relations among the eastern nations.

Pakistan and Russia had both put their back to 1971 and 1979. Relations were on the upswing, and the only setback had been a last-minute cancellation of Vladimir Putin's visit to Pakistan scheduled for 27 September 2012.

Foreign Minister Sergey Lavrov rushed to Islamabad to contain the damage. It took four years for the Russian Ambassador Alexey Dedov to explain that ceremonies alone do not warrant a presidential visit, there had to be 'substance'. The substance was not elaborated upon by the ambassador, but later, Russia let it be known that Pakistan's inability to go ahead with the Iran–Pakistan Gas Pipeline project had caused the cancellation. It was the US which had forced Pakistan to drop the project, and Russia felt making futile agreements at the presidential level could prove to be an embarrassment.

Any increased military commitment would be resisted by both America and India. However, terror and militancy, universally condemned gave the two countries an opening to form a panel to increase military cooperation. The growing footprint of the Islamic State (Daesh) in Afghanistan and the indifference to this menace by the NATO-led forces caused closer cooperation between Russia and Pakistan. With the US having lately withdrawn from its 2015 Treaty with Iran, the presidents of Iran, China and Russia met in Qingdao, China. President Xi Jinping hailed the unity of the security bloc headed by Russia. President of Pakistan, Mamnoon Husain, and Prime Minister of India, Narendra Modi, were also present for the 9 June 2018 Shanghai Cooperation Organization summit.

On the same day, President Xi Jinping gave China's First Friendship Medal to President Vladimir Putin to symbolize the profound friendship between the two giants. Shortly after Russia and China began war games by mobilizing more than 300,000 Russian troops. On 27 March 2019, Pakistan's Foreign Secretary Tehmina Janjua at an Islamabad Conference described Pakistan's relations with Russia as 'an emergent partnership with tremendous scope'. She recommended that Pakistan resolve the issue of $200 million due to Russia. Tehmina Janjua proposed free bilateral trade and the deepening and augmentation of mutual strategic and defence relations. She publicly called for Russia's participation in the China–Pakistan Economic Corridor (CPEC).

This clearly meant distancing Pakistan from the Western bloc. On 23 March 2021, in Beijing, foreign ministers Sergey Lavrov and Wang Yi not only reaffirmed their close ties, but also rejected Western criticism of their policies, and sanctions against their countries and called upon the US to rejoin the Iran Nuclear Agreement of 2015. On 6 April 2021, Russian Foreign Minister Sergey Lavrov arrived in Islamabad and met both Prime Minister Imran Khan and COAS General Bajwa. They agreed that opportunities for joint work had significantly expanded following Pakistan's membership of the Shanghai Cooperation Organization in 2017.

Thereafter, President Putin on Christmas Eve 2021 issued a statement that insulting the Holy Prophet Muhammad (PBUH) does not constitute artistic freedom but is rather a violation of religious freedom. In an ideological conflict Muslims, Pakistanis in particular, were sure to contrast the Russian President's views with the virtual EU Summit in Paris following the *Charlie Hebdo* affair.

The China Factor. The resurgence of Russia, as we have been constantly seeing since the end of the Cold War has been due to the rise of China as the main rival of the US due to size, population, and scientific and industrial progress. Although China has never formally shed its communist ideology, it realizes that the Cold War hostility had no real basis after the transformation of the USSR into the Russian Federation. Even after shedding its Central Asian and East European possessions, Russia is still large and full of resources. The 1971 breach healed long ago, and geopolitics has triumphed over ideology. China and Russia have formed a bloc, hailed mainly by countries disenchanted with the West, notably Iran. When the Ukraine crisis heated up, Chinese President Xi Jinping supported President Putin in seeking guarantees that would preclude NATO's eastward expansion (15 December 2021). As earlier stated, Russia's alliance with China is natural even economically interdependent, while Russia's alliance with India is traditional. Russia did ask India to line up behind China's One Belt One Road (OBOR) initiative the extension of which is CPEC on 11 December of 2017. Sergey Lavrov told his Indian counterpart that India should not let political problems deter it from benefitting from a billion-dollar investment. The final outcome of a Russia–Pakistan *entente* shall rest on the outcome of whether the Russian alliance with China can prevail over the Russian alliance with India.

The India Factor. The main reason behind Russia's alliance with India was perceived as the Russian desire to keep India from falling in the US camp. This expectation was frustrated on 1 October 2008 the US and India signed a Nuclear Cooperation Pact. Russia had never needed to re-arm, but about a decade of economic dislocation during the transition from a planned economy to a price economy had made it vulnerable. Although Russia could never have been happy with the final choice made by India, its reaction was muted and only rarely did it find expression. On 1 October 2017 in St. Petersburg, President Putin told an Indian correspondent: 'We do not have tight relations with Pakistan—no binding alliance—with the US you do have close relations.'[59]

India and Russia had a difference of opinion over the presence of America-led troops in Afghanistan, but the joint communique issued at the end of their meeting made only an oblique reference to these.[60] The main reason is Russia's economic dependence on India. India financed one-fourth of the $20 billion the Russian Stealth fighter T-50 PAK FA which was deemed superior to the US Lockheed F-22. For Pakistan, this means that not only shall India receive one-fourth of the T-50 PAK FA aircraft direct from the assembly line, but it shall also benefit from technology transfer.

Post-Tashkent 1966 Russia has thrice offered to mediate the Kashmir dispute, on 30 June 1999, 16 June 2017, and on 28 February 2019 yet when in the same year on 5 August 2019, India revoked its Article 370 and increased its suppression of Kashmiris. Russia issued a statement saying that the Kashmir issue be settled bilaterally.

One month after the signing of the Pakistan–Russia Defence Cooperation Pact, stated on 10 December 2014—while visiting India—that the scope of the Pakistan–Russia Pact was limited to improving Pakistan's anti-terrorism and anti-drug operations: 'In my view, this kind of co-operation served the long term interests of all countries in the region, including India.'[61] On 14 November 2021, India began receiving Russian S-400 missiles despite the risk of American sanctions. When the Ukraine war broke out both Pakistan and India abstained from voting after the UN General Assembly debate. Predictably Pakistan, not India, bore the brunt of Western censure.

The Ukraine War. Imran Khan the prime minister of Pakistan was holding talks with President Putin when the Ukraine war broke out. It was not unforeseen, because the US and EU's dicta about Ukraine being a sovereign state had become resounding, as indeed Cuba had been a sovereign state in the 1962 missile crisis. Having supported the US in 1962, Pakistan on principle had to support Russia because President Putin had clearly spelt out that if NATO shared the Ukraine border with Russia, Moscow could be hit within four minutes. On 4 February, Russia and China declared a 'no limits partnership' and assailed US policies.

Imran Khan's talks with Putin ended without any agreement and before leaving Moscow, Imran Khan stated that the Ukraine dispute should be resolved through dialogue and diplomacy, but simultaneously the US told Pakistan that 'every responsible country should voice concern over Ukraine. Ironically the Soviet prime minister at the 1962 Cuban Missile Crisis had been Nikita Khrushchev, a native of Ukraine.'[62] The European Union followed with a joint statement critical of Pakistan's neutrality. On 5 March, Foreign Minister Shah Mahmood Qureshi urged Russia to find a diplomatic solution. That was the extent to which Pakistan could go, but the next day on 6 March the diplomatic front got heated when Imran Khan hit back at the European Union calling its demarche undiplomatic. At the end of the month, on 30 March, Sergey Lavrov said that 'Russia and China were moving towards a multipolar, just democratic world order.'

On 1 April 2022, Imran Khan said that his Russian visit had angered a powerful country. The allusion was clear, yet the no-confidence movement against Imran Khan could not have been engineered by the US. The intention was there, but there were other issues like hyperinflation and mounting fuel prices which had caused disenchantment. A far easier and traditional way would have been to accelerate judgment in the Foreign Funding case. Still, the next day on 2 April a statement by COAS General Bajwa lent credence to the prime minister's accusation: 'Russia's aggression against a smaller nation cannot be condoned.'

Russia was viewing these developments with deep interest on 5 April its Foreign Office issued a statement that the US wanted to punish a disobedient Imran Khan and condemned the US's 'shameless interference in Pakistan's affairs.'

Nevertheless, President Vladimir Putin congratulated Shehbaz Sharif, the incoming prime minister. Later reports revealed that Putin and Shehbaz Sharif had quietly exchanged letters reflecting the desire of both sides to strengthen mutual relations. However, both countries tried to keep this correspondence from the media's eyes.[63]

In a New York press conference, the incoming Foreign Minister Bilawal Bhutto-Zardari said: 'I defend former Prime Minister Imran Khan's visit to Russia. Imran Khan visited Russia as per Pakistan's Foreign Policy.'[64] Next to follow was a meeting between President Vladimir Putin and Prime Minister Shehbaz Sharif at Samarqand on 15 September 2022, on the sidelines of the Shanghai Cooperation Organization Conference. These overtures were having an effect. On 9 October 2022, President Putin issued a statement: 'I would like to note that we see Pakistan as a priority partner in South Asia, as well as the continent as a whole. Relations between our countries are developing positively and we are pleased about it.'

The year 2023 saw more positive developments. The US relieved pressure by stating that: 'Pakistan can buy Russian oil despite restrictions.'[65] A few days later Bilawal Bhutto-Zardari visited Russia at the invitation of his counterpart Sergey Lavrov on 29 and 30 January 2023. Addressing a joint press conference, the Pakistani foreign minister expressed the hope that the strong tradition of Russian diplomacy would achieve a peaceful resolution to the (Ukraine) crisis. 'Pakistan desires to strengthen cooperation with Russia in the fields of trade, security, defence, counterterrorism, education, and people-to-people contacts.' Foreign Minister Lavrov said Russia was satisfied with its military cooperation with Pakistan. Both the countries, he added, were holding regular military contacts, including joint exercises and military training.[66] Bilawal Bhutto-Zardari added: 'As far as interference by other countries are concerned, I expect that they will not interfere in bilateral relations between Pakistan and Russia.'[67] In view of the US reconciliation to oil trade between Pakistan and Russia, the allusion seems directed against India.

The following month Pakistan abstained from voting on a UNGA resolution condemning the Russian invasion of Ukraine. Pakistan's Permanent Representative Munir Akram explained that while Pakistan adhered to the principle enshrined in the resolution it did not believe in selective implementation.[68] That is Pakistan showed that while the UNGA was vociferous in upholding Ukraine's right of self-determination, seventy-five years had gone by without UNGA and UNSC resolutions on Jammu and Kashmir having been implemented. India, too, despite being the Nuclear Strategic Partner of the US, abstained.

Two days later, President Putin called the Ukraine war an existential battle for the survival of Russia. He said that the West wanted to divide Russia and then control the world's largest producer of raw materials. Russia was facing NATO: 'They are sending tens of billions of dollars in weapons to Ukraine. This is really participation.'[69]

On 21 March 2023, Chinese President Xi Jinping and President Vladimir Putin jointly called upon the US to 'stop undermining global strategic security.'[70] Thus, the stakes were high for Pakistan, but this time, as against 1979 and 2003, Pakistan had been successful in keeping a distance. Rather, in Kazan, Russia, during a three-day conference of eighty-five countries, Russia and Pakistan signed a bilateral agreement trade agreement on 19 May 2023, aimed at facilitating and reducing the cost of trade between the two countries. This protocol also offers a substantial custom-duty discount for Pakistani products entering Russia.[71]

In a related development, Pakistan and Belarus signed on 30 May 2023, a visa waiver agreement for those holding diplomatic or official passports. The Foreign Minister of Belarus Sergei Aleinik said: 'We see Pakistan as a very valuable and reliable partner in South Asia and the Muslim World.'[72] The foreign minister also had a very cordial meeting with Prime Minister Shehbaz Sharif. This is significant as Belarus is an important Russian ally in the Ukraine war.

On 10 June 2023, Foreign Minister Bilawal Bhutto-Zardari told Al Jazeera TV that Pakistan, while retaining neutrality in the Ukraine war seeks enhanced engagement with the Russian government, through meaningful ties. Then, oil again became a cementing factor. The prime minister of Pakistan announced on 11 June 2023 the arrival of oil crude from Russia. State Minister for Petroleum Musadik Malik revealed that the first consignment of 45,000 tons was paid for in Yuan, the Chinese currency.[73]

The Gaza crisis has brought China and Russia closer to each other adding to the isolation of United States.

PAKISTAN AND PEOPLE'S REPUBLIC OF CHINA.—China was established in 1949, two years after Pakistan's creation. No ideological restraint marked Pakistan's relations with Communist China, as it had with Communist Russia. Pakistan was one of the first countries to recognize China, diplomatic relations had been established by 1951. The Pakistani leadership had had an unhappy exchange with Chiang Kai-shek and was more receptive to the regime headed by Mao Zedong. The relations were initially formal, and China was not pleased with Pakistan joining SEATO and CENTO, yet there was no bitterness. The Pakistani Prime Minister, Mohammad Ali Bogra, was able to strike a rapport with the Chinese Premier Zhou Enlai during the Bandung Conference of 1955,[74] which Pakistan had co-sponsored. Bogra's successor, H.S. Suhrawardy, visited China on Zhou Enlai's invitation in October 1956 and Zhou Enlai paid a return visit to Pakistan in March 1957. Unfortunately, Suhrawardy, on his visit to the US, not only played down relations with China but also voiced criticism of the Chinese regime: 'described the Chinese posture as one of aggressive expansionism that threatened peace and freedom in Asia.'[75]

This damage was contained due to China's diplomatic maturity, but an episode occurred which had greater potential for misgivings. At the start of the Sino–Indian conflict in 1959, President Ayub most injudiciously offered India a joint defence against China, which the Indian Premier, Jawaharlal Nehru, inexplicably refused. At this stage, the Foreign Minister, Mohammad Ali Bogra, who, as prime minister, had established first contacts with China, was able to nullify Ayub's indiscretion and cement ties with China.

On 2 March 1963, the Sino–Pakistan border was demarcated, and later agreements on trade, and much more significantly, direct air communications were signed. China was culturally insular and diplomatically isolated; therefore, air links were a boon to both countries. During the 1965 War, China offered Pakistan military support, reportedly on the condition that Pakistan sustain the conflict and not accept a ceasefire precipitously. On 16 September, when the war was at its height, China issued an ultimatum to India to return some border outposts, yaks, and other chattels. Alarmed by Chinese support for Pakistan, the British High Commissioner, Sir Morrice James, played on Ayub's conservatism and dissuaded him from accepting Chinese help. China issued another ultimatum to India on 6 January 1966, while the Tashkent Conference was in progress, but Ayub again succumbed to Soviet pressure.

In the 1965 war, when Pakistan had a sizeable arsenal, it did not seize the offer of Chinese help; in 1971, when Pakistan had a depleted arsenal, China fell short of promising armed intervention. We have seen earlier in the chapter how in the US eyes Chinese intervention had room for manoeuvre despite their postures. In 1971, an active Sino–American partnership could not result in gains for Pakistan. In 1970, President Yahya Khan helped the US establish links with China, but China was too cautious and unable to decide between the mixed signals it was receiving from the White House and the State Department to commit troops to Pakistan, especially in the face of Russian deployment. In 1965, since China was not in contact with the US, Russia did not raise the stakes as it did in 1971. Even before the 1971 war, Pakistan actively supported China's bid to regain its seat in the UN and opposed the American Two Chinas formula. It voted for the draft resolution which seated China in the UNSC and expelled Taiwan from the UN.

Z.A. Bhutto regarded Sino–American relations as an important factor in consolidating Pakistan's position in Asia and visited China in January 1972, May 1974, and May 1976. China became one of the main suppliers of arms to Pakistan. This continued despite the death of Zhou Enlai, and Mao Zedong in 1976 and the execution of Zulfikar Ali Bhutto in 1979.

During the 1980–90s, relations between China and Pakistan remained stable and friendly. In November 1989, Li Ping, head of the Chinese government, visited Pakistan when China promised to help Pakistan in the development of nuclear energy including provision of technical equipment for a nuclear plant. In 1990, Pakistan launched a satellite from Chinese territory.

At the end of the Cold War, Sino–American relations were strained but had not broken down. Russo–Chinese relations also improved when ideology was no longer a key factor. Thus no power required Pakistan to encircle China. The year 2003 marked a number of developments showing that even in changed circumstances China was helpful to Pakistan. On 19 June 2003, when India blocked Pakistan's membership of the Association of South East Asian Nations (ASEAN), China strongly supported Pakistan. President Pervez Musharraf visited China on 4 November 2003, when Prime Minister Hu Jintao agreed to enhance defence cooperation.

Pakistan's pro-Taliban policy cast its shadow over its relations with China. The nuclearization of North Korea caused adjustments on a global scale. The incursion of Islamic militants into the Xinjiang province with a Uighur Muslim majority became a source of Chinese concern. Sino–Indian relations, even amidst heavy rhetoric, improved. On 20 January 1995, China, though loudly declared by India to be the main reason for Indian nuclearization, gave India thirty tonnes of uranium. On 22 October 2003, China and Pakistan conducted joint naval exercises, the first China had conducted with any country. On 15 November 2003, China conducted similar naval exercises with India. By the beginning of 2005, Indian Foreign Minister Natwar Singh said that China was no longer regarded as an adversary.[76]

On a more serious note, China expelled 700 Pakistani traders from Xinjiang, albeit under a 1985 agreement. Both China and Pakistan have decried US sanctions[77] on them for the alleged transfer of nuclear technology. In mid-January 2005, American sources revealed that the US had constantly urged China not to help Pakistan in its quest for nuclearization citing documents dated from 1977 to 1997.[78] While China has reaffirmed its commitment to non-proliferation, its discretion in the face of such pressure has shown that China still values Pakistan's friendship.

Several Pakistani projects have been undertaken with Chinese help and are still continuing. CPEC shall be discussed separately below.

The relations between China and Pakistan have continued to grow despite changes in the imperatives. Nevertheless, the imperatives have to be considered, for though mutual relations have apparently not changed, the world around has changed, and we shall consider these under different headings.

The Russian Factor. Pakistan–China relations began when China and Russia were formally allies, but by 1971 the Sino–Soviet split had occurred. The US and the USSR headed the blocs emerging after the Second World War, i.e., they made the world bipolar. This phase lasted till 1989 when the USSR began disintegrating. Thereafter, the US-dominated a unipolar world; till the rise of China and the resurgence of Russia. These two developments changed the world's configurations till a change was heralded in December 2014 when Russian President Vladimir Putin spoke of the 'Strategic Balance of Power'. Today China and Russia have shed their sub-ideological baggage and are much closer to each other than they were during the Cold War. Why this should be so has been explained by Edward Crankshaw: 'China existed for the revolution, the revolution existed for Russia.'[79]

China underwent a Cultural Revolution from 1966 for about a decade while the Soviet Union under President Mikhail Gorbachev floated Glasnost and Perestroika, instruments of liberalization. Though opposite in nature, repression in China and liberalization in Russia had the same effect, weakening their polities. Now China and Russia stand united in confronting the West.

The American Factor. The US stance is not clear-cut. The US and China were outright enemies since the establishment of China in 1949, the Korean War of the 1950s, the Vietnam War of the 1960s and of course the status of Taiwan are reminders, that for America and China, the Cold War was hot. However, the Sino-Soviet split had occurred before the 1965 India–Pakistan War and was absolutely in the open when the US and China colluded against the Soviet Union and India during the 1971 war. However, the Sino-American *entente* gradually weakened with the disintegration of the USSR in the early 1990s. There has been an ambivalence in US–China relations because economic imperatives competed with strategic imperatives. These have been spelt out by President Barack Obama: 'US corporations and their shareholders liked the reduced labor costs and soaring profits that resulted from shifting to China. US farmers liked all the new Chinese customers buying their soybeans and pork. To pull ourselves and the world out of recession, we needed China's economy growing, not contracting. In the run-up to our China trip my team and I settled on a strategy to thread the needle between tough and not tough enough.'[80]

The American war in Afghanistan proved to be of common concern. From 10 to 12 November 2014, President Xi Jinping received President Barack Obama, and among the host of issues discussed Afghanistan proved to be the least contentious. 'In the context of the Heart of Asia Conference, they also cannot support economic development projects and frameworks to foster Afghanistan's regional integration and build government capacity.'[81]

In the aftermath of President Obama's visit US Defence Secretary Ashton B. Carter stated that the US did not see China as an adversary.[82] However, this was in stark contrast to what Secretary of State Hillary Clinton said on 2 March 2011, after the visit of President Hu Jintao to the US: 'The US is in direct competition with China.'

In the wake of the Ukraine war, a State Department spokesperson made the following statement: 'Pakistan is a strategic partner of the United States.

We have an important relationship with the government in Islamabad, and it is a relationship we value across a number of fronts. Islamabad does not have to strain its relations with China to maintain ties with Washington.'[83] This latitude in the attitude of the US has been late in coming, but it is a source of assurance in the strife-torn era.

The India Factor. The Sino–Indian relations began with the slogan *Hindi-Cheeni Bhai Bhai* (Indians and Chinese are brothers) but with the development of border disputes India and China became rivals for Asian supremacy. After the 1962 Sino–Indian War till the breakthrough during the 1971 war, China and America had relations which were hotter than the Cold War. The wars in Korea in the 1950s in Vietnam in the 1960s and of course the status of Taiwan kept the US at loggerheads, leading even to a softening of relations between the US and USSR in the mid-1960s. China has been supportive of Pakistan in its most radical phase. After China gained its seat in the UNSC and saw a rise in the same period of economic transition from a planned economy to a price economy that Russia was going through, China felt that it must develop a global and not regional vision. It was in this context that China sought to establish equal relations with India and Pakistan.

In June 1980, Deng Xiaoping stated that Kashmir was a bilateral issue between India and Pakistan which should be resolved peacefully.[84] In December 1996, President Jiang Zemin failed to mention Kashmir explicitly. He favoured seeking a just and reasonable settlement in his address to the Pakistani Senate. Jiang Zemin indicated that if some issues cannot be resolved, they should be shelved temporarily.[85] Chinese Foreign Ministry spokesperson Hua Chunying clarified that China's position on Kashmir has not been changed by CPEC. It needs to be properly settled through dialogue and consultation between the two sides.[86] The following report was even more explicit: China's Ambassador to India Luo Zhaohui reminded an Indian audience in May 2017 that China had changed its position: 'We supported the relevant UN resolutions before the 1990s. Then we supported a settlement through bilateral negotiations in tune with the Shimla Agreement.'[87]

This stance was not productive. In the aftermath of the 11 May 1998 Indian nuclear tests, Indian Prime Minister Atal Bihari Vajpayee's letter to President Bill Clinton was carried by *The New York Times*. It cited Chinese presence on India's borders and China's nuclear aid to Pakistan as the justification for the Indian explosions. This reflection was heightened by the signing of the US–India Nuclear Co-operation Treaty 2008. As Andrew Small has stated China understood that: 'India was not merely the short-term ally, it was the like-minded successor which the United States would help become a major world power in the Twenty-first Century…But China had a tried and tested solution to hand. If the US was going to smoothen the path for India's ascent, Pakistan would be the means for China to hold it down.'[88]

Thereafter China reverted to citing the relevant UNSC resolutions though a reference to bilateral means was retained: (i) The Kashmir issue is a dispute left from colonial history. It should be properly resolved based on the UN Charter, relevant UNSC resolutions and bilateral agreements. China believes that unilateral actions (5 August 2019) that will complicate the situation should not be taken.[89] (ii) A Chinese spokesperson said that the Kashmir issue between India and Pakistan had always been on the UNSC agenda and as a Permanent Member of the UNSC, China would continue to play a constructive role in upholding regional peace and stability.[90] (iii) China during the talks re-affirmed its support for a peaceful resolution of the Kashmir conflict and regretted unilateral actions (5 August 2019) Kashmir dispute should be resolved peacefully and properly with the UN Charter, relevant UNSC resolutions and bilateral agreements.[91]

Other Issues. One writer assures us that there were behind-the-scenes Sino–Pakistan tensions over Kosovo and Xinxiang.[92] Why there should have been concern over Kosovo is not clear. After the break-up of Yugoslavia, the Christian Serbs set up on the Muslim Bosnians, both in Kosovo and Bosnia-Herzegovina itself. Though there had been quite a distance between Russia and Yugoslavia, the Russians seemed to favour the Serbs, while the US sympathized with the Bosnians as the victims of genocide. Finally, the US stepped in to stop the massacre of the Bosnians. It is, however, within the bounds of possibility differences over Kosovo were privately expressed as at this time China was seeking a rapprochement with India.

Xinxiang. The US and EU have been waging a war against Islamic militancy since the collapse of the Soviet Union, but they seem to make an exception in the case of the East Turkistan Islamic Movement, which is situated in Kashghar and in Xinxiang among the Uighur Muslim population. Islamic militancy has been met by State suppression, and behold, Xinxiang has far outstripped Kashmir as the region Muslims are subject to repression. China having cordial relations with Muslim countries sought their understanding over this issue. As Xinxiang borders with Kashmir including Gilgit and Hunza they are directly in the line connecting China to Pakistan.

On 14 June 2008 China announced that seven terror cells being run by the militants seeking the separation of Xinxiang from China were closed down. By 2015 East Turkistan Islamic Movement had established cells within Pakistan. By 3 September, the Government of Pakistan claimed that all such cells within its territory had been wiped out.[93] There was a campaign, incendiary in Pakistan where Taliban and Al-Qaeda were claiming responsibility for acts of terror, claiming that China was preventing its Muslims from practising their religion. A four-member Ulama delegation was invited to the region and reported that they had found no evidence that the Chinese authorities had banned fasting during Ramadan. On 6 February 2017, Pakistan assured China of support in its efforts against Separatists.[94] During the Hajj of 2018, this writer saw a very large delegation from China.

Nevertheless, Western propaganda would not cease and in November 2018, China faced harsh criticism over alleged crackdowns on Uighur camps during the United Nations Human Rights Council. American and French delegations led the attack.[95] In Pakistan, a new issue was unfolded. Pakistani men who had married Uighur or Kazakhs complained that the Chinese authorities had interred their spouses in camps which they call schools. This report stated that 'millions of Muslims' were being re-educated away from Islam. However, only two such cases were reported where the borders separated a husband from his wife.

In February 2019, the Chinese authorities incensed by such criticism assembled eighty delegates from countries and Human Rights associations, from all over the world. They said their re-education facilities were turning people away from militancy, but Rights groups termed them internment camps. Chinese officials emphasized that theirs was a more humane, non-violent method of combating terrorism and militancy.[96]

The notch was raised when the Pakistani FIA off-loaded five passengers. There were complaints that Pakistani women married to Chinese citizens were being forced either into prostitution or human organ sale. The Chinese Ministry of Public Security investigated these charges but found no evidence.[97] The Pakistani FIA nevertheless sought judicial remand of eleven Chinese citizens.

In view of such propaganda hurtful to mutual relations, the Chinese Ambassador to Pakistan, Yao Jing wrote a press article on Xinxiang. He mentioned how peaceful and multi-ethnic Xinxiang was and reminded readers that delegates from Pakistan, Malaysia, Saudi Arabia, and Turkey, among other Muslim countries had met the trainees face-to-face. The trainees were being imparted vocational education to make them self-reliant.[98] Within a week, on 12 July 2019, representatives of thirty-seven countries including Saudi Arabia Algeria, Nigeria, the Russian Federation, and North Korea wrote a joint letter to the UN defending Chinese actions in Xinxiang. A month later on 26 September, criticism of Uighur internments was being coupled with criticism of Chinese projects in Pakistan. On 1 July 2021, Prime Minister Imran Khan backed Beijing's version of Xinxiang. The Pakistani Prime Minister did not fail to mention Human Rights violations in Indian-occupied Kashmir where nine million people had been put in an open prison yet failed to find mention in Western media.[99]

Security Issues. Since all groups who are out to subvert the State of Pakistan understand that China is the mainstay of Pakistan's security, they have adopted the device of attacking Chinese working in Pakistan. During a terrorist strike on the naval base Mehran, Chinese technical staff were taken hostage.[100] In Quetta, two teachers who were not even connected to CPEC were kidnapped and taken hostage by gunmen posing as policemen; the Chinese and Pakistani governments were working together for their recovery.[101] The next outrage—claimed by the Baloch Liberation Army (BLA)—was an attack on the Chinese Consulate in Karachi.[102] Fortunately, the attack was thwarted, leaving three heavily armed militants dead; two policemen and two visa applicants were also killed.[103] The same militant outfit attacked the Pakistan Stock Exchange, and shortly after released a statement that 'its purpose was to simultaneously target Pakistan's economy and China for its involvement in Balochistan'.[104]

The next major incident (14 July 2021) was the Dasu bus tragedy in which nine Chinese and four Pakistanis were killed when the bus carrying them fell into a ravine after an explosion. This has a sinister aspect because this was the project over which Chinese and Pakistani parties had litigation. On 25 October 2016, a Chinese firm Messrs. Power Construction Corporation of China was not allowed to join a bid for the tender floated. This was due to the World Bank's condition imposed upon the Water and Power Development Authority (WAPDA). In January of the following year, WAPDA cancelled Rs 5.4 billion worth of Dasu Project contracts to Chinese firms who were incensed and vowed to seek arbitration.[105] Therefore, the Dasu Bus blast represents some induction of Chinese firms in the project. The Chinese Embassy issued a statement asking its nationals in Pakistan to remain on the alert.[106] Two days later Chinese Prime Minister Li Keqiang called Imran Khan on the telephone demanding punishments for the elements responsible for the Dasu blast.[107] Two days later the foreign minister rushed to Dasu while a Chinese team concluded its own investigation into the blast.[108] This was not the end of the matter on 19 August 2021 there was a suicide attack on a motorcade carrying Chinese nationals to the Gwadar Eastbay Expressway. The Chinese Ambassador Nong Rong met with Pakistan's Interior Minister Sheikh Rasheed to take up the issue of safety for Chinese nationals working in Pakistan.[109] This Expressway is a major component of CPEC to which the next section is devoted.

Another incident took place on 26 April 2022 when three Chinese teachers at the Confucius Institute, University of Karachi were killed by a veiled suicide bomber, a mother of two called Shari Baloch. The BLA accepted responsibility. Security at the Karachi University Campus was tightened. Other teachers from China returned home. On 15 May 2022, Foreign Minister Bilawal Bhutto-Zardari held a memorial meeting at the Foreign Office to express grief.[110]

CPEC. The China–Pakistan Economic Corridor (CPEC) is a major component of China's One Belt One Road Initiative to provide transport and other infrastructure over many countries to provide connection. CPEC connects China to Pakistan, or to put it in other words, it connects Kashgar (the most irksome region of China) to Gwadar (the most irksome region of Pakistan). Kashgar is the base of the East Turkistan Islamic Movement, and Gwadar is the base of the Baloch Liberation Army. Both sides hope that the economic uplift of the two destinations shall end feelings of disgruntlement among the militant groups. Though CPEC has been proclaimed to be devoid of military components, Henry Kissinger has pointed to a consideration which cannot have been ignored: 'China's greatest strategic fear is that an outside power, or powers will establish military deployments around China's periphery capable of encroachments on China's territory or its domestic institutions.'[111]

Such being the reality, both sides have tried to show that there is nothing sinister to this two-nation initiative. American concerns may have considerably lessened when the Russian Federation announced that it was secretly negotiating to join CPEC.[112]

To alleviate objections China invited India to join CPEC.[113] France also offered to join OBOR/CPEC in the second phase on the condition of transparency.[114] After the NATO withdrawal from Afghanistan, China offered to extend its membership to this strife-torn country, although Afghanistan shall need time to put its house in order. Unfortunately, the US proved to be the only other country, besides India, to object to the CPEC. Russia had urged India to line up behind China's OBOR initiative. Russian Foreign Minister Sergey Lavrov said: 'New Delhi should not let political problems deter it from joining the project, involving billions of dollars of investment and benefiting from them'.[115]

However, the US Assistant Secretary of State Alice Wells said in Islamabad on 23 November 2019 that CPEC would increase Pakistan's debt burden, and slighted CPEC's feasibility.[116] Although three days later (26 November 2019), the State Department said that Pakistan had the sovereign right to take any decision and that Alice Wells only wished to give rise to a debate, China would not let her comments be disregarded and warned the US against its efforts to spoil Pakistan–China ties.[117]

There were Pakistani legislators as well who wanted a full parliamentary briefing on the project. A CPEC Authority bill was passed by parliament, but in 2022 it was done away with on the grounds that its work had been unsubstantial, and the responsibility was given to the Planning Commission of Pakistan.

The CPEC project was visualized during a meeting between Chinese Prime Minister Li Keqiang and Pakistan's Prime Minister Nawaz Sharif in 2013. The Pakistani Prime Minister called it a game-changer.[118] The CPEC was planned to be in two phases, the short term, from 2015 to 2020, and the longer term taking ten to fifteen years. China included CPEC in its fifth Five-Year Plan. What CPEC has achieved in its first phase can be taken from China's rejoinder to Alice Wells: 'Major progress has been achieved... with 32 projects achieving early harvests. This has... improved local transportation infrastructure and power supply, created over 75,000 jobs directly and contributed one to two per cent of the GDP growth in Pakistan... CPEC is playing an important role in boosting Pakistan's socioeconomic development and improving people's livelihood... According to... the State Bank of Pakistan, the total foreign debt... is [$]110 billion... Loan for the CPEC is about [$]5.8 billion ..., accounting for 5.3% of Pakistan's total foreign debt, with a repayment period of 20–25 years and an interest rate of approximately 2%... repayments will start in 2021, with annual repayments of about [$]300 million... It will never be a burden to Pakistan.'[119]

The first phase was dominated by government-to-government, or government-to-business corporations in the fields of roads, highways, and energy infrastructure. The second phase, now begun, is expected to revolve around the private sector. A business reporter recommended that the CPEC Authority be revived to provide a one-window facility.[120]

Allied Ventures. The following Pakistani projects have been undertaken with Chinese help: the Karakorum Highway; the Heavy Mechanical Complex at Taxila; the Heavy Electrical Complex at Kot Najibullah; the Thermal Power Station at Guddu; SPARK, an agricultural cooperation programme; the Saindak Metallurgy Project; the ongoing development of Gwadar Port; and a jointly developed fighter aircraft, the JF-17.

It was a joyous day when two JF-17s were delivered on 12 March 2007. On 19 April 2007, Prime Minister Shaukat Aziz said in Chengdu that Pakistan would recover investment by selling the aircraft.[121] It was stated on 13 May 2007 that China would supply F-22P frigates. These frigates would have six helicopters each.[122] Nevertheless, Sino–Indian relations had also grown. There was speculation that China would also sign with India a nuclear cooperation treaty.[123] Despite all confidence-building measures, it has surfaced that China has not given up its claim to the territory that India calls Arunachal Pradesh.[124]

Prospects. The pattern of Sino-Pakistan relations remains the same—with the same vulnerability. The Ukraine war has brought these relations into closer focus. With the US and NATO seeking to box in the Russian Federation, the stakes were raised. Just as in the 2007 Lal Masjid Operation, militants targeted Chinese citizens to create cracks in the defence of Pakistan. A Chinese national at the Dasu Hydropower Project was taken into custody on the charge of blasphemy. Religious parties immediately blocked the Karakorum Highway. However, it proved to be a case of not blasphemy, but discipline.[125]

When India hosted the G20 meeting in Srinagar (the capital of occupied Kashmir), China took the lead in opposing and boycotting the session. Only Western countries participated.[126] Regional compulsions were driving relations. Russia and Iran signed an agreement in May 2023 for a 164 km railway connection between Astara in Russia and Rasht on the Azerbaijan border. It would later extend to India.[127] The very next day, Chinese President Xi Jinping told a meeting of eighty-five countries that strengthening ties with its Central

Asian neighbours was a 'strategic choice'. Central Asia is key to China's trillion dollars OBOR initiative.[128] Central Asia is the world's second-largest energy producer while China is the world's second-largest energy consumer. This augurs well for Pakistan.

With regards to foreign policy formulations we have three statements, not easy to reconcile: (1) 'The United States doesn't ask Pakistan to choose between it and China, but rather wants countries to have a choice.' Derek Chollet a State Department Counsellor said Washington was not afraid of competing with China but would like to have a fair competition.[129] (2) *The Washington Post* published a leak from Pakistan; a Memo from the Minister of State Hina Rabbani Khar. From the Memo it was clear that Pakistan was not taking the American assurance at face value: 'Pakistan can no longer try to maintain a middle-ground between China and the United States. Islamabad should avoid giving the appearance of appeasing the West.' It warns that the instinct to preserve Pakistan's partnership with the US would ultimately sacrifice the full benefits of the country's real strategic partnership with China.[130] (3) Pakistan rejected speculation that it had joined the China bloc. The FO spokesperson Mumtaz Zehra Baloch said: 'I would like to refute any such speculation that Pakistan has joined one bloc or another. Pakistan has a consistent policy that we do not believe in bloc politics.' She added that Pakistan had an 'All Weather Strategic Cooperative Partnership' with China. '…Our relations with the United States are perhaps as old as Pakistan itself. Pakistan-US relations are multidimensional with several areas of cooperation with Pakistani Americans acting as a bridge between Pakistan and the United States. We have no desire to take sides or to join one bloc or the other.'[131] There the matter apparently rests.

BRITAIN-PAKISTAN RELATIONS.—Pakistan was created when it gained independence from Britain. The last Viceroy, Lord Mountbatten, was given a brief to partition India only if unavoidable. Even before Lord Mountbatten, arrived, it was decided to concede a Pakistan in which Punjab and Bengal, Muslim-majority provinces, were to be divided. It was decided more than a year before independence that Pakistan, in the event of its creation, would not be given the Muslim-majority district of Gurdaspur.[132] Herbert Christopher Beaumont later confessed that a further gift of Ferozepur and Zira was made to India by Sir Cyril Radcliffe. Thus, all the disadvantages with which Pakistan was born were due to British manipulations. In a way, this was to be expected as India was a larger market and was strategically more important to the east of Suez interests of the British Empire.

The Labour Party's commitment to the Indian National Congress was so firm that it was a wonder that partition was at all conceded. Sardar Patel complained to Richard Symonds that Winston Churchill was responsible for the creation of Pakistan.[133] This was a manifest exaggeration, but the basic fact remained that there was a powerful and influential Conservative element better represented in the House of Lords, which was mindful of British promises to the minorities. Churchill's speech in the House of Commons, following the announcement of the Cabinet Mission Plan, is an example of this.

Pakistan came into existence as a Dominion of the British Commonwealth and even when it became a republic in 1956, it retained its membership of the Commonwealth. In the 1956 invasion of Egypt, Pakistan angered its population by siding with Britain and France against Egypt. At the initial stage, there was also tension between Britain and the US over the exercise of influence over Pakistan. British influence remained strong till the 1965 war. The statement of Prime Minister Harold Wilson in 1965, that India was the aggressor was the highest point in mutual relations. Subsequent to his announcement, he received inadequate support from the Foreign Office and scaled down his rhetoric. The British High Commissioner, Sir Morrice James, was able to persuade President Ayub Khan against accepting Chinese aid, promising never to let the Kashmir issue be side-lined, but when Ayub took him at his word, he betrayed that trust.

When the 1971 war broke out, Harold Wilson was still prime minister, and he led the charade against Pakistan. When a deputation of British parliamentarians under Mrs Jill Knight gave a favourable report on Pakistan, he despatched another delegation under Arthur Bottomley to obtain a second, adverse report. In January 1972, Pakistan left the Commonwealth in protest against Britain's recognition of Bangladesh as an independent state. In July 1973, Zulfikar Ali Bhutto visited Britain and in January 1978 Prime Minister James Callaghan visited Pakistan. The Afghan crisis caused by the Russian invasion saw Prime Minister Margaret Thatcher visit Pakistan, but cooperation was confined to the Afghanistan crisis.

In October 1989, Prime Minister Benazir Bhutto restored Pakistan's membership of the Commonwealth. Britain–Pakistan relations came under mild strain as a result of Pakistan's nuclear tests, and severe strain during the 1999 Kargil crisis. When the military government of General Pervez Musharraf took over, the Commonwealth suspended Pakistan's membership. Since Pakistan joined the anti-terror coalition, relations have thawed to a degree that can be called cool but correct. A sizeable Pakistani population has made Britain its home and this, in addition to some commercial interests, keeps Britain–Pakistan relations on an even keel.

British Prime Minister Tony Blair visited Pakistan, and on 19 November 2007, signed an accord with President Musharraf and Prime Minister Shaukat Aziz to strengthen cooperation to fight terrorism, drug trafficking, illegal immigration, and trans-national organized crime.[134]

Tony Blair announced that Britain had doubled development assistance, as well as pledged £20 million to reduce poverty. There was a plea for greater British market access for Pakistani goods on which the British prime minister was non-committal.

In the Honours list issued on Her Majesty's Birthday, a knighthood was awarded to Salman Rushdie, author of the blasphemous *Satanic Verses* (London, 1988). Previously a knighthood had been awarded to V.C. Naipaul, author of *Among the Believers: An Islamic Journey* (1982), a book which is unsympathetic to Muslims. The foreign secretary said that the reason for the award was self-evident. It was hardly that since an internationally celebrated author, Colin Wilson was consistently passed over. When the Beatles were awarded the OBE in 1962, a number of recipients returned their awards. So soon after the cartoon fiasco, why the sentiments of Muslims had to be injured is not self-evident. So while hopes for better relations had been raised in November 2006, in June 2007 they have been dashed.

In the period from 2009, what we mainly see are meetings between the prime ministers or foreign ministers of both sides urging Pakistan to cooperate with India and take other measures to fight militancy, only three events stand out, the Birmingham race riots of 10 August 2011, British parliament members support for the Kashmir cause 6 April 2017, and the resumption of British Airways flights to Pakistan after a break of eleven years 3 June 2020.

The Birmingham riots began when Asian youth, mainly Pakistanis were guarding shops when three of them were run over by a car. The resulting riots caused 805 arrests showing the magnitude of feeling which had developed between the White British and Asians, especially Pakistani immigrants to Britain. However, Tariq Jahan whose 21-year-old son Haroon had been killed in the car incident stood up in Birmingham and pleaded with the Asians not to seek revenge from the car's occupants.[135] His speech had the effect of sending the protestors home and was duly appreciated by Prime Minister David Cameron.

A six-member group of British parliamentarians visited Azad Kashmir and called themselves, 'advocates of Kashmir'. Royston Smith said: 'Indeed, this issue needs to be resolved by the UN. If the UN could not resolve it in the past 70 years, then my question is what role does the UN have? Henry Smith said: 'Somebody who is a democrat, someone who is the beneficiary of the elected democratic process should realize that the future of the region should be decided by you—people of Kashmir.' The other delegates made similar speeches, but they have been in the minority, still, their support should be appreciated.[136]

The resumption of British Airways flights to Pakistan came as a boon, especially to the Pakistani migrants.

Notes

1. K. Arif (ed.), *American–Pakistan Relations* (Lahore: Vanguard, 1984), p. 3.
2. Dennis Kux, *Disenchanted Allies* (Karachi: Oxford University Press, 2001), excerpts *Dawn* 25 September 2001.
3. Francis Robinson, *Islam, South Asia and the West* (New Delhi, 2007), p.275.

4. *Dawn*, 23 August 2017.
5. *Dawn*, 24 August 2017.
6. *Dawn*, 27 August 2019.
7. *Dawn*, 4 August 2019.
8. *Dawn*, 22 August 2019.
9. *Dawn*, 8 October 2019.
10. *Dawn*, 24 October 2019.
11. *Dawn*, 24 August 2017.
12. General Mirza Aslam Beg, *Compulsions of Power* (Lahore: Adabiyat, 2021), p. 273.
13. *The New York Times*, 18 April 2022.
14. *Dawn*, 4 February 2022.
15. *Dawn*, 2 April 2022.
16. *Dawn*, 25 February 2022.
17. *The Express Tribune*, Karachi, 27 April 2022.
18. *Dawn*, 25 April 2009.
19. Michael Krepon, *The New Friday Times*, Lahore, 8 August 2003, p. 6.
20. *The Times*, London, 3 December 1971.
21. Pran Chopra, *India's Second Liberation* (Cambridge, Massachusetts: MIT Press, 1974), p. 100.
22. *Dawn*, 5 June 2000.
23. Suroosh Irfani (ed.), *Fifty Years of the Kashmir Dispute: Based on the Proceedings of the International Seminar Held at Muzaffarabad, Azad Jammu and Kashmir August 24–25, 1997* (Muzaffarabad: University of Azad Kashmir, 1997), pp. 83–88.
24. *Dawn*, 26 December 2007.
25. *The News*, 10 February 2004.
26. *The News*, 11 February 2004.
27. *Dawn*, 10 and 11 August 2005.
28. *Dawn*, 24 December 2006.
29. Eric Margolis, *War at the Top of the World: The Struggle for Afghanistan, Kashmir and Tibet* (New Delhi: Roli Books, 2001), p. 9. See also, General S. Padmanabhan, *The Writing on the Wall: India Checkmates America 2017* (New Delhi: Manar Publications 2004), written by a former Chief of the Indian Army Staff.
30. *Dawn*, 23 January 2005.
31. *Dawn*, 2 June 1999.
32. *Dawn*, 4 June 2004.
33. Roedad Khan (ed.), *The British Papers: Secret and Confidential Documents India-Pakistan-Bangladesh 1958–1969* (Karachi: Oxford University Press, 2002), p. 276.
34. Ibid., p. xix.
35. Ibid., p. 372.
36. Ibid., p. 384.
37. Paul Bracken, *Fire in The East: The Rise of Asian Military Power and the Second Nuclear Age* (New York: Perennial, 2000), p. 102.
38. Mahir Ali, *Dawn*, 11 December 2002.
39. *Dawn*, 31 October 2003.
40. *Dawn*, 1 December 2022.
41. *Dawn*, 14 February 2023.
42. *Dawn*, 28 April 2023.
43. *Dawn*, 8 June 2023.
44. *Dawn*, 10 June 2023.
45. *Dawn*, 9 June 2023.
46. *Dawn*, 25 May 2002.
47. *Dawn*, 7 June 2002.
48. *Bolshevik* Moscow, No. 3, 1946, reproduced in Mahboob A. Popatia, *Pakistan's Relations with the Soviet Union1947–1979* (Pakistan Study Centre, University of Karachi, 1988), p. 14.

49. See, Muhammad Reza Kazimi, *Liaquat Ali Khan: His Life and Work* (Karachi: Oxford University Press, 2003) for references to the Russian invitation.
50. *Dawn*, 4 June 2005.
51. *Dawn*, 10 February 2021.
52. Madeleine Albright, *Memo to the President Elect: How We Can Restore America's Reputation and Leadership* (New York: Harper, 2008), p. 209.
53. Zulfikar Ali Bhutto, *The Myth of Independence* (Karachi, Oxford University Press, 1969), p. 126.
54. *Dawn*, 29 November 2011.
55. *The Express Tribune*, Karachi, 17 January 2017.
56. *Dawn*, 24 September 2016.
57. *Dawn*, 25 April 2018.
58. *Dawn*, 6 November 2018.
59. *Dawn*, 10 June 2017.
60. *Dawn*, 19 November 2011.
61. *Dawn*, 11 December 2014
62. For his version of the 1962 Cuban Missile Crisis see, Nikita Khrushchev, *Khrushchev Remembers*, translated and edited by Strobe Talbott (New York: Bantam Books, 1971).
63. *The Express Tribune*, 6 May 2022.
64. *The Express Tribune*, 20 May 2022.
65. *Dawn*, 25 January 2023.
66. *The Express Tribune*, 30 January 2023.
67. *Dawn*, 31 January 2023.
68. *Dawn*, 25 February 2023.
69. *Dawn*, 27 February 2023.
70. *Dawn*, 22 March 2023.
71. *Dawn*, 20 May 2023.
72. *Dawn*, 31 May 2023.
73. *Dawn*, 13 June 2023.
74. Qutubuddin Aziz, *Exciting Stories to Remember* (Karachi: Islamic Media, 1995), p. 54.
75. Anwar H. Syed, *China and Pakistan Diplomacy of an Entente Cordiale* (Karachi, Oxford University Press, 1974), p. 73.
76. *Dawn*, 28 January 2005.
77. *The News*, Karachi, 22 November 2000.
78. *Dawn*, 15 June 2005.
79. Edward Crankshaw, *The New Cold War: Moscow v. Pekin* (Harmondsworth: Penguin, 1963), p. 69.
80. Barack Obama, *A Promised Land* (New York: Crown, 2020), pp. 475–76.
81. White House Fact Sheet, 11 November 2014.
82. *Dawn*, 7 April 2015.
83. *Dawn*, 4 February 2022.
84. Ghulam Ali, *China–Pakistan Relations: A Historical Analysis* (Karachi: Oxford University Press, 2017), pp. 110–11.
85. Andrew Small, *The China–Pakistan Axis: Asia's New Geopolitics* (London, Hurst & Co. 2015), p. 49.
86. *Dawn*, 18 March 2017.
87. *Dawn*, 10 June 2017.
88. Andrew Small, op. cit., p. 52.
89. *Dawn*, 10 August 2019.
90. *Dawn*, 18 January 2020.
91. *Dawn*, 22 August 2020.
92. Ghulam Ali, op. cit., p. 148.
93. *Dawn*, 3 September 2015.
94. *Dawn*, 7 February 2017.

95. *Dawn*, 7 November 2018.
96. *Dawn*, 18 December 2018.
97. *Dawn*, 25 February 2019.
98. *Dawn*, 11 May 2019.
99. *Dawn*, 2 July 2021.
100. *The New York Times*, 25 May 2011.
101. *Dawn*, 26 May 2017.
102. *Dawn*, 24 November 2018.
103. *Dawn*, 30 June 2021.
104. *Dawn*, 15 July 2016.
105. *Dawn*, 23 January 2017.
106. *Dawn*, 17 July 2021.
107. *Dawn*, 19 July 2011.
108. *Dawn*, 23 August 2021.
109. *Dawn*, 23 August 2021.
110. *The Express Tribune*, 16 May 2022.
111. Henry Kissinger, *On China* (London: Penguin, 2012), p. 540.
112. *Dawn*, 30 November 2016.
113. *Dawn*, 9 May 2017.
114. *Dawn*, 22 October 2018.
115. *Dawn*, 12 December 2017.
116. *Dawn*, 23 November 2019.
117. *Dawn*, 23 January 2020.
118. *The Express Tribune*, 19 August 2013.
119. *Dawn*, 23 January 2020. See also Statement by the Spokesperson of the Chinese Embassy in Pakistan in response to US Views on CPEC on the website of the Embassy of the People's Republic of China in the Islamic Republic of Pakistan.
120. *The Express Tribune*, 16 May 2022
121. *Dawn*, 20 April 2022.
122. *Dawn*, 14 May 2007.
123. Ibid.
124. *Dawn*, 15 November 2007.
125. *Dawn*, 18 April 2023.
126. *Dawn*, 20 May 2023.
127. *Dawn*, 18 May 2023.
128. *Dawn*, 19 May 2023.
129. *Dawn*, 1 September 2022.
130. *Dawn*, 1 May 2023.
131. *Dawn*, 26 May 2023.
132. Penderel Moon (ed.), *Wavell: The Viceroy's Journal* (Karachi, 1974), p. 245.
133. Richard Symonds, *In the Margins of Independence* (Karachi: Oxford University Press, 2001), p. 92. See also, Andrew Roberts, *Churchill: Walking with Destiny* (New York, Viking, 2018), p. 857.
134. *Dawn*, 20 November 2006.
135. *Dawn*, 11 August 2011.
136. *Dawn*, 7 April 2017.

CHAPTER 43

Pakistan's Relations with the SAARC States

South Asian Association for Regional Cooperation (SAARC) was founded in Dhaka in December 1985, then comprising Bangladesh, Bhutan, India, Maldives, Nepal, Pakistan, and Sri Lanka as members. The then total population of South Asia was more than a thousand million. SAARC was established to enhance economic relations among the member countries in what has been termed as no-conflict areas, which exclude bilateral issues. Relations of South Asian states with the outside world are beyond the scope of SAARC. The Thirteenth Summit, scheduled for February 2005, was postponed. The King of Nepal, Gyanendra Bir Bikram Shah Dev, dismissed his cabinet, and India took this as an affront and refused to attend. When the Summit was belatedly held in November 2005 at Dhaka two important developments took place. Afghanistan was made a member, and China was given observer status. Till the Addu (Maldives) Seventeenth Summit concluded on 11 November 2011, measures were taken to give effect to Free Trade. SAARC finance ministers were directed to prepare a proposal 'to allow for greater flow of financial capital and intra-regional long-term investment', but then politics took the driving seat and SAARC lost its pace. The Nineteenth Summit was scheduled to be held in Islamabad in November 2016, however, on 27 September, India conveyed it would not attend, citing the 18 September attack at Uri (located on the left bank of the Jhelum River, about 10 km east of the Line of Control with Pakistan) in which eighteen Indian soldiers were killed. Despite Pakistan denying its involvement, Afghanistan, Bangladesh, and Bhutan joined India in boycotting the summit. The summit was cancelled. Pakistan sought a larger SAARC to counter India's influence. Senator Mushahid Husain sought to include China, Iran, and neighbouring Central Asian republics. This was in line with India's insistence that Afghanistan join SAARC which it did in April 2007. Afghanistan lies at the junction of the Middle East and Central Asia, its induction had already distorted the geographical basis for cooperation, but the proposed alliance was too large and too unwieldy to take shape, considering that Economic Cooperation Organization too had not been a vibrant organization. It was the turn of Pakistan to nominate the SAARC secretary-general for the tenure from 1 March 2017 to 28 February 2020, but India made objections, as a result, the only confidence-building forum available to India and Pakistan became moribund.

RELATIONS WITH INDIA.—Relations between India and Pakistan remain contentious on both sides. After Partition, state-to-state relations did not turn a new leaf but rather remained a continuation of the relations between the Indian National Congress and the All-India Muslim League. Some of the rancour comes from the frustration caused by missed opportunities. Even after securing an electoral endorsement for Partition in 1946, the Muslim League compromised by accepting the Cabinet Mission Plan which provided for a central power between the Hindustan and Pakistan areas, controlling defence, foreign affairs, and communications.

Some writers have defended Nehru's rejection of the Cabinet Mission Plan by asserting that it would have resulted in the creation of Pakistan. This argument would have been forceful, had its rejection prevented the emergence of Pakistan. Even if the Muslim League had the desire to create Pakistan from the Cabinet Mission Plan, it did not have the means.

After the creation of Pakistan, the next issue to sour India–Pakistan relations was Kashmir. In the matter of integrating the princely states, India did not display the patience required to tackle the issue. If India had not forcibly resisted the accession of Junagadh to Pakistan, it would have had a more convincing case over Kashmir. India not only resisted the accession of Junagadh, a strategically negligible state with a Hindu majority ruled by a Muslim prince but characterized the accession of Junagadh to Pakistan as being 'against the principle of partition'. Then finally, Prime Minister Nehru rejected President Ayub's offer of a joint India–Pakistan defence against China. Thus three decisions by Nehru eventually resulted in the emergence of a nuclear Pakistan.

After Kashmir, the next issue was the sharing of the Indus waters between India and Pakistan. This problem was considered permanently solved, but since 2004, the spectre of the Baglihar Dam built on the Indian side has reopened the issue and again brought the World Bank into the scene. Kashmir, however, has not been the only problem. The 1971 war was caused by the crisis in East Pakistan, an integral part of Pakistan under International Law. Kashmir came to be discussed only during the 1972 Simla Conference.

Another problem between India and Pakistan was the valuation of the Pakistani rupee in the face of Indian devaluation. The communal riots that broke out between Hindus and Muslims were addressed in the Liaquat–Nehru Pact of 1950. These agreements, together with the arbitration over the Rann of Kutch in 1965, show that when there has been a political will, there has been a way and that the outstanding disputes are not dictated by nature.

In the political development chapters, we have already discussed the three wars and the Kargil crisis. The 1998 nuclear stand-off cut through the posturing and resulted in the visit of the Indian Prime Minister, Atal Bihari Vajpayee, to Lahore. This was overtaken by the 1999 Kargil crisis. Relations worsened because of a terrorist attack on the Indian parliament on 13 December 2001 which resulted in military confrontation at the border for two years before it was called off on 12 October 2002. This crisis caused a break in diplomatic relations since India recalled its envoy and threatened to send back the Pakistan envoy. Simultaneously, over-flights were banned. This has been remedied: diplomatic relations have been re-established, over-flights have been restored, and both armies have withdrawn from offensive positions. However, confidence-building measures and meetings between India's and Pakistan's leaders have not yet led to the resolution of any outstanding dispute, least of all Kashmir.

Kashmir. Reasons for India's Diplomatic Success in the Kashmir Dispute. While the arguments are in favour of Pakistan, Kashmir is in the possession of India. It is necessary to explain why. (1) India has done well by following the golden rules of unity, faith, and discipline. It has worked at building its country's image. Nehru was a chain smoker, but it would be difficult to find a photograph showing him smoking, because the patriotic Indian press did not publicise even what was a fashionable practice in those days. They revere Nehru for his role in securing India's freedom and disregard his errors of judgement that resulted in Partition. On our part, we ridicule Prime Minister Liaquat Ali Khan and persistently perpetuate a completely baseless myth, that he solicited an invitation from Russia, and used it instead to manoeuvre an invitation from the USA. Instead of showing appreciation we revel in criticizing him. (2) Every Indian is united on the claim that Kashmir is an integral part of India, while our own intellectuals and politicians create confusion. Some advocate a compromise on the LoC, even giving up Kashmir altogether, and some press for a neutral or independent Kashmir. It is because of the unity of the Indian people that the Kashmir problem is viewed internationally not as an unfulfilled UN resolution, but as a case of cross-border terrorism. This is India's greatest diplomatic success and Pakistan's greatest diplomatic failure. It was this failure that led to Pakistan's withdrawal from Kargil in 1999, although the comparable Indian occupation of Siachen in 1985 occasioned no international outrage. (3) Hardly any Indian ever blames his government for invading an integral part of Pakistan in 1971 and violating the principle of non-interference in the internal matters of Pakistan. On the other hand, our own newspapers are replete with biased stories of genocide in 1971. Our intellectuals constantly complain that power was not transferred to the Awami League, the majority party in 1971, but no one advocates giving Six Points to NWFP (Wana) or Balochistan (Sibi) which would give these provinces separate currencies and provincial militias, as well as placing the responsibility for international aid and trade directly in the hands of provinces, completely bypassing the central government. Whether these writers are aware of it or not, whether they are doing this with honest intent or not, it amounts to propaganda. What is the purpose of this propaganda? Its purpose is to take away the will to fight. Reference will be made to some writers and their suggestions but before we come to that stage, we need to examine all aspects of the Kashmir dispute.

The Origins of the Kashmir Dispute. Kashmir was one of more than 500 princely states in India. It was ruled by a Hindu Maharaja, Hari Singh, but the population was overwhelmingly Muslim. It had a very strategic location. Most other states were completely surrounded by either India or Pakistan but because of the division of the Punjab, Kashmir had equal access to India and Pakistan. The ruler was inclined towards India, and the people towards Pakistan. The importance of Kashmir was clear to all, and even before the division of India was agreed upon in principle, efforts were afoot to block the accession of Kashmir to Pakistan.

Pre-Partition Moves. On 23 January 1946, the Reforms Commissioner, V.P. Menon wrote to George Abell that Gurdaspur be excluded from Pakistan.[1] On 15 April 1946, the brief prepared by the Cabinet Mission for talks with Jinnah proposed a Pakistan without Gurdaspur.[2] The importance of Gurdaspur was that it provided India with all-weather access to Kashmir. It was a Muslim-majority district. On 14 June 1947, Krishna Menon wrote to Lord Mountbatten that 'there might be dire consequences for the future of Anglo–Indian relations if Kashmir were permitted to go to Pakistan'.[3] Menon had asked Mountbatten not to keep this letter, but he preserved it.[4] On 17 June 1947, V.P. Menon again favoured Gurdaspur becoming part of India.[5] The correspondence shows that preparations for preventing the accession of Kashmir to Pakistan began even before Lord Mountbatten arrived as governor-general.

The Boundary Award. We have seen in the section on the national struggle that Arthur Henderson, H.C. Beaumont, Sir Ian Scott, and others gave evidence that Radcliffe altered the awards at the behest of Lord Mountbatten. In the first instalment, Gurdaspur was given to India and in the second instalment Ferozepur and Zira were added. All three were Muslim-majority districts. When Liaquat Ali Khan sent Chaudhry Mohammad Ali to Lord Ismay to protest, he blandly denied any such changes.

The Outbreak of Fighting. The conflict began when the Dogra state forces started terrorizing Muslims in the Poonch district of Kashmir. Tribal Pathans who had relatives in Poonch, mounted an attack to rescue the Muslims. This is what is described as Pakistan's invasion of Kashmir. The genocide at Poonch is suppressed from all accounts published in India. It is alleged that the people of NWFP had not wanted accession to Pakistan, but here we see them trying to rescue Muslims in Kashmir. The Pakistan Army had yet to complete its reorganization, and it could not risk interfering with the Tribal Pathans. Indeed, their progress was ultimately barred by the Indian army. We must reflect that whatever areas of Kashmir we have, are the result of these tribal incursions.

The Instrument of Accession. It is alleged that frightened by the tribal reprisal, Maharaja Hari Singh signed an Instrument of Accession to India.

After it was signed, the Indian Army entered Kashmir to combat the tribals. Alastair Lamb has established that the Maharaja never signed an Instrument of Accession and that such a document does not exist. Nevertheless, as we have seen above, when the Muslim ruler of Hindu majority Junagadh acceded to Pakistan, India militarily blocked the accession, saying that such an accession was against the principle underlying Partition. Having made such an assertion, India could not have accepted the accession of Kashmir.

Promises of a Plebiscite. At the time India accepted the supposed accession of Kashmir, it also stated that the final disposition of Kashmir would depend on a free and impartial plebiscite of the people of Jammu and Kashmir. India made this promise not only to the people of Kashmir but to the international community as well.[6] The dates on which Nehru repeated his promise of a plebiscite were 26 October 1947; 27 October 1947; 30 October 1947; 2 November 1947; 12 February 1951; 27 June 1952; and 7 August 1952. Despite these repeated promises it is now claimed by India that Kashmir is its integral part. On 3 November 1947, Nehru assured Liaquat that 'we have agreed to an impartial international agency like the UN supervising any referendum'. Thus, any internal election held by India is not valid. Nehru went back on his solemn pledges on 24 February 1955 with the excuse that Pakistan had become a military ally of the USA.

UNSC Resolutions. The United Nations Security Council Resolution which says that the accession of Kashmir will be decided by a free and impartial plebiscite was passed on 21 April 1948 and reiterated on 5 January 1949. Any election held by Indian authorities in Kashmir cannot replace the provision of a free and impartial plebiscite. Hence, it cannot be asserted by India that Kashmir is its integral part. Such an assertion is not upheld by International Law. In 1957, the UN resolved that this step was in conflict with a plebiscite.

The cause of the 1965 war was Kashmir. The Indian parliament had taken steps to integrate Kashmir into India constitutionally. Before 1965 India had kept up the pretence of the autonomy of Kashmir. The head of the Kashmir administration had been designated prime minister, now he was designated chief minister, like the head of any province in India. Pakistan sent infiltrators inside Kashmir, just as President John Kennedy sent infiltrators inside Cuba, with equally disastrous results. Most of the infiltrators were arrested. Pakistan took this desperate step because if it had remained silent it would have acquiesced to the integration of Kashmir into India. As Ayub had replied, India had no legal title to Kashmir, hence intrusion was not aggression.

When friction along the ceasefire line increased, Kargil fell to India. As stated earlier, Kargil was part of Pakistan until 1971. The course of the war and the Tashkent Declaration have been discussed in the chapter on Ayub Khan. The only point to stress is that Pakistan's reoccupation of Kargil in 1999 set off a crisis whereas the 1965 fall of Kargil to India did not.

The 1971 war did not take place because of Kashmir, but at the Simla Summit, India tried to take advantage of Pakistan's military defeat to impose a unilateral solution for Kashmir. The Simla Agreement could also be concluded because, in a skirmish after the ceasefire in 1971, Pakistan was able to take the Lipa Valley in Kashmir. On 5 February 1973, Zulfikar Ali Bhutto called for a strike which was observed on both sides of the Line of Control. This was a signal that Pakistan had not surrendered in Kashmir.

If we exclude the allegations of ceasefire violations on both sides, there was no momentous development until 1985 when Indian troops occupied the Siachen Heights. In a similar action, Pakistan occupied Kargil in 1999, but because of hostile world opinion had to pull out.

Since the conflict has remained unresolved for more than fifty years, certain commentators have offered different solutions. One solution has been to establish an independent Kashmir. It is forgotten that Alexei Kosygin had turned down this option in Tashkent. An independent Kashmir, he told Ayub, would fall under the influence of third parties.[7] An American representative identified the third party as China.[8] It is again fortunate that Kosygin did not let Ayub proceed with this proposal. Once Pakistan itself floats independent Kashmir as a solution, the only tangible result would be the renunciation of Pakistan's claim to its side of Kashmir. India's initial promise to hold a plebiscite had also appeared as a reassuring and reasonable solution, but when sufficient time had elapsed after the ceasefire, that solution proved elusive.

How long a united and independent Kashmir can remain free depends on factors much beyond Pakistan's control. When the dismissal of his prime minister by the king of Nepal can cause India to feel affronted, when it claims that Bangladesh is harbouring terrorists, a much more innocuous development in an independent Kashmir may cause India to intervene. This could spell the end of Kashmir's neutrality and this time round there may be no UN resolutions in Pakistan's favour.

Then there are politicians who favour accepting the Line of Control as the permanent international border. Again, such acceptance by Pakistan cannot result in India's renunciation of her claim over Pakistan's Northern Areas. Hunza and Chitral would provide India with a springboard to enter Afghanistan; a foothold in Afghanistan would enable India to drive a strategic wedge between China and Pakistan.

President Pervez Musharraf also tried to propose a satisfice solution to Kashmir. On 18 December 2003, he said that Pakistan could move halfway from demanding a plebiscite under UN resolutions; he thought both countries could move from their stated positions. Reacting, the peace activist Pervez Hoodbhoy proposed accepting the Line of Control as the border.[9] Perhaps Pervez Musharraf was fazed by the US describing his willingness to set aside the UN resolutions as a 'constructive development'. He clarified that flexibility has to be mutual. At present such prospects are bleak. Nevertheless, there is no reason for Pakistan to blink first. If India compromises, it compromises an outpost, if Pakistan compromises on Kashmir, it compromises its sovereignty.

There was scarcely any urgency when President Pervez Musharraf gave an exclusive interview to Prannoy Roy, on 5 December 2005. The president reiterated his four-point solution to Kashmir. He had put it forward in an October 2005 interview also, but he interrupted, watching the unfolding of his plan. The four-point formula is clearly mentioned in the 5 December 2005 interview: (1) Kashmir will have the same borders, but people will be allowed to move freely back and forth in the region. (2) The region will have self-governance or autonomy, but not independence. (3) Troops will be withdrawn from the region in a staggered manner. (4) A joint supervision mechanism will be set up, with India, Pakistan, and Kashmir represented.

The president was still asked just as he unfolded these four points, whether he was giving up the plebiscite and giving up the UN resolution, although that is inherent in the four points. Explaining the first point he had stated: 'Therefore the solution lies in making the line of control irrelevant and this is a term I am borrowing from your leadership; this is the word they used, and I keep saying it now.'

It needs to be realized that from making the Line of Control irrelevant to making the international border irrelevant is but a short step. When the Indian leadership asserts that 'redrawing of boundaries is out of the question',[10] it clearly means that it makes no such distinctions. This too, is a position which has solidified gradually. Previously Swaran Singh had complained that Pakistan had not reciprocated on this point: 'India had proposed ceding to Pakistan 110,000 square kilometres of a total of 275,000, whereas Pakistan had not even ceded Jammu—a state where there was a majority of Hindus.'[11]

So not only was a redrawing of borders proposed but it was also proposed to be redrawn on religious lines. The second point, autonomy, has been tried at least constitutionally, on both sides, but it had led nowhere near a solution. The third point, demilitarization, was the point on which the earliest Kashmir negotiations had failed. The fourth point is impractical as it was also ruled out, even though the British Commonwealth prime ministers had offered the troops and money necessary to inaugurate this idyllic arrangement.

Indian Muslims. Khurshid Mahmud Kasuri, Pakistan's Foreign Minister at the time of the Kargil crisis revealed that Dilip Kumar (1922–2021) the Peshawar-born film icon told Nawaz Sharif: 'Mian Sahib, we did not expect this from you, since you have always claimed to be a great supporter of peace between Pakistan and India. Let me tell you as an Indian Muslim that in case of tension between Pakistan and India, the position of Indian Muslims becomes very insecure, and they find it difficult to even leave their homes. Please do something.'[12]

Atal Bihari Vajpayee, the Indian Prime Minister was listening in, as he was using Dilip Kumar to reiterate Jawaharlal Nehru's threat that in case of a Kashmir settlement, the Muslims of India would suffer. Indeed Kargil or no Kargil, Kashmir or no Kashmir, Indian Muslims have been held hostage by India. Communal riots against Muslims have never ceased, only their pauses have been irregular.

The Delhi riots began on 23 February 2020 when the ruling Bharatiya Janta Party forcibly ended the sit-in by women to protest against the Indian Citizenship (Amendment) Act 2019 which was widely viewed as discriminatory by all minorities. Initially, twenty-four deaths were reported with four mosques burnt. The figure rose to fifty-four, two-thirds of whom were Muslims. The Congress President, Sonia Gandhi called for Home Minister Amit Shah's resignation. One day after Justice S. Murlidhar of the Delhi High Court had criticized the police for inaction against the ruling party provocateurs, he was transferred to the Punjab and Haryana High Court.[13]

The Indian Citizenship (Amendment) Act 2019 was not resented by Muslims alone, the Dalit leader Chandrashekhar Azad Ravan led a massive protest at the historic Jamia Masjid, Delhi. There were riots in two provinces Uttar Pradesh and Madhya Pradesh, with at least fifteen persons reported dead.[14] It is fair to note that not only Parsis, but Upper caste Hindus joined in protesting against this discriminatory law.[15]

Indian Reprisals in Indian Illegally Occupied Jammu and Kashmir. Muslims are spread out in India but concentrated in Kashmir where since 1989 an uprising has been taking place. Years of oppression and humiliation have caused the Kashmiris to raise the Pakistani flag. There were some like Masarat Alam Bhat who were acquitted of the charge, but Pakistani flags were openly displayed during a rally held by Shabir Shah in Nowhatta (known as Navyut in Kashmiri). This was in advance of talks scheduled between the National Security Advisers of India and Pakistan.[16]

Rajmohan Gandhi's Centre for Dialogue and Reconciliation prepared a report, which included inputs from the Bharatiya Janata Party. Its findings: 'Young Kashmiris have lost their fear of Indian forces and they are evermore eager to die resisting routine high-handedness than submit to a life of discrimination and humiliation.'[17]

India responded by using pellets, such as are loaded in airguns but loaded in shotguns. They did not directly kill, but they permanently blinded protestors, at least 6,000 of them. It was after the killing of Burhanuddin Wani, the young charismatic revolutionary Kashmiri freedom fighter, in July 2016 that protesters became reckless, and police fell back on pellets.

Six Kashmiris were killed in the Shopian district, and in the resulting demonstrations, troops fired tear gas shells on them for defying a curfew.[18] Twenty Kashmiris were killed on 1 April 2018. Described as a day of funerals, the demonstrations led to the reinforcement of curfews and the shutting of schools and internet services.[19]

The recklessness of the Kashmiris would not abate. They defied restrictions to attend the funeral of Sabzar Ahmad Bhat, a senior leader of the Hizbul Mujahideen group, who had been killed in a gunfight with Indian forces. Although the demonstrations coincided with the first of Ramadan, Kashmiris broke through the barricades to attend the funeral of Bhat and a 16-year-old youth along with him.

Some atrocities were too reprehensive for the authorities to ignore. Prime Minister Narendra Modi called the rape and murder of 8-year-old Asifa Bano of the nomadic Muslim Bakkarwal tribe in Kathua 'a matter of shame for India'. This came after a candlelight vigil led by Congress President Rahul Gandhi.[20] The growing defiance of the Kashmiris led an Indian body Concerned Citizens' Group to issue the following statement: 'Within the Kashmir valley despite the success of the Security forces in eliminating top militant leaders, the recruitment to the militant ranks was on the rise with even highly educated youngsters choosing to pick up the gun. Suicide attacks were unknown in the Kashmir Valley earlier.'[21] On the following May, ten protestors, including a Kashmir University Professor of Sociology, Mohammad Rafi Bhat, were killed in a series of gun battles.[22]

Violations of the Line of Control. Another recurring feature of the conflict was the violation of the Line of Control (LoC) established under the 1972 Simla agreement. The original cease-fire line was drawn on 27 July 1949, and a cease-fire agreement on the LoC was signed in 2003. India mainly used unmanned drones for surveillance. Pakistan's vigilance too remained high, and some drones were downed. One spy drone intruding into Pakistan near Bhimber was shot down.[23] Ten days later, on 26 July 2015, the Inter-Services Public Relations (ISPR) recovered photographs and videos from the internal memory of the quadcopter providing irrefutable evidence that it was flown by the Indian Army for reconnaissance inside Pakistan territory.[24] One month later, India's Border Security Force (BSF) resorted to shelling Sialkot border villages along the Working Boundary, killing at least eight people including a lady and a child, damaging houses and killing and wounding livestock. Over the three previous months, India violated the ceasefire 143 times with 24 casualties.[25] This was an instance of the Indian Army attacking civilian targets; the following year Indian shelling killed seven Pakistani soldiers in the Bhimber District.[26] The next major targets were again civilians when India used cluster munitions in the Neelum Valley. This was in gross violation of International Law. One small boy was a victim when India claimed to have smashed four terror launch pads. Pakistan's Foreign Office called upon the P5 (Permanent Members of the UNSC) to ask India for evidence and showed its willingness to invite a P5 delegation to visit the locations, India had claimed were terrorist pads.[27] India lost nine troops in reprisal. There were as many as 2,900 cease-fire violations during the Covid-19 lockdown, with casualties swelling to 59. However, back-channel negotiations were reported on 29 May 2022 to have brought a lull in cease-fire violations.

Executions and Encounters. Indian authorities have executed Kashmiri leaders, the hanging of Afzal Guru in Delhi's Tihar prison on 9 February 2013, began a new round, but these executions and encounters instead of instilling fear in the masses have inspired more and more acts of valour. Prem Shankar Jha author of *Kashmir, 1947: Rival Versions of History* (New Delhi: Oxford University Press, 1996) who had challenged Alastair Lamb's contention that Maharaja Hari Singh had never signed an Instrument of Accession, on 23 August 2016, made the following observations: (i) 'But no amount of money or exhortations could have made 1.5 lakh people from all over South Kashmir rush to Tral within hours of (Burhanuddin) Wani's death (8 July 2016) to catch a last glimpse of him and offer no less than 40 prayers for his soul. And Pakistan did not even learn of Wani's death or instigate it (the uprising) before the people of South Kashmir.'[28] (ii) 'It happened to us in 2008 because of the Amarnath land scam in Shopian double rape and murder agitation; in 2010 because of the Macchil fake encounter killings. It happened again after your forces killed Burhanuddin Wani.'[29]

The following discussion has the effect of controverting the arguments Prem Shankar Jha made in 1996: 'The International Commission of Jurists (ICJ) passed a resolution in 1993 in Geneva, proclaiming Kashmir's accession to India null and void. India has never produced the original copy of the Instrument of Accession on any international forum, claiming in 1995 that the original document was lost or stolen.'[30]

Indian forces arrested Yasin Malik, Chairman of the Jammu Kashmir Liberation Front the same day that Burhanuddin Wani was killed.[31] The next to share this fate was Sabzar Ahmad Bhat with two others. This encounter also led to widespread protests in Kashmir. The demonstrators chanted: 'Go India go back. We want freedom'. The security forces retaliated with indefinite lockdowns. The internet services recently restored were shut off again. Asiya Andrabi, founding leader of Dukhtaran-e-Millat (Daughters of the Nation) has been under illegal and inhuman incarceration for more than fifteen years on fabricated charges under draconian laws aimed at perpetuating India's occupation of Indian Illegally Occupied Jammu & Kashmir (IIOJK) through the brutalisation of Kashmiri people.[32] Mohammad Ashraf Sehrai died in police custody at the age of 77.[33] These are only the high-profile cases, as attempts to silence the media have abounded. Every execution, every encounter now results in demonstrations. A.S. Dulat, the former RAW chief noted: 'School girls and women are coming out to throw stones. The Kashmir situation has never been so bad.'[34]

Spies and Strikes. The first instance of an Indian spy captured in Balochistan came to light on 3 March 2016. The Indian High Commissioner was summoned to receive a démarche over the capture of Kulbhushan Jadhav (Indian Navy, Engineering Corps Service #41558Z) from Chaman. The spy had the cover name of Hussain Mubarak Patel. The DG ISPR Lt.-Gen. Asim Bajwa said Jadhav's capture was proof of Indian interference in Balochistan. 'This is no less than State-sponsored terrorism.'[35] When Jadhav was sentenced to death, India appealed on 8 May 2017 to the International Court of Justice (ICJ).[36] The ten-member ICJ restrained Pakistan from executing 'Kulbhushan Sudhir Jadhav of Indian nationality'. The implications of this order were noted in India. Markandey Katju, a former judge of the Indian Supreme Court said: 'Pakistan must be happy that we went to the ICJ for a single individual's fate, as they can now raise all kinds of issues, particularly Kashmir, in international fora to which we had always objected.'[37] Read between the lines, the eminent jurist's dictum means that India has no case on Kashmir that can stand in the International Court of Justice. The Indian lawyer Harish Salve mocked: 'All Pakistan has is a passport. Jadhav had travelled to Pakistan on a passport containing his assumed Muslim name. The Joint Secretary of the India External Affairs Ministry, Deepak Mittal, altered India's demand from Jadhav's acquittal to a re-trial in a civilian court.[38] In July 2019 the ICJ rejected the Indian plea for Jadhav's acquittal and release but asked Pakistan to provide him with consular service under the Vienna Convention.[39] The Pakistani *ad hoc* judge, former Chief Justice Tassaduq Hussain Jillani wrote a dissenting note: 'Since 31 May 2017 Pakistan has sent six requests to India for necessary co-operation in the investigation of the criminal case and about the passport issue, but these were of no avail. Pakistan even offered to extradite Mr Jadhav to India, if India was prepared to indict him under Indian laws.'[40] Kulbhushan Jadhav received a reprieve when under the Pakistan Tehreek-e-Insaf regime, on 10 June 2021, the ICJ (Review and Re-consideration) Bill, 2020 was bulldozed through the National Assembly to provide him with the right of appeal. The rules of business had been suspended and Opposition members charged that the Bill had been included in the heavy legislative agenda to provide relief to the spy.

India claimed that its troops made a surgical strike across the LoC against 'terrorist launch pads', a charge denied by Pakistan. In the Hotspring sector, Pakistan lost two soldiers, Havildar Jumma Khan and Naik Imtiaz. The UN secretary-general urged restraint on both sides.[41] This strike was said to be in response to the Uri incident in which 'Pakistani terrorists' were blamed for Indian casualties.

In a similar incident at Pulwama on 14 February 2019 eight Indian aircraft intruded four nautical miles into Pakistani airspace. The intrusion lasted four minutes. This was in Jabba tehsil of Balakot. When on 27 February 2019 two Indian jets were downed by Pakistan, the US response was to inquire whether its F-16 jets had been deployed in the air battle. Pakistani sources said JF-17 an aircraft co-produced with China had been employed.[42] High-resolution images produced by Planet Lab, San Francisco showed the purportedly destroyed targets at Jabba/Balakot intact.[43] A few days later, foreign media persons, including those from India, ambassadors and defence attachés of different countries were taken to Jabba/Balakot, showing the madrassah that India had claimed targeting, was intact.[44]

In this strike as well, two Indian fighter jets were downed, and a pilot Wing Commander Abhinandan Varthaman was captured alive.[45] On 1 March 2019, both the Treasury and Opposition benches agreed to release the captured pilot. Just before returning home, the Indian pilot in a video message disclosed that he was trying to 'find a target' when the Pakistan Air Force shot his aircraft down. 'Then I ejected and when I fell many people surrounded me. I had a pistol but I dropped it seeing so many charged people. I tried to run to save my life. Then two Pakistan Army captains came there and rescued me. I was taken to their unit where I was provided with first aid and later shifted to hospital. The Pakistani Army is a very professional service. I have spent time with the Pakistan Army and I am very impressed.'[46]

Revocation of Article 370. The Indian government's revocation of Article 370 (and a key provision added under it, known as Article 35A) of its Constitution was preceded both by a court ruling and mounting violence. The Article had been enacted in the early stages of the conflict to give a special status to Jammu and Kashmir and the High Court of Indian-held Kashmir had ruled that Article 370, granting special status to the state, has assumed a place of permanence in the Constitution and the feature is beyond amendment, repeal, or abrogation.[47]

When violence and protest continued, the practice of riddling demonstrators with pellets was not confined to causing blindness. Nasir Shafi an 11-year-old schoolboy who died from pellet injuries caused outrage in Harwan. The killing of a schoolboy led to demonstrations causing a death toll of 81; the worst violence since 2010.[48] A.S. Dulat the former RAW Chief said the armed militancy and the intensity of violence witnessed in 1990 was not there now. 'There were more guns then... Actual militancy was more then, but today the situation is scarier. When stone-pelting is done by youths, and girls, it's abnormal... Today, they are proud of being stone-pelters. They are no longer hiding. Schoolgirls and women are coming out to throw stones. The Kashmir situation has never been so bad... I am sorry to say but it's easier to talk to Pakistan than to Kashmiris.' The uprising after the killing of Burhan Wani surprised Pakistan.[49]

Thus, when India offered a truce for the month of Ramadan (2018), Kashmiri leaders were sceptical. Chairman of a faction of the All Parties Hurriyat Conference Mirwaiz Umar Farooq asked: 'What next after this temporary relief? What is the vision, the path ahead? Will they kill us again after one month? Will they again use bullets, pellets, pepper gas, chilli powder and tear gas shells against us after a month?'[50]

Finally, on 5 August 2019, India annulled Article 370. Ahead of this move, Indian authorities arrested political leaders and cancelled the Amarnath Yatra (Amarnath is located in Jammu and Kashmir and is one of the most important pilgrimages in India for the worshippers of the Hindu god Shiva) and internet services. In retaliation, Pakistan suspended all trade with India (10 August 2019). Anchar a densely populated area of Srinagar was ringed by steel barricades and razor wires. The situation inside became grimmer when the besieged themselves put up barricades of fallen trees, electric poles and barbed wire to keep police out. Young, masked men spent the night outside near bonfires.[51] After three weeks, as many as 500 demonstrations had taken place. In his speech to the UN General Assembly 74th session, Pakistani Prime Minister Imran Khan warned of a 'bloodbath' in Kashmir and warned that war was possible over India's actions in the region.

Kashmiris continued to defy curbs. Stones hurled by protestors were met with tear gas, chilli grenades and pellets. By 15 September 2019, the number of protests had increased to 700. However, Prime Minister Narendra Modi claimed his siege operation was successful. The Kashmir Chamber of Commerce and Industry said that the shutdown caused losses of over $1 billion.[52]

Amnesty International criticized the controversial and repressive Public Safety Act for circumventing the justice system and respect for human rights in Jammu and Kashmir. As a result, the Indian human rights activist and Chair of Amnesty International India Board, Aakar Patel, was prevented from leaving the country. India predictably clamped an information lockdown and also blocked the streaming of Pakistan Broadcasting Corporation's bulletins on Kashmir. Facebook censored dozens of posts on Kashmir and Twitter followed suit. Al Jazeera revealed that one million tweets had been removed since 2017.

On 18 September 2019, Imran Khan said that 'until they lift the curfew in Kashmir and reverse the revocation of (Article) 370, there is no chance of talks with them.' As far as creating the atmosphere for parleys is concerned, this demand is fair; however, the restitution of Article 370 should never be characterized as the resolution of the Kashmir dispute.

The United Nations Again. It was after the term of Kofi Annan (1938–2018) as the seventh Secretary-General of the UN (1997–2006) had ended that the UN woke up to its responsibility with regard to the Kashmir dispute. On 11 December, Secretary-General Ban Ki-moon offered his offices for the resolution of the dispute—an offer that Pakistan accepted. On 20 July 2015, the UN Military Observers Group visited the villages near Sialkot that had been the target of cross-border Indian shelling in which four Pakistanis had died. On 29 August 2015, observers from UN headquarters met the bereaved families. In September 2015, Pakistan's Permanent Representative to the UN, Maleeha

Lodhi, complained to the UN Security Council (UNSC) about India's plans to construct a wall along the Line of Control allegedly to convert it 'into a quasi-international border'. On 13 September 2016, at the 33rd session of the Human Rights Council, the UN Human Rights Chief Zeid Ra'ad Al Hussein (2014–2018) lamented: 'I believe an independent, impartial and international mission is now needed crucially and that it should be given free and complete access to establish an objective assessment of the claims made by the two sides.' On 16 October 2017, Pakistan was elected to the UN Human Rights Council. Pakistan had polled 151 votes when only 97 had been necessary. On 17 November 2017, the UNGA adopted Pakistan's sponsored resolution on self-determination.

In 2018, the UN Human Rights Chief released a 49–page document covering both sides of Kashmir. From July 2016 to April 2018, i.e. after the killing of Burhanuddin Wani, 130 to 145 civilians had been killed by India's security forces. The use of pellet-firing shotguns found special mention, along with arbitrary arrests of children, torture, enforced disappearance, and reprisals against human rights defenders. The finding related to Azad Kashmir and Gilgit-Baltistan were limited to the constitutional and legislative, restrictions on the freedom of expression and association and the impact of counter-terrorism operations on human rights. The report contains no instance of state violence on the Pakistani side.[53] In 2019, the Jammu Kashmir Coalition of Civil Society also released a report to the effect that India was using torture as a matter of policy. Torture is the most unreported human rights violation perpetrated by the State.[54] In 2020, the UN again followed through with another report on human rights in Kashmir and the details were similar.[55]

On 16 August 2019, the UNSC held a meeting on Kashmir after a break of fifty-four years. This was caused by the revocation of Article 370 and the resulting disturbances. The ninth UN Secretary-General António Guterres asked India not to change the status of Kashmir. He went on to challenge India's interpretation of the 1972 Simla Agreement as binding the two parties to a bilateral mechanism. He stressed that the agreement 'calls for the final status of Jammu and Kashmir to be settled by peaceful means in accordance with the Charter of the United Nations.'[56] The Secretary-Generals' reference to the UN Charter is meaningful as it does not allow the suspension of human rights. In a report published from Geneva, the Kashmir State Human Rights Commission said it had evidence of 2,730 bodies buried in forty mass graves.[57] The following month, at the 42nd session of the UN Human Rights Council, the UN Human Rights Chief Michelle Bachelet (2018–2022) in her address to the body: 'While I continue to urge the Governments of India and Pakistan to ensure that human rights are respected and protected, I have appealed particularly to India to ease the current lockdowns or curfews; to ensure people's access to basic services; and that all due process rights are respected for those who have been detained.'[58] She said it is important that the 'people of Kashmir are consulted and engaged in any decision-making processes' that have an impact on their future.

In October, France as a permanent member of the UNSC caused a postponement of its meeting: 'Our position has been very clear: Kashmir issue has to be treated bilaterally.' This was an acceptance of India's interpretation of the Simla Agreement 1972, an interpretation at odds with the interpretation of the UN secretary-general. Finally, at the prompting of China, a UNSC meeting on Kashmir was held on 15 January 2020. Chinese Ambassador Zhang Jun told journalists that China's position is very clear. China recognises Kashmir as a territory disputed between India and Pakistan and openly supports Islamabad's demand for a plebiscite to enable the Kashmiri people to decide their own future.[59]

Noting that the people of Kashmir had been facing a lockdown since 5 August 2019 Pakistan's Prime Minister Imran Khan called for the UN to send military observers to the LoC. Secretary-General António Guterres criticized the Indian citizenship laws, saying they would render Indian Muslims stateless. He was critical of the veto as five permanent members were hampering the ability of the UN to deliver the very object it was created for—conflict resolution.[60]

On 20 February 2020, at the anti-Citizenship Amendment Act (CAA) rally in Bengaluru, India, a 19-year-old undergraduate student Amulya Leona Noronha raised the 'Pakistan zindabad' slogan. The *Hindu* reported that BJP supporters threw stones at the house of Leona's parents.[61] Despite the curfew, the killing went on. Nine Kashmiris and three Indian soldiers were killed in gun battles on 4 and 5 April 2020. On the anniversary of the Article 370 revocation, the UNSC held a closed-door meeting to review the human rights situation. In August 2020, the UNGA President for the 75th session Volkan Bozkir called for the resolution by giving multilateralism a chance. The UNGA adopted a Pakistan-sponsored resolution on self-determination.[62] The situation was further inflamed when Indian forces opened fire upon a UN vehicle carrying two military observers on a routine monitoring mission (18 December 2020) the observers were unhurt, but the UN vehicle was damaged. The next day (19 December 2020) the UN confirmed that its vehicle was damaged by 'an unidentified object.'

In 2021, António Guterres issued a statement regarding the revocation of Article 370, urging India to refrain from steps that could affect the status of Jammu and Kashmir. The UN position, the secretary-general said, was governed by the charter of the UN and applicable UNSC resolutions.[63] Pakistan's envoy Munir Akram said that the siege of Kashmir beginning on 5 August 2019 has caused the occupied territory a loss of $3.5 billion.[64] Secretary-General António Guterres issued a statement asking India to end the use of pellets against Kashmiri children: 'I am alarmed at the detention and torture of children and concerned by the military use of schools.'[65]

Even on India's assumption of the UNSC presidentship in August 2021, the UN position on the Jammu and Kashmir dispute has not changed. When prodded Stéphane Dujarric, spokesperson for the UN secretary-general, said 'You will find it in relevant resolutions. I'm not going to go and repeat it, but ours is unchanged'.[66]

India maintains at a conservative estimate, 50,000 troops in Kashmir. In the month of October, twelve Kashmiris were killed without provocation, the last being a milk seller.[67] Against this backdrop, Kashmiri groups urged for the release of prominent human rights activist Khurram Parvez from the Rohini Jail Complex in Delhi. In 2022, Jammu and Kashmir Liberation Front (JKLF) chief Yasin Malik was awarded a life sentence. A joint Kashmiri and Sikh protest in front of the Indian Consulate General in Chicago, US vehemently denounced the unjust life sentence given to Kashmiri leader Yasin Malik by an Indian court.

Pakistan has long suffered UN indifference to the Kashmir cause, now that the UN is active, Pakistan must match its efforts.

Foreign Condemnation. Before the revocation of Article 370, apart from the world body itself, many individual members of the UN condemned Indian atrocities in Kashmir. Italian Defence Minister Roberta Pinotti (2014–2018) in a meeting with President Mamnoon Hussain (1940–2021) stated: 'Italy has criticized brutalities and atrocities of Indian Armed Forces against innocent Kashmiris who have been demanding their right of self-determination in accordance with the United Nations resolutions'.[68]

In 2017, a member of the EU parliament, Julie Ward, Canadian human rights activist Ken Stone, and Manchester City Council member Yasmin Dar called the situation in Kashmir the worst kind of human rights violations. Julie Ward said that the UN resolutions were the bedrock of the Jammu and Kashmir issue, and the international community should settle this dispute in the larger interest of the people of South Asia. 'The use of pellet guns in Kashmir against the innocent youth and women highlights the violent image of India which should be condemned.'[69]

On 14 September 2018, Turkey pledged to support Pakistan at the UN on Kashmir. On 5 October 2019, a candlelight vigil marked the two-month lockdown in Kashmir in London. The demonstrators were mostly British Kashmiris. King Carl Gustaf XVI of Sweden stated on Indian soil his feelings on the Kashmir situation.[70] One week before the visit Swedish Foreign Minister Ann Linde told the Riksdag (the legislature and the supreme decision-making body of Sweden) that a long-term solution must involve the inhabitants of Kashmir.[71]

On 8 December 2019, a four-member delegation of Human Rights from Canada met Mushaal Hussein Mullick the wife of Yasin Malik and voiced concern at his incarceration.

Members of the British parliament adopted on 5 February 2019 a joint statement on the Kashmir dispute. On 28 September 2019, Mahathir Mohamad, Prime Minister of Malaysia said that 'despite UN resolutions on held Jammu and Kashmir, the territory has been invaded and occupied.'

On 22 October 2019, a group of twenty-three diplomats was taken to Jura to witness the targets and the damage caused by the Indian shelling from across the LoC. On 29 January 2020, the European Parliament proposed a resolution that criticized the Citizenship Amendment Act, 2019 and the lockdown of the disputed territory of Kashmir. The European Parliament intended to vote on this resolution on 30 January 2020. Instead, the voting on the resolution was deferred until after the visit by India's Prime Minister Narendra Modi on 13 March for the 15th EU–India summit.

On 17 February 2020, a UK Labour MP Debbie Abrahams was denied entry into Indian Territory on the ground that her visa was not valid. She was critical of the Indian government and wrote to the UK foreign secretary, saying the parliamentary group was 'gravely concerned' about the decision to strip the disputed region of its special status, adding that it 'betrayed the trust of the people of Jammu and Kashmir'.

In London itself, Labour MP Sarah Owens protested the Kashmir lockdown. She compared it with the Covid-19 lockdown, saying that the Kashmir lockdown was not about safety but about control.[72]

The United States and Kashmir. The official and historical position of the US is that Kashmir is a disputed territory awaiting disposition following a UNSC-sponsored plebiscite. However, even after the end of the Cold War, the US sees China as an adversary and is trying to build up India as a democratic counterpoise to China. This consideration often pushes American Kashmir policy to the side, most notably by President Bill Clinton during the Kargil crisis of 1999.

The reasons are not very clear to outsiders. In 2015, Ashton Carter, US Secretary of Defence, listed a number of Chinese activities that caused concern to the US but conceded: 'The US and China are not allies, but we don't have to be adversaries. A strong constructive US relationship is essential for global security and prosperity.' Acknowledging that US–Sino relations would be 'complex' as both nations sought to 'compete and co-operate'.[73]

A few months later, in September 2015, President Xi Jinping visited the US and urged both nations to better understand each other's strategic intentions and avoid tensions: 'We want to see more understanding and trust; less estrangement and suspicion... Should they enter into conflict or confrontation, it would lead to disaster for both countries and the world at large.'[74]

Thus, though awareness is mutual, it is not enough to shape policy as the US is unable to shed its suspicions. US–Pakistan relations, as we have seen, are more complex, as their interdependence is always short-term, and the worst sufferers of this standoff are the people of Jammu and Kashmir. The US acknowledges that Pakistan has been trying to meet its concerns. Pakistan has deployed at least 140,000 troops to FATA—the terror war theatre. This unprecedented deployment and thinning of the lines against India indicate that Pakistan is giving attention to its 'domestic insurgent threat'.[75] The previous year the US Secretary of State had admitted which country was responsible for the domestic threat.

Against this backdrop, Indian atrocities in Kashmir though hurting the sensibility of a very liberal society, evinced a very limited response. When it was reported that India claimed to have killed militants, the State Department spokesperson John F. Kirby urged all sides to find a peaceful solution.[76] The violence following the revocation of Article 370 could not be brushed aside and in September 2019 seven US lawmakers wrote to the US administration: 'The reports we are receiving [from Kashmir] are harrowing with allegations including forced disappearances, mass detentions, rape and sexual assault, and the targeted detention of political, economic and social leaders.'

Pramila Jayapal and Jim McGovern demanded international media and independent human rights observers be allowed into Jammu and Kashmir to investigate reports of abuses.[77] Concerns were heightened when photographs of children blinded by pellets were seen in the US. India claimed that it had discontinued the use of these weapons, but in fact, their use increased after 5 August 2019.[78] In November, the situation in Kashmir came up for discussion again. Congresswoman Pramila Jayapal of Indian origin wanted Washington to send a clear message to India to reconsider its policies in held Kashmir. Her endeavours show the limit of remonstrance. She first wrote to Secretary of State Mike Pompeo on 10 September 2019, with little effect. High profile, though it was, Pramila Jayapal's resolution on Kashmir gained only 29 co-sponsors in a house of 435 members (7 January 2020). For her efforts, she earned the wrath of the large and influential Indian lobby. Her efforts were seconded by Senator Bernie Sanders: 'India's action is unacceptable.... The communications blockade must be lifted immediately, and the United States government must speak out boldly in support of international humanitarian law and in support of UN-backed peaceful resolution that respects the will of the Kashmiri people.'[79] But Bernie Sanders could not even secure a presidential nomination. There are voices of conscience in America, but they are in the minority. Still, on 15 November 2019, a human rights panel of the US Congress reminded India that it can never give up supporting the Kashmiris' right to self-determination because it seems difficult to implement it at this stage. Kashmir kept echoing in Congress. Brad Sherman asked Alice Wells: 'Have US diplomats been permitted to visit Kashmir since 5 August 2019? What are the reasons the Indian Government has given for refusing US diplomats permission to visit Kashmir?[80]

In a letter dated 12 February 2020, US Senators Lindsey Graham, Dick Durbin, Chris Van Hollen, and Todd Young wrote to Secretary of State Mike

Pompeo requesting an assessment of the human rights situation in Jammu and Kashmir and of the rights of religious minorities in India.[81]

A month later, the US State Department's *Country Reports on Human Rights* noted 703 incidents of religious violence in India for the period 2016–2017. *The New York Times* reported in March 2020 that since the Delhi riots of February 2020, videos had surfaced showing police assaulting Muslim protesters and urging Hindus to join them. These reports, these concerns are doubtlessly heartening, but whether they have any influence on US policy shall be determined by how US–India relations stand; for it is the US championship of India's regional status that is preventing the resolution of the Kashmir dispute.

Indian Critics. Both India and the US are democracies. Both during their struggle for independence from Britain emerged with democratic and liberal values. There is a body of concerned Indian citizens who would like to see these ideals put into practice, but here too, they remain in a minority. Pakistan has its own critics of its Kashmir policy. Pervez Hoodbhoy, as related above, favours a solution that makes the LoC the border. I.A. Rehman (1930–2021) called for circumventing disputed regions,[82] a solution that would leave us upholding human rights in Pakistan and withholding them in Kashmir. S. Akbar Zaidi wrote: 'It is Pakistan's political economy of defence which keeps the *status quo* as it is.'[83] Documents reveal the opposite. The Indian Army prevented Prime Minister Manmohan Singh from solving the Siachen issue.[84] Such being the case, it should not be surprising that some Indians too are critical of their country's Kashmir policy.

The most prominent critic is a renowned Indian novelist and political activist Arundhati Roy,[85] who has been the most outspoken about the situation in Kashmir: 'Kashmir is one of the most protracted and bloody occupations in the world, and one of the most ignored.' Roy attributed the apathy towards Kashmir, especially in the Western world, to their pursuit of commercial interests in India, 'where they are more eager to sell their goods than human rights.'[86] Two years later Arundhati Roy deplored the execution of Afzal Guru. He had been hanged for an attack on the Indian Parliament which left eight security personnel and a gardener dead. All five attackers were killed on the spot. Arundhati Roy cites the Indian Supreme Court judgment: 'As is the case with most conspiracies, there is and could be no direct evidence amounting to criminal conspiracy... The incident which resulted in heavy casualties had shaken the entire nation, and the collective conscience of society will only be satisfied if capital punishment is awarded to the offender.'[87] While all perpetrators were killed on the spot, the enormity of the crime compelled the Indian Supreme Court to hang a person who was not present at the scene of the crime but was arrested from a fruit market in far-away Srinagar. Thus, Indian investigators themselves linked the attack on the Indian Parliament to the Kashmir dispute.

Similar was the case of India's Deputy Inspector General of the Coast Guard B.K. Loshali. He blew up a suspected Pakistani boat off the Gujarat coast on the night of 31 December 2014. However, Defence Minister Manohar Parrikar had said that the Pakistani crew had set it on fire and blown up the boat. Loshali faced a court martial and was sacked for passing remarks that contradicted the government's stand over the sinking of a Pakistani boat.

Indian academia too was not silent. Professor Nivedita Menon of the Jawaharlal Nehru University told a gathering of students on 22 February 2016: 'Everyone knows that India is illegally occupying Kashmir.' Kanhaiya Kumar, President of the Student's Union, was also arrested along with the lady professor.[88] In another incident on 2 January 2016, terrorists stormed an Indian Air Force base at Pathankot, leaving seven persons dead. On 2 June, Sharad Kumar, director general of the National Investigation Agency said that there was no evidence of Pakistan's complicity, and the incident was used to scuttle the impending talks between the foreign secretaries of the two countries.[89]

In 2017, journalist Prem Shankar Jha said that the Indian steel tycoon Sajjan Jindal visited Pakistan at the invitation of Nawaz Sharif, not at the instance of Narendra Modi.[90]

On 30 July 2017, India-held Kashmir's Chief Minister Mehbooba Mufti called for the reopening of all routes to Azad Kashmir to let the 'caged Kashmiris free'.[91] On 16 September 2019, Farooq Abdullah the former Chief Minister was formally arrested under the Public Safety Act (PSA) and his home turned into a 'judicial lockup'; he was later released after seven months in March 2020. In a London meeting, A.S. Dulat former RAW chief blamed his country for the crisis in Kashmir: 'heavy-handedness has never worked in Kashmir...actually it doesn't work anywhere as we have recently seen in Spain.'[92]

There are other instances. Transcripts reveal that Arnab Goswami of Republic TV knew two days in advance of the 26 February 2021 attack on Balakot, officially ascribed to Pakistan but actually carried by Indian forces.[93] In conclusion, we can say that while Indian dissidents are arrested or ostracized, Pakistani dissidents are applauded.

> **INDIAN LEADERS ON KASHMIR**
>
> Although now every leader in India insists that Kashmir is an integral part of India, this was not the position early in the conflict. Below are some statements of Indian leaders. One sample statement of Pandit Jawaharlal Nehru, the first Prime Minister of India was:
> 'We have declared that the fate of Kashmir is ultimately to be decided by the people. That pledge we have given, not only to the people of Kashmir, but to the whole world. We want it to be a fair, just referendum and we shall accept the verdict.'
> – Nehru AIR Broadcast, 2 November 1947
>
> 'Those who accepted the partition of India—the Congress—on the basis of communal majority should have agreed to the inclusion of Kashmir in Pakistan, as undeniably Kashmir has a Muslim majority.'
> – Dr N.B. Khare, President, Hindu Mahasabha, APP, 3 May 1951
>
> 'If the Muslims of Kashmir do not want to remain with us, let them go away, but Kashmir must and will be ours.'
> – Shyama Prasad Mukherjee's Speech, Patiala, 20 April 1953
>
> 'The Mahasabha is convinced that an overall plebiscite will mean loss of both Jammu and Kashmir to India.'
> – V.G. Deshpande, General Secretary, Mahasabha, Bombay, 14 September 1953
>
> 'Knowing that Kashmir is predominantly Mussalman, it is one day bound to become a Mussalman State.'
> – Mahatma Gandhi, 5 May 1934
>
> Source: Prem Nath Bazaz, *The History of the Struggle for Freedom in Kashmir* (New Delhi: Kashmir Publishing Co., 1954), p. 343.

RELATIONS WITH BANGLADESH.—The tragic and bloody circumstances in which Bangladesh seceded from Pakistan have already been recounted. We can start from 22 February 1974 when Pakistan recognized Bangladesh and Sheikh Mujibur Rahman, president of Bangladesh, attended the Lahore Islamic Summit of 1974. On 9 April 1974, representatives from Pakistan, Bangladesh, and India met in Delhi to agree to normalise relations. The repatriation of Bangladeshis from Pakistan, and the repatriation of some non-Bengalis to Pakistan (mainly divided families) took place under this declaration. On 27 June 1974, Prime Minister Zulfikar Ali Bhutto was given a popular and tumultuous reception in Dhaka, 'Let us forget the enmity and bitterness of the past and inaugurate a new chapter of hope and prosperity' said President Sheikh Mujibur Rahman, the founder of Bangladesh.

In 1978, President Ziaur Rahman of Bangladesh was heartily welcomed by President Ziaul Haq of Pakistan. Quite astoundingly, there were demonstrations in Dhaka on 5 April 1979 to protest against the execution of Zulfikar Ali Bhutto. In 1983, Foreign Minister Sahibzada Yaqub Khan, who as Commander, Eastern Command in East Pakistan had resigned rather than take military action in 1971, visited Dacca (now Dhaka) and addressed two outstanding issues between the two countries, the division of assets and the repatriation of non-Bengalis to Pakistan. Neither of these issues has been resolved to the satisfaction of Bangladesh, nor have they become impediments to improved relations.

Ties with India took centre stage. The Indian government did not take a sympathetic view of the plight of Bangladesh caused by the 1974 completion of the Farakka Barrage and later the linkage of thirty-seven rivers which blocked flows into Bangladesh, affecting fish stocks and navigability. An Indian spokesperson said his country had shown a 'great deal of generosity to Bangladesh by signing the Ganges Water Treaty of 1996'.[94]

In June 1986 and in July 1987, President H.M. Ershad visited Pakistan. Prime Minister Benazir Bhutto visited Dhaka in 1989. Tributes were paid to Sheikh Mujibur Rahman at an Islamabad meeting on 17 March 1998. On 27 November 2000, the deputy high commissioner to Bangladesh said at a Dhaka seminar that Pakistan would not apologize to Bangladesh because the violence had been initiated by Awami League 'miscreants'. Although Pakistan had announced his withdrawal, the Bangladesh government expelled the deputy high commissioner. Two years later on 29 July 2002, President Pervez Musharraf apologized in Dhaka for the army action. Since the induction of Khaleda Zia's government in October 2001, relations improved and this position was maintained till the Awami League, under Sheikh Hasina Wazed (also spelt Wajed) returned to power. During her term, debates on who initiated the killings were re-ignited, especially after the publication of two books written by Bengalis themselves: Sarmila Bose, *Dead Reckoning* (London: Hurst Publishers, 2011) and Yasmin Saikia, *Women, War and the Making of Bangladesh* (London: Duke University Press, 2011).

The issue did not remain academic. Ethnic Bengalis opposed to secession were set upon by the Bangladesh government. In 2013, Jamaat-e-Islami Secretary-General Ali Ahsan Mohammad Mojaheed was hanged, causing an outcry from the people and a protest by the Government of Pakistan. The executions went contrary to the India–Pakistan–Bangladesh Tripartite Agreement 1974 which had provided for amnesty. In 2000,[95] there was a mutual withdrawal of diplomats.[96]

The execution which caused outrage and demonstration both in Pakistan and Azad Kashmir was that of Amir Jamaat-e-Islami Motiur Rahman Nizami[97] on 11 May 2016. All the demonstrators cited the 1974 Tripartite Agreement. On the very same day, the National Assembly of Pakistan passed a unanimous resolution condemning the act. The Senate met on 13 May and condemned the execution of Nizami; condemning punishments for acts purported of having taken place forty-five years ago.[98] Turkey too recalled its ambassador from Bangladesh in protest.

Matters had subsided when the abrogation of Article 370 and then the religious profiling of minorities in India caused demonstrations in Bangladesh. Nur Hossain Kasemi of the Hefazat-e-Islam Bangladesh body called upon Sheikh Hasina to cancel plans for inviting Narendra Modi to the 50th Anniversary of Bangladesh.

On 12 April 2020, Captain Abdul Majed was executed for the 1975 assassination of Sheikh Mujibur Rahman. This prevented the cooling of nationalist sentiments but not snuffing them out. The Golden Jubilee of Bangladesh liberation was the occasion for a flood of books, articles, films, and documentaries: with India boasting of its military prowess, Bangladesh highlighting atrocities against Bengalis and Pakistan drawing attention to the ethnic cleansing of the non-Bengali minority which by and large, it refuses to accommodate.

Narendra Modi arrived in Dhaka, on 26 March 2021, to attend the celebrations of the golden jubilee of Bangladesh. Imran Khan, the Prime Minister of Pakistan, extending felicitations wrote: 'On my own behalf, and on behalf of the Government and people of Pakistan, I have great pleasure in extending our felicitations on the 50th anniversary of the People's Republic of Bangladesh.'[99]

RELATIONS WITH AFGHANISTAN.—The Muslims of India used to look to the Afghans for help against the Hindu majority. Ahmad Shah Abdali's defeat of the Marathas in 1761 is symbolic of that sentiment. During the Khilafat Movement, there was also a migration movement. Muslims migrated to Afghanistan but soon found its gates barred. At Independence, Pakistan's membership in the UN was challenged only by Afghanistan. However, due to Jinnah's personal diplomacy, the Afghan envoy presented his credentials to him. Yet Afghanistan did not recognize the Durand Line which had been established in 1893 by an Anglo-Afghan treaty; it claimed Pakistan territory up to Attock.

The Afghanistan stance has no basis, Pakistani scholars have made two main points: (i) There exists a doctrine *uti possidetis juris* applied when a colonial power transforms its rule to independent states. The administrative lines that were in practice during colonial times remain valid. (ii) The Amir after signing the (Durand Line) Agreement called a meeting of the Loya Jirga where he endorsed the contents of the agreement.[100]

From 1961 to 1963 diplomatic relations between Pakistan and Afghanistan remained broken and were revived only due to the mediation of the Shah of Iran. However, during the 1965 and 1971 wars, in spite of its hostile posturing, Afghanistan did not embarrass Pakistan. On 13 December 1971, King Zahir Shah was in Moscow but, as foreign diplomats noted, did not endorse President Nikolay Podgorny's condition of transfer of power to the Awami League as a requirement of a ceasefire.

Shortly after, King Zahir Shah was ousted in a coup, a number of pro-Russian regimes ruled, finally culminating in the 1979 Russian invasion of Afghanistan. At first, Pakistan joined the US in its efforts to counter the Russian invasion. After an interlude, Pakistan joined the war against terror in Afghanistan. The situation across the Afghan border worsened after President Hamid Karzai assumed power in Kabul. Unable to stem the resurgence of the Taliban, Karzai's government constantly blamed 'cross-border terrorism' from Pakistan for their anarchy. Their dilemma is that they want Pakistan to secure a border (Durand Line) that they do not wish to recognize. Those crossing over from Pakistan are not Pakistan but Afghan nationals. On 20 November 2006, Foreign Office spokesperson Tasnim Aslam said that: 'The only solution to Afghanistan's complaints of cross-border terrorism is that it should take back the three million Afghan refugees who live in Pakistan.'[101] She added that Afghanistan would not allow fencing or sealing of the border which had as many as ninety-seven posts.

Afghanistan is not willing to take back its citizens who are mostly armed and have the potential to destabilize the host country. On 31 March 2007, the UNHCR had to suspend repatriation after the killing of an Afghan national near its verification centre. 15 April had been set as the deadline for the registration of Afghans.

Previously when US/NATO forces bombed sites within Pakistan, killing civilians, only Pakistan protested. Hot pursuit into its territory was where Pakistan drew the line. On 23 June 2007, a barrage of artillery killed sixty civilians whom the NATO command described as 'insurgents'.[102] However, many children were killed, and one person seeing nine members of his family dead, committed suicide. Since the 'insurgents' included Afghans, Karzai also criticized 'indiscriminate and imprecise' operations by US/NATO forces.

The ever-present tension was because of Indian intrusion. Yashvardhan Kumar Sinha the Indian diplomat told the American counsellor: 'We will not leave Afghanistan because we have strategic interests there.'[103] What could the strategy be other than to apply pressure on Pakistan?

Afghan Refugees. Afghan refugees have been the greatest source of trouble for Pakistan. Their presence has rendered Pakistan helpless in combating terrorism. Tasnim Aslam's statement given above shows the extent of Pakistan's exasperation.[104] Head of the UNHCR sub-office Peshawar Jacques Franquin said that Pakistan has been insisting on the repatriation of those Afghans whose Proof of Registration cards would expire after 31 December 2015. Franquin stated that the situation for the Afghan refugees had changed since the 16 December 2014 Army Public School massacre: 'We have been working to convince Pakistani authorities to open the door a little bit for the integration of a certain number of refugees, but Pakistan says this is not an option.'[105]

Pakistan relented to the extent that it agreed to a one-year delay for 1.6 Afghans with registration cards. On 6 December 2015, Lt.-Gen. (retd.) Abdul Qadir Baloch the Minister for States and Frontier Regions said that Pakistan could not forcibly send back Afghan refugees, because they were living in Pakistan under an international agreement and convention. Lt.-Gen. Baloch said 281,000 Afghan refugees are living in Balochistan.[106] Gen. Baloch set 20 July 2016 for a tripartite meeting between Afghans, Pakistanis, and UNHCR to determine a timeline for their repatriation. He warned that any refugee who overstays in the country beyond the 31 December 2016 deadline would be treated as illegal.[107] On 14 November 2016, a decision was taken to extend the deadline to 2018.

Pervez Khattak the Chief Minister of Khyber Pakhtunkhwa said: 'There had to be a deadline—the issue of repatriation cannot be left open-ended'. Less than ten days later, the US released $207 million for re-settling those returning to Afghanistan.

Just weeks before the deadline, on 7 December 2016, Col. Umar Farooq said Afghanistan had installed machines for making fake Pakistan identity cards, the detection of which was not immediately possible. This was impeding border management.[108]

In a bilateral meeting on 7 November 2018, Afghanistan and Pakistan agreed to follow a timeline for the return of the refugees. Although the timeline was not revealed, President Ashraf Ghani had in February 2018 pledged to ensure the return of all refugees in Pakistan in the next twenty-four months.[109] The European Commission allocated €40 million for Afghan refugees on 23 November 2019, however, the next year saw the Covid-19 epidemic, and the necessary lockdown caused a crisis, as the refugees who could not step out of Pakistan appealed to the UN for food parcels.[110] The UN too had sought help for the refugees but the Americans withdrew and the Taliban came in. On 15 February 2022, Pakistan asked the UNSC to stop attacks on its soil from Afghanistan. The UNSC on 6 March sought the world's help to catch the masterminds of an attack on a Shi'ite Muslim mosque in Peshawar. The UNSC it seems, was helpless.

Border Fencing. The 1893 Durand Line has always been a source of strife, mainly because of Afghanistan's irredentist claims. The then Foreign Minister Hina Rabbani Khar said since 2009 a fresh crop of Afghan refugees had caused the property prices in Peshawar to rise by 300 per cent. She observed: 'One major objective of foreign presence in Afghanistan was to reduce the ideological space that exists for extremist mindset. I think if you look at the last 10 years, the ideological space for extremists has only increased.'[111] She went on to say that before 2001 there had been only one suicide bombing in Pakistan, but the last few years have seen 300 attacks causing 3,000 casualties, meaning that the borders are not well managed.

Border-fencing of the 2,611 km porous border was to be done in phases. Rs 12 billion had been sanctioned for this purpose.[112] Under the Sir Mortimer Durand Line, Afghanistan relinquished Swat, Chitral and Chaghey; but it gained areas not before under its control notably Nuristan and Asmar. Afghanistan recognised the border in 1893, 1905, and 1919. In October 2017, at Angoor Ada village, the Afghans complained that the barbed wires would create 'hatred and resentment'.[113] Two years later, the Pakistan Army had completed the fencing of 900 km by 28 January 2019.

Border fencing became a more contentious exercise after the American exit and the entry of the Taliban into Afghanistan. Taliban forces stopped Pakistani soldiers from fencing the border. Although Pakistan has prudently refrained from recognising the Taliban regime, this time, the role played by Pakistan in evacuating American forces and their collaborators was seen as a sign of cooperation. On Christmas Day 2021, it was announced that the fencing issue had been resolved, but it was a manifest exaggeration. On 4 January 2022, Foreign Minister Shah Mahmood Qureshi conceded that discord existed over the fencing and the Taliban had pulled down part of the fencing. Thus, at the end of the Afghan wars, the hosting of 5 million refugees had not created any goodwill for Pakistan. The Afghan Defence Minister, Mullah Yaqub, son of Taliban founder Mullah Omar, said that Afghanistan was willing to send its troops to India for training.[114] Apparently, Taliban puritanism stopped at the destruction of the Bamiyan statues.

When former COAS General Mirza Aslam Beg had stated in 2001 that the Taliban would win, he was greeted with laughter[115] but as the longest war in American history prolonged, this result became progressively apparent. *The Washington Post* sifted through 2,000 pages of documents and announced the US was losing the Afghan war for lack of clear objectives.[116] The US war veterans launched a drive for a complete American pull-out: 'Keeping American troops in isolated bases is no longer critical to our security'.[117] Finally, pursuant to the American withdrawal the Taliban took over Kabul on Pakistan's Independence Day.

What did Pakistan gain from the two Afghan wars? Instability, insecurity, and insolvency. Pakistan would have been made the scapegoat for the American failure but for Senator Chris Van Hollen. Here's the exchange between Van Hollen and Anthony Blinken at the Senate Foreign Relations Committee hearing[118] on Capitol Hill:

> Van Hollen: 'Is it not the fact that the Trump administration asked the Pakistani government to release three top Taliban commanders as part of that process?'
> Blinken: 'That's correct'.
> Van Hollen: 'And one of them is now number two in the Taliban government, [Abdul Ghani] Baradar, right?'
> Blinken: 'That's correct.'

> Van Hollen: 'Now, let's see what the negotiation was: the US will leave by a certain date in May this year, right?'
> Blinken: 'Correct.'
> Van Hollen: 'You can't attack American forces, but you can attack the Afghan forces with impunity, right?'
> Blinken: 'That's correct.'
> Van Hollen: 'And so, we pick a date. We say to the Taliban you can attack Taliban forces and then we say, now let's negotiate the future of Afghanistan. Isn't the way it was set up when you walked in?'
> Blinken: 'That's essentially, yes.'

Pakistan should be grateful to Senator Van Hollen to avoid a greater reckoning than that awaits us. Another instance of truth, the most ironic confession that underpins a half-century of Pakistan's abject misery is the last interview given by Khan Abdul Ghaffar Khan, to an Indian journalist and carried by an Indian newspaper:

> Q. You mean the idea of Greater Pakhtoonistan is dead? Or do you mean that the concept does exist but that it's not causing any problems?
> A. The idea never helped us. In fact, it was never a reality. Successive Afghan governments just exploited it for their own political ends. It was only towards the end of his regime that Daoud Khan had stopped talking about it. And Taraki in the early part of his regime also didn't mention it. So when I met him, I thanked him for not raising the issue. But later, even he raised the issue because he wanted to continue the problem for Pakistan. Our people suffered greatly because of all this.[119]

Let us thank Khan Abdul Ghaffar Khan also, for all his services.

OTHER SAARC COUNTRIES.—With other SAARC countries, Sri Lanka, Nepal, the Maldives and Bhutan, Pakistan enjoys normal relations. They have no disputes with Pakistan and the SAARC meetings, especially the Summit meetings, have brought these countries closer than otherwise would have been the case.

Notes

1. S.M. Burke and S.A.D Qureshi, *The British Raj in India* (Karachi: OUP, 1995), pp. 563ff.
2. Penderel Moon (ed.), *Wavell: The Viceroy's Journal* (Karachi: OUP, 1974), p. 245.
3. Alastair Lamb, *Incomplete Partition* (Karachi: OUP, 1992), p. 108 vide. *Transfer of Power Papers* (London: HMSO), Vol. xi, No. 201.
4. Ibid., p. 118.
5. Burke and Qureshi, op. cit., p. 587.
6. Alastair Lamb, *Kashmir: A Disputed Legacy* (Karachi: OUP, 1992), p. 182.
7. Iqbal Akhund, *Memoirs of a Bystander* (Karachi: OUP, 1997), p. 118.
8. Roedad Khan (ed.), *The British Papers* (Karachi: OUP, 2002), p. 411.
9. *Dawn*, Karachi, 23 December 2003.

10. Ibid., 15 January 2007.
11. Jean Alphonse Bernard, *From Raj to Republic: A Political History of India,1935–2000* (New Delhi: Hara Anand Publications, 2001), p. 241. Also for a confirmation that India was willing to redraw boundaries in Kashmir, see Kuldip Nayar, *India: The Critical Years* (New Delhi: Vikas, 1971), p. 195.
12. *Dawn*, 14 October 2015.
13. *Dawn*, 28 February 2022.
14. *Dawn*, 22 December 2019.
15. *Dawn*, 26 December 2019.
16. *Dawn*, 22 August 2015.
17. *Dawn*, 8 January 2017.
18. *Dawn*, 6 March 2018.
19. *Dawn*, 3 April 2018.
20. *Dawn*, 14 April 2018.
21. *Dawn*, 16 March 2018.
22. *Dawn*, 7 May 2018.
23. *Dawn*, 16 July 2015.
24. *Dawn*, 26 July 2015.
25. *Dawn*, 29 August 2015.
26. *Dawn*, 15 November 2016.
27. *Dawn*, 21 October 2019.
28. *The Wire*, 23 August 2016.
29. Ibid., p. 6.
30. Ibid., pp. 13, 14.
31. *Dawn*, 2 October 2016.
32. *Dawn*, 28 May 2017.
33. *Dawn*, 6 May 2021.
34. *Dawn*, 4 May 2017.
35. *Dawn*, 30 March 2016.
36. *Dawn*, 19 May 2017.
37. *Dawn*, 26 May 2017.
38. *Dawn*, 21 February 2019.
39. *Dawn*, 18 July 2019.
40. *Dawn*, Ibid.
41. *Dawn*, 30 September 2016.
42. *Dawn*, 4 March 2019.
43. *Dawn*, 7 March 2019.
44. *Dawn*, 11 April 2019.
45. *Dawn*, 28 February 2019.
46. *Dawn*, 2 March 2019.
47. *Dawn*, 17 October 2015.
48. *Dawn*, 18 September 2016/
49. *Dawn*, 4 May 2017.
50. *Dawn*, 18 May 2018.
51. *Dawn*, 28 September 2019.
52. *Dawn*, 20 November 2019.
53. *Dawn*, 15 June 2018.
54. *Dawn*, 21 May 2019.
55. *Dawn*, 9 July 2019.
56. *Dawn*, 9 August 2019.
57. *Dawn*, 22 August 2019.
58. *Dawn*, 10 September 2019.
59. *Dawn*, 16 January 2020.

60. *Dawn*, 19 February 2020.
61. *Dawn*, 27 February 2020.
62. *Dawn*, 18 December 2020.
63. *Dawn*, 30 January 2021.
64. *Dawn*, 13 March 2021.
65. *Dawn*, 29 June 2021.
66. *Dawn*, 5 August 2021.
67. *Dawn*, 25 October 2021.
68. *Dawn*, 20 September 2016.
69. *Dawn*, 9 January 2017.
70. Dawn, 5 December 2019.
71. *Tribune India*, 29 November 2019.
72. *Dawn*, 15 January 2021.
73. *Dawn*, 7 April 2015.
74. *Dawn*, 24 September 2015.
75. *Dawn*, 30 April 2010.
76. *Dawn*, 3 July 2016.
77. *Dawn*, 16 September 2019.
78. *Dawn*, 30 October 2019.
79. TRT World, 3 September 2019.
80. *Dawn*, 24 November 2019.
81. *Dawn*, 15 February 2020.
82. *Dawn*, 2 March 2017.
83. Moonis Ahmar (ed.), *Challenge of Confidence-Building in South Asia* (New Delhi: Har Anand Publications, 2001), p. 346.
84. *Dawn*, 2 June 2011.
85. Arundhati Roy is the author of Soviet Intervention in *Afghanistan: Causes, Consequences, and India's Response* (New Delhi: Stosius Inc/Advent Books Division, 1987) and ten years later her Booker Prize-winning novel *God of Small Things* (New Delhi, 1997).
86. *Dawn*, 13 November 2011.
87. Cited in Arundhati Roy, *My Seditious Heart: Collected Nonfiction* (Chicago: Haymarket Books 2019).
88. *Dawn*, 10 March 2016.
89. *The Express Tribune*, 3 June 2016.
90. *Dawn*, 16 May 2017.
91. *Dawn*, 31 July 2017.
92. *The Express Tribune*, 8 October 2017.
93. *Dawn*, 17 January 2021.
94. *Dawn*, 24 August 2003.
95. *Dawn*, 23 November 2015.
96. *Dawn*, 7 January 2016.
97. Motiur Rahman Nizami was a very close friend of this writer and a class-fellow for three years and he cannot even imagine Nizami committing any of the un-Islamic crimes of murder, arson, and rape.
98. *Dawn*, 14 May 2016.
99. *Dawn*, 26 March 2021.
100. Quratulain Jaffar and Sadia Saeed, 'Pakistan and Afghanistan Claim over the Durand Line,' *Pakistan Journal of History and Culture*, vol. xli, no. 2, July–December 2020, pp. 244, 245.
101. *Dawn*, 1 April 2007.
102. *Dawn*, 24 June 2007.
103. *Dawn*, 8 June 2011.
104. *The Daily Times*, 21 November 2006.
105. *Dawn*, 15 April 2015.

106. *Dawn*, 7 December 2015.
107. *The Express Tribune*, 19 July 2016.
108. *Dawn*, 8 December 2016.
109. *Dawn*, 8 November 2018.
110. *Dawn*, 6 April 2020.
111. *Dawn*, 18 January 2013.
112. *Dawn*, 27 June 2017.
113. *Dawn*, 19 October 2017.
114. *The Express Tribune*, 5 June 2022.
115. General Mirza Aslam Beg, *Compulsions of Power* (Lahore: Adabiyat, 2021), p. 273.
116. *Dawn*, 10 December 2019.
117. *Dawn*, 21 January 2020.
118. *Dawn*, 16 September 2021.
119. Haroon Siddiqui, 'Everything in Afghanistan is done in the name of religion: Khan Abdul Ghaffar Khan', *India Today*, Issue Date: 31 March 1980, Reprinted: 19 November 2014.

Chapter 44
Pakistan, the Non-Aligned Movement, and the Muslim World

NON-ALIGNED MOVEMENT.—Pakistan was a non-aligned country from 1947 to 1954 and allied with the West from 1954 to 1979. From 1979 onwards it became once again non-aligned. In the first phase, the Cold War was raging and both America and the USSR were actively inducting allies. The American Secretary of State, John Foster Dulles, (1888–1959) under President Dwight D. Eisenhower (1890–1969), had a dictum that 'those who are not with us are against us.' It was against this background that Pakistan joined SEATO and CENTO. In the second phase, pacts had less to do with the conduct of foreign policy; NATO is still maintained though the Soviet counterpart, the Warsaw Pact, has disappeared. NATO now serves as a US superimposition upon the European Union (EU) states.

Pakistan co-sponsored the Bandung Conference in 1955 even after joining CENTO and SEATO, but its non-aligned status was challenged, and it could not continue. CENTO and SEATO petered out when both sponsors and client states considered them redundant; Pakistan after its breakup and Iran after its Revolution in 1979. Pakistan joined the Non-Aligned Movement (NAM) during its 1979 Havana Conference. Now there are so many economic configurations such as ASEAN, G8, etc., that the NAM no longer has the cohesiveness to be very active. At present, the North/South division between developed and developing countries has become a more prominent issue.

THE MUSLIM WORLD.—After the demise of CENTO it could be observed that all Muslim countries were non-aligned. After 1969, Muslim countries started becoming members of the Organization of Islamic Conference (OIC). In the last quarter of the 20th century, NAM and OIC had come to overlap. The unity and the glory of the Muslim world is one of the most sentimental concerns of Pakistani citizens, yet Pakistan's entry into the Muslim world was resisted and delayed.

1947–1967. At the time of its creation, Pakistan was the largest Muslim nation in terms of population. During the Freedom Movement, Indian Muslims had been blamed by their Hindu compatriots for looking outside India for inspiration. This referred not only to the religious duty of Muslims to look toward Makkah but also to their greater interest in the fortunes of the Middle East.

Although the Khilafat Movement had ended in failure, it showed the extent to which pan-Islamic sentiments could politically galvanize the Muslims of India. Quite naturally, on creation, Pakistan approached the Muslim world with its long-nurtured feelings of brotherhood and voiced sentiments echoing Muslim solidarity. Its leadership had, from time to time, called Pakistan a 'fortress of Islam' and a laboratory for Islamic statecraft. These Pakistani sentiments did not strike a responsive chord in the Muslim world.

The outcome was that the stress on Islam did not obtain for Pakistan a foothold in the Muslim world (especially the Middle East) but had a contrary effect. Sultan M. Khan, who was posted to Cairo, said that Pakistan had put forward proposals for an Islamic banking system, an Islamic Steamship Company, an Islamic news agency and an Islamic Conference to discuss important issues. This was considered trespassing on the preserves of the Arabs who felt that non-Arab Muslim countries would form a bloc with Pakistan.[1]

These were not merely racial feelings, it corresponded with the historical enmities in the Middle East. Arab countries led by Egypt had lost their independence to Britain and other Western countries. Therefore, on attaining freedom, Arab countries were averse to the West and looked to the USSR, the new enemy of the West. Non-Arab countries, particularly Turkey and Iran had a centuries-old conflict with Russia. They also shared frontiers with the USSR, and for their preservation, they looked to the US, its post-war enemy. With the Cold War dividing the Muslim world, Pakistan could not cater to a unified Muslim world. Its welcome in the non-Arab camp led to its being mistrusted in the Arab camp.

India had succeeded in portraying the creation of Pakistan as a British conspiracy, which is the opposite of the truth. However, after the assassination of Liaquat Ali Khan, Pakistan signed military pacts with Britain and America. This in itself was not too harmful. What happened was that in the first test of solidarity, Pakistan failed the Arabs. In July 1956, Britain, France, and Israel invaded Egypt because President Gamal Abdel Nasser had nationalized the Suez Canal. Pakistan sided with Britain against the Arabs, reinforcing the Indian propaganda that Pakistan was a British creation. First President Iskandar Mirza (on 26 July 1956), and then Prime Minister H.S. Suhrawardy explained to an indignant Pakistani public that, since the Arab world was of no consequence, Pakistan was siding with the invaders. 'Zero plus zero plus zero is equal to zero.'

This was adding insult to injury. Relations with Arab countries became bitter, a far cry from October 1951 when Pakistan had tried to form a block with Iran and Egypt, both countries then having anti-British administrations. One year later King Saud of Saudi Arabia visited Pakistan and India.

In 1956, despite its anger with Egypt, the USA forced Israel to vacate most of its Arab territory as did the USSR. After the war, there were changes in the region. There was a revolution in Iraq. Although Pakistan was allied to the West, due to its experience in the 1962 Sino–Indian war and the 1965 India–Pakistan war, Pakistan firmly sided with the Arabs in the 1967 Arab–Israeli war. The Six-Day War in 1967 was disastrous for the Arabs, but it was only in this war that Pakistan was able to rehabilitate itself in the Middle East.

1968 to 2009. After the 1967 war, neither was the USA inclined, nor the USSR able, to have the Arab lands vacated. 1968 saw the Arab world trying to return to normalcy after its trauma. In 1968 there were widespread student demonstrations in France as well as in Pakistan; both President Charles de Gaulle and President Ayub resigned. In 1969 a fanatic Jew set fire to the Al-Aqsa Mosque in Jerusalem. This outrage brought Muslim countries onto a single platform after centuries of division. The first Islamic Conference was held in Morocco. An Indian delegation was initially invited on the plea that India had a large Muslim minority, but when President Yahya Khan threatened a boycott, the Indian delegation was forced to withdraw. It was during the Ayub era that Pakistan began to woo the Arabs and it was in 1969 that this effort produced results. Had the first Islamic conference been held in the 1950s, India would have ousted Pakistan.

The second Islamic Conference was held in the aftermath of the 1973 Arab–Israeli war, in Lahore. It was a grand success but, on another level, the heightened relations with Arab nations resulted in a sliding of relations with non-Arab nations. Because Anwar Saadat of Egypt and Muammar Qaddafi of Libya came, neither the Shah of Iran nor his prime minister attended. It is rumoured that Pakistani Prime Minister Zulfikar Ali Bhutto had advised Middle Eastern countries to use the oil weapon; to withhold oil from supporters of Israel and sell it for a high price generally. The Organization of Petroleum Exporting Countries (OPEC) was not made up exclusively of Muslim countries but was dominated by them. The assassination in 1975 of King Faisal of Saudi Arabia, the co-host of the 1974 Lahore Conference, and the overthrow of Zulfikar Ali Bhutto in 1977 removed two of the most dynamic leaders of the Muslim world.

RCD/ECO.—Iran's cold response to the Lahore OIC was a new development. Turkey and Iran were Pakistan's partners in CENTO as well as in the Regional Cooperation for Development (RCD). Later, it was revealed that the RCD comprising Pakistan, Iran and Turkey was set up in 1964 to counter the influence of China over Pakistan. Neither CENTO nor RCD survived the 1979 Iranian Revolution, but the RCD was later transformed into a larger-based but low-key organization called the Economic Cooperation Organization (ECO). ECO signified Pakistan's approach to the newly independent Muslim Central Asian States. Turkey, Iran and Pakistan, the original RCD members, joined the Central Asian States Azerbaijan, Kyrgyzstan, Tajikistan, Turkmenistan, and Uzbekistan in February 1992 to form the ECO. A number of joint projects have been undertaken and trade barriers have been removed. The leaders of the Central Asian States (CAS) all accepted the invitation of Pakistan's Prime Minister, Nawaz Sharif, in 1991 to visit the country with a view to fostering closer relations between the states. The next important step was the visit, from 24 November to 18 December 1991, of a delegation led by Sardar Assef Ahmad Ali (Minister of State for Economic Affairs) to the Central Asian States.

A number of trade agreements were signed and an opportunity for a new vista in foreign relations was being opened up. Pakistan was willing to extend credit and provide facilities for privatizing Central Asian economies. This was a sound basis, but then relations cooled after 25 May 1997 when Pakistan recognized the Taliban regime in Afghanistan. Since Afghanistan lies between Pakistan and the ECO countries, this step had a cataclysmic effect. To Central Asian countries, the Taliban projected a militant and fanatical image of Islam. Even Iran and China, the closest neighbours of Pakistan, did not appreciate Pakistan's step and felt that friendship with Pakistan would bring Taliban-like regimes to their countries.

Even before the Taliban insurgency, the Central Asian States signed a mutual pact in 1996 to reduce armed forces along the former USSR and Chinese borders. In the Shanghai Cooperation Organization (SCO) set up in the same year, the CAS joined hands with Russia and China. This removed the thrust of their development from the South. Russia, from which CAS had gained freedom, gained a partial comeback because of unresolved disputes. Previously the Amu Darya and Syr Darya flows were controlled by the USSR; after independence, the northern states began hampering the flow of water to the southern states. Russia was called upon for the purpose of coordination, resulting in further loss of influence by Pakistan.

Big power rivalry surfaced briefly in 2001 when the US set up military bases at Manas in Kyrgyzstan and Khanabad in Uzbekistan. Russia later on (25 October 2003) opened an airbase in Kant, 35 miles from the US base. It publicly demanded that the US pullout from its Central Asian bases. This, in conjunction with Pakistan's post-9/11 anti-Taliban, volte-face afforded an opportunity to improve relations with the Central Asian States and revitalise the ECO.

2010 to 2022. The resurgent Taliban Movement, which has distinct sectarian overtones, moved into neighbouring Iran. A sound bomb exploded in Zahedan on 15 June 2005. In an almost unprecedented move, the foreign office summoned the Pakistani ambassador, Shafqat Saeed, 'to give explanations'.[2] It is quite apparent that Iran is adding its voice to the voice of the US/NATO forces to 'do more'. Suspicions were raised by the Iraq war, an Arab, non-Arab polarization raised concerns when Islamabad hosted a mini OIC Foreign Ministers summit on 25 February 2007. On 9 March, President Pervez Musharraf telephoned President Mahmoud Ahmadinejad assuring him 'that Pakistan would always guard Iran's interests' and reassuring Iran that the mini-summit was not directed against it.[3] In the meanwhile, the President of Iran visited Saudi Arabia on 4 March 2007 and agreed with King Abdullah that the sectarian violence stalking Iraq and Lebanon be jointly countered.[4]

The scene changes when we approach the present decade. First, the NAM became non-functional. When Egypt recognized Israel in 1979, when Yugoslavia broke up in 1992 and when India signed a Nuclear Defence Partnership with the US in 2008 all the three original proponents of the NAM had left. A bipolar world had been replaced by a multilateral world and the incentive for the NAM declined.

ARAB SPRING.[5]—The second decade of the 21st century was momentous. December 2010 saw populism ending in the Arab world: Tunisia's President Zine al-Abidine Ben Ali was forced by demonstrations to leave Tunisia on 14 January 2011; on 20 October 2011; NATO forces killed the President of Libya Muammar Gaddafi (20 October 2011); and following massive demonstrations in Tahrir Square, Cairo, President Hosni Mubarak resigned on 11 February 2011. However, the fruits of populism didn't last. Tunisia and Libya suffered instability and, in July 2013, General Abdel Fattah al-Sisi overthrew the elected President of Egypt, Mohamed al-Morsi (1951–2019).

We can reduce the events of the present era by marking the following events: (1) the failure of the Arab Spring; (2) the Yemen war and its sectarian fallout; (3) the replacement of Al-Qaeda by Daesh; (4) the preference given to Sufi Islam over Salafi Islam; (5) the Indian and Israeli footprints in the Gulf States and weakening of the OIC; (6) Saudi Arabia's dissonance with the UAE over OPEC+[6]; (7) unexpected Arab reaction over blasphemy in India; and (8) Chinese entry in OIC.

The only result of the Arab Spring, which ostensibly began to bring democracy and liberal values to Muslim countries, was massive waves of migrants entering Europe. The ideals cherished by the West could not flourish despite regime change in Tunisia, Libya, and Egypt. The reason being that within the Muslim world, the United States has closer relations with monarchies and dictatorships than with democratic countries.

The Yemen war broke out because of a coup launched by the Houthis. The Houthis follow a rare sect called the Zaidis who occupy a position in between Sunni and Shia Islam. They believe in the primacy of the descendants of the Prophet (PBUH) but revere the first two caliphs.[7] This still makes them heretics by Salafi standards and Saudi Arabia accuses Iran of being behind the Yemen war. This war led to the first contention between Pakistan and the UAE.

The UAE had expected Pakistan to join their war militarily and diplomatically. To its surprise, the parliament of Pakistan passed a resolution (11 April 2015) backing its government's commitment to protecting Saudi territory from the Houthis but declined the request of Riyadh to send Pakistani troops, ships, and warplanes inside Yemen. The reaction came from the UAE Foreign Minister Anwar Gargash: 'Iran was more important to Turkey and Pakistan, although they relied on investment from Arab states.' Talking to *Khaleej Times* the UAE foreign minister said he meant to warn Pakistan that it would have to pay a heavy price for its ambiguous stand.[8]

The Pakistani response was incendiary. Maulana Fazl-ur-Rehman accused the UAE of fomenting unrest in Balochistan and Karachi.[9]

The next day, Pakistan's Interior Minister Chaudhary Nisar Ali Khan stated: 'This is not only ironic but thought-provoking that a Minister of UAE is hurling threats at Pakistan.'[10] The response of Saudi Arabia, the country directly concerned was more sober. Saudi minister Saleh bin Abdul Aziz arrived in Pakistan to discuss the crisis: 'The resolution on Yemen is Pakistan's internal matter.'[11]

Since the Arab states had openly accused Iran of fomenting the Yemen crisis, this created a market for books on the sectarian divide in Pakistan.[12] Such publications ensured that those beliefs that are contested by the other sect, loom largely in the public eye.

The Al-Qaeda, considered responsible for 9/11, was replaced by an even more militant and puritan group known as the Islamic State of Iraq and Syria (ISIS) and by its Arabic acronym Daesh, which jumped into the strife, threatening shrines in both countries. Michael F. Scheuer, the former head of the CIA's Bin Laden Unit and one of the soberest analysts of Middle East affairs, described in an interview with UK's Channel 4 the ISIS advance on Baghdad as a development most beneficial to the US: '…our best hope right now is to get the Sunnis and Shias fighting each other and let them bleed each other white.' In Western academia, favour was bestowed on Salafi Islam while Afghanistan was occupied by the Soviet Union, but when the US occupied Afghanistan, Sufi Islam was promoted because of its pacifist nature.

The OIC which had been very active in the 1970s became an inconsequential body. The OIC was vociferous in supporting the Kashmir and Palestine causes, but at the OIC Foreign Ministers Conference on 1 and 2 March 2019, in Abu Dhabi the Indian Foreign Minister Sushma Swaraj was invited as a guest of honour. Pakistan apprised the OIC Secretary-General Yousef Al-Othaimeen that Pakistan would boycott the conference if the invitation to the Indian Foreign Minister was not withdrawn. There was a precedence. In the first OIC at Morocco in 1969, the Indian delegate Gurbachan Singh had his invitation withdrawn at Pakistan's instance. This time, with Pakistan's 'ambiguous' stand on Yemen, the invitation stood.[13]

Pakistan's Foreign Minister Shah Mahmood Qureshi kept away but stated that some officials of his ministry would participate to prevent India from being granted an observer status.[14] Next, the OIC led by Saudi Arabia, prevented Imran Khan from participating in the Kuala Lumpur Summit on Kashmir in December 2019. During a later visit to Malaysia, Imran Khan expressed his regret at missing the summit, attributing his absence to a 'misconception.'[15] The presidents of Iran and Turkey among others had attended.

On 13 August 2020, the United Arab Emirates (UAE) and Bahrain signed the Abraham Accords (mediated by the US under the Trump administration), officially recognizing the State of Israel.[16] Other Arab and Muslim-majority countries soon followed suit.[17] On 10 December 2020, Morocco signed a normalization agreement with Israel, becoming the second North African country—after Egypt in 1978 with the Camp David Accords—to recognize the Jewish State. Iran and Turkey deprecated the move. Saudi Arabia held back insisting on the 2002 peace plan proposed by the then Crown Prince Abdullah bin Abdul Aziz[18] which meant that Israel should go back to its pre-1967 frontiers in the implementation of Security Council Resolutions 242 and 338. Palestine applauded Pakistan's stand. Imran Khan said that Pakistan would not recognize Israel unless the State of Palestine was established[19]—a reference to the Camp David Accords. The recognition of Israel did nothing to change ground realities, and just one year later the OIC was urging the UNSC to stop Israeli violence in Palestine.[20]

The next UAE step was to relax Islamic laws to boost tolerance, allowing extra-marital affairs, relaxing alcohol restrictions, and criminalizing honour killings.[21] These steps also proved insufficient. The UAE's reaction to Indian politician Nupur Sharma's blasphemous remarks against the Holy Prophet (PBUH) caused outrage in Muslim countries. Saudi Arabia, Qatar, Jordan, Afghanistan, Iran, Indonesia and of course, Pakistan lodged protests with the Government of India.[22] Kuwait shopkeepers removed Indian products from their shelves and OIC as a body also registered its protest.

Oil diplomacy took the lead shortly after. A year before the Ukraine war (24 February 2022), an OPEC+ meeting was called off because the Covid-19 pandemic had reduced oil demand causing oil prices to plummet. Russia had demanded an increase in oil output, while Saudi Arabia had resisted it; but in January, all countries led by Saudi Arabia agreed to cut oil production by 1 million barrels per day.[23] Only the UAE had held back. The Saudi Energy Minister Abdulaziz bin Salman Al Saud commented: 'It is the whole group versus one country which is sad to me.' Such differences between UAE and Saudi Arabia were unprecedented.[24]

Another turn was witnessed during the Islamabad OIC Foreign Ministers Conference. It was addressed by Wang Yi the Foreign Minister of China. Senator Mushahid Husain Saiyid described the development as the emergence of a triangle between China, Saudi Arabia, and Pakistan.[25]

THE GAZA WAR.—On 7 October 2023, the situation underwent a significant change when Hamas, a Palestinian resistance group, initiated a large-scale attack on Israel. In their initial assault, Hamas launched 5,000 rockets, some of which successfully evaded the Iron Dome defence system, reportedly killing 200 Israelis. Despite being caught off guard, Israel retaliated on the same day, resulting in the death of 230 people in Gaza.[26]

The first international reaction came from US President Joe Biden who said that the US will always have Israel's back.[27] Thus emboldened, the Israelis continued their assault, resulting in the death of more than 370 people, including 20 children, the following day. On 18 October, Israel escalated its targeting to include hospitals in Gaza, with the al-Ahli Arab Hospital being struck, resulting in the tragic death of 500 Palestinians.

On 26 October, Israel initiated a comprehensive invasion of the Gaza Strip, leading to Palestinian casualties surpassing 7,000, and causing significant damage to healthcare facilities. Toward the conclusion of October, Israel declared that Phase II of its invasion was in progress.[28]

By 3 November, the death toll in Gaza had surpassed 9,000. Two days later, Israel targeted its first school in Gaza,[29] leading to hand-to-hand fighting. Subsequent attacks hit more hospitals and schools, with Israeli ground troops storming Al-Shifa Hospital, resulting in 24 casualties and the medical superintendent being held hostage.[30] Israeli claims that the hospital's basement served as Hamas headquarters were contradicted. The pause in war crimes, particularly the killing of children, occurred on 24 November 2023.

The United Nations and Gaza. Within two days of the Hamas attack, the United Nations Security Council (UNSC) convened, but no resolution was reached. The US insisted on including a condemnation of Hamas in the resolution,[31] causing an impasse. The UNSC reconvened on 17 October, and a Russian resolution condemning escalating violence in the Middle East was vetoed by the US.[32]

Addressing the UNSC on 24 October 2023 the UN Secretary-General Antonio Guterres said: 'I have condemned unequivocally the horrifying and unprecedented 7 October acts of terror by Hamas in Israel ... It is important to also recognize the attacks by Hamas did not happen in a vacuum. The Palestinian people have been subjected to 56 years of suffocating occupation. They have seen their land steadily devoured by settlements and plagued by violence; their economy stifled; their people displaced and their homes demolished. Their hopes for a political solution to their plight have been vanishing. But the grievances of the Palestinian people cannot justify the appalling attacks by Hamas. And those appalling attacks cannot justify the collective punishment of the Palestinian people. ... Even war has rules.' The Israeli response to this speech was to call for the resignation of the Secretary-General.[33]

Two days after the deadlock in the UNSC, the issue was brought before the United Nations General Assembly (UNGA). Ayman Safadi, the deputy prime minister of Jordan and spokesperson for Arab nations, highlighted that Israel had cabinet members advocating for the eradication of Palestinians. Sidi Mohamed Laghdaf, the Ambassador of Mauritania and spokesperson for the Organization of Islamic Cooperation (OIC), expressed regret that the lack of consensus had empowered Israel to pursue its illegal policy of colonial settlement and annexation with impunity.

Hossein Amir-Abdollahian, the foreign minister of Iran, stated at the UNGA that Hamas is prepared to release civilian hostages, but emphasized that the international community should also support the release of 6,000

Palestinians held in Israeli prisons. He criticized the characterization of Palestinian freedom fighters as terrorists.[34]

On 6 November 2023, the UN Secretary-General urgently called for an immediate cease-fire, stressing that all parties must adhere to their obligations under international humanitarian law. This urgent meeting of the UNSC had been convened by China and the UAE. Martin Griffiths, the Under-Secretary-General for Humanitarian Affairs and Emergency Relief Coordinator, conveyed to the UNSC that 'enough is enough; this must stop now.'[35] When the UNSC reconvened, it called for an extended humanitarian pause and the establishment of corridors through the Gaza Strip. However, many UN agencies rejected these plans for safe zones unless they were approved by both sides.[36]

Subsequently, the UNGA adopted six resolutions in favour of the Palestinians. By this time, over one hundred UN staff members had been reported killed. The resolutions included the following: (1) Authorizing a UN Committee to investigate Israeli actions against Human Rights—85 in favour, 13 against, and 32 abstentions. (2) The UN should demand that Israel cooperate with the Special Committee in implementing its manual. Israel must cease the exploitation, damage, etc. of the natural resources of Palestine. Also, Palestine would have the right to seek restitution for any such damage. The voting results for these demands were 151 in favour, 6 against, and 11 abstentions.

The US representative said: '… one-sided resolutions, whether put forward in the Security Council or here in our General Assembly's Fourth Committee, will not help to advance peace.'[37] Addressing the UNGA, Munir Akram speaking on behalf of a number of countries called for reforms to end UNSC stalemates.[38]

The US Factor. The US was the one that vetoed the Gaza cease-fire resolution in the UNSC. Israel's ability to resist global opinion has been sustained by the backing of the US, but this support is now showing signs of weakening. The American-Israel Public Affairs Committee (AIPAC), a highly influential organization, appears to have exerted significant influence on Middle East policy since the conclusion of President Dwight D. Eisenhower's term. Former US Presidents Jimmy Carter and Barack Obama have both voiced criticism of AIPAC,[39] as have some American authors.[40]

On 1 November 2023, in the US Congress, there was a request for approval of an additional $106 billion for Israel by the Secretaries of State and Defence. The most vocal opposition to this proposal came from Jewish Voice for Peace, as red hands were raised in protest.[41] The increasing civilian casualties in Gaza, including disturbing scenes of children being buried in large numbers, were evoking strong revulsion among the American public. While media had previously been controlled to shape public opinion, the rise of social media has made such control no longer feasible. Israeli spokespeople were also making aggressive statements, prompting a discerning segment of American society to become vocal in response.

A group of fourteen US Senators collectively advocated for a humanitarian pause in the conflict. Certain members of the Democratic Party co-authored a statement asserting that the $14.3 billion allocated to Israel was inconsistent with the Leahy Law. This was attributed to Israel's retaliatory attacks on Gaza, which were deemed to disproportionately harm civilians.[42] When Congresswoman Rashida Tlaib was censured for her anti-Israel remarks,[43] Pramila Jaypal rose to her defence.

LEAHY LAW

The 'Leahy Law,' also known as the Leahy Amendment, is a US law with two parts that stop the government from using money to help foreign security forces if there is good evidence, they have committed serious human rights violations (GVHR). One part applies to the State Department, and the other applies to the Department of Defense. The State Department Leahy law became permanent under section 620M of the Foreign Assistance Act of 1961, 22 U.S.C. 2378d. This law considers actions like torture, extrajudicial killing, enforced disappearance, and rape under the colour of law as GVHRs. Its goal is to prevent the US government from supporting foreign security forces involved in human rights violations, ensuring that US assistance doesn't endorse actions against human rights standards.

The stance of the US administration also started to toughen. US National Security Advisor Jack Sullivan emphasized that his country would not tolerate the Israeli reoccupation of Gaza.[43] Up to 400 government employees placed 10,000 carnations on the steps of Capitol Hill, symbolizing the reported number of casualties at that point. Their accompanying letter urged an immediate cease-fire, de-escalation, and the release of hostages.[44]

According to a Reuters/Ipsos poll, 68 per cent of Americans expressed a desire for peace, while 43 per cent were against sending weapons to Israel.[45] The NBC News poll indicated a significant decline in President Biden's approval ratings. Senator Bernie Sanders expressed the view that while Israel has the right to target Hamas, it does not have the right to engage in almost total warfare against the Palestinian people. This perspective, particularly prevalent among the youth, was evident as a substantial 70 per cent of voters aged 18 to 34 disapproved of President Biden's handling of the Gaza crisis.[46] On Saturday, 18 November, President Joe Biden authored an article in *The Washington Post*, emphasizing the necessity of reunifying the West Bank and Gaza under the Palestinian Authority. UN Secretary-General Antonio Guterres echoed the sentiments of the US President, advocating for a bolstered Palestinian Authority.[47]

Gaza Crisis and Pakistan. The Gaza crisis not only directly impacts Pakistan but also highlights a global unity based on humanity, which is reassuring for

Pakistan. Notably, China and Russia have taken a leading role in advocating for human rights in Gaza, despite both nations recognizing Israel. The crisis has also brought Russia and China closer to Iran and Turkey, traditional Cold War adversaries, which is likely to provide reassurance to Pakistan. In a significant move, Russian President Vladimir Putin, addressing the G-20 on 22 November, expressed the need to consider halting the tragedy of the war in Ukraine, emphasizing Russia's openness to peace talks with Ukraine.

Pakistan's Response. The Senate of Pakistan unanimously called for a Gaza cease-fire and lifting of the Israeli blockade of Gaza.[49] However, a problematic development ensued when President Arif Alvi, while speaking with Palestinians on the phone on 10 November 2023 said: 'If [the] two-state solution is not acceptable to Israel, then [a] one-state solution is the only way where Jews, Muslims and [a] good percentage of Christians could live to exercise equal political rights.' Within a few hours, the President retracted his statement.[50] The caretaker foreign minister Jalil Abbas Jalbani clarified that the President's one-state proposal did not align with the country's foreign policy.[51] President Arif Alvi, in subsequent discussions with the Imam of Ka'ba, reiterated that he had withdrawn his one-state solution proposal for Palestine.[52]

Munir Akram, the Permanent Representative of Pakistan, represented over eight countries when addressing the UNGA. "For more than a month now, a brutal war has raged in Gaza, with blatant war crimes and genocide being perpetrated by Israel against innocent Palestinian women and children. ... The primary reason for the Council's frequent failure to respond effectively ... is the inability of its permanent members to agree on decisive action.'[53] This situation echoed Z.A. Bhutto's 1971 statement at the UNSC, where he had vehemently criticized the veto system: 'We have been frustrated by the veto. Let's build a monument for the veto. Let's build a monument for impotence and incapacity.'[54] Munir Akram, in a matter-of-fact manner, reiterated the same point, emphasizing that this time Pakistan was aligning its stance with Russia.

Pakistan and Israel

Should, or should not Pakistan recognize Israel—this is the most debated question about Pakistan's relations with the Muslim World. There are two sides to the question: Ideological and Practical.

Ideologically Pakistan should refrain from recognizing Israel, as it is a country which is set up on usurped and occupied land. It has a bad human rights record and is the cause of the displacement of millions of Palestinians who have been stateless since 1948. Pragmatically, Pakistan should recognize Israel because it would neutralize US and Western objections to Pakistan's nuclearization and end the discrimination that Pakistan's nuclear programme faces. This is all the more urgent in view of the A.Q. Khan scandal. Libya has suffered no obloquy for exposing A.Q. Khan. It is not probable that the Arab world would criticize Pakistan for such a measure. India has suffered no dent in Arab relations because of its ties with Israel. The case of Palestine and Kashmir also, are not parallel, as Egypt and Jordan already recognize Israel.

A third factor is opportunity. Z.A. Bhutto recognized Bangladesh under the cover of the Islamic Summit. Pakistan has had only one such opportunity. The recognition of Israel should have been announced alongside the attainment of nuclear status. The Israeli ambassador to the US was desperately trying to contact his Pakistan counterpart in May 1998, to assure him that Israel had no intention of attacking Pakistan's nuclear facilities. Perhaps the lack of contact between two nuclear states is not good for world security.

The demilitarization of the Gaza strip provided an opportunity, and on 1 September 2005, the Israeli Foreign Minister Silvan Shalom (2003–2006) met his Pakistani counterpart, Khurshid Mahmud Kasuri, in Istanbul. After Musharraf, the leaders who subsequently rose to power in Pakistan did not embrace his strategic thinking regarding Israel. As of early 2023, Israel and Pakistan do not have diplomatic relations.

Notes

1. Sultan M. Khan, *Recollections and Reflections of a Pakistani Diplomat* (London: Centre of Pakistan Studies, 1997), p. 65.
2. *Dawn*, 19 February 2005.
3. *Dawn*, 9 March 2007.
4. *Dawn*, 18 March 2007.
5. A wave of pro-democracy protests and uprisings that took place in the Middle East and North Africa beginning in 2010 and 2011, challenging some of the region's entrenched authoritarian regimes.
6. Organization of the Petroleum Exporting Countries (OPEC) and its allies led by Russia, is known as OPEC+.
7. John L. Esposito, *The Oxford Dictionary of Islam* (New York: Oxford University Press, 2003), p. 347.
8. *Dawn*, 11 April 2015.
9. *Dawn*, 12 April 2015.
10. *Dawn*, 13 April 2015.
11. Ibid.
12. Works on the topic published before the Yemen war, S.H.M. Jafri, *The Origins and Early Development of Shia Islam* (London: Longman, 1979) and Wilferd Madelung, *The Succession to*

Muhammad: A Study of the Early Caliphate (Cambridge University Press, 1997) were works of high scholarship, but three books, all published in 2017 trailed behind. John McHugo, *A Concise History of Sunnis and Shi'is* (Georgetown University Press, 2018); Laurence Louër, *Sunnis and Shi'a: A Political History* (New Jersey: Princeton University Press, 2019); and Frederic Wehrey (ed.), *Beyond Sunni and Shia: The Roots of Sectarianism in a Changing Middle East* (New York: Oxford University Press, 2017).

13. *Dawn*, 28 February 2019.
14. *Dawn*, 2 March 2019.
15. *Dawn*, 5 February 2020.
16. *Dawn*, 14 August 2020.
17. *Dawn*, 14 September 2020.
18. Statement at the Council of the League of Arab States at the Summit Level, 14th Ordinary Session.
19. *Dawn*, 20 August 2020.
20. *Dawn*, 17 May 2021.
21. *Dawn*, 8 November 2021.
22. *The Express Tribune*, 7 June 2022.
23. *Dawn*, 10 January 2021.
24. *Dawn*, 6 June 2021.
25. *The Express Tribune*, 23 March 2022.
26. *Dawn*, 7 October 2023, p. 1.
27. *Dawn*, 8 October 2023.
28. *Dawn*, 30 October 2023, p. 1.
29. *Dawn*, 6 November 2023, p. 1.
30. *Dawn*, 18 November 2023, p. 1.
31. *Mideast Daily News*, online 9 October 2023.
32. *Dawn*, 18 October 2023, p. 11.
33. Consortium News.com, 25 October 2023.
34. *Dawn*, 27 October 2023, p. 11.
35. *Dawn*, 7 November 2023, p. 11.
36. *Dawn*, 17 November 2023, p.11
37. *Dawn*, 11 November 2023, p.11
38. *Dawn*, 18 November 2023, p. 12.
39. Jimmy Carter, *Palestine: Peace, Not Apartheid* (New York: Simon & Shuster, 2006); Barack Obama, *The Promised Land* (New York: Crown, 2020), pp. 628, 629.
40. John Mearsheimer & Stephen Walt, *The Israeli Lobby and US Foreign Policy* (New York: Farrar, Strauss and Giroux, 2007).
41. *Dawn*, 1 November 2023, p. 11.
42. *Dawn*, 5 November 2023, p. 11.
43. *Dawn*, 13 November 2023, p. 11.
44. *Dawn*, 15 November 2023, p. 11.
45. *Dawn*, 16 November 2023, p. 11.
46. *Dawn*, 21 November 2023, p. 11.
47. *Dawn*, 22 November 2023, p. 11.
48. *Dawn*, 25 May 2023, p. 1.
49. *Dawn*, 2 November 2023, p. 12.
50. *Dawn*, 11 November 2023, p. 12.
51. *Dawn*, 22 November 2023, p. 12.
52. *Dawn*, 24 November 2023, p. 12.
53. *Dawn*, 18 November 2023, p. 12.
54. Henry Tanner, 'Bhutto denounces Council and Walks Out in Tears', *The New York Times*, 16 Dec. 1971.

Part 9
Economic History

Chapter 45

Economic Development

The first objection to be made to the creation of Pakistan was that the state would not be economically viable, i.e., it would not have the finances to survive. After Pakistan was created, the Government of India refused to give its share of financial assets. The excuse that Nehru gave was that since there was a war over Kashmir, by handing over the financial resources, India would be helping Pakistan to defeat it. Gandhi, however, saw the injustice of this stance. He went on a hunger strike against the Government of India, forcing it to hand over 17.5 per cent of Pakistan's share. Gandhi was killed by Nathuram Godse, a member of the Rashtriya Swayamsevak Sangh; one of the reasons for his anger with Gandhi was the fact that he had helped Pakistan.

Yet, despite the amount that was received, which was just one instalment of the amount due, Pakistan was seriously short of finances. As has been mentioned before, the Nizam of Hyderabad sent a cheque for a large sum of money, but Nehru did not allow it to be encashed. Pakistan overcame this financial crisis, the worst in its history, with the help of its businessmen.

Pakistan's economy was indeed very weak at the time. It was too dependent on agriculture, which contributed 60 per cent of its income. The savings rate was as low as 5 per cent of the gross domestic product (GDP), which is very low. GDP means the total value of the goods and services produced by the country in one year. To take an example, suppose a country produces 100 tons of bananas which sell for Rs 50,000 a ton, the income from the domestic product, bananas, is Rs 50 million in a year. The country now also offers tourism, which fetches Rs 20 million a year. Tourism is a service and like bananas it is also a 'product' since it is marketed by the people of the country. The GDP of this country is then, Rs 70 million.

The financial system was very basic and at Independence, Pakistan had no central bank. A central bank is required to control a country's money supply, which helps in determining the buying power of money. A central bank fixes monetary policy which includes the rate of interest. This further helps people in calculating the risks and gains of their ventures. A central bank is also required to regulate other, mostly private banks. A central bank is subject to political control. Therefore, under those hostile circumstances, it was even more necessary for Pakistan to set up its own central bank which could issue its own currency notes if its economic independence was to be upheld. This was the reason why Jinnah, despite his severe illness, travelled from Ziarat to Karachi to open the State Bank of Pakistan on 1 July 1948.

In the agriculture sector, the land tenure system and the low level of agricultural technology were responsible for low productivity. The only redeeming feature was that Pakistan had inherited part of a well-developed irrigation system. Industries were inadequate, rather informal, and at that time could not be optimally utilized because of riots and mass migration. There was a small nucleus of industrial units around Lahore; diesel engines were being manufactured, electric fans were being produced, and the machine tool factories had actually started exports in 1942. The Darra Adam Khel Arms factory, although efficient, was considered to be outside the formal sector of the economy. The withholding of military assets by India had raised disappointment to a level that even these available resources were not visible, even during the Kashmir war.

Pakistan survived, as Richard Symonds has observed, because the harvest in 1947 was good, and there were sufficient peasants to harvest it. The two initial years involved the management of the economy on a daily basis and there was no real development except for the establishment of the State Bank during Jinnah's lifetime.

In those early years, industrialization was seen as the only road to progress, therefore, Liaquat Ali Khan set up two corporations in the public sector, one for heavy and one for light industries. Under these corporations, the government would provide financing to an extent not forthcoming from the private sector. As a priority, it planned to set up three jute mills in East Bengal. This need can be understood when we recall that it had a large crop of jute fibre but no mill at all to process it. There were a few cotton mills in the western wing, but hardly in proportion to the size of the cotton crop in Sindh and Punjab.

However, once the economy stabilized there was progress. All governments gave priority to development. Gross national product (GNP) increased on an average by 5 per cent a year. Undeniably there have been setbacks, there have been lapses, but Pakistan survived not only the partition of the Punjab in 1947 but also the loss of East Pakistan in 1971.

ECONOMIC HISTORY.—The economic history of Pakistan can generally be divided into five phases: (i) The initial era of crisis management: this corresponds to the first democratic era from 1947 to 1958. (ii) The era of determined planning: this characterizes the Ayub era. (iii) The re-orientation of growth strategy: This covers the first PPP regime 1971–77. (iv) Distancing the economy from state capitalism: the Zia era reaction to Bhutto's policy, and finally (v) Attempting structural reforms; the current phase.

The establishment of the State Bank of Pakistan in 1948 proved to be the first symbol of Pakistan's economic independence, and in the following year, Pakistan asserted itself by refusing to fall in line with Britain and India when they devalued their currencies by 37 per cent. This was not rancour on the part of Pakistan as imagined. Devaluation, a political decision to decrease the value of one's currency in relation to other currencies, may have enhanced exports but would also have increased the domestic price of imported goods on which Pakistan relied much more than India did. In retaliation, instead of paying higher prices to Pakistan for the same goods, India suspended all trade links. Among those who exported raw materials to India, the most important were the jute growers of East Bengal. If India did not buy jute, they would have no other means of subsistence. Liaquat Ali Khan approached the jute growers and undertook to buy the whole crop to prevent it from being sold at devalued rates.

As an indication of how Pakistan weathered the crisis, the per capita income increased by 1.4 per cent. Per capita income means the income of a country divided by the number of its inhabitants. Agriculture increased by 2.6 per cent and the manufacturing sector by as much as 23.5 per cent. External factors were responsible for constricting Pakistan's economy, but the Korean War (1950–53) proved to be a factor highly conducive to growth. The Korean War created a demand for raw materials at enhanced rates. Pakistan's decision not to devalue in 1949 paid off, since it was able to sell at a higher exchange rate. It was also able to sell to different countries, which meant, in other words, diversifying the market.

Along with the Korean War boom, planning was needed to deal with the recession that would follow, when the war ended, and the demand ceased. Pakistan had two choices. The first involved devaluation coupled with the rationing of imports. Rationing meant fixing the amount of a particular item that could be imported. The second was to re-impose trade and foreign exchange controls. The Government of Pakistan exercised the second option, with the expectation that the manufacture of goods that were previously imported, would grow. The government-imposed tariffs, a tax on imports and exports, which meant that consumer goods would become more costly. Since rising costs could reduce profits it was thought that investing in such industries that produced goods already in demand, would increase.

The government decided to make the process of imports a category of reward for the companies which had imported during the crisis period. In other words, to those firms who placed reliance on the government and had imported goods when the prospects were not bright, the government issued licences to import. Ultimately, this step led to the sale of licences. Uneven management skills or confidence in firms induced them to sell their licences to other parties who were more confident of making a larger profit on those licences. This system had the effect of engendering rent-seeking, a practice which became entrenched and still persists. Rent seeking means that instead of trying to improve the quality of the goods and services they provide, businessmen approach the government to enact legislation to make their businesses more profitable.

When countries set priorities, it means that some sectors of the economy perform better than others. But those segments of the economy which were earlier neglected, also need to be developed. If a country has the resources, it can allow all segments of the economy to develop together, but when the resources are limited, some segments are neglected. Thus initially, while industry progressed, agriculture lagged behind. It was also felt, at that time, that investment in education and social development had been too low, and this neglect would have an impact on other sectors of the economy. For example, if there were not enough educated people who could perform their functions in a commercial firm, or if healthcare facilities were not provided, it would reduce the commitment and efficiency of the workforce.

One reason for the concentration on the industry was that Western countries had been extremely reluctant to sell Pakistan, components for those industries which already existed in India. In their scheme of business, Western countries wanted Pakistan's industry to be subordinate to the Indian industry. In practical terms, it meant that Pakistan must depend on Indian industries to purchase its raw material at prices of their choice. Pakistan needed to avoid this. In these circumstances, only some East European countries, strapped for hard cash, were ready to sell industrial units or components to Pakistan. Since these countries were also Soviet satellites, political exigencies prevented this market from expanding.

The decision to promote import substitution industrialization was based on the premise that the terms of trade would, in the long run, prove unattractive to producers of primary commodities, and also on the premise that the capitalist sector had a greater propensity to save. It was hoped that the aggregate savings ratio could be enhanced by incentives for capital formation.

This brings us to planning, which is covered separately in the next chapter, but here we need to outline the initial efforts and the delay in beginning to plan. The Pakistan Planning Board was set up in 1951 but did not prove to be very active. Before 1955, no serious planning was undertaken. Even when the First Five-Year Plan (1955–1960) was made, the objectives were too ambitious, therefore, only a modicum of them could be achieved. The Plan sought to reduce regional disparities, increase both agricultural and industrial production, increase exports, and increase the rate of savings.

Naturally not all of these objectives could be achieved, at least, not at a uniform rate. Nevertheless, the exercise in planning was essential since it was long overdue. The exercise had begun a full eight years after the creation of Pakistan. This exercise accelerated the process of consolidation and experimentation. The Plan did provide incentives, to industry, but not to agriculture or education. This was not surprising as agriculture had been allocated only 11 per cent of the total investment. This stagnation of agriculture naturally constrained other sectors of the economy.

AYUB KHAN ERA.—After the first democratic phase of Pakistan's history there came the first military regime of Ayub Khan. A Green Revolution was set in force, during the Second Five-Year Plan (1960–1965), by increasing irrigation and introducing mechanized farming and fertilizers. The growth rate of agriculture increased from 1.43 to 5.1 per cent. To boost exports the Ayub regime introduced, in 1959, a Bonus Voucher Scheme which was intended to provide price incentives to the exporters of selected manufactured goods. Within three years, the net export of commodities covered by the Bonus Voucher Scheme saw a 40 per cent increase.

The Second Five-Year Plan was viewed as successful, and Pakistan was held up as a model for other countries, for, contrary to the socialist trend in Asia, Pakistan was setting up units in the public sector and then selling them to the private sector. Of course, as noted when priorities are set, they are achieved at a cost. In this case, the cost was social and ideological. When Dr Mahbub ul Haq, a bureaucrat during the Ayub era, stated that the wealth of Pakistan was concentrated in the hands of twenty-two families, people turned their focus away from the production of wealth to its distribution. The flow of production had to be slowed down due to the 1965 war. Thereafter, production decreased, and wealth continued to be distributed unevenly.

The 1965 war proved to be a serious economic setback, not only because foreign aid was curtailed but also because the crops failed that year. This forced Pakistan to change its development strategy, especially as far as sectoral allocations were concerned. Agriculture was given greater importance. Greater attention was given to installed industries and consumer goods because they required less foreign exchange and had better export prospects.

The 1971 war proved far more calamitous. It is often asserted that the 1971 war had its origin in the economic deprivation of the East wing. The eastern wing had greater resources such as jute, but these were exploited mainly by non-Bengali investment and enterprise. This not only caused resentment but led to attacks on non-Bengali jute workers.

ZULFIKAR ALI BHUTTO ERA.—Zulfikar Ali Bhutto's nationalization programmes are widely regretted today, but they were an inevitable outcome of Mahbub ul Haq's pronouncement that twenty-two families controlled the country's economy, and, of a sense of ethnic deprivation. Bhutto's nationalization received great condemnation, but Sheikh Mujibur Rahman's simultaneous nationalization did not receive any condemnation although it was more disastrous. Bhutto at least had the excuse of the massive dislocation caused by the war. Two essential items, matchboxes and paper were exclusively supplied by the eastern wing. West Pakistan was also the largest market for tea from East Pakistan. As the residual, Pakistan had to arrange its emergency imports at high costs.

By 1972, the PPP government had nationalized thirty-two large manufacturing units in eight major industries. On 1 January 1974, Bhutto nationalized local banks and all life insurance companies as well. During Bhutto's term, there was a 50 per cent reduction in private investment; the capital that could not be transferred abroad was used to finance small-scale industry. Syed Akbar Zaidi has shown that these small units, unafraid on the account of nationalization, came forward and were proved to be expanding the economy.[1]

When PPP nationalized, it was forgotten by its opponents that the unmitigated dependence on the private sector, the pro-industry bias, the increasing dependence on foreign aid and the neglect of human development had led to some distortions and regional imbalances which had come to the political forefront. The reliance on the private sector was based on the expectation that the capitalists had a better propensity to save, but Pakistani capitalists were not as frugal as had been expected.

On the other hand, since a substantial part of the saving was done by the twenty-two families, they were able to pre-empt credit facilities from commercial banks and specialized financial institutions. It was this factor which led to the clamour for better income distribution that Bhutto had to deal with.

Zulfikar Ali Bhutto re-oriented growth strategy in the face of East Pakistan's secession, to take the edge off the more abrasive aspects of development planning, and, in doing so, he had to redefine the concept of a mixed economy. Unfortunately, Bhutto began this process in a most unseemly manner by arresting the two leading industrialists of Pakistan. This set off a war of attrition between the political and economic forces of the country, and worse, Bhutto referred to his tenure as commerce minister in a manner which indicated industry-agriculture rivalry. Thus his economic policies encountered more resistance than was warranted by his reforms.

Bhutto was justified in giving the government a greater share in economic planning. He scaled down economic planning and nationalized it according to political strategy. For example, after leaving the business community in suspense, he nationalized banks and insurance companies on 1 January 1974. Meanwhile, he consolidated the nationalization of industrial units.

Since Bhutto had been blamed for being softer on the agricultural sector than on the industrial sector, he overreached himself by nationalizing small agro-based industries. This was an important reason why the small-town businessman participated in the 1977 upheaval against Bhutto. It is also forgotten that Bhutto's reforms had an unlucky start; his announcement of reforms was greeted by massive floods and exceptionally high oil prices, which were keenly felt because Bhutto had devalued the Pakistan rupee by 57 per cent.

However, since Bhutto was adept at both granting and withholding concessions, he removed all official bottlenecks for a wave of temporary migration to Arab countries. This improved the employment opportunities in the urban centres which had been polarized because of the language controversy and increased the income of the lower and middle classes. Another feature was that, at a time when slow growth in output had increased inflation, the home remittances gave a fillip to price pressure since they increased the demand for consumer goods.

In a similar development, we see that because of the nationalization, the sustainability of large-scale industry allowed small-scale industries to emerge as a major economic factor. It was the small-scale industries which benefited from the devaluation which offset the excessive fiscal advantage that accrued to large-scale industries. On the political level, it was increased trade union activity which led businessmen to move towards smaller units. The government had simplified import procedures, and this also contributed to the greater advantages of the smaller units.

Between 1969–70 and 1976–77, the Yahya and Zia years, the commodity-producing sector grew by 2.2 per cent per annum as against the 6.4 per cent output growth in the service sector. This increased price levels. In the 1970s the consumer price index rose, on average, by 12.5 per cent per annum, up from 3.2 per cent in the 1960s. Although the PPP's economic performance was marred by a slow output rate and high inflation, objectively viewed, it was not dismal. It was cruel and ridiculous for Bhutto's opponents to claim that they would be able to reduce prices to pre-1970 levels when Bhutto was removed. Although this may not sound like an achievement, Bhutto not only laid the foundations of the capital goods industry, but he also protected the incomes of the industrial labour force and low-wage earners in the public sector. The performance of the nationalized industries was not as bad as alleged, and the banks showed a profit until lending large sums of money without collateral became a means of patronage in the Zia era.

ZIAUL HAQ ERA.—The two defining trends of the Ziaul Haq era (1977–88) were the Soviet invasion of Afghanistan, and the sharply rising fiscal deficits. Fiscal deficits mean that the government was granting more subsidies than it was collecting taxes, leading to a deficit. The Afghan war led to a large increase in aid inflow since Zia had wisely refused to accept 'peanuts' from the USA. On an ideological basis, the government made some attempts at denationalization and privatization, but despite a sense of triumph over Bhutto's removal, capital remained shy, and even now it has not regained confidence. The rate of savings at 9 per cent average was quite low, therefore foreign exchange was far more welcome than Zia had claimed.

Pakistan's economy grew in this period by 6.5 per cent and the rate of inflation averaged 7.3 per cent. The growth of public debt remained under control under the PPP in the 1980s, though the domestic debt grew far too high. On the other hand, Pakistan, during the 1980s, became self-sufficient in all types of foods except edible oils.

Structural Reforms 1988. By the time democratic regimes were reinstalled, debt-servicing comprised 80 per cent of the GDP. This growth of public debt was caused by neglect of financial discipline, poor use of fiscal resources and the high cost of borrowing. External debt also rose sharply but this was not due to internal slackness, but because international capital was available on extremely onerous terms. From 1972 to 1999, the percentage of concessional aid had fallen from 73 to 53 per cent. The official rate of interest increased, bringing it close to the market rate.

The 11 September 2002 terrorist attack on the US brought Pakistan to the right side of the war on terror. Pakistan again became a front-line state. It received short-term debt relief, debt forgiveness, and debt restructuring. Trade concessions and an increase in formal home remittances provided further respite. Fortunately, this time round, Pakistan had effective policies to reduce external debt and liabilities. These were structural adjustments which will be explained. During the Pervez Musharraf regime, and for the last three consecutive years, Pakistan had a current account surplus. (Current accounts are where transaction means income for the recipient. This is in contrast with capital accounts where no actual rise in income takes place, but the form in which assets are held, changes).

Apart from home remittances, exports also increased, and after a long time, foreign exchange reserves were high. External debt and liability considered as a percentage of GDP fell from 51.7 per cent in the financial year 1990–2000 to 37.8 per cent in 2003–4. Considered as a percentage of foreign exchange earnings they have decreased from 297.33 to 168.7 per cent during the same period. It is because of a hostile security environment that these figures have not been heartening.

Structural Adjustment Programme 1988. Realizing that a mere reversal of the PPP's nationalization programme was not enough, a structural adjustment programme was put into effect which basically means the encouragement of the private sector's participation in the expansion of the rural/agricultural sector. The government not only abolished regulatory restrictions such as making businesses dependent on government licences but also provided infrastructure like roads and ports so that the private sector could benefit from government measures. Power generation was opened to private enterprise with government subsidies on power and grains being withdrawn. Tax exemptions, previously extended to urban areas, have been extended to rural areas since 1995.

The Structural Adjustment Programme has come in for some criticism. Firstly for its belief that marketization is the only route to economic progress. This, in other words, means that markets are allowed to govern economic decisions. This system disregards the external forces which loom large in Pakistan. Monopolies can distort the market because of a collective decision like any taken by any government department, and income distribution is affected, as was witnessed at the end of the Ayub era.

Pakistan has gone for budget cutting, i.e., removing items from the budget due to financial constraints, exchange rate depreciation, interest rate liberalization, realistic prices without subsidies and trade liberalization. These are positive features but were considered ill-timed. Trade liberalization was premature because it resulted in de-industrialization. An estimated 4,000 industrial units have closed down. Budget cutting at a time when Pakistan was faced with a recession made economic revival more remote. The exchange depreciation increased the rupee value of external debts without enhancing exports. An interest rate liberalization meant that the government had to borrow at a higher rate of interest.

What is important is that this fallout was managed soundly because of the support of international institutions, local political support, consistency, and transparency of policies. In 2003–4, the GDP grew by 6.4 per cent, per capita income by 4 per cent and the manufacturing sector registered a growth rate of 17 per cent. During 2005, the fiscal deficit was contained at 4 per cent of the GDP and the government was able to repay more than 1.6 billion dollars to its foreign lenders.

Since Pakistan had achieved macroeconomic stability over the last five years, many economists expect the government to enlarge the Public Sector Development Plan, while others argue that the base is not broad enough.

There is an argument that the private sector should be encouraged to increase expenditure. Here the focus is on the textile industry. Apart from its large size, the textile industry is notable for two features: firstly, it was not touched by nationalization, and secondly, it has had to cope with the industry-agriculture tension: while cotton growers wanted to export directly at a higher price, cotton mill owners claimed primacy over crops.

Since 2000, more than $4 billion have been invested in the textile sector, but overall private investment has been languid, at a rate of about 11 per cent of the GDP during this time. The principal reason cited for this is that there is considerable excess capacity in some industries. This fact underscores the need for a modicum of planned economy. As the Multi Fibre Agreement (MFA), which ensured a share in exports, has expired, the only way to survive is to be competitive.

The Challenge of Globalization. Globalization of the economy means free international trade and free movement of capital across the globe. This is based on common information which enables multinational firms to calculate the widest parameters for their products and to select the cheapest locations for any product in terms of labour, availability of raw materials or transport.

We can survive globalization by being competitive which means that we make technological progress, develop our human resources by imbuing the working force with better knowledge and skills, encourage flexibility and adaptability in organizations and ensure that the role of capital and finance is positive. In Pakistan, firms are generally small, and technologically they are underdeveloped, they have unskilled workers and, of course, an undeveloped financial sector.

Firms by themselves are unable to remedy these defects. The government will have to help, chiefly by investing in public infrastructure, providing low-cost transportation, and facilitating exports. Experience has shown that sound economic policies without sound economic institutions are not very effective. The government could help by removing infrastructural bottlenecks, for example by repairing the irrigation system. Water supply dominates the discourse of the present (ninth) Five-Year Plan and future agricultural development will have to rely on greater efficiency in water management. With the ideological debate now behind us, we can pursue pro-poor policies. This could be done by building a network of institutions at the village level. The devolution of power scheme can be instrumental in achieving this. There is a need to focus on infrastructure projects that can provide greater employment. The growth of small industries must be accelerated and greater education opportunities and expanding health care can help to achieve this goal.

The Rise and Fall of the BCCI

One of the most spectacular successes of private enterprise in Pakistan was the establishment of the Bank of Credit and Commerce International (BCCI). Its fall, therefore, proved most confounding. At its height, the BCCI had 398 branches in 72 countries. The moving spirit behind the bank was Agha Hasan Abedi (1922–95) Obtaining an MA in English Literature and a Law degree, Abedi joined the Habib Bank in 1946. In 1959, he received financial backing from the House of Saigols to set up the United Bank Ltd. in 1959. The United Bank became synonymous with push and drive, or to put it in less staid terms, ambition. The United Bank in time set up 912 branches in Pakistan, and 24 branches in foreign lands. The opening of a new bank branch was perceived as a repository of more deposits and more capital. The Habib Bank remained conservative; insisting for example, that its staff acquire academic expertise in banking, the United Bank, allegedly waived this requirement if the employee under reference was able to attract sizeable deposits. Symptomatically, Habib Zurich the second largest international bank did not have a sensational success, nor did it suffer a dramatic decline and still carries on.

Although the incoming PPP regime was to nationalize banks on 1 January 1974, Abedi, as head of the United Bank anticipated the move, and as early as 1972, he had founded the BCCI in cooperation with the Bank of America. This institution ran anti-clockwise to the socialist direction of the economy. Just as employment in the Gulf and Middle Eastern countries, offset the constricting elements of nationalization; obtaining employment in the BCCI was considered striking bonanza because the pay scale and perquisites were much higher than those prevailing then in Pakistan. The cream of the Pakistani banking talent was recruited, but the recruitment went on till after the Bank was incurring losses.

Abedi was not neglectful of the demands of philanthropy. On the one side, he inducted former US President Jimmy Carter into Global 2000, one of its benevolent institutions. He set up the Orangi Pilot Project in 1980, a project to take up city planning to sanitation, in the largest urban area in Karachi. The BCCI Foundation set up two prestigious educational institutes in Pakistan, the Foundation for Advancement of Science and Technology (FAST), now a university specializing in Information Technology and the Ghulam Ishaq Khan Institute of Engineering Sciences and Technology at Topi, Khyber Pakhtunkhwa. These are flourishing despite the closure of the BCCI.

What could cause such a massive enterprise to fail? Only a massive lack of collateral. *The Wall Street Journal* reported that huge loans were given to the Gokal brothers, the shipping magnates: $30 million in 1978, $70 million in 1979, and $71 million in 1981. Although no direct connection can be proved, this was around the time that Mustafa Gokal was a member of Zia cabinet. Testifying before the US Senate, Masihur Rahman, an employee, pinpointed the Gokals as the biggest reason for the bank's downfall.[1] The salaries and emoluments of the employees were also a major reason. BCCI showed an operational loss of $40 million in 1988, but instead of retrenchments, new appointments continued.[2]

The year 1988 proved to be an inauspicious year. Agha Hasan Abedi suffered a heart attack and had to withdraw from the bank's affairs. In October of the same year, drug money laundering charges were brought against the BCCI. There was some discrepancy between the roles of the employers and the employees who were indicted at Tampa. The prosecutors conceded in December 1988 that the defendants 'did not receive any personal monetary gain from this alleged money laundering, neither did they accept the bribes offered by the undercover agents.'[3]

Was it a bubble that had burst on the pin of laundering charges, or was it an exercise to liquidate an institution that could stand in the way of imposing World Bank/IMF conditionalities? It was, it seems, a little of both. The BCCI pleaded guilty to the charges. Other banks charged simultaneously with the BCCI were treated more leniently. The American Bank of Dade County confessed to laundering $90 million. more than six times the amount the BCCI was accused of laundering. Banco de Occidente, Panama had to pay a fine of $5 million for laundering $411 million, which is a slap on the wrist compared to the liquidation of the BCCI.

A crucial factor was the US endeavour to charge Manuel Noriega (d. 2017) for drug money laundering. The New World Order had begun. Meanwhile, in February 1991 Agha Hasan Abedi was set to launch his third venture. It was to be called the Progressive Bank.

Notes

1. *Newsline*, Karachi, September 1991, p. 56.
2. Ibid., June 1990, p. 100.
3. *Herald*, Karachi, March 1991, p. 125.

THE ECONOMY OF PAKISTAN, 2008-2022.—From 2008 to 2018 the economy of Pakistan declined; from 2018 to 2022 the decline accelerated. Why it declined is apparent. Dr Shahida Wizarat said that governments in Pakistan went to the International Monetary Fund (IMF) for budgetary support without studying the sustainability of debts. Pakistan's debts have become unsustainable.[2]

The framework within which Pakistan's economy declined remains a matter of debate. It is difficult to determine whether the decline of the Pakistani economy is a triumph of Capitalism or its failure. With the collapse of Communism, only the traditional Capitalism headed by the United States or State Capitalism headed by China remains. Neither has been able to provide a solution to Pakistan.

It can easily be projected that the nationalization under the first PPP regime (1971-77) alienated capital and since then investment has been shy. Why State-Owned Enterprises (SOE) are running at a loss is not as clear. Be it Pakistan International Airlines, Pakistan Steel Mills, and the Pakistan Railways have been run profitably in the past but are now being regarded as White Elephants. Pakistan Railways, till the 1970s had warranted a separate budget. In the passages that follow, we shall, in sequence seek some explanations, but speaking broadly we see some factors being commonly blamed: the complacency of the staff brought about by security of service; overstaffing and corruption.

There is a clamour that we privatise SOEs. Latent in that clamour is the belief that the SOEs are by themselves feasible, but that their management has failed. But has privatization succeeded? The power sector is a case in point. The distribution systems have worsened after privatization. Copper wires have been replaced by cheap aluminium wire. The tariff has gone on increasing while the quality of service has gone on decreasing, leading to power outages and power riots.

Some of the ailments are not peculiar to Pakistan. Oxfam reported that the richest 1 per cent owned 82 per cent of the wealth created in 2017. Oxfam noted: 'The billionaire boom is not a sign of a thriving economy but a symptom of a failing economic system.'[3] *Foreign Affairs* published a section on Capitalism in which it was pointed out that Globalization had provided plutocrats with tax havens to locate their capital. In any case, Globalization meant the globalization of capital, not labour. In Pakistan, the tax base is woefully narrow. Moreover, it is met by the argument that taxation lessens profits, or it makes Pakistani goods uncompetitive in the global market.

IMF loans began in 1959 when the Pakistani economy was flourishing. During the PTI regime from 2018 to 2022, it peaked. Every IMF loan is accompanied by demands for structural adjustments, such as: (1) closing the loopholes and improving tax collection domestically; (2) privatizing SOEs, and deregulating state-controlled industries in order to attract foreign investment; (3) cutting public sector employment subsidies and other spending to reduce budget deficits.

TAXATION.—Because the period of economic decline coincides with democratic regimes, it is widely held that legislators protect their own sectors from taxation (clearly, it means Agricultural Income Tax). It is a very contentious issue. Those who favour imposing Agricultural Income Tax (AIT) have the following arguments:

(1) Agriculture constitutes nearly a quarter of Pakistan's GDP but only one per cent of tax revenues. Farmers enjoy all manners of subsidized inputs. In truth, hundreds of billions are transferred from the urban to the rural sector, much of it ending in the pockets of big and powerful landowners. At harvest times the demand for expensive cars increases.[4]

(2) In 2020, agriculture contributed Rs 11.5 trillion to the GDP, yet the total AIT collection was less than Rs 3 billion or 0.02 per cent of agriculture GDP. In 2019–20, the national AIT was Rs 2.75 billion; Punjab paid 74 per cent, Sindh 22 per cent, Khyber Pakhtunkhwa and Balochistan together paid three per cent. Section 41 of the Income Tax Ordinance 2001 exempts agricultural income from the federal income tax, leaving it to the provinces. Taxpayers claiming an exemption from the Federal Bureau of Revenue (FBR) have to declare such income and confirm that they have paid provincial tax on agricultural income. FBR data shows that 165,000 individuals claimed exemption from AIT, but while a number of taxpayers are claiming exemption, they are not paying provincial dues, taking advantage of different jurisdictions and enforcement agencies.[5] This argument places the loss on discordant administration. The laws are there but separate statements provide a loophole. This is compounded by the rule that while tax evasion is illegal, tax avoidance is legal. This thin line too, is blurred because of the outmoded system of collection. Provincial land tax and land administration systems have been in place since the colonial period. AIT is effectively a tax on land and not a tax on income, and provinces have not revised the land rates to reflect changes in the income potential from land.[6]

(3) Feudal lords prefer to pay the tax calculated by measuring the area under cultivation and yield per acre as calculated by revenue officials. Thus it is clear that administrative obsolescence and dysfunction are responsible for poor tax collection. In view of the fact that AIT in 2020–21 was Rs 3 billion or merely two per cent of agricultural GDP, state institutions like NADRA can help in comparing and reconciling federal and provincial revenue records.

Arguments against levying agricultural tax are mainly that: With over 96 per cent of farmers owning less than 12.5 acres does the government think that they can make money out of land? In 2015, Rs 100 billion Kissan Package and in 2016 Rs 100 billion as interest-free loans. Subsidy and taxation together do not make sense.[7] This means that four per cent of farmers who have larger holdings are liable to pay AIT. It is simply a matter of taxing the rich, but how to identify them.

Benazir Bhutto a year after her second ouster revealed in a videotaped interview that out of a population of 130 million (30 years ago), only 800,000 pay taxes and out of these 500, 000 are government servants whose tax is deducted at source. She proposed a survey in which owners of Land Cruiser cars or houses built over an area of 1000 square yards or above be identified and taxed. The 'machinery' as she termed the income tax bureaucracy did not heed her. Then she forwarded a proposal to privatize tax collection. A party had asked her for a Lahore market and guaranteed a thirty-time increase over current receipts. She was told this was illegal as the department would first have to float tenders and award the assignment to the highest bidder. In such a case the guarantee would be taken out.[8]

That the majority of farmers are poor is no argument against taxing the rich. It is only a question of fixing a threshold. The urban/rural divide bias theory also does not hold water because for non-agricultural income the first Rs 400,000 are exempt while for agricultural income only Rs 80,000 are exempt.[9] An advocacy group has contended that the largest gap in revenue collection is in corporate income tax which is 3.7 per cent of the GDP. Only 40 per cent of companies registered with the Securities and Exchange Commission of Pakistan (SECP) file returns and only 60 per cent of those who file returns declare any profit.

In Punjab, the revenue potential in urban immovable property tax is almost Rs 25 billion. If collected a ten-time increase could be realized.[10] The IMF and some federal ministers are demanding that AIT become a federal cess, but it should be apparent from the above figures that this would be a cosmetic exercise.[11] Another practice to cause the economic landslide was writing off bank loans, apparently against political support as they were advanced without collateral. It was reported in 2012 that Rs 112.305 billion were written off in the previous four years. A number of 1,434 clients benefited from both public and private banks.[12]

Six years later the Supreme Court summoned the representatives of 222 firms and companies for their role in getting non-performing loans worth millions of rupees written off. Soon after the October 2002 elections President Pervez Musharraf and Finance Minister Shaukat Aziz allowed the State Bank of Pakistan to have loans written off. A Commission headed by former Justice Syed Jamshed Ali Shah released a report stating that Rs 87 billion in loans were written off (1971 to 2009).[13]

In the next hearing the Chief Justice observed: 'We are surprised to learn that despite making default on returning the loans, the companies are still functioning and running their business.'[14] The loans were written off under Banking Policy Department (BPD) Circular No. 29 of 2002. The Syed Jamshed Shah Commission examined 740 cases and regretted that despite its efforts, banks, and development financial institutions (DFI) had not provided information about the loans sanctioned or written off on 'other than business considerations'.[15] Legally, since the banks were reluctant to prosecute, recovery of these loans would be difficult.

AMNESTY SCHEMES.—From time to time, the Government of Pakistan launches amnesty schemes in the hope of recovering undeclared or ill-gotten wealth. In 2018, more than 55,000 individuals availed of this scheme as it would render the balance of their holdings legal. In 2019, another amnesty scheme was launched which allowed real estate investors to pay one per cent tax on 1.5 per cent of the Deputy Commissioner's value of the land. This rate was less than one-fifth to one-tenth of the market value.[16]

EX-PAKISTAN INVESTMENT.—While real estate income remained lucrative at home, as the above-mentioned amnesty scheme shows, the investors sought new pastures. The dismemberment of Pakistan towards the end of 1971 and the independence of the oil-rich Trucial States in 1972 provided employment and investment opportunities to Pakistanis in what was renamed the United Arab Emirates.

By 2015 Pakistanis had bought property worth 16 billion dirhams in Dubai alone when the one dirham was equal to Rs 27. However, by this time, Indian investment had exceeded the investment of Pakistan.[17] Only two years later in Pakistan, a National Assembly Panel was set up to track the loopholes in the system that allowed massive investment abroad, especially in Dubai. An FIA team told the panel that they had a list of 100 Pakistanis who owned properties in Dubai. The FIA and the FBR failed to elicit information from UAE authorities.[18]

Early the next year (2018) Ashraf Malkham a journalist briefing the National Assembly claimed that he had a soft copy of an FBR document listing 3,363 Pakistanis who had properties in Dubai. The FBR spokesman present said that he was not aware his office had such a list.[19]

The Supreme Court also took *suo moto* notice and tried to develop guidelines and ways to retrieve money from Pakistanis who had stashed money illegally in foreign bank accounts or property. The Committee could suggest only an amnesty scheme as the only way to recover the money.[20] In the next hearing, while the Supreme Court received a report to the effect that $15.25 billion were sent abroad in a single year (2016–17) both through normal banking channels as well as through promissory notes that were illegal tender, the only progress reported was the promulgation of the Foreign Assets (Declaration and Repatriation) Ordinance 2018. The significant feature of the Ordinance was immunity promised from taxation or penal action on the declaration of foreign assets. The Committee did note the adverse impact of this practice on the Pakistani economy.[21] As a member noted on 8 November 2017: 'The most powerful and the strongest people have properties abroad.'

THE UNTOUCHABLES.—A year later the FIA made a high-profile arrest. Hussain Lawai, then Chairman of the Central Depository Company and Vice-Chairman of the Summit Bank and his associates were arrested in a case the FIA was investigating transactions of Rs 35 billion in twenty-nine 'fake' bank accounts for the purpose of money laundering. The report added that Hussain Lawai was believed to be close to former President Asif Ali Zardari, who at that space of the report was described as Chief Executive of the Institute of Bankers, Pakistan. The advanced age and the record of Hussain Lawai caused his arrest to be seen as a part of a political vendetta and eventually, he was released.

The power of capital was nevertheless asserted. A delegation of industrialists and businessmen called on Prime Minister Imran Khan and demanded that exported goods be untaxed. The same goods the Prime Minister countered would be taxed if sold in the local market. The zero-rating of export commodities ran from 2005 to 2009 when the PPP withdrew the facility. The PML (N) revived it in 2015. The meeting was inconclusive, but the delegation was told that tax would be levied on all products, but products that are exported would have the dues refunded on the provision of full details.[22]

In October of the same year, two news items were published. The first describes a meeting of businessmen with the COAS General Qamar Javed Bajwa. The Federal Minister for Economic Affairs Hammad Azhar said the businessmen were upbeat after their meeting with the army chief. The same issue carried an item stating that the National Accountability Bureau (NAB) would not investigate cases of tax evasion and bank default and that such cases shall be the jurisdiction of the FBR.[23]

PRIVATIZATION.—Were the units founded originally in the public sector, or those nationalized in 1972–77 running at a profit? They were not. Therefore there was a demand that the once prestigious and profitable units like PIA, PSM, and Pakistan Railways be privatized. Their sale would offset the debt accruing to the government. The clear implication was that government servants with their services secure had no incentive to deliver; while private parties with a smaller workforce would have an incentive to earn profits.

We have stated above that with the collapse of Communism in 1991, the rivalry was between Capitalism and State Capitalism. How have SOEs led China to world power status and Pakistan to ruination? Branko Milanović observed that: 'production is generally organized in the most hierarchal fashion, not the most democratic. Workers do not vote on the products they would like to produce, or on how to produce them.'[24] Concentration of wealth is also not the culprit as even in the US, the top 10 per cent own more than 90 per cent of the financial assets.²⁵

In late November, Finance Minister Ishaq Dar said that 90 per cent of the privatization proceeds would be utilised to clear debts. Dar put the total domestic debt at Rs 18,093 billion and revealed that in the previous financial year 2014–15, Rs 1,304 billion was spent on debt servicing. Dar explained that the IMF loan of $18 billion by September 2015 was meant exclusively to build foreign exchange reserves and had not been used for budgetary support. Both profit-making and loss-incurring units were to be privatized.²⁶ The loss incurred while running SOEs was becoming unsustainable, but was privatization viable? The Asian Development Bank reported in 1998 that only 23 per cent of SOEs were doing better in private hands and the number of units that had shut down was high.²⁷

PAKISTAN RAILWAYS.—Chief Justice of Pakistan Gulzar Ahmed (2019–2022) while hearing a plea for the regularization of 76,000 railways employees, turned around and said the railways were suffering from over-staffing and incompetence. Not only were the overstaffed employees preventing profits, but their incompetence also caused horrible rail accidents.²⁸ On the surface, this was puzzling. Passengers had to book seats fifteen days in advance and even then, the trains were overcrowded. While the overcrowding nullified the quality of railway service, the loss can be explained only by over-staffing and pilferage. Chief Justice Saqib Nisar had ordered an audit of the Railways account by a private firm.²⁹ The closure of two luxury trains—Shalimar Express and Sir Syed Express—led to an inquiry. The ticket checkers were surprisingly not approached, but the train drivers said that track rehabilitation was needed. Instead of repairing the old railway tracks, railway authorities were forcing drivers to run on defective tracks; a practice that led to accidents.

Railways are one of the oldest SOEs. Railway stations brought civilization in the midst of wilderness and rail travel was prestigious. The railways are acquiring new bogeys essential to enhance service quality, but railway tracks are not receiving commensurate attention.

PAKISTAN STEEL MILLS (PSM).—Senator Lt.-Gen. (retd.) Abdul Qayyum said that during his tenure as PSM Chairman (2004–2006), he had inherited liabilities of Rs 7.8 billion, but in three years the PSM earned a gross profit of about Rs 18 billion and paid Rs 6 billion in taxes.³⁰

According to a usually reliable source, the turnaround came out because of drastic measures. Firstly a massive consortium bank loan was retired, and then a very low-interest loan was taken for bridge financing. An eye was kept on the international steel market, and progressively prices were increased. The increased prices were below that of imported steel. The demand always exceeded the supply, so the profit margin went on increasing. The PSM initiated maintenance, and despite the fact that the machinery had become obsolete, value addition was achieved. Some slab production was retained because the railways needed them, but cold rolling and hot rolling made the products a fast-selling item. Financial discipline was ensured, and over-staffing was firmly resisted. These measures went into the turnaround mentioned by Lt.-Gen. Abdul Qayyum.

This is a case study that shows that once profitable SOEs can be made profitable again if administered honestly and efficiently. It also shows that such a turnaround needs to be sustained. Chief Justice Iftikhar Muhammad Chaudhry forbade its sale in 2006, after which the downslide resumed. The PSM's debt liability in November 2012 exceeded Rs 82 billion.[31] For three years the PSM faced a gas shortage (see Circular Debt). It had two real options, either to pay Sui Southern Gas Company Limited its bill of Rs 35 billion or execute a plant shutdown. Neither of the options was exercised and the PSM was kept in heating mode.

Insiders revealed that there was a problem with the plant, despite being run on off-specification raw material and non-maintenance since 2007 but the new chief executives and his directors had no relevant background and experience, and this took its toll on the PSM. Yet the management expected that a Rs 5 billion bailout would be effective.[32]

Senator Aitzaz Ahsan had a simple explanation. Since Prime Minister Nawaz Sharif owned Ittefaq Foundries (Pvt) Ltd., it was an open and shut case of conflict of interest between the Sharif family and the State, and the PSM was forcibly made to underperform.[33] One year later the import bill of iron and steel scrap had risen to Rs 1 billion. It was stated that heavy taxation was imposed on the shipbreaking sector which provided cheap scrap. Although the PSM was not in production, its semi-finished and finished products billets and slabs were substitutes for the scrap needs of the steel industry.[34]

The next year the Government of Pakistan attempted to lease out the PSM for forty-five years, but nothing came of it. With privatization had come the hope that the machinery would be replaced.[35] The very next day the Privatization Committee decided to float a company to run the PSM for thirty years on the basis of sharing the revenue. The land would be retained while the plants and machinery would be handed over.[36]

One year later Senator Taj Haider complained that the gas connection to the PSM was cut exactly on the day it had broken even: 'In the last meeting I had proposed that iron billets[,] of a quantity enough to produce coils worth Rs 5 billion[,] were lying in the PSM and these coils could be produced if gas supply...to that sector was restored. The ministry would not agree.'[37]

During the Covid-19 pandemic, China showed an interest in running the PSM, figures were shared, but no progress was reported.[38] In the next step, 9,350 employees were removed at a total cost of about Rs 20 billion.[39] Two days later the estimate had gone up to Rs 40 billion.[40] On the same day, the Senate was told that SOE losses were exceeding the Defence budget of Pakistan. Thus, the PSM remained in a state between functioning and privatization, with a punch line yet to come. It was reported that assets worth Rs 10 billion were stolen from the PSM. On the night of 27 July 2022 about fifty robbers had entered the steel mill and looted copper wires.[41] The following day the action of the PSM was to dismiss engineer Abdul Rahman who had prepared the report of the theft.[42] The upshot was that when on 25 October 2023. The PSM was offered for sale, there were no buyers.

PAKISTAN INTERNATIONAL AIRLINES (PIA).—Overstaffing is a feature that runs through all SOEs. Democratic regimes pressed to alleviate unemployment but could not offer openings in private entities, so the only recourse was the over-staffing of SOEs. From the 1950s to the 1970s PIA was one of the world's leading airlines. Its revenue allowed it to accommodate sportsmen, even to build a Squash Complex and to make strides in poultry farming. It had China as a destination which it shared with very few airlines. Air Marshals Nur Khan and Asghar Khan headed it in succession. When nationalization began in 1972, PIA actually flourished. Mian Mohammad Rafique Saigol a member of the twenty-two families became managing director. In 1974 Air Marshal Nur Khan was re-appointed managing director, but his second stint was not as successful as his first.

The ultimate result was that the financial foundations of PIA were shaken. Workers went on strike when conditions deteriorated and on 2 February 2016, two PIA employees were killed while protesting. The decline was gradual, and the causes were many. The PML (N) government had introduced an Open Skies policy, which took away the home space advantage from PIA. The oil-rich Gulf countries formed their own airlines, which provided competition to PIA over its most lucrative routes.[43] When Parliament debated the plight of PIA, Senator Farhatullah Babar suggested code-sharing with other airlines to share traffic. This would increase the number of destinations and revenue.[44] A fault was found with the type of aircraft. Four DC-10 aircraft had been replaced by Boeing 747 which lacked fuel efficiency.

The 2016 crisis and the strike lasted till April when PIA withdrew termination letters issued to striking employees.[45] It was then revealed that over the decade, PIA had sustained a loss of Rs 400 billion. A business plan was prepared to obviate the necessity of privatization. The Government of Pakistan was providing PIA guarantees against loans, not the loans themselves. The financial cost was Rs 3 billion per month including the Rs 1 billion markup. PIA requested an interest write-off, not the principal, but the request, although quite reasonable was not heeded.[46]

The Covid-19 pandemic starting in January 2020 affected most airlines, as travel was restricted, and air routes closed. PIA already staggering was hit hard. A PIA spokesperson said the losses and debts had become too much for the airline to handle. An option suggested was that the Government of Pakistan include debt-to-equity swaps and issuance of long-term bonds.[47]

This grim outlook showed that PIA had no need for further crises, but more were on the way. Commenting on the PIA air crash in Karachi on 22 May 2020, Aviation Minister Ghulam Sarwar Khan stated that 40 per cent of Pakistani pilots held fake licences. How many passengers and routes this single indiscretion costs can only be imagined. The Director General of the Civil Aviation Authority Hasan Nasir Jamy clarified that all licences issued by it were genuine and valid.[48] How much of the damage was controlled, is a matter of conjecture.

Then Malaysian authorities seized a PIA Boeing 777 aircraft on 15 January 2021 because of a case pending in a British court.[49] A Malaysian court released the aircraft after Peregrine Aviation Charlie Limited withdrew its suit.[50] Mercifully PIA won the case in the UK Supreme Court. The judgment was delivered on 18 August 2021.[51]

CIRCULAR DEBT.—As mentioned earlier, Sui Southern Gas Co. Ltd. (a government entity) stopped supplying gas to Pakistan Steel Mills (another government entity) for non-payment. Each entity needs to show a profit, otherwise, it shall be shut down and this shall be deemed a loss to the whole economy. Circular Debt is formally defined as a situation which occurs when one entity facing problems with cash inflows, holds back payment to its suppliers and creditors.

Earlier, electricity was at the head of circular debt. The Asian Development Bank attributed circular debt to the inefficiency of the Distribution Company (DISCO) = 31 per cent delayed tariff adjustment 35 per cent financial costs and unbudgeted subsidies 16 per cent.[52] However, privatised components like K-Electric (Karachi) are making huge profits through frequent power shutdowns. The private party did not fulfil its promise of re-vamping the distribution system, and copper wire has been largely replaced with aluminium wire.

TEXTILE INDUSTRY.—The textile industry never touched by nationalization complains of the lack of power to run its mills. In January 2017, when the textile industry became crisis-ridden, a report bemoaning the shortage of electricity had also this observation: 'Only those manufacturers which invested heavily in their own energy production survived.' The same report says, 'the biggest manufacturers have been provided power without interruption.'[53]

The textile sector is the largest export-oriented sector, which moreover employs the largest amount of labour. It has been enjoying subsidies, but two questions emerge. Why was power production not replicated by the whole industry? Second, why were Faisalabad units given uninterrupted power supplies while units located elsewhere were not given priority? Ever since it has been revealed that Bangladesh which does not even produce cotton has overtaken the Pakistani textile industry in terms of exports, the local industry has come to be viewed unsympathetically. Their second complaint is valid, that is the delayed refunding of extra tax.

Another report six months later from Lahore reported that both owners and workers of textile mills observed Black Day. Their demand was the release of a Rs 180 billion package, abolition of turnover and general infrastructure developments taxes, quick refunds of sales tax, fixed electricity, and gas tariffs, and to do away with the extra tax of Rs 3.63 per unit on electricity. They also demanded an end to textile imports from China and India. All these demands are fair because concessions could be treated as investments. However, according to the same report: 'In Faisalabad meanwhile, many of the factory workers who were taking part in protests against the government didn't really know why they had been asked to take to the streets.'[54]

The government relented and announced an export sector support package. The trouble was that even after the passage of a year there had been no implementation. The electric distribution companies not only charged the agreed 7.5 cents per unit till June but also started charging a quarterly adjustment of Rs 1.8 over and above the agreed rate. Electricity and gas charges had gone on increasing despite assurances.[55] Only fifteen days later the textile industry was facing a liquidity crunch.

After removing five export-oriented sectors from zero rating on 1 July 2019 under IMF pressure, the government imposed a 17 per cent sales tax on export on the assurance that refunds would be paid in 72 hours, but that had never materialized. Rs 80 billion was outstanding and because of the liquidity crunch, they could neither disburse salaries nor purchase raw material for new orders.

The textile industry has its critics. As far back as 2007 a correspondent claimed that more than seventy leading textile units posted loss worth Rs 100 million, but only seven textile mills had shown Rs 100 million profit. In the same year (2005–6) exports increased from $14.41 billion to $16.5 billion—a 15 per cent growth.[56] Such criticism of the textile industry remained valid only till the export figures showed an increase. In February 2020, textile exports increased by 17 per cent. However, during the Covid-19 pandemic, it declined by 64.5 per cent by April.[57] Whatever the IMF demands, whatever the complaints, the Government of Pakistan should enable the country to compete with Bangladesh and Vietnam, with all the resources at its command, including tax-free import of fibre.

SILK INDUSTRY.—Till 1993, Swat alone had 400 silk mills. During the operations against the militants by 1994 the number had come down to 100. The replacement of manual power looms with new technology helped silk mills to survive although it cost massive unemployment. What broke the industry's back was the import of Indian silk. One mill owner complained that Indian units were getting electricity at Rs 7 per unit, as against Rs 20 charged from Pakistani mills. The new technology—water jet looms—caused a decline in quality. The report clearly says that Indian silk was imported, it does not say that it was smuggled. This means bureaucratic neglect has its share in the economic plight of Pakistan.

SUGAR INDUSTRY.—The Pakistan Sugar Mills Association published an advertisement saying that they did not want a subsidy but only a policy enabling export. Their case was that in 2017 and 2019 farmers produced a record crop taking sugar production 7.1 metric tons, while the consumption was 5.1 mt. When the world market was $550 the government disallowed export. It allowed exports only when the prices went down to $325. The main complaint of the association was that despite a crash the Government of Pakistan maintained a support price of Rs 180 per 40 kg which meant the cost of sugar was Rs 63 per kg. This rendered the export price below the cost of production.[58]

The main point of contention is pricing by sugarcane farmers and the export or equity price of refined sugar. In 2021, the Ministry of Industries calculated that at Rs 200 per maund, the retail price of sugar should have been between Rs 75 to 80, but the rates in Sindh were Rs 300, in Punjab Rs 270 and Rs 290 in Khyber Pakhtunkhwa. Smuggling and the role of middlemen were ascribed as the cause of the cost increase between agriculture and industry. Another complaint is that sugarcane crops consume a very large amount of water which could be diverted to other crops and sugar imported on a net saving. Stevia the organic sugar substitute has been grown successfully in Pakistan. Dr Kaiser Bengali has described Pakistan's sugar industry as artificial.[59]

INTERNATIONAL MONETARY FUND (IMF).—We have given the example of two industries to show that privatization is not a panacea. The IMF demands it, but no creditor in the world has the welfare of the debtor in mind. Creditors impose conditions that either ensure the return of their money or enslave the debtor. Why should we expect a different treatment from the IMF?

We can make a beginning by at least closing the loopholes. Rs 423 billion lapsed in 2017–18 because ministries did not return the unspent money on time. Thus an administrative lapse proved costly.[60] Over Rs 60 billion untaxed foreign income was detected by the Large Taxpayers' Office. Pakistani individuals were paid through a US-based company Payoneer. Another novel way of avoiding tax was depositing money in bank accounts far from commercial centres.[61]

FEDERAL BUREAU OF REVENUE (FBR).—The FBR is the body responsible for collecting cash and other cess. Whether the Bureau was ineffectual, or the chairman was ineffectual is a question that is answered by saying that in three years we have had six chairpersons of the FBR. One Chairman Mohammad Javed Ghani revealed that Rs 1.856 billion were stuck up because of litigation. Litigation was in turn stuck up because vacant positions in the relevant tribunals were not being filled.[62] Another Chairman Asim Ahmad was removed because of a cyber-attack on the FBR database. 'He did not install sufficient security to protect the data of the taxpayers.'[63] The reason why Syed Shabbar Zaidi resigned as Chairman is the most interesting of all. In a television interview, Shabbar Zaidi mentioned the theory of elite capture of power and resources in Pakistan. He added that this phenomenon coupled with unbridled corruption in state institutions had assured that he could not deliver as chairman, and that is why he resigned.[64]

* * * *

14 August 2022, the 75th anniversary of Independence, Pakistan's economy has come full circle. In 1947 plutocrats jumped in to save Pakistan from insolvency when India had withheld Pakistan's share of financial assets. In 1968, came Dr Mahbub ul Haq with the intelligence that the wealth of Pakistan was held by twenty-two families. In 1972, Zulfikar Ali Bhutto arrested leading industrialists and threatened to keep hostages if money stashed abroad was not brought back.

In 2023, such a threat shall not be necessary. In view of the present financial crisis, with hyperinflation, the sovereign status of Pakistan is in danger. If God forbid, such a situation arises, all of Pakistan's wealth stashed abroad shall be forfeited to the Government of India. Plain business sense makes that clear.

Notes

1. Syed Akbar Zaidi, *Issues in Pakistan's Economy* (Karachi: Oxford University Press, 2005), p. 131.
2. *The Express Tribune*, 1 August 2022.
3. *Dawn*, 23 January 2018.
4. *Dawn*, 30 May 2016.
5. *The Express Tribune*, 31 August 2021.
6. Anjum Nasim, *Dawn*, 4 April 2021.
7. *Dawn*, 31 October 2016.
8. *The Economist*, 21 August 1997.
9. *Dawn*, 31 October 2016.
10. *The Express Tribune*, 3 May 2016.
11. *Dawn*, 23 September 2019.
12. *Dawn*, 8 September 2012.
13. *Dawn*, 19 May 2018.
14. *Dawn*, 9 June 2018.
15. Ibid.
16. *Dawn*, 23 May 2019.
17. *Dawn*, 17 February 2015.
18. *Dawn*, 9 November 2017.
19. *Dawn*, 10 February 2018.
20. *Dawn*, 15 March 2018.
21. *Dawn*, 23 June 2018.
22. *Dawn*, 3 June 2019.
23. *Dawn*, 7 October 2019.
24. *Foreign Affairs*, Jan/Feb 2020, p. 20.
25. Ibid., p. 14.

26. *Dawn*, 28 November 2015.
27. *Dawn*, 5 March 2015.
28. *Dawn*, 13 June 2020.
29. *Dawn*, 29 April 2018.
30. *Dawn*, 6 June 2020.
31. *Dawn*, 10 November 2012.
32. Dawn, 6 August 2015.
33. *Dawn*, 19 September 2015.
34. *The Express Tribune*, 25 July 2016.
35. *Dawn*, 17 January 2017.
36. *Dawn*,18 January 2017.
37. *Dawn*, 18 March 2018.
38. *Dawn*, 5 April 2020.
39. *Dawn*, 4 June 2020.
40. *Dawn*, 6 June 2020.
41. *The Express Tribune*, 1 August 2022.
42. *The Express Tribune*, 2 August 2022.
43. *Dawn*, 9 February 2016.
44. *Dawn*, 11 February 2016.
45. *Dawn*, 7 April 2017.
46. *Dawn*, 3 November 2017.
47. *Dawn*, 28 March 2020.
48. *Dawn*, 16 July 2020.
49. *Dawn*, 18 January 2021.
50. *Dawn*, 28 January 2021.
51. *Dawn*, 19 August 2021.
52. *The Express Tribune*, 18 July 2022.
53. *Dawn*, 9 January 2017.
54. *Dawn*, 21 June 2017.
55. *Dawn*, 30 September 2019.
56. *Dawn*, 18 March 2007.
57. *Dawn*, 14 May 2020.
58. *Dawn*, 15 April 2020.
59. *Dawn*, 27 November 2012
60. *Dawn*, 20 February 2020.
61. *Dawn*, 25 January 2020.
62. *Dawn*, 14 October 2020
63. *Dawn*, 25 August 2021
64. *Dawn*, 1 December 2020

Chapter 46
Economic Planning

Why do countries need to plan ahead? To ensure that the available resources of a country are utilized to their maximum advantage. Planning means deciding how to best organize the factors of production. The factors of production are land, which includes all natural resources employed in production; labour, which includes all mental and physical human resources; and capital which includes money and other goods and services utilized in the production of goods.

Planning means taking decisions about what and how much to produce, and how to distribute what is produced. To take these decisions, economists must have a comprehensive knowledge of what a country possesses and what a country requires. Planning has to be long-term, and this is what differentiates it from annual budgets. Economic development, as Parvez Hasan states, 'must be sustainable'. Manufacturing should not be at the cost of depleting natural resources.

Planning is a governmental not private activity. Classically, its main objectives are positive growth in GDP, i.e., an increase in a country's total level of output; control levels of unemployment; setting a target rate of inflation; ensuring that the current account balance is surplus, and lastly ensuring that the exchange rate is stable, i.e., the value of the local currency does not fluctuate sharply in relation to other currencies.

A planned economy meant the socialist economy of communist states, most of which had collapsed by 1990. A price economy means that market forces determine the price of commodities; this corresponds to the capitalist economy. We must be clear that planning in the context of Pakistan, is not planning as an ideological entity but a practical entity.

Economic planning began late in Pakistan, a full eight years after independence. It is possible that the government did not believe that it had a sufficient resource base to undertake economic planning.

THE FIRST FIVE-YEAR PLAN (1955–60).—The First Plan set out the following targets: (1) a 15 per cent increase in GDP and a 7 per cent increase in per capita income; (2) create employment opportunities for 20,000,000 people; (3) a 13 per cent increase in food production, and ultimately autarchy and self-sufficiency in food; (4) improve 6,000 villages by providing power, water, sanitation and communications; (5) irrigate 3,000,000 acres of land; (6) produce 580,000 kilowatts of electricity; (7) establish 1,500 new post offices; (8) add Rs 250,000 hospital beds; (9) earn Rs 50 crores worth of foreign exchange.

However, none of these targets were achieved. One reason is that the plan was sanctioned in 1957 and three years was too short a time for implementation, even if all the resources had been available. Thus, instead of 15 per cent, only an 11 per cent increase in GDP was achieved. The per capita income was increased by 3 per cent instead of 7 per cent because the population increased faster than the rate of development. The plan failed, partly because the effort seems to have been half-hearted, and partly due to inexperience. On the other hand, a great increase in economic activity is featured in the second plan.

THE SECOND FIVE-YEAR PLAN (1960-65).—This Plan had as its goal a 24 per cent increase in the GDP, a 12 per cent increase in per capita income, a 6 per cent increase in heavy industry and a 30 per cent increase in light industry. It aimed at food autarchy and the removal of regional imbalances. This plan held out encouragement to private entrepreneurs to participate in profit-making activities, while the public sector moved into those activities which had little attraction for the private sector. This impetus to the industry, alongside the Green Revolution which undertook to increase irrigation, enlarge mechanized farming and supply fertilizers, had an overall effect on development, and during the Ayub era all the economic indicators were positive. Towards the end of the plan period, the 1965 war broke out and resources from other sectors had to be diverted to defence. On the whole, the plan was considered very successful.

THE THIRD FIVE-YEAR PLAN (1965-70).—The Third Plan had been designed on the lines of the Second Plan but proved unsuccessful because of the two wars. The Third Plan also showed that foreign aid was an important factor in development, and if withheld or curtailed, it had an adverse effect on development. As against a 37 per cent target in GDP, 36 per cent was achieved. In agriculture, the target was 5 per cent whereas 4 per cent was achieved. The export target of 9.5 per cent was actually achieved to the extent of 6.5 per cent. The greatest shortfall was a poor performance in savings and capital development, and as Faruq Aziz has pointed out, this was the main reason for the economy not progressing at the desired rate. He also says that private enterprise in East Pakistan remained dormant, and the target of removing inter-wing disparity was not achieved. During the Ayub era, private enterprise was the key to development, but because it was in the hands of non-Bengalis, private enterprise was locally resented. The economists of Dhaka University came up with a two-economy theory, saying that the economies of the two wings were organically different. This made capital shy in East Pakistan, and it is possible that the steel mill planned for Chittagong was withheld on political grounds.

THE FOURTH FIVE-YEAR PLAN (1970-75).—This Plan had to be abandoned because of the 1971 war and the secession of East Pakistan. When Zulfikar Ali Bhutto took over, he abandoned five-year plans and opted for annual plans. These too were not acted upon, consequently, the Bhutto years came to be known as the non-plan years. However, this was the period when nationalization took place, and this agenda lasted throughout the Bhutto years, affecting future planning in Pakistan.

THE FIFTH FIVE-YEAR PLAN (1978-83).—This Plan laid the foundation for long-term economic planning. The small agro-based units Bhutto had nationalized towards the end of his term, were denationalized. Zia did not undertake large-scale denationalization, therefore those capitalists who were hit by nationalization remained wary. This provided an opportunity for a new class of entrepreneurs who wished to move from trade to industry. The Zia regime gave impetus to cement and fertilizer factories, a development this new class found conducive. One notable feature was that half the amount of public sector funding was allocated to the recently established steel mill in Bin Qasim town. This was a major step in basic industry development in Pakistan. The same period saw an increase in defence expenditure. The influx of Afghan refugees had both a financial and social cost with drug mafias acquiring a presence in Pakistan. Although the foreign aid in view of the Afghan influx was large, the balance went against Pakistan since a section of entrepreneurs, mostly centred around Karachi, though otherwise willing to invest, was inhibited by the law-and-order situation. It must be noted that during this planning period, Pakistan became self-sufficient in all basic food items except edible oils.

THE SIXTH FIVE-YEAR PLAN (1983-88). The Sixth Five-Year Plan was essentially a continuation of the previous plan. It was aimed at maintaining the rate of economic development, harnessing modern technology, and also avoiding the neglect of the social sector. Private investment in petrochemicals and fertilizers fell short of the expected levels. On the other hand, investment in agro-based industries, textiles and pharmaceutical industries was between 2 to 8 per cent higher than the expected level. A growth of 6.5 per cent was registered. Severe droughts in 1986 and 1987 impeded a better growth rate.

THE SEVENTH FIVE-YEAR PLAN (1988-93).—The Seventh Five-Year Plan corresponded roughly with the induction of the first Benazir Bhutto and Nawaz Sharif democratic regimes. Benazir Bhutto tried to signal clearly that her regime did not intend to return to the nationalization of her father's regime and encouraged private enterprise. Free enterprise, open markets, privatization, and deregulation were to form the basis of a new economic framework. There was great emphasis on growth, though during the plan period, there was no success in generating additional resources and even less success in curbing day-to-day expenditure. The delay in the stabilization of the Afghan situation after the Soviet withdrawal, the breakup of the USSR, and the Gulf War of 1991 were external factors that slowed progress. At home, ethnic strife and strikes took their toll. Between 1989 and 1993 there were two floods that affected progress.

THE EIGHTH FIVE-YEAR PLAN (1993–98).—The Eighth Five-Year Plan was actually approved on 31 May 1994 by the National Economic Council. In 1991, the government had inducted representatives from the private sector to seek guidelines for a programme. A balance was sought between the public and private sector, between existing capital and new enterprise. The plan had a three-pronged strategy which meant privatization, promotion of a free market and the development of small-scale industries. No great interest was shown during the period under review and the Five-Year Plan somehow went out of fashion.

One problem facing the economy during the Pervez Musharraf regime was that successive governments had been experimenting with privatization, but this had not proved a panacea for the economy. The economic crisis is paralleled by a moral crisis. To concede that only incentive and insecurity can make the wheels of the economy move means that the economic process can proceed only on the basis of the baser instincts of mankind. Viewed ideologically private property needs protection. The only solution is to make the industries originally founded in the public sector more competitive.

The Pakistan Steel Mills is a major example. By 30 June 2000, the Pakistan Steel Mills had registered a colossal loss. The government formed a Restructuring Committee, and its recommendations were carried out by cutting all unessential expenditures. A corporation forming a separate legal entity has been made responsible for all auxiliary duties including education. PSM was operating successfully against imported steel products, despite the fact that its existing capacity of 1.1 million is an uneconomic size which makes the production costs higher. This, being an administrative problem, was capable of resolution, but then the Supreme Court halted the sale of the PSM.

Water has become the most serious resource problem and the issue of building a dam at Kalabagh has divided the nation politically. The people of Sindh are wary, saying that since insufficient water is being allowed to flow into the sea, the sea is claiming more and more upstream areas. On the other hand, if storage facilities are neglected, the whole area could suffer. This is the old struggle between the production and distribution of wealth.

VISION 2030.—This is a plan which has a long-term perspective. Approved by Prime Minister Shaukat Aziz on 3 March 2005, its key feature, predictably a key feature was a Rs 293 million allocation for increasing water availability from 135.68 million acre-feet to 150.35 million acre-feet. The strategic direction as stated by Akram Sheikh, Deputy Chairman of the Planning Commission was to be a developed, industrialized, just and prosperous Pakistan through rapid and sustainable development in a resource-constrained economy by employing knowledge inputs. This focus on knowledge inputs needs not only a reordering of the administrative structure but the social structure itself. The experience is that allocation is not enough, the teaching force needs both monetary and authority incentives coupled with empowered parents' bodies. Human resource development, discussed further on, will have a more prominent role to play.

THE MEDIUM-TERM DEVELOPMENT FRAMEWORK (2005–10).—This is a component of Vision 2030, for both a short-term and long-term plan are needed to set priorities, five-year plans are envisaged as a whole, naturally dependent on previous successes. A promising feature is that except for institutions and finance, the main objectives are more social than economic. They are Education, Justice, and Health. The imperative of Education planning we have already discussed. Under Justice, reengineering of police has been proposed. This was attempted under local government, but the police were not willing to have their powers made subservient. With the political ends of justice having erupted in crisis, a new approach needs to be applied. Health needs the greatest attention, not only by extending facilities to rural areas but by combating, on a war footing, the unsanitary challenge in hospital management. Under institutions, allocations of resources to achieve social justice are mentioned emphasis is placed on ending corruption and increasing accountability. Food, shelter, and clothing have been conceded as requirements. How this can be achieved along with the structural adjustment plan is not clear. Under finances, the necessity of promoting a just and non-regressive regime of taxation is mentioned. The tightening of the tax net is proposed, and a legal system to stop tax evasion by the corporate sector is emphasized. The spreading of the tax net should be given equal emphasis. It is proposed to improve the infrastructure of the corporate sector. Infrastructure needs in the agriculture sector are also important. This framework had a mixed success.

THE KALABAGH DAM PROPOSAL

The most burning controversy in the domain of economic planning is whether a dam should be built at Kalabagh or not. Representatives of the most populous province, the Punjab, are vehement that it should be built. The representatives of all other provinces are equally vehement that it should not. For the Punjab, it means greater irrigation, greater yield and greater prosperity. The other provinces argue that it would cause inundation of large areas, lead to the dislocation of thousands of persons and cause large areas to go barren. This topic has not remained confined to discussions among engineers or economists but has become a political issue, the topic of many slogans. The World Bank has tried to bring about consensus between contending parties, and undeniably, it has a right to intervene, since it was the World Bank which brokered the 1960 Indus Badin Water Treaty. Lately, it arbitrated over Pakistan's objections to the design of the Indian-built Baglihar Dam. Pakistan's objections to the Baglihar, the objections of Bangladesh to the Farakka Barrage in India, and the conjoining of Indian rivers around Bangladesh show how far the era of the Mangla and Tarbela dams have been left behind when their construction was held up as a sign of progress. The World Bank Report was prepared by John Briscoe and his associates and contains interesting new material: (1) there is only one industrial common effluent treatment plan for the whole country; (ii) there is no modern Asset Management Plan for any major infrastructure; (iii) the silt now causes the Indus River to shift vertically, not horizontally; (iv) 20 to 30 per cent of water in the Indus Badin is consumed by weeds; (v) there are 20 million tons of salt accumulating in the system every year. There are grave developments and unless remedied, the prospects for our economy are bleak.

What is contended is whether storage will reduce silt and salinity, or will it increase them. The World Bank experts recommend storage and dams. They also prophesy that investment in water infrastructure will reduce poverty. These recommendations are based on ecological studies. The melting of glaciers, which has already started in Pakistan, will cause a water glut, inevitably to be followed by water scarcity. They hold that midstream there is 20 per cent less flow of water, and downstream 20 per cent less than midstream. This brings us to the Sindhi objection to the Kalabagh. There is a minimum amount of river water which needs to flow to the sea. The alternative is that the sea climbs up, filling the gap. Sea water being saline would render the present fertile area barren. Sindhi experts say that 10 million MAF is the minimum amount required for preventing sea intrusion. This estimate was contested but no alternative estimate was forwarded. As far as Balochistan and NWFP are concerned, the Government of Pakistan can, as per the World Bank's recommendation, give priority to developing storage infrastructure, but unless this complaint of Sindh is redressed, opposition to the Kalabagh Dam will not die down. Perhaps, the World Bank should have advanced the quantum of water required to flow downstream, and not have left the issue to political recrimination.

The IMF asked Pakistan to resume 5 year plans.[1]

Note

1. *Dawn*, 20 November 2023.

M AHBUB UL HAQ (b. Jammu, 22 February 1934–d. New York, 16 July 1998) was one of the most influential economists that Pakistan has produced. He had the benefit of being educated at the universities of the Punjab, Cambridge, Yale, and Harvard. His brilliant academic accomplishments in Economics led to Mahbub ul Haq's induction into the Planning Commission of Pakistan, and in the 1960s, he rose to be its chief economist. It was in this latter position that Mahbub ul Haq delivered an address that changed the face of politics and development in Pakistan: 'The wealth of Pakistan was held by twenty-two families only.'[1]

This was at the height of the Ayub Khan era when all economic indicators were positive. This speech was highlighted by the socialist parties of Pakistan to offset the effects of the Ayub era boom. The East Pakistan fallout was wider. The economists of the University of Dacca, led by Dr Abu Nasr Mahmud, had formulated a Two Economies theory whereby the economy of the two wings had two separate bases. Since the overwhelming number of the twenty-two families belonged to non-Bengali entrepreneurs who had invested in East Pakistan, 'Twenty-two Families' became a slogan with Maulana Abdul Hamid Khan Bhashani (1880–1976), president of the National Awami Party, and in the western wing with Zulfikar Ali Bhutto, chairman of the PPP. Mahbub ul Haq provided these parties with support through another speech, made two years later: 'A mere reform of the capitalist system is no longer viable. The reforms cannot be built in Pakistan through an evolutionary process.'[2]

Mahbub ul Haq was taken at his word, and while the two socialist parties were rampant in both wings, in East Pakistan, the ingredients of '*gherao, jalao*' (surround, burn) were added to the heady mixture of revolution. The ouster of Ayub led to nationalization in Pakistan under Zulfikar Ali Bhutto, and in Bangladesh under Sheikh Mujibur Rahman, but it was only in Pakistan that capital shied away from investment.

Meanwhile, in 1970, Mahbub ul Haq left Pakistan and until 1982, he was the director of the Policy Planning Department at the World Bank. To his credit, here also, he advocated the restructuring of the World Bank itself. In 1982, during the Zia era, Mahbub ul Haq returned to Pakistan and joined the Federal cabinet, serving in turn as minister of Finance, Planning and Development, Commerce, and Economic Affairs. He stood for tax reforms, poverty alleviation, and deregulation of the economy. In none of these could he claim success.

From 1989–95, that is, during the democratic interregnum, Mahbub ul Haq left Pakistan to serve as special adviser to the UNDP administrator. He was the creator, chief architect, and principal author of the Human Development Reports of the UNDP. It was shortly after leaving this assignment that Mahbub ul Haq made his second celebrated observation: 'The magnitude of corruption in Pakistan, exceeds Rs.100 billion a year.'[3]

The corrupt have been more resilient than the capitalists in Pakistan, and Mahbub ul Haq had to concede that the incidence and volume of corruption had Economic Planning gone up. Mahbub ul Haq can be held up as an example of the brilliant economists produced by Pakistan, who, despite having power and responsibility, were unable to influence the economy of their country in the direction and to the extent they desired.

Notes

1. Speech to Pakistan Management Association, vide *Pakistan Observer*, Dacca, 3 May 1968.
2. 'Pakistan's Choice for the 1970s'. Paper presented at the University of Rochester, 29–31 July 1970.
3. 'Ethics and Government'. Statement at the State of the World Forum, 21–23 November 1996, Guanajuato, Mexico.

Chapter 47
Energy

Pakistan did not strike oil, but in 1952 at Sui in Balochistan, natural gas was discovered. By the 1980s gas was supplied all over Pakistan through pipes. In the last years of the Pervez Musharraf regime, two developments took place simultaneously. First, commercial banks started advancing loans for purchasing cars. A whole social stratum, was by this means enabled to own cars, adding to the number of cars on the road. Secondly, Concentrated Natural Gas (CNG) was opened which offered fuel much cheaper than petrol, consequently, CNG pumps saw much longer lines than petrol pumps.

Ishrat Hussain Usmani (1917–1992) the nuclear scientist would bemoan the fact that natural gas, nature's bounty was being wasted by being used to cook food. The CNG supply to cars was a much greater loss in terms of comparative advantage. The result was that the gas reserves expected to last thirty years, were depleted in three years. Inflation hit Pakistan when oil prices began to rise after the 1973 Middle East war, Arab states did favour Pakistan, but even concessional rates pushed transport prices up, which meant every good that had to be transported became expensive.

The upshot was that gas reserves fell at the same time as the major dams of Pakistan, Tarbela, Mangla, and Warsak began to silt. Both sources of power production fell. Furnace oil or gas was used to generate electricity, Pakistan began to suffer first, power outages and thereafter power riots Continued till 2022. Industrial production fell as it ceased to be competitive, with American sanctions having precluded Pakistan from buying cheap gas from Iran, Central Asian states are willing to supply gas to Pakistan but since such routes need to traverse Afghanistan which even after the American withdrawal, is hostile to Pakistan such plans have remained on paper.

HYDEL PROJECTS.—The proposal to build a dam at Kalabagh and the political debate that followed, have been already outlined. A compromise location Diamer-Bhasha Dam in the Gilgit-Baltistan region. In October 2011, Prime Minister Yusuf Raza Gilani laid the foundation of the Diamer-Bhasha Dam. It was estimated to cost $12 billion, produce over 4500MW of electricity and be able to store 8 million acre-feet (9.864 billion m3) of water, Gilani said that he had consulted various sources to ensure that this dam would not suffer the same fate as the Kalabagh Dam proposal.[1]

The Diamer-Bhasha Dam project was too expensive. The Chief Justice of Pakistan Saqib Nisar opened the Diamer-Bhasha Dam account for donations towards that end, and the money is still in the Supreme Court account. It is not known how much was contributed to this fund, after the retirement of Chief Justice Saqib Nisar, and as recently as April 2022, the Lahore Chambers of Commerce and Industry was demanding its construction.[2]

Climate change threatens to melt glaciers and there is a dire need to store water. In addition hydel is the cheapest source of electricity. With no quarrel in its feasibility, funds are lacking to undertake construction. The American CENTCOM Chief, General Kenneth F. McKenzie Jr., and the US Ambassador Paul Jones visited Tarbela[3] and the WAPDA Chairman Lt.-Gen. Muzammil Hussain said that the US offer of $41 million will pay for the fifth extension of the Tarbela Dam which would add another 1410MW to the generation capacity of the Dam and the life of the powerhouse would be extended up to twenty years.[4]

The only silver lining is the Neelum-Jhelum Hydropower Project which generated, 1040MW beyond its formal capacity of 969MW. The project started operation with the commissioning of the first unit on 13 April 2018.

GAS.—After the initial discovery of Gas at Sui in 1952, new reserves were also discovered. The OGDCL announced in May 2007 that five wells had been discovered in Thora, Sindh which would push up the output of oil being 1746 barrels and gas 44.12 million cubic feet.[5]

Good news continued to emanate from Sui. The Minister of Petroleum and Natural Resources Asim Hussain informed the National Assembly that there was a reservoir of tight gas. The figures indicated otherwise. The minister put the country's gas reserves at 100 million cubic feet compared to the previous report of 29 trillion cubic feet.[6] Just in one year, the sale of gas as car fuel had raised an alarm.

Three industrial associations: All Pakistan Textile Mills Association (APTMA), Fertilizer Manufacturers of Pakistan Advisory Council (FMPAC), and Independent Power Producers Advisory Council (IPPA) published an advertisement asking whether conversion of 3.5 million cars to CNG is needed or the precious resource of 500 million cubic feet per day (MMcf/d) gas should be saved to spend on productive sectors and saving cost of Rs 300 billion. They contented: (1) The curtailment of gas to the electricity-producing units is the main cause of expensive electricity and load shedding, as they are running on diesel/furnace oil costing Rs 22 per unit instead of Rs 5 on gas. (2) Due to gas curtailment to fertilizer manufacturers for 180 days in a year, the government has to import fertilizer at double the price with more than Rs 100 billion impact on the national economy. (3) The curtailment of gas to the textile industry for 180 days annually is costing the country a $4 billion loss in exports with the employment of 10 million Pakistanis threatened. A textile industry worth $16 billion will be saved from bankruptcy with a continuous supply of gas, and there will be an increase of $4 billion in exports.[7]

Thus after the exit of military rule, and three years into the PPP regime under President Asif Ali Zardari further developments show that populist policies won, and the economy of Pakistan started suffering a setback. It was revealed in November 2012 that the 400 MMcf/d discovered in Sindh had not been connected to the main transmission line five years after discovery.[8] A discovery of crude oil, condensate, and natural gas in Kalabagh-1 A STI well. Mari Petroleum has a 40 per cent Hungarian share. Its first discovery was in the Halini Well-1 in 2011. The discovery five years later on 20 March 2015 was valuable: 'The gas discovery has an excellent heating value of 1144 BTU/SCF and its Condensate API is 52 @600F.'[9] Mari Petroleum announced another significant discovery in the same area one year later.[10]

The latest discovery of Mari Petroleum (in association with the Fauji Foundation) is in the Bannu-West Block in Northern Waziristan. The well was initially tested at the rate of around 25 MMSCFD and 300 barrels per day (bpd) on condensate.[11] This promises to be a real breakthrough and may make up significantly for the oil gap, provided that the earlier Pakistan Petroleum Ltd. discovery of gas in Matiari, Sindh is also taken into account.[12]

There were two other sources, shale for one, Shahid Khaqan Abbasi said that Pakistan has recoverable reserves of around 200 trillion cubic feet of natural gas and around 58 billion barrels in its shale structure.[13] Shale oil was considered expensive, but the US has preceded Pakistan in tapping shale reserves. The other source, biogas and biomass gasification was highlighted at a NED University seminar in 2019. It was recommended that biodiesel from non-edible resources be used in Pakistan. The total consumption of diesel in Pakistan is approximately 13 million tonnes of which 88 per cent was being used in transport. The consumption of mineral diesel can be reduced by using 10 per cent blended biodiesel fuel. Agricultural waste was also a source of bioenergy.[14]

While the overriding concern in Pakistan is about the gas shortage, sometimes supply outstrips demand, creating passing hiccups. Rain was responsible for the drop in demand. This condition causes pipelines to face extreme backpressure of Liquefied Natural Gas (LNG) causing pipeline rupture.[15]

How successfully these deposits are harnessed is the $64 million question, because what the country is facing currently is long power outages and violent power riots. The Minister for Energy Omar Ayub Khan said in 2020 that the country was facing a shortfall of 35 billion cubic feet a day, and by 2021 Sindh would become a gas-deficit province.[16] The Chief Minister of Sindh Murad Ali Shah said that Sindh would run out of natural gas in twelve years.[17] However, some of the gas discovered may be later utilized.

COAL.—Coal has been the earliest source of fuel since colonial times and was used to run railway trains and light people's ovens. This gave a respite to wood. Pakistan has vast coal reserves in Thar, but for ecological reasons, the public representatives of the area are resisting its exploitation. The European Union in the face of gas curtailment from Russia has been forced to reconsider its position on coal as a source of fuel. This may give an incentive to Pakistan.

SOLAR ENERGY.—Solar energy is considered perennial because scientifically, life on Earth shall vanish long before the sun cools down. For a country like Pakistan which lies in the tropical region most areas see sunshine throughout the year.

As far back as 2010 a European Union solar project invited attention in Pakistan. The project called DESERTEC would cost $560 billion. The planned solar panels, called mirrors, would be set up in the deserts of North Africa. The sunlight would be concentrated on water pipes which would turn the power to steam.

Pakistan was not dependent on foreign countries. The Thar Desert would provide more than sufficient room. Meanwhile, solar panels would directly convert sunlight to electricity without water and steam intervening. Initially, quality concerns were aired mainly by Chinese companies themselves because they were being pressed to reduce costs.

A solar panel has a photo voltaic cell which converts sunlight into electricity, the most critical component is a film which protects the cell from moisture and the capsule which seals the cell within layers of glass. American and Australian consumers found their panels lasting barely two years instead of the promised twenty-five years.

By this time, Pakistan was well into using panels to reduce the misery caused by electricity failures. It was proposed that installing solar panels on use for domestic consumption would be a minor investment, solar farms to energize industries were proposed. The Government of Pakistan exempted tax on solar panels for tube wells, consumer's desired exemption on all components of solar panels across the economy. The main concern was pilferage, especially from solar panels installed on streetlights.[18] No one can say their concern was unreal.

Solar energy as an energy source received a boost towards, the end of 2014 when the Russian Federation offered to establish a 100MW generation plant in Sialkot, the city that exports surgical and sports goods.[19] Such offers and even individual efforts were not bearing fruit, because it was necessary to obtain the permission of local power companies for installation. Second, since solar panels were a new commodity, customers were forced by dealers and sometimes second-hand products were passed off as new.[20]

That trade practice was a hurdle was demonstrated by the success of the Quaid-i-Azam Solar Park in Bahawalpur which was producing 12 per cent more power than the minimum requirement set by the National Electric Power Regulating Authority (NEPRA) The first phase of the plant was completed in March 2015 with 100MW solar park only required capital expenditure in the form of loans because the production did not require any fuel while its maintenance cost was negligible. Solar energy can be the cheapest mode of power in Pakistan if commercial loans are available on early terms.[21]

The Chinese installed solar panels in the tube wells in Quetta. Three solar tube wells would provide about 450 tankers of water daily and the city. The deputy chief of the mission said that China is committed and providing maximum possible assistance to Balochistan.[22]

In Lahore, the Alternative Energy Development Board (AEDB) was pursuing twenty-two solar projects with a combined capacity of 890.8MW but demanded the removal of taxes from solar capacity.[23] A group of foreign investors sought the intervention of Prime Minister Imran Khan to remove roadblocks to cheap power. The Pakistan Foreign Investors Forum (PFIF) a group of wind and solar energy sponsors made the plea. In spite of NEPRA having cleared their generation tariffs the Ministry of Energy despite the passage of months had not notified it.[24]

The State Bank of Pakistan doubled the scope of its renewable energy re-financing from Rs 1 billion to 2 billion since the introduction of the scheme in June 2016, the total outstanding finances reached Rs 5.6 billion for 217 projects having the potential of adding 292MW of energy supply.[25]

The Prime Minister of Greece Kyriakos Mitsotakis took the decision to de-couple gas prices from electrical prices.[26] However, there is a serious downside to developing solar energy that is, a threat to the environment.

Farhan Ahmed Memon in November 2020 wrote that solar panels generate 300 times more toxic waste per unit of energy than nuclear power plants. Memon said that the waste included lead, cadmium and other toxic even carcinogen chemicals which cannot be removed without breaking apart the entire panel. There is a vast increase in nitrogen trifluoride while constructing solar panels.[27]

In a later communication, Farhan Ahmed Memon mentioned solar energy without lasting its drawbacks. He emphasized how even: 'Pakistan has coastal belts with a consumable potential of generating 50,000MW electricity through wind turbines.'[28]

For the reason that Wind power cannot be attached to houses or even located near industries, they are not receiving as much attention as solar energy.

NUCLEAR POWER.—Dr Ansar Parvez called for the expansion of nuclear power generation from the current 8 per cent capacity to 20 per cent of the capacity: 'Once 20pc of your capacity is on secure baseload, you can build as many of solar, wind, and hydel plants.' Dr Parvez said that solar, wind and other renewables were being prioritized over nuclear fuel because they were cheap.[29]

On 21 May 2021, Prime Minister Imran Khan inaugurated the Karachi Nuclear Power Plant Unit-2 (K-2). The Pakistan Atomic Energy Commission (PAEC) announced that it had successfully hooked K-3 to the national grid, adding 1100MW. PAEC is now running six nuclear power plants in the country. Two of them are located in Karachi and are named K-2 and K-3, while four in District Mianwali are named Chashma Nuclear Power Plant Unit 1–4.[30]

Pakistan engineers and technicians had completed a re-fuelling outage at C3, in record time. All six PAEC nuclear power plants are operational with optimum capacity factor, generating 3560MW in total and providing it the national grid thus the future of Pakistan is bright, but what is bleak is the present.

Notes

1. *Dawn*, 19 October 2011.
2. *The Express Tribune*, 19 April 2022.
3. *Dawn*, 10 April 2019.
4. *Dawn*, 8 September 2019.
5. *Dawn*, 24 May 2007.
6. *Dawn*, 21 June 2011.
7. *Dawn*, 9 June 2012.
8. *Dawn*, 18 November 2012.
9. *Dawn*, 19 September 2015.
10. *Dawn*, 31 March 2014.
11. *The Express Tribune*, 26 June 2022.
12. *Dawn*, 16 December 2015.
13. *Dawn*, 24 November 2012.
14. *Dawn*, 25 August 2019.
15. *Dawn*, 25 July 2019.
16. *Dawn*, 11 August 2020.
17. *Dawn*, 13 January 2021.
18. *Dawn*, 25 June 2013.
19. *Dawn*, 10 December 2014.
20. *Dawn*, 14 July 2015.
21. *Dawn*, 5 November 2015.
22. *Dawn*, 22 July 2019.
23. *Dawn*, 8 November 2020.
24. *Dawn*, 4 January 2021.
25. *Dawn*, 23 July 2020.
26. *The Express Tribune*, 14 April 2022.
27. *Dawn*, 24 November 2020.
28. *Dawn*, 26 February 2021.
29. *Dawn*, 15 December 2021.
30. *Dawn*, 5 March 2022; 6 April 2022.

Chapter 48
Environment

Energy runs the economy but ruins the environment. Progress is measured by industrialization, and the industrial units of Pakistan have little ecological room for progress. Of all the fuels we surveyed in the previous chapter, only hydel and wind energy are safe. Science is trying to contain, isolate, and deposit at safe places the pollutants that result from human exploitation of nature. The major types of pollution are climatic, domestic, industrial, and medical waste. To these are added the cutting and burning of forests and the poaching of wildlife.

CLIMATIC POLLUTION.—The northern mountainous and snow-bound region is a cause of concern for Pakistan. Climate change was unobtrusive at first. A snow leopard has not been spotted there since 2013,[1] however, the residents, especially of Gilgit-Baltistan, informed the World Bank of the heavy reliance on wood, in the absence of natural gas, due to which deforestation was taking place. The Gilgit-Baltistan government complained about the lack of investment. Such investment, the Gilgit-Baltistan government contended, could unlock the immense hydro-power potential of the province.[2] Reports later emerged of remedial measures being counter-productive. New saplings planted in Chitral are spreading their disease to other plants.[3]

The main and overriding concern, in the wake of climate change, is the melting of glaciers. People in Swat noted that glaciers had become thinner. Out of the thirty glaciers surrounding Jabba, only five remain. Two small lakes near Godar Lake had disappeared. The annual flow of the Swat River declined by 0.03 cubic m/s.[4]

Glaciers alone are not exposed to melting. In 2010, a massive landslide blocked the Hunza River, creating Attabad Lake. Seven years later, the same effect was produced by the Khurdopin Glacier shifting and blocking the Shimshal River completely. Downstream settlements were threatened.[5]

During the construction of the Khunjerab Pass which was to link China to Pakistan, it was found that development and climate were at odds. Road traffic would increase, which would exude carbon, a gas that causes glaciers to melt. The Karakoram Highway was built in 1982, but later China upgraded it to a 15 feet wide paved road.[6] Gilgit-Baltistan legislators urged the federal government to erect walls along rivers. The legislators held that rapid deforestation was the cause of massive floods.[7] One of the legislators admitted that global warming was an international problem. He was right, as a giant iceberg had broken away from Antarctica.[8] Still, deforestation was not as rampant a problem as in the Northern Areas of Pakistan. The cutting of trees is illegal, but in the absence of alternative sources, it is the only life-saving option. If all of the country combines to provide gas and electricity to the snow-capped regions, it shall benefit the whole country.

In recent years, the problem has accelerated. On 30 May 2019, the Gilgit-Baltistan government and the United Nations Development Program (UNDP) launched a five-year project designed to contain glacier outbursts. This project was unable to prevent a Chitral glacier flood, which caused damage of Rs 330 billion in the Golain Valley in July of that year.

The following year (June 2020) the Shisper Glacier melted, a threat to the people of Hunza. At least 3,000 lakes were formed. Implementation of the Gilgit-Baltistan–UNDP agreement was hampered by the spread of Covid-19 in the area. The mountains and lakes thus created are very scenic and attract tourists; a major source of livelihood in the area, but which unfortunately also causes climatic decay.

The World Bank prepared a study on the environmental challenges with regard to solid waste management which could cause improvement in the mountain areas (22 April 2021), but another glacial outburst was threatening Chitral villages. Two Glacial Lake Outburst Floods (GLOF) were recorded in the Rabat Goal area of Lower Chitral district. The floods washed away forests and embankments, even an Ismaili Jama'at Khana. This is the current situation.

PLASTICS AND RIVER POLLUTION.—Of all human inventions the plastic bag promised to be the most convenient, light, and cheap mode of packaging—but it proved to be the deadliest. The World Economic Forum in a report called *New Plastics Economy* said that the 2016 rate of plastic flowing into the ocean shall outweigh fish and other marine creatures by 2050: 95 per cent of the value of packaging material, worth $80 billion to $120 billion is being lost to the sea after a short first use.[9]

At a seminar organized by the National Institute of Oceanography, it was asserted that Clifton Beach (Karachi) was badly hit by sewage. Apart from animal waste, plastic pollution was blamed. One delegate pointed out that freshwater constituted only 2.5 per cent of all the world's resources, whereas 97.5 per cent is salty: 'One can make use of desalination technology, only if we have clean coastal water.'[10] The University of Karachi's Institute of Environmental Studies also pointed out the hazards of ocean pollution. Its study showed that 80 per cent of ocean pollution comes from land and is located around the coasts of low and middle-income countries.[11]

On the positive side, Chinese scientists discovered a new strain of microalgae capable of absorbing 90 per cent of the greenhouse gas and industrial fumes that are the components of smog. At the Institute of Hydrology, Chinese Academy of Sciences Dr Wang Qiang said, 'Our micro algae's highest consumption efficiency for nitrogen oxides can reach around 96 per cent'.[12]

Research on air pollution led to research on ocean pollution. A joint China–Pakistan research team had discovered a plastic-eating fungus.[13] Plastic, long considered imperishable was in fact perishable as shown by the plastic-eating fungus. Sino-Pakistani scientists found a fungus on land; Japan found plastic-eating bacteria in the ocean.[14] These findings are a breakthrough, but one does not know how much more laboratory research is required to dent the world's plastic waste.

Most of the pollutants reach the oceans through rivers. McGill University conducted a survey which found that dams built at great labour and expense have an adverse impact on water purity. An UN-sponsored study showed that there were 60,000 large dams at least 15 meters tall. The blocking or damming of rivers disrupts the flow of nutrients vital to replace those lost through agriculture and diminishes the amount of river-borne species that can complete their lifecycles. The study also identified 3,700 hydropower projects. Professor Bernhard Lehner of McGill University said, 'Hydro-power has more complex environmental impacts than the oft-cited positive effects of avoiding fossil fuels.'[15]

A shocking piece of news emerged that people around Sukkur used to poison fish to catch them. The fish after taking the (unspecified) poison die and float on rivers. The poison affects other river life, as well as the lives of unsuspecting human consumers. The whole Indus River is affected by such a heartless practice.[16]

Reports of the Ravi River being polluted have also surfaced. One study conducted by the University of York detected paracetamol, nicotine, caffeine, even epilepsy and diabetes drugs, in the Ravi; human and industrial waste are in addition.[17] In a follow-up study, the Water and Sanitation Agency (WASA) reported that it had been trying to install water treatment plants for the last twenty years but lacked the funds to do so. Apart from harming human health, the contaminated river had become devoid of aquatic life. WASA had however purchased land needed for the setting up of treatment plants. Currently, work is in full swing on the Babu Sabu Wastewater Treatment Plant which would absorb 40 per cent of the water discharged from Lahore.[18]

SEA INTRUSION.—A Senate Committee was told in 2015, by the National Institute of Oceanography that if the rate of intrusion was not checked, Badin and Thatta would drown by 2050 and Karachi by 2060.[19] Sea intrusion occurs because of a lack of river water flowing downstream, as we saw in the section on the Kalabagh Dam proposal. Upper riparian of the country call rivers flowing into the sea, a waste, while the lower riparian worry that curtailment of fresh water causes sea intrusion. A body of experts gathered by the Pakistan Fisher Folk Forum said that the minimum requirement of 35 trillion million acre (MAF) was not being released downstream Kotri, as a result of which 1.8 MAF of fertile land in the coastal districts of Thatta, Badin, and Sujawal had been eaten up by the sea. The participants then marched to mark 14 March 2017—the International Day of Rivers.[20]

A decrease in freshwater leads to an increase in tainted water. At Kot Asadullah near Kasur, tainted water was causing people deformities. The Lahore Chamber of Commerce and Industry itself said that 90 per cent of factories in or around the city dump their waste in open pits or discharge untreated water in the streams.[21]

In Quetta, the situation is far worse. Dr Zahoor Ahmad Bazai of the Balochistan University revealed that vegetables were grown by using contaminated water. Quetta-based botanists explained that water from the drains is cheaper than fresh water; secondly, produce grows faster in contaminated water as there is no need for fertilizers.[22]

The most contaminated is the effluent or waste discharged by mills and factories; the effluents from leather factories are the deadliest. However, the Korangi Association of Trade and Industry asked the Sindh Environmental Protection Agency for financial aid, pleading that small to medium size industries did not have the resources to set up effluent treatment plants.[23]

The problem extended beyond the industrial areas. The Chief Minister of Sindh Murad Ali Shah told a World Bank delegation that he has assigned the NED University the task of (1) inspecting the drainage system of Karachi, and (2) removing the design defects of the Left Bank Outfall Drain (LBOD). The drainage system of Karachi would be re-designed as per the recommendation of the NED University. Explaining the design defects in the LBOD which was 385 meters long, Murad Ali Shah said that at high tide, seawater started flowing back. Instead of disposing of saline water or rainwater, the LBOD submerges nearby lands. The World Bank promised support for both projects.[24]

Members of the Sindh Assembly complained that not a single effluent treatment plant was functioning in the entire province. The SEPA Director, N.A. Mughal said that 470 million gallons per day (mgd) were directly disposed of without any treatment. Of the total, 80 per cent was sewage and 20 per cent was industrial waste. The Director said that over the last three years, 209 treatment plants were installed in Karachi, and a further 50 more were being installed; none of them was functional.[25]

The SEPA Director issued notices to the Defence Housing Authority, seven cantonment boards and even Navy Housing Schemes to install wastewater treatment plants. The Supreme Court at that time was hearing a case of pollution in coastline areas. Hospital waste was a greater hazard as it infected diseases. N.A. Mughal said 130 notices were issued to Karachi hospitals which were violating the Hospital Waste Management Rules 2005.

The University of Karachi and the Pakistan Maritime Security Agency (PMSA) had agreed to collaborate in research and conservation along the 1,046 km coastline.[26] As against this re-assuring news, the stunning disclosure came that Pakistan was the top destination of waste from ten countries including the US, the UK, UAE, and many European countries. This caused a shock to the Senate Standing Committee on Climate Change. Not having been aware of this, the Senate asked why this practice had not been stopped.[27]

DEFORESTATION.—The Supreme Court, citing a document from the National Information System regretted that Pakistan had the highest deforestation rate in the world. The rate was between 0.2 and 0.5 per cent per annum. The natural forest cover had gone down to 3.32 hectares, at an average of 27,000 hectares annually, a rate at which the complete forest area of Pakistan would be denuded by 2024.[28]

Deforestation is caused by the cutting of trees by timber barons. Surprisingly, there are some types of wood Pakistan imports, but the rare types of trees are being cut, pointing to the fact that Pakistan must be exporting timber either as logs and planks or fashioned as furniture and other living-style goods.

As far back as 2015, the Chief Minister of Balochistan, Dr Abdul Malik Baloch alerted the country of the deforestation of juniper trees in Ziarat which were the world's second-largest juniper forest. Dr Baloch deprecated the chopping of the trees of which some were centuries old. He called for legislation to declare this practice illegal.[29] Six years later Balochistan Finance Minister Noor Muhammad Dummar asked the Sui Southern Gas Co. to restore the supply and pressure to Ziarat: 'People have no option but to cut down juniper trees to keep their homes warm amidst freezing temperature.'[30] The Sui Gas Company undertook to restore the supply and pressure, but the gas load shedding which is ongoing (July 2022) could worsen by winter, and the juniper forest would have to compete with human survival. If the juniper forest is lost due to lack of gas, Ziarat will ultimately be emptied of human habitation as well.

The juniper forest presents a hardship choice, there are other cases where it is a matter of choice. The Supreme Court ruled against the Balochistan Communications Department for its plan to extend the 10 km Pishin-Yaroo link Road, as it would involve the uprooting of 2,200 trees. The communication department pleaded that the alternative, constructing a road on the right side of trees entailed an expenditure of Rs 1.1 billion. The original plan had a provision for planting 5,150 trees at an additional cost of Rs 25 million. The Supreme Court turned down the plan that involved the felling of trees.[31]

At a seminar on Earth Day at Sindh Agricultural University, Tando Jam the issues of paucity of water, the toxicity of water and the deforestation and resulting damage to mangroves was highlighted.[32] A much more severe problem struck Karachi. When vegetable beds were uprooted from mid-road by the Karachi Municipal Corporation, on the plea that an Urban Forest Project had failed to take off.[33]

Then there was an incidence of disease which caused deforestation. Deodar (Cedar) trees were drying up in Chitral due to some mysterious disease. A resident revealed that the trees had been attacked by a herd of oval medium-sized insects. Samples from the affected trees were sent to the Pakistan Forest Institute, Peshawar for diagnosis.[34]

Sheesham (Rosewood) trees were dying near Khanewal and Gujrat. One expert said that Rosewood had been brought in from Nepal, and since Pakistani soil was not native to it, it was struck by a disease called dieback. This was due to continuous inbreeding between the same species of trees.[35] Apart from the felling and disease of trees, the third and most devastating enemy was fire. A vast forest of over 45 acres was burnt in the Lower Dir district between Amlook Darra and Gumbat. The trees thus gutted, included hundreds of old pine trees.[36]

In 2020, the Food and Agricultural Organization (FAO) of the United Nations prepared a report based on the laid down criteria, which identified numerous habitat and plant criteria as hot spots for priority action: the pine nut (Chilghoza) forests of Suleiman Range in Zhob, and Sheerani in Balochistan and Dera Ismail Khan, in North and South Waziristan and Chitral were threatened due to excessive grazing, cutting for fuel and timber, excessive collection of seeds and the lobbing of branches which contain future cones.[37]

According to FAO, Pakistan was a forest-poor country with a small area of 4,478 million ha (51 per cent) under forests. This amounts to 0.021 ha per person, compared to the world average of 1 ha per person. Awareness has not stopped depredation. About 145 acres of rich land had been encroached upon by powerful chieftains and land-grabbers, while provincial governments over the last thirty years (in 2018) had allotted another 64,500 ha to their favourites. Muhammad Nawaz Khuhro said that Sindh forests are classified as riverine, irrigated plantations and mangrove forests. Riverine forests declined to 0.05 million ha (0.35 per cent) irrigated forests to 0.082 million ha (0.14 per cent) and mangrove forests to 0.2 million ha (1.41 per cent) till October 2017. The overall forest cover had fallen to 1.9 per cent.[38]

In 2015, a tree plantation drive was associated with an association called Shehri-Citizens for a Better Climate (CBE) which planted fruit trees in Karachi. Tree plantation along Mai Kolachi Road was planned. The Sindh government launched a Green Karachi Programme. The efforts of Muslim Raza Syed towards conservation in Karachi deserve recognition.

The only positive development has been an increase in the mangrove cover in the Indus Delta. The Sindh Forest Department and the World Wildlife Fund have together added a significant 14,000 ha. Arif Ali Khokhar, Sindh Forest Conservator revealed that mangrove cover was reduced to 80,000 during the 1980s, but with the joint efforts of many organizations, it has increased to 200,000 ha.[39]

WILDLIFE.—Houbara Bustard hunting is the favourite sport of our Arab neighbours. Houbara Bustard is an endangered species in Pakistan which results in contentions between the laws of hospitality and the laws of nature. Although its hunting through Falconers has been going on since the early 1970s, it was in 2015 that the Supreme Court admitted a petition seeking the cancellation of licenses to Arab royals. One applicant from Balochistan pleaded that dignitaries who hunt the birds bring prosperity and welfare to their hunting fields. The Supreme Court recalled that under the Third Schedule of Pakistan Wildlife Ordinance 1971, there was a complete ban on Houbara Bustard hunting.[40]

Notwithstanding, a special hunting permit for Houbara Bustard had been issued to a Qatari prince. The special license is for hunting 100 birds in ten days.[41] Apart from Houbara Bustard, another favourite of hunters is the partridge. The hunting of partridges is generally prohibited in the Punjab, says a report, but is allowed in winter under certain conditions: a valid shooting license and a permit from the Punjab Wildlife and Parks Department. The bag limit for one hunter is ten birds a day, and automatic weapons are strictly forbidden.

The hub of the partridge is the Salt Range, which is also the hub of the Urial. A census conducted in 2008 claimed that the Urial population was increasing, but the partridge population was decreasing. This was due to 'influential poachers'.[42]

It was in Cholistan that the Houbara Bustard found respite. Brigadier Mukhtar Ahmed, chief of the Houbara Foundation, said that the birds were bred in captivity by the UAE International Fund for Houbara Conservation, and after one year witnessed Houbara Bustards hatch.[43] The Gulf states are making efforts to preserve their favourite spoil. Brigadier Mukhtar Ahmed stated that 1,700 Houbara Bustards had been bred and raised in the UAE by the above-named facility. Earlier 500 and then 1,000 Houbara Bustards were released in the Cholistan desert. The International Fund for Houbara Conservation in collaboration with the Pakistan Army had aerially spread seeds of desert vegetation to make desert life hospitable.[44]

In an opposite climate in the freezing Kurram Agency in Gilgit-Baltistan, the Palla cat which has grey, long, and dense fur—considered highly threatened—has been caught on camera. Generally, however, illegal hunting has reduced the population of many endangered animals in Gilgit-Baltistan.[45]

Another source of anxiety is the smuggling of rare turtles and tortoises. A Karachi pet shop was raided yielding 129 freshwater turtles, nine marine green turtles, and ten living and three dead tortoises were recovered and released back to their habitat.[46]

There are concerns over the declining population of predators. Pakistan has 144 species of sharks and rays. The Sindh government undertook to save its shark population along the coastline.[47] In a very tragic event, lions at the Lahore Safari Zoo killed a 17-year-old grass reaper, Bilal Hussain. The poor teenager climbed over a fence to what looked like a thick jungle, but four lions rushed out to devour him.[48]

As against predators, deer have become endangered because of excessive hunting. The area from Fort Abbas to Khairpur Tamewali was the habitat of the black deer, but in 1967 it was reported extinct. The Pakistan Army helped the conservation cadre and for the first time, after a lapse of fifty-three years, the black deer population registered an increase.[49] Thus, efforts are underway to save all the flora and fauna of Pakistan.

OUTER SPACE.—Pre-human history has been written by geologists. Post-human history shall be written, if at all, by astronomers. Space travel and life on other planets are the stuff of science fiction. These were classified as fantasy or curiosity. Environmental degradation has made it a matter of exploration. Our astronomers are already on the lookout, trying in the first instance the physics of space: from the Expanding Universe of Albert Einstein to the dissipating Black Holes of Stephen Hawkins. In May 2016, scientists discovered three potentially habitable planets. These are a mere thirty-nine light years away.[50] A star named TRAPPIST-1 is located forty light years away and has seven earth-size planets orbiting it.[51] To reach them shall require the conquest of Time, not the conquest of Space.

Note

1. *Dawn*, 3 April 2020.
2. *Dawn*, 12 February 2014.
3. *Dawn*, 16 February 2015.
4. *Dawn*, 7 September 2016.
5. *Dawn*, 1 June 2017.
6. *Dawn*, 4 November 2016.
7. *Dawn*, 11 March 2018
8. *Dawn*, 13 July 2017.
9. *Dawn*, 20 January 2016.
10. *Dawn*, 22 September 2017.
11. *Dawn*, 18 January 2022.
12. *Dawn*, 27 December 2017.
13. *Dawn*, 20 September 2017.
14. *Dawn*, 23 October 2018.
15. *Dawn*, 9 April 2019.
16. *Dawn*, 31 January 2020.
17. *Dawn*, 10 February 2022.
18. *The Express Tribune*, 21 March 2022.
19. *Dawn*, 10 February 2015.
20. *Dawn*, 8 March 2017.
21. *Dawn*, 12 May 2018.
22. *Dawn*, 6 February 2019.
23. *Dawn*, 23 April 2019.
24. *Dawn*, 5 November 2020.
25. *Dawn*, 23 December 2021.
26. *The Express Tribune*, 1 July 2022.

27. *The Express Tribune*, 1 July 2022.
28. *Dawn*, 4 September 2019.
29. *Dawn*, 8 September 2015.
30. *Dawn*, 22 December 2021.
31. *Dawn*, 12 April 2018.
32. *The Express Tribune*, 23 April 2022.
33. *Dawn*, 12 September 2019.
34. *Dawn*, 17 July 2017.
35. *Dawn*, 13 November 2017.
36. *Dawn*, 9 November 2016.
37. *Dawn*, 10 March 2020.
38. *Dawn*, 18 April 2018.
39. *The Express Tribune*, 29 April 2022.
40. *Dawn*, 20 August 2015.
41. *Dawn*, 20 November 2016.
42. *Dawn*, 6 December 2016.
43. *Dawn*, 8 April 2020.
44. *Dawn*, 13 October 2020.
45. *Dawn*, 20 January 2018.
46. *Dawn*, 23 February 2018.
47. *Dawn*, 28 February 2019.
48. *Dawn*, 27 February 2020.
49. *The Express Tribune*, 30 March 2022.
50. *Dawn*, 3 May 2016.
51. *Dawn*, 23 February 2017.

Part 10
Cultural History

Chapter 49
Culture and Society

What is culture? The search for a satisfactory answer to this question has given rise to a great deal of discussion and debate. What is Pakistani culture is another difficult question for which no completely acceptable answer has yet been evolved, but towards which we can draw closer by discussing and debating the question.

    T.S. Eliot (1888–1965) the celebrated poet and critic called his treatise, *Notes Towards the Definition of Culture*.[1] In other words, Eliot does not claim to have arrived at a definition of culture but can only point to a definition. Then again, the reader must be warned that not only does the term culture have different meanings for different writers, but that it is used interchangeably with another term, civilization. The word civilization is of French origin (1734). It meant according to Michel Boivin,[2] to improve the social state of a community. Later, it denoted the higher state of humanity. In its origin, it is quite compatible with culture. We can see this in the writings of two theorists of history. For Oswald Spengler (1880–1936) culture meant: 'Nobility, church privileges, dynasties, convention in art, and limits of knowledge in science.'[3] In other words, Spengler has used the word 'culture' as an extranational unit of society in which common features transcending national boundaries are highlighted. His contemporary, Arnold Joseph Toynbee (1889–1975) employed the term civilization in almost the same sense. Toynbee found that a national state was not an intelligible field of study in isolation; and that 'a civilization is an intelligible field by comparison with its component communities—nations, city-states, millets, castes etc.'[4] In Eliot we find no attempt to determine the frontier between culture and society.[5]

    A more recent author, Shireen Hunter, is more forthcoming: 'Culture, which subsumes civilization as its outward manifestation of itself.'[6] Oswald Spengler, the most influential exponent of culture as a unit of historical study states that: 'The Civilization is the inevitable destiny of the Culture.'[7] We ourselves speak of a Pakistani culture and an Islamic civilization. As an illustration, we can take the example of Faiz Ahmed Faiz (1911–84), the most internationally acclaimed poet of Urdu, who complained that Urdu was an imposition since only 8 per cent of Pakistani babies listen to lullabies in the national language.[8] We can deduce that for Faiz, culture is defined by the mother tongue, which in 92 per cent of cases means regional languages. It follows that civilization is defined by Urdu since Faiz not only composed the bulk of his poetry in Urdu, but he even, on occasion strayed into Purbi, a Hindi dialect having no territorial representation in Pakistan.

The *Oxford English Dictionary* defines culture 'as the customs, institutions and achievements of a particular nation, people or group'. Sir Edward Taylor defines culture as 'that complex whole which includes knowledge, belief, art, morals, law, custom, and any other habits acquired by human beings as members of society'. The United Nations Economic, Social and Cultural Organization UNESCO (2002) has defined culture as: 'culture should be regarded as the set of distinctive spiritual, material, intellectual and emotional features of society or a social group, and that it encompasses, in addition to art and literature, lifestyles, ways of living together, value systems, traditions and beliefs. In short, it requires unity in diversity.'

THE MAIN COMPONENTS OF CULTURE.—The four elements that can be considered to be the main components of culture are (1) Values, (2) Norms, (3) Institutions, and (4) Artefacts.

Values can be described as ideas of what seems important in life to a group of people or a society. They are ideals that guide or qualify conduct and interaction among people. They help to distinguish what is right from what is wrong and serve as a guide on how to conduct life in a meaningful way. Culture is greatly influenced by values, and most often the ideas they generate are brought together in religion from which society derives its values. For example, honesty is a value shared by all religions, while honouring one's ancestors is a value present in some religions but not in all. According to A.L. Kroeber, 'culture embodies values'.⁹

Norms consist of what society considers normal behaviour. Eating with one's fingers is considered normal behaviour in South Asia but not in Europe. Each culture has methods or sanctions, for making sure that people live and respect its norms. If you eat with your fingers in a European city, people may look at you with disapproval, so you may stop eating that way. Sanctions may be strict or not, depending upon the importance of the norm. Norms that a society enforces in a formal manner because it considers them important, become the laws of that society. For example, drinking alcohol is legally prohibited in Pakistan.

Institutions are the structures of a society within which values and norms are practised and transmitted. Some institutions are exclusive to South Asian society, such as *mushairas*. However, marriage is an institution of our society which prevails in many other societies as well. In all these societies having a family and providing stability for them is considered an important norm. The rituals that are legal are religious, and those that are cultural are social.

Artefacts are shaped by a culture's values and norms. A society's arts and crafts come under this heading. Geometrical design, for example, has grown out of Islamic culture as a substitute for the artistic depiction of human bodies which is not acceptable in culture. This is an example of how a culture's values influence its artefacts. Some are developed by convention. The earliest mosque, at Madinah, had no dome or minaret, but now a dome and minaret are the most recognizable features of the mosque.

Culture has also been described as the result of 'the best that has been thought and said in the world'. In a progressive, developing and evolving culture, all achievements and accomplishments improve with time. In such a culture, improvement is given a great deal of importance, and since improvement becomes a value, people are open to listening to and acting upon the views of others.

Thought, and respect for ideas are forces inherent in the development of a culture's artefacts, just as thought and research are reflected in scientific advancement. Those who are courteous, tolerant, and calm are considered cultured, as are those who are interested in the artefacts and institutions of their own and other cultures.

CULTURE AND CLASSES.—It is often said that culture is the collective behaviour of the educated segment of society. Education is conceived to be a vital ingredient of culture. When we call a man 'cultured' we presuppose a certain level of education; when we speak of 'cultured pearls' we mean pearls have all the natural ingredients and are produced in a shell, but whose production has been artificially induced. Therefore, we can confidently state that education is an important element in the diffusion of culture. We can relate our observation to the class structures of Pakistan.

We can say that the appreciation of art and the patronage of art belong to the Pakistani upper class, although the creation of art itself may be outside the purview of the upper class. Apart from the arts, as far as customs, manners and behavioural norms go, they belong more to the middle and lower classes. Dress and food vary from class to class in style, but in propriety, there is unity. Education is an important element in relation to the arts as well. There are many arts which cannot be appreciated naturally. They develop from an acquired taste. For example, in Pakistan, classical music and modern art can be appreciated only by those who know the intricacies of these arts. Folk music and pop music have separate but overlapping audiences. People who can appreciate representational art far outnumber people who can appreciate abstract art.

Snobbishness in art is at an ebb. There is an effort by established artists to embrace the crude and garish artwork on trucks and buses. Literature is the only art, that is available to all classes, but even here there is a distinction between serious and popular literature. However, taste distinction and class distinction are not congruent. Popular literature is devoured more by the middle class. Cinema has not yet found its bearings, in spite of three or four high-class films. Television drama which played a formative role in fostering cultural awakening has seen technical advance and artistic decline at the same time.

CULTURE AND POLITICS.—Culture acquires a political dimension when the culture of the conqueror is perceived to be higher than the culture of the conquered. Sir Percival Spear observes that a situation like this can bring about a real revolution and give rise to rethinking. Since Pakistani culture cannot be divested of its British content, the clothes we wear, the language employed both by this writer and his readers and other technological improvements (or intrusions) into our life, mention must be made of three Englishmen who had a pronounced influence over us, Edmund Burke, Sir William Jones, and Lord Macaulay.

Edmund Burke's impeachment of Warren Hastings transmitted British ideals to India, Sir William Jones made Indians aware of the grandeur of their early civilization, and on the opposite side, Lord Macaulay made them aware of their shortcomings. Education in English overcame the separatist tendency of vernacular languages and provided an outer shell to culture. In other words, acting as a common language among speakers of various regional languages, English brought them closer, giving their cultures a better chance to merge.

In Pakistan, cultural varieties have been given a political meaning. It is reiterated that by neglecting regional cultures we are threatening the federation. One of the reasons why East Pakistan broke away was the issue of not giving Bengali its rightful place. On the breakup of Pakistan two Russian historians, Yuri V. Gankovsky and L. R. Gordon-Polonskaya, popularized the notion that Pakistan was composed of four nationalities, relating to the four provinces. Z.A. Bhutto, who took over after the secession of East Pakistan and was then engaged in military operations in Balochistan, banned this notion. It rarely serves to ban a concept. As an example, in order to show the failure of federation in Pakistan Syed Jaffar Ahmed highlighted the differences among the people of Pakistan: 'A people who have not coalesced into a nation, and are a disjointed lot'.[10] Writing in a very different context, at least three authors, Intizar Hussain, Bapsi Sidhwa, and Attiya Dawood, coincidentally in the same issue, noted the similarities between India and Pakistan.[11] There is much to be said on the issue of federal myopia having fostered regionalism, but against this, we note that Yusuf Haroon had warned against provincialism before the creation of Pakistan.[12] Since regional tensions deal with language hegemony we shall resume this discussion in Chapter 49: Language and Literature.

CULTURAL HERITAGE AND MODERN CULTURE.—Although culture is the term most used to interpret history, the historical component of culture is not unanimously acknowledged. Clifford Geertz defines culture as 'a historically transmitted pattern of meaning embodied in symbols.'[13] On the other hand, Philip Bagby defines culture as: 'Regularities in the behaviour, internal and external, of the members of a society, except those regularities which are clearly hereditary in origin'.[14] People wishing to reform, are mostly hampered by hereditary or historical norms; like the Mughal and British attempts to abolish the Sati custom. The cultural scene in Pakistan attests to the compartmentalization of the historical and current.

In the domain of art, Abdur Rahman Chughtai (1897–1975) represents cultural heritage, Sadequain (1930–1987) represents modern culture; in music, Roshan Ara Begum (1917–1982) represents cultural heritage, Fuzön (a Pakistani pop rock band) represents modern culture; in literature, Hafeez Jalandhari represents cultural heritage, N.M. Rashid (1910–1975) represents modern culture. Apart from personalities, the Badshahi Mosque in Lahore is our cultural heritage, and the Tooba Mosque in Karachi is a product of modern culture.

In historical terms, it should be clarified that the possession of a great cultural heritage, to belong to a religion which has had a great cultural impact is not the same as possessing a great culture. A great culture is one that can overcome military superiority. The Hindus were able to assimilate conquerors like the Huns and the Scythians, and Muslims were able to convert Mongols and Tartars who were their conquerors, to their own religion.

When the British invaded India, European culture was in a dynamic state; scientific discoveries, political theorizing and literature were receiving an impetus, and at the same time, the Muslims were reflecting on their decline. We mentioned earlier Edmund Burke, Sir William Jones, and Lord Macaulay. Sir William Jones translated Kalidasa's *Shakuntala* and founded the Asiatic Society of Bengal. It was his mission to discover and propagate the glory of Hindu civilization. Lord Macaulay, on the other hand, remarked that one shelf of Western books contained more wisdom than whole libraries in Oriental languages. Both Jones and Macaulay were right. Jones was concerned with cultural heritage, the past which was indeed glorious. Macaulay was concerned with the present, with what was, in his time, modern culture.

Gradually the mould of South Asian culture will become obsolete. The mould of modern Pakistan will come into play. Perhaps the present is not equal to the past, but nevertheless, it will point to the future, to a Pakistan which is perforce nuclear, a Pakistan which is threatened, a Pakistan which, in addition, is beset with environmental hazards, which has serious gender inequalities, and which is sitting on a population time bomb. These are to be the future parameters of Pakistani culture regardless of whether we overcome these challenges, or whether they overwhelm us. If these trends are a danger, they are equally so to all Pakistanis and in that sense, they have a unifying effect, for they call for all of us to put our heads together in order to evolve values and a mode of life acceptable to all.

Notes

1. T.S. Eliot, *Notes Towards the Definition of Culture* (London: Faber and Faber, 1961).
2. Michel Boivin, *Jihad* (Chambery: Universite de Savoie, 1999).
3. Oswald Spengler, *The Decline of the West* (New York: Vintage Books, 2006), p. 25.

4. Arnold J. Toynbee, *A Study of History*, Vol. XII: Reconsiderations (Oxford University Press, 1961), pp. 284 and 286.
5. T.S. Eliot, op. cit., p. 15.
6. Shireen Hunter, *The Future of Islam and the West: Clash of Civilizations or Peaceful Coexistence?* (Westport: Praeger, 1998), p. 8.
7. Oswald Spengler, op. cit., p. 24.
8. Faiz Ahmed Faiz, *Meezan* (Lahore: Minhas, 1962).
9. A.L. Kroeber, *The Nature of Culture* (Chicago: University of Chicago Press, 1952), p. 104.
10. Syed Jaffar Ahmed, *Dawn*, Sunday Magazine, 10 August 2003, p. 1.
11. Ibid., Books and Authors, pp. 1-4.
12. Ibid., 28 July 1947.
13. Clifford Geertz, *Interpretations of Culture* (New York: Basic Books, 1973), p. 89.
14. Philip Bagby, *Culture and History: Prolegomena to the Comparative Study of Civilizations* (London: Longman, 1958), pp. 84 and 195.

Chapter 50
Language and Literature

We have already noted how languages evolved. The evolution of speech is due to mimesis in a child, but the evolution of language has another dimension. Sanskrit was the language of the Aryans, and since Hinduism was common to South Asia, there could have been no ideological or political forces to promote regional languages. Regional languages like Pushto and Bengali, correspond to the climates in which they were nurtured. However, the spread of language does not follow the same process as the evolution of language. If a language contains knowledge required by other people, or if a language is championed by a politically dominant people, that language spreads far beyond the confines of its birthplace. In both instances, English is the prime example. The language of a small island on the fringes of Europe has become not only the educational but literary language of people around the globe.

Then there are languages that are religiously sanctified. Sanskrit was the language of prayers and rituals for Hindus and spread all over the subcontinent. Yet, because regional languages evolved and Sanskrit became too difficult for common use, it became a dead language and was replaced by Prakrit and eventually by modern Hindi. There is also the case of Latin. It was the educational and religious language of the whole of Europe, but even in the country of its origin, it was replaced by Italian which became an important literary language and produced great poets like Dante and Petrarch who are as revered as Latin writers, such as Lucretius and Virgil. Arabic remains the living language of the Middle East, much beyond its original home in the Arabian Peninsula; but in other Muslim lands where the Holy Quran and daily prayers are recited in Arabic, Persian, Turkish, and Urdu evolved as distinct languages which not only produced great literature but expounded the themes of Islam. It is in this light that we must view the relations between Urdu, the national language, and the regional languages of Pakistan. Since they have all been developed over time and reflect the disposition, the circumstances and the fortunes of the people who use them, we must acknowledge them as our treasures, just as we value the natural resources of our provinces.

URDU.—When we view the language scene of Pakistan, we see a scene both stormy and complex. Urdu is the national language of Pakistan, but its position has never remained unchallenged. In 1867, there was a conflict between Hindi and Urdu, in 1952 there was a conflict between Bengali and Urdu and, in 1972, there was a conflict between Sindhi and Urdu, and in every conflict,

Urdu proved to be the language of the minority. How then did Urdu become the national language of Pakistan? One reason is that all conflicts took place within three different borders. The Urdu-Hindi conflict took place within British India, the Bengali-Urdu conflict took place within divided India and the Sindhi-Urdu conflict took place within divided Pakistan.

In South Asia, there was no true national language which was universally spoken, read, and understood. Both Hindi and Urdu were actually inter-provincial languages, spoken in the same provinces: United Provinces (UP), Central Provinces (CP), and Bihar. However, there was one difference, Hindi was spoken all over, whereas Urdu was concentrated in the cities. Because Urdu was an urban language, it was used more in the urban centres than in rural areas. Urdu became associated with the Muslims and Hindi with the Hindus. Muslims, who had for a long time made Persian their official language, were confident that Urdu, the result of Hindu-Muslim interaction, would be equally acceptable to both communities, therefore, it came as a shock, when Babu Shiva Prasad, a poet of Urdu, led a movement in Benares in 1867 to replace Urdu with Hindi. It was this movement that led Sir Syed Ahmad Khan to articulate the Two-Nation Theory. Sir Syed said that the dissension between Hindus and Muslims originated with the language issue.

Why should there have been any resistance to Hindi at all since it was the language of the majority? This question must be answered if we are to trace the history of Muslim nationalism in India. The answer is provided by Farman Fatehpuri: 'It was because the birth of Modern Hindi was not the result of natural or linguistic evolution.... It was brought forth at the instigation of the Fort William College authorities'[1] who commissioned Lallu Lal to write *Prem Sagar*, and in the process remove Arabic and Persian words and replace them with Sanskrit. This was carried to such extremes that even Shiva Prasad was shocked. Tara Chand's comment on *Prem Sagar* was that: 'Modern Hindi was till then unknown, for no literature existed in it'.[2] As late as 1937, the UP Minister of Education had refused to promulgate Hindi, which he considered 'rustic'.

In 1949, N.V. Gadgil, speaking in the Indian parliament on 13 September, admitted that 'Hindi today is admittedly a provincial language, and there are other provincial languages far richer in literature'.[3] R.R. Divakar, Information and Broadcasting Minister said in 1950 that he was receiving numerous complaints from people that the Hindi of All-India Radio was not intelligible to them and they had to listen to the Urdu of Radio Pakistan to follow the news.[4] Urdu became a political cause with Muslims because, more than Hindus, the British seemed bent on championing Hindi. In 1873, the Lt. Governor of Bihar, Sir George Campbell banned Urdu from educational institutions and the courts. The Lt. Governor of UP, Sir Antony MacDonnell passed a resolution replacing Urdu with Hindi.

The Muslims of India, alarmed at this turn of events formed, an Urdu Defence Committee under Sir Syed Ahmad Khan on 9 December 1873 at Allahabad. In 1900, first Nawab Mohsinul Mulk and then Nawab Viqarul Mulk led another Urdu Defence Association. In 1903, the Society for the Progress of Urdu was formed, and in 1910 when Aziz Mirza was honorary secretary, the society came under the aegis of the All-India Muslim League and the promotion of Urdu became one of the Muslim League's responsibilities. From then on Urdu became one of the symbols of Muslim League aspirations. In 1937, the possibility of compromise on Urdu, nurtured by the Nehru family, was finally ended when Gandhi ruled: 'Urdu was the religious language of the Muslims; it was written in the Quranic script; Muslim rulers had devised and spread it. Muslims, if they wish can keep it and spread it.' It was at this juncture that Allama Iqbal offered his support to Maulvi Abdul Haq.

This culminated in the AIML legislator's convention in Delhi in 1946, when M.A. Jinnah proclaimed that 'only Urdu would be the national language of Pakistan because it is the repository of Muslim culture, civilization and intellectual cohesion'. Jinnah's reiteration of this stand at Dhaka in 1948, could not have come as a surprise. However, for that independence year, the Federal Public Service Commission had allowed different languages in its examination including even Hindi, but Bengali was not included, and this was the real reason that the language issue was raised.

This brings us to Urdu's relations with Bengali. At the time the rivalry between Hindi and Urdu began, it was clear that both languages were being backed by religious sentiments; regional considerations took second place. It was also a fact then, that no language confined to a province, no matter how rich, could challenge the hegemony of either Urdu or Hindi. Babu Deena Nath Ganguly and Pandit Navin Chandra (or Nobin Chunder) Roy (who created the first Brahmo Samaj in Lahore in 1861) were the first of a complete cadre of Bengali writers who espoused the cause of Hindi. Presiding over the All-India Urdu Conference at Calcutta on 9 January 1936, A.K. Fazlul Haq reassured the delegates that the Muslims of Bengal were not against Urdu. A Calcutta meeting addressed by both Fazlul Haq and H.S. Suhrawardy, president and secretary of the Bengal Muslim League, on 8 April 1939, had stressed the 'need for protecting and promoting the Urdu language and script in Bengal'. Even now the Bengali-speaking Muslims of the Purnia district in India insist that their mother tongue is Urdu. Attitudes changed only when borders changed. Urdu was challenged only when Hindi was removed from the scene.

There is another factor which led to Urdu becoming the national language of Pakistan. In history, people have worked for the consolidation and advancement of other languages. Persians have served the cause of Arabic, Indians have served the cause of Persian, and Punjabis have served the cause of Urdu. This has not been confined to writers but has extended to publishers. Not only

Muslim publishers who are many, but the Hindu publishers also played a pivotal role in the promotion of Urdu. Then Urdu acquired a national status because of its role in the Freedom Movement. Ninety per cent of the poems confiscated by the British were in Urdu.

When Pakistan came into being, the echoes of classical poetry were still strong and three classical poets—Seemab Akbarabadi (1880-1950), Arzoo Lakhnavi (1872-1951), and Natiq Lakhnavi (1878-1950)—migrated to Pakistan when they were on the verge of death. The immigration of Josh Malihabadi (1895-1982), the poet of revolution, was felt deeply because he believed in Indian nationalism. Josh wrote most of his masterpieces in Pakistan and justified his stay in cultural terms.

Initially, the Progressive Writers Association was favoured because the Communist Party had supported partition, but because of its lukewarm response to the Indian occupation of Kashmir, eminent writers like Muhammad Din Taseer (1902-1950)—one of its founders—parted company with it. Extreme ideological exclusiveness and factional strife had already weakened the association when it was banned in the wake of the Rawalpindi Conspiracy when Faiz Ahmed Faiz and Syed Sajjad Zaheer (1905-1973) were incarcerated. The two literary figures standing outside the Progressive Writers Association were Sa'adat Hasan Manto (1910-1955) and N.M. Rashid (1910-1975).

Sa'adat Hasan Manto illuminates his scenes and defines his theme sharply, and as far as the etching of his characters, the depiction of the shadowy world of harlotry, and his cynical exposé of bestiality, during communal riots is concerned, Manto is beyond the pale of comparison. He displays a dramatic flair, giving artistic credence to his surprise endings. Following closely is Ghulam Abbas (1909-1982) whose stories are known not only for artless and unobtrusive depicture, but also for delicacy and finesse.

Writers of the right-wing also felt the pressure of religious groups; as a result Qurratulain Hyder (1927-2007) resentful of the tirade against her masterpiece, *Aag ka Darya* (1959), re-migrated to India. Soon after, Shaukat Siddiqui (1923-2006) published *Khuda ki Basti* which became an overnight success because of its strong social realism. By 1960, the experimental short story became dominant under Intizar Hussain (1923-2016), Enver Sajjad (1934-2019), Masood Ashar (1931-2021), and Arsh Siddiqui (d.1997). Khalida Hussain (1937-2019) received recognition rather late, but her mysterious and inscrutable treatment and choice of themes have left a lasting impression on Urdu fiction. The next generation, headed by Muhammad Mansha Yaad (1937-2011) has original writers, Asif Farrukhi (1960-2020) and Ali Haider Malik (1944-2014). While Mansha Yaad has drawn his symbols from rural myths and folk tales, another prominent contemporary, Rasheed Amjad (b.1940), has sought to break both the plot and linguistic structure.

Turning to poetry we encounter N.M. Rashid (1910-1975), a sceptic with deep metaphysical insight, he transformed blank verse into abstract illuminations and formations, projecting the enigmatic, bizarre, and weird aspects of life, absorbing into poetry the themes that had been the preserve of prose. His contemporary, Miraji (1912–1949) became a cult figure and far more influential. (Faiz Ahmed Faiz (1911–1984) wrote on all themes even ideological in a deep lyrical mode).

Side by side with a generation of neoclassical poets, a generation of post-modern poets started attracting attention. These were led by Iftikhar Jalib (1936–2000), Qamar Jamil (1927–2000), and Mubarak Ahmed (d.2001). Some even penetrated the hitherto impregnable fortress of the hidebound *ghazal* and turned it into an avant-garde art form. They were led by Javed Shaheen (b.1932), Zafar Iqbal, and Anwar Shaur (b.1943), but before they could displace the earlier generation, the 1965 war broke out. The demands of national solidarity were catered to. Himayat Ali Shair's (1926–2019) *Blood* conveyed solemnly the sentiments of the nation. Anthems were contributed by Jamiluddin Aali (1925–2015) and Rais Amrohvi (1914–1988).

The Tashkent Declaration (1966) was viewed as a betrayal and gave rise to protest poetry. Habib Jalib (1929–1993) led the revolutionary chorus followed by Yunus Sharar (b.1946).

The 1980s decade saw the flowering of feminist love poetry. Ada Jafri, Parveen 'Fana' Syed, and Zehra Nigah gained respect for breaking the male monopoly over lyricism. Their poetry turned feminist only with the advent of Kishwar Naheed (b.1940), and Fahmida Riaz (1946–2018). Feminist issues and grievances were amplified by Sara Shagufta and Azra Abbas.

The ingredient of glamour remained elusive till the advent of Parveen Shakir (1952–1994), a poet of exceptional sensibility and erudition, she added literary lustre to the genre of feminine poetry. Their inhibitions have diminished, and a number of poets have held the field without being avowedly feminist. They are Shahida Hasan (b.1953), Tanvir Anjum (b.1956), Ishrat Afreen, Wazahat Nasim, Fatima Hasan (b.1952), and Fouqia Mushtaq (b.1968)

Iftikhar Arif (b.1943) as an eminent poet has served as Chairman of the Pakistan Academy of Letters. The Chairman of the National Language Authority, Fateh Muhammad Malik (b.1936), represents both historians and literary critics.

PUSHTO.—Pushto literature dates back to the 8th century AD and the legendary ruler of Ghur, Amir Kror Suri (aka Jahan Pahlawan) who is reputed to be the first poet of this language. A warrior, his poetry consisted of war and battle themes. There is some gap between the legendary and historical period, but the historical period had been neatly chalked out into three eras, each with its distinctive features, according to M.M. Kalim, (1) from the earliest times to the 16th century, (2) from the 16th century to the coming of the British, and (3) from 1840 to the present.[5]

During the second era, the literary scene was dominated by Khushal Khan Khattak (1613–1689) contemporary and adversary of Aurangzeb. He not only immortalized his struggles but gave philosophical content to Pushto poetry. His poetry was noted for its realism as well. His symbol, Shaheen (Falcon), was adopted by Allama Iqbal. Among the junior contemporaries of Khushal Khan were Abdul Hamid, noted for his lyrics, and the celebrated Rahman Baba whose mystical poetry, though less appealing than Khushal Khan's still has a large number of votaries. A major influence on Pushto poets was Pir Roshan who was a pantheistically inclined mystic.[6]

In the post-Partition era, a People's Literary Society was founded by Sanober Husain and included stalwarts like Dost Mohammad Kamil, Amir Hamza Shinwari and Samundar Khan Samundar. A major contribution was made by Abdul Wahid Thekadar (1910) of Mardan who wrote *Maidan-i-Jang* (The Battlefield) a daily diary of events of the 1965 war between Pakistan and India. Ajmal Khattak a poet and Abdul Ghani Khan a scholar are writers who have a political profile. Raza Hamdani (1910–1999) and Farigh Bukhari (1917–1997) were poets who served as a bridge to Urdu poetry as well.

Hashim Babar, Taqi Hashmi, Fozia Anjum and others among poets, and Tahir Afridi, Gul Afzal, Abdul Kafi Adeeb, and Zaitun Bano among fiction writers have made major contributions to Pushto literature.

SINDHI LITERATURE.—Sindhi is one of the oldest languages of the subcontinent. According to Shamsul Ulama U.M. Daudpota, it descended from the Virachada dialect of the Prakrit languages.[7] Sindhi was recognized as a distinct language by many early scholars including al-Biruni (973 CE–c. 1052). It initially had many scripts according to the regions in which it was used but came to be standardized in a script derived from Arabic. It is visible as such in the couplets of Shah Abdul Karim Bulri (1536–1623). Scholars identify a gap of about two hundred years between Shah Karim and Shah Inayat. It is possible that manuscripts dating from that era will one day be discovered and scholars will maybe be able to bridge the gap. Shah Inayat's disciple was the literary luminary Shah Abdul Latif Bhittai (1689–1752).

Shah Abdul Latif is the 'sun' in the firmament of Sindhi literature and gave Sindhi an internationally acclaimed stature. He is credited with being the originator of *Wai* or *Kafi*. His romance *Umar–Marvi* is enchanting and well-known and lends itself to modern interpretation. Shah Abdul Latif's poetry is multifaceted, but, in the words of Umar Muhammad Daudpota; 'the poet's mind is always attuned to his Maker. His divinely inspired ecstasy, his melody and imagery have made his poetry unrivalled'. He is a classical poet who rules the hearts of the common man.

Another poet of this era was Khwaja Muhammad Zaman Luari (1713–74) who also had a mystical dimension to his verse, and his most illustrious contemporary was Sachal Sarmast (1730–1828). Sachal Sarmast was an original thinker and a free thinker as well. The spiritual quality of his poetry has attracted many devotees.

In the 20th century, the most famous traditional poet was Makhdoom Muhammad Zaman Talibul Moula (1919–93) and among the modern poets was Shaikh Mubarak Ayaz (1922–97). Shaikh Ayaz is for the modern age what Shah Abdul Latif was for the early Sindhi era. His poetry is in its essence, protest poetry expressing the sentiments of a deprived people. Sindhi language teaching was actively banned by the first military regime and Sindh suffered most from an effort at cultural regimentation. The other poets of this school were Tanveer Abbasi (1934–1999), Shamsher-ul-Hyderi (1931–2012), Tufail Bewas, Badar Abro, Taj Baloch, Niaz Humayuni and others. Ustad Bukhari has only been recognized as a great poet since his death.

The sense of deprivation in Sindh found expression in fiction with Jamal Abro's *Pishu Pasha Ain Biyoon Kahanyoon* and Ghulam Rabbani Agro's (1933–2010) works which portray the travails of peasants and workers. There have emerged notable writers to comment on gender imbalance, a major social theme. Nurul Huda Shah, Samira Zarin, and Mahtab Mahbub are the most prominent writers in this respect. Criticism and scholarship by the late Durre Shahwar Syed and Fehmida Husain are a lasting contribution.

PUNJABI LITERATURE.—Punjabi literature, from the beginning, was attuned more to rural sensibilities than city life. It has its basic expression in folklore.[8] This began with short poems and songs, but soon extended to what are called romances; long poems, all on love themes. There are five major romances Heer-Ranjha, Sassi-Punnu, Sohni-Mahiwal, Mirza-Sahiban, and Puran Bhagat. Heer-Ranjha went from ballad to romance, in the hands of many poets, until finally, Waris Shah provided a version of such excellence that earlier versions were discarded. Waris Shah's version also underwent variations, until an authorized edition was presented by the historian Abdul Aziz. Waris Shah's *Heer* is also valuable as social history because it vividly portrays the ravages caused by the invasions of Ahmad Shah Abdali.

Sassi-Punnu and Sohni-Mahiwal also ran a similar course. Sassi-Punnu had many authors, but Hashim Shah's version was judged the best; Sohni-Mahiwal found its poet in Fazal Shah. The themes of these perennial romances are explained by the fact that, though on the surface they were the Romeo and Juliet type of romances, below the surface they were expressions of the mystical love for God, and the longing of lovers stood for the mystic's love of God.

According to Ahmad Salim, classical Punjabi poetry had the following traits: it was committed to the masses and aloof from royal courts, it was intelligible to both the local peasant and the university professor, and it was attuned to the villages, and not to cities.[9]

Apart from the romances mentioned above, there were other forms, including the *Kafis* of Madholal Hussain. Another epoch-making poet was Sultan Bahu (1631–91), the author of the *Si Harfi*. He did not use the cover of romance and presented high ethics in a straightforward manner, and because they have sincerity their appeal is direct. Another great poet, Bulleh Shah (1680–1758), wrote poetry replete with spiritual ecstasy.

One historical figure who became the subject of romance was Dulla Bhatti. His father was killed when he defied Mughal forces over the forcible exaction of taxes. Dulla Bhatti avenged his father and began a peasants' movement. Ultimately, he was overpowered, captured, and executed. It is said that Saint Madholal Hussain was present at Dulla Bhatti's execution.

The Sikh period is generally considered a period of stagnation in Punjabi literature and only under the British was a revival witnessed. Post-partition Punjabi poetry was dominated by Ahmad Rahi. He wrote the most moving revolutionary poetry using folk songs. He was followed by Nawaz who wrote stories under the heading *Donghiyan Shaman*. The later generation of Punjabi writers is represented by Afzal Randhawa and Najm Husain Syed, followed by Nasrin Anjum Bhatti, Mushtaq Sufi and others. Ustad Daman, with his protest poetry, loomed large in the public eye, and today Baba Najmi has gained recognition as a representative Punjabi poet.

BALOCHI LITERATURE.—The Baloch have a timeless literary lore but only a modern literary history. The Baloch have been basically a nomadic society which explains why the Balochi script is still not standardized. Balochi has its presence in three countries, Pakistan, Iran, and Turkmenistan, with a lesser presence in Afghanistan and the Gulf States. The development of Balochi as a literary language is a recent phenomenon: 'Baloch literary activities have been concentrated in Pakistan and the development of Balochi as a written language is a very recent phenomenon.'[10]

Another factor retarding the development of Balochi compared to other languages of Pakistan, relates to the location of its users. In Turkmenistan, Balochi was actively suppressed, in Iran, there was covert suppression and in Pakistan, because of the radical tone of Baloch poetry, it found an opportunity for development in Karachi, rather than in Balochistan itself.

'There came about a great change in Baloch society after the creation of Pakistan,' says Abdullah Jan Jamaldini (1922–2016).[11] Literary history was made when Maulana Khair Mohammad Nadvi launched a monthly journal, *Oman*, in 1950. Both Gul Khan Naseer (1914–83) and Mohammad Husain Anka (d.1977), the luminaries of Baloch poetry, received an impetus to publish their poetry. Gul Khan Naseer was the author of the first-ever published Baloch book, *Gulbang* (Quetta, 1952). It was closely followed by Azad Jamaldini's (1912–81) *Masteen Tawar* (1953). A new generation of poets includes Ata Shad, Malik Tooqi, Mubarak Qazi, and others.

Fiction flowered in the writings of Mir Amanullah Gichki, Sher Mohammad Marri, Aziz Bugti, and others. The Baloch novel made its debut with Syed Zahur Shah Hashmi's *Nazuk*. Baloch literature has always been strongly responsive to political and social crises, and though it may not have had a very illustrious past, it has a very bright future.

Notes

1. Farman Fatehpuri, *History of the Pakistan Movement and the Language Controversy* (University of Karachi, BCCT, 2001), p. 43.
2. Tara Chand, *The Problem of Hindustani* (Allahabad, 1944), pp. 32, 33.
3. Prem Nath Bazaz, *The History of the Struggle for Freedom in Kashmir* (New Delhi, 1954), p. 348.
4. Ibid., p. 335.
5. M.M. Kalim in S.M. Ikram and Percival Spear (eds.), *The Cultural Heritage of Pakistan* (Karachi: Oxford University Press, 1955), p. 145.
6. Ibid., p. 150.
7. Ibid., p. 155.
8. Ibid., p. 157.
9. S.H.M. Jafri and Ahmad Salim (eds.), *Pakistan Society and Literature* (Urdu) (Karachi: Pakistan Study Centre, 1987), p. 205.
10. Carina Jahani, 'Poetry and Politics', in Paul Titus (ed.), *Marginality and Modernity* (Karachi: Oxford University Press, 1996), p. 205.
11. S.H.M. Jafri and Ahmad Salim, op. cit., p. 153.

HAFEEZ JALANDHARI (b. Jalandhar, 14 January 1900–d. Lahore, 21 December 1982) born Mohammad Hafeez, was the national poet of Pakistan, by virtue of having written the national anthem. Allama Iqbal is our ideological poet, but it was Hafeez who lived through the literary contentions in independent Pakistan. Poetical endeavours in Pakistan have been directed towards protest and a struggle for democracy and human rights against successive military regimes. In this struggle, progressive stalwarts like Faiz Ahmed Faiz, Habib Jalib, and Ustad Daman occupied centre stage. In contrast, Hafeez Jalandhari became identified with the establishment, basking under the sun of patronage.

This, however, is an unfair appraisal. Literary historians by and large have turned a blind eye to Hafeez Jalandhari's struggles in his early life. In 1921, Hafeez launched a literary journal, *Ejaz,* from his native Jalandhar. To raise the capital he had to mortgage the family residence—for which his father hit him in front of his wife and child. Next, he accepted the editorship of *Shabab-i-Urdu*, Lahore. When the promised salary remained outstanding for many months, Hafeez was expelled from his house by his father-in-law.

What is not emphasized is that whilst most of the progressive stalwarts (like Josh Malihabadi, Faiz Ahmed Faiz, and Syed Sajjad Zaheer) came from aristocratic and affluent families, Hafeez came from the lower middle class. While progressive poets championed the cause of the workers and labourers; Hafeez—in order to support his family—often had to work as a common labourer, sometimes having to go to bed hungry. This struggle aroused the resentment and not the sympathy of the progressive writers. Syed Sajjad Zaheer made it a point of ideological correctness that Hafeez should be rated below Faiz Ahmed Faiz.

In the last year of his life, a controversy was created when on the death of Josh, Hafeez referred to the former's scepticism. It was, indeed, an unfortunate utterance, but while the controversy raged, no one had cared to recall that on Fani's death, similar unkind words had been published by Josh.[1] Since the diatribe of Josh had no effect on the intrinsic worth of his poetry, the diatribe of Hafeez does not detract from his own intrinsic worth.

In 1919, while Hafeez was still in his teens, Hafeez recited a revolutionary poem in a Congress meeting at the request of Dr Saifuddin Kitchlew and was promptly jailed. From the chronology of the events, it can be deduced that Hafeez was released on the same day that the Jallianwala Bagh tragedy took place.

The critical notices of Hafeez are sparse, but they are meaningful and are reflective of the early recognition he gained. In 1925, Firaq Gorakhpuri broadcast a talk on Hafeez and focused on the euphony of his poems and lyrics. Not surprisingly, Firaq was disdainful of the *Shahnama-i-Islam*. In 1942, Hafeez received the praise of two critics, who were acclaimed as the best in those days: Niaz and Majnun. According to Niaz: 'The basic muse of Hafeez is fixed on the ghazal, which has led him into songwriting. He has simplicity and euphony imbued in equal measure…whatever he says carries weight, has insight, but in all his gravity we find not a trace of artifice.'[2] According to Majnun: 'The whole of the poetry of Hafeez, has as a permanent quality the exultation and loftiness which can be ascribed only to youth. The numbers of artistic qualities that have come together in Hafeez, are not seen in any other Urdu poet.'[3]

Hafeez had a sharp tongue, but he was also maligned. In his old age, Hafeez basked in glory, but in his youth, he had to suffer a hard struggle. He has given us an inspiring anthem—let us pay him reverence.

Notes

1. *Humayun*, Lahore, January 1942.
2. *Nigar Annual*, Lucknow, 1942.
3. *Bouquet War Publicity Mushaira*, Gorakhpur, 1942.

Chapter 51
Human Resource Development and Education

The development of education in Pakistan has been in double jeopardy. On the one side is the *zamindar* (feudal landlord) who actively resists education for fear that education will emancipate his peasants. The peasant, on the other hand, seeing the poor quality of education, considers school a burden and is reluctant to lessen the workforce at his disposal. This situation is very bleak, but a recent survey by Shahrukh Rafi Khan has recommended that the promotion of education be made a criterion for legislative ability, just as the graduation clause was applied in the 2002 elections. For the peasants, the survey observed that the formation of Parent Teacher Associations has the potential to maximize the benefits of existing school facilities, especially if mothers, rather than fathers, are represented. This is a very small step, but a step in the right direction, and kindles hope for human resources development.

When Pakistan came into being, it was actively supported by an educational society, the All-India Muslim Educational Conference. Subsequently, however, education has been given a low priority in Pakistan. During the era of highest productivity in our history, in the Ayub Khan era, the value of imported books per person per year was limited to Rs 150; at the end of ten years, the limit was raised to Rs 500. President Ayub Khan told the Raja of Mahmudabad that all the trouble in the world was caused by people who read books. Thus, the attitude that held centre stage was that of the peasant who considered education to be a burden. To regard education as a process of human development, and human development as a means of economic development seems almost to have been an afterthought.

It was a matter of some satisfaction, therefore, that in June 2002, a National Commission on Human Development (NCHD) was formed on the directive of President Pervez Musharraf, as a public-private partnership to promote development in the fields of health, education, and microfinance. Under the NCHD, 481 non-formal education centres have been established where 12,900 children have achieved literacy.

THREE STREAMS OF EDUCATION.—In Pakistan, there are three streams of education, one represented by schools that prepare students for Cambridge or London University 'O' and 'A' Level Examinations, the second represented by government or privately run schools that prepare students for Secondary School Certificates issued by the boards of education in the provinces, and the third are the *madrassas*, where religious and traditional education is taught.

There is a political demand to have a single, uniform system of education throughout the country. Due to a confused language policy, the general expertise in English at the time of Independence has been voluntarily foregone, and to regain expertise in English, an international language necessary for scientific progress, there is an uphill struggle to reclaim lost ground.

POLICIES.—Pakistan had a number of National Education Policies beginning with the Fazlur Rahman Conference of 1947 in which all the right recommendations were made without any means of implementation. The Sharif Report of 1959 was the first to focus on vocational institutes. This Report recommended that secondary education be a distinct stage, not merely preparation for higher education. The undergraduate course was extended from two to three years, but because of student agitation, the extra year was dropped.

The Nur Khan Report of 1969 became the basis of the 1970 and 1972 education policies. It recommended the nationalization of all colleges and most schools. Nationalization of educational institutions was not a part of the PPP manifesto but because of teacher lobbying it had to implement the recommendations of the Nur Khan Report.

The National Education Policy of 1978, under President Zia, recommended the opening of mosque schools. Islamic learning and Arabic were introduced as compulsory subjects. An important feature was the establishment of a Special Education structure. Under Prime Minister Mohammad Khan Junejo (1985–88), Nai Roshni schools were set up in remote corners of the country but barely lasted beyond the architects' tenure.

The Education Policies of 1990–95 during the two democratic regimes, introduced the Social Action Programmes (SAP). These were intended to develop primary education and deliver crash literacy programmes aimed primarily at remote and underdeveloped areas. These had only a limited impact.

The latest policy is the 2017 National Education Policy. Its declared goals are the pursuit, use and evaluation of knowledge. It also embraced upbringing students on moral and ethical principles and the purification of their souls. This was to have been done under Article 25(A) of the Constitution. It has not been achieved. The third goal was to increase the education budget to 4 per cent of the GDP. The present allocation is 2 per cent.

SCHOOLS.—According to the *Pakistan Economic Survey 2004–05* there are 164,970 primary schools. The enrolment figures for 2004 for primary schools is 19.795 million students. There are 28,728 middle schools with an enrolment of 4.318 million students. There are 9,819 higher secondary schools with an enrolment of 1,497,496 students. By 2021, the number of primary schools was 132,079—87 per cent in the public sector and 13 per cent in the private sector.

COLLEGES.—Arts and Science: 939, Law: 53, Commerce: 87, Home Economics: 4, Teacher Training: 103, Engineering: 13, Agriculture: 5, Computer, Fine Arts Homeopathy and Tibb Colleges: 162, Medical: 28. In 2022 the number of affiliated colleges stands at 2,900.

PUBLIC SECTOR UNIVERSITIES.—In 2008, the figures were Federal Area: 11, Punjab: 18, Sindh: 10, NWFP: 10, Balochistan: 3, Northern Areas: 1, Azad Jammu and Kashmir: 1. In 2022, the figures are Islamabad 16; Punjab 54; Sindh 29; Khyber Pakhtunkhwa 33 universities out of which 10 are private; Balochistan 7; Azad Jammu and Kashmir 6 in the public sector; Gilgit-Baltistan 2, both public. Total 73.

PRIVATE SECTOR UNIVERSITIES.—Federal Area: 3, Punjab: 11, Sindh: 21, NWFP: 8, Balochistan: 1, Azad Jammu and Kashmir: 2. In 2022 Islamabad 8; Punjab 26; Sindh 31; Khyber Pakhtunkhwa 10; Balochistan 1; Azad Jammu and Kashmir 1; Gilgit-Baltistan none. Total 59. University education, which was previously regulated by the University Grants Commission, is now regulated by the Higher Education Commission of 2002.

AREAS OF EDUCATION.—There are three that merit special mention:

(1) **Computer and Information Technology.** Pakistani students have adapted swiftly to computer technology. Courses in IT are offered at the most prestigious universities and institutes in both the public and private sectors, such as the Petroman Institutes, under the federal government; the Institute of Business Administration, Karachi; the University of Karachi; the NED University, Karachi; and the Lahore University of Management Sciences (LUMS), have prestigious departments of computer sciences. Earlier they were providing teaching aid material now they have search engines that have widened the horizon of knowledge access.

(2) **Distance Learning.** The People's Open University, Islamabad, was established in 1974 (renamed Allama Iqbal Open University in 1977) as one of the earliest distance learning centres to be set up globally. It provides services to remote parts of the country where schools and colleges are not present or are insufficient. It is complementary to formal education and allows students who have dropped out to resume education after long absences. The AIOU caters to all levels, from secondary schools to Ph.D. At present, the AIOU offers 1,054 subjects in 91 programmes at 9 levels. Apart from Open and Virtual universities, Distance Teaching became widely prevalent because of the Covid-19 outbreak in January 2020 in which online teaching had to be resorted to on a very large scale even in private institutions. Online teaching has the advantage of being able to go beyond prescribed textbooks; it can be accessed from any location of choice and its outreach is extended. It has the further advantage that lectures or lessons can be recorded, archived, and shared. A software catering to all-

in-one management is Fedena. The disadvantages: focusing on computer screens for a long time strains the eyes; in Pakistan, internet connections are unreliable and cannot reach remote areas; and studying in isolation becomes psychologically constricting.

(3) **Special Education.** The Zia regime gave importance to Special Education in its 1978 Education Policy. A national policy for special education was drafted in 1985 and reviewed in 1988. Teacher training facilities were first set up by the University of Karachi in 1988. The University of Punjab and the AIOU, Islamabad subsequently opened facilities. The University of Karachi has granted affiliation to two special colleges, Ida Rieu College, and DEWA College. At first, only mental retardation, visual impairment and hearing impairment were the subjects of teacher training and instruction, but now Autism and Learning Disability are also being catered to.

The latest trend (2022) is to shift from special to Inclusive Education. This aims to provide education to normal and special children in a single classroom. Such an environment is beneficial to special children but is being resisted by parents of normal children.

BUDGET ALLOCATION.—At present, the most notable feature is the large budget allocation to Education and the high number of national and international scholarships awarded to students and faculty members. The most recent figures showing the public sector allocation for Education in 2004–05 in million rupees are:

	Current	Development	Total
Federal	16,548.420	14,416.464	30,969.884
All Provinces	94,142.970	33,616.388	127,759.358

TEACHER EDUCATION.—The earlier degrees and certificates, B.Ed. C.T., are now considered obsolete. The qualification for teaching elementary and primary classes is a four-year B.Ed. (Hons.) Elementary deemed equal to a BA/BSc plus the old B.Ed. course. For the higher 16–year plus classes a five-year B.Ed. (Hons.) Secondary is now prescribed.

HIGHER EDUCATION COMMISSION.—Under the Eighteenth Amendment, Education is a provincial subject, but under a Supreme Court ruling on 9 April 2017, the HEC shall continue to function as a federal body. A major innovation was to replace the traditional bachelor's and master's programmes with a four-year Associate Degree Programme (ADP). The policy framers say that the ADP has been inspired by the Community College Model introduced in the United States, United Kingdom, and other developed countries. Critics, mainly teachers' bodies, are wary of the dislocation this may cause and that seeking its equivalence to centuries-old degrees shall be cumbersome. Still, this new curriculum may help in state-building.

Chapter 52
Human Rights in Pakistan

In every political entity, citizens have both rights and responsibilities, but it is more common to see responsibilities being imposed than to see rights being upheld. Asian nations have struggled valiantly and successfully against colonialism, and subsequently as valiantly but less successfully to secure human rights. In Pakistan, too, the attainment of human rights, which came on the tail of the struggle for democracy, has proved elusive. The pursuit of freedom inherently involves the quest for human rights, yet, after gaining freedom, the seamless extension of these rights to citizens has not been consistently realized.

What are human rights? The UN defines human rights, as 'those rights which are inherent to our nature, and without which we cannot live as human beings'. Human rights have been conceptualised at two levels, (1) legal and formal articles, and (2) social and cultural values. Legal and formal articles are necessary to save human beings from unwarranted arrests and torture, while social and cultural values are necessary to save human beings from, for example, honour killings (*karo kari*) and forced marriages.

Human rights are such that they are valid for all, without distinction of gender, age, nationality, religion, possessions, race and/or origins. Human rights are based on universal values of dignity, freedom, equality, and justice. Since they are universal, these values can act as standards to regulate the life of all human beings. Human rights are also specific and characterize certain activities such as enslavement, torture, and unlawful confinement of persons to be inhuman.

Human rights are not only universal, but they are indivisible. By indivisibility is meant their inalienability. For example, economic, political, and civil rights cannot be undermined for the cultural and social rights of individuals and societies. It may be part of a people's culture to suppress women's or workers' rights, but it is, nevertheless, an infringement of human rights.

Pakistan is a signatory to the Universal Declaration of Human Rights, and its representative served on the committee that drafted the Declaration. Since 1986, Pakistan has had its own Human Rights Commission (HRCP). This is an independent, voluntary, non-political, non-profit making and non-government organization registered under the Societies Registration Act. HRCP is a member-based organization, with an elected council, and a number of office bearers (a chairperson, four vice-chairpersons, a secretary general, and a treasurer). The highest organ is the General Body comprising all HRCP members. It has its main secretariat in Lahore headed by a director. Its main affiliation is with the International Commission of Jurists (ICJ). The aims and objectives of the HRCP are: (i) Spreading awareness of Human Rights among people. (ii) Exposing wrongs and disseminating knowledge about them. (iii) Motivating communities for collective response against local wrongs. (iv) Mobilizing public opinion against bigger or systemic ills. (v) Intervening where important and possible, for redressal of individual injustice or fear of injustice. (vi) Information collection, in order to track incidents and tendencies on a day-to-day basis.

I.A. Rehman (1930–2021), a director and later secretary-general of HRCP, traced the process of framing constitutions in Pakistan, against the standards of the Human Rights Declaration. He said that the Universal Declaration of Human Rights (UDHR) were not ignored but was never wholly incorporated. Social rights like education and health, economic rights like equal pay for equal work, the right of protection against inhuman treatment or the right to participate in government were not incorporated. According to I.A. Rehman: 'Some of the reservations against total acceptance of the UDHR were plainly rooted in religious beliefs... The Constitution of 1973 not only retained the provisions of the earlier Constitutions in respect of the State's name, the exclusion of non-Muslims from Presidential election, and the Islamization of laws, [but] offered further concession to the religious lobby. A new Article 2 declared Islam to be the State religion of Pakistan, and Article 91 reserved the office of the Prime Minister for Muslims.'[1]

I.A. Rehman goes on to list the Second Amendment declaring Ahmadis to be non-Muslims. His comments on the implication of these constitutional provisions are most instructive: 'The title of the State (Islamic Republic of Pakistan) had no effect on fundamental rights. The Objectives Resolution was not enforceable. The exclusion of non-Muslims from the offices of the President and Prime Minister did in theory smack of discrimination on the basis of beliefs, but in practical terms, the impossibility of a non-Muslim becoming head of state or government was generally conceded. The process of Islamization of laws through the agency of elected representatives was not considered in conflict with fundamental rights. Even the proclamation of Islam as the State religion was not seen to undermine fundamental rights because [,] at that time, no conflict was perceived between Islam and Socialism.'[2]

According to Uzma Qureshi, 'In the modern world, guarantees regarding human rights are afforded primarily by international institutions... It was natural then, that the prime international institution, the United Nations should have highlighted the issue of Human Rights, consequently, they were included in the Charter of the United Nations on 20 June 1945. The next step was taken by a subsidiary body United Nations Economic, Social and Cultural Organization (UNESCO) while adopting its constitution on 16 November 1945. UNESCO concerned itself with peace and security. It was only expected that after the ravages and devastations of the Second World War [,] the Universal Declaration of Human Rights was made on 10 December 1948 by the UN General Assembly... Formally Human Rights became part of Pakistan's Constitution by virtue of its adherence to the Universal Declaration of Human Rights. In the current 1973 Constitution, there is Part II of Chapter 1 dealing with 'Fundamental Rights and the Directive Principles of State Policy'. The fundamental rights which have been spelt out are security of person, safeguards against arrest and detention, prohibition of slavery and forced labour. Freedom of movement, of association and speech, Freedom of religion and safeguards to religious institutions were enshrined.'[3]

Education is also guaranteed under Article 37. 'Unfortunately [,] these guarantees have suffered erosion due to political exigencies. The right to private ownership was abridged due to the nationalization policy of the first PPP Government. When this policy was reversed, the labour laws suffered. More scandalous has been the violation of Women's rights and Children's rights. The HRCP has brought to light many violations and afforded legal help to the victims.' According to the HRCP report 1998, 'Women's subordination remained so routine, by custom and by tradition that much of the endemic violence against her was considered normal behaviour.' In the HRCP 2000 report, it is stated that even the government accepts there is gender disparity in education.

In Pakistan, it is generally conceded that women's rights are human rights. Sadly these rights are upheld more in the breach than in the observation. The human rights most blatantly and most commonly trampled upon are women's rights. They are trampled upon in unspeakable ways. It has to be realized, and, moreover, implemented, that unless women are empowered and their status is upheld, no values can flourish in society. Women's rights are hampered by legislation, the least of which are the divorce laws. Children's rights are trampled upon in spite of existing laws. According to Asma Jahangir, child marriages take place even though they are illegal under the Child Marriage Restraint Act 1929.[4]

One aspect of children's rights that has attracted international attention is child labour, which exists despite protective laws. Article 11 (3) states that: 'No child below 14 years shall be engaged in any factory or mine, or any other hazardous employment.' Article 37 (e) provides greater cover: 'The state shall make provisions for ensuring that children are not employed in vocations unsuited to their age.' Despite these provisions, children are employed in carpet weaving and football manufacturing. Others begin their working lives as unpaid apprentices to motor mechanics. The acts of violence against and abuse of children and women are too numerous to be listed here. Suffice it to say that abuse is rampant and real. In a patriarchal set up women and children are the most vulnerable members of society.

Abuse offends human dignity, and the greatest enemy of human dignity is 'terror'. It is terror, not greed, that principally threatens the rights of all citizens. Crime has proliferated, especially after 1981. Drug abuse and Kalashnikov culture need to be controlled and prevented since the maintenance of law and order is the basic responsibility of the state. Yet these are mostly individual (or gang) acts. 'Terror' also includes violence motivated by ethnic, religious, or sectarian prejudice. Perpetrators of crimes know and recognize that their actions are wrong. Those who spread terror in the name of race or religion, especially religion, do so because they imagine their acts to be meritorious.

The HRCP is pressuring the government to protect people held under the Blasphemy Act. This act is a relic of the British Indian criminal law of 1860. The application of this law is a real cause of concern. A person has only to be accused, and his life is lost. Not only have members of the minority communities been victimized—but even orthodox Muslims have been killed in custody by fellow prisoners. Judges who acquit such accused, are killed. Lawyers who defend people charged with blasphemy are constantly threatened. First individuals, mostly physicians, were targeted, and now worshippers in the act of prayers are killed. To put it mildly, the government's role in protecting the rights of all its citizens has been ineffective.

The human rights dictum for social and economic development is 'Equal wages for equal work'. Social stratification is measured by a person's socioeconomic status. It is unlikely that this standard will ever fail. The only remedy is to provide equal opportunity to all citizens to attain a socio-economic status that is in keeping with human dignity. The socialistic measures have given place to market forces. Labour laws are in place, but there is a need to offer incentives and a need to provide workers with security of service. Where these have been absent there has been a marked deterioration in economic productivity. Economic status determines social status. The role of human rights should be to implement workers' rights to education, health, and social welfare.

Human rights are those inherent rights of human beings that derive from a general sense of morality. They may be inspired by or opposed by particular religious beliefs. In that sense, the rise of Jainism and Buddhism, with their cardinal belief in the sanctity of human and animal life, of all creatures capable of feeling pain or terror, can be characterized as the first historical movement for human rights in South Asia. In the context of South Asia, it needs to be noted that Hinduism as a religion is not intrinsically against human rights, but since it is a religion where orthopraxy outpaces orthodoxy, abuses have found their way into social norms. In Islam, we have two lists the rights of God and the rights of worshippers. This meant that if a man had done injury to another human being, God would not forgive the sin unless the injured party forgave it. A conceptual framework of human rights was welcomed when recognized by a conquering horde.

The British, though they initially trampled on all human rights, nevertheless professed a notion of the White Man's Burden—a mission of civilizing the peoples they conquered and introducing laws that upheld human rights. There were certain practices in Indian society pertaining to gender that were viewed with moral ambivalence mainly *jauhar* and *sati*. What were the original and authentic Hindu precepts that surfaced when the British tried to lay down laws concerning Hindu practices.

In the matter of *sati* the immolation of the widow on the funeral pyre of the husband, there were conflicting authorities. *Agni Purana* promised paradise to volunteer widows, while *Medhātithi* declared *sati* to be suicide and against the Shastras.[5] *Sati* could not have been universal otherwise the related issue of the re-marriage of widows would not have arisen. A.L. Basham has cited *Narada* pages xii and 97 and *Parasa* LV:30 as the text allowing the re-marriage of widows.[6] Basham held that such practices were not prevalent in the Vedic ages, or even until 1000 BC. The *Code of Manu*, however, forbade the re-marriage of widows.

Widow re-marriage found a venerable champion in Ishwar Chandra Vidyasagar (1820–1891). With his support, the British could pass the Hindu Widow Re-Marriage Act on 2 July 1856. Another gender-related piece of legislation was the Age of Consent Act (signed on 19 March 1891). This had followed a protest at the plight of child brides. The Brahmo Samaj was cast out of the pale of Hinduism, but they had been able to advance scriptural arguments.

These were more or less in the domestic domain, but similar resistance was faced in the public sphere. Allopathy was initially resisted both by Hindus and Muslims who had hitherto relied on traditional medicine. The outbreak of plague in the port city of Bombay (now Mumbai) led to sanitation measures against which Hindus rioted.[7] When W.M. Haffkine (1860–1930) discovered an effective anti-plague vaccine, Bal Gangadhar Tilak (1856–1925) challenged the theory that diseases were caused by germs in the body. Tilak hinted that the British were using Indians as guinea pigs.

The same mentality can be witnessed in contemporary Pakistan where lady health workers have been shot dead for administering anti-polio drops. Even more, resistance was witnessed against lockouts and then against vaccines during the Covid-19 pandemic. Thus, it is not a particular system of belief, but a fanatical mindset which causes disruption. Such being the case, we have to find an appeal to human rights that transcends particular religious prescriptions. This was the problem faced by the British, who were not only a minority but also an alien race. Vincent Smith explains that 'These steps marked a new feature of British rule; for they avowedly interfered with social and religious customs. The ground of interference was the universal law of humanity; it was now maintained that not even religious sanction could stand against the universal moral law.'[8]

The same concept was highlighted by Mrinalini Sinha while explaining the reforms initiated by Lord Landsdowne: 'Despite their avowed concern to avoid unsettling Indian religious belief, British reformers were in no doubt that there existed an absolute standard of morality, and where, as Landsdowne insisted in the debate on the Age of Consent Act, if religion and morality were in conflict, the former had to give way.'[9]

This was not an arbitrary standard. It is floating but palpable. In the initial propagation of beliefs, an appeal is made to universal moral values. The Holy Quran warns of the time 'when baby girls, buried alive, are asked for what crime they were put to death' (81:8-9). Since female infanticide was practised by pagans, the Quran is protesting over the female infanticide of non-Muslims. Again: 'This is how We make Our revelations clear for people of knowledge' (7:32). Pakistan inherited a number of British era laws, indeed a British legal system, but it also inherited a tribal system with its novel notions of justice, in which religion was not allowed a say. The resistance to the Soviet invasion of Afghanistan because it mobilized the tribal areas ended up strengthening tribalism more than religious fanaticism.

MINORITIES RIGHTS.—Independence in 1947 was accompanied by a fresh bout of communal riots. Two provinces had been partitioned simultaneously with India, which harmed official efforts to contain the killing and the mayhem. The after-tremors of the partition riots—mostly in the East wing were felt till 1951 when the Liaquat–Nehru Pact was signed. This was to ensure the protection of minorities in both India and Pakistan. Pakistan despite complaining of the discriminatory nature of the Indian Citizenship (Amendment) Act 2019 has so far not invoked the Liaquat–Nehru Pact 1951, which would protect it from the charge of interfering in the internal affairs of India.

During the Islamization Movement of 1977, religious sentiments were heightened but directed more against those considered heretics than the followers of other religions. In December 1992, in the wake of the destruction in India of the Babri Mosque, there were retaliatory attacks on Hindu temples in Pakistan, but these were swiftly contained. Since the secession of East Pakistan in 1971, the Hindu population of Pakistan was significantly reduced, making them more vulnerable.

Some disputes were of a civil nature. The Hindu cremation ground on Tipu Road, Rawalpindi was reduced from 10 to 2 kanals; but on the appeal of the President of the Pakistan Hindu-Sikh Social Welfare Council, Jagmohan Kumar Arora, the Punjab Revenue Board accepted the appeal and the original allocation was restored.[10] Two years later there was violence and the patron-in-chief of the Pakistan Hindu Council, Ramesh Kumar Vankwani, listed the destruction of temples and idols.[11] The Supreme Court ordered restitution. On Ramesh Kumar's plea, the Supreme Court ordered the Khyber Pakhtunkhwa government to protect and preserve the Karak Temple, which Muslim fanatics had dismantled in 1997.[12]

When the draft of the Hindu Marriage Bill was presented, Clause 12 (iii) was contested because it provided for the annulment of marriage in case any one of the spouses converted to Islam. In Islamic law, such annulment would be unavoidable, but Ramesh Kumar Vankwani explained the presentiments of the Hindu community: 'There are fears the clause would be misused for forced conversions of married women the same way young girls are being subjected to forced conversions.'[13]

Since this was a problem on the ground, Sindh Assembly Member Nand Kumar Goklani tabled a Bill criminalizing forced conversions. On 24 November 2016 the Sindh assembly passed the Criminal Law (Protection of Minorities) Bill 2015. This made forced conversion a crime with a punitive clause.[14] Finally, the Hindu Marriage Bill was passed in the National Assembly in September 2015 and approved by the Senate two years later. This was the first personal law for Hindus across the country.[15] Within the week, it was found that the vote bank of the minorities had reached almost 3 million. Among them, Hindu voters have a dominating majority (1.49 million), followed by Christian voters (1.32 million). There were 1,634 Buddhist voters mostly living in Sindh and Punjab.[16]

Matters did not remain peaceful for long and in February 2019 Prime Minister Imran Khan took notice when unidentified people attacked a Hindu temple in Kumbh, Khairpur District and fled after setting statues and Hindu holy books on fire.[17] The Supreme Court on 4 October 2019 constituted a special bench for speedy implementation of its 2014 verdict. Drafted by Justice Tasadduq Hussain Jilani, to promptly register criminal cases for the desecration of places of worship of minorities, or on the violation of any of their rights guaranteed under law.[18]

Similarly, the Islamabad High Court disposed of all pleas against the construction of a Hindu temple in Islamabad Sector H-9/2, and the disbursement of Rs 100 million for its construction. The construction had been opposed by the Capital Development Authority on technical grounds, but the Supreme Court overruled them.[19]

The Parliament formed an Implementation Committee for the Sindh Minority Rights Commission Bill 2019 and the Criminal Law (Protection of Minorities Bill) 2019 when apprised of six controversial cases of conversions of Hindu girls. Thereafter the scene shifted to Khyber Pakhtunkhwa when on the first day of 2021, the Chief Justice of the Supreme Court Gulzar Ahmed (2019–2022) sought a report on the burning and vandalization of the shrine of Hindu Saint Shri Param Ram Hansji Maharaj in Karak district on 30 December 2020. On 5 January 2021 the Supreme Court ordered the re-construction of the shrine and to recover the expenses from Maulvi Mohammad Sharif who had instigated the mob to desecrate the shrine.[20]

Not only the law but the Sharia came into action when the Council of Islamic Ideology condemned a mob attack at Ganesh Temple, at Bhong Sharif on 4 August 2021: 'Demolishing any of their religious places of worship is a clear violation of Islamic law and Pakistani law.[21] Earlier, the National Assembly had condemned the attack on the Bhong temple. The resolution was unanimously adopted.[22] The matter lingered on, and the Supreme Court asked the police to arrest the culprits behind the Ganesh Mandir attack and twenty suspects were taken into custody.[23] The Karak Temple contention ended when 215 Hindu Yatris (pilgrims) including 159 from India performed their religious rituals there.[24]

CHRISTIAN COMMUNITY.—The first major incident of violence involving the Christian community of Pakistan took place in All Saints' Church, Peshawar. On 22 September 2013, 127 worshippers were killed by twin suicide bombers. Heightened fanaticism and heightened militancy were having unexpected consequences in the Pashtun capital. Terror attacks are listed in Chapter 53, here we are mentioning how innocent and vulnerable minority communities have suffered violence leading to feelings of insecurity.

On 4 November 2014, a Christian couple, Shama and Shahzad Masih were lynched, dragged to a brick kiln in Kot Radha Kishan, and burnt to death. The Supreme Court of Pakistan summoned the police officers beginning with the Inspector General to explain their lax attitude and failure to protect Shama and Shahzad Masih. Blasphemy was alleged which was sufficient to enrage a mob.[25] The Supreme Court's strictures had their effect.

In Makli village the police saved an illiterate couple from being lynched and later arrested a maulvi for inciting the violence.[26] The police had no opportunity to intervene in the next such outrage when the Muslim classmates of a 17–year-old Christian boy, Sharoon Masih, lynched him in Burewala, Vehari because he drank water from the same glass as the Muslim boys.[27]

In December 2017, nine people were killed in Quetta at the Bethel Memorial Methodist Church in a suicide attack. However, the police arrived within fifteen minutes, killed the remaining suicide bombers, and averted a much larger tragedy.[28] Matters reached a new height when on 3 December 2021, Priyantha Kumara, a Buddhist Sri Lankan manager of Rajco Industries in Sialkot, was dragged to the road, beaten with stones and iron rods, and after he was killed, his body was burnt. Three policemen had reached the spot, but they were hopelessly outnumbered.[29] Four days later a delegation of ulama representing all sects called on the Sri Lankan High Commissioner and called the murder un-Islamic. On 31 January 2022, a Christian priest William Siraj was shot dead after Mass, in a typical attack mounted by gunmen on a motorcycle.[30]

Cause Celebre. The *cause celebre* was that of Aasia Bibi, a Christian lady arrested for blasphemy and sentenced to death on 8 November 2010. When the

Governor of Punjab, Salman Taseer, demanded that she be pardoned, one of his own guards Mumtaz Qadri shot him on 4 January 2011. Qadri said that he killed the Governor for opposing the Blasphemy Act.

The Lahore High Court upheld her death sentence on 16 October 2014, but the Supreme Court stayed her execution and heard her appeal. The verdict and the sentence were overturned. Chief Justice Saqib Nisar defended the Supreme Court judgment asserting that the bench had a love for the Holy Prophet (PBUH) but asked: 'If there is no proof against someone, how can we punish them?'[31]

Mumtaz Qadri, meanwhile, had been convicted and hanged for the murder of Salman Taseer on 29 February 2016. A review petition challenging Aasia Bibi's acquittal was dismissed in January 2019. Aasia Bibi left Pakistan to ensure her safety.

In 2012, an 11-year-old Christian girl Rimsha Masih reportedly suffering from Down's Syndrome was charged with blasphemy. On 20 November 2012, Rimsha was cleared of all charges by the Islamabad High Court and her acquittal was subsequently confirmed by the Pakistan Supreme Court in January 2013.

AHMADIS.—In 1974, the National Assembly designated the Ahmadiyya community as non-Muslim. Theologically, all Muslim sects consider Ahmadis non-Muslim and Ahmadis also consider all non-Ahmadis non-Muslim. However, bringing legislation to that effect rendered a subject of religious polemics a matter of human rights.

The members of the Ahmadiyya community routinely face assassination and terror. On 8 November 2020, Mahboob Khan (75) was killed. The Ahmadiyya community called it the result of a hate campaign. On 26 March 2022, the Supreme Court overturned the verdict of the Lahore High Court which had endorsed blasphemy charges against Ahmadis. According to *The Express Tribune* 27 March 2022, the Supreme Court observed: 'To deprive a non-Muslim (minority) of our country from holding his religious beliefs, to obstruct him from professing and practicing his religion within the four walls of his place of worship is against the grain of our democratic Constitution and repugnant to the spirit and character of our Islamic Republic.' The court noted that even though Article 260(3) of the Constitution declared Ahmadis as non-Muslims, it neither disowned them as citizens, nor deprived them of their entitlement to their fundamental rights.

CHILDREN'S RIGHTS.—In Pakistan, children suffer because they are deprived of freedom, or because they are deprived of education. Sometimes parents are too poor to provide sustenance or education, but many a time, children are kidnapped and inducted either into forced unpaid labour or as beggars.

A forced labour camp was discovered on 11 May 1967 at Ghorghushti.[32] It was discovered when an 11–year-old boy Azad managed to escape. Azad had been kidnapped from Lawrencepur Railway Station. The Hazro police recovered nine prisoners including teenagers who had all been kidnapped from different places. They were being forced to construct a road under the most terrifying conditions, including torture. The Hazro police arrested four slave drivers.[33]

As late as 1 April 2018, the Supreme Court took up a petition about brick kiln workers, who were bonded labourers denied wages and the facilities allowed to workers under the Constitution. In brick kilns not all bonded labourers were young boys but many adults too. The petition complained that the kiln workers were being denied education, a basic right.[34]

Roshaneh Zafar the Managing Director of Kashf Foundation reported the ILO's figures for Pakistan that there are 12.5 million children below the age of 14 in the labour force. ILO also noted that half of them are less than 10 years old, while 264,000 children are employed as domestic workers. Meanwhile, data on informal employment is difficult to come by.[35]

The occasion for the report was the plight of a minor girl servant Tayyaba, who was subject to ill treatment by her employers, an additional district and sessions judge Raja Khurram Ali Khan and his wife Maheen Zafar. Within two hours of being convicted, the couple was released on bail. The Islamabad High Court said that the prosecution could not prove the charge of torture. However, Roshaneh Zafar adds the Supreme Court took *suo moto* notice of the case and sent the employers to jail for one year.

Boys fare no better, and it is not uncommon to receive news of boys being subject to police torture such as 18–year-old Adeel Nazir of Malipura. While the police registered a case against the owner of the factory where Nazir worked, his mother accused the police not only of subjecting Adeel Nazir to torture but also of poisoning him.[36] In another case, the Station House Officer, Dost Mohammad and *moharrar* (scribe) Ismail were remanded into custody for the custodial death of Shah Zeb, a student at Racines School in Peshawar.[37]

Street children fared no better. At the auditorium of Sindh Boy Scouts, both girls and boys complained of being subject to abuse. Laws against such abuses were passed in 2011 but were not implemented. The plight of school-going children is no better, i.e., students are tortured and abused by their teachers, not only in religious seminaries but in modern schools as well.

RIGHTS OF WOMEN.—As far as legislation is concerned, Pakistani women are well-protected. According to the Protection of Women Act (2006) complaints of rape were treated as admissions of adultery. The Act was amended to remove this anomaly. A Bill to declare Domestic Violence a crime was passed in 2009. Protection against Harassment of Women at Workplace Act. 2010 and the Prevention of Anti-Women Practices Act 2011 are comprehensive.

The complication is that there is religious and social resistance to such legislation. On the one hand, are the ulama who voice dissent over such laws. On the other is the supersession of Islamic laws by tribal and social customs that cause death and injury to our women. We have seen above, how a girl worker Tayyaba was treated by a member of the lower judiciary; in rural and tribal areas, the situation is far worse. Village headmen at a meeting called Panchayat, deal out punishments such as gang rape, which under Islamic law are cardinal crimes.

Some girls have been killed for dancing at weddings, a routine practice in Pakistan, while some have been killed for demanding a divorce, a right guaranteed in Islam, but considered a stigma in tribal societies. Public assertions of Women's Rights are opposed. An Aurat (Woman) March organized by Dr Farzana Bari on International Women's Day (8 March 2020) was pelted with stones. The religious parties had been allowed to hold their own Haya (Modesty) March at the same time and place. The Haya March participants were well-supplied with stones and chilli powder, with which they pelted the Aurat March participants. A judicial inquiry was demanded by the Aurat March organizers, but it is not known that one took place. In 2022, the Minister for Religious Affairs Maulana Noorul Huq Qadri requested Prime Minister Imran Khan to convert International Women's Day to International Hijab Day. This was to prevent another Women's Rights procession.

The Council of Islamic Ideology (CII) meanwhile, has been taking a moderate stand. CII Chairman Maulana Mohammad Khan Sheerani said that any woman over the age of 40 could become a judge or a *qazi*, but only if she observes *purdah/hijab* (veil). When asked to explain the age limit, the CII chairman said, 'This is a mature age, when women no longer remain attractive or marriageable.' CII also announced that the practice of pronouncing 'talaq', or the intention to divorce, three consecutive times should be deemed an offence. This is a measure that offers unprecedented relief to Muslim women.[38]

In the matter of *hijab* too, the CII adopted a moderate stance ruling that it was not necessary for a woman to cover her face, feet or hands up to the wrists.[39] The Federal Shariat Court, on its part, ruled that fixing a minimum age for marriage was not un-Islamic. Previously orthodox circles had been opposing the fixation of a minimum age for marriage as un-Islamic and a petition against such fixation filed by Omar Farooq Bhoja was turned down.[40]

It is in the traditional Panchayat, made up of village elders and traditional Jirga made up of tribal leaders that deal out punishments which are actually offences under Islamic law. In retaliation for a rape attempt, the Panchayat ordered the gang rape of the married daughter of the suspect. The victim committed suicide after she got pregnant due to the rape.[41] A 17-year-old girl whose brother had committed rape in Multan was sentenced to 'revenge rape' by the Panchayat.[42] This report recalled the most widely reported case of this nature; the gang-rape of Mukhtaran Mai by a Muzaffargarh Panchayat in

2002. While the military court had sentenced six of the accused to death, in March 2005, the Lahore High Court overturned the verdict, acquitting five and commuting the death sentence of the sixth to life imprisonment. The Supreme Court upheld the acquittal in a two-to-one majority judgment in April 2011.

The perpetrators of the extrajudicial and un-Islamic rape which undoubtedly took place are still at large. In the same town of Muzaffargarh, some police officers were accused of abetting and participating in the gang rape of a job-seeking lady at Faisal Stadium in July 2015. At around the same time, on 13 October 2015, a lady who complained that the police gang-raped her, immolated herself in front of the police station.

Kohistan Wedding Dance. Rape is not the only punishment that is awarded but outright murder takes place for very innocuous acts. In 2011, In Sartai, a video surfaced in which five girls were shown dancing at a wedding in a remote village in Kohistan. It was alleged they were dancing with boys, but the video frame does not show them. It was alleged by Dr Farzana Bari of the Quaid-i-Azam University, Islamabad, that all five girls had been killed by the tribals. In November 2016, the Supreme Court ordered the Kohistan Sessions judge to visit the village and submit a report. A witness Muhammad Afzal contended that the girls had been killed on the orders of the Jirga. A prayer leader from the area, Muhammad Javed Azad belied him. Dr Farzana Bari sought an order from the Supreme Court to have the girls seen in the video, produced in court for identification. The Supreme Court replied that being a constitutional court it was not its job to call the girls for an in-camera appearance. Habibur Rahman, an uncle of the five girls assured the court that the girls were alive.[43] The commission headed by the Kohistan Sessions judge suspected that the five girls were dead. Two girls were produced by the locals who did not resemble the girls in the video.[44] The witness Muhammad Afzal was gunned down in Abbottabad in 2019. He was shot five times on a busy road and died on the spot. An activist Benazir Jatoi said that witness protection was almost non-existent.[45] About a week later Farzana Bari said that initially eight men after confessing to Afzal's murder had been nominated in the First Information Report (FIR). She criticized the last two commissions for failing to do justice.[46] The multiple murder of the girls was allegedly ordered by the local cleric, although no capital punishment is prescribed by the Shariah for festive dancing.

Saima Sarwar Murder. Another high-profile case was the murder on 6 April 1999, of Saima Sarwar for demanding a divorce, a right sanctioned in Islam. Saima's father, Ghulam Sarwar Mohmand, was president of the Sarhad Chamber of Commerce and Industry. Saima's mother, Sultana Sarwar (a doctor), had her shot dead in the chambers of Asma Jahangir and Hina Jilani while visiting there on the pretext of giving her the signed divorce papers from her

(Saima's) husband. The gunman was shot dead by a policeman while trying to escape. The other defendants were forgiven by Saima's father. Captain Nadir Mirza (Saima's suitor) named as co-respondent was discharged from the army. It was plain that Islamic law would not be allowed to stand between a citizen and a tribal custom.

Qandeel Baloch. Fouzia Azeem, known by her stage name Qandeel Baloch, was a Pakistani model, actress, social media celebrity and activist. She was the country's first social media celebrity. She was seen in a video carousing with a respected cleric Maulvi Abdul Qavi. The video went viral and on 15 July 2016, her brother Muhammad Waseem killed her for honour. Maulvi Abdul Qavi was acquitted. Muhammad Waseem had confessed to the murder the next day, but all prosecution witnesses resiled from their original statements. On 21 August 2019, the parents of Qandeel Baloch forgave their son for the murder of their daughter.[47]

Those who murder their wives are not easily acquitted, because they have different parents. A Sindh High Court Bench directed the provincial chief secretary to have the Domestic Violence (Prevention and Protection) Act 2013 implemented in letter and spirit. The Court observed that as per a Human Rights Watch study, 5,000 women were killed every year. The court deprecated the fact that despite complaints of torture and mistreatment of women by their husbands and in-laws, parents forced their daughters to go back to their husbands which resulted in their murders.[48]

Jail Conditions. Prime Minister Imran Khan ordered the implementation of SC Order 299/2020, which meant the release of women who could not afford to pay the fines for petty crimes.[49] A clear gender bias was witnessed in jail conditions. It was reported that over 3,500 women and children interned in jails across Pakistan were living in deplorable conditions. A Jails Reforms Committee formed on the orders of the Supreme Court said in its report that apart from 1,600 women and 1,500, there were 425 children living in jails with their convicted mothers. It was recommended that jail conditions be improved. The Committee Chairperson Asma Jahangir said that compared to the 1980s and 1990s the complaints of sexual abuse by female prisoners have seen a drastic decline, but the issue still persists in some jails.[50]

In September 2015, a *suo moto* action by two judges took up the pathetic conditions of prisoners, especially women. In an earlier order of 28 May 2015 the Supreme Court had taken the position that it was not sufficient for ombudsmen to address just individual complaints, rather they should address the systematic failures that were the root cause of maladministration. It also noted overcrowding in jails.[51] In July 2018 the Supreme Court ordered provincial governments to end overcrowding in jails. Senior Counsel Hafiz Ahsaan Ahmad Khokhar reported that in total 98 jails accommodate a total of 78,160 inmates against the sanctioned capacity of 56,353 prisoners. Out of these, women prisoners made up 1,955 inmates both convicts and those undergoing trial.[52]

Two years later the situation had not improved. The number of jails had increased to 116, but there were 79,603 inmates against the sanctioned capacity of 64,099 prisoners. Hafiz Ahsaan Khokhar and his committee recommended that special attention be given towards the supply of clean drinking water to all prisoners and visitors, seating arrangements for visitors, establishments of proper toilets and provision of health care facilities.[53]

In 2022, the Lahore High Court sought a report on remissions given to minority prisoners. Counsel Shahbaz Akmal Jandran pointed out that Rule No. 215 provided remission under the category of education for those convicted Muslim prisoners who completed their reading of the Holy Quran. He pointed out that non-Muslim convicts were not given such remission which was in violation of six articles of the Constitution.[54]

There are some jails that paint a contrary picture. A search operation in Larkana jail caused unrest when mobile phones and other prohibited items were recovered from prisoners. The prisoners complained of inhuman treatment. The issue was later resolved peacefully when jail authorities decided to defer the search operation and the shifting of inmates to other jails.[55] Even recently the Larkana jail underwent an eight-day crisis when seven policemen were held hostage by prisoners. The Larkana Central Jail Superintendent Liaquat Ali Pirzada was suspended on 7 July 2021 and the very next day, a riot broke out. The jail was undoubtedly overcrowded and on 12 January 2022, thirteen troublemakers were shifted to other jails. The inmates demanded a supply of illicit drugs, alcohol and 'possibly weapons'. They wanted both prisoners and jailors of their choice.[56]

Women prisoners no matter how hardened, were unable to adopt such tactics against burly jail superintendents. Outside too, in some areas, women were disenfranchised. In Khyber Pakhtunkhwa women under an agreement, reached among male contestants, were not allowed to vote. Both the UNDP and the EU asked the provincial government to ensure that women voted in the then-coming local government elections.[57] The Election Commission of Pakistan noted that in seventeen constituencies 95 per cent of women did not vote in the 2013 general elections. This was on 31 December 2016. One year later, during the local government by-elections, not a single woman cast her vote in the districts of Dir.[58]

RIGHT OF EXPRESSION.—Journalists also form a category of persons vulnerable to interference. Journalists belong to political parties or are employed by media houses partial to political parties, or an ideology. The Pakistan Press Foundation released the figure of journalists who faced violence or other obstructions. In the report prepared by Tooba Masood for the years 2002 to 2019, about 699 Press Freedom cases were monitored. In 2018, twenty-two physical assaults took place, and thirty media workers were attacked. Forty-eight journalists became victims of targeted murder, and twenty-four were killed in the line of duty. Eighteen journalists were arrested, twenty-six detained; thirty-seven had cases registered against them. Twenty-six were kidnapped, five were harassed six faced defamation cases. Journalists attacked in media house premises were thirty-two, and those attacked in their residences were eleven.[59]

It would be unfair to blame the governments of the day alone for such infringement of human rights, as political parties, pressure groups, and some professional bodies have been known to mount attacks. In times of military dictatorships, censorship was easily enforced, rather a culture of self-censorship was nurtured. But even during such times, journalists responded boldly. When the renowned Urdu poet Josh Malihabadi was banned from the official media under the Zia regime in 1979, the Karachi Press Club made him an Honorary Member.

In democratic regimes, highhandedness takes place because election campaigns are hard-hitting and personal; politicians become unusually sensitive to media pinpricks. Normally it is the crime reporter or the city reporter that is picked up, but when stakes are high media house owners are also held. The prime example is that of Mir Shakilur Rahman the owner of the Jang/Geo group. On 12 March 2020, the National Accountability Bureau (NAB) arrested him in a 34-year-old case. The NAB ruled that the Lahore Development had allowed fifteen plots measuring one kanal each to be 'exempted.' Mir Shakilur Rahman, through a Power of Attorney allegedly secured 'exemption' on fifty-four plots measuring one kanal each. Journalist Hamid Mir alleged that following the arrest of Mir Shakilur Rahman, PEMRA had asked cable operators to block the Geo TV channel and subsequently it was blocked.[60] The chief justice of the Islamabad High Court said the judiciary would not allow the government to ban the media.

Matiullah Jan, a senior journalist, was abducted from G-6/1-3, Islamabad. The scene was caught on Closed Circuit Television (CCTV) causing outrage. After about twelve hours Matiullah Jan returned safely home.[61] Another journalist Ali Imran Syed, of the *Jang* group, went missing from his house but returned home after protests.[62]

A *Dawn* Special Report stated that between 3 May 2020 and 20 April 2021, there were 148 instances of violence against journalists. These included six murders and seven failed assassination attempts.[63] These figures show that though journalism may be a profitable profession, it is also a hazardous one.

FORCED DISAPPEARANCES.—Perhaps forced disappearances began because of poor prosecution rates, and poor witness protection, but soon the clandestine removal of persons without having to account for their disappearance in court was the beginning of this practice. Or perhaps it began under the Z.A. Bhutto regime when political rivals were interred in Azad Kashmir.[64] By 2007 an association of missing persons was functioning. Amina Masood

Janjua, Chairperson of Defence of Human Rights Trust alleged that action had been taken against Chief Justice Iftikhar Muhammad Chaudhry because of his having taken *suo moto* notice of missing persons: 'His commitment to providing justice to the missing people has perhaps upset the Government.'[65]

Continuing, Amina Masood Janjua stated that twenty-three victims of forced disappearance had been released, while sixty new cases were filed during the past four months, with only thirteen left. Their continued detention at undisclosed locations was a clear violation of law. Next Amina Janjua announced that about a hundred relatives of missing persons wearing orange-coloured jackets shall march to the National Assembly on International Human Rights Day.[66] This was seven years later than her previously mentioned statement. It took one year more before the Senate of Pakistan took notice of the missing persons' outcry.

The Senate on 22 December 2015 unanimously approved measures to address the phenomenon of enforced disappearances. Senator Farhatullah Babar said missing persons represented a section of society having no access to justice 'no matter how expensive and how slow.'[67] A Commission of Inquiry on Enforced Disappearances was formed, but the Supreme Court expressed its disappointment over its performance. Later, Amina Janjua revealed that out of 749 cases pending before the Supreme Court, she had categorized 55 cases as per earlier directions of the Court where there was concrete evidence about the disappearance of a missing person. Ms Janjua submitted a letter by Dr Imran Munir dated 21 December 2015 that indicated that her husband was being held in Westridge, Rawalpindi.[68]

The Supreme Court asked the registrar of the Commission of Inquiry on Enforced Disappearances, founded in March 2011, to submit a report about 'perceptible progress' in locating missing persons. The Commission contended that it had disposed of 3,000 cases while 1,577 cases are still pending.[69] At the Eighth Judicial Conference, it was declared that enforced disappearance is a crime.[70] The next month Chief Justice Saqib Nisar of the Supreme Court directed law enforcement agencies to set up a special cell to ascertain information about missing persons. He also threatened the distraught relatives of missing persons with contempt proceedings for their unruly behaviour.[71]

Next, Chief Justice Saqib Nisar while presiding over a high-profile meeting of stakeholders that the Supreme Court would not tolerate such illegalities regarding the life and liberty of citizens.[72] By this time, Prime Minister Imran Khan had taken notice and instructed an amendment to the Pakistan Penal Code in order to criminalize any attempt by an individual or an organization to make someone disappear by force.[73] Within a week, on the assurance of Zia Langove, the Home Minister of Balochistan, twenty-eight missing persons returned.[74]

In a very important development, Maj.-Gen. Asif Ghafoor, of the ISPR issued the following statement: 'Our hearts beat with the family of every missing person. We share their pain, and we are in the process of tracing them.' The same day, relatives of missing persons ended a two-week sit-in before the Karachi residence of President Arif Alvi, after four more missing persons were released. Sajid Gondal, Joint Secretary of the Securities and Exchange Commission of Pakistan, went missing on 3 September 2020 and later returned home after a week.[75] The Islamabad High Court imposed a fine of Rs 10 million for being unable to discover one Ghulam Qadir who had been missing for six years.[76]

Shireen Mazari, the Minister for Human Rights assured the protesting families of missing persons that Prime Minister Imran Khan would meet them 'next month'. Most of the protestors were from Balochistan and had been sitting for a month on 20 February 2021. A month later, the Sindh High Court criticized the federal government for taking no interest in the missing person's case. The Sindh High Court granted a last chance to the federal secretaries of Defence and Interior to collect reports from the internment centres about missing persons and submit them before the next hearing.[77]

The phenomenon of missing persons took a new turn, when after the 19 February 2021 Daska by-polls twenty presiding officers went missing. This presumably was done to manipulate the results. On 1 December 2021, Chief Justice Athar Minallah addressed the prime minister and members of his cabinet. The Chief Justice, Islamabad High Court noted: 'The practice of enforced disappearances has existed in Pakistan over a considerable time. The existence of this phenomenon is intolerable in a society governed under the Constitution.'[78]

This homily was occasioned by the disappearance of a journalist Mudassar Mahmood Naaru, who had gone missing on 19 August 2018. The Islamabad High Court while still seized of the petition in Mudassar Naaru's case proposed that state functionaries responsible for providing protection to citizens should be tried for high treason.[79] The Islamabad High Court asked Attorney-General Khalid Javed Khan to take steps to prosecute officials responsible for the abduction of citizens. The Attorney-General replied that during dictatorship there might be tacit approvals of such acts but elected prime ministers would not approve of such high-handedness by any state institution.[80]

After the kidnapping case of Sobia Batool was taken up by the Supreme Court, Punjab police statistics revealed that 40,000 had been abducted in the last four years, and the police were clueless about the whereabouts of 35,000 women.[81] The Commission of Inquiry on Enforced Disappearances said since it was formed (March 2011) 8,463 citizens had gone missing out of which only 3,284 had returned home. The Supreme Court remarked that the Commission had not taken action against any person responsible for enforced disappearances.[82]

Still seized of the petition of Mudassar Naaru, the Islamabad High Court called enforced disappearances an Act of Treason. The chief justice asked why the chief executive shouldn't be held responsible. The new Prime Minister

Shehbaz Sharif promised the people of Balochistan that he would broach the cases of missing persons with 'powerful quarters'.[83] The Islamabad High Court told the Interior Secretary to take up the issue of seventy-six persons, missing since March with Prime Minister Shehbaz Sharif.

Chief Justice Islamabad High Court, Athar Minallah, directed the federal government to issue notices to all chief executives from Pervez Musharraf to Shehbaz Sharif asking why proceedings should not be initiated against them for subversion of the Constitution, in the context of State Policy on Enforced Disappearances.[84] Chief Justice Athar Minallah said that the Commission of Inquiry on Enforced Disappearance was a burden on the exchequer and asked it to justify its continued existence.[85] There the matter rests at the time of writing.

Notes

1. I.A. Rehman, 'Human Rights', in Rafi Raza (ed.), *Pakistan in Perspective* (Karachi: Oxford University Press, 1997), p. 311.
2. Ibid., p. 312.
3. Uzma Qureshi, *Human Rights* (Islamabad: Higher Education Commission, 2003), p. 4.
4. Asma Jahangir, *Newsline*, August 2002, p. 22.
5. Kirk Straughan, 'The Abolition of Sati in India', *Investigator*, January 2008, p. 3.
6. A.L. Basham, *The Wonder That Was India*, 3rd ed. (London: Sidgwick and Jackson, 1967), p. 186.
7. Vincent A. Smith, *The Oxford History of India*, 4th ed. (Oxford University Press, 1981), p. 691.
8. Ibid., p. 588.
9. Mrinalini Sinha, 'The Age of Consent Act: The Ideal of Masculinity and Colonial Ideology in Late Nineteenth Century Bengal,' in Tony Stewart (ed.), *Shaping Bengali Worlds: Public and Private* (East Lansing, MI: Asian Studies Center, 1989), p. 100.
10. *Dawn*, 2 March 2013.
11. *Dawn*, 17 February 2015.
12. *Dawn*, 17 April 2015.
13. *Dawn*, 14 February 2016.
14. *Dawn*, 25 November 2016.
15. *Dawn*, 3 January 2017.
16. *Dawn* 8 January 2017.
17. *Dawn*, 7 February 2019.
18. *Dawn*, 4 October 2019.
19. *Dawn*, 8 July 2020.
20. *Dawn*, 6 January 2021.
21. *Dawn*, 10 August 2021.
22. *Dawn*, 7 August 2021.
23. *Dawn*, 7 August 2021.
24. *Dawn*, 3 January 2022.
25. Ibid.
26. *Dawn*, 3 July 2015.
27. *Dawn*, 12 September 2017.
28. *Dawn*, 17 December 2017.
29. *Dawn*, 4 December 2021.
30. *Dawn*, 31 January 2022.
31. *Dawn*, 1 November 2018.
32. Ghorghushti is a town of Chhachh in Attock District and is on the border of North-West Punjab, and Hazara in Khyber Pakhtunkhwa province.

33. *Dawn*, 12 May 1967.
34. *Dawn*, 2 April 2018.
35. *Dawn*, 30 January 2019.
36. *Dawn*, 14 October 2011.
37. *Dawn*, 16 March 2021.
38. *Dawn*, 22 January 2015.
39. *Dawn*, 20 October 2015.
40. *Dawn*, 29 October 2021.
41. *Dawn*, 13 November 2016.
42. *Dawn*, 26 July 2017.
43. *Dawn*, 11 November 2016.
44. *Dawn*, 2 December 2016.
45. *Dawn*, 9 March 2019.
46. *Dawn*, 15 March 2019.
47. *Dawn*, 15 February 2019.
48. *Dawn*, 20 April 2019.
49. *Dawn*, 3 September 2020.
50. *Dawn*, 6 August 2016.
51. *Dawn*, 16 September 2015.
52. *Dawn*, 4 July 2018.
53. *Dawn*, 12 November 2020.
54. *Dawn*, 8 March 2022.
55. *Dawn*, 2 January 2021.
56. *Dawn*, 11 February 2022.
57. *Dawn*, 1 January 2017.
58. *Dawn*, 26 December 2017.
59. *Dawn*, 3 May 2019.
60. *Dawn*, 15 March 2020.
61. *Geo News*, 21 July 2020.
62. *Dawn*, 25 October 2020.
63. *Dawn*, 3 May 2021.
64. Mehmood Chaudhry, *Ba Yad-i-Yar-i-Mehrbanan* (Lahore: Classic, 2001), p. 79.
65. *Dawn*, 12 March 2007.
66. *Dawn*, 9 December 2014.
67. *Dawn*, 23 December 2015.
68. *Dawn*, 8 April 2016.
69. *Dawn*, 27 February 2018.
70. *Dawn*, 6 May 2018.
71. *Dawn*, 25 June 2018.
72. *Dawn*, 3 August 2018.
73. *Dawn*, 30 January 2019.
74. *Dawn*, 7 February 2019.
75. *Dawn*, 9 September 2020.
76. *Dawn*, 2 January 2021.
77. *Dawn*, 23 March 2021.
78. *Dawn*, 2 December 2021.
79. *Dawn*, 14 December 2021.
80. *Dawn*, 19 January 2022.
81. *Dawn* 25 January 2022.
82. Dawn 12 March 2022.
83. *The Express Tribune*, 1 May 2022.
84. *The Express Tribune*, 30 May 2022
85. *The Express Tribune*, 24 June 2022.

Chapter 53
The Judicial History of Pakistan

When Pakistan was established, it initially did not have a Supreme Court. Instead, the oath of office to the Governor-General Mohammad Ali Jinnah was administered by Sardar Abdul Rashid (1889–1979), the most senior judge of the Punjab High Court. Following the Indian Independence Act of 1947, an interim constitution was put in place. This constitution led to the establishment of a Federal Court, two High Courts in Lahore and Dhaka, a Chief Court in Sindh, and a court of the Judicial Commissioner in Peshawar. Later, the Federal Court was elevated to the status of the Supreme Court. Additionally, the Chief Court and the Court of the Judicial Commissioner were raised to the position of High Courts. Notably, Sindh and Balochistan shared the same High Court.

CONSTITUTIONAL CASES.—The decisions of the superior judiciary which shaped the political course of Pakistan were constitutional in nature. The first landmark case was the Tamizuddin Khan Case. Governor-General Ghulam Mohammad had dissolved the Constituent Assembly, upon which the Speaker, Maulvi Tamizuddin Khan, approached the Sindh Chief Court.

Tamizuddin Khan Case. The full bench of the Sindh Chief Court unanimously declared the Governor-General's act of dissolution illegal and decided in favour of the Speaker. The entire panel of the Sindh Chief Court came to a unanimous decision, ruling that the Governor-General's action of dissolution was unlawful and sided with the Speaker's stance. The crux of the matter was the validity of Section 223–A, which granted the Constituent Assembly the authority to issue writs of *mandamus* and *quo warranto*. This section hadn't yet become law as it lacked the Governor-General's assent, rendering the legislation invalid. *Mandamus* refers to directions from a higher court to a lower court, while a *Quo Warranto* writ serves to investigate the basis or authority behind a functionary's issued order. Furthermore, the Governor-General raised an objection to Section 10, which restricted his discretion in selecting Ministers. The Chief Court held that the 'Indian Independence Act did not contain any express rule for the dissolution of the Constituent Assembly. It was a sovereign body created for a special purpose and it was to function till that purpose was achieved.'

The Governor-General appealed to the Federal Court which on 21 March 1955 overturned the judgement of the Sindh Chief Court by a 4 to 1 majority. The judgement was reversed on the main point that the Sindh Chief Court had struck it down. The Federal Court ruled that Section 223–A was not yet law as it had not yet received the assent of the Governor-General (the respondent).

According to Inam Aziz, Chief Justice Munir was closeted with the Governor-General on the eve of the judgement. When *Jang* showed that story to Chief Censor M.H. Askari, he held back the copy and demanded to know the source of the story.[1] The one dissenting judge A.R. Cornelius ruled, 'The Constituent Assembly was to be placed over the Governor-General the Chief Executive, because the Constituent Assembly was a sovereign body, and it was under its competence to amend the status under which the Governor-General was required to function.'[2]

It is not the fact that the dissenting judgement has been applauded, but the fact that the author of the majority judgement, Chief Justice Muhammad Munir, tried to explain his judgement five years later, in 1960, 'Situations such as these are not for the Court to deal with, unless the courts know that their writ would be restored and enforced.'[3] In other words, if a verdict is not enforceable, it is not valid.

Usif Patel Case. Following the above judgement of the Federal Court, the Governor-General Ghulam Mohammad promulgated the Emergency Powers Ordinance IX of 1955, which granted him the powers to (1) make provisions for framing the Constitution of Pakistan and (2) validate laws that had been passed by the Constituent Assembly but had not received the assent of the Governor-General, among other provisions.

In *Usif Patel vs. The Crown* (13 April 1955) the same Federal Court held that the power to make provisions to the Constitution could not be exercised by the Governor-General by means of an Ordinance. This judgement of the Federal Court held that only the Constituent Assembly was vested with the power to make provisions for the Constitution, to the exclusion of any other functionary.

The State vs. Dosso. The two previous judgements, in the Tamizuddin Khan case and in the Usif Patel Case were pronounced before the promulgation of any Constitution in Pakistan. The next such case came up after the 1956 Constitution had been abrogated and Martial Law was proclaimed on 7 October 1958. Ultimately, the validity of military rule was called into question. Citing Hans Kelsen's *General Theory of Law and State*, Chief Justice Muhammad Munir maintained that a successful resolution or a successful *coup d'état* is an internationally recognized *legal* method of changing a constitution. After the change, the national legal order must for its validity depend on the new law-creating organ (i.e. Martial Law).

It is true that the 1958 Martial Law faced no public resistance, and people despairing of stability, even welcomed it. The question was of restoring fundamental human rights because the reference to government in the cited Article II was to the structure and outline of government. Again, Justice A.R.

Cornelius dissented. He said that Fundamental Rights did not derive their entire validity from constitutional formulation and, being essential, human rights inherently belonged to every citizen.

Mehdi Ali Khan Case (1959). This was a case related to the East Wing. The Dacca High Court issued a writ mandamus asking the provincial government to withdraw the notification whereby it had acquired *Waqf* (Trust) property. When the Government of East Pakistan appealed to the Supreme Court, it upheld the appeal on the same grounds as in the Dosso Case. The Supreme Court ruled that fundamental rights are not a part of the law of the land and cannot be enforced. Both in the Tamizuddin Khan and Mehdi Ali Khan cases, the provincial courts upheld fundamental rights and the Supreme Court denied them.

Mir Hasan Case (1969). This case was filed in 1969 after the 1962 Constitution had been abrogated. This time certain provisions of the abrogated Constitution were retained as the Provisional Constitution Order. A certain Malik Mir Hasan with others, was to stand trial before the Central Special Judge at Rawalpindi. The defendants filed for quashment on the grounds that the actions they were deemed to have taken, did not constitute offences. Meanwhile, Martial Law authorities passed orders to transfer the case to a special military court. The West Pakistan High Court ruled that the order transferring the case to a military court was defective and without jurisdiction. The High Court contended that the Provisional Constitutional Order could not be subject to Martial Law Regulations and Orders and thus upheld the jurisdiction of the higher judiciary.

Asma Jilani Case. After the resignation of General Yahya Khan, following the fall of Dacca, Martial Law was initially retained as Basic Law by the incoming PPP regime. The new government ordered the arrest of Malik Ghulam Jilani and Altaf Gauhar. The Lahore High Court dismissed the petitions of the defendants citing the Dosso Case. The Supreme Court on appeal overturned the verdict in the Dosso Case on the ground that it did not find support from any principles of International Law. Their lordships held that Field Marshal Ayub Khan under the 1962 Constitution (that he had himself promulgated) had no option other than to transfer power to the Speaker of the National Assembly. The Supreme Court further found that General Yahya Khan was a usurper whose acts were illegal and illegitimate. When the defendants were released, General Yahya Khan was himself in detention.

The Nusrat Bhutto Case. This constitutional petition was filed after the PPP government had successfully framed a constitution in 1973. Keeping before itself the ruling of the Supreme Court in the Asma Jilani Case, the legislators introduced Article 6 which said that any step to disrupt, abrogate or abridge the Constitution of Pakistan would constitute high treason, an offence punishable by death.

After the 5 July 1977 coup by General M. Ziaul Haq, the Constitution was put into abeyance. Prime Minister Zulfikar Ali Bhutto with others was arrested and Martial Law was promulgated. Begum Nusrat Bhutto wife of the deposed prime minister filed a petition seeking the restoration of the 1973 Constitution and nullification of Martial Law.

The Supreme Court relied not on case law, but ruled upon facts following the general elections of 1977, observing that the widespread agitation had justified Martial Law as a State necessity. In its ruling Chief Justice Anwarul Haq held that 'The 1973 Constitution still remained the supreme law of the land subject to the condition that certain parts thereof had been held in abeyance on account of State necessity'.[4]

However, in paragraph iii (a) the Supreme Court gave the chief martial law administrator (CMLA) the power to amend the constitution. Since General Zia had undertaken to hold elections within three months, the Supreme Court noted that one of the reasons given for validating the extraconstitutional step was the solemn pledge of the CMLA to restore order, hold free and fair elections leading to the restoration of the democratic order.

A notable feature was that despite there being no dissenting judgement, a number of the honourable judges wrote separate judgements on 10 November 1977. Another feature was, that when approached, high courts were more guarded in their judgements. The Peshawar High Court while ruling on the necessity of military courts noted 'the political implications of this or that action will be an argument to which we cannot subscribe.' The Sindh High Court held detention without trial illegal as the same authority would be both prosecutor and judge.

Z.A. Bhutto's murder trial and execution shall be discussed under a separate heading. Suffice it to recall that after Z.A. Bhutto's execution, his daughter Benazir Bhutto led his mission. General Zia who had shied away from holding his promised elections made amendments to the Political Parties Act to the effect that anyone who had held public office between 1 December 1971 to 5 July 1977 would be ineligible to stand for elections. In plain terms, all PPP members were disqualified.

In this situation, Benazir Bhutto, the Co-Chairperson of the PPP challenged the amendments in the Supreme Court. This constitutional petition was accepted, and two major objections of the military regime were overruled. The first plea was that Benazir Bhutto was not an aggrieved party under the amendments; the second was that Benazir Bhutto should have approached the High Court first. The Supreme Court ruled that the moment a prejudicial order was passed, citizens could be deemed an aggrieved party; a political party could be deemed an aggrieved party. Secondly, the Supreme Court held that the principle of invoking a lower court was not inviolable. Thus, the

Supreme Court during the military regime of General Zia ruled on 20 June 1988 in favour of the PPP.

Before he lifted Martial Law in 1985, Zia extracted the condition that the Eighth Amendment be adopted. This amendment contained Article 58(2)(b) which empowered the president to dismiss the prime minister and dissolve the assemblies. Under this proviso, on 30 December 1985, Martial Law was lifted. General Zia continued as president.

Muhammad Khan Junejo was Zia's handpicked prime minister. Inherently honest and conscientious, Muhammad Khan Junejo started asserting himself. Three actions were prominent. He concluded the Geneva Agreement allowing the USSR to exit Afghanistan, probing the Ojhri camp incident and more than that forcing austerity by having high officers allocated small cars. Ultimately, the crisis blew over and Zia on 29 May 1988 dismissed Muhammad Khan Junejo under Article 58(2)(b) of the Eighth Amendment.

Muhammad Sharif and Haji Saifullah Cases. In the Lahore High Court, one Muhammad Sharif challenged the dismissal of the prime minister and the dissolution of the National Assembly. The Lahore High Court held the action unconstitutional but refused to provide relief—to restore Muhammad Khan Junejo as prime minister—on the grounds that preparations for new elections were already underway.

In the *Federation of Pakistan vs. Haji Muhammad Saifullah* case, the Supreme Court upheld the verdict of the Lahore High Court on both counts. The dissolution was illegal, but the prime minister would not be restored to office. Thus, though not in law, but in effect Article 58(2)(b) had drawn first blood.

On 1 December 1988, Benazir Bhutto was sworn in as prime minister, and on 6 August 1990, her government was dismissed on grounds of misrule and corruption. All the assemblies were dissolved. The dissolution order was challenged before the High Courts of Lahore and Sindh and, before both, the dissolution order was upheld. The dissolution of provincial assemblies was also challenged. The Peshawar High Court upheld the appeal and ordered the restoration of the Provincial Assembly and the chief minister. However, before the verdict could be given effect, the Supreme Court overturned the ruling of the Peshawar High Court. The ground given by the Supreme Court was that the Attorney-General had not been given sufficient notice before deciding important constitutional questions.

As a consequence of the dismissal of Benazir Bhutto new elections were held in 1990. These elections were still before the Supreme Court as the Asghar Khan Case. Evidence was given that the PML (N) was favoured by the government, largesse was distributed among adversaries of the PPP, and her party obtained a surprisingly low number of 45 seats. However, sidelining the PPP was not sufficient to ensure stability and President Ghulam Ishaq Khan dismissed the Nawaz Sharif government as he had dismissed the Benazir

Bhutto government under Article 58(2)(b). This time the Supreme Court rallied.

On 18 April 1993, Nawaz Sharif was dismissed. Both the Speaker Gohar Ayub Khan and the prime minister filed appeals under Article 184(3) of the Constitution. Headed by Chief Justice Dr Nasim Hasan Shah, an eleven-member bench delivered a verdict with a majority of 10 to 1, in favour of the prime minister. Nawaz Sharif and the National Assembly were restored—for the first time. Paragraph 7 of the judgement was the most interesting, 'The allegations of corruption, maladministration, incorrect policies being pursued in matters of financial, administrative and international, were held to be neither independently decisive, nor within the domain of the President for action under Article 58(2)(b).'[5]

The sole dissenting judge, Sajjad Ali Shah held that the same yardstick should be applied as was applied on the dismissal of Muhammad Khan Junejo and Benazir Bhutto. The relations before a dismissing president and restored prime minister became unworkable and the upshot was that both the president and prime minister were asked to resign, and fresh elections were ordered. These were held on 6 October 1993 and the PPP was elected with Benazir Bhutto as prime minister.

President Farooq Ahmed Leghari although a PPP nominee dismissed Benazir Bhutto on 5 November 1996 under Article 58(2)(b). Army action against the MQM, first taken under Nawaz Sharif, continued till the second term of Benazir Bhutto. This time she was dismissed for custodial deaths and fake police encounters. This included the murder of her own brother Mir Murtaza Bhutto in a police encounter on 20 September 1996. Paragraph (e) of the judgement passed against her stated, 'There was sustained assault on the judicial organ of the state by proposing a law under which a judge could be removed through a vote of No-Confidence.'

Benazir Bhutto may have presumed that the Supreme Court would be bound by precedent and like the Nawaz Sharif government, her government would also be restored. The Supreme Court dismissed Benazir Bhutto for the second time on the grounds among others of 'ridiculing the judiciary'. The Nawaz Sharif government which was brought back into power as a result of this judgement stormed the Supreme Court on 28 November 1997.

Nawaz Sharif had prudently passed the Thirteenth Amendment which did away with Article 58(2)(b) as well as the Fourteenth Amendment which put a ban on floor crossing. A divided bench prevented contempt proceedings. Nawaz Sharif and succeeding prime ministers were to learn that Article 58(2)(b) was a convenient but not necessary device for sending elected governments home. The second regime of Nawaz Sharif was removed through a *coup d'état*.

When after the resignation of General Pervez Musharraf a democratic government was installed, the first act of the newly elected Prime Minister Yusuf Raza Gilani was to release the judges incarcerated by General

Musharraf. Still, they were not restored, and Chief Justice Iftikhar Muhammad Chaudhry was restored last. President Asif Ai Zardari was vocally reluctant to restore him.

The NRO (National Reconciliation Ordinance) Case. Two veteran founders of the ruling party (PPP) Dr Mubashir Hasan and Abdul Hafeez Pirzada filed a suit against the legality of the NRO. The Supreme Court thereupon struck down the NRO and ordered re-opening proceedings against President Asif Ali Zardari and ordered the prime minister to write to the Swiss authorities to reopen the case. This, Prime Minister Yusuf Raza Gilani refused to do, claiming constitutional immunity for the president.

Chief Justice Iftikhar Muhammad Chaudhry did not accept this plea and, on 26 April 2012, Prime Minister Yusuf Raza Gilani was convicted of Contempt of Court. The parliament gave a ruling through the Speaker on 24 May 2012 that despite the Supreme Court verdict there was no ground for action against the prime minister. The Supreme Court differed, 'The Speaker, by interfering with a concluded judgement in the matter of Contempt of Court, went beyond her jurisdiction. She is bound to make a reference to the Election Commission and cannot sit in judgement over it in the garb of exercise of power under Article 63 (2) of the Constitution.'

When a letter, drafted by the Supreme Court was finally sent, the Swiss authorities refused to entertain it on the ground that it was time-barred. The Parliament on 9 July 2012 passed a new contempt law which saved the new Prime Minister Raja Pervez Ashraf from court proceedings.

Arsalan Case. This was a case pertaining to the allegation of one Malik Riaz that he had financed a holiday in Europe enjoyed by Arsalan Iftikhar son of the Chief Justice. The Supreme Court set up a Commission under Dr Shoaib Suddle to investigate the matter, but after the investigations were complete, the Supreme Court ordered the dissolution of the Suddle Commission. One notable feature of this case was that Justice Jawwad Khwaja upbraided Attorney General Irfan Qadir, holding him responsible for the deference shown by the Supreme Court employees to Malik Riaz.

The Panamagate Case. Papers of an offshore company in Panama revealed that many businessmen and politicians had deposited money there. The list included Prime Minister Nawaz Sharif. The Supreme Court, in a unanimous verdict on 28 July 2017 declared Nawaz Sharif as 'dishonest' and disqualified him from parliamentary membership. As *Dawn* reported, 'A five-judge Supreme Court bench headed by Chief Justice Asif Saeed Khosa disqualified the Prime Minister, not on corruption allegations or the issues highlighted by the petitioner in the Panama Papers Case, but on the basis of new evidence unearthed by a specially constituted Joint Investigation Team (JIT).[6]

It was unearthed that the prime minister was the Chairman of Capital FZE, a UAE-based company run by his son. Under the Iqama (work visa) he was entitled to a salary which he had not disclosed in his nomination papers for the 2013 elections. The defence was that Nawaz Sharif had not drawn the salary.

Nawaz Sharif's outburst against the Supreme Court was true to character as his storming of the Supreme Court under Chief Justice Sajjad Ali Shah shows. In Gujranwala he decried before a crowd; 'Conspirators desecrating the sanctity of votes cast by 200 million Pakistanis.' A remark that was clearly contemptuous.[7] In another speech, in Jhelum, Nawaz Sharif noted that no prime minister was allowed to complete his term. Nawaz Sharif went on to remind the crowd that dictators broke the law and constitution, but it was the judiciary that accorded them legitimacy.[8]

Nehal Hashmi Case. Contempt proceedings were faced by Senator Nehal Hashmi, who on 28 May 2018 had delivered a speech which the Supreme Court called, '...improper, unwise and imprudent. The offending words... admitted and not denied by him, were nothing but an effort to obstruct, interfere with and prejudice the proceedings pending before this Court.'[9] The Supreme Court did not accept Nehal Hashmi's 24 January 2018 apology which it termed 'belated.' The defendant, himself a lawyer, lost his party membership and resigned from the Senate. Imran Khan, the PTI Chairman was exultant, but the Karachi Bar Association protested, pointing out that the Supreme Court had accepted the apologies of Altaf Hussain (MQM), Nawaz Sharif (in an earlier case) and Imran Khan but had made an exception in the case of Nehal Hashmi.

Following a one-month suspended jail term, Nehal Hashmi had another outburst. The Chief Justice of the Supreme Court mentioned a new FIR in response. Nehal Hashmi's explanation was unique: he claimed he had been 'acting' and mentioned that he was not in a mentally sound state. He also appealed that he should not lose his license to practice law, as it was his sole source of income.

The Contempt of Court committed by the ousted prime minister and his supporters showed one aspect, while an *obiter dictum* by another Supreme Court judge showed another. Justice Qazi Faez Isa remarked on a lawyer's reference to the Panamagate case, 'The Panama Papers Case was about London flats, but the judgement came on the Iqama.'[10]

The Lawyer's Movement. We have touched upon this Movement briefly, but we still need to put it in context. On 23 June 2006, Chief Justice Iftikhar Chaudhry delivered a verdict that forbade the sale of the Pakistan Steel Mills, Karachi. It is speculated that it was this verdict that led to the suspension of Chief Justice Iftikhar Chaudhry on 9 March 2007. This was followed by, not preceded by, a reference to the Supreme Judicial Council. On 26 July 2007, a full bench of the Supreme Court struck down the reference and restored Chief Justice Iftikhar Chaudhry to his position. Chief Justice Iftikhar Chaudhry heard a number of sensitive cases, especially those of missing persons. It was believed that as a consequence on 3 November 2007 General Pervez Musharraf suspended the Constitution, imposed a State of Emergency, and again removed judges from the Supreme Court.[11]

The judges of the Supreme Court were subjected to differing treatment. While some judges were released and reinstated, the restoration of Chief Justice Iftikhar Chaudhry's position was delayed. This situation paralleled what occurred during the NRO cases. The PPP government took a slow approach, and eventually, Chief Justice Iftikhar Chaudhry was reinstated for the second time on 24 March 2009. Notable figures like Aitzaz Ahsan, Ali Ahmed Kurd, and Tariq Mehmood played significant roles in leading this movement.

As mentioned earlier, old stalwarts of the PPP, Dr Mubashir Hasan and Abdul Hafeez Pirzada, challenged the NRO on 12 October 2007 as the NRO gave politicians immunity from prosecution in criminal cases. The NRO, promulgated on 5 October 2007 was struck down on 16 December 2009. Asma Jahangir a former Bar Council president, criticized the judgement on the basis of its being violative of Article 62(1)(f) which requires a Member of Parliament to be sagacious, righteous, and non-profligate, honest and Ameen (trustworthy) the stringiest standards set by the Zia regime.[12] The two PPP founders congratulated each other for bringing down a PPP prime minister.

Pervez Musharraf Case. Ibrahim Satti representing General Pervez Musharraf in the treason (Article 6) case reminded the judiciary of its role in validating martial laws and said that while his client was prepared to face treason charges, he alone should not be blamed.[13] Later, while paying tribute to Asma Jahangir, Chief Justice Mian Saqib Nisar proclaimed that there would be no more validation of Martial Law.[14]

Finally, a Special Court comprising three High Court judges awarded Pervez Musharraf the death sentence (in absentia) for suspending the Constitution on 3 November 2007.[15] Both the Inter-Services Public Relations (ISPR) and the government expressed pain and anguish over the verdict. Paragraph 66 of the judgement recommended the desecration of the body.[16] The Pakistan Bar Council criticized the military's objections to the judgement.[17] But it remains intriguing why the Special Court delivered a verdict against the 3 November 2007 action, instead of his initial takeover of 12 October 1999.

INTRA-JUDICIARY CASES

Justice Qazi Faez Isa Reference. A controversy arose when a (single judge) judicial commission headed by Justice Qazi Faez Isa submitted its inquiry report on the 8 August 2016 carnage at the Civil Hospital, Quetta in which over seventy lawyers had been killed. The basic finding of the 110–page report was that government inaction against militant bodies was responsible for the spread of terrorism. The Commission held that it was illogical for the National Anti-Terrorism Authority (NACTA) to seek verification from the ISI whether the two named organisations had carried out the attack when both banned outfits had claimed responsibility.[18]

The Justice Faez Isa Commission went on to regret that Interior Minister Chaudhry Nisar Ali Khan had on 21 October met Maulana Muhammad Ahmed Ludhianvi, the head of three banned organisations, viz. Sipah-i-Sahaba, Pakistan, Millat-i-Islamia, and Ahle Sunnat Wal Jamaat, and had, according to media reports, conceded to his demands. The Commission held that the Anti-Terrorism Act (ATA) was equally applicable to public functionaries, and they should not be seen as cavorting with proclaimed members of banned outfits.

The following day the interior minister retaliated, calling the Justice Faez Isa Commission Report one-sided. Chaudhry Nisar Ali claimed that the questionnaire that the Commission had sent to him was 'irrelevant'. He also explained that he was not aware that Maulana Ludhianvi was part of the delegation. Chaudhry Nisar Ali threatened to confront the Justice Faez Isa Report at all forums.[19]

Predictably, opposition parties came out against the Interior Minister. Shah Mehmood Qureshi PTI Vice-Chairman ridiculed the contention of Chaudhry Nisar Ali that he was not aware of Maulana Ludhianvi's identity, 'How a member of a banned outfit managed to enter the office of the Interior Minister?' Likewise, the PPP Secretary-General Sardar Abdul Latif Khosa said his party would file a contempt petition against the interior minister.[20]

The Interior Minister Chaudhry Nisar repeated his allegations against the Faez Isa Report, 'Responding to the objection to his meeting with a delegation of banned outfits, the Interior Minister said that outlawed sectarian organisations should not be equated with those of terrorist outfits. He also stated that unfortunately, sectarian violence had been continuing for 1300 years.' This statement led to a walkout in the Senate.[21] PPP Senator Farhatullah Babar retorted that to assert that banned sectarian outfits could not be equated with banned terrorist organisations, betrayed ignorance of the violence created by *Takfiri* (excommunicating) rhetoric of sectarian groups.[22]

The recriminations over the 8 August 2016 terrorist attack had not yet died down when Justice Faez Isa along with Justice Mushir Alam Khan was placed on a bench to consider the twenty days long Faizabad sit-in by the Tehreek-e-Labbaik, Pakistan. The sit-in ended after an agreement with the Punjab government. The Supreme Court not only deprecated the use of filthy language by the leader of the sit-in, ostensibly a religious scholar, but it also went on to observe that the people of Pakistan were entitled to know the extent of loss of lives and property caused by the sit-in.[23] Petitions were filed against the legality of Qazi Faez Isa's elevation to the higher judiciary, but the Supreme Court dismissed them on 5 April 2018. Justices Isa and Alam also wanted to know the financial resources of the protesters. An ISI report said that the

Tehreek-e-Labbaik had collected funds from 45,000 persons. Justice Isa remarked that it must be assumed that State enemies had provided them with funds. The Supreme Court inquired how the banners of the protestors remained hanging for twenty days. 'Are we complicit in projecting a particular point of view?'[24]

Next, the Supreme Court rejected the reports of the Faizabad sit-in submitted by the Defence Ministry and the Election Commission of Pakistan. The Supreme Court wanted to know whether Pakistan was a functional state or should be determined by street power.[25] Later, Justice Faez Isa observed in the background of the Faizabad sit-in that the supremacy and sovereignty of Parliament are continuously being undermined and asked whether the country's future will be determined by Parliament or insidious forces.[26]

On 28 May 2019, it was learnt that President Arif Alvi had sent a reference against Justice Isa to the Supreme Judicial Council. Bar Associations across the country pressed for impeaching the president for sending a reference against Justice Isa. The basis of the reference was that Justice Faez Isa had not disclosed the wealth and property of his wife and children in his income tax return. The cause of the outrage was that legally, the confidentiality of any income tax return cannot be breached. Moreover, the requirement of providing details of the wealth and property of one's family was under electoral law and not income tax law. The case dragged on because Justice Isa's lawyer, Munir A. Malik, had had to undergo heart surgery.

In June the Law Ministry and the Assets Recovery Unit (ARU) of the prime minister's office in a joint statement claimed to have received certified copies from the land registry of the assets in the UK owned by learned judges of the superior courts, on the basis of which references had been filed against them before the Supreme Judicial Council.[27] In late July, Justice Faez Isa wrote to Chief Justice Asif Saeed Khosa to provide the evidence against him so he could reply to the show cause notices issued to him. He also called for making public his earlier reply submitted to the Supreme Judicial Council, as allegations against him had been made public.[28]

Though two references were pending against him, it was decided that Justice Isa would resume hearing cases on 11 September 2019. A week later, two judges of the Supreme Court, Justices Sardar Tariq Masood and Ijaz-ul-Hasan, recused themselves. Earlier, the Supreme Court had observed that *prima facie* the submissions of the lawyers representing the judges under reference did not carry weight.[29]

However, come September, the Supreme Court issued notices to the president and prime minister among others. Rasheed A. Rizvi argued against the immunity claimed by the president and prime minister by citing the Supreme Court's ruling in Chief Justice Iftikhar Chaudhry's 2010 case that immunity did not extend to acts that were *coram non judice* or malafide in nature.[30]

The plaint of Attorney General Anwar Mansoor Khan was that the Supreme Judicial Council was immune from judicial review, though he simultaneously pleaded that the allegations against the Supreme Judicial Council were wrong.[31] While the government asked the Supreme Court to reject Justice Isa's challenge to the reference, Munir Malik said properties mentioned in the reference had no bearing on Justice Isa as they were owned by his children who were not his dependents.[32]

When the hearing resumed, Qazi Faez Isa contended that the government wanted a subservient judiciary. Munir Malik argued that a Benami[33] property he was accused of owning, was not mentioned in the original reference, the accusation did not carry even one of the many legal texts to prove Benami ownership, and thirdly, he argued that if a Supreme Court judge did not enjoy immunity, how was the prime minister exercising his immunity in giving details of his own income.[34] The next day Justice Faez Isa said 'inconvenient truths emerging in his judgement in the Tehreek-e-Labbaik *dharna* (sit-in) case led to references against him.[35]

The next step taken was to reconstitute the bench. Justice Isa countered that once the hearing of the case had commenced with a ten-member bench, the same judges must hear these part-heard cases till its conclusion.[36] Munir Malik contended that the reference was based on unlawful surveillance of the judge's family members, reiterating that the 6 February Tehreek-e-Labbaik sit-in verdict had prompted the move.[37]

After this development, the Pakistan Bar Council inquired why Justice Isa's case was taken up out of turn. Abid Hasan Manto (He was a cousin of Sa'adat Hasan Manto) and I.A. Rehman argued that out-of-turn reference was an arbitrary and malafide exercise of power by the secretary of the Supreme Judicial Council.[38] When the secretary pleaded that he had acted within the law; Justice Isa's rejoinder (through his counsel) was that though his role was secretarial in nature, the secretary had issued show cause notices in two references. The date of the hearing had been fixed while Justice Isa was abroad, taking a relative for medical treatment; furthermore, when the last day of filing (31 July 2019) arrived, the secretary, A.M. Arif was absent.[39]

Justice Mansoor Ali Shah asked under what law the ARU held power to collect evidence against a judge. Justice Maqbool Baqar interpreted Malik's contention. 'You mean to say that though the methodology was different, the collateral purpose both in the Iftikhar Chaudhry case and Justice Qazi Isa were the same.'[40] Babar Sattar held that the Income Tax Department should have first issued notices to the family of Justice Isa before filing references.[41]

Senator Raza Rabbani made the argument that the president can only forward a tentative opinion and the decision stands with the Supreme Judicial Council (SJC). Only the SJC can initiate a reference.[42] Continuing the next day Rabbani contended that under Article 175-A the recommendations of the parliamentary committee and Judicial Commission were sent directly to the president, implying that the prime minister's role was not sustainable. Raza Rabbani read the notification of the Terms of Reference for the ARU, arguing that it was functioning without any enabling law. No. 7 of the Terms of Reference empowered the ARU to request any intelligence agency at the federal government level to assist in the collection of material particularly against judges.[43]

Attorney General Anwar Mansoor Khan made a remark that the bench forbade the media from reporting. The Supreme Court called the attorney general's remark 'uncalled for' and 'too serious'.[44] The following day, the Supreme Court asked Attorney General Anwar Mansoor Khan to either substantiate his remark or withdraw it. Without knowing what the exact remark was, we should be content to learn that Anwar Mansoor Khan resigned at the behest of the Pakistan Bar Council.[45]

The Law Minister Dr Farogh Naseem resigned, to represent the government in the case. Farogh Naseem filed a paper missing from the previous hearings. He shifted the burden of the non-production of the document on the former Attorney General Anwar Mansoor Khan. The lawyers representing Justice Isa objected to the introduction of new evidence at this stage.[46] The ARU head Shahzad Akbar said he received no salary or other benefits. He pleaded that he was not making disclosures as the owners of property in the United Kingdom could be accessed through websites like 192.com and UK phonebook.com.[47]

The bench on its part observed that Justice Faez Isa had filed returns of Rs 37 million in 2009, and in 2011 he had money obtained from his law practice. Justice Munib Akhtar asked whose 'bright idea' was to file a reference against Justice Isa. Justice Yahya Afridi noted that Shahzad Akbar was appointed ARU chairman on 20 August 2018, the same day a summary was placed, and Terms of Reference of the ARU were finalized. Questioning Shahzad Akbar's appointment as well as the constitution of the ARU, Justice Afridi asked why a special person was brought to do a duty already assigned to statutory bodies like the FIA.[48] Justice Maqbool Baqar reminded Farogh Naseem that one of the democratically elected governments was sent packing on charges of surveillance of judges in 1996.[49]

Since the case hinged around the property owned by Mrs Isa (Zarina[50] Montserrat Carrera Khoso), she herself testified that she had vast properties and had earned a handsome salary from the American School. She testified that she bought the properties between 2003 and 2013 and transferred a total of £700,000 through the Standard Chartered Bank which reports every transaction to the State Bank. Serena Isa stated that she had been filing income tax returns for the properties in Pakistan and in England. The Supreme Court asked Farogh Naseem to furnish the reply of the Federal Board of Revenue (FBR) in a sealed envelope about Mrs Isa's complaint that she had disclosed the properties in her returns for 2018–2019 but the FBR had still issued a notice to her.[51]

Despite this complaint, though the Supreme Court quashed the reference against Justice Isa, they added a rider asking the FBR to seek explanations from his family members about the nature and source of funding for the offshore properties they held in their name. Justices Maqbool Baqar, Mansoor Ali Shah, and Yahya Afridi did not endorse the order of sending a query to the FBR. The remaining judges sought an explanation from the wife and children of Justice Isa on how they had acquired three London properties.[52]

The Supreme Court Bar Association (SCBA) too wanted a deletion of the directives to the FBR. They argued that after the quashing of the reference against Justice Isa, it was beyond the jurisdiction of the Supreme Judicial Council to take notice of any future report against the judge. The SCBA asked under what law and constitution, the matter relating to the properties held by the wife and children of Justice Isa had been referred to the FBR.[53] In her own petition, Mrs Isa complained of discrimination, the FBR acting on 'instructions' and that she should not be blamed if she asked for the record of the petitioner, that is the prime minister, the former law minister and the former attorney general.[54]

She repeated her demand on 29 August. Mrs Isa also reiterated that the FBR had not explained under what proviso she was required to furnish details of the foreign income and assets for the period before it had become mandatory. She further accused the FBR of disregarding her agricultural income tax returns. On 22 October Justice Isa and his wife voluntarily released income tax and asset details most of which had been acquired before his elevation as a judge.

Since reference had made the assets of Mrs Isa and their children to undermine Justice Isa, she now remained centre-stage. Four Bar Associations questioned why a seven-member bench would hear her review petition, while the bench passing the original order had contained ten. As a consequence, the three Supreme Court judges who had opposed submitting her assets to the FBR were excluded.[55] Mrs Isa continued to write unanswered letters to President Arif Alvi asking why her husband was considered a security threat. She referred to acts of terrorism in Quetta, Karachi, and the Rawalpindi sit-in. Mrs Isa objected to the exclusion of the very three judges Justices Maqbool Baqar, Syed Mansoor Ali Shah, and Yahya Afridi who had dissented from the order to submit her records to the FBR.[56]

The Supreme Court set 13 April 2021 for taking up pleas in the Justice Isa case. On that day, the Court dismissed Justice Isa's plea for a live telecast of the hearing by a 6 to 4 majority.[57] Justice Isa openly claimed that the government wanted to remove him from his post because of his judgement in the Faizabad sit-in case.[58] Next, Justice Faez Isa questioned why FBR Chairperson

Nausheen Javaid Amjad had been removed after only four months in office, in violation of the ruling in the Anita Abu Turab case.[59]

Finally, the Supreme Court in a 6 to 4 majority judgement accepted the review petitions thus rendering all the FBR probe into the finances of Mrs Isa null and void.[60] Although the Supreme Court decided not to proceed against Justice Isa, there was an after-tremor when a former director general of the FIA, Bashir Memon, stated on a television show that the ARU head Shahzad Akbar had pressurized him to file a reference against Justice Isa. Shahzad Akbar has issued a libel notice to Bashir Memon.[61]

The Pakistan Bar Council demanded a judicial probe into Bashir Memon's allegations. In a subsequent television interview, Bashir Memon exonerated Prime Minister Imran Khan for having directly referred to Justice Isa.[62] In its detailed judgement, the Supreme Court declared that the direction to the FBR in the Justice Isa case was against natural justice.[63] Imran Khan, removed as prime minister by this time, admitted that the reference against Justice Isa had been a mistake.[64] The new cabinet decided to withdraw the reference against Justice Isa.[65] Thus, the long drawn-out procedure which had dissenting judgements in both the original and subsequent verdicts came to an end.

It is to be noted that throughout the trial, Bar Associations had been supportive of Justice Isa with one exception. The Punjab Bar Council justified the reference as Justice Isa in his judgement in the Faizabad sit-in case had ridiculed the armed forces and cast aspersions on intelligence agencies. The resolution also hailed the removal of Justice Shaukat Aziz Siddiqui by the Supreme Judicial Council, a similar case demanding our attention.[66]

Justice Shaukat Aziz Siddiqui Case. This case began not with a report or a verdict but with a speech delivered on 21 July 2018 by Justice Shaukat Aziz Siddiqui of the Islamabad High Court to the Rawalpindi Bar Association. The judge accused the ISI of manipulating judicial proceedings. He went on to allege that ISI officials managed to 'constitute benches of their choice'. Specifically, Justice Shaukat A. Siddiqui said the ISI wanted to ensure that Nawaz Sharif and Maryam Nawaz Sharif were not released before the coming elections.

Maj.-Gen. Asif Ghafoor, DG ISPR, urged Chief Justice Mian Saqib Nisar to take notice of Shaukat Siddiqui's speech. The chief justice expressed surprise and said, 'None can dare put pressure on judiciary'. At this Justice Shaukat Siddiqui asked the chief justice to constitute an independent commission to probe the authenticity of presented facts.[67]

Chief Justice Saqib Nisar asked the chief justice of the Islamabad High Court, M. Anwar Kasi, to obtain material/evidence to substantiate these allegations.[68] Chief Justice of Pakistan said attempts were being made to defame the judiciary. On 30 July the Supreme Judicial Council met. The charge was that Justice Shaukat Siddiqui had allegedly renovated his official residence beyond entitlement. Shaukat Siddiqui submitted three applications: (1) seeking information about expenditures incurred on the maintenance of each official accommodation occupied by Supreme Court judges; (2) asking for the records of the expenditure incurred on the houses personally owned by the judges but declared as 'official' accommodation; (3) seeking particulars of superior court judges who were receiving house rent allowance of Rs 65,000 every month. The Supreme Judicial Council (SJC) rejected all three applications and ruled that these applications had no relevance to the charge he was facing.[69]

Shaukat Siddiqui challenged, before the Supreme Court, the dismissal of his applications and insisted the documents he sought were necessary and relevant for the preparation of his defence. Thereafter, followed a notification, 'The President of Pakistan has been pleased to remove Mr Justice Shaukat Aziz Siddiqui, Judge Islamabad High Court with immediate effect.'

The SJC headed by the chief justice of the Supreme Court ruled, 'In the matter of making his speech before District Bar Association on 21 July 2018, Mr Justice Shaukat Aziz Siddiqui, Judge, Islamabad High Court had displayed conduct unbecoming of a judge thus guilty of misconduct.'[70]

The following day the chief justice of the Islamabad High Court who had been facing charges of misconduct had the charges against him dropped by the SJC.[71] While filing an appeal to the Supreme Court, Shaukat Siddiqui did not retract the substance of his 21 July 2018 speech, rather he added details. The dismissed judge complained that 'The SJC considered the letter of the Islamabad High Court Chief Justice as gospel truth against him, despite the fact that it was not an affidavit. It said later that the Chief Justice IHC was exonerated from all allegations he was facing.'[72]

On 10 November 2018, former judge Shaukat Siddiqui moved two applications in the Supreme Court against his removal from service. One, asking for an early hearing of his appeal, and the second, to put his original plea before a judge who had earlier not dealt with the matter. The dismissed judge insisted upon the veracity of his allegations in his 21 July 2018 speech.[73] Rasheed Razvi, on behalf of the Karachi Bar Association, asked for the SJC's order, leading to Siddiqui's removal, to be set aside.[74] The Supreme Court admitted the appeal.[75] In April 2021, Shaukat Siddiqui once more approached the Supreme Court, urging them to consider his plea against the 11 October 2018 notification that led to his removal, and he also asked for a suspension of the notification.[76]

In a three-page fresh application, Shaukat Siddiqui asked for his plea to be heard before his superannuation.[77] When the hearing commenced, Justice Ijaz-ul-Ahsan observed that the moot point was whether it was appropriate for a judge to make allegations, regardless of their veracity, in a courtroom[78] the federal government denied, and declared as misleading the assertions made by Siddiqui when he mentioned a specific ISI officer.[79]

After three dates of hearing were fixed but postponed, Shaukat Siddiqui saw a ray of hope in the Chief Justice of Pakistan Gulzar Ahmad's assurance that the 'judiciary never takes dictation'.[80] No headway was made despite an outburst of the dismissed judge which displeased the presiding judge, Umar Ata Bandial.[81] Shaukat Siddiqui urged the Supreme Court to resume hearing his appeal.[82] After ten days Shaukat Siddiqui wrote his third application, seeking the provision of certified copies and complete order sheets in the four references that had been moved against him by the chief justice of the Islamabad High Court.[83] There presumably matters still stand.

Arshad Malik Case. It was Maryam Nawaz who, during a press conference, screened a video of Justice Arshad Malik telling Nasir Butt that he had ruled against Nawaz Sharif in the Azizia (Panama) case because he had been blackmailed. Justice Arshad Malik called the tape fabricated. Pakistan Electronic Media Authority (PEMRA) issued notices to twenty-one television channels.[84] Prime Minister Shahid Khaqan Abbasi referred to the discrepancies found in Arshad Malik's statement and his subsequent affidavit which mentioned another recording called 'The Multan Video.'[85] In a video that Arshad Malik said was fabricated he was taped *flagrante delicto* (in the very act of committing a misdeed). As a consequence, the Islamabad High Court removed the judge.[86]

Since Justice Arshad Malik's repatriation to his parent institution, the Lahore High Court had been delayed, the Chief Justice asked the Attorney General whether the government was protecting the judge. The Attorney General Anwar Mansoor Khan assured Chief Justice Asif Saeed Khosa that Arshad Malik would be repatriated. The strictures passed by the Supreme Court on that occasion are being passed over.

Rana Shamim Case. Rana Muhammad Shamim former Chief Judge of Gilgit-Baltistan alleged that he had heard Mian Saqib Nisar, the chief justice of the Supreme Court, instruct a judge of the Islamabad High Court not to release Mian Nawaz Sharif and his daughter before the 2018 elections. On 20 January 2022, the Islamabad High Court accused Rana Shamim of Contempt of Court. Since a recording had been produced, an American forensic firm sought permission to examine the purported audio leaks. Former Chief Justice Mian Saqib Nisar said that the audiotape was fabricated.[87]

Finally, after a flurry of statements from political parties, the Islamabad High Court indicted Rana Shamim for contempt. The attorney general assured the court that at the next hearing, scheduled for 15 February 2022, the former judge would be given every opportunity to submit evidence or proof to establish his innocence.[88]

Rana Shamim, unable to substantiate his allegations against former Chief Justice Saqib Nisar, submitted an unconditional apology. The acceptance of his apology was deferred.[89]

JUDICIAL ACTIVISM.—As stated in the section on Economic history, Pakistan needs a new dam—a need heavily underscored by the 2022 floods—but its location at Kalabagh had been politically opposed. In this background, a petition was filed by Zafrullah Khan, Barrister at Law, for the construction of the Kalabagh Dam.

During the hearing, Chief Justice Saqib Nisar clarified that he was not asking for the construction of the Kalabagh Dam *per se* but was looking for a way to build a comparable dam. The chief justice had also taken *suo moto* notice of a report published by the Pakistan Council of Research in Water Resources which had warned of impending water scarcity. Chief Justice said that the court would take the dam issue 'very seriously because it was its duty to ensure the provision of fundamental rights.' During the hearing, the chief justice noted that the displacement of persons would be higher at Kalabagh than it had been at Mangla and Tarbela. The Supreme Court was informed that a 4500 MW Diamer-Bhasha Dam could have been built in 2001, but it was opposed by the Kalabagh Dam lobby. The Supreme Court decided to focus on this project.[90]

Only two months later, school buildings in the Diamer district of Gilgit-Baltistan were attacked. The chief justice attributed the attacks to elements opposed to the construction of the Diamer-Bhasha Dam. The chief justice also informed the audience that his 8–year-old granddaughter had donated Rs 7000 for the construction of the dam.[91] Chief Justice Saqib Nisar set up Diamer-Bhasha and Mohmand Dam funds. He said that critics of the dam project would be taken to task.[92] On the same day, five companies submitted bids for the construction of the Diamer-Bhasha Dam.

Regardless, criticism of the project mounted. Chief Justice Saqib Nisar said he was examining the scope of Article 6 of the Constitution (pertaining to treason), to determine if it could be applied to the critics of the dam proposals.[93] During the same hearing, the chief justice sought a rationalization of profits by companies selling groundwater.

The dam had not been built by the time of Justice Saqib Nisar's superannuation. Former foreign minister and second-generation legal luminary, Khurshid Mahmud Kasuri, wrote a letter to the incoming Chief Justice Asif Saeed Khosa, he respected the integrity, legal expertise and well-meaningness of the outgoing Chief Justice Saqib Nisar, but he deprecated the recent judicial interventions in economic and fiscal market spheres. Such judicial manipulations of the market and regulatory mechanisms have chilled investor and business confidence.[94]

JURISDICTION.—In Pakistan, there are traditional assemblies of elders that dispense justice parallel to the constituted judiciary. They are called Panchayats or Jirgas. Their verdicts often disregard both the Criminal Procedure Code and Islamic law. The most notorious case is that of Mukhtaran Mai who was sentenced to gang rape by a Jirga. Later, however, the defendants were found not guilty by the Supreme Court. On the query of the National Commission on the Status of Women, the Supreme Court declared that such Jirgas or Panchayats violated Articles 4, 8, 10–A, 25 and 175(3) of the Constitution of Pakistan. They were also held to be violative of Pakistan's international commitments: the Universal Declaration of Human Rights and the Convention on the Elimination of all Discrimination against Women.[95]

The judiciary's equation with the legislature is another aspect. When Article 58(2)(b) had lapsed with the passage of the Eighteenth Amendment, the Supreme Court had sent Prime Ministers home for contempt (Yusuf Raza Gilani) or corruption (Mian Nawaz Sharif) but it had not been able to send parliaments packing as under the old law. It is common that courts can strike down laws on the basis of being *ultra vires* of the Constitution. Even Constitutional Amendments are struck down if they are found to have violated the basic principles of the Constitution, but Chief Justice Saqib Nisar asked whether an 'incompetently passed law' could be annulled.

Farooq H. Naek replied that the courts cannot 'read in' or 'read out something' in the Constitution unless an amendment was made by parliament. The chief justice persevered. 'Instead of destroying the law we can read down a law' Farooq Naek replied, 'But I will still humbly state that the court has no authority to read into the Constitution'. Not fully satisfied, the Supreme Court issued notice to the attorney general and adjourned the hearing to 7 March 2019.[96]

The Senate Chairman, Raza Rabbani, had shown his concern at 'judicial scrutiny of the legislative process.' He cited the issuance of a Contempt of Court notice to the Speaker of the Khyber Pakhtunkhwa assembly. Raza Rabbani cited *Zulfiqar Ahmad Bhutta vs. The Federation of Pakistan* in which the Supreme Court had shown restraint in going beyond the veil of 'internal proceedings' in terms of Article 69 of the Constitution.

Senator Farhatullah Babar was more outspoken. He contended that the judiciary refused to submit to accountability, thus creating a state within the state. 'We must resolve this contradiction of state within the state if Pakistan is not to be devoured by it.' The PPP distanced itself from Senator Babar's opinion.[97]

Two years later, Bilawal Bhutto-Zardari, Chairman of the PPP, complained that the judiciary had taken away parliament's power to appoint judges. The judiciary had forced its government in 2010 to pass the Nineteenth Amendment which did away with the parliamentary committee's role in the appointment of judges in the superior courts. The issue in question was the powers enjoyed by the National Accountability Bureau (NAB). Bilawal held that the NAB is holding accountable the rivals of the PTI government. He underscored that Prime Minister Imran Khan, through an executive order excluded businessmen and bureaucrats from the accountability mechanism.[98]

The next day, the Islamabad High Court seized petitions filed by the removed director general and director of Pakistan Telecommunication Authority (PTA) stating that unchecked NAB powers were against fundamental rights.[99] Ten days later chief justice of the Islamabad High Court, Athar Minallah, accused NAB of attempting to blackmail Islamabad High Court judges. The NAB had implied that some housing of judges may be irregular Chief Justice Athar Minallah observed. If there was any discrepancy, then why NAB did not file a reference of misconduct before the Supreme Judicial Council?

PERFORMANCE OF THE JUDICIARY.—Perhaps in no country other than Pakistan has the phrase 'justice delayed is justice denied' been cited with sickening regularity. This happens mostly in the lower judiciary where adjournments are regularly granted, the backlog increases, and litigants spend half their lives obtaining a decree and the other half seeking its implementation. If two judges have delivered a judgement, one of them can go on leave before a certified copy of the judgement is issued. As a result, these cases drag on, and despite the accumulation of numerous files, the dispensation of justice remains elusive.

Legislators blamed the judiciary for not allowing reforms in institutions. A MNA complained, 'Earlier the President of Pakistan had powers to appoint judges, but this power was snatched. Similarly, a parliamentary committee was empowered to appoint judges under the 18th Amendment, but it was also made helpless.'[100] The burden of the argument was that since judges were not accountable, they were not efficient. The judiciary though does not lack introspection. Chief Justice Saqib Nisar blamed the incompetence of judges for the delay.

The chief justice regretted that the knowledge of judges even about basic laws was not adequate and they were getting salaries more than what officials of other government institutions received. A single judge cost the government Rs 55,000 per day, he said, adding that the delay in court proceedings had become a menace.

He said that the Supreme Court restored possession of a house to an elderly woman, who had been seeking justice for the past sixty-one years, within fifteen days by taking notice of human rights jurisdiction.[101]

Chief Justice Asif Saeed Khosa attributed the backlog of cases to a shortage of judges. The chief justice bemoaned that almost 25 per cent of seats in the judiciary of Pakistan were vacant. For a population of 210 or 220 million people, there were only 3,000 judges and magistrates available from top to bottom.[102]

JUDICIARY AND THE EXECUTIVE.—Chief Justice Anwar Zaheer Jamali held politicians responsible for the failed Pakistan. 'Insincere and dishonest politicians, as legislation done out of vested interest.'[103]

Unfortunately, sometimes acrimony goes public. Chief Justice Asif Saeed Khosa rejected a statement by the sitting Prime Minister Imran Khan that the chief justice of Pakistan and Justice Gulzar Ahmed should come forward and 'restore public trust by ending the impression about favouring the powerful against the poor.' The chief justice of Pakistan gave statistics of relief provided to weak litigants and referring to a specific decision said that permission to Nawaz Sharif was granted by Prime Minister Imran Khan himself as the Lahore High Court only set modalities in this regard.[104]

The PDF government came into being because the Supreme Court ensured that its orders that the National Assembly proceed with the No Confidence Movement were carried out. The ousted Prime Minister Imran Khan had complained (9 April 2022): 'Why did the courts open their doors at midnight?' 'Everyone should know that this is not the Pakistan of the 1970s when the US conspired to remove Zulfikar Ali Bhutto.'[105]

Although by 14 November 2023, Imran Khan ceased blaming the US for his ouster, the allusion was a costly one. The PPP was a coalition partner which was reminded how its other Prime Minister Yusuf Raza Gilani was sent packing by Chief Justice Iftikhar Chaudhury. The parliament passed a law protecting the prime minister from the chief justice of Pakistan's stricture, but the chief justice struck down that law as well on 24 May 2012. The coalition understood, that to protect its domain it would have to become active and treat the judiciary as hostile.

The Public Accounts Committee (PAC) Chairman, Noor Alam Khan, summoned the registrar of the Supreme Court to explain whether it was lawful on the part of former Chief Justice Saqib Nisar to open an account to collect funds for the construction of the Diamer-Bhasha and Mohmand dams.[106] During the next hearing, the deputy registrar appeared, but not the registrar. The PAC Chairman was not satisfied and insisted that the audit of the Diamer-Bhasha and Mohmand dam funds was necessary.[107]

Pointedly, the incoming Prime Minister Shehbaz Sharif withdrew the curative reference against Justice Faez Isa (filed in May 2019) as 'baseless and politically motivated.' Despite this clear directive, on 8 April, Chief Justice Umar Ata Bandial scheduled a hearing to take up the government's directive to withdraw the reference. On 11 April, judgement was reserved.

Later, on 9 June, Supreme Court Justice Sardar Tariq Masood, not while allowing a plea, or hearing a review petition, but merely as an *obiter dictum*, raised a question of why only one family (Sharif) was segregated from the total of 436 parties named in the Panama Papers and proceeded against?[108]

The Supreme Court's willingness to countenance a reference to Justice Faez Isa, a sitting judge made it open to criticism. A former Attorney-General Irfan Qadir had observed as early as July 2022: 'The Supreme Court is not the Chief Justice of Pakistan alone.' He argued that the judiciary would be independent when individuals are not able to prevail upon it.[109]

The government had two responses to the judiciary. It assigned an investigation on audio leaks concerning Supreme Court judges to the second most senior judge, Qazi Faez Isa. The other was to bring about an amendment through parliament curtailing the individual powers of the chief justice, delegating them to the three seniormost judges of the Supreme Court.

The Audio Leak Commission was formed under Section 3 of the Pakistan Commission of Inquiry Act 2017 comprising Justice Qazi Faez Isa, Balochistan High Court Chief Justice Naeem Akhtar Afghan and Islamabad High Court Chief Justice Aamer Farooq. They would have 'all the power to fix responsibility against the delinquents for their alleged role behind phone tapping.' *Dawn* was told that Chief Justice Umar Ata Bandial was not privy to the move.[110]

Five days later, former prime minister Imran Khan and the Supreme Court Bar Association challenged before the Supreme Court, the Audio Leaks Commission.[111] In consequence, the Supreme Court suspended the federal government's notification: 'In the circumstances, till the next date of hearing, the operation of the impugned notification No.SRO.596(I)/2023 dated 19.05.2023 issued by the Federal Government is suspended as is the order dated 22.05.2023 made by the Commission and in consequence thereof proceedings of the Commission are stayed.'[112] Later, the Commission itself put itself on the back-burner, but not before Justice Faez Isa had made detailed analyses of the Supreme Court stay order on 27 May 2023.

That the Supreme Court stayed the proceedings of a Commission comprised entirely of the higher judiciary, was perhaps, a new precedent. The federal government sought the 're-constitution of a five-member bench. It asked Chief Justice Umar Ata Bandial, Justice Ijazul Ahsan, and Justice Munib Akhtar to recuse themselves from the five-member bench as they had been mentioned in the audio leaks. Such lack of confidence within the bench emboldened the government to ask for 'impartial judges.'[113]

When challenges to the Commission to be headed by him continued, Justice Isa responded that the Supreme Court (Practice & Procedure) Act 2023 required that every appeal, or case set before it be heard by a bench comprising the chief justice and the two next senior-most judges of the Supreme Court. The petitions challenging the Audio Leaks Commission couldn't be heard until the Committee determined the members to sit on the bench. The Supreme Court had already passed on 13 April 2023 an order staying the proceedings of the Supreme Court (Practice & Procedure) 2023, though Justice Isa referred to this in his response. Thus, the Audio Leaks Commission became an issue that would determine whether the legislature or the judiciary was supreme.

On 30 May 2023, Chief Justice Umar Ata Bandial said that the Supreme Court did not want to axe the Commission led by Justice Faez Isa and the stay was 'merely aimed at protecting the judiciary.' Chief Justice Bandial said that the government should have consulted him before inducting judges in the judicial commissions in line with convention. Chief Justice Bandial added that he obviously would not have become part of the Commission.[114]

Thereafter the Supreme Court took up the issue of *how* audio leaks implicating members of the higher judiciary were obtained. The chief justice asked whether the government, with all its resources, could find out from where and how these audio leaks are coming forward and who is behind all this. Attorney-General Mansoor Usman Awan replied that it was to put all such issues at rest that the federal government had wanted the three-member Commission to probe all aspects. The attorney-general clarified that the government's plea was not related to any 'bias' on the part of any judge, but due to 'conflict of interest'. The chief justice responded to this argument by saying that it was his responsibility to decide which judges could be spared even if the government presumed that the chief justice of Pakistan was conflicted: 'Do you agree to this, or disagree with this settled law?'[115]

The Pakistan Bar Council called for the Audio Leaks Commission headed by Justice Isa to work independently and present its report to the government, despite the Supreme Court having suspended it. The Pakistan Bar Council: 'Resolved that the Supreme Court (Practice and Procedure) Act 2023 has been duly enacted by Parliament and it is the outcome of the legal fraternity's struggle spanning two decades. Therefore, the Supreme Court should withdraw its 13 April restraining order for its implementation.'[116]

The Senate approved the Supreme Court (Practice & Procedure) Act 2023 on 30 March 2023. The bill also retroactively granted the right to appeal against all verdicts delivered in *suo moto* cases. The National Assembly also passed the bill, but when President Arif Alvi declined to sign it into law, the option of a joint parliamentary session was considered to enact it. In this process, the bill would be resubmitted to the president for signing, and if he didn't sign it within ten days, under constitutional provisions, his assent would be considered granted. Azam Nazeer Tarar said: 'We have increased their (judiciary's) powers and brought transparency to the affairs of the Supreme Court through this bill.'[117]

The gravity of this bill can be imagined by recalling the events of 13 April 2023. It was on that day that an eight-member bench of the Supreme Court had put on hold the Supreme Court (Practice & Procedure) Act 2023 passed by a joint sitting of Parliament. It was still awaiting the assent of the president and would become law on 20 April when the Supreme Court struck it down in an 'anticipatory injunction.'[118]

The National Assembly rejected the Supreme Court decision and defied its order to provide funds for provincial assembly elections in Punjab and Khyber Pakhtunkhwa. The National Assembly went on to pass a resolution against the alleged 'attempts by the judiciary to usurp the authority of the Parliament to legislate and interfere in its constitutional jurisdiction.'[119]

Justice Isa observed that with regards to *suo moto* powers, Article 184(3) holds that the 'Supreme Court shall (as) it considers a question of public importance with reference to enforcement of fundamental rights...' His point was that the Act mentioned the Supreme Court and not the chief justice as the authority. Regardless, President Arif Alvi once more refused assent.[120]

On 21 April the bill was sent to the Printing Corporation of Pakistan to publish the Act in the official gazette. About a week later, on 27 April, Prime Minister Shehbaz Sharif sought and obtained a vote of confidence rendered by 180 members. Thereafter, the Supreme Court sought the record of the relevant National Assembly proceedings. The chief justice simultaneously turned down the application for the formation of a full court and the exclusion of Justice Mazahir Ali Naqvi who had been charged in the Supreme Judicial Council for living beyond his known means. On 2 May, the Pakistan Democratic Movement (PDM) government asked Chief Justice Bandial to step down for giving undue facilitation to Imran Khan.

Joint sittings of parliament passed the National Accountability (Amendment) Bill 2023 which asserted that no individual or court can restrain parliament from legislation. The next day the National Assembly passed a Contempt of Parliament Bill 2023.[121]

Irfan Qadir former attorney-general and special advisor to the prime minister, not content with re-asserting that legislation was the preserve of Parliament said that Supreme Court judges could face 'NAB trials for graft' if they were found to have been corrupt! On the same day, Attorney-General Mansoor Usman Awan sought more time from the Supreme Court to review laws regulating the court's affairs.[122]

On 16 June, the chief justice said that the government should have consulted the attorney-general before enacting laws like the Supreme Court (Review of Judgements and Orders) Act 2023. Attorney-General Awan argued on 16 June 2023 that being the court of last resort the Supreme Court must not limit the re-hearing of *suo moto* cases [Article 184 (3)].

With regard to this Act, the Supreme Court reserved its judgement, with the Chief Justice Bandial adding that the decision on the Supreme Court (Review of Judgements and Orders) Act 2023 shall also determine the fate of the Election Commission having had fixed 14 May 2023 as the date for holding Punjab Assembly elections. Chief Justice Bandial said: 'Remedies should be crafted within the Constitutions by adding valid grounds rather than 'ordinary legislation.'

There was an expected scene when on 22 June 2023 the Supreme Court took up the matter of whether civilians could be tried under military courts. As the proceedings began Justice Faez Isa asked Attorney-General Awan to come to the rostrum and observed that Article 175(2) of the Constitution gives the courts the right to hear, and the oath expects judges to decide matters in accordance with the law. Justice Isa who one day previously had been designated by President Arif Alvi to take over as chief justice on 17 September, cited the Supreme Court (Practice & Procedure) Act 2023 as the reason for the whole tension between the legislature and the judiciary saying that Section 2 requires petitions under Article 184(3) of the Constitution (relating to the review of verdicts in *suo moto* cases) to be placed before a Committee of three senior-most judges to determine which bench consisting of which judges should proceed with the matter, 'I am not recusing myself but I will not sit either and therefore rising.' Justice Sardar Tariq Masood also agreed with Justice Isa and left the bench wondering why petitioners never questioned the violation of Human Rights when the Pakistan Army Act was in existence since 1952 and despite the 1973 Constitution, many people were tried under the same law. Why did not the petitioners invoke Article 199 under which petitions could be filed before high courts? At issue was the trial of persons accused of vandalization of the corps commander's residence and other military installations. The remaining seven members of the Supreme Court bench went on with the hearing.[123] Justice Mansoor Ali Shah stepped down on 25 June 2023 over the objection that he was related to the litigant former Chief Justice Jawwad Khwaja. Justice Shah had offered to step down at the outset but then, no objection had been raised. Later, on 27 June 2023, Justice Yahya Afridi also recused himself, calling for a full bench.

There were two unusual features of this case, one political, and one judicial. Politically, Aitzaz Ahsan (a PPP stalwart, former law minister and leader of the 2007 Lawyers Movement) became a complainant, appearing through his lawyer Abdul Latif Khosa (a former attorney-general and governor of Punjab under the PPP government). Both went against party policies. Judicially uncommon was that former Chief Justice Jawwad Khwaja appeared as a complainant in the Army Act case. According to Irfan Qadir, Article VI of the Code of Conduct for judges requires them to avoid litigation as far as possible.[124]

MISCARRIAGE OF JUSTICE.—The trial and execution of Zulfikar Ali Bhutto over the murder of Nawab Muhammad Ahmad Khan Kasuri has been the most discussed. A convention of international jurists in the trial of Zulfikar Ali Bhutto on 6 and 7 April 1979 was convened, and its proceedings were published as *Zulfikar Ali Bhutto Judicial Murder* (Lahore, 2016).

John Matthew QC, who had observed the proceedings, provided his testimony, primarily focusing on the inconsistency in the ballistics evidence. The prosecution's claim that sub-machine guns were used was contradicted by the fact that no automatic rifles had been discharged. This assertion was supported by the absence of significant damage to the vehicle. Instead of the anticipated structural harm caused by automatic rifles, only pellets were employed, leaving distinct markings on both the windshield and the car's side. Despite the defence's desire to inspect the vehicle, they were informed that it had already been destroyed. Additionally, the photographs depicting the car's damage were not presented as evidence.

There exists no record to illustrate the modifications made to the witness's testimony, a pattern that occurred repeatedly. This presented a significant issue, as John Matthew comprehended that the chief justice was declining to include the defence's submitted applications onto the official record, consistently rejecting them.[125]

Benazir Bhutto in her memoirs recalled, 'The positions the assailants claimed to have fired from did not match the bullet holes in the car. Moreover, the FSF guns which the confessing accused claimed to have used in the murder attempt did not match the empty cartridges found at the scene. We have won the case! Rehana Sarwar, the sister of one of my father's lawyers and a lawyer herself said to me jubilantly in the courtroom.'[126]

The verdict was announced at 11 a.m. on 6 February 1979. Four judges found Zulfikar Ali Bhutto guilty of murder: Anwarul Haq, Mohammad Akram, Karam Elahi Chauhan, and Nasim Hasan Shah. Judges who gave him a clear acquittal, were Ghulam Safdar Shah, Dorab Patel, and Abdul Haleem. Thus, there was also a divided bench.

The intriguing part is that while the main Supreme Court judgement was split, the rejection of the review petition was unanimous. Nasim Hasan Shah one of the convicting judges explains how, 'The proposal put forward by Anwarul Haq CJ was that a unanimous verdict may be handed down (so) as to obviate all provincial acrimony. According to him, the fairest solution would be if the Punjab judges could be persuaded to agree to the awarding of a lesser sentence to Mr Bhutto (thus saving his life) while the pro-Mr Bhutto judges might agree to hold him guilty of the death of Nawab Ahmed Khan.'[127]

According to the law, there have to be mitigating circumstances for handing down a lighter-than-usual sentence. The proposal of Anwarul Haq amounted to a plea bargain. Only after the guilt has been established can the question of sentence arise. To ask the acquitting judges to find the defendant guilty on the promise of a lighter sentence might be viewed as an extraordinarily deceptive manoeuvre.

Most miscarriages of justice cause misery and penury, but the totally irremediable are death sentences. Consider the following. Mazhar Farooq was found not guilty by Chief Justice Asif Saeed Khosa due to weak evidence twenty-four years after his initial arrest.[128]

Another defendant Shafqat Husain was acquitted after fifteen years in jail. When in a case the prosecution sought an adjournment, the lawyer for the defendant said he had no objection since his client Lal Khan had died two years ago in prison.[129] The most pathetic case was that of Mohammad Anar. The Supreme Court exonerated him when it found that the purported witnesses had arrived at the scene of the crime after it had been committed, a point which should not have escaped the notice of even the trial court. When the release of two brothers, Ghulam Sarwar and Ghulam Qadir was ordered, it was found that they had already been executed.[130]

A retired Inspector General of Police Tariq Khosa came out against executions, 'Based upon about four decades of experience as a police officer, I can confidently state that it is the certainty rather than the severity of punishment that creates a difference and promotes the rule of law...Harsh punishments never deter criminals.'[131]

Capital punishment is prescribed in Islamic law, but it is rare that the stringent rules of evidence under Islamic law are applied.

Notes

1. Inam Aziz, *Stop Press* (Karachi: Oxford University Press, 2008), p. 7.
2. Hamid Khan, *Constitutional and Political History of Pakistan*, 3rd ed. (Karachi: Oxford University Press, 2018), p. 83.
3. Ibid., p. 84.
4. Ibid., p. 329.
5. Ibid., p. 587.
6. *Dawn*, 29 July 2017.
7. *Dawn*, 12 August 2017.
8. *Dawn*, 11 August 2017.
9. *Dawn*, 1 February 2018.
10. *Dawn*, 21 March 2018.
11. Moeen H. Cheema and Ijaz Shafi Gilani (eds.), *The Politics and Jurisprudence of the Chaudhry Court 2005–2013* (Karachi: Oxford University Press, 2015), p. 18.
12. *Pakistan News Home*, 15 January 2012.
13. *Dawn*, 30 April 2013.
14. *Dawn*, 6 April 2018.
15. *Dawn*, 18 December 2019.
16. *Dawn*, 20 December 2019.
17. *Dawn*, 26 December 2019.
18. *Dawn*, 16 December 2016.
19. *Dawn*, 18 December 2016.
20. *Dawn*, 19 December 2016.
21. *Dawn*, 11 January 2017.
22. *Dawn*, 19 January 2017.
23. *Dawn*, 3 December 2017.
24. *Dawn*, 26 April 2018.
25. *Dawn*, 17 November 2018.
26. *The Express Tribune*, 25 November 2018.
27. *Dawn*, 3 June 2019.
28. *Dawn*, 27 July 2019.
29. *Dawn*, 19 September 2019.
30. *Dawn*, 25 September 2019.
31. *Dawn*, 8 October 2019.
32. *Dawn*, 9 October 2019.
33. 'Benami' means 'no name' or 'without name'. Benami properties are those that are held by an owner through proxies. The property is purchased in the name of or held in the name of a person who has neither paid for it nor actually enjoys it. It may even be held in the name of a non-existent person.
34. *Dawn*, 14 October 2019.
35. *Dawn*, 15 October 2019.
36. *Dawn*, 22 October 2019.
37. *Dawn*, 16 October 2019.
38. *Dawn*, 19 October 2019.
39. *Dawn*, 20 October 2019.
40. *Dawn*, 5 November 2019.

41. *Dawn*, 12 November 2019.
42. *Dawn*, 21 January 2020.
43. *Dawn*, 23 January 2020.
44. *Dawn*, 19 February 2020.
45. *Dawn*, 21 February 2020.
46. *Dawn*, 3 June 2020.
47. Ibid.
48. *Dawn*, 5 June 2020.
49. *Dawn*, 12 June 2020.
50. Justice Isa's wife Zarina Montserrat Carrera is half Spanish, is a Spanish citizen and has always had a Spanish passport. In Spanish Zarina is spelt as 'Cerina', hence she is referred to as Sarina/Serena in the media.
51. *Dawn*, 19 June 2020.
52. *Dawn*, 20 June 2020.
53. *Dawn*, 16 July 2020.
54. *Dawn*, 31 July 2020.
55. *Dawn*, 29 October 2020.
56. *Dawn*, 11 November 2020.
57. *Dawn*, 14 April 2021.
58. *Dawn*, 16 April 2021.
59. *Dawn*, 22 April 2021.
60. *Dawn*, 22 April 2021.
61. *Dawn*, 27 April 2021.
62. *Dawn*, 29 April 2021.
63. *Dawn*, 3 May 2021.
64. *Dawn*, 30 January 2022.
65. *Dawn*, 18 April 2022.
66. *Dawn*, 27 July 2022.
67. *Dawn*, 21 April 2019.
68. *Dawn*, 23 July 2018.
69. *Dawn*, 24 July 2018.
70. *Dawn*, 31 July 2018.
71. *Dawn*, 12 October 2018.
72. *Dawn*, 13 October 2018.
73. *Dawn*, 27 October 2018.
74. *Dawn*, 11 November 2018.
75. *Dawn*, 29 March 2019.
76. *Dawn*, 17 September 2019.
77. *Dawn*, 7 April 2021.
78. *Dawn*, 29 April 2021.
79. *Dawn*, 1 June 2021.
80. *Dawn*, 11 June 2021.
81. *Dawn*, 25 November 2021.
82. *Dawn*, 7 December 2021.
83. *Dawn*, 8 February 2022.
84. *Dawn*, 18 February 2022.
85. *Dawn*, 8 July 2019.
86. *Dawn*, 11 July 2019.
87. *Dawn*, 23 November 2021.
88. *Dawn*, 21 January 2022.
89. *The Express Tribune*, 13 September 2022.
90. *Dawn*, 28 June 2018.
91. *Dawn*, 5 August 2018.

92. *Dawn*, 13 September 2018.
93. *Dawn*, 16 September 2018.
94. *Dawn*, 18 January 2019.
95. *Dawn*, 17 January 2019.
96. *Dawn*, 2 March 2019.
97. *Dawn*, 7 March 2018.
98. *Dawn* 7 March 2020.
99. *Dawn* 8 March 2020.
100. *Dawn*, 3 March 2018.
101. *Dawn*, 13 October 2018.
102. *Dawn*, 9 March 2019.
103. *The Express Tribune*, 20 May 2016.
104. *Dawn*, 21 November 2019.
105. *Dawn*, 13 September 2022.
106. *Dawn*, 17 May 2023.
107. *Dawn*, 10 June 2023.
108. Ibid.
109. *The News International*, 28 July 2022.
110. *Dawn*, 21 May 2023.
111. *Dawn*, 26 May 2023.
112. Ibid.
113. *Dawn*, 31 May 2023.
114. *Dawn*, 30 May 2023.
115. *Dawn*, 7 June 2023.
116. *Dawn*, 8 June 2023.
117. *Dawn*, 11 April 2023.
118. *Dawn*, 14 April 2023
119. Ibid.
120. *Dawn*, 20 April 2023.
121. *Dawn*, 17 May 2023.
122. *Dawn*, 9 June 2023.
123. *Dawn*, 23 June 2023.
124. *Arab News*, 22 June 2023.
125. *Zulfikar Ali Bhutto Judicial Murder* (Lahore: Bhutto Legacy Foundation 2016), pp. 74–7.
126. Benazir Bhutto, *Daughter of the East* (London: Hamish Hamilton, 1988), p. 107.
127. Nasim Hasan Shah, *Memories and Recollections* (Islamabad: Alhambra, 2002), p. 191.
128. *Dawn*, 26 November 2016.
129. *Dawn*, 17 February 2021.
130. *Dawn*, 7 December 2016.
131. *Dawn*, 11 April 2021.

Chapter 54
History of Terrorism in Pakistan

INTRODUCTION.—Before 1980, there were no incidents of terrorism in Pakistan, only crimes. At one time a murder case would make headlines, however, now murder cases routinely merit a mention on the city page of a newspaper. All this changed after the Soviet invasion of Afghanistan in 1979 and intensified after the American invasion of Afghanistan in 2001. Both conflicts caused Afghans to seek refuge in Pakistan. Figures keep on changing but three million Afghan refugees is a fair average. Larry Pressler[1] mentions how it all began as follows: '… on 24 December 1979, the Soviet Union invaded Afghanistan and everything changed. President Carter and President Reagan put their concerns about Pakistan's development of a nuclear weapon on the back burner. They now needed Pakistan to bolster the resistance fighters trying to oust the Soviets in Afghanistan. These resistance fighters were Islamic fundamentalists, the same we are fighting all over the world today.'[2]

The Americans succeeded. The Afghan Taliban now used Google Earth to pinpoint targets. Their targets changed, however, and now they began attacking the Afghan National Army (ANA). A report written by Kenneth Katzman computed ANA strength at 185,000 out of whom 5,300 were commandos. Taliban fighters were estimated to be 25,000, including 3,000 Haqqani network and other Hizb-i-Islami fighters.[3]

At the end of 2014, General Raheel Sharif, Chief of the Army Staff said with reference to terrorists: 'The enemy lies within us and looks like us.'[4] On 16 December 2014, the Army Public School (Peshawar) massacre took place and Lt.-Gen. (retd.) Abdul Qadir Baloch, Minister of States and Frontier Regions rejected a perception that after the tragedy, Afghan refugees shall involuntarily be sent back. Lt.-Gen. Baloch, contradicting the COAS, claimed that the registered Afghan refugees had never been found involved in terrorist-related incidents in the country.[5]

Thus, Pakistan's attitude towards Afghan refugees was ambivalent. Sardar Sanaullah Khan Zehri, the Chief Minister of Balochistan, urged Afghan refugees to get themselves registered.[6] He asked a delegation of the United Nations High Commission for Refugees (UNHCR) for help in this regard. When the legal stay of Afghans in Pakistan expired, Lt.-Gen. (retd.) Abdul Qadir Baloch informed the Senate that the extension of the Afghan refugees' stay was being considered. He said that the repatriation of Afghan refugees would be guided by 'voluntarism' as required under the UNHRC, Afghanistan and Pakistan tripartite agreement. General Baloch said that the Afghan government could not accommodate three million refugees without proper infrastructure and other required arrangements.[7] A further extension of six months was granted by Prime Minister Nawaz Sharif. He however asked for the gradual relocation of refugee camps from Pakistan to Afghanistan.[8]

In contrast, the Khyber Pakhtunkhwa was not in favour of any extension. They said that the federal government should have taken the adjacent provincial government on board.[9] Later, the Interior Minister of State, Baligh Ur Rehman informed the Senate that foreign agencies were funding groups to destabilize Pakistan.[10] The UNHCR expected a modest return of Afghan refugees in 2018.[11] When 2018 came, it was seen that the return would not be even modest.

Despite claiming that terrorists could easily mix in Afghan refugee camps, the Cabinet gave a two-month extension to Afghan refugees.[12] The extension seemed permanent when Prime Minister Imran Khan allowed them to open bank accounts.[13] But fifteen days after the body of SP Tahir Khan Dawar, who had been kidnapped from Islamabad, was discovered in Nangarhar province of Afghanistan,[14] the Peshawar High Court directed the federal and Khyber Pakhtunkhwa governments to restrict the activities of the Afghan refugees in the country in line with the law of the land.[15]

The 27th Report of the UN Analytical and Monitoring Team showed that the Tehreek-e-Taliban, Pakistan (TTP) was based in Afghanistan and had carried out more than a hundred cross-border attacks in only the preceding three months.[16] Only four days earlier armed attacks on Nushki and Panjgur districts in Pakistan had left seven security personnel and thirteen terrorists dead, in attacks from across the border. The Pakistan Army said that the terrorists had handlers in Afghanistan.[17]

TERRORIST ATTACKS

The Hangu School Attack. On 6 January 2014, terrorists turned to a soft target, the Hangu Public School, Khyber Pakhtunkhwa. Their attempts were thwarted by the courage of a 15-year-old ninth-grader, Aitzaz Hasan Bangash. He was a bit late, so he could see the attacker approaching the school. Aitzaz Hasan grabbed the attacker preventing him from entering the school. In the scuffle, the explosives went off, killing both, the student and the terrorist. Aitzaz Hasan was awarded a posthumous Sitara-i-Shujaat for his courage, which saved the lives of all other students in the school. In December, it was discovered that this act of heroism had not deterred the terrorists.

The Army Public School, Peshawar Massacre. The most terrible attack in the history of Pakistan took place in Peshawar on 16 December 2014. Terrorists belonging to TTP attacked the Army Public School (APS). The Taliban commander, Omar Khorasani, was giving directions from Afghanistan. The militants torched a vehicle as a diversion before entering the school and opening fire on students who were giving an examination. They also targeted teachers. One teacher was set on fire for the students to witness. Six militants blew themselves up while three were taken down by the Pakistan Army. Seven soldiers, including two officers, were injured in the operation.

The casualty would rise to 150. We have graphic scenes from survivors. A 16-year-old boy Shahrukh was shot in both legs, but he played possum and escaped a fatal bullet. Students spoke of a class fellow 13-year-old Uzair Ali who was shot thirteen times trying to save them. The TTP spokesman, who claimed responsibility said: 'We targeted the school because the Army targets our families. We want them to feel our pain.'[18]

The Principal Mrs Tahira Qazi was rescued safe and sound, but she went back into the school, to be with 'her children'. Students were forced by the militants to see their principal being killed. Much greater courage was displayed by the victims than by the suicide bombers.

'The state of denial and capitulation has allowed militants to gain further space; wrote journalist Zahid Husain. To illustrate that despite years of terror attacks there was no clear-cut policy with the state, he wrote that 6000 alleged militants arrested in Swat and Waziristan have been languishing in army detention camps without being produced before a court of law.[19]

A judicial commission was appointed to probe the APS tragedy on 5 October 2018, four years after the tragedy. Justice Muhammad Ibrahim Khan completed the report on 26 June 2020 but released it in September. It found inertia on the part of Askari Guards and deputed static guards to the early firing. It was only when the Mobile Vigilance Team and the Quick Response Team arrived that the militants were countered. The porous Pakistan-Afghanistan border was blamed. The Commission went on to report: 'Above all the assistance provided to the fanatics from the inhabitants of (the) locality, especially in this particular episode was palpable and unpardonable.' The Commission concluded that inside help caused the militants to succeed.[20]

On the first anniversary of the tragedy, the Tamgha-i-Shujaat was awarded to the courageous and conscientious Principal Prof. Tahira Qazi. In 2021, grieving parents insisted on filing an FIR against those who had been responsible for security: 'We don't want any compensation, but only action against those responsible for the APS tragedy.'[21] A student on the seventh anniversary of the tragedy wrote: 'Our fear was thus replaced by a determination to prove to the world that no matter what, we will keep learning'.[22]

In an apparent reference to the reports and announcement by the government that it was holding negotiations with the TTP, former President Asif Ali Zardari said that the state had no right or authority to pardon the killers of innocent school children.[23] The grieving parents also moved the Peshawar High Court on 15 July 2022 against the Government of Pakistan's negotiations with the TTP.

The director of the APS tragedy Omar Khorasani was killed on 7 August 2022 by a roadside mine. Ehsanullah Ehsan the spokesman who claimed responsibility for the APS tragedy as well as a failed attack on Malala Yousafzai offered terms for surrender. A house in Rawalpindi where he and his family could initially stay as well as a huge sum with which he could start some business. He also wanted relocation to a Middle Eastern country.[24]

Ehsanullah Ehsan whose real name was reported to be Liaquat Ali surrendered to a Pakistan security agency on 5 February 2017. Later, in an audio message Ehsanullah Ehsan disclosed that 'With the help of Allah' he had escaped from Pakistani custody on 11 January 2020, he said he was in Turkey. Ehsanullah claimed that he had faced hardship in Pakistani custody where his terms for surrender were not honoured.[25]

Mohsin Dawar a leader of the Pashtun Tahaffuz Movement (PTM) sought an explanation for Ehsanullah Ehsan's escape in the National Assembly. Syed Naveed Qamar (PPP) sought the reason for the government's silence on the escape. PPP Chairman Bilawal Bhutto-Zardari also questioned how such a criminal was allowed to escape.[26] Seven days later the Interior Minister Ijaz Shah confirmed that Ehsanullah had escaped, leading Bilawal Bhutto-Zardari to call the escape a proof of the PTI government's incompetence and failure.[27]

The reaction of the Pakistan Army was more severe and more forthright. Maj. Gen. Babar Iftikhar the Director-General of the Inter-Services Public Relations said that Ehsanullah's escape was a serious matter and action had been taken against the military officers involved in the escape. Though in the custody of Pakistan for three years, Ehsanullah was never formally charged for the APS massacre.[28]

The Supreme Court sought the government's reply to the six-volume judicial report. Parents present during the Supreme Court hearing sought an explanation of why Ehsanullah who financed and planned the massacre was never tried and how he had managed to escape.[29]

Civil Hospital, Quetta Carnage. On being informed of a terrorist attack in Quetta, people have come to assume that the victims were Shia Hazara. However, in one of the most horrible incidents, it was the lawyers who were victims. On 8 August 2016, two motorcyclists shot dead Bilal Anwar Kasi, president of the Balochistan Bar Association. When lawyers and other mourners gathered in the Civil Hospital, where the body had been taken, a suicide bomber blew himself up killing 70 persons. Half of them were said to be lawyers. It became standard procedure to kill a prominent person to lure people to the funeral and kill all the mourners in one stroke.[30]

Later, in the same month, the Supreme Court under Chief Justice Anwar Zaheer Jamali took *suo moto* notice of the carnage. This, actually, was at the instance of a 13 August 2016 Pakistan Bar Council Resolution. The inspector-general of police and the chief secretary were required to explain the security lapse. The registrar of the Supreme Court wrote: 'Lack of security arrangements, despite past precedents points to the miserable failure of the provincial government and law enforcement agencies to avert the tragic incident.' It went on to observe that such negligence constituted a violation of the fundamental right to life and liberty guaranteed under Article 9 of the Constitution.[31]

Soon after, the Senate took up the issue of intelligence failure and sought a thorough investigation to fix responsibility. Fiery speeches and walkouts from the Senate did not help.[32] In a meeting held at the Prime Minister's House, COAS General Raheel Sharif was quoted as saying that simply ridding the country of terrorists was not enough, and law enforcement agencies needed to get hold of the financiers, abettors, and facilitators of terrorists. The National Action Plan (NAP) drawn up after the APS tragedy was found to lack implementation.[33]

Military Installations. After the Soviet withdrawal (1989), militants ceased to be allies of Pakistan, and they began attacking military installations. By way of illustration, the three most deadly attacks are given below.

On 10 and 11 October 2009, militants attacked the General Headquarters, Rawalpindi. The militants were able to take control because of the prohibition of soldiers bearing arms within the complex. The gunmen who opened fire were in military uniform. The casualties suffered during the operation were ten soldiers and two civilians against nine militants killed. One militant, Mohammad Aqeel aka Dr Usman,[34] was captured. The militants were able to take twenty-two civil and military men hostage. The SSQ Division and Army Special Forces rescued the hostages. They were led by Brig. Gen. Anwarul Haq Ramday. The responsibility was claimed jointly by Lashkar-i-Jhangvi and TTP. They said their attack was in retaliation for Pakistan military operations in Waziristan. The operation lasted 22 hours.

Militants stormed PNS Mehran a naval facility in Karachi on 22 May 2011. The attackers were probably six in number, who killed eight Navy men and two Rangers. They went on to destroy two US-supplied P-3C Orion aircraft costing $30 million each. The eleven Chinese and six Americans who were at the base remained safe. The militants used ladders and pliers to cut wires. Naval commandos responded within three minutes, but the militants had taken position and the battle lasted 16 hours. Lt. Syed Yasir Abbas[35] commanded the response. The TTP spokesman Ehsanullah Ehsan said: 'The fighters do not want to come out alive.' The TTP claimed responsibility 'in revenge for the 2 May 2011 operation that had killed Osama bin Laden.'[36] This was not clear as on 13 May 2011, the TTP had already exacted revenge for the attack killing Osama bin Laden. They had attacked the Frontier Constabulary Training Centre. Two suicide bombers succeeded in killing ninety-eight persons, mostly recruits. One terrorist blew up his car at six in the morning when the recruits had gathered to return home after their training was over.[37]

Miscellaneous Attacks. Other attacks included an attack by the TTP on an army camp at Sarai Naurang *tehsil* of Lakki Marwat District, Khyber Pakhtunkhwa on 2 February 2013. First, a suicide bomber blew himself up in a nearby residential area killing eleven civilians. Thirteen soldiers and twelve militants were killed. TTP spokesman Ehsanullah Ehsan said the attack was carried out to avenge the killing of two Taliban commanders, Toofani and Faisal, in a US drone attack.[38]

One year later, it was learnt that the TTP had killed twenty-three Frontier Constabulary (FC) men they had captured three years ago in 2010. This was claimed to be revenge for twenty-three TTP men killed in government custody. The Government of Pakistan called off talks that had been scheduled.[39]

Three Frontier Constables were killed when a roadside explosive device went off. Two FC vehicles were also destroyed.[40]

A suicide blast in Karachi on 20 March 2015 killed two Rangers and injured two.[41]

Two Civil Aviation Authority men were killed in an attack on Jiwani Airport near Gwadar. Around twelve men on motorcycles stormed the airport at 3:30 a.m. on 30 August 2015. No security personnel were present at that time. The installation in charge Mehmood Ahmed Niazi was captured and killed. Another officer electronics engineer Khalil Ullah was killed in the attack. The responsibility was claimed by Meerak Baloch of the Baloch Liberation Army.[42]

Afghan Taliban killed twenty-nine Pakistan Air Force (PAF) personnel at Badaber Airbase, close to the north-western city of Peshawar on 18 September 2015. The TTP claimed the attack saying it was carried out from an Afghan base.[43] In this attack, no one had worn a suicide jacket, but all fourteen TTP men were killed. On 19 September 2015, it was disclosed that the TTP fighters had been armed with grenades, rocket launchers Kalashnikov rifles among other weapons apparently expecting a long battle. The death toll had been twenty-two PAF officers, including army Captain Asfandyar Bukhari with two of his men. Four civilians were also killed. Omar Khorasani of the TTP claimed responsibility.

Tehreek-e-Taliban, Pakistan (TTP). The rise of the Taliban is shrouded in some mystery. The purpose of the United States had been served by the withdrawal of Soviet forces from Afghanistan. At their withdrawals, neither the USSR nor the US seemed to care what they were leaving behind. In the interregnum between the Soviet withdrawal in 1989 and the American invasion in the wake of 9/11, Afghanistan was going through anarchy. Warlords were fighting each other, causing the Mujahideen created by the United States to overstay their welcome. Salafi Islam was discarded and now Sufi Islam was to be favoured.

The only way to bring stability to Afghanistan seemed to side with the strongest party. The Taliban set up under the jihadist period had the upper hand. The Taliban were organized as such during the term of Benazir Bhutto.

Talking later to the Voice of America, Benazir Bhutto said that the Taliban formed during her regime had no links with Al-Qaeda. What was more, they had American support. She recounted that as Leader of the Opposition she had asked the Treasury benches to use their influence on the Taliban 'otherwise the entire region would face a catastrophe.'[44]

The White House also had shades of ambiguity. As late as 2015, its Press Secretary was saying that 'the Afghan Taliban were armed insurgents, not terrorists. The Pakistani Taliban, Al-Qaeda and ISIS are terrorists.' A journalist asked: 'Was the attack on a Pakistani school (APS, 2014) that killed 140 kids not a terrorist attack?' The Press Secretary replied: 'Yes, it was a terrorist attack carried out by the Pakistani Taliban, and these are two different groups.'[45]

Two different groups with the same name and the same mission. The 'Good Taliban' and 'Bad Taliban' confusion led to more and more bloodshed, as the Taliban that carried out the APS attack were guided by Omar Khorasani stationed in Afghanistan. With such ambivalence, no wonder the eventual American withdrawal from Afghanistan proved chaotic.

This also explains why there were attempts by the Pakistani government to negotiate with the Tehreek-e-Taliban, Pakistan (TTP). Their spokesman Ehsanullah Ehsan set two conditions for talks: (1) the release of its seven leaders held by Muslim Khan and Maulvi Umar, and (2) the PML (N), the JUI (F) and the Jamaat-e-Islami to act as guarantors on behalf of the Pakistan Army. The TTP claimed that previous agreements signed with political forces were not honoured. The TTP spokesman also attacked the MQM in a public meeting, killed its MPA, and threatened more attacks.

The Jamaat-e-Islami lost no time in pulling out. They said that the Jamaat-e-Islami cannot become a guarantor because they had nothing to do with the Taliban and that the TTP too had not contacted them to get their opinion.[46] The ruling PPP tabled a resolution seeking an amendment to the Anti-Terrorism Act of 1997: 'If any or all office-bearers of a proscribed organization form a new organization under a different name, upon suspicion of their involvement in similar activities, the said organization shall also be deemed to be proscribed and the government may issue formal notification of its proscription.'[47]

A few days later, the All-Parties Conference hosted by Maulana Fazlur Rahman adopted the following resolution: 'In order to restore peace in Pakistan, especially in Fata and Khyber Pakhtunkhwa, the APC completely supports the efforts of a 17-member grand jirga and suggests the following steps: The jirga should be expanded by giving representation to all political and religious parties (having different schools of thought) of the country. A trust should be set up for the welfare of the injured and the families of those killed (in terrorism-related incidents). The jirga should start a dialogue with the stakeholders under the guidance of the leadership of all political and religious parties attending today's APC. Practical steps should be taken to eliminate lawlessness in the country and that we all support the dialogue that could result in the enforcement of the Constitution and law of the country. All the religious and political parties and Fata elders participating in today's APC announce that the present, interim and the next elected government and the (future) opposition will be bound to implement all the steps agreed upon.'[48]

VICTIMS OF TERRORISM

Polio Vaccinators. Terrorists target para-medical workers who administer anti-polio drops to children. Because babies are in the care of mothers, lady health workers are employed for this task, as a result, most of the victims are women. They are counted in the hundreds. The occurrence is highest in Balochistan and Khyber Pakhtunkhwa where tribal culture prevails. A mother-and-daughter team of polio workers was shot down in Quetta, Balochistan on 18 January 2018.[49] Two lady health workers were shot dead in Swabi, Khyber Pakhtunkhwa.[50]

A superstition has taken hold that anti-polio drops cause sterility, which means their population is sought to be controlled. At the onset of Covid-19 in Pakistan (February 2020) a similar suspicion had spread, and the dread disease could be controlled only by punitive measures.

Sunni Muslims. Sunni Muslims constitute the overwhelming majority in Pakistan, yet they have not been immune to terror attacks by extremists. On 11 April 2006, a Milad-un-Nabi[51] celebration organized at Nishtar Park in Karachi was bombed. One of the two suicide bombers reached the dais on which almost all the Sunni Tehrik leaders were present and then blew himself up. Among the martyrs were Maulana Abbas Qadri, Maulana Ikram Qadri, and Maulana Iftikhar Ahmad Bhatti. A total of fifty-seven lives were lost in this carnage. Later they started taking safety measures.

Twelver Shias. The Shias of Pakistan are the world's second-largest Shia community after that of Iran but comprise only 10–15 per cent of Pakistan's population.

Sindh. The first major massacre took place in Thehri on 3 July 1963. At least 118 Shia Muslims were killed. This area of Sindh was one where due to the influence of Sufi saints, Shi'i Imams were venerated by the Sunnis too. Till after the Musharraf Era, this remained an isolated incident. Later two acts of violence stand out. A mosque in Shikarpur was attacked at the time of Friday prayers killing around sixty Shia worshippers.[52] Ten months later, in Jacobabad, a procession of Shia Muslims on Eid Milad-un-Nabi was attacked killing at least twenty-one participants.

Karachi. Karachi is the capital of Sindh, but since most migrants from India (and now Afghanistan) made it their home, its ethnic profile has changed. Muslims from all sects came from India. As during Colonial times there were disputations, sermons, polemics, and pamphlets, but all these remained well below incitement to violence. In the early years of the Zia era, in February 1978, Ali Basti, a Shia locality was attacked, leaving five dead. On 14 August 1978, Independence Day which coincided with Ashura, the procession was attacked, and twenty-two mourners were shot dead. In 1983, Shia localities were attacked on Eid Milad-un-Nabi with ten Shias killed and ninety-four houses set on fire. In 1985, a month-long riot from 27 September to 26 October raged in which mosques and Imam Bargahs were burnt, especially in the Liaquatabad area. Exact casualty figures were not available but were large. Ten years later, on 25 February 1995, there was a carnage of Shia Muslims gathered for dawn prayers at Mehfil-e-Murtaza, PECHS. Eighteen worshippers were lined up and shot; one, despite being shot survived. The killers were identified as Mansoor Ali Babar, Umar Hayat, and ten more. From Mehfil-e-Murtaza they went to Mehfil-e-Abul Fazl-il-Abbas in PIB Colony and killed six more worshippers. On 26 December 2009, corresponding with the eighth of Muharram, a procession was targeted in the Paposh Nagar neighbourhood, drawing blood. Two days later (28 December) on Ashura the main procession was attacked with bombs and bullets and over fifty were killed on the spot. Since then, high security has been ensured on procession routes. This was the deadliest attack in the history of Karachi, and though perpetrators were identified, the trial dragged on for eleven years, witnesses were relocated, files went missing, and no verdict was delivered. Another major incident was a gun and bomb attack on worshippers at Friday prayers at the Shia Mosque within the compound of the Sindh Madrassa Science College. Initially, 14 were killed and 125 injured. This was located near the most office premises; the State Bank and many private banks had their head offices in the vicinity. On 21 Ramadan, the Youm-i-Ali procession came under attack at Saddar where the main markets are located.[53] The next major incident was when an Imam bargah at Orangi Colony was bombed with two dead and seven injured. Abbas Town a largely Shia locality witnessed an attack on the imam bargah with worshippers killed in the dozens.[54] The following year the whole residential area of Abbas Town was hit. About 45 died and 135 were injured many houses and apartment houses were damaged. In Nazimabad a mourning assembly was attacked killing five men.[55] Masjid Baab-ul-Ilam, North Karachi saw two major incidents. Firstly, three mourners, all young, were killed by guns fired from outside.[56] Then, when Doctor Ibn-e-Hassan was killed in Malir, his funeral proceeded from Baab-ul-Ilam to Sakhi Hasan Graveyard, but the funeral turned into a protest and public property was damaged in August 2003.[57] Even academia was not spared. Dr Shakil Auj, Dean of Islamic Studies at the University of Karachi, was assassinated on 18 September 2014. He was a Sunni but against violence. Syed Waheedur Rahman, Assistant Professor of Mass Communications, was killed on 13 April

2015. Hasan Turabi, a prominent cleric from Gilgit-Baltistan, was killed along with his nephew in Karachi on 14 July 2016.

Quetta, Balochistan. Quetta is home to Hazaras who were expelled by Amir Abdul Rahman from Afghanistan. When they settled in Quetta, they became a flourishing business community. Twelver Shia by belief, the Hazaras are ethnically Mongoloid, which marks out their identity. The Hazara built two localities in Quetta, and they had to traverse Spiny Road to commute between the two localities. Here too, the killing of Osama bin Laden exponentially increased the number of terrorist attacks, which however had begun in the early years of the 21st century. In the holy month of Ramadan, seven Hazaras were gunned down in Quetta. This was a prelude to a veritable carnage in Quetta on 3 September 2010 to mark Al-Quds Day[58] organized by the Imamia Students Organisation (ISO), a subsidiary of the Tehreek-e-Jafaria. A suicide bomber blew himself up in the middle of the procession, killing 56 persons and wounding 160. Both TTP and Lashkar-i-Jhangvi claimed responsibility.[59] Another major incident was when 29 members of the Hazara community were killed at Mastung on 20 September 2011. Three Hazaras travelling on Spiny Road in a taxi were killed.[60] Thirteen Hazaras died when their bus was bombed when they were going by road to Mashhad, Iran for pilgrimage.[61] Five Hazaras were off-loaded from a bus, lined up and shot dead. Two other Hazaras were shot dead at Taftan at the border entry into Iran. Seven Hazaras were killed by six terrorists, who as the police reported, managed to escape.[62] In 2013, a major carnage took place on Alamdar Road, Quetta in which 81 perished, and 120 persons were injured which included ten personnel of the Pakistan Army and the FC.[63] This caused 5000 protesters to sit in vigil despite the mid-January cold. The vigil was called off when Prime Minister Raja Pervez Ashraf came to Quetta on 13 January 2013 and imposed Governor's rule in Balochistan. Barely a month had passed when, on 16 February 2013, there was a massive bomb blast in Hazara Town. A water tanker, loaded on a tractor trolley was filled with explosives which killed 67 Hazaras on the spot. The explosion left a crater 6 feet deep and 18 feet wide. The Supreme Court took *suo moto* notice and a hearing took place on 26 February. The Supreme Court rejected a report presented by the Balochistan police.

In late June, in Karachi, Justice Maqbool Baqar of the Supreme Court was targeted in a near-morning attack. No deaths were reported.[64] There was a respite as far as major incidents were concerned. Two Hazara shopkeepers in the Quetta market were shot dead in late May 2015 and the assailants fled on a motorcycle.[65] Two days later two pilgrim buses were stopped at Mastung, and 19 passengers were taken to the nearby mountains and killed.[66] Another bus, in October 2015, within the city was bombed killing ten which included two children.[67]

Travelling even short distances had become hazardous. Four Hazara ladies were killed when they were commuting in a coach.[68] This too, was a prelude to a blood bath in Quetta. A gun and bomb attack on the Police Training College killed 62 cadets and 2 soldiers. Both the outfits claiming responsibility were sectarian: Islamic State of Iraq and Syria (ISIS) and Lashkar-i-Jhangvi.[69] Captain Roohullah Mohmand threw himself on a bomber; he died but saved the lives of at least 12 recruits.[70]

In 2017, suicide bombings took place across the country. In Balochistan only, the number of attacks were 183, which killed a total of 308 persons.[71] Nine days later, the Hazaras called for the Supreme Court to appoint a judicial commission to probe their genocide.[72] There were sporadic attacks in April 2018. On the last day of April, two demonstrations were held in Quetta. The protestors said that they would call off their sit-in only when General Qamar Javed Bajwa, Chief of the Army Staff visited them.[73] Over 125 people perished in a suicide attack in Mastung.[74]

One year later suicide bombers killed twenty persons in Quetta of which eight were Hazaras, including two children. The TTP claimed to have collaborated with the Lashkar-i-Jhangvi. The same day, the Senate took up the issue and sought a comprehensive report on the action taken against banned outfits.[75] The Minister of State for Interior Affairs, Shahryar Khan Afridi, said that external forces were involved.[76] Later Shahryar Afridi with the Chief Minister of Balochistan, Jam Kamal Khan Alyani, came to the camp of the protestors and assured them that the National Action Plan would be fully implemented.[77] But only three days later the banned outfits killed fourteen security personnel in Gwadar. The martyred included members of the Navy, Air Force, and Coast Guards. The Baloch Liberation Army claimed responsibility for the outrage.[78] Later that year, the Supreme Court rejected the police report on the Hazara killings.[79]

In January 2021, eleven coal miners at Mach were captured and killed.[80] The protesters refused to bury their dead or call off their vigil until the then Prime Minister, Imran Khan, himself came to them.[81] Two opposition leaders Bilawal Bhutto-Zardari (PPP) and Maryam Nawaz (PML-N) visited the heirs of the coal miners. She slated the Prime Minister's comment that 'politics is being done on the corpses'[82] Prime Minister Imran Khan said he would not be 'blackmailed' by the protesters and shall visit the protesters only after they had buried their dead.[83] Arrangements for burial began when the Prime Minister finally arrived. He blamed India for the attack. He added, 'To end this divide we have tried to remove differences between Saudi Arabia and Iran.'[84]

As early as 2009 a former Capital City Police Officer, Quetta, Rafi Ahmad Pervez Bhatti wrote of his experience to explain why the insurgency was not being controlled. When this officer was posted, Quetta was under curfew after 43 people had been killed. In 2003, Quetta had witnessed over 200 sectarian killings The officer wrote, 'The Lashkar-i-Jhangvi and not the Baloch Liberation Army (BLA) was behind these killings. The BLA had its own separate agenda of eliminating "Punjabi" settlers. The Quetta police took up the challenge and as a result, not a single incident of sectarian attack and BLA members were arrested in coordination with the ISI and MI. The coordination of the police, the intelligence agencies and community leaders was such that suicide bombers were identified and raided before they could operate... I received intelligence reports that Lashkar-i-Jhangvi was planning to ambush DSP Nisar Kazmi who was interrogating the arrested. 'I tried my best to get an official residence allotted to him in the Police lines for his safety, but the Police Department refused it.' The DSP was attacked and injured. His assailant was killed, but DSP Kazmi got himself transferred to Punjab. Sub-Inspector Shahid Raisani who was interrogating BLA men was also refused official quarters and as a result, he was killed by the BLA. Taking a lesson from all this several police officers who had participated in Rafi Ahmad Pervez Bhatti's campaign were scared and demoralized, how can an unarmed shopkeeper, school teacher or lawyer gather courage?' Lashkar-i-Jhangvi and the Baloch Liberation Army now co-ordinated their activities. Bhatti complained of a lack of commitment in his estimate only 45 to 50 terrorists needed to be arrested.[85] With such a successful outreach of intimidation, it is not surprising that the BLA attacked the Pakistan Stock Exchange, Karachi. The attackers arrived in a car and hurled a grenade. One policeman and three security guards were martyred, but within eight minutes all insurgents had been killed.[86]

The Punjab. This is the province where the most ancient shrines of Shia saints are located, and which has a long history of Muharram observations. The first terrorist attack took place at Mominpura graveyard in Lahore on 11 January 1998. Twenty-five mourners were killed on the spot. Three months later three Shias were targeted in Multan.[87] On 2 September 2010, a major bombing took place in Lahore. Then came a more violent incident in the same city. At the Ashura procession (26 January 2011) in Karbala Game Shah a suicide bomber killed 25 on the spot and injured 80. Muharram processions became a soft target. During Ashura observance, Imambargah-i-Hefazat Ali was torched. Deadly bombings at the same site took place on 11 January 2015. Next terrorists attacked Qasr-i-Sakina, killing three and wounding many more.[88] A wider terror attack occurred at Gulshan-i-Iqbal Park, Lahore, killing over seventy members of the general public and injuring many more.[89]

Khyber Pakhtunkhwa and Northern Areas. The first major incident is traced to 1 September 2012 at Maltiani Market, Peshawar, where a bomb loaded on a truck exploded killing 8 adults and 3 children. Another suicide bomber on 2 February 2013 killed 26 worshippers and injured 62 outside a Hangu mosque, just as they were emerging after prayers. Later that year, 15 worshippers were killed at the Arif Husaini Mosque in Peshawar. This was the mosque where Syed Arif Hussain Al-Hussaini leader of the Tehreek-e-Jafaria had been killed in 1988. In this attack, his grandson, Syed Mehdi also became prey to terror.[90] A mosque in Parachinar was bombed on 14 December

2015.⁹¹ The next year, 20 persons including DSP Naveed Bangash were killed; six were killed in a Shia mosque in Hayatabad, Peshawar on 24 January 2016. In an attack on Shabqadr Mosque, Charsadda two soldiers and one suicide bomber with his family were killed on 3 March 2016.⁹² Another attack followed on 18 March 2016. The most devastating attack to date took place at the Turi Market, Parachinar, when 75 were killed and 300 injured in early June 2017.⁹³ The survivors staged a sit-in, which only ended when COAS General Qamar Javed Bajwa visited them.⁹⁴ These attacks have not stopped due to their proximity to the Afghan border. A large number of men were killed at Kurram Imam Bargah in a bomb blast on 6 May 2020.⁹⁵ In 2022, an attack on a Shia mosque in Peshawar claimed 57 lives.⁹⁶ Among the prominent ulama of this sect who were assassinated were Aftab Jafri, Taqi Hadi, Abbas Nasir, and Mazharul Haq Deobandi.

Ismailis, Khojas. The Khoja Ismailis, followers of the Aga Khan have suffered one but major carnage. On 13 May 2015, residents of Azhar Gardens commuted to their places of business in a bus. A very peaceful community with contributions in the health, education, and welfare circles, the Khojas were seemingly immune. ISIS had their eyes on them. Their bus was intercepted near Safoora Goth. Eight gunmen led by Saad Aziz and Tahir Saeen opened fire killing at least forty-six. An ISIS pamphlet was left which declared that all Shias were infidels and as such liable to be killed.

Dawoodi Bohras. The Dawoodi Bohras follow the Fatimi Ismaili Tayyibi school of thought and are guided by their leader known as the *al-dai al-mutlaq* (absolute missionary). Twin blasts took place in Barkat-i-Hyderi, a locality in North Nazimabad, Karachi first founded by them. Seven including a girl and an infant were among those killed in the blasts. The next attack took place in Hyderabad on 3 November 2012 when two Bohris, Murtuza and Shabbar were killed instantly. The third attack by an internal explosive device took place on Swaleh Mosque killing two on 20 March 2017. The last took place in a field when Bohras were hosting a reception for their al-Dai al-Mutlaq Syedna Mufaddal Saifuddin on 13 April 2017.

Sufi Shrines. The first shrine to be attacked was Bari Imam in Islamabad on 28 May 2005. The second was at the shrine of Rahman Baba, Peshawar 5 March 2009; Data Durbar, Lahore, 2 July 2010 (a second attack took place on 9 May 2019); Abdullah Shah Ghazi Mazar, Karachi on 7 October 2010. The Shrine of Baba Farid Ganj-i-Shakar in Pakpattan 25 October 2010. The shrine of Sakhi Sarwar, Dera Ghazi Khan18 April 2011. The Shah Noorani shrine in Balochistan was bombed on 13 November 2016. In all of these attacks, many lives were lost, but the largest number of casualties took place at the Shrine of Sakhi Shahbaz Qalandar, Sehwan Sharif, in which a female suicide bomber killed 75 and injured more than 250 devotees in February 2017.⁹⁷

Salafis Losses. Although all terrorist outfits professing Islam have Salafi roots, and hence are violent were in no danger of being attacked themselves, though it may have been in reprisal. A DSP was among the martyrs when ISIS attacked a Sunni Mosque; seven others were killed. Then a rally by the Ahl-i-Sunnah wa'l Jama'at (a reincarnation of Sipah i-Sahaba) was attacked by a suicide bomber on 5 November 2011. The leaders of their various anti-Shia organizations have mostly died violently, though no organization has come forward to claim responsibility: Ihsan Ilahi Zaheer on 24 March 1987; Haq Nawaz Jhangvi on 22 February 1990; Maulana Yusuf Ludhianvi on 18 May 2000; Riaz Basra on 14 May 2002; Azam Tariq on 6 October 2003; and Maulana Nizamuddin Shamzai on 30 May 2004.[98]

Militants Killed. Other militants who have been killed include Waliur Rahman, the Deputy Chief of the TTP in a drone attack on North Waziristan on 30 May 2013.[99] Forty, mostly Uzbek fighters killed in North Waziristan on 22 January 2014. Pakistan Air Force struck at members of the Islamic Movement of Uzbekistan on 21 February 2014. This was a reaction after 23 Frontier Corps members had been kidnapped and killed. Ten militants including Gul Nawaz TTP leader, were killed in an air raid.[100] Forty terrorists were killed in North Waziristan on 16 August 2015. The Al-Qaeda Karachi chief and one accomplice were killed in August 2015. The report gave no names.[101] On 19 September 2015, eighteen terrorists were killed in Tirah. In a Gilgit-Baltistan incident, when a terrorist Hazrat Noor on being cornered, blew himself up with his wife and daughter. Most of the militants were killed in the operation known as Zarb-i-Azb which was launched in June 2014. By 2017, the operation had cost $1.9 billion to Pakistan.[102]

Ahmadis. Ahmadis were first targeted in Lahore in 1953 when the first, though localized Martial Law was declared. In 1974, the National Assembly of Pakistan declared them non-Muslim. The incidents are too many to recount, but we give one incident by way of example. Two Ahmadi worship places in Lahore were attacked leaving ninety people dead on 28 May 2010.

Christian Community. A suicide attack on a US consular vehicle in Peshawar killed two Americans in September 2012. TTP killed ten foreign climbers and one local guide at Nanga Parbat camp in July 2013.[103] On 15 March 2015, two explosions took place at the Roman Catholic Church and Christ Church during Sunday service in Youhanabad, Lahore. In the same city, suicide bombers killed seventy-five worshippers on Easter on 26 March 2016. In Karachi, a Christian Foundation on M.A. Jinnah Road was attacked killing most of the volunteers. In December 2021, a mob in Sialkot tortured to death a Sri Lankan Christian mill manager over blasphemy allegations before burning his body.

Daniel Pearl. Daniel Pearl, 38, a reporter for *Wall Street Journal* was reported missing on 23 January 2002. The arrested suspect Ahmed Omar Saeed Sheikh confirmed his death on 13 February 2002. Anti-Terrorist Court awarded death sentence to all defendants. The Sindh High Court overturned the verdict of the Anti-Terrorist Court for want of sufficient evidence on 2 April 2020. The Supreme Court of Pakistan also found the defendants non-guilty on the basis of 'prosecution flaws.'[104]

The parents of Daniel Pearl, Ruth and Judea Pearl in a heart-rending appeal protested the release of the defendants: 'As parents, we know, regardless of differences parents everywhere want to raise their children in a safe society free of the violence and terror that took Daniel's life.'[105]

Social Workers. Perween Rahman, Director of the Orangi Pilot Project was murdered on 13 March 2013. She had been campaigning against land grabbers. Among those arrested included her neighbour Raheem Swati, Ahmad Khan, Amjad Husain and Azam Swati. All of them were given life terms.[106]

The next such incident took place on 24 April 2015 when Sabeen Mahmud, who was running a forum called The Second Floor was shot down on a road. Those arrested included Saad Aziz (also wanted in the Safoora carnage case), Tahir Husain Minhas, Asadur Rahman, Hafiz Nasir and Majid. Sabeen Mahmud was targeted because she had celebrated St. Valentine's Day and because she was pursuing a case against the Lal Masjid cleric Abdul Aziz. The Army Chief upheld the death penalty for all accused.[107]

Another person to pursue cases against Maulana Abdul Aziz was Khurram Zaki. He was killed by two men. His supporters rallied and staged a demonstration as a result of which the police registered cases against Abdul Aziz and Aurangzeb Farooqui head of the ASWJ.[108]

Terrorism in Pakistan is not at an end, but we can rationally nurture hope.

Notes

1. As chairman of the US Senate's Arms Control Subcommittee, Larry Pressler advocated the now-famous Pressler Amendment, enforced in 1990.
2. Larry Pressler, *Neighbours in Arms: An American Senator's Quest for Disarmament in a Nuclear Subcontinent* (Gurgaon: Penguin/Viking, 2017), p. 17.
3. *Dawn*, 23 February 2014.
4. *Dawn*, 5 December 2014.
5. *Dawn*, 24 December 2014.
6. *Dawn*, 29 January 2016.
7. *Dawn*, 19 February 2016.
8. *The Express Tribune*, 30 June 2016.
9. *Dawn*, 28 August 2015.
10. *Dawn*, 20 January 2017.
11. *Dawn*, 17 November 2017.
12. *Dawn*, 1 February 2018.
13. *Dawn*, 26 February 2019.
14. *Dawn*, 15 November 2018.
15. *Dawn*, 30 November 2019.
16. *Dawn*, 8 February 2021.

17. *Dawn*, 4 February 2019.
18. *Dawn*, 17 December 2014.
19. *Dawn*, 7 January 2015.
20. *Dawn*, 6 September 2020.
21. *Dawn*, 21 October 2021.
22. *Dawn*, 16 December 2021.
23. *Dawn*, 16 December 2021.
24. *Dawn*, 6 September 2017.
25. *Dawn*, 8 February 2020.
26. *Dawn*, 11 February 2020.
27. *Dawn*, 18 February 2020.
28. *Dawn*, 25 February 2020.
29. *Dawn*, 5 August 2020.
30. *The Express Tribune*, 9 August 2016.
31. *Dawn*, 1 September 2016.
32. *Dawn*, 6 September 2016.
33. *Dawn*, 11 September 2016.
34. Mohammed Aqeel, also known as Dr Usman, a member of Lashkar-i-Jhangvi, a banned Punjabi militant outfit with strong links to the main Pakistan Taliban faction and al Qaeda. Aqeel also led the attack on the military headquarters in Rawalpindi, officials say, and was captured in the attack.
35. Lt. Syed Yasir Abbas was an aeronautical engineer in the Pakistan Navy, and an Officer on Duty at PNS Mehran on the day of the Mehran Attack. He attained martyrdom at the age of 24.
36. *Dawn*, 26 August 2016.
37. *Dawn*, 24 May 2011.
38. *Dawn*, 3 February 2013.
39. *Dawn*, 18 February 2014.
40. *Dawn*, 2 March 2014.
41. *Dawn*, 21 March 2015.
42. *Dawn*, 31 August 2015.
43. *Dawn*, 19 September 2015.
44. *Daily Times*, 23 August 2006.
45. *Dawn*, 31 January 2015.
46. *Dawn*, 4 February 2013.
47. *Dawn*, 26 February 2013.
48. 'Declaration,' Dawn.com, 28 February 2013, http://www.dawn.com/news/789399/declaration.
49. *Dawn*, 19 January 2018.
50. *Dawn*, 30 January 2020.
51. The Islamic observation of the day when Prophet Muhammad (PBUH) was born.
52. *Dawn*, 31 January 2015.
53. *Dawn*, 2 September 2011.
54. *Dawn*, 19 November 2012.
55. *Dawn*, 4 March 2013.
56. *Dawn*, 5 June 1992.
57. *Dawn* 8 August 2003.
58. Al-Quds Day takes place annually on the last Friday of Ramadan. The event began in Iran in 1979 to show support for the 'liberation' of Jerusalem and to protest the Israeli occupation of the Palestinian Territories.
59. *Dawn*, 4 September 2010.
60. *Dawn*, 28 August 2012.
61. *Dawn*, 29 June 2012.
62. *Dawn*, 2 September 2012.
63. *Dawn*, 11 January 2013.

64. *Dawn*, 27 June 2013.
65. *Dawn*, 28 May 2015.
66. *Dawn*, 30 May 2015.
67. *Dawn*, 20 October 2015.
68. *Dawn*, 5 October 2016.
69. *Dawn*, 26 October 2016.
70. *Dawn*, 27 October 2016.
71. *Dawn*, 1 January 2018.
72. *Dawn*, 9 January 2018.
73. *Dawn*, 1 May 2018.
74. *Dawn*, 11 July 2018.
75. *Dawn*, 13 April 2019.
76. *Dawn*, 17 April 2019.
77. *Dawn*, 16 April 2019.
78. *Dawn*, 19 April 2019.
79. *Dawn*, 2 October 2020.
80. *Dawn*, 4 January 2021.
81. *Dawn*, 5 January 2021.
82. *Dawn*, 8 January 2021.
83. *Dawn*, 9 January 2021.
84. *Dawn*, 10 January 2021.
85. *Dawn*, 6 July 2009.
86. *Dawn*, 30 June 2020.
87. *Dawn*, 30 March 1998.
88. *Dawn*, 19 February 2015.
89. *Dawn*, 28 March 2016.
90. *Dawn*, 22 June 2013.
91. *Dawn*, 2 February 2013.
92. *Dawn*, 25 January 2016.
93. *Dawn*, 24 June 2017.
94. *Dawn*, 1 July 2017.
95. *Dawn*, 6 May 2020.
96. *Dawn*, 5 March 2022.
97. *Dawn*, 17 February 2017.
98. Andreas Rieck, *The Shias of Pakistan: An Assertive and Beleaguered Minority* (London: Hurst and Co., 2015), *passim*.
99. *The Express Times*, 30 May 2013.
100. *Dawn*, 28 February 2014.
101. *Dawn*, 19 August 2015.
102. *Dawn*, 18 January 2017.
103. *Dawn*, 24 July 2013.
104. *Dawn*, 27 March 2021.
105. *Dawn*, 6 May 2020.
106. *The Express Tribune*, 17 December 2017.
107. *Dawn*, 12 May 2016.
108. *Dawn*, 9 May 2016.

Chapter 55
75 Years of Pakistan: A Summary

When the Lahore Resolution was passed, it was said that Pakistan would not come into being. When it came into being it was said that Pakistan could not last. Now when Pakistan is celebrating its Diamond Jubilee it is said that Pakistan should not have come into being. It is undeniable, however, that when we mark 75 years of our existence, we are in an economic crisis. We are also in a deluge. We cannot stop people from asking whether our present plight is incidental or structural in nature, and to answer that question we shall have to re-visit the 1947 Partition, the Pakistan Movement; for introspection, but also to arrive at a solution.

In one sense, after the Delhi Riots of 2019, it was not necessary to explain why Pakistan came into being. The survivors were openly questioning the wisdom of Maulana Abul Kalam Azad, not the foresight of Mohammad Ali Jinnah. Questions are academic in nature too, and I need to place on the record of your seminar, the various criticisms of the Pakistan Movement. In the course of introspection, Dr Kaiser Bengali stated publicly at a Pakistan Institute of International Affairs Seminar that the economy of Pakistan is being brought to such a pass that we have to surrender our nuclear arsenal.[1]

That is seen as our contradiction, we are a nuclear state, but we are a poor state. We can now better understand why Zulfikar Ali Bhutto said that we must have a nuclear shield even if we have to eat grass. Once bereft of our nuclear arsenal we shall lose the very independence that we are celebrating. Either way, it is not a matter of choice, it is a matter of survival. Pakistan came into being after the Cold War had started, and today the Ukraine crisis seems to have brought us full circle. What we are undertaking to do is not to provide the background, but to set the context.

When I was asked why Muslims did not formulate a Two-Nation Theory when they were rulers, instead of when they were in decline and a minority. As a matter of record, they did. What else did the puritanism of Mujaddid Alf Thani and Shah Waliullah signify? Even Akbar the Great Mughal when he invaded Chittor in 1568, called it a victory of Islam over Hinduism, broke idols, destroyed temples and killed 30,000 Rajputs.[2] Akbar also renamed Prayag as Allahabad. It was Akbar's tolerance which was urged on Mohammad Ali Jinnah by Lord Mountbatten.[3]

Let us then see how this theory evolved.

A HISTORY OF THE TWO-NATION THEORY

- 'Hindus and Muslims are two separate nations' (Sir Syed Ahmad Khan, 1867)
- 'Every community is entitled, even bound to organize itself, if it is to live as a separate entity' (After inspecting RSS Sabarmati Camp, Mahatma Gandhi, *Young India*, 6 January 1929)
- 'There is one point which has been troubling me of late and one about which I want you to think carefully, and that is the question of Hindu-Muslim unity. I have devoted most of my time during the last six months to the study of Muslim history and Muslim Law and I am inclined to think it is neither possible nor practicable' (Lala Lajpat Rai to C.R. Das. Cited in Indra Prakash, *A Review of the History and Works of the Hindu Mahasabha and the Hindu Sanghatan Movement*, New Delhi, Akhil Bharatiya, Hindu Maha Sabha, 1938)
- 'The Hindus and Muslims belong to two different philosophies, social customs and literature' (Mohammad Ali Jinnah, Lahore, 23 March 1940)
- 'Let us bravely face the unpleasant fact. There are two nations in India, the Hindus and the Muslims' (Vinayak Damodar Savarkar, cited in Beverly Nichols, *Verdict on India*, Bombay, Thacker & Co. 1944, p. 185)
- 'There was no chance of Hindus there agreeing to put themselves under permanent Muslim domination' (Pandit Jawaharlal Nehru in Nicholas Mansergh et al. (eds.), *The Transfer of Power*, London, HMSO, 1981, Vol. X, p. 1013)

Regardless of who promoted the Two-Nation Theory, we need to ask, is it intrinsically valid, or could it become the basis of nationhood? Among all the proponents of the Two-Nation Theory, it was Jinnah alone who did not see it as water-tight compartmentalization, he saw it as the basis of two federations: one with a Hindu and one with a Muslim majority. He made this clear to H.V. Hodson the Reforms Commissioner: 'Each minority, whether Hindu or Muslim will have its essential rights of language and so forth protected, but it will have to reconcile itself to being a minority. The strain will be relaxed because the Hindus in Muslim areas will no longer feel that they have this enormous mass behind them, nor will the Muslims feel that they have no one behind them and must always be ruled by a Hindu majority.'[4]

Now we come to what can be called the Unionist Party version of the Pakistan Movement. Critics, including the British, held that Pakistan would prove economically unviable. Dr Shahid Javed Burki says Pakistan was created for economic reasons by the Muslim minority states and that the Muslim majority states had no reason to demand Pakistan: 'The Movement was led by a group of people who belonged to the Muslim minority areas of British India and who felt that their economic future would be threatened in a state in which the Hindu majority would rule. However, they created a state in the part of India in which Muslims constituted the majority and felt secure about their economic future even after the departure of the British from India.'[5]

This assertion fails to explain why the Muslims of Punjab were against the Delhi Muslim Proposals 1927 which would be based on a joint electorate. Why were the Muslims of the majority areas in need of separate electorates? Because they knew that a national majority could neutralize a regional majority. The 1945 elections were won by the Muslim League from both the majority and minority areas. On an All-India basis, the Muslims were a minority, which is why the Chief Ministers of the Punjab, Bengal and Assam attended the October 1937 Session of the All-India Muslim League despite its having lost the recent elections. The Muslim political elite was led by the Unionist Party in Punjab and by the National Agriculturist Party in the United Provinces, the largest Muslim majority and Muslim minority provinces respectively. The latest broadside has come from Mazhar Abbas of the GCU, Faisalabad, who says the Muslim landlords learnt that Congress would introduce land reforms.

Now land reforms were on the manifesto of both the Congress and the Muslim League in 1937 when they had an electoral understanding against the British-sponsored National Agriculturist Party. The only difference was that the Muslim League would pay compensation while the Congress would not. Sailesh Kumar Bandopadhyay, who accuses Jinnah of being in need of his lucrative law practice, still in the context of the 1937 elections concedes: 'There is also no edge in the plea that the League leadership was especially pro-landlord interests; to be honest to facts, the class character of the bulk of the leaders was elitist, the difference being that of Tweedledum and Tweedledee. Further, both parties rallied together to confront the Agriculturist Party.'[6]

The All-India Muslim League did not join the provincial ministries until the Congress did so, Liaquat Ai Khan told the Nawab of Chattari that it would be undemocratic to form a minority government.[7]

As for inducting the religious elite Mazhar Abbas holds that they were equally divided between the Congress and Muslim League. He names only the Jamaat-i-Islami and the Khaksars as opponents of the Muslim League. This is not true as the Jami'at-ul-Ulama had said that they could cooperate with the Congress but not with the Muslim League. Other ulama also sided with Congress, not forgetting Abul Kalam Azad who was constantly buffeted by Mahatma Gandhi during his tenure as Congress President. In fact, Jinnah told the Muslims that the Muslim League 'had freed you from the undesirable elements of Maulvis and Maulanas.'[8]

In my book, *M.A. Jinnah The Outside View* I've dedicated an entire chapter to Dr Pervez Hoodbhoy's speech at the Karachi Adab Festival in 2020. In this chapter, I address two specific objections he raised, and I'd like to highlight them here: Dr Hoodbhoy claimed that 'Jinnah never wrote an essay in his life.' However, there is a book titled *Writings of the Quaid-i-Azam*, edited by Ahmed Saeed and published by the Nazaria-i-Pakistan Trust in 2014. This book contains twenty essays written by Jinnah, which clearly refute the assertion that he never wrote an essay. Another objection raised by Dr Hoodbhoy was that 'Jinnah had no plans for Science and Technology.' To counter this, I refer to the book *Quaid-i-Azam's Unrealized Dream* by Khalid Shamsul Hasan, published by Royal Book Co. in 1991. This book contains minutes of the Planning Committee, with pages 24 to 26 listing the Sub Committees on Fuel and Power, Mining and Metallurgy, Chemical Industries, and Manufacturing and Engineering Industries. On 1 November 1944, M.A. Jinnah addressed the AIML Planning Committee, emphasizing that their purpose was not to further enrich the wealthy but to uplift the general standard of living among the masses. He stressed that their ideal should be Islamic rather than Capitalistic, and they should always prioritize the interests and welfare of the entire population.[9]

So much for an elitist state which Shahid Javed Burki and Mazhar Abbas alleged Pakistan was. Let us also recall the 1943 speech of Mohammad Ali Jinnah: 'There are millions of people who hardly get one meal a day. Is this civilization? Is this the aim of Pakistan? Do you realize that millions have been exploited and cannot get one meal a day, if that is Pakistan, I would not have it.'[10]

Another tact used by Jawaharlal Nehru was to claim that Jinnah knew that Pakistan could never stand up to scrutiny and therefore he was determined that it should not be subject to it. By this, he implied that Jinnah never defined Pakistan, so whatever he gained, he would describe it as Pakistan. This too is not true. On 8 November 1945, in answer to a query from an Associated Press of America correspondent, M.A. Jinnah defined Pakistan geographically, politically, and economically. Geographically he named Sindh, Balochistan, NWFP and Punjab (whole) and Assam and Bengal (whole). Politically, he said Pakistan would be a democracy; economically he personally hoped its major industries and services would be socialized. Mr Jinnah said that he would oppose one-party rule: 'An opposition party or parties are good correctives for any party that is in power.' The Muslim League leader said that Hindu minorities can rest assured that their rights shall be protected.[11]

The harshest criticism has come from Ishtiaq Ahmed who called Mohammad Ali Jinnah 'the villain of the piece who bears most responsibility for the bloody partition of India which claimed more than a million Hindu, Muslim and Sikh lives.'[12] Ishtiaq Ahmed persists with the illusion that riots were the result of the Partition, while in fact, the Partition was a result of riots. As far as personal responsibility is concerned, even those contemporaries who have candidly said they did not like Jinnah have recorded the following.

The Secretary of State Lord Pethick-Lawrence who had an unseemly scene with Jinnah over Clause 8 of the Cabinet Mission Plan writes: 'He was coming to believe that Gandhi did not care whether 2 or 3 million people died and would rather that they should than he should compromise.'[13] Then there is the account of the Viceroy Lord Wavell, who in the aftermath of the Great Calcutta Killing in August 1946 asked Gandhi and Nehru to conform to the Cabinet Mission's interpretation of its own plan. Nehru got very heated,

Gandhi said if a blood bath was necessary, it would come about despite non-violence.[14]

Then there is the statement of Jawaharlal Nehru: 'I would rather have every village in India put to the flames than to keep the British Army here after 15 August.'[15] Finally, see the report of Brigadier Desmond Young: 'British officers—infantrymen from the desert battles—have told me that three weeks from August 15 in the Punjab were worse than anything we experienced in war...They blamed the Sikhs most...It is undeniable that from the day of Master Tara Singh's speech, if not before, the Sikhs began their preparations. In making them they had [the] covert assistance of some, at least, of [the] rulers of Sikh states who supplied them with arms. It is equally certain that the massacre of Muslims in Delhi in September was the result of a carefully planned Sikh conspiracy, and it was not, as the Hindu press tried to make out, a spontaneous act of revenge by Sikh refugees from Western Punjab.'[16]

Thus, the shoe is on the other leg, contrary to what Ishtiaq Ahmed in his most voluminous denunciation of Jinnah tries to establish.

With so much concerted opposition it is not a surprise that not all aspirations were fulfilled. When Pakistan came into being, the provinces of the Punjab and Bengal were divided, and of Assam, Pakistan could get only Sylhet. Democracy lasted barely a decade, and socialism became taboo. Since India had withheld the financial assets of Pakistan and Muslim Plutocrats intervened, the socialist economy could not be given effect too. Still, in 1948, M.A. Jinnah spoke of Islamic Socialism and Liaquat Ali Khan called Islamic Socialism the state policy of Pakistan.

Now we face two questions. Why did not Pakistan collapse, as predicted, and why Pakistan did not find stability? For the first question, we owe our survival to the selfless devotion, dedication, and honesty of our first batch of government servants from the Secretary-General down to the lowest-ranking peon. We had no place to begin our government. Our office workers made workplaces for themselves, wherever they could find shade or shelter bringing furniture and stationery from their home. Thus, we forestalled the short-term danger, but even this was not tension-free.

The Sindh Muslim League went into opposition when Karachi was declared to be the capital of Pakistan. Then the Sindh government wanted financial compensation at a time when Pakistan's coffers were empty.[17] At first, they refused to accommodate more than 100,000 refugees and relented to the extent of allowing 200,000. Liaquat Ali Khan saw off two trains taking would-be migrants back to India.

Despite such discouraging circumstances, the government machinery was given a push start, so much so that when Britain and India devalued their currency Pakistan refused to follow suit and started purchasing industrial machinery from East European countries against hard cash as the West would not sell us the machinery for industries already established in India, making us subservient as perhaps we were, in their perception, to India.

There were two long-term pincers put in our path. You have seen in the section on the Two-Nation theory and how Jawaharlal Nehru employed it to deny Bengal the independence their leaders, both Hindus and Muslims sought, although Mohammad Ali Jinnah and the AIML had agreed. This has been recounted among others by Sheikh Mujibur Rahman in his memoirs. Why Nehru took this stance is also revealed in *The Transfer of Power Papers*. Nehru said: 'East Bengal would be a source of embarrassment for Pakistan.'[18]

On the other side, when Sri Prakasa the first Indian High Commissioner to Pakistan, proposed that Pakistan be allowed to have Kashmir for the sake of peace, Jawaharlal Nehru was indignant: He wrote back 'Kashmir will be a drain on India's resources, but they would be a greater drain on the resources of Pakistan.'[19] This means his promises of the plebiscite were totally insincere from the beginning, and it is on these two issues Kashmir and Bangladesh that Pakistan has had to face aggression. The 1965 War on Kashmir and the 1971 war on Bengal. You know that I have written books and papers covering these events, but here I shall try to tell you briefly the internal story of these wars.

The first question often asked is, why didn't Pakistan take Akhnur? Why was the command transferred midway from General Akhtar Husain Malik to General Yahya Khan? For the simple reason that the British High Commissioner Sir Morrice James made the request.[20] Why China refrained from helping Pakistan? For the simple reason that President Ayub told them not to. Why did Pakistan accept a precipitate cease-fire? You guessed it. Because Sir Morrice James asked President Ayub.[21] The Americans despite the anger of President Lyndon B. Johnson were more accommodative. Under Secretary George Ball and Assistant Secretary William Bundy hoped that China would take some mild harassing action that would give the US some leverage over India.[22] Secretary of State Dean Rusk issued a statement upholding the principle of self-determination.[23]

What happened thereafter in Tashkent was another letdown. It was India that was beholden to the USSR for arms, not Pakistan. Therefore, it was an anomaly that Pakistan and not India should succumb to Soviet pressure. What happened in Tashkent is best told by Altaf Gauhar: 'When Ayub was relating how Shastri kept saying he was answerable to the people, Bhutto interrupted him and said, quite sharply: "But you too are answerable to the people. You don't have a heavenly mandate".'[24]

What is more, over the typed draft of the Tashkent Declaration, where it was written that: 'all disputes between the two countries should be settled by peaceful means' President Ayub had added in his own hand: 'Without recourse to arms.'[25] Z.A. Bhutto had an unpleasant exchange with Alexei Kosygin to have Ayub's concession removed. A war widow appeared at the gate of the University of the Punjab when the Tashkent Declaration was published, with her two children to ask whether this was the result for which soldiers had laid down their lives.

Now to address the unseemly controversy regarding whether 1971 was a military or a political failure. In terms of gallantry, if anything, the Pakistan Army fought more bravely than in 1965. The arms embargo had assured a defeat and surrounded on all sides by enemy territory and hostile and trained saboteurs they gave a sterling performance. Prime Minister Morarji Desai's admission that India had lost more than 5,000 regular soldiers is a fact to be weighed in. At the strategic level, foreign commentators held that if instead of defending the whole of East Bengal the Pakistan Army had withdrawn to the triangle created by rivers surrounding Dacca they could have held on for months.

Now, this is only a rumour, but a rumour I heard when the conflict was raging, that either General Tikka Khan or Lt.-Gen. A.A.K. Niazi had suggested that the Pakistan Army take over Assam, which had a border with China with civilians on both sides coming under occupying forces. Such a decision required vision which was wanting. It was not a military failure, but an individual failure. The Six Point programme had been floated in 1966 and its implications had been commented upon again and again. General Yahya Khan had been urged by his military colleagues to impose a two-thirds majority condition to frame a constitution, but he refused even to countenance a 60 per cent majority condition.[26]

The Communications Minister in Yahya Khan's cabinet G.W. Choudhury had been Professor and Head of the Department of Political Science at Dhaka University. His assessment of the situation was a bit different from West Pakistan analysts: 'Thanks to the naiveté and incompetence of Governor Ahsan, Mujib and his followers had a free hand and were able to preach secession without the least hindrance. Bhashani told me that if the Government were leaving Mujib free to preach the idea of Bangladesh, he had no option but to speak in terms of an independent East Pakistan.'[27]

Regarding the role of Zulfikar Ali Bhutto so many lies have been told, it is necessary to underline that Bhutto had never said *Hum Idhar, Tum Udhar* This was a headline in the *Azad* (Lahore, 15 February 1971). The sub-headline of the same issue quoted Bhutto as saying Pakistan shall remain united. In fact, it was Sheikh Mujibur Rahman who told *The New York Times* (4 March 1971) that both wings should have separate prime ministers. It is *The New York Times* (16 December 1971) that reveals that the Polish Resolution had not even been on the agenda, and what Bhutto tore up was the Agenda. An Anglo-French Resolution was under consideration. The Polish Resolution had been rejected earlier because it required the Pakistani Armed Forces first to vacate its own territory while India would vacate it later at an unspecified date. Also left unspecified, was the ultimate destination of the Pakistan

Armed Forces, though the preceding clause had clearly said that the civilian population would be allowed to go home.

It should also be remembered that in 1971, Pakistan had no constitution, but only basic law which was Martial Law. Zulfikar Ali Bhutto could not have been transferred the office of President without first transferring authority to him as the Chief Martial Law Administrator. Pakistan withstood defeat, and the loss of territory but still survived. The developments take us to *The Crash of '79*.[28] A work of fiction written years before the designated year, but it nevertheless proved to be a bad omen. Three major events took place that year. The execution of Zulfikar Ali Bhutto, the Revolution in Iran and the Soviet invasion of Afghanistan. What happened next, is best told by Secretary of State Hillary Clinton: 'Let's remember here, the people we are fighting today, we funded 20 years ago, and we did it because we were locked in a struggle with the Soviet Union. They invaded Afghanistan and we did not want to see them control Central Asia, and we went to work. It was President Reagan in partnership with Congress led by Democrats, who said, you know what; it sounds like a pretty good idea. Let's deal with the ISI and the Pakistan military and let's go recruit these mujahidin. And great, let them come from Saudi Arabia and other countries importing their Wahhabi brand of Islam so that we can go beat the Soviet Union. And, guess what? They (Soviets) retreated, they lost billions of dollars and it led to the collapse of the Soviet Union. So there is a very strong argument which is it wasn't a bad investment in terms of the Soviet Union. But let's be careful with what we sow because we will harvest. So, we left Pakistan. We said okay fine. You deal with the Stingers we left all over your country, you deal with the mines that are along the border, and, by the way, we don't want to have anything to do with you. In fact, we are sanctioning you. So we stopped dealing with the Pakistan military and ISI and now we are making up for a lot of time.'[29]

The upshot was that Pakistan entered the Reign of Terror and Drugs. After 9/11 Pakistan urged us to do more in combating the militants. The State Department continuously accused Pakistan of playing a double game. However, there was no subterfuge. General Ashfaq Parvez Kayani told Anne W. Patterson the US Ambassador on 23 September 2009 that unless Pakistan was sure of the outcome, it could not afford to completely cut off contact with the Taliban 'General Kayani was utterly frank about this', she wrote home. Her recommendation was for the US to actively pursue the resolution of the Kashmir conflict; the obvious solution that the US would not look at.[30]

Pakistani diplomacy does not lack finesse. Therefore communication does not translate to collaboration. Had it been so, Pakistan would have been spared the violence inflicted on the most harmless targets. To name a few attacks claimed by the Tehrik-i-Taliban (TTP), Pakistan, the Hangu School attack, 2013 the Army Public School, Peshawar 2014 massacre and the Civil Hospital, Quetta mass bombings 2016.

After years of sanctioning Pakistan and raining Drone attacks on its civilians, the US awoke on 4 February 2022 to the realization that Pakistan was a strategic partner. Months later, the US spelt out its policy on South Asia: 'India is a global partner, while Pakistan is a valuable partner in a sensitive region. India is an invaluable partner, not just in the region, but as it relates to a lot of the United States' shared priorities across the world…The US values our long-standing co-operation with Pakistan and has always viewed a prosperous and democratic Pakistan as critical to US interests.'[31]

When the TTP announced on 28 November 2022 that it was ceasing its truce with Pakistan because of its 'unabated' action in the Khyber Pakhtunkhwa province.[32] The US immediately pledged support for Pakistan's anti-TTP efforts. The State Department spokesperson recalled that the Pakistani people have suffered tremendously from terrorist attacks in the last two decades. 'We support the Pakistan Government's efforts to combat terrorism in all its forms.'[33]

The TTP showed that its threats were not empty when a suicide attack took place against a truck carrying policemen who were to protect anti-polio workers from terrorists. Four lives were outright lost, one of a police officer, a lady and her two children. At least twenty-four suffered injuries.[34] The American assurance was welcomed because of being issued despite Pakistan's neutrality in the Ukraine war. The US did not applaud the identical stance of India and Pakistan on the Ukraine War. Both abstained, but India was more vocal on the reason for its neutrality.

The Indian Minister for External Affairs Subrahmanyam Jaishankar stated in Australia that: 'India has had a long-standing relationship with Russia including military co-operation, dating back to the times when Western countries didn't supply weapons to India and saw Pakistan as the preferred partner.'[35] It is not certain at which country this statement was directed. At the US for showing it the limit of Nuclear Strategic Partnership, or at Russia whose President Vladimir Putin had stated only five days before that: 'I would like to note that we see Pakistan as a priority partner in South Asia as well as the continent as a whole. Relations between our countries are developing positively and we are pleased about it.'[36]

Pakistan's position was based on principle. The Ukraine War is a mirror image of the 1962 Cuban Missile Crisis when the Soviet Union placed missiles in Cuba, a sovereign country within striking distance of the US. Now read what President Vladimir Putin said on 26 December 2021 months before the outbreak of the war: 'We have nowhere to retreat. NATO could deploy missiles in Ukraine that could take just four or five minutes to reach Moscow.'

Spheres of influence have been a courtesy in the era of conventional warfare, their retention in the nuclear age makes them a matter of survival. One lesson from the 1962 Cuban Missile Crisis is forgotten. It is an observation of President John F. Kennedy: 'They were in the wrong and they knew it. So when we stood firm, they backed down. But this doesn't mean at all that they would back down when they felt they were in the right and had vital interest involved.'[37]

There was sufficient opportunity to assure the Russian Federation that NATO would not extend to Ukraine and to forestall the Ukraine war. If International Relations are bereft of morality, they are also bereft of rationale.

It is worth recalling the words of Nikita Khrushchev: 'When we put our ballistics missiles in Cuba, we had no desire to start a war. On the contrary, our principal aim was only to deter America from starting a war. We were well aware that a war that started over Cuba would quickly expand into a World War. Any idiot could have a war between America and Cuba.'[38]

On 24 February 2022 when the Ukraine War broke out, the Prime Minister of Pakistan Imran Khan was in Moscow. The nature of relations between Russia and Pakistan did not admit to any postponement of the visit to Moscow. It is heartening therefore that the Foreign Minister of the succeeding administration, Bilawal Bhutto-Zardari, defended on American soil, Imran Khan's visit to the Russian Federation and the relations between Pakistan and Russia remain on the upswing. On 11 October 2022, just one day after the Indian External Affairs Minister had railed against the United States, India abstained from voting on a UNGA resolution condemning Russia's 'illegal annexation' of four regions of Ukraine, but so did Pakistan.[39]

There was no comment on this rare assent between India and Pakistan. The US was treating India and Pakistan differently, but Pakistan and India were treating the US similarly. This was the second time in seven months that Pakistan had resisted Western pressure by abstaining from condemning Russia's actions in Ukraine.[40] There was a mild and curious hiccup when Senator Igor Morozov on 2 November 2022 shared the concern that Pakistan and Ukraine scientists had discussed the technology for making nuclear weapons. The Pakistan Foreign Office responded by terming this claim as 'without any rationale and is entirely inconsistent with the spirit of Pakistan-Russia relations.'[41]

Within the fortnight Pakistan (and India) abstained from voting on a UNGA resolution calling upon Russia to pay reparations to Ukraine.[42] On 28 November 2022, Pakistan's Minister for Oil was proceeding to Moscow for talks on oil and gas supply from Russia. On 6 December 2022, the results of the negotiations were shared.[43] India's Minister for External Affairs Subrahmanyam Jaishankar has also spoken of the need to increase trade with Russia.

This situation developed because NATO tried to impose a Treaty of Versailles on a nation that did not even need to re-arm. Western scholars are now weighing in the power equation between China and Russia as well as between India and Russia. Professor Matthew Sussex of Griffith University, Australia, has said: 'It is an unequal partnership. China is in the dominant position in the relationship. Russia needs China more than China needs Russia.'[44] Similarly, *The Economic Times* (30 March 2022) is of the opinion that: 'Russia will not support India in a stand-off against ally China.'

This equation is reassuring. However as I have had occasion to point out before, Russia is dependent on India. Russia built its stealth jet fighter TA-50 PAK-FA, with 25 per cent financing from India.[45] This means that not only India shall obtain the jets directly from the assembly lines, but a transfer of technology has been taking place. Every country in the range of the TA-50 PAK-FA is potentially threatened and this includes the United States. However, a Sino-Indian standoff is not imminent. It goes back to the same year that the Cuban Missile Crisis developed. On the other side, the primary victims of the gulf between the US policy towards India and Pakistan are the people of Kashmir.

The critics of our 'Kashmir First' policy assume that if a fire has broken out on the ground floor, the people on the first floor have no cause to worry. Mine is not a rhetorical but an empirical plea. The 'Kashmir First' policy was set aside when the Prime Minister of Pakistan Imran Khan refused to attend the Summit on Kashmir called at Kuala Lumpur (18–20 December 2019). Thus, the fact that Kashmir is potentially a very incendiary issue is not a Pakistani obsession. Despite Pakistan's relegation of the Kashmir issue, it has still garnered the world's attention after India's action on 5 August 2019.

On 8 August 2019, António Guterres Secretary-General of the United Nations refused to treat the Simla Agreement of 1972 as an impediment to the resolution of the Kashmir issue. He recalled that according to the Simla Agreement: 'The final status of Jammu and Kashmir is to be settled by peaceful means in accordance with the Charter of the United Nations.' The Secretary-General concluded that the Kashmir issue should be settled in conformity with the relevant UNSC Resolutions.

On 30 January 2021, Secretary-General Guterres stressed the need to fully respect Human Rights in the Indian-occupied regions of Jammu and Kashmir and on 29 June 2021 the Secretary-General urged India to 'end the use of pellets against children.' India has not examined this option primarily because of the obsession of Jawaharlal Nehru, but if India wishes to regain the world position it held when Buddhism spread across Asia, it needs to examine it. Buddha is not smiling.

Notes

1. Nausheen Wasi and Kaiser Bengali, 'Contemporary Economic and Security Issues in Pakistan', in Masuma Hasan (ed.), *Pakistan Horizon*, Vol. 73, No.1, January 2020, p. 28.
2. Iqtidar Alam Khan, 'Akbar's Personality Traits and World Outlook', in Irfan Habib (ed.), *Akbar and his India* (New Delhi: Oxford University Press, 2000), pp. 79–96.
3. *Jinnah: Speeches and Statements 1947–1948* (Karachi: Oxford University Press, 2000), pp. 33–34.
4. Waheed Ahmed (ed.), *The Nation's Voice* (Karachi, Quaid-i-Azam Academy, 1999), Vol. 4, pp. 831–843.
5. Shahid Javed Burki, 'History must not Lie', *Dawn*, Karachi, 9 November 2010.

75 Years of Pakistan: A Summary   513

6. Sailesh Kumar Bandyopadhyay, *Quaid-i-Azam Mohammad Ali Jinnah and the Creation of Pakistan* (New Delhi: Sterling, 1991), p. 131.
7. Pran Chopra (ed.), *Towards Freedom 1937–1947* (New Delhi, 1985), Vol. 1, p. 313.
8. Yasser Latif Hamdani, *Jinnah A Life* (New Delhi: Macmillan, 2020), p. 195.
9. Khalid Shamsul Hasan, *Quaid's Unrealized Dream* (Karachi: Royal Book Co.,1991), p. 33.
10. Ahmed Hasan Dani (ed.), *World Scholars on Quaid- i- Azam Mohammad Ali Jinnah* (Delhi, 1943; Islamabad, Islamabad University, 1979), p. 362.
11. *Dawn*, Delhi, 9 November 1945.
12. Ishtiaq Ahmed, *Jinnah His Successes, Failures and Role in History* (Gurgaon: Penguin Random, 2020), p. 1.
13. Peter Clarke, *The Last Thousand Days of the British Raj* (London: Penguin, 2008), p. 453.
14. Penderel Moon (ed.), *Wavell: The Viceroy's Journal* (Karachi: Oxford University Press, 1974), p. 341.
15. Leonard Mosley, *The Last Days of the British Raj* (New York: Harcourt, Brace and World, 1962), p. 149.
16. *Dawn*, Delhi, 7 December 1947.
17. Naumana Kiran Imran, 'Politics in Sindh and the Federal Cabinet of Pakistan', *Quarterly Journal of the Pakistan Historical Society*, Vol. 69, no. 4, pp. 89–107.
18. Nicholas Mansergh et al. (eds.), *The Transfer of Power* (London: HMSO, 1982), Vol. 11, p. 3.
19. S. Gopal (ed.), *Selected Works of Jawaharlal Nehru* (New Delhi: Orient Longmans), Second Series Vol. 4, pp. 346–347 (letter dated 25 November 1947).
20. Roedad Khan (ed.), *The American Papers* (Karachi, Oxford University Press, 1999), p. 44.
21. Roedad Khan (ed.), *The British Papers* (Karachi: Oxford University Press, 2002), p. 398.
22. Aziz Ahmed, 'The First Round A Rejoinder,' *Dawn*, 22 June 1979.
23. Khan, *The British Papers*, p. 410.
24. Z.A. Bhutto (Foreign Minister's) Speech, UNSC, 22 September 1965.
25. Altaf Gauhar, *Ayub Khan: Pakistan's First Military Ruler* (Lahore: Sang-i-Meel, 1993), p. 382.
26. Kuldip Nayar, *Distant Neighbors* (New Delhi: Vikas, 1972), p. 136, (Photographic Image).
27. G.W. Choudhury, *The Last Days of United Pakistan* (Karachi: Oxford University Press, 1993), p. 87.
28. Paul E. Erdman, *The Crash of '79* (New York: Simon & Schuster, 1976).
29. Ibid., p. 117.
30. *Dawn*, 25 April 2009.
31. *Dawn*, 29 May 2011.
32. *Dawn*, 21 November 2022.
33. *Dawn*, 29 November 2022.
34. *Dawn*, 30 November 2022.
35. *Dawn*, 1 December 2022.
36. *Hindustan Times*, 10 October 2022.
37. Arthur M. Schlesinger Jr., *Journals 1952–2000* (New York: The Penguin Press, 2017), p. 177.
38. Strobe Talbott (ed.& tr.), *Khrushchev Remembers* (New York: Bantam Books, 1971), p. 549.
39. *The Express Tribune*, 12 October 2022.
40. *The Express Tribune*, 14 October 2022.
41. *Tribune News Service*, 2 November 2022.
42. *CNBC*, 18 September 2022.
43. *Dawn*, 1 December 2022.
44. Lee Ying Shan, ' "No limits" relationship between China and Russia has limitations, professor says', *CNBC*, 16 September 2022.
45. Gautam Datt, 'T-50 PAK-FA fighter jet project with Russia hits turbulence', *India Today*, 31 August 2014.

Acknowledgements

The author and the publisher would like to thank the following:
- Ahmed Faruqui and Ashgate for quoting from *Rethinking National Security of Pakistan*
- David Page and Oxford University Press, Pakistan for quoting from *Prelude to Partition*
- G.W. Choudhry and Oxford University Press, Pakistan for quoting from *The Last Days of United Pakistan*
- Hasan Zaheer and Oxford University Press, Pakistan for quoting from *The Separation of East Pakistan*
- I.A. Rehman and the Oxford University Press, Pakistan for quoting from *Pakistan in Perspective*
- I.H. Qureshi and BCCT for quoting from *The Muslim Community of the Indo-Pakistan Subcontinent*
- J.H. Gense and Macmillan for quoting from *History of India*
- Kalikaranjan Qanungo and Orient Longmans for quoting from *Sher Shah and His Times*
- Matiur Rahman and Luzac for quoting *From Consultation to Confrontation*
- Nazrul Islam and Vanguard for quoting from *A Study in National Integration*
- Olaf Caroe and Oxford University Press, Pakistan for quoting from *The Pathans*
- Peter Hardy and the Cambridge University Press for quoting from *The Muslims of British India*
- Prem Nath Bazaz and the Kashmir Publishing Co. for quotes from *The Struggle for Freedom in Kashmir*
- Qayamuddin Ahmad and Manohar for quoting from *The Wahabi Movement*
- Richard Eaton and the University of Arizona Press to quote from *Approaches to Islam*
- Sir Ian Scott and the Radcliffe Press for quoting from his *Memoirs*
- Stanley Wolpert and the Oxford University Press, Pakistan for quoting from *Jinnah of Pakistan* and *The Encyclopedia of Pakistan*
- Sultan M. Khan and the London Centre for Pakistan Studies for quoting from *Recollections and Reflections*
- T.S. Eliot and Faber and Faber for quoting from *Notes Towards the Definition of Culture*
- Tara Chand and the Indian Press for quoting from *The Influence of Islam on Indian Culture*
- Usha Sanyal and Manohar for quoting from *Muslim Communities of South Asia*
- Uzma Qureshi and the Higher Education Commission for quoting from *Human Rights*
- Z.H. Zaidi and Oxford University Press, Pakistan for quoting from *Jinnah Papers*

Bibliography

Afzal, M. Rafique, *Pakistan: History and Politics 1947–1971*, Karachi, Oxford University Press, 2007.
Ahmad, Aziz, *Islamic Culture in the Indian Environment*, London, Oxford University Press, 1964 reprint, OUP India, 1999.
Ahmad, Qayamuddin, *The Wahhabi Movement in India*, second edition, New Delhi, Manohar, 1994.
Akhund, Iqbal, *Memoirs of a Bystander*, Karachi, Oxford University Press, 1997.
Alam, Muzaffar and Subramanyam, Sanjay (eds.), *The Mughal State*, New Delhi, Oxford University Press, 2000.
Alavi, Seema, *The Sepoys and the Company*, New Delhi, Oxford University Press, 1999.
Arif, K., (ed.) *American–Pakistan Relations*, Lahore, Vanguard, 1984.
Arif, K.M., *Working with Zia*, Karachi, Oxford University Press, 1995.
Azad, Abul Kalam, *India Wins Freedom: The Complete Version*, London, Sangam, 1988.
Aziz, K.K., (ed.), *Muslims Under Congress Rule*, Islamabad, NIHCR, 1978.
Aziz, K.K., *The Khilafat Movement*, Karachi, Pakistan Publishers, 1972.
Aziz, Qutbuddin, *Exciting Stories to Remember*, Karachi, Islamic Media, 1995.
Bandopadhaya, Sailesh Kumar, *Quaid-i-Azam Mohammad Ali Jinnah and the Creation of Pakistan*, New Delhi, Sterling, 1991.
Bazaz, Prem Nath, *The History of the Struggle for Freedom in Kashmir*, New Delhi, Kashmir Media, 1954.
Bhargava, G.S., *Success or Surrender? The Simla Summit*, New Delhi, Sterling, 1972.
Bhutto, Zulfikar Ali, *The Great Tragedy*, Karachi, Pakistan Peoples Party, 1971.
Bhutto, Zulfikar Ali, *The Myth of Independence*, Dacca, Oxford University Press, 1969.
Boivin, Michel, *Jihad*, Chambery, Universite de Savoie.
Bracken, Paul, *Fire in the East*, New York, Perennial, 2002.
Brown, Percy, *Indian Architecture (The Islamic Period)*, Bombay, Taraporevalas, 1942.
Burke, S.M., and Qureshi, S.A.D., *The British Raj in India*, Karachi, Oxford University Press, 1995.
Caroe, Olaf, *The Pathans*, London, Macmillan, 1965.
Chamberlain, M.E., *Britain and India*, Devon, 1974.
Chand, Tara, *Influence of Islam on Indian Culture*, Allahabad, The Indian Press, 1946.
Chand, Tara, *The Problem of Hindustani*, Allahabad, The Indian Press, 1944.
Chandra, Satish, *Parties and Politics at the Mughal Court*, Aligarh, Peoples Publishing House, 1959.
Cheema, Pervaiz Iqbal, *The Armed Forces of Pakistan*, Karachi, Oxford University Press, 2003.
Chopra, Pran, *India's Second Liberation*, second edition, Cambridge, Massachusetts, MIT Press, 1976.
Choudhry, G.W., *The Last Days of United Pakistan*, Karachi, Oxford University Press, 1998.
Clarke, Peter, *The Cripp's Version*, Harmondsworth, Penguin, 2003.
Cohen, Stephen, *The Pakistan Army*, Los Angeles, University of California Press, 1984.
Dreher, Diane Sansevere, *Benazir Bhutto*, New York, Bantam-Skylark, 1991.

Eaton, Richard M., *Essays in Islam and Indian History*, New Delhi, Oxford University Press, 2000.
Eliot, T.S., *Notes Towards the Definition of Culture*, London, Faber and Faber, 1961.
Fallaci, Oriana, *Interview with History*, Boston, Houghton and Muffin, 1976.
Faruqui, Ahmad, *Rethinking the National Security of Pakistan*, Aldershot, Aldergate, 2003.
Fatehpuri, Farman, *History of the Pakistan Movement and the Language Controversy*, University of Karachi, BCCT, 2001.
Feldman, Herbert, *Pakistan: An Introduction*, Karachi, Oxford University Press, 1961.
Frankel, Joseph, *International Relations*, London, Oxford University Press, 1964.
Friedmann, Yohanan, *Shaykh Ahmad Sirhindi*, New Delhi, Oxford University Press, 2000.
Gense, James H., *A History of India*, Madras, Macmillan, 1957.
Habib, Muhammad, *Politics and Society during the Early Medieval Period*, New Delhi, Peoples Publishing House, 1981.
Haeri, Munira, *The Chishtis*, Karachi, Oxford University Press, 2000.
Hardy, Peter, *The Muslims of British India*, New Delhi, Cambridge University Press, 1998.
Hayes, Louis D., *The Struggle for Legitimacy in Pakistan*, Lahore, Vanguard, 1986.
Hodson, H.V., *The Great Divide*, second edition, Karachi, Oxford University Press, 1989.
Hunter, Shireen, *The Future of Islam and the West*, Westport, Praeger, 1998.
Husain, S. Irtiza, *Compromise with Conciliation*, Karachi, Pak-American Commercial, 1997.
Husain, S. Ishtiaq, *The Life and Times of the Raja of Mahmudabad*, Karachi, Mehboob Academy, 1990.
Irfani, Suroosh, (ed.), *Fifty Years of the Kashmir Dispute*, Muzaffarabad, University of Azad Jammu and Kashmir, 1997.
Islam, Nazrul, *A Study in National Integration*, Lahore, Vanguard, 1990.
Jafri, Syed Husain Mohammad and Ahmad Saleem, (eds.), *Pakistan Society and Literature*, (Urdu), University of Karachi, Pakistan Study Centre, 1987.
James, Sir Morrice, *The Pakistan Chronicle*, Karachi, Oxford University Press, 1993.
Javed, Qazi, *Barr-e-Sagheer Mein Muslim Fikr Ka Irtiqa*, (Urdu), Lahore, Nigarishat, 1986.
Jinnah, M.A., *Speeches and Statements as Governor-General*, Karachi, Oxford University Press, 2000.
Judd, Denis, (ed.), *A British Tale of Indian and Foreign Service: The Memoirs of Sir Ian Scott*, London, The Radcliffe Press, 1999.
Kazimi, Muhammad Reza, (ed.), *M.A. Jinnah: Views and Reviews*, Karachi, Oxford University Press, 2005.
Kazimi, Muhammad Reza, *Liaquat Ali Khan. His Life and Work*, Karachi, Oxford University Press, 2003.
Kazimi, Muhammad Reza, *M.A. Jinnah The Outside View*, Lahore, Peace Publications, 2022.
Khan, M. Asghar, *The First Round*, London, Islamic Information Services, 1979.
Khan, M. Ayub, *Friends Not Masters*, Karachi, Oxford University Press, 1967.
Khan, Muin-ud-Din, *The Faraidi Movement*, Karachi, Pakistan Historical Society, 1965.
Khan, Roedad, (ed.), *The American Papers: Secret and Confidential India-Pakistan-Bangladesh Documents, 1965–1973*, Karachi, Oxford University Press, 1999.
Khan, Roedad, (ed.), *The British Papers: Secret and Confidential Documents India-Pakistan-Bangladesh 1958–1969*, Karachi, Oxford University Press, 2002.
Khan, Salahuddin, (ed.), *Speeches, Messages, and Statements of Mohtarma Fatima Jinnah*, Lahore, Research Society, University of the Punjab, 1976.
Kissinger, Henry, *The White House Years*, London, Weidenfeld and Nicholson, 1979.
Kux, Dennis, *Disenchanted Allies*, Karachi, Oxford University Press, 2001.

Lamb, Alastair, *Incomplete Partition*, Karachi, Oxford University Press, 2002.
Lamb, Alastair, *Kashmir: A Disputed Legacy*, Karachi, Oxford University Press, 1992.
Mahmood, Safdar, *Pakistan Divided*, Lahore, Jang Publications, 1981.
Malik, Muhammad Aslam, *The Making of the Pakistan Resolution*, Karachi, Oxford University Press, 2001.
Margolis, Eric, *War at the Top of the World*, New Delhi, Roli Books, 2001.
Martin, Richard C., (ed.), *Approaches to Islam in Religious Studies*, Tuscon, University of Arizona Press, 1985.
Matiur, Rahman, *From Consultation to Confrontation*, London, Luzac, 1970.
Minault, Gail, *The Khilafat Movement*, New Delhi, Oxford University Press, 1999.
Moon, Penderel, (ed.), *Wavell: The Viceroy's Journal*, New Print, Karachi, Oxford University Press, 1997.
Moon, Penderel, *Divide and Quit*, Delhi, Oxford University Press, 1998.
Moulvi, Ghulam Abbas, *Hindustani Musawwari Ka Irtiqa* (Urdu), Bombay, np. 1942.
Naim, C.M., (ed. and tr.), *Zikr-e-Mir*, New Delhi, Oxford University Press, 1999.
Nayar, Kuldip, *India: The Critical Years*, New Delhi, Vikas, 1971.
Nixon, Richard M., *Memoirs of Richard Nixon*, New York, Grosset and Dunlap, 1978.
Page, David, *Prelude to Partition*, Karachi, Oxford University Press, 1987.
Popatia, Mahboob A., *Pakistan's Relations with the Soviet Union*, Karachi, Pakistan Study Centre, University of Karachi, 1988.
Qanungo Kalikaranjan, *Sher Shah and his Times*, Calcutta, Orient Longman's, 1965.
Qureshi, I.H., *Muslim Community of the Indo-Pakistan Subcontinent*, Karachi, BCCT, 1999, University of Karachi, 1999.
Rabbani, Ata, *I was the Quaid's ADC*, Karachi, Oxford University Press, 1996.
Raza, Rafi, *Zulfikar Ali Bhutto and Pakistan 1971–1977*, Karachi, Oxford University Press, 1997.
Rizvi, Hasan-Askari, *The Military and Politics in Pakistan*, New Delhi, Konark, 1988.
Seervai, H.M., *Partition of India: Legend and Reality*, Karachi, Oxford University Press, 2005.
Shah, Mansoor, *The Gold Bird*, Karachi, Oxford University Press, 2002.
Shah, Mehtab Ali, *The Foreign Policy of Pakistan*, London, IB Tauris, 1997.
Siddiqi, A.R., *East Pakistan: The Endgame*, Karachi, Oxford University Press, 2004.
Singh, Khushwant, *Truth, Love and a Little Malice*, New Delhi, Viking, 2002.
Spengler, Oswald, *The Decline of the West*, New York, Vintage Books, 2006.
Syed, Anwar Husain, *China and Pakistan: Diplomacy of an Entente Cordiale*, Amherst: The University of Massachusetts Press, 1974.
Symonds, Richard, *In the Margins of Independence*, Karachi, Oxford University Press, 2001.
Symonds, Richard, *The Making of Pakistan*, second edition, Islamabad, National Book Foundation, 1976.
Toynbee, A.J., *The Study of History*, 12 vols. London, Oxford University Press, 1934–61.
Vincent, Arthur, *The Defence of India*, Bombay, 1922.
Wolpert, Stanley, *A New History of India*, 7th ed. New York, Oxford University Press, 2004.
Wolpert, Stanley, *Gandhi's Passion*, New York, Oxford University Press, 2001.
Wolpert, Stanley, *Jinnah of Pakistan*, Karachi, Oxford University Press, 1989.
Wolpert, Stanley, *Roots of Confrontation in South Asia*, New York, Oxford University Press, 1982.
Wolpert, Stanley, *Zulfi Bhutto of Pakistan*, New York, Oxford University Press, 1993.
Zaheer, Hasan, *The Separation of East Pakistan*, Karachi, Oxford University Press, 1994.
Zia, Shakeel Ahmad, *Sindh Ka Muqaddama* (Urdu), Karachi, 1987.
Ziring, Lawrence, *Bangladesh: From Mujib to Ershad*, Karachi, Oxford University Press, 1997.

Index

A

Abbasi, Shahid Khaqan, 232, 402, 472
Abdali, Ahmad Shah, 20, 46, 48, 50, 51, 346, 428
Abdul Latif, Dr Syed, 124
Abdul Qayyum, Lt.-Gen. (retd.), 384, 385
Abdul Qayyum, Nawab Sahibzada, 74, 150
Abdul Wahhab, Shaikh Muhammad bin, 70
Abell, George, 142, 327
Act for the Better Government of India 1858, 244
Afghanistan, 2, 12, 14, 16, 46, 51, 72, 93, 108, 160, 168, 176, 205, 210, 211, 214, 218, 219, 227, 228, 231, 236, 264, 272, 285, 288, 289, 290, 292-294, 297, 300, 301, 304, 305, 311, 316, 319, 324, 329, 346-349, 350, 357, 359, 360, 374, 400, 429, 442, 460, 485, 486, 490-492, 494, 509
Afridi, Yahya, 468, 469, 480
Afzal, Muhammad, 448
Aga Khan III, 79, 83, 110, 497
Agartala Conspiracy, 185, 199, 202
Ahsan, Aitzaz, 18, 385, 464, 480
Aibak, Qutbuddin, 20
Ajatashatru, 11
Ajmeri, Syed Muinuddin (Khwaja Gharib Nawaz), 33, 34
Akbar, 25, 26, 35, 36, 37, 42, 44, 45, 192, 502
Akbar, Muhammad, 274
Akbar, Shahzad, 468, 470
Akram, Mohammad, 481
Akram, Saleh Muhammad, 142
Alcock, Leslie, 5
Alexander the Great, 4, 12, 14, 55
Alexander, Albert V., 131
Ali, Chaudhry Mohammad, 95, 143, 166, 174, 175, 204, 251, 267, 327

Ali, Chaudhry Rahmat, 108, 109
Ali, Maulana Zulfiqar, 69
Ali, Muhammad, 140
Aligarh College, 68, 76, 79, 81
Aligarh University, 124
Aligarh, 62, 66, 68, 69, 70-73, 76, 80, 87, 104, 108, 153, 187
All-Bengal United Muslim Conference 1936, 130
All-India Communist Party, 140
All-India Khilafat Conference, 91
All-India Muslim League (AIML), 68, 70, 73, 76, 80, 81, 83, 85, 88, 89, 90, 91, 93, 96-99, 100, 104, 105, 108, 110, 112, 114, 115, 117-119, 120, 121, 124, 126-129, 130, 132-136, 138, 139, 140-142, 145-149, 150-153, 157, 158, 163, 168, 169, 170, 172, 174, 202, 221, 244, 250, 263, 298, 325, 424, 504, 505, 507
All-India States Muslim League, 151
All-India Urdu Conference 1936, 424
All-India(n) Muhammadan Educational Conference, 68, 83
Al-Qaeda, 160, 227, 313, 358, 359, 491, 498
Alvi, Arif, 237, 238, 241, 364, 453, 466, 469, 478, 479
Al-Zarqawi, Abu Musab, 160
Amitabha, 10
Anjuman Himayat-i-Islam, 72, 73
Anjuman-i-Ittehad-i-Balochistan, 152
Anka, Mohammad Husain, 429
Arab-Israeli War 1967, 355
Arab-Israeli War 1973, 205, 250, 287, 356, 400
Army Public School (APS), 231, 232, 257, 347, 485-489, 491, 509
Article 370, 235, 291, 306, 335-339, 341, 346
Ashoka, 10, 13, 14, 23
Ashraf, Raja Pervaiz, 226, 223
Association of South East Asian Nations

Index 519

(ASEAN), 310, 354
Atharva Veda, 7
Atlee, Clement, 98, 131, 134, 143, 168, 282
Auchinleck, Field Marshal Sir Claude, 166
Auliya, Shaikh Nizamuddin, 30, 31, 34, 36
Aurangzeb, 35, 37, 42, 44, 45
Aurangzeb, Marriyum, 237
Awadh, 4, 26, 34, 42, 43, 60, 61, 62, 64
Awami League, 184, 190, 191, 193, 194, 195, 197, 199, 202, 204, 253, 326, 345, 346
Ayub, Gohar, 184, 188, 296, 461
Azad Kashmir, 2, 181, 198, 214, 288, 297, 320, 337, 343, 345, 451
Azad, Maulana Abul Kalam, 37, 88, 92-94, 100, 134, 135, 136, 140, 147, 151, 163, 502, 504
Azad, Muhammad Javed, 448
Aziz, Sartaj, 230, 302
Aziz, Shaukat, 217, 219, 301, 317, 319, 381, 395

B

Babar, Akbar S., 237
Babur, 20, 42
Bactria, 12, 13
Bahadur Shah I, 42, 59, 61
Bahadur Shah II, 42, 59, 61, 62, 64
Bahadur, Nawab Sir Khwaja Salimullah, 83
Baiju Bawra, 26
Bajwa, Qamar Javed, 239, 303, 304, 306, 383, 495, 497
Balban, Sultan Ghiyasuddin, 30, 36
Ball, George, 183, 296, 507
Balochistan Bar Association, 488
Balochistan Muslim League, 152, 153
Balochistan University, 409
Balochistan, 2, 3, 4, 12, 21, 27, 96, 99, 100, 101, 104, 108, 126, 152, 153, 168, 169, 189, 191, 193, 205, 220, 226, 232, 250, 254, 258, 274, 300, 315, 326, 334, 348, 359, 380, 397, 400, 404, 410, 411, 412, 419, 429, 435, 452, 453, 454, 456, 477, 485, 492, 494, 495, 497, 505
Bangash, Aitzaz Hasan, 486
Bangladesh, 190, 193, 194, 198, 200, 202, 205, 284, 319, 324, 329, 344-346, 365, 387, 388, 396, 398, 507, 508
Bank of Credit and Commerce International (BCCI), 377, 378
Bannerjee, Sir Surendranath, 78, 86
Bannerji, R.D., 6
Barelvi, Sayyid Ahmad, 51, 52, 54, 70, 146
Battle of Balakot 1831, 52
Battle of Buxar 1764, 43, 44
Battle of Plassey 1757, 43, 44, 46, 60
Bay of Bengal, 15
Beas River, 12, 143
Beg, Mirza Aslam, 182, 213, 278, 292, 349
Begum of Awadh (Hazrat Mahal), 61, 62, 64
Bengal Councils Act 1892, 82
Bengal Legislative Assembly, 193
Bengal Muslim League, 139, 424
Bengal Pact, 94
Bengal, 4, 20, 21, 27, 30, 34, 42, 43, 54, 56, 60, 66, 76-79, 80, 83, 84, 89, 94, 100, 101, 102, 105, 108, 109, 116, 117, 119, 121, 125, 126, 130, 132, 138, 139, 142, 145, 146, 174, 175, 177, 192, 193, 198, 247, 283, 318, 424, 504, 505, 506
Bengali Language Movement 1948, 130, 174, 175, 202
Bengali(s), 28, 54, 61, 66, 83, 94, 122, 125, 130, 170, 174, 175, 189, 192, 193, 195, 196, 200, 202, 249, 250, 251, 297, 345, 346, 419, 422-424
Bengali, Dr Kaiser, 235, 242, 389, 502
Bengali-Urdu conflict, 423
Bhagavad Gita, 9
Bhashani, Maulana Abdul Hamid Khan, 159, 174, 175, 196, 398, 508
Bhat, Mohammad Rafi, 332
Bhutto, Begum Nusrat, 213, 458, 459
Bhutto, Benazir, 212 213, 214, 220, 222, 224, 225, 274, 283, 289, 300, 319, 345, 381, 394, 459, 460, 461, 481, 490, 491, 502, 507, 508
Bhutto, Mir Murtaza, 214, 274, 461
Bhutto, Sir Shahnawaz, 73, 146
Bhutto, Zulfikar Ali, 159, 184, 186, 187, 191-193, 197-199, 202, 204-209, 210, 214, 220, 253-255, 260, 261, 268, 278, 284, 288, 289, 290, 295, 299, 309, 319, 329, 344, 356, 364, 365, 369, 372-374,

390, 393, 394, 398, 419, 451, 459, 476, 480, 481, 509
Bhutto-Zardari, Bilawal, 241, 307, 308, 315, 474, 488, 495, 511
Biden, Joe, 292, 360, 363
Bihar Riots 1946, 202
Bihar, 9, 51, 57, 61, 76, 79, 116, 117, 119, 134, 146, 151, 192, 193, 423
Bihari/s, 192, 195, 202
Bilgrami, Syed Hasan, 80, 84
Bimbisara, 11
Bindusara, 13
Birkenhead, Lord, 98, 99
Bogra, Mohammad Ali, 174, 250, 288, 308, 309
Bolan: River, 5; tunnel, 2
Bonnerjee, Womesh Chandra, 82
Brahman, Chandra Bhan, 28
Brahmanas, 7
Brahmin, 16, 24, 55, 86, 112
Brahmo Samaj, 66, 424, 441
Britain, 62, 82, 86, 91, 98, 114, 126-128, 131, 134, 172, 175, 176, 181, 183, 186, 194, 216, 253, 259, 267, 276, 284, 286, 318, 319, 320, 342, 355, 369, 506
British Commonwealth, 88, 127, 138, 143, 175, 194, 245, 251, 319, 330
British India, 4, 62, 63, 77, 152, 244, 245, 260, 423
British Indian criminal law 1860, 440
Buddha, 10, 24, 102
Buddhism, 8, 9, 10, 11, 13, 14, 16, 20, 21, 24, 440, 512
Bugti, Nawab Akbar, 220
Burma (Myanmar), 60, 108, 126, 128, 244
Bush Jr., George, 221, 289
Bush Sr., George, 197, 289

C

Cabinet Mission Plan 1946, 112, 126, 131-139, 142, 147, 166, 319, 325, 327, 505
Calcutta (Kolkata), 55, 64, 67, 76-78, 88, 92, 94, 98, 100, 117, 126, 130, 134, 136, 165, 174, 175, 177, 195, 196, 202, 424
Campbell, George, 76, 423
Canning, Lord Charles John, 60, 62
Carter, Jimmy, 221, 288, 289, 362, 378, 485

CENTO, 180, 205, 284, 287, 308, 354, 356
Chandragupta I, 15
Chandragupta II, 15
Chaudhry, Iftikhar Muhammad, 220, 222, 225, 385, 452, 462
Chelmsford, Lord, 91
China, 2, 13, 113, 178, 180, 183, 185, 186, 197, 198, 218, 231, 236, 239, 278, 284-288, 292, 296, 301-306, 308, 309, 310-318, 324, 325, 329, 335, 338, 340, 356, 357, 360, 362, 364, 379, 383, 385, 386, 388, 404, 406, 408, 507, 508, 511, 512
China-Pakistan Economic Corridor (CPEC), 272, 304, 305, 310, 312, 314-317
Chitral, 2, 4, 329, 349, 406, 407, 411
Chotani, Haji Jan Muhammad, 93, 140
Chughtai, Abdur Rahman, 27, 420
Chundrigar, I.I., 176, 251
Churchill, Sir Winston, 116, 126, 127, 129, 131, 318, 319
Civil Disobedience Movement, 110, 111, 192
Clinton, Bill, 215, 289, 294, 312, 340
Clinton, Hillary, 228, 290, 293, 311, 509
Clive, Lord, 43, 44, 46
Cold Start Doctrine, 278
Constitution 1956, 175, 176, 179, 245, 251, 259, 457
Constitution 1962, 180, 189, 252, 458
Constitution 1973, 211, 245, 248, 253, 254, 255, 258, 260, 438, 439, 458, 459, 480
Cornwallis, Lord, 54
Covid-19 pandemic, 233, 242, 273, 333, 340, 348, 360, 385, 386, 388, 407, 435, 441, 492
Cripps Mission 1942, 126
Cripps, Sir Richard Stafford, 126-129, 131, 132, 134
Curzon, Lord, 77, 78, 83, 86, 150
Cyrus the Great, 12

D

Dalhousie, Lord James, 60, 62
Darius I, 12
Darius III, 12
Darul Uloom Deoband, 69

Das, Chittaranjan, 94
Daudpota, Dr Umar Muhammad, 73, 427
Day of Deliverance, 120
Deccan, 4, 42, 45, 59, 62, 124, 169, 263
Dehlavi, Shaikh Abdul Haq Muhaddith, 36, 38
Delhi, 23, 30, 34, 43, 45, 59, 61, 62, 79, 88, 91, 108, 142, 143, 151, 168, 298, 331, 339, 342, 344, 424, 506
Delhi Durbar 1911, 88, 89, 1911
Delhi Muslim Proposals 1927, 96-99, 100, 145, 146, 163, 503
Delhi: Riots 2019, 502; Sultanate, 4, 35; Sultans, 21, 34
Dhaka, 58, 76, 78, 83, 84, 88, 168, 170, 180, 191, 192, 195, 199, 202, 260, 324, 344-346, 393, 424, 456; University, 190, 202, 508
Direct Action 1946, 134
Doctrine of Lapse, 60, 62
Dudhu Miyan (Mohsinuddin Ahmad), 56-58
Dummar, Noor Muhammad, 410
Dupleix, Joseph-François, 44
Durand Line, 346-349

E

East Bengal, 21, 56, 77, 78, 79, 126, 134, 168, 170, 175, 177, 191, 193, 202, 249, 250, 285, 294, 369, 370, 507, 508
East India Company, 43, 44, 59, 60, 61, 62, 64, 82, 114, 244, 276
East Pakistan, 112, 176, 179, 180, 184, 189, 191, 195, 196, 198, 199, 208, 249, 250, 283, 288, 294, 299, 300, 325, 345, 369, 372, 373, 393, 398, 419, 442, 458, 508
Eaton, Richard M., 20, 21
Effendi, Hasan Ali, 74, 146
Ehsan, Ehsanullah, 488, 489, 490, 491
Eisenhower, Dwight D., 288, 354, 362
Elizabeth II, Queen, 194, 195

F

Fahim, Muhammad, 227
Faiz, Ahmed Faiz, 6, 416, 425, 426, 431
Faraidi Movement, 56, 57, 77, 94

Faraz, Shibli, 236, 237
Farooqui, Aurangzeb, 499
Farrukhsiyar, 44
Fatimi, Syed Qudratullah, 18
Fazlul Haq, Abul Kasem, 119, 125, 126, 130, 174, 196, 202, 424
Ferozepur Headworks, 167
Fort William College, 67, 423
Fourteen Points 1929, 100, 111, 145, 146
Fuller, Joseph Bampfylde, 78, 79, 81, 83

G

Gandhara, 13, 14
Gandhi, Indira, 196, 207, 294
Gandhi, Mohandas Karamchand, 8, 9, 65, 90-92, 94, 97, 99, 102, 103, 110, 111, 112, 117, 119, 125, 127-129, 132, 133, 136, 137, 140, 147, 150, 157, 163, 166, 175, 177, 193, 276, 344, 368, 424, 503-506
Gandhi, Rahul, 332
Gandhi, Sonia, 331
Gangohi, Maulana Rashid Ahmad, 69, 70
Gautama, Indrabhuti, 9
Gaza War, 360, 361, 363, 364
Ghani, Mohammad Javed, 389
Ghose, Motilal, 78
Ghuri, Sultan Moizuddin, 20, 21, 34
Gilani, Yusuf Raza, 222, 225, 226, 301, 400, 461, 462, 474, 476
Gilgit, 2, 3, 313, 337
Gilgit-Baltistan, 400, 406, 407, 412, 435, 472, 473, 494, 498
Godse, Nathuram, 102, 166, 368
Gokhale, Gopal Krishna, 78, 82, 86, 87, 90, 125, 163
Government of India Act 1919, 97, 115, 244
Government of India Act 1935 (GOI Act 1935), 115, 116, 127, 129, 134, 138, 146, 150, 244, 245, 266
Great Calcutta killings, 134, 175, 177, 505
Gujarat, 15, 36, 343
Gupta dynasty, 15, 16
Guterres, Antonio, 207, 235, 337, 338, 361, 363, 512
Gwadar seaport, 2, 220, 315, 317, 490, 495

H

Habib, Mohammad Ali, 166
Habibullah, Isha'at, 121, 58
Haji Dawood, Sir Adamjee, 166
Haji Shariatullah, 56, 57, 70
Haleji, 2
Hamas, 360, 361, 363
Hameed ud Din, Qazi Khalifa, 72
Hamilton, Alexander, 253
Hamoodur Rahman Commission Report, 194, 195
Haqqani, Hussain, 228, 272, 273
Harappa, 5
Hardinge, Lord, 79
Haroon, Lady Nusrat, 152
Haroon, Sir Abdullah, 73, 124, 146
Haroon, Yusuf, 170, 298, 419
Harsha, 16, 192
Hasan, Sir Wazir, 88, 89
Hasan, Syed Zafarul, 124
Hasina, Sheikh, 345, 346
Hayat, Sir Sikandar, 119, 145, 148, 149
Hidayatullah, Sir Ghulam Hussain, 73, 139, 146, 147
Hindi, 28, 29, 67, 76, 119, 417, 422, 423, 424
Hindi-Urdu conflict, 76, 77, 83, 423
Hindu Gram Moorchana Paduti, 25
Hindu Mahasabha, 97, 99, 344, 503
Hindu Marriage Bill, 443
Hindu: religion, 3, 28, 66; society, 3, 9, 23, 24, 25
Hindu Widow Re-Marriage Act 1856, 441
Hindu(s), 3, 4, 6, 7, 8, 9, 15, 20-29, 30, 31, 33-37, 42-45, 48, 51, 54, 56, 57, 59, 60, 62, 67, 68, 73, 76-79, 80, 81, 83, 86, 88, 89, 90-94, 96, 97, 99, 100, 102, 104-106, 108, 110, 111, 114, 117, 119, 120, 124, 125, 128, 130, 133-136, 145-147, 149, 150, 151, 157, 163, 165, 166, 168, 175, 192, 193, 195, 196, 247, 249, 276, 277, 298, 325, 327, 328, 330, 331, 336, 342, 346, 354, 420, 422, 423, 425, 441-444, 503, 505, 506
Hinduism, 4, 7, 8, 10, 15, 16, 23, 24, 28, 29, 36, 45, 66, 70, 72, 422, 440, 441, 502
Hindukush mountains, 13
Hindustan, 6, 7, 120, 132, 133, 152, 300, 325

Hodson, H.V., 115, 168, 503
Hoti, Nawab Akbar, 150
Hujjat ullah al Baligha, 49
Hujveri, Syed Ali (Data Ganj Bakhsh), 33
Hume, Allan Octavian, 67, 77
Hunza, 2, 313, 329, 407; River, 406
Hyderabad, 4, 62, 121, 124, 141, 169, 212, 497
Hyderi, Sir Akbar, 111

I

Ibn Arabi, 33, 37, 38, 40, 41, 49
Ibrahim, Shaikh Abu Tahir Muhammad bin, 49
Ikramullah, Shaista, 130, 172
India Councils Act 1909, 84, 244
India, 2, 3, 4, 6, 9, 10, 11, 12, 15, 16, 19, 20, 23, 23, 24, 26, 27, 29, 32-35, 37, 39, 43-46, 51, 57, 59, 61, 62, 64, 67, 68, 70, 73, 76, 77, 79, 80, 82, 83, 85, 86, 88, 89, 90, 91, 97-99, 100, 102, 104, 105, 108, 110, 111, 112, 114, 115, 117, 120, 124-129, 131-136, 138, 139, 140, 142, 143, 147-149, 153, 157, 163-169, 170, 172, 173, 180-187, 193, 196, 197, 198, 205-208, 210, 212, 214-216, 218, 221, 227, 230, 235, 242, 244, 247, 266, 267, 276, 277, 278, 283-289, 291, 294-299, 300, 302-309, 310, 312, 313, 316-319, 320, 324-329, 330, 331, 333-339, 340-346, 349, 354, 355, 356, 358, 359, 360, 365, 368, 369, 370, 371, 388, 389, 396, 419, 420, 423, 424, 425, 427, 442, 444, 492, 495, 503, 505-508, 510, 511, 512
India-held Kashmir, 235, 291, 294, 314, 317, 335, 343
Indian Citizenship (Amendment) Act 2019, 331, 338, 442
Indian Civil Service (ICS), 266
Indian Councils Act of 1861, 244
Indian Councils Act of 1892, 244
Indian Illegally Occupied Jammu & Kashmir (IIOJK), 331, 333
Indian Independence Act of 1947, 138, 245, 247, 456
Indian Legislative Assembly, 96, 129, 135
Indian Muslim/s, 39, 80, 88, 91, 92, 129,

Index   523

136, 152, 330, 331, 338, 346, 354, 424
Indian National Congress, 67, 77, 78, 82, 94, 117, 131, 136, 318, 325
Indian Statutory Commission, 97
Indian/s, 8, 12, 13, 19, 21, 24, 60, 64, 66, 67, 68, 79, 82, 83, 85, 86, 88, 89, 91, 92, 97-99, 101, 102, 108, 110, 111, 112, 115, 126, 127, 129, 132, 141, 152, 163, 166, 167, 169, 170, 174, 176, 177, 181-186, 196, 198, 200, 207, 215, 218, 219, 230, 235, 236, 242, 244, 266, 267, 272, 273, 280, 283, 284, 287-289, 291, 292, 294, 295, 296, 297, 299, 300, 301, 302, 305, 309, 310, 312, 314, 325, 326, 328, 330-336, 339, 340, 341, 342, 343, 345, 347, 350, 355, 356, 358, 359, 360, 371, 382, 388, 389, 396, 419, 423, 424, 425, 441, 442, 507, 510, 511, 512
Indian: airs, 25; compositions, 25; independence, 81, 120, 131; historian, 59, 67, 164; Federation, 101; empire, 12; music, 25, 30; princes, 62; religion, 20; Revolt, 82; society, 12, 24; troops (army), 43, 44, 60, 91, 120, 181, 182, 199, 235, 253, 276, 278, 294, 324, 327, 328, 329, 331-333, 338, 339, 342, 343, 344
India-Pakistan Defence Pact, 288, 325
India-Pakistan war 1965, 180, 181, 182, 185, 187, 196, 197, 284, 288, 296, 299, 309, 311, 319, 328, 355, 372, 393, 426, 427, 507
India-Pakistan-Bangladesh Tripartite Agreement 1974, 345
India-US nuclear agreement 2006, 208, 236, 297
Indonesia, 167, 181, 182, 284, 360
Indus Valley, 5, 6, 13
Indus Water Dispute, 167, 325
Indus Water Treaty 1960, 113, 167, 180
International Monetary Fund (IMF), 212, 220, 234, 239, 241, 279, 298, 378, 379, 381, 384, 388, 389, 397
Iqbal, Javed, 237
Iqbal, Sir Muhammad, 27, 72, 73, 97, 99, 101, 104-107, 110, 111, 140, 148, 161, 204, 424, 427, 431
Iran Nuclear Agreement 2015, 304

Iran, 2, 12, 14, 19, 27, 35, 45, 52, 108, 180, 182, 191, 218, 231, 233, 236, 263, 264, 285, 301, 302, 304, 305, 317, 324, 346, 354-359, 360, 361, 364, 400, 429, 492, 494, 495, 509
Iranian Revolution 1979, 218, 356
Iran-Pakistan Gas pipeline, 301, 304
Iran-Pakistan-India pipeline, 220
Iraq, 2, 19, 92, 213, 219, 283, 287, 295, 355, 357, 359
Irwin, Lord, 98, 111, 266
Isa, Qazi Faiz, 463-469, 476, 477, 479
Isa, Qazi Muhammad, 152, 153
Islamia College, 72, 73, 74, 150, 202
Islamic State of Iraq and Syria (ISIS), 359, 491, 495, 495, 498
Ismay, Lord, 142, 143, 327
Ispahani, M.A.H., 130, 133
Israel, 175, 212, 219, 235, 283, 355, 356, 358, 359, 360-365

J

Jadav, Kulbhushan, 334
Jalandhari, Mohammad Hafeez, 431
Jamaat-e-Islami, 157, 248, 249, 263, 345, 491, 504
Jamali, Mir Zafarullah Khan, 217, 221
Jammu, 167, 181, 184, 206, 207, 307, 328, 330, 331, 333, 335-339, 340, 341, 342, 344, 398, 435, 512
Jarrige, Jean-Francois, 5
Jauhar, Maulana Mohammad Ali, 88, 93
Jaunpuri, Sheikh Adnan, 26
Jehangir, 26, 35, 36, 39, 42
Jhelum, 12, 463; River, 324
Jinnah, Fatima, 140, 158, 180, 204
Jinnah, Mohammad Ali, 37, 68, 73, 86, 88, 89, 90-92, 96-99, 100, 102-105, 108, 109, 110-112, 115, 117, 119, 120, 121, 122, 124-126, 128, 129, 130-136, 138, 139, 140-149, 150-153, 158, 163-165, 168, 169, 170, 172, 175, 177, 193, 204, 208, 245-247, 249, 259, 276, 277, 284, 298, 299, 327, 346, 368, 369, 424, 456, 498, 502-507
Jinping, Xi, 231, 304, 305, 308, 311, 317, 340

Jintao, Hu, 310, 311
Jogezai, Nawab Mohammad Khan, 153
Johnson, Lyndon B., 183, 507
Junagadh, 166, 325, 328
Junejo, Muhammad Khan, 211, 434, 460, 461
Jaunpur, 4, 25, 35
Jainism, 8, 9, 11, 24, 440

K

Kabir Das, 29
Kalachakra, 10
Karachi, 73, 74, 84, 92, 121, 122, 146, 147, 158, 165, 167, 168, 169, 172, 180, 184, 204, 213, 214, 219, 221, 224, 232, 237, 270, 274, 279, 299, 301, 302, 315, 359, 368, 378, 387, 394, 404, 405, 407-409, 410-412, 420, 429, 435, 436, 451, 453, 463, 469, 471, 489, 490, 492-494, 496-498, 504, 506
Karakoram Highway, 2, 277, 406
Kargil, 181, 182, 186, 198, 215, 235, 285, 289, 294, 319, 325, 326, 328, 329, 330, 331, 340
Karzai, Hamid, 347
Kashful Mahjub, 33
Kashmir, 4, 15, 62, 108, 115, 138, 142, 143, 166, 167, 170, 181-186, 206, 207, 212, 215, 228, 230, 235, 263, 272, 283-285, 287, 291, 292, 294, 296, 297, 299, 306, 307, 312, 313, 319, 320, 325-329, 330-339, 340-344, 359, 365, 368, 425, 435, 507, 509, 512
Kashmir War, 166, 167, 369
Kashmiri(s), 112, 182, 216, 235, 291, 306, 331-333, 335, 336, 338, 339, 341, 343
Kasuri, Khurshid Mahmud, 330, 365, 473
Kasuri, Mian Mahmud Ali, 253
Kasuri, Nawab Muhammad Ahmad Khan, 480
Kayani, Ashfaq Parvez, 222, 228, 280, 302, 509
Kayqubad, Sultan Moizuddin, 30
Kennedy, John F., 181, 293, 328, 510
Keqiang, Li, 315, 316
Khaliquzzaman, Chaudhry, 121, 126
Khalji, Ikhtiaruddin, 20

Khalji, Sultan Alauddin, 20
Khan, Abdul Qadeer, 219, 287, 295, 365
Khan, Abdul Wali Khan, 191, 253
Khan, Azam, 179, 180, 195
Khan, Chaudhry Nisar Ali, 359, 465
Khan, Chin Qilich (Nizam-ul-Mulk Asaf Jah I) 45
Khan, Field Marshal Mohammad Ayub, 69, 176, 179, 187, 189, 252
Khan, Ghulam Ishaq, 211, 212, 213, 230, 255, 378, 460
Khan, Imran, 226, 229, 232-239, 241, 242, 273, 291-293, 304, 306, 307, 314, 315, 336, 338, 346, 359, 360, 383, 404, 333, 447, 449, 452, 453, 463, 470, 474-477, 479, 486, 495, 511, 512
Khan, Khan Abdul Ghaffar, 150, 350
Khan, M. Asghar, 181, 204, 227, 386, 460
Khan, Maulana Ahmad Raza, 70
Khan, Maulvi Tamizuddin, 174, 249, 250, 456, 457, 458
Khan, Muhammad Amir Ahmad (Raja of Mahmudabad), 87, 98, 100, 105, 119, 121, 128, 147, 148, 158, 204, 433
Khan, Muhammad Ibrahim, 487
Khan, Muhammad Saifullah, 211, 460
Khan, Nawabzada Muhammad Liaquat Ali, 69, 89, 103, 105, 115, 118, 119, 124, 133-135, 139, 147-149, 153, 158, 159, 166, 169, 170-175, 177, 178, 193, 204, 246, 247, 277, 284, 287, 299, 326-328, 355, 369, 370, 504, 506
Khan, Sahibzada Yaqub, 212, 344
Khan, Sardar, Aurangzeb, 150, 151, 426
Khan, Sir Syed Ahmad, 66-69, 70-73, 76, 79, 82, 83, 136, 423, 424, 503
Khan, Sir Zafarullah, 142
Khan, Tikka, 192, 195, 278, 508
Khan, Yahya, 122, 182, 189, 190-194, 197, 198, 202, 204, 205, 252, 268, 299, 309, 356, 375, 458, 507, 508
Khan-i-Khanan, Abdur Rahim, 28
Khatami, Muhammad, 264
Khilafat Movement, 88, 91, 92, 94, 96, 102, 117, 140, 146, 150, 163, 346, 354
Khosa, Asif Saeed, 228, 462, 466, 472, 473, 475
Khosa, Sardar Abdul Latif, 465, 480, 481

Index   **525**

Khrushchev, Nikita, 288, 299, 306, 511
Khudai Khidmatgars, 117, 150
Khuhro, M. Ayub, 147
Khuhro, Muhammad Nawaz, 411
Khunjerab Pass, 2, 406
Khusro, Amir, 25, 26, 28, 30, 31
Khyber Pakhtunkhwa, 2, 3, 13, 258, 270, 274, 348, 378, 380, 389, 435, 442, 443, 450, 474, 478, 486, 490, 491, 492, 496, 510
Kili Gul Muhammad, 4, 5
King George V, 88, 110
King George VI, 132, 138
Kissinger, Henry, 197-199, 294, 295, 297, 316
Kitchlew, Dr Saifuddin, 93, 97, 98, 431
Konakamana, 10
Kosygin, Alexei N., 184, 185, 186, 197, 299, 329, 507
Kot Diji, 5
Kshatriya/s, 11, 24
Kumaragupta, 15
Kushan: Empire, 13, 14, 15; period, 6, 14

L

Laden, Osama bin, 227, 228, 230, 280, 290, 302, 359, 489, 494
Lahore Resolution, 108, 124, 125, 147, 157, 502
Lahore, 33, 72, 73, 98, 103, 105, 124, 125, 148, 151, 158, 182, 184, 187, 191, 205, 213, 215, 230, 231, 260, 263, 278, 290, 301, 302, 325, 344, 356, 369, 381, 388, 404, 408, 420, 424, 431, 438, 445, 448, 451, 456, 458, 460, 472, 476, 480, 496, 497, 498, 503, 508
Lakshmi Bai (Rani of Jhansi), 62, 64
Lal Masjid, 221, 263, 264, 317, 499
Lavrov, Sergey, 302, 304-307, 316
Lawrence, Sir Henry, 61
Legal Framework Order (LFO), 189, 190, 252, 256, 257
Leghari, Farooq, 214, 255, 461
Leonard, Karen, 44
Liaquat-Nehru Pact, 151, 325, 442
Linlithgow, Lord, 120, 127, 129
London, 79, 80, 84, 86, 105, 110, 111, 121, 122, 135, 196, 267, 276, 320, 339, 340, 343, 345, 433, 463, 469, 503
Luari, Khwaja Muhammad Zaman, 427
Lucknow, 61, 64, 71, 76, 89, 90, 100, 108, 119, 120, 121, 124, 140, 145, 163
Lucknow Pact, 87, 89, 90, 93, 96, 130, 145
Ludhianvi, Maulana Muhammad Ahmed, 465

M

Macaulay, Lord, 68, 69, 419, 420
Macdonald, Ramsay, 102, 110, 111
Madhopur Headworks, 167
Madrassa Manzar-e-Islam, Barelvi, 70
Magadha, 9, 11, 12, 13
Mahabharata, 9, 18
Maharashtra, 15
Mahavira, 9, 10, 15
Mahbub ul Haq, 180, 269, 372, 390, 398
Makli, 2, 444
Makran, 2, 19, 153
Malaviya, Pandit Madan Mohan, 110
Malaysia, 182, 235, 314, 340, 359
Malik, Fateh Muhammad, 426
Malik, Musadik, 308
Mangla Dam, 180, 396, 400, 473
Manto, Abid Hasan, 467
Manto, Sa'adat Hasan, 165, 425
Marathas, 42, 45, 46, 50, 51, 53, 59, 62, 346
Marri, Sher Mohammad, 429
Marshall, Sir John, 6
Martial Law, 176, 179, 189, 192, 194, 204, 211, 217, 251, 253, 255, 260, 278, 457-459, 460, 464, 498, 509
Maududi, Syed Abul Ala, 38, 247, 249, 263, 264
Mahmud, Sultan, 20, 33
Mahmud-ul-Hasan, Maulana, 69
Maurya Chandragupta, 11, 12, 13
Maurya(s), 4, 13, 14, 15
Mazhar, Mohammad, 76
McDonnell, Anthony, 76, 78
Megasthenes, 13
Mehrgarh, 5
Mian Tansen, 25, 26
Minto, Lord, 78, 79, 80, 81, 84
Mir Jafar, 43

Mirza, Iskander, 122, 175, 176, 251
Modi, Narendra, 230, 231, 291, 304, 332, 336, 340, 343, 346,
Moenjo Daro, 5, 6
Mohammad, Din, 142
Mohammad, Ghulam, 174, 176, 250, 251, 284, 287, 456, 457
Mohammadan Association, 76
Mohammadan Literary Society, 76
Mohammadan Political Organization, 76
Mohani, Maulana Hasrat, 92, 93, 98, 139, 140, 158, 204
Mojaheed, Ali Ahsan Mohammad, 345
Mongeri, Maulana Muhammad Ali, 71
Montagu-Chelmsford Reforms, 94, 97, 150, 244,
Morley, Lord John, 79, 80, 81, 84
Morley-Minto Reforms, 84, 89, 244
Mountbatten, Lord, 135, 138, 139, 142, 143, 151, 153, 164-166, 168, 245, 318, 327, 502,
Movement for the Restoration of Democracy (MRD), 211
Mughal, N.A., 409
Mughal/s, 4, 20, 23, 25-27, 35-37, 42, 44, 45, 59, 68, 149, 419, 429, 502
Muhajir Qaumi Movement (MQM), 212-214, 221, 461, 463, 491
Muhammad, Arif, 13
Muhammad, Habib, 45
Muhammad, Jalaluddin, 35
Muhammad, Prince, 30
Muhammad, Prophet (PBUH), 16, 32, 34, 38, 40, 41, 66, 70, 71, 161, 181, 233, 304, 358, 360, 445
Muhammad, Syed, 35
Mujaddid Alf Thani (Shaikh Ahmad Sirhindi), 32, 35-39, 40, 44, 49, 106, 502
Mukti Bahini, 196, 294, 300
Mulk, Nawab Mohsinul, 76, 79, 81, 83, 84, 87, 424
Mulk, Nawab Viqar, 83, 84, 424
Mundaka Upanishad, 8
Munir, Muhammad, 142, 157, 457
Musharraf, Pervez, 160, 195, 215, 217-219, 220-225, 230, 235, 255-257, 261, 269, 270, 278, 279, 280, 290, 300, 301, 310, 319, 329, 330, 345, 357, 365, 375, 381, 395, 400, 433, 454, 461, 462, 464, 492
Muslim University, Aligarh, 67, 68, 74
Muslim, Qutaybah bin, 20

N

Nadir Shah, 20, 45, 46
Nadvat-ul-Ulama, Lucknow, 71
Nadvi, Maulana Khair Mohammad, 429
Nadvi, Maulana Syed Suleman, 71
Naidu, Sarojini, 86, 90
Nana Sahib Peshwa II, 62
Nana Sahib, 62
Nanotvi, Maulana Muhammad Qasim, 69, 70
National Awami Party (NAP), 159, 191, 204, 220, 253, 398
National Mohammadan Association, 77
National Reconciliation Order (NRO), 226, 462, 464
Nawab Sirajuddaulah, 43, 46
Nazimuddin, Sir Khwaja, 117, 174, 175, 177, 246, 250
Neelum-Jhelum Hydropower Project, 401
Nehru Report 1928, 88, 89, 99, 100, 136, 145
Nehru, Motilal, 94, 97, 99, 110, 112, 163
Nehru, Pandit Jawaharlal, 67, 94, 99, 102, 103, 110, 112, 113, 117, 120, 125, 127, 128, 132-134, 136, 138, 139, 143, 147, 149, 151, 153, 163, 164, 166, 167, 175, 181, 193, 209, 242, 284, 299, 309, 325, 326, 328, 331, 343, 344, 368, 424, 503, 505-507, 512
New Delhi, 91, 102, 112, 136, 138, 165, 316, 333, 503
Nisar, Mian Saqib, 228, 384, 400, 401, 445, 452, 464, 470, 472-476
Nixon, Richard M, 197
Nizam of Deccan, 62
Nizam of Hyderabad, 72, 108, 166, 242, 368
Nomani, Shibli, 68, 71, 72
Non-Aligned Movement (NAM), 354, 358
Non-Bengali, 192, 193, 200, 344, 345, 346, 372, 393, 398
Non-Cooperation Movement, 92, 94, 128,

Index 527

136, 141, 150, 163
Noon, Sir Feroz Khan, 176, 251, 266
North Waziristan, 402, 498
North-West Frontier Province (NWFP), 2, 21, 53, 59, 73, 96, 99, 100, 104, 108, 116, 117, 121, 126, 139, 149, 150, 151, 153, 168, 170, 176, 189, 191, 193, 205, 244, 250, 254, 258, 276, 300, 326, 327, 397, 435, 505
Nusayr, Musa bin, 20

O

Obama, Barack, 227, 228, 290, 311, 362
Objectives Resolution 1949, 157, 169, 247, 248, 249, 259, 260, 263, 438
Olivieri, Dr Luca Maria, 14
One Belt One Road (OBOR), 305, 316, 318
One Unit, 174, 189, 191, 194, 250, 251
Organization of Islamic Conference (OIC), 355, 356-359, 360, 361

P

Pak-China Investment Company (PCIC), 272
Pakistan Army Act 1952, 258, 480
Pakistan Army, 166, 167, 181, 192, 194, 199, 231, 277, 278, 279, 327, 335, 349, 412, 413, 486-488, 491, 494, 508
Pakistan Democratic Movement (PDM), 241, 479
Pakistan Hindu Council, 442
Pakistan Hindu-Sikh Social Welfare Council, 442
Pakistan Muslim League (N) (PML N), 213, 225, 229, 232, 237, 241, 255, 293, 383, 386, 460, 491
Pakistan Muslim League (Q) (PML Q), 221, 222, 225
Pakistan National Alliance (PNA), 159, 205, 206, 208, 210, 260
Pakistan People's Party (PPP), 159, 187, 191, 204, 206, 210, 212, 213, 221, 222, 225-227, 229, 232, 233, 236, 237, 253, 260, 268, 272, 273, 290, 369, 372, 373-375, 377, 379, 383, 398, 401, 434, 439, 458, 459, 460-462, 464, 465, 474, 476, 480, 488, 491, 495
Pakistan Tehreek-e-Insaf (PTI), 229, 232, 236, 237, 239, 241, 242, 298, 334, 379, 463, 465, 474, 488
Pakistan-Afghanistan border, 487
Pal, Bipin Chandra, 78
Palestine, 360, 362, 364, 365; Authority, 363; cause, 168, 235, 359
Palestinian/s, 361-365
Panama Gate, 232, 462, 463
Panama Papers, 232, 462, 463, 472, 476
Panikkar, K.M., 24, 43
Partition Plan 3 June 1947, 138, 139
Pasha, Ahmed Shuja, 228, 280
Pataliputra, 11, 13, 51
Patel, Aakal, 336
Patel, Dorab, 481
Patel, Hirubhai M., 166
Patel, Hussain Mubarak, 334
Patel, Sardar Vallabhbhai, 128, 135, 139, 153, 163, 318
Patel, Usif, 457
Patel, Vitthal Bhai, 110
Permanent Settlement 1793, 54
Persian, 15, 25, 26, 28, 30, 33, 48, 76, 104, 105, 108, 422, 423, 424; Empire, 12, 152
Peshawar, 14, 15, 20, 52, 73, 74, 150-152, 169, 191, 229, 231, 232, 299, 330, 347, 348, 411, 444, 446, 456, 459, 460, 485-487, 490, 496-498, 509; University, 262
Pethick-Lawrence, Lord Frederick, 131-133, 505
Pitt's India Act 1784, 244
Podgorny, Nikolai, 197, 299, 346
Porus, 12
Princely States, 4, 72, 114, 115, 138, 165, 169, 193, 325, 327
Punjab, 3, 21, 51, 52, 59, 72, 73, 89, 98, 99, 100, 101, 104, 105, 108, 109, 117, 121, 126, 132, 138, 142, 143, 145, 147-149, 150, 165, 170, 172, 174, 181, 183, 189, 191, 212-214, 229, 232, 247, 250, 258, 274, 276, 283, 318, 327, 331, 369, 380, 381, 389, 396, 398, 412, 435, 436, 442, 443, 445, 453, 456, 465, 470, 478, 479, 480, 481, 495, 496, 503-506, 508

Pushyamitra, 13
Putin, Vladimir, 238, 239, 292, 293, 300, 301-308, 311, 364, 510

Q

Qadri, M. Afzal, 124
Quetta, 5, 152, 168, 169, 213, 229, 232, 314, 404, 409, 429, 444, 464, 469, 488, 492, 494, 495, 509
Quit India Movement, 128, 129, 132, 136
Qunavi, Sadruddin, 33
Qureshi, Shah Mahmood, 227, 306, 349, 359, 465
Qasim, Mohammad bin, 19, 20, 24

R

Radcliffe, Sir Cyril, 142-144
Rahman, Maulana Fazlur, 69, 76, 434, 491
Rahman, Sheikh Mujibur, 177, 184, 187, 190, 191, 193, 194, 199, 202, 203, 252, 344, 345, 346, 372, 398, 507, 508
Rai, Lala Lajpat, 78, 86, 125, 150, 503
Ramayana, 9, 18
Rashidi, Sibghatullah Shah (Pir of Pagaro), 146
Rashtriya Swayamsevak Sangh (RSS), 125, 165, 166, 368, 503
Reagan, Ronald, 288, 293, 485, 509
Regional Cooperation for Development (RCD), 180, 356
Rig Veda, 7, 18
Rishabh, 9, 10
Roosevelt, Franklin Delano, 126
Roos-Keppel, George, 73, 150
Round Table Conferences (RTCs) 1930-1932, 101, 108, 110, 111, 114, 115, 140, 146, 151, 202
Roy, Raja Ram Mohan, 66, 68
Russia, 236, 238, 239, 283, 284, 286, 292, 293, 296-298, 300-309, 310-313, 316, 317, 326, 355, 357, 360, 364, 402, 510, 511, 512
Russia-Ukraine War, 238, 239, 293, 297, 301, 303, 305-308, 311, 317, 360, 364, 502, 510, 511

S

Saadullah, Sir Muhammad, 119
Safdar, Captain Muhammad, 274
Saigol, Mian Mohammad Rafiq, 271, 386
Sama Veda, 7
Samudragupta, 15
Sassanid, 15, 19
Saudi Arabia, 214, 218, 231, 235, 273, 293, 314, 355, 356-359, 360, 495, 509
Scott, Sir Ian Dixon, 74, 327
SEATO, 204, 284, 287, 308, 354,
Seleucus, 12
Sen, Rai Bahadur Norendranath, 78
Shafi, Sir Muhammad, 72, 97, 98, 100, 110, 140, 145
Shah Waliullah, 38, 39, 46, 48, 49, 50, 51, 69, 70, 502
Shah, King Zahir, 205, 346, 347, 479
Shah, Qutbuddin Mubarak, 31
Shah, Wajid Ali, 62, 64, 65
Shahjahan, 39, 42, 44
Shakyamuni, 10, 11
Shamazai, Maulana Nizamuddin, 498
Shamim, Rana Muhammad, 472
Shanghai Co-operation Organization (SCO), 230, 231, 301, 303, 357
Shapur I, 15
Shapur II, 15
Sharif, Maryam Nawaz, 470
Sharif, Maulvi Mohammad, 443
Sharif, Muhammad, 460
Sharif, Nawaz, 160, 212-215, 217, 220-222, 225, 230, 231, 232, 256, 261, 278, 283, 291, 303, 316, 330, 343, 356, 385, 394, 460, 461-463, 470, 472, 474, 476, 486, 489
Sharif, Raheel, 485
Sharif, Shehbaz, 229, 232, 237, 241, 242, 293, 307, 308, 454, 476, 479
Sharqi, Husain Shah, 25
Shastri, Lal Bahadur, 181, 184, 185
Sheerani, Maulana Mohammad Khan, 447
Shishunaga, 11
Shudra, 24
Siddhartha, 9, 10, 11
Siddiqui, Shaukat Aziz, 470-472
Sikh/s, 51, 52, 53, 60, 62, 64, 114, 138, 143,

146, 149, 151, 165, 244, 277, 339, 429, 505, 506
Simla, 79, 80, 81, 83, 129, 206, 207; Agreement, 206, 207, 329; Conference, 129; Deputation 1906, 76, 79, 80, 81, 83, 84, 145; Summit/Agreement 1972, 283, 325, 329, 332, 337, 338, 512
Simon Commission 1927, 88, 97-99, 100, 110, 140, 145, 163
Simon, Sir John, 97
Sindh Madressatul Islam, 73, 74, 146
Sindh Minority Rights Commission Bill 2019, 443
Sindh Muslim League, 124, 147, 165, 506
Sindh, 3, 19, 20, 27, 52, 73, 96, 99, 100, 101, 104, 108, 116, 117, 121, 139, 145, 146, 147, 165, 170, 172, 174, 189, 191, 204, 213, 214, 229, 244, 258, 270, 274, 369, 380, 389, 395, 397, 401, 404, 409, 411, 412, 428, 435, 443, 446, 449, 453, 456, 459, 460, 492, 493, 499, 505
Sindhi, 139, 146, 147, 204, 397, 422, 423, 427, 428
Sindhia, Daulat Rao, 51
Sindhi-Urdu conflict, 423
Singh, Maharaja Ranjit, 51, 52
Sino-Indian War 1959, 309
Sino-Indian War 1962, 180, 299, 312, 355
Six Point programme, 184, 189, 190, 191, 192, 194, 196, 199, 252, 253, 326, 508
Skandagupta, 16
South Asian Association for Regional Cooperation (SAARC), 231, 324, 350
South Waziristan, 218, 411
Sri Lanka, 181, 215, 350, 444, 498
State-Owned Enterprises (SOEs), 271, 272, 379, 383-386
Sufism, 32, 37, 49
Suhrawardy, Huseyn Shaheed, 94, 130, 134, 174, 175, 177, 178, 179, 180, 193, 202, 247, 251, 309, 355, 424
Sukkur, 2, 147, 408
Svetasvatara Upanishad, 8
Syed, G.M., 124, 128, 147

T

Tagore, Jatindramohan, 78

Tajikistan, 2, 356
Taliban, 160, 214, 218, 227, 228, 231, 232, 235, 264, 280, 289, 290-292, 300, 310, 343, 347-349, 350, 357, 485, 486, 490, 491, 509
Talibul Moula, Makhdoom Muhammad Zaman, 428
Tara Chand, 20, 24, 27, 28, 67, 423
Tarar, Azam Nazeer, 478
Tarar, M. Rafiq, 217
Tarbela Dam, 2, 396, 400, 401, 473
Taseer, Muhammad Din, 425
Tashkent Declaration (1966), 182-187, 197, 206, 283, 299, 406, 309, 328, 329, 426, 507, 508
Taxila, 12, 13, 14, 317
Tehreek-e-Labbaik Pakistan, 273, 465, 466, 467, 486
Tehreek-e-Taliban, Pakistan (TTP), 486, 487, 489, 490, 491, 494, 495, 498, 509, 510
Thanvi, Maulana Ashraf Ali, 71
Thapar, Romila, 7, 13, 16
Thar Heritage site, 15
Thar, 2, 402, 403
Tharparkar, 4
Third Battle of Panipat 1761, 46, 48, 50
Tilak, Bal Gangadhar, 78, 89, 91, 276, 441, 442
Tirthankara, 9, 10, 15
Titu Mir (Mir Nisar Ali), 54-57, 70, 77
Treaty of Sèvres, 91
Truman, Harry, 282
Trump, Donald, 235, 291, 298, 349, 359
Tughlaq, Sultan Muhammad bin, 34, 45
Turkey, 91, 92, 180, 182, 191, 236, 314, 339, 345, 355, 356, 358, 359, 360, 364, 488
Two-Nation theory, 71, 76, 124, 125, 157, 175, 193, 263, 423, 502, 503, 507
Tyabji, Badruddin, 67

U

Union of Soviet Socialist Republics (USSR), 127, 168, 172, 173, 180, 183, 185, 186, 196-198, 205, 219, 284-289, 298, 299, 300, 301, 305, 310, 311, 312, 354-357, 394, 460, 490, 507
United Arab Emirates (UAE), 2, 214, 218,

235, 273, 280, 358, 359, 360, 362, 382, 410, 412
United Nations Economic, Social and Cultural Organization (UNESCO), 417, 438
United Nations Security Council (UNSC), 186, 197, 199, 215, 224, 286-288, 291, 300, 307, 309, 312, 313, 328, 332, 337-339, 340, 348, 361, 362, 364, 512
United Nations, 168, 184, 198, 199, 206, 207, 224, 235, 284, 287, 297, 306, 307, 309, 312-314, 328, 329, 336-339, 340, 341, 347, 348, 361, 362, 398, 407, 411, 437, 438, 485, 486, 511, 512
United States of America (US), 126, 178, 180, 183, 186, 197, 198, 202, 204, 212, 214-219, 220, 222, 227, 228, 231, 233, 239, 280, 282, 283, 286-289, 290-299, 300-302, 304-309, 310-312, 318, 329, 340, 341, 342, 347, 348, 354-357, 359, 360, 362, 363, 374, 375, 400, 401, 490, 507, 509, 510, 511, 512
Upanishads, 7, 8
Urdu Defence Association 1900, 76, 424
Urdu, 67-69, 76, 104, 105, 108, 119, 137, 168, 177, 195, 202, 204, 250, 251, 416, 417, 422-425, 427, 432, 451
US-India Nuclear Co-operation Treaty 2008, 312
US-India Nuclear Strategic Partnership, 235
Usmani, Ishrat Husain, 400
Usmani, Maulana Shabbir Ahmad, 69, 70, 249

V

Vaishya, 24
Vajpayee, Atal Bihari, 207, 215, 312, 325, 331
Victoria, Queen, 61, 62, 64, 68
Vikramaditya, 15

W

Wahdat-ul-Wajood, 28, 32, 33, 37, 38, 49, 51
War of Independence 1857, 58, 59, 60, 61, 62, 64, 66, 67, 76, 82, 277
Warsak Dam, 180, 400
Waseem, Muhammad, 448
Water and Power Development Authority (WAPDA), 315, 401
Wavell, Lord, 129, 131, 132, 135, 142, 505
Waziristan, 149, 487, 489
West Bengal, 56, 77
West Pakistan, 179, 189, 195, 198, 199, 249, 250, 288, 297, 372, 458, 508
Wheeler, Sir Mortimer, 6
Willingdon, Lord, 111
Wilson, Harold, 182, 319
Wilson, Woodrow, 283
Wolpert, Stanley, 28, 91, 102, 209, 219
Wyllie, Sir Curzon, 79

X

Xiaoping, Deng, 312
Xinxiang, 312, 314

Y

Yaad, Muhammad Mansha, 425
Yajur Veda, 7
Yaqub, Sir Muhammad, 98, 140
Yemen War, 273, 358, 359
Yi, Wang, 304, 360
Yousuf, Kaniz Fatima, 18
Yusuf, Hajjaj bin, 19

Z

Zaidi, Shabbar, 234, 242, 390
Zaidi, Syed Akbar, 342, 373
Zakaria, Shaikh Bahauddin, 34
Zardari, Asif Ali, 220, 224-228, 278, 290, 383, 401, 462, 487
Zedong, Mao, 308, 309
Zemin, Jiang, 312
Zhob, 4, 5, 411
Zhou Enlai, 178, 182, 308, 309
Ziarat, 2, 169, 368, 410
Ziaul Haq, General Muhammad, 125, 159, 160, 206, 210, 211, 218, 224, 230, 255, 260, 288, 300, 344, 369, 374, 378, 394, 398, 434, 436, 451, 452, 459, 460, 464, 493
Ziyad, Tariq bin, 20